PROPHETS OF DOOM

The Unauthorised and Unofficial Guide to *Doomwatch*

PROPHETS OF DOOM

The Unauthorised and Unofficial Guide to *Doomwatch*

Michael Seely & Phil Ware

Published in 2020 by Telos Publishing Ltd
139 Whitstable Road, Canterbury, Kent CT2 8EQ

www.telos.co.uk

Telos Publishing Ltd values feedback. Please e-mail us with any comments
you may have about this book to: feedback@telos.co.uk

Prophets of Doom: The Unauthorised and Unofficial Guide to Doomwatch
© 2012, 2020 Michael Seely and Phil Ware

Originally published in 2012 by Miwk Publishing.

ISBN: 978-1-84583-141-7

Cover Art: © 2019 Iain Robertson

Contents

Acknowledgements

I would like to acknowledge and thank the family of Dr Kit Pedler: his widow, Una Freeston; and his children, Carol Topolski, the late Mark Pedler, Lucy Pedler and Justin Pedler.

I would also like to thank Jonathan Alwyn, John Archibald, Hilde Dudley-Attwood, Nigel Barrett, Judy Bedford, Richard Bignell, Darrol Blake, Anthony Brown, David Brunt, Scott Burditt and all the contributors and readers of doomwatch.org, Elizabeth Coe, readers of the Craven Herald, Mark Cooper, Richard Cross, Ian Curteis, Allen Dace, John Dare and the Plymouth Lifeguard, Tony Derbyshire, Keith Dewhurst, Stephen and Sue Dudley, Glyn Edwards, Scott Frankton, Rob Hammond, Alan Hayes of Avengers Declassified, Eric Hills, David J Howe, Brookes Irvine, Alexandra Mann, Richard Marson, Bob Meades, the late Peter Miles, MIWK, Louise North of BBC Written Archives Centre, Andy Priestner, Peter Neill, Andrew Pixley, Elizabeth Rowell, Don Shaw, Hope Smith, Vivien S Smith, Elaine Spooner, Jean Trend, ukCaving.com, Stephen James Walker, Phil Ware, Matt West, Jennifer Wilson, Adele Winston and Martin Worth.

And a special thank you to the readers of the original 2012 book and its brief reprint in 2016, both published by MIWK Publishing Ltd.

NOTE

In the case of those supporting artists who appeared in multiple episodes but were uncredited on screen, there may be inconsistencies in the spelling of their names. These variations reflect the original documentation of the time that has been used as reference. This is also true for uncredited production personnel.

This book is respectfully dedicated to the memories of Kit Pedler, Gerry Davis and Terence Dudley.

Introduction

'The days when you and I marvelled at the miracles of science … are over.
We've grown up now – and we're frightened. The findings of science are still
marvellous, but now is the time to stop dreaming up science-fiction about
them and write what we call "sci-fact". The honeymoon of science is over.' –
Gerry Davis, 1970

'I feel that one of the best and most effective ways of making the public
aware of the problem is dramatically. Talk a lot of dry, dusty facts and they
couldn't care less, but absorb those facts into a dramatic, fictional work and
they start to take notice.' – Kit Pedler, 1972

'Terry Nation … is always quoting Sam Goldwyn's dictum that "messages
are for Western Union", but I've always liked drama that has something to
say. *Doomwatch* may have added a new word to the language, but also it did
make a point.' – Terence Dudley, 1975

It is not often that a television programme puts a word into the English
language, but *Doomwatch* did. The language had been needing a short,
snappy description to embrace a growing concern for some time now.
Throughout the 1960s, there was a lot of doom being foretold, and the
prophets were legion. We were on the verge of destroying our planet and
ourselves. The end of the world was nigh – due at any point before the next
millennium. It wasn't just the atom bomb that was exercising concerns, it
was what was being done in the name of progress by science. Do we need a
car to go a little bit faster if it means more lead in the atmosphere? Do we
need supersonic craft and their noise pollution just to get businessmen
across the Atlantic a bit quicker? Do we need to put hormones into chicken
feed to make the animal plumper? Did we have to kill off life in a river
simply to make plastic things? Did we have to destroy the ecology of an area
to protect one crop? Objectors were regarded as cranks or, at worst,
subversives.

Governments were not keen to explore these issues during a turbulent
period of social, economic and global problems. These were the necessary
side effects of economic growth, forged in the white heat of technology, to
coin a phrase. Business was not keen to spend money on cleaning up the
mess before or after they made it if the expenditure involved cost them a
slight economic advantage. As for the people who came up with the ideas,
carried out the research and made it all possible, the side effects of use or
misuse were someone else's problem.

Doomwatch was conceived at the beginning of that turbulent year 1968, when the student protests against Vietnam and the atomic bomb awoke an interest in ecology and the protection of the environment, and apocalyptic predictions were made over what would happen if the growing populations of Third World countries (and ours in the West) were not controlled. The series went into production during 1969, when it looked possible that a baby could be conceived in a test tube outside of a mother's womb, when biologists were seeking to prove blacks were inferior to whites and that an extra chromosome predisposed a male to violence. In February 1970 *Doomwatch* was launched on BBC1. America was about to celebrate its first Earth Day, to bring awareness of the need to protect the environment of Spaceship Earth. When *Doomwatch* finished in August 1972 there wasn't any doubt about the importance of tackling pollution, from the simple dumping of industrial waste in landfills to the poisonous soup being created in the Mediterranean, and the United Nations had hosted a global conference in Stockholm on the environment.

Because a popular BBC drama was tackling subjects that had previously gained only a minimal smattering of press or TV documentary coverage, it suddenly gave viewers and the media a hook for discussing what became known as 'Doomwatch' issues. One of the programme's creators, Dr Christopher 'Kit' Pedler, became seen as a wise soothsayer, our prophet of doom ('Doctor Doom', one interviewer called him in 1972). Not only did he pose the problem in dramatic form, he would soon look for an answer in redirecting scientific enquiry and steer a path towards a post-industrial age.

If Kit Pedler was a prophet then the other creator, writer Gerry Davis, was a very willing disciple who fought for the message of the programme against the 'forces of conservatism' within the BBC – and lost. He never gave up in trying to take *Doomwatch* to other TV companies both in the UK and in America. He believed in the message.

Producer Terence Dudley was not one of those conservative forces, at least not to begin with. After all, he wrote one of the most controversial episodes of the first series, *Tomorrow, the Rat*. Dudley was not a wrecker. Outwardly an Establishment man, he understood the message Pedler wanted to give the programme and approved of it. Where he differed with Pedler and Davis was on how to tell a story, how to keep it down to earth and away from fantasy, to make it as real as possible. He would argue that *Doomwatch* was not science-fiction, but an intelligent extrapolation of how current scientific research could go wrong if misapplied. He had to obey the laws of drama in his own way – possibly an old-fashioned set of laws, but ones that the BBC felt comfortable with. He also had to deal with the wishes of his superiors in BBC management, who were certainly Establishment types and nervous ones too, bruised by earlier controversies emerging from the drama department.

Regardless of the conflicts, which this book will explore in detail, the programme was a huge success when it was launched. The word entered the language, and this is why I believe *Doomwatch* to be one of the most important television programmes of the 1970s. It wasn't another recreation of what had happened in a nicely distanced history. It was relevant to now. It chimed with what was going on in the world and in our lives. It exercised the imagination and made people ask: 'Could it happen?' 'Do we need a real Doomwatch?' It even attracted the attentions of politicians from both left and right. It pleased and infuriated the scientific world. It had a lasting impact and remains fresh in people's memories. The three years *Doomwatch* was on screen saw a huge shift in opinion on matters environmental. We only had the one world, and we were willingly poisoning it and ourselves for the sake of progress.

Doomwatch begins with one of the technological marvels of the age – transatlantic flight – and a man-made virus designed to deal with a man-made problem. And it all goes horribly wrong ...

Part One
The Creation Of *Doomwatch*

1
When Kit Met Gerry: 'A Radical Thinker'

'Scientific research has now advanced to the stage where, unless carefully monitored, mankind's greatest hazard may well be from his own discoveries … Already we have the nuclear bomb, rising radiation levels, the risks of poisoning by insecticides. How many other scientific advances will prove double edged weapons unless handled with great vision and restraint.' *Doomwatch* Format Document

'The most immediately surprising impression of the Doctor is that he looks nothing at all like a Prophet of Doom.' Lorna O'Connell in *Building Services and Environmental Engineer* 1979

Kit Pedler (or Christopher Magnus Howard Pedler) was born in London in 1927 and grew up in rural Suffolk, the son of a Medical Officer of Health, before enduring ten unhappy years at a boarding school in Ipswich. He went to Chelsea Polytechnic as a medical student, trying to follow in the footsteps of his ancestors in Victorian London who achieved high levels of success within their own medical fields. His academic results were not good enough for any hospital to take him, and thus Pedler could not avoid being drafted into a short spell of National Service. His time at the Royal Army Medical Corps took him from Aldershot to the Middle East. Despite his intense dislike for the army, it helped him a great deal with its courses in anatomy (which accompanied his training to become a physiotherapist) and awoke a genuine interest.

Following his discharge Pedler resumed his studies, gaining a place at Westminster College, and here began an unbroken run of success as he achieved his first doctorate and virtually any prize going. By this time he had married Una Freeston, the daughter of Sir (Leslie) Brian Freeston, who had been Governor of Fiji and the Leeward Islands. Dr Pedler continued his career as a house surgeon at Westminster and then became a house doctor at Kingston for six months before he briefly sampled general practise, which he disliked for its mundanity. A chance meeting with Professor Norman Ashton from the newly created Institute of Ophthalmology sparked an interest in Dr Pedler to specialise in research. Ashton had only recently discovered the link between oxygen levels and blindness in premature babies by experimenting on kittens, whose eyes followed a similar development to that of human infants.

From 1953 onwards, Dr Pedler pursued his researches and contributed towards scientific papers on causes of disease in the infant eye. Achieving his second doctorate in 1960, he became Head of Anatomy at the institute and decided to specialise in the study of the retina, using an early electron microscope, pioneering various techniques in interpreting what they were actually seeing. These pictures of almost invisible slices of retina revealed features never seen before, which fascinated him. He came to believe that the retina was far more than just another part of the eye: it acted as the eye's computer, decoding and knitting together thousands of images. He realised that if he could replicate the retina's complex circuitry in electronic form he could discover more about how the real thing worked.

Pedler and his staff made polystyrene models of the eye's retinal cells, and by 1965 he was applying the new science of cybernetics to his work. His unusual but visual work was beginning to get him noticed; the *Guardian* and the *Illustrated London News* did features on his studies, the BBC World Service interviewed him and he eventually appeared on television, and the BBC's *Tomorrow's World* filmed Pedler at the Institute on 22 and 26 November 1965.

Pedler was a man of many talents as well as an imaginative and visual scientist; he was a sculptor, painter, home-made racing car enthusiast, musician and would-be writer. He enjoyed and devoured science fiction and harboured a desire to write his own, and perhaps enjoy a secondary career alongside his more serious research work, which was beginning to lose its attraction. Department heads, like Pedler, were spending as much time trying to fundraise to cover the shortfalls generated by cuts in government funding, or play politics in endless committee meetings. 'I love my work here,' he told the *Evening News* in 1967, 'but the thought that I might be a scientist – and only a scientist – for the rest of my life began to bother me. I wanted to explore other facets of myself. There were so many subjects racing through my mind ...'

So when the chance came to submit ideas and give advice to the BBC's most popular science fiction series of the time, he seized it. Here, he met the man who would shape his ideas and help him find his authorial voice.

Gerry Davis

Born in 1930, Gerry Davis was encouraged to write by his father. One of his idols was H G Wells, and at the age of 16 he set up the Wellsian Youth Club in his honour. After a period in the Merchant Navy, Davis became an actor but found he preferred directing and stage management. By the age of 22 he had begun writing plays for Canadian radio before moving on to television and then the National Film Board, where he worked under future ITV and BBC legend Sydney Newman, and it was in television

Davis wanted to work. He returned to England in 1960 with his young wife, who was dying from leukaemia. He got a job at Granada TV, helping to nurse *Coronation Street* through its early days, but did not feel he could contribute much since he had hardly been in England, least of all Salford, for a large part of his life.

Following the death of his wife, Davis left England and writing behind for a while, taking a scholarship to go to Italy and become an opera singer. However, the writing bug soon began to itch. Returning to England, he started to write for the BBC in a freelance capacity. In March 1965 Gerald Davis (as he was then known) was invited to write an episode of *Dr Finlay's Casebook*, a successful series about a general practice in Scotland, which had been running since 1962. Unfortunately Davis' episode 'Art or Science' was not accepted by the programme's producer, Gerard Glaister, who considered it 'an improbable melodrama'.

Nevertheless, on the strength of creating a course on television script writing for international correspondence schools, Davis was offered a job as a script editor at the BBC, and his first task was winding up an unsuccessful soap opera called *199 Park Lane* before editing *United!*, a series about a football team. Not much of a football fan himself, Davis was rather keen to work on a drama based in London, rather than Birmingham where *United!* was recorded. Having remarried, and with a daughter on her way, he asked to be transferred to *Doctor Who*, a programme which fascinated him.

Doctor Who had been running since 1963 and was going through a change in behind-the-scenes personnel. Outgoing producer John Wiles and script editor Donald Tosh had found it increasingly difficult to put their own vision of the programme on screen whilst faced with an awkward leading man in William Hartnell, as well as having been saddled with a three-month Dalek epic which they had wanted nothing to do with. Davis was soon joined by Innes Lloyd, a tough new producer who had his own ideas and the ruthlessness to put them into practice. He wanted to take the programme away from historical dramas and fantasy and put in something more identifiable. Lloyd had a scientific background himself and decided that the programme needed to be more science fiction ideas, and who better to provide the fiction than a scientist. This person could provide the programme with 'real information and who could show us where science was perhaps going'.

Combining a scientist to formulate ideas with a dramatist to create science fiction was not an unusual idea for the BBC. The early 1960s saw two serials, *A For Andromeda* and *The Andromeda Breakthrough*, written by John Elliot, with scientist and astronomer Fred Hoyle contributing the plots and the ideas. They concerned themes of global disaster brought about by impatient, unstoppable and greedy scientific research, with

17

political and business interests fighting over a computer which could create life. It ended with a rather usual science fiction device of the time: a warning from another world of the catastrophe that awaited this fledgling one. Hoyle believed that life on Earth could not have been created by accident; he took the human eye as an example of something far too complicated to have come about by chance or even by evolution over millions of years. He believed the template of life came from existing forms somewhere in outer-space.

Davis had a number of false starts with people like astronomer Patrick Moore, Professor Eric Laithwaite from Imperial College and scientist, pacifist, poet and novelist Alex Comfort (still yet to find his ultimate fame as author of *The Joy of Sex*). They only thought in what was possible and scientifically accurate, and did not let their imaginations run riot. Then, Innes Lloyd contacted his former colleagues at the Outside Broadcast Unit to see if someone in the 'science slot' knew anyone who had an imaginative and creative mind. Aubrey Singer was Head of Television OB Feature and Science Programmes, based in Kensington House, Richmond Way. He had been involved with the creation of a series called *R3*.

R3

The *R3* series followed the exploits of a team of scientists at a government funded research centre. *R3* was an attempt to break away from the old dramatic formulas and clichés which revolved around the scientist. The 'Boffins' were usually to be found solving crimes, inventing gadgets, defeating alien menaces or if they had a strong European accent, trying to take over the world. *R3* wanted to do to the scientist what *Z Cars* did for the policeman, take a realistic and hard look at their professional lives. Producer Andrew Osborn told a syndicated reporter who came down to watch the camera rehearsals for the second episode 'We are not concerned with the domestic lives of the people involved, or with the conventional dramatic situations. We do not go in for suspense as such nor can we dramatise science. The major advances – the discovery of antiseptic, chloroform, the X-ray, penicillin – are few and far between. So we are working on the things which happen to scientists, because they are scientists – the problems in which human beings are caught up in their pursuit of work … Our net is very wide but the scientific content is as accurate as our advisors can make it. This programme is an honest endeavour to be intelligent and entertaining at the same time.'

The article did not name any advisors. The *Radio Times* feature which launched the series in the autumn of 1964 did not name any advisors; neither did it explain that the concept and the majority of the storylines was the result of collaboration between a dramatist and an occasional BBC documentary presenter and broadcaster, Dr Stephen Black, who was currently directing a seven year ergonomic survey into the relationship between motor vehicles and drivers in order to improve safety. Unlike astronomer Fred Hoyle who contributed the ideas for *A For Andromeda,* or Kit Pedler, who was more than happy to become the public face of *Doomwatch*, the co-creator of *R3* was very comfortable to remain anonymous, even though his face was widely known on television at the time.

After a break, Black had resumed occasional broadcasting, making a series of documentaries beginning with *The Prizewinners* where he interviewed four British and one American Nobel prize winners for Chemistry and Medicine winners. In 1963, it was the turn of four cosmologists including Professor Hoyle and Professor Sir Bernard Lovell. Future series looked into atomic physicists, surgeons and mathematicians. There were few other people who could get under the skin of a scientist as well as Dr Stephen Black.

As well as co-authoring the format, Black was employed to provide storylines, vet scripts for accuracy and generally give advice. His co-author was Norman J Crisp, who had previously worked on the BBC's popular soap opera *Compact*. The first episode, 'A State of Anxiety', had the following plot:

Doctor Peter Travers has an idea for a complex experiment to study the effects of stress on the human body. The members of Travers' team like the idea, but Doctor May Howard wonders if it is all that safe. Doctor Fratton the Deputy Director of R3 is decidedly hesitant and cautious about it. Travers appeals to the Director, Sir Michael Gerrard (played by Quatermass actor John Robinson), who gives qualified permission – provided the right experimental subject can be found. Gerrard has just had a difficult session with Pomeroy from the Ministry. The grant for R3 is insufficient for Gerrard to complete the Molecular Biology section on which he has set his heart, and Gerrard wants one man to head it – Calvos. Unless Calvos has an early decision, he will go to Caltech in California. Pomeroy has agreed to present Gerrard's case again to the expert committee, though Gerrard has little faith in Pomeroy's abilities.

Travers has difficulty in finding his subject. The medical student who at first agreed proves not to be available. Preparations are far advanced, and, in desperation, Travers decides to be his own subject. Jill, Travers wife, discovers this, and asks Gerrard, through Miss Brooks, his personal secretary, if he knows that Travers was ill after a previous, rather similar, experiment. Gerrard vetoes Travers as a subject – and appoints himself. He is an ideal subject, but the team have not considered him because of his position. While the experiment, carried out under full surgical conditions, is going on, Pomeroy is arguing with the expert committee. Travers, who has inferred the importance of the expected phone call to Gerrard, is using the passage of time to create his state of anxiety in Gerrard. When a non-committal phone call comes through, the readings are, as Doctor Jack Morton says, 'beautiful.' But Gerrard collapses on the operating table. Travers takes emergency action. Gerrard is all right but, when he does take his phone call from Pomeroy, he finds that he has only half the additional money he wanted. He blames Pomeroy for not trying, but phones Calvos and confirms his appointment just the same. He knows that he will have to make economies elsewhere, but – he wanted Calvos, and now he has got him.

The series had been difficult to write, and many scripts and ideas fell through, and the storylines were handed over to different writers. Generally, the episodes were about the scientists. In 'The Patriot', one scientist wants to stop researching nuclear physics which he feels is endangering the world, and transfer his skills into cancer prevention, but pressure is put onto him to stay where he is. Another episode looked into what happens when a line of drugs is discovered to have unpleasant side effects and the lobbying involved to reverse the decision. This episode, 'Against the Stream', caused a letter of complaint from the pharmaceutical industry on the rather jaundiced characterisation of one of their number. The series ended with Dr Travers emigrating to America where science was better funded, a victim of the Brain Drain.

The second series saw R3 broaden its scope (and ditch most of its cast). It now featured a trouble-shooting consultancy, which allowed its new cast (although still headed by John Robinson as R3's boss) into more exciting, and dangerous areas, discovering why machines breakdown, the stresses put on the human being in a technological environment, such as high-atmospheric balloon tests or a deep sea bathysphere. It looked into, and ridiculed, faith-healing. The second series also saw R3 turn towards issues Doomwatch would embrace, such as pollution, nerve gas experiments and pesticide misuse.

From Aubrey Singer's point of view, R3 had to convince an audience which would include scientifically and technically orientated people, especially members of the BBC's own Scientific Consultative Committee, chaired by Professor Haddow, head of the Chester Beatty Research Institute, which studied cancer at the Royal Cancer Hospital on the Fulham Road. The view of science in 1964 was still positive, and the scientist, if not always a hero, remained within the traditional scope of a scientist.

R3 finished in 1965. The episode was about Dr Richard Franklin, played by Oliver Reed, turning his back on research and become a television pundit. He is talked out of it by professors he deeply respects, and that the television producers wanted him to generalise too much. The accusation of being a populist stings him back to 'his senses'. This was the environment Kit Pedler worked in, and later escaped from.

Later in 1965, someone in Kensington House, possibly Singer himself, or the producer of *Tomorrow's World*, suggested 'quite a radical thinker in their books': Dr Kit Pedler. The invitation by Lloyd and Davis to submit ideas for *Doctor Who* and act as its science *fiction* adviser was just the opening Pedler was looking for. Not only was it a chance to write, and perhaps make some extra money to support his family of four children, it also gave him an opportunity to explore and imagine the future, and draw upon views he was developing as a scientist of scientists, which might not have sat well with Haddow. It wasn't an altogether positive picture.

Doctor Who and the Cybermen
Pedler and Davis hit it off straight away and quickly developed an imaginative idea based on a new landmark Pedler could see growing from his laboratory window in Judd Street – the newly built Post Office Tower, a view which was also visible to Gerry Davis. They conceived of a computer that could hypnotise people through the telephone, which constructed massive War Machines (which were originally based on a human form, but translated by the designer into a more conventional and easier-to-operate tank). This idea was given first to Pat Dunlop to dramatise (who had been script editor on *Dr Finlay's Casebook* when Davis tried to write for it) and then to Ian Stuart Black.

Davis had a gift of getting the best out of his adviser, who loved science fiction in all its forms, from the comic strip antics of Dan Dare to the more literary end of the spectrum. He wanted proper science fiction ideas, based on today. 'I used to try and get him off the familiar themes and get back to what were basics. In other words, he was a scientist and I would say, "Okay, tell me something exciting that's happening in science," (like the thinning of the ozone layer) and I would take it from there and say, "Well, what could happen about this in time?" and build up the stories rather than saying, "Well, let's do a transmutation of matter story" or another familiar sci-fi cliché.'

Pedler wanted to write his own scripts. So far, he had only written a few book reviews for academic publications, and to craft four 25-minute scripts of affordable television, with each episode attempting to follow its own thread, is a skill many an experienced writer has fallen down upon. Nevertheless, after a lot of discussion with Davis, a *Doctor Who* story called 'The Tenth Planet' was born, and with it, the Cybermen. Pedler thought up the idea of the Cybermen in his large back garden at 119 Parkhill Road in Clapham whilst talking with his wife, Una. She recalled how the Cybermen were an expression of his own fear of himself – all intellect and no heart. Davis remembered it as a view of what would happen if spare-part surgery went too far: dehumanising medicine.

Pedler was a man who had spent a great deal of time in hospitals for a mystery ailment that had been only correctly diagnosed by the time he was rewriting his first four scripts. Davis helped Pedler to shape his drafts and visited him in hospital to discuss a writing partnership. Pedler had no agent at this point but fought back from his hospital bed in Tooting Bec when the BBC mistakenly assumed he had not delivered all of the scripts and had therefore not paid him his full fee. Davis made sure that he earned some extra money from the deal but took over the revisions and insisted on a co-credit and a fee.

'The Tenth Planet' featured a space-shot gone wrong, dehumanised medicine, technological quick-fixes, doomsday weapons and a dying world, crippled by its own scientific advances that had gone too far – *Doomwatch* in embryonic form. Indeed, an early idea for Pedler's script would eventually be made as a *Doomwatch* episode.

Gerry Davis learned through the experience of 'The Tenth Planet' Kit's strengths and weaknesses as a writer so by the time of *Doomwatch*, he knew how they could work together. 'Kit Pedler was flexible and he could write, not dramatically, but very movingly and well about science, and that's where we were sort of able to come together because he didn't really interfere with my dramatic side, and I didn't interfere with his scientific side. We both respected each other's abilities whereas if you get two writers together they've both got different ideas of drama and characters and you sometimes get a conflict going on and the same thing happens if you get two scientists together.'

Recovered from his operation to remove the lower gut, during which he technically 'died' on the operating table, Pedler wrote two more Cyberman serials with Davis. The first of these, 'The Moonbase', was credited solely to Pedler, and it gave him some publicity in the *Guardian* and on television in the form of *Late Night Line Up*. The BBC sought his advice on other projects, such as a BBC2 programme called *The Paradise Makers* script edited by Roger Parkes. This was a thriller written by Arden Winch about a physicist and a former spy infiltrating a corrupt scientific establishment. Pedler was also invited by Head of Series Andrew Osborn to comment on the pilot episode of the BBC1 science fiction series *Counterstrike*.

Pedler and Davis' third and final *Doctor Who* serial, 'The Tomb of the Cybermen', upset enough viewers for it to feature in the pilot edition of *Talkback*, where Kit Pedler fought his corner against criticisms from angry parents of too much horror and violence in a children's programme. This was in September 1967, and by now Gerry Davis had moved on from *Doctor Who* and was script editing *The First Lady* with his favourite producer, David Rose. Created by Alan Plater for actress Thora Hird, *The First Lady* was a Sunday night series about an independent councillor in a northern town, which explored the current social issues of its day. It was meant to be a hard-hitting and political programme but was toned down for its second series, moving towards human relationship issues.

Kit Pedler was still submitting ideas to *Doctor Who* whenever the production team wanted to use the popular Cybermen. With no Gerry Davis available to write the scripts with, he knew he couldn't do the job on his own; the ideas were again farmed out to other writers. His fifth and final submission was treated by the production team as mere formality in order to get the Cybermen back again; although they did not intend to use all of his ideas, they were trying to make him feel more involved after he complained about being used as a think-tank.

This was in the spring of 1968. Since leaving *Doctor Who* Davis and Pedler had continued meeting at their favourite fish-and-chip shop in Kensington to discuss future ideas. Gerry Davis remembered how 'Kit would come back from … conferences and say, "Do you realise what's happening?" and tell me about some dreadful ecological disaster that had been hushed up.' The lack of social and political awareness in scientists was an active idea in the air at the time, and it was beginning to bother Pedler, a man who had been re-evaluating his own life since his near-death experience in 1966: 'I looked outside my laboratory door and didn't like what I saw.' As the writer of a piece in a 1971 edition of *New Scientist* put it, 'He objected to what he felt was the way science and technology had got away from serving the human race, and instead was serving the advancement of individual careers (in the case of science) and company profits (in the case of technology).'

Early Voices of Dissent
Pedler wasn't the only one concerned by what was going on outside his own door. In 1967, Dr Maurice Henry Pappworth (who would be an adviser on the third series of *Doomwatch*) published a book called *Human Guinea Pigs*, based on an article he had written in 1962 for *Twentieth Century* magazine. He wrote that 'During the last twenty years clinical medicine, especially in the teaching hospitals, has become dominated by research workers whose primary interest is the extension of medical knowledge. Their concern with patients as such, that is individual people who are sick, tended to suffer as a result.' He was unsettled by articles from teams engaged in research in which 'extremely unpleasant and often dangerous experiments are performed on unsuspecting patients.' Doctors were concerned but felt powerless to stop it, and the public, he maintains, were unaware of what was happening to them. There was no informed consent. The Nuremberg Codes, drawn up in 1947 after the revelations of Nazi experiments on Jewish prisoners, was supposed to prevent such a thing happening again.

By 1968 there was a lot to be concerned about. Since the Second World War, the world had lived under the shadow of the ultimate scientific expression – the Bomb. An escalating arms race nearly led to the Third World War in 1962 during the Cuban Missile Crisis. The testing of these weapons was adding to the background radiation of the world, and testing was halted, at least in theory, in the early 60s. It was ironic that, now the world had a method with which to destroy itself quite comprehensively, the standard of living, especially in the West, was improving at least superficially. The age of mass production and consumption had arrived; life expectancies were increasing; technology was providing amazing leisure and business opportunities.

In 1962 the American journalist and anarchist theorist Murray Bookchin published *Our Synthetic Environment* under the pseudonym Lewis Herber. He had been studying the effects of the revolution on ordinary life by its invisible and visible consequences. He covered topics such as chemical hazards to human food supplies from pesticides (including DDT), synthetic hormones, antibiotics and additives. He advocated a rejection of industrialisation, centralisation, the profit motive and 'the most pernicious laws of the market place given precedence over the most compelling laws of biology'. The book flopped, barely noticed or reviewed, and when it was, it was dismissed.

Three months after *Our Synthetic Environment*, Rachel Carson attacked the pesticide culture in America. Her treatise, *Silent Spring*, was published in three issues of the *New Yorker* magazine and then as a book. The counter-attack had begun.

Another post-war concern was the population explosion, and with the publication of *The Population Bomb* by Paul Ehrlich in 1968 the issue became almost as big a concern as nuclear ones. The world had finite resources, not enough for the three billion people of the planet to share. He envisaged the next decade to be one of wars, riots, famines and invasions as more and more people fought over what there was to be had. Also published in 1968 was Gordon Rattray Taylor's *The Biological Time Bomb*. It studied theories and findings in genetic engineering and asked what did all this research into test-tube babies, heart transplants and so on mean for the future of mankind. Would the family unit become a thing of the past? Were there enough controls? Who was investigating the ethics of the matter? What will we turn into? Do we want this?

1968 contributed psychoanalyst Erich Fromm's *The Revolution of Hope: Towards A Humanized Technology*, in which he made a stark prediction of the future based on current trends. This time the focus wasn't on biology but on a relatively new development in computers. 'A spectre is stalking our midst whom only a few see with clarity. It is not the old ghost of communism or fascism. It is a new spectre: a completely mechanised society, devoted to maximal output and consumption, directed by computers; and in this social process, man himself is transformed into a part of the total machine, well fed and entertained, yet passive, unalive, and with little feeling. With the victory of the new society, individualism and privacy will have disappeared; feelings towards others will be engineered by psychological conditioning and other devices, or drugs which also serve a new kind of introspective experience.'

Pedler's Views

Pedler made similar comments in newspaper interviews in 1967 and developed them into a piece of speculative fiction for *The Listener* in 1969 called 'Deus Ex Machina?' The individual is losing his voice and is becoming irretrievably immersed in the complex system of increasingly intelligent artefacts around him ... Each day they flock to empty cubicles, take places, produce their required function, eat identical luncheon meat in their sandwiches, and talk about their identical subjects – the Cup final, knitting or last night's TV. Battery buildings for battery peoples ... Their lives and personalities are computerised, their output compared to a 'norm', even the time they spend in the lavatory is measured and allowed for ... He will be nothing.'

Pedler thought he could see the manipulation of ordinary people to accept what was being done for them in the name of science, progress and convenience, ignoring the long term and potentially lethal side effects. 'In my view, the most dangerous *Doomwatch* theme at present is the extent to which ordinary people have become conditioned to accept an intolerable environment.' In other words, where there's muck there's brass, but science could always be depended upon to come up with a quick technological fix as a solution – should it go wrong.

At this stage, Pedler was primarily concerned with the role and direction of the scientist, who he believed should come down from their ivory towers, forget their detachment and comment on the way their work was being used. Some were doing just that, as we have seen. They were yet to become the environmentalists as we would understand the term today, but something was starting around this time. In 1968, out of the student campuses and from the various campaigns against the end product and result of chemical weapons being used in the war in Vietnam, and the waste product generated by industrial and technical society. The word 'pollution' crept in. Environmentalism as a movement was conceived. The first Ecology Action group formed in America at the beginning of the year on the Berkeley campus in California. Pedler believed that 'the scientist is a citizen, and as such he has a complete responsibility as a citizen for the work he does. I don't think he can ever say, "Of course, it's up to a politician," or it's up to people or something. He is the people, he is concerned with politics.' Pedler later developed a mantra: 'No scientist shall by his professional ability harm a human or by inaction in this sphere allow a human being to come to harm.' Today's research, with its pure motives, could be tomorrow's killer – by design or by accident.

Gerry Davis realised that 'gradually, we began to find we thought alike about what was happening in the world. Without being aware of it, we were quietly cutting our throats.' Davis found that the fears he wanted to tap in Pedler for *Doctor Who* could make for an excellent drama series. The pair of them began to keep scrapbooks of worrying scientific advances, environmental hazards and disasters as reported in the press and journals – apparently thousands of them. 'It is quite clear to us', said Pedler, 'that there already is a real and deep-seated fear of science and technology and that this is firmly based on real life experience.'

There wasn't a better time to submit an eleven-page treatment to Gerry Davis' current boss at the BBC, the Head of Drama Series, Andrew Osborn, and call it *Doomwatch*.

2
'A Kind Of Science Fact-Fiction'

'We were not climbing on the environmental bandwagon. We felt a genuine concern about the crisis and wanted a dramatic format to bring it home to people because they were tired of documentaries which were preaching to the converted anyway.' Kit Pedler quoted in *Bath Chronicle* circa 1976.

'First of all, we set out to write entertaining stories, because if you want to preach a sermon people just switch off, but if you embed it in a dramatic story, they may stay listening.' Kit Pedler in *Hospital Times* 1970.

In early 1968 Dr Kit Pedler and Gerry Davis realised that they had the genesis of a good, original TV series, and Davis was positioned to sell formats to the BBC. This could be an exciting drama with a serious message to impart. It wasn't just a message for the public, but perhaps for some of Pedler's colleagues too. As a series on BBC1, it had a potentially huge audience to go out to. A documentary on BBC2 would attract a fraction of the viewers of a BBC1 drama. 'The man who impressed me most at the BBC', Davis told *The Listener* in 1988, 'was Huw Wheldon. He used to give us pep-talks, and ran home the message that the way to get information across was by telling a story.' Since the invention of kitchen sink drama, television was no stranger to giving a voice to playwrights who wanted to make a point. Indeed, it was encouraged to some extent.

Pedler told BBC Radio 4 listeners the basics in a programme recorded in January 1969 and broadcast in July called *Of Ombudsman and Cybermats*: 'It's about the first three scientific ombudsmen put out by a government to look into possible harmful effects of scientific research, and in it we find that our three characters keep coming up against all the various vested interests politically in the government, vested interests in science itself, and we try to write stories around this general theme … I think this is the function of the arts, to utter a warning and be imaginative about future prospects … It's certainly one function of the science fiction writer, in the best sense of it anyway.'

Kit Pedler recalled the thinking behind the name for *Doomwatch* in a paragraph cut from his introduction to a *Dan Dare* anthology in 1979: They needed to create a short, snappy title that would grab attention. After spending an afternoon by a blackboard experimenting with a combination of words such as 'monitor' and 'protector,' they put together two of the words already selected. 'We based part of our thinking on the psychology behind the OMO detergent logo. "Doom" looked good, it had the two eyes and an apocryphal ring, but its sound was two (sic) soft and soothing so we added on "-Watch" which had a clipped, whip-like sound. The two syllables matched well together, fell easily off the tongue and above all looked right.' *Doomwatch* made more than a perfect, if downbeat, title. 'And now we have just discovered, with some amazement, that we have put a new word into the Oxford Dictionary.'

The Original Format
Pedler and Davis needed to write a format first. How would the programme work? What would be its dynamics? It ran as follows:

> Scientific research has now advanced to the stage where, unless carefully monitored, mankind's greatest hazard may well be from his own discoveries. Already we have the nuclear bomb, rising radiation levels, the risks of poisoning by insecticides. How many other scientific advances will prove double-edged weapons unless handled with great vision and restraint?
>
> The time will certainly come when a measure of governmental control will have to be devised to keep tabs on the long range effects of the various discoveries made in private and public work shops and laboratories.
>
> To perform this task a group of exceptional men must be assembled. In the wrong hands, administered with too much power, such a check could be as disastrous as the effect of the Inquisition upon Galileo. The group must therefore be much more than trained scientists – they must be men of vision, able to estimate the long term implications of an investigation. They must process the capacity for taking quick decisions and, occasionally, direct action to avert a possible disaster.
>
> They will probably operate as a semi-secret department under a code name.
>
> This series takes a look forward at the possible situations that could evolve.
>
> We call our group "DOOMWATCH".

The series is set in present day Britain. A newly formed Government have been elected on a main platform of concern for the individual against the encroachment of the State and technological advance. The people of Britain have become increasingly disturbed about many of the after-effects of current industrial, medical and fundamental scientific-research.

The "Ombudsman" department has been enlarged but is clearly incapable of dealing with increasing complaints on the lines of "Silent spring", destruction of wild life, pollution of the seas with atomic wastes, tanker oil fouling the beaches, missing H-bombs, etc.

For this reason, the Cabinet, through the Ministry of Defence, have decided to set up a small group to study the effects of ethical/moral problems arising from specific research activities.

On the surface, the group, code-named "Doomwatch", is a little more than the equivalent of a Royal Commission and is quickly forgotten by the public since it is clear that any information they might produce will not be forthcoming for some months or years.

What has not been made public, however, is the fact that the group is very well financed and has been given the brief not only of investigating and making reports but also taking action. Thus, if any technological danger arises they are empowered to put it right.

When the series opens, several months after the inauguration of the Department, it has become obvious to Dr QUIST, the Head of Doomwatch, that the Government have had cold feet about the amount of freedom and initiative to be allowed him and his team. The pressures of both private industry and Governmental research installations, alarmed at the reports circulating regarding the powers of Doomwatch, have resulted in the Minister (of Defence), who is responsible for the Department, clamping down in the project and trying to clip their wings.

This process proves much more difficult than anticipated,

however, because they have failed to take into account the full character and calibre of Dr QUIST.

As one of Britain's Nobel Prize winners, he was carefully picked for the job and his appointment received the maximum amount of publicity.

Once given his mandate, he refuses to be influenced by the blow hot, blow cold currents of higher politics. He has been given a job to do and he intends to carry it through – no matter what.

He remains impervious to either threats or the bribes of a title, or a higher paid job, and his dismissal would lead to exactly the kind of searching publicity as to the function and effectiveness of Doomwatch that the Government are so anxious to avoid.

The Minister, therefore, starts a steady campaign of attrition to wear QUIST down, demolish his enthusiasm for the post and drive him to resign.

But in QUIST they have chosen the last man ever to submit to threats, pressure or bribes. A man of fanatical dedication to his job, and a deep-seated personal reason for wanting to make a success of it.

The format then runs through the character story of Dr Spencer Quist, Dr John Paul Ridge and Toby Wren, with brief notes on Colin Bradley and the secretary Pat Hunnisett.

The group is housed in a converted, but closed, church in Westminster. On the outside of the building there are 'Keep Out' 'Dangerous Building' notices. Inside and down in the crypt, there are offices, bedsitters, a laboratory and a communications room.

In the laboratory is a combined analogue-digital computer. This looks on the outside to be conventional but has 'graphic' read-out facilities: that is, any item of information that is recalled from it can be displayed on the screen. Print-out facilities also exist thus, given certain co-ordinate information about events, the machine can formulate strategies in much the same way as the war game machine of the Rand Corporation.

Thus the activities of the group can, when necessary, be planned by the machine, although the members may not necessarily take the advice of the machine.

Further Notes: -
The men of Doomwatch are by no means omnipotent supermen. There are many failures on their files. On two occasions the computer "Doomwatch" has broken down or its messages jammed with disastrous results.

Sometimes their on-the-spot evaluation of a situation causes them to disregard the computer's advice. WREN habitually follows his own line of enquiry with varying results.

All too often they work against the direct instructions., or prohibitions of their official brief. This puts not only their jobs in jeopardy but, confronted with police, troops etc. they could face a possible prison sentence or bullet.

One of the minor irritations of being, even loosely, a government department means that right in the middle of an urgent investigation they are apt to be side-tracked by trivial cases sent on from other departments.

They are apt to retaliate by using the latest scientific discoveries to create confusion among the more parasitic and time-wasting of their colleagues. For example, a carefully administered paper-destroying virus planned to eradicate files shortly to be passed over to them.

These activities provide a little light relief from the high tensions of their main job besides identifying them in the Civil Service as a department to be left strictly alone.

As described, the team investigate the moral and ethical implications in scientific research with a thriller element attached. The format did not describe the intention of having a strong scientific basis towards each episode, nor that they would be looking at current issues and giving them a science fiction twist. Also lacking is any example of the type of story the series would present.

The format for *Doomwatch* was submitted to Andrew Osborn in May 1968 with the encouragement of Davis' current producer, David Rose. The previous month, the Club of Rome had been created. This was a think tank of 'a group of world citizens, sharing a common concern for the future of humanity'.

Andrew Osborn

Series was one of the three departments within the drama group created by Sydney Newman in 1963. Its head, Andrew Osborn, was born in 1910, starting off as an actor before moving over, like so many others, into production at the BBC. The last of the many series that he produced was the first series of *R3*, after which he was promoted to his current position. He had also produced *Doctor Finlay's Casebook*, and earlier, the successful French detective series *Maigret*.

As Head of Series, Osborn was effectively an executive producer of many different programmes on both BBC1 and BBC2. He is remembered with great affection by those who worked under him as a very supportive man, but one who brooked no nonsense. Judy Bedford, Terence Dudley's secretary, remembered how Osborn would sometimes need to bring order to his band of producers and staff. 'Andrew Osborn was a former actor and seemed to miss having an audience, so he'd often summon an all-staff meeting where he'd address us in his rather histrionic style, peppering his speech with lots of standard phrases that he used all the time. ("We don't want any mavericks in the pack; we're not running a little show at the end of Brighton Pier – this is the biggest programme making organisation in the world"; and others I've forgotten). All delivered in a resonant tone with big gestures as he paced up and down.'

Andrew Osborn liked the *Doomwatch* format and saw its potential despite apparent misgivings about the gloomy title. On Monday, 13 May, Osborn contacted John Henderson, the assistant head of copyright, to commission a pilot script and iron out any difficulties over Gerry Davis collaborating with Kit Pedler. Henderson replied the next day that, like a similar situation with a programme being developed called *The Regiment*, Davis could assign all his rights to Pedler, with whom the BBC could then deal. Henderson needed to check with BBC staff regulations before he could go any further. As with his *Doctor Who* scripts and the rights to the Cybermen, Gerry Davis wanted a 50/50 split, which Pedler felt reflected the creative collaboration.

'If I had attempted to write the series on my own I would have been bogged down by boring details and my characters would have been involved in talking rather than action situations,' Pedler told a Lincoln newspaper at the end of February 1970. 'I had a head full of knowledge and Gerry has an intuitive dramatic instinct.'

On 24 June 'Gerald Davis' was cleared to collaborate on writing the first script since he 'is the most obvious and suitable person to collaborate with [Pedler] on this pilot script.' When the script was commissioned, Pedler would receive £137. 10s. out of his £275 writing fee in advance (which in this case was authorised on 23 July) and the rest on delivery, whilst Gerry Davis would be paid his full £275 on the script's acceptance, which was on 8 August.

Pedler was busy with his academic life, which he was starting to find was losing its appeal despite some of the exciting work he was currently engaged with, pioneering new understandings of how vision worked. He would write late at night until around two o'clock in the morning and do more thinking before he left home for work in one of his sports cars. He would write with Gerry at the weekends, often with a bottle of wine or two.

As the pilot episode was being written, Davis continued with his day job as script editor on *The First Lady*, and in July was commissioned to write a script for it called 'Take-Over Bid'. David Rose, who might have produced *Doomwatch*, had left and like Osborn, entered management. Davis had a new boss to work with.

Terence Dudley

Born in Hong Kong in 1919, Dudley spent the Second World War on one of the occupied Channel Islands, After the war he left Guernsey and spent a fulfilling eighteen months with his wife, the Jersey born Marjorie Baker, as a producer at the Connaught Theatre in Worthing where he produced some seventy plays. In 1950, he moved to the Ventnor in the Isle of Wight and then from 1952, he became assistant to Maude Edwards and her repertory company at the Grand Theatre in Swansea. At one point he apparently rented a shed at the bottom of Dylan Thomas' garden, probably in the garden of his birthplace in Swansea. Following Edwards' dismissal by the theatre over a row about money, Dudley was invited to take over the company and soon found himself in direction competition with Edwards at the Palace Theatre. Dudley became something of a one-man band during his repertory days, sometimes performing and directing his own written plays.

Swansea wasn't big enough to support two repertory companies, and despite some good notices, neither venture lasted more than a couple of years. Dudley's was the first to go under in 1955, the year independent television started. Together with his wife, he settled in London and while he carried on in the theatre, she got a job as a production assistant at ABC Television [which later became Thames Television] and worked her way up to become a features producer. His final theatrical production was directing a Victorian musical called *Meet Me By Moonlight* which transferred from Salisbury to the Aldwych Theatre, which featured a young Jeremy Brett in the cast. A forty-five minutes excerpt was broadcast on the BBC in September 1957 as part of their *Theatre Night* strand, presumably designed to encourage more people to go back to the dying theatres.

Dudley saw the future and joined the BBC in 1958. With his excellent background in theatre, Dudley entered the BBC's producer-director training course. These were the days when a director and a producer were often the same man, and scripts were handled by the Script Department. This would soon be phased out and replaced by the production team format of a director and script editor being overseen by a producer. He earned a reputation for being a decent thriller producer, who could also write. Dudley's writing credits included the six-part Sunday thriller *The River Flows East* in 1962

In 1962, Dudley directed and produced a science fiction serial with a *Doomwatch* flavour. *The Big Pull* was written by actor Robert Gould, who was inspired by recent high atmospheric nuclear explosions conducted by the Americans who wanted to see their effects upon the Van Allen Belt which encircles our planet. A first-time writer, Gould's script was recommended to Dudley who immediately saw its potential. It could have been a remake of *The Quatermass Experiment* with its plot featuring an American astronaut who dies after returning to Earth, yet his memories are absorbed by the capsule designer.

He produced and directed episodes from the espionage series *The Mask of Janus* starring Simon Oates, which featured location filming in Malta, before a spell of regional dramas such as *Dr Finlay's Casebook*, the Yorkshire detective *Cluff*, and then *The First Lady*. He was still able to write, direct and produce the same episode. He also wrote a play for BBC2's Theatre 625 called *A Piece of Resistance*, concerning the German occupation of Jersey. This was a comedy shown on Boxing day in 1965.

While certainly talented, he wasn't always an altogether easy man to work with, something he would blame on a childhood attack of meningitis. During this period, he divorced his wife. Their marriage had been childless. Judy Bedford who worked for him at the BBC remembers he was a very particular man. 'In all honesty Terry could be difficult. He had very strong likes and dislikes – he either liked a person or definitely didn't. If he liked you he'd be endlessly supportive, patient, encouraging and generous. If not then [he] could be judgemental – generally he would avoid people he didn't like rather than engage in open confrontation. He had very firm views about proper grammar and English usage – if a letter contained a grammatical error he would refuse to read it and throw it in the bin. A person could damage their reputation for ever with Terry by using a split infinitive. But he knew his own deficiencies and could be very open about his shortcomings with trusted associates. He had a sophisticated sense of humour, and enjoyed irony – often at the expense of those he saw as arrogant or bombastic. He disliked anyone who he felt was full of their own importance and loved to deflate them.'

As we have seen, he found Andrew Osborn's 'prep talks' a great source of amusement. 'This made Terry collapse with laughter the minute the performance started, so we had to sit at the back and try to hide him. Terry had a word-perfect imitation of Andrew and would perform his version at the slightest opportunity.'

Interviewed by Anthony Howe in the late 1980s (reproduced in the third volume of *Talkback: The Unofficial and Unauthorised Doctor Who Interview Book*) Dudley remembered in later years that it was Gerry Davis who came to him with the *Doomwatch* format through Andrew Osborn. *The First Lady* had attracted Dudley as it 'allowed for a certain amount of serious social comment.' It may have been this that made Gerry Davis and Andrew Osborn think that Dudley could be the ideal producer for a programme like *Doomwatch* and its concerns; he also had experience in thrillers and science fiction. In Dudley's own words, the format captivated him, as indeed did Kit Pedler. 'Dr Pedler was, in my view, a great man with a gut mission in life, which I admired and respected.' If it was to go ahead, it would be developed concurrently with *The First Lady* until the current (and, as it turned out, last) series finished production.

Doomwriters

By the middle of September 1968, the Head of Series was about to engage in serious discussions about the pilot script – now called 'The Plastic Eaters' – which he thought it needed considerable revision: 'That is not to say that I do not believe the idea to be an excellent one or that there is anything in the script which cannot be put right. This is a strong contender for a pilot slot early next year.' He was keenly interested in the programme and its potential, and had recently told Gerry Davis so. Encouraging words indeed for Dr Pedler, who had written to Osborn on Friday, 13 September 1968, having just returned from the Fourth European Regional Conference on Electron Microscopy in Rome:

> 'Although what I am going to write may seem to be an unashamed plug, I feel I must tell you about it. I have just returned from a conference of biologists and physicists in Rome. I went there to give a lecture. During the various meetings I brought up the question of *Doomwatch* to groups of scientists … The response was really quite remarkable. Everyone would immediately flood the conversation with ideas. It was as if the collective guilt of the scientific

community was suddenly unleashed and the most ingenious and in some cases appalling ideas were put forward. For example, an immunologist suggested a specific antigen which would attack the germ-plasma of a particular race: result – sterility. Given a racist immunologist in say Alabama and the colour problem would cease to exist in one and a half generations – and so on. The enthusiasm of the people in Rome for the idea of the series – I didn't mention it by name – was so extraordinary that I felt you might be interested.'

Soon, the series was given a tentative go-ahead. Production would not start for at least a year. By early November news of the project was spreading across the BBC writers' grapevine. Script editor Roger Parkes suggested to writer Jan Read (who had written episodes of *The Mask of Janus*) that he should contact Gerry Davis about writing for *Doomwatch*. Other writers already working on *The First Lady* were being sounded out, such as Harry Green and Hugh Forbes, although Davis did not want to start briefing writers until mid-December at the earliest. Forbes was sent a copy of the pilot script and saw at once difficulties and exciting possibilities. 'I think the whole idea is very difficult and very exciting,' he wrote on 4 December. 'The pilot script seems to solve all the problems admirably, with great drive, and the running characters are an intriguing bunch. Various thoughts arise, such as: Do lots of subjects have to be left out because they can't be personalised (such as industrial waste killing off fishing grounds)? Can the Minister always be involved as strongly and neatly as this, or who is our adversary? But no doubt part of the battle is to solve things like that. I look forward very much to working on it, and the sooner we can agree on a couple of subjects for me to mull over the better, as far as I'm concerned.'

For a start, there was a second script which he and Pedler were going to write together. This was commissioned in late November and was called 'Operation Neptune' which was about a sunken nuclear submarine and its effect on fish, turning them into man-eaters. On their contract, the theme of the series is expressed – as it would be on all subsequent writers' contracts: 'Adventure in the responsibilities implicit in scientific advancement when it ignores the human condition. A kind of science fact-fiction.'

Style of an episode
Plastic-eating viruses, embryo experiments, escaped nerve-gas cylinders, man-eating rats, killer sounds, lethal pesticides, food stuffs poisoned by pollution or by a banned wartime chemical and finally, a nuclear bomb lost in an air collision – unrecognised and counting down … Kit Pedler said in 1971: 'In each episode we take what seems to be a reasonable jump

forward from a real contemporary event and create an exciting story around it.'

The Doomwatch team act as scientific detectives and have to fight to discover the truth and act upon it as a given situation escalates. Here is an effect, what is the cause and thus what was the reason? Normally, an effect in *Doomwatch* is someone dying, falling ill or acting out of character. The effect is misdiagnosed to begin with by the authorities or even by the Doomwatch team themselves as something that is within the known sphere of things: perhaps suicide, drugs overdose or food poisoning. However, something does not add up correctly or an association with a project rings an alarm bell in the team, and they investigate to find out the true cause and the reason behind it: sloppy labs, ruthless business, cost-cutting and so on.

Doomwatch would investigate, not always willingly, and not always initiated by Quist. But once he got the scent that this was Doomwatch territory, he would launch an official enquiry, to be faced with obstructions from ministers or from the responsible parties themselves before a showdown, often akin to an Agatha Christie drawing-room scene. The answer would be found, but a solution to the problem was not always offered, or if it was, not always followed through by the authorities.

The series was not anti-science, but instead wanted to present a realistic view of how scientists would operate within such a field. Animal experimentation was the norm, and no-one on the team questions it or raises a moral objection, although a voice of dissent might be heard from secretary Pat Hunnisett. The authentic view in favour of such experiments was that it was either 'them or you', an attitude Kit Pedler once told his daughter Carol long before he too started to question and lobby to have them abolished. The subject of animal experimentation was one idea vetoed by Andrew Osborn when he was effectively the executive producer of *R3*. The script by David Chantler was called 'Leave My Dog Alone', featuring the concerns of the animal handler at *R3*, a disgruntled non-scientist. He worries about whether the dogs in his charge and suffering, and despite the actions of a bitter scientist on the verge of dismissal, his fears are demonstrated not to be true. The storyline went out of its way to present the scientist as caring and responsible. Osborn did not want to risk creating an out-cry from animal lovers by bringing such controversial subject matter to the screen. Not in the first year of his job, anyway.

The series was set not so much in the present day, but next Tuesday, as Gerry Davis once described it. There would be no visi-phones, experiments in transmats or scientists dabbling in hard science-fiction concepts. It would have to be based on real, current research or concerns that had the potential of being harmful to mankind. 'Our objective was to base every *Doomwatch* subject on something real, something that could happen and probably would in time if nobody took steps to stop it', Terence Dudley told the *Radio Times* in December 1970.

The Storylines
Naturally Davis and Pedler wanted control over the writing and direction of the series. They persuaded Terence Dudley to authorise an exclusivity in their interest in the matter of storylines. Osborn did not like this idea, despite practising something similar in the first series of *R3* with Dr Stephen Black and NJ Crisp. It had worked well in the first series, but the problems started in the second series when Black was side-lined in favour of different advisors, and started claiming fees when he spent a couple of hours in an office discussing ideas with the production team. The fee agreed for each storyline was a reflection on the Black incident, and was never as high. The situation did deteriorate into unpleasantness. History couldn't repeat itself, could it?

Dudley agreed to the idea, feeling that it would be in the best interests for the series as it would help with the factual nature of the science content of the stories. Each storyline begins with a statement of the theme and its relevance, such as dumping chemical weapons at sea. They then set up the story, introduce relevant characters and explore the incident which brings in Doomwatch. The storylines did allow enough scope and space for a writer to bring in his own imagination, and in the few that exist in Kit Pedler's surviving archive, the way a story ends is not described.

As well as writing the storylines and two of the scripts, Pedler would be on hand to offer scientific advice, should the writers need it, and comment on every script. Pedler waived any fee for being the programme's scientific adviser since 'his advice would be implicit in each storyline'.

By 18 December Terence Dudley had accepted the first four storylines, which would be handed out to writers who would then select a theme favourable to themselves. These were 'Check and Mate', 'The Logicians', 'The Devil's Sweets' and 'The Battery People'. The day before, Hugh Forbes, having just finished work on an episode of *The First Lady*, became the first outside writer commissioned to turn one of these storylines into a *Doomwatch* script. This would be 'Check and Mate'.

On 20 January 1969 the BBC drew up an agreement with Pedler's and Davis' agent, Harvey Unna, for *Doomwatch* – which had still yet to be confirmed for production. The BBC recognised that the sole copyright for *Doomwatch* lay in the hands of Unna's clients as a science fiction writing partnership and set out the agreements for publication, film and, merchandising rights. The BBC also agreed that both on screen and in the BBC's own weekly listing magazine, the *Radio Times*, the writers would have the credit 'Series created by Kit Pedler and Gerry Davis'.

On 29 January, Gerry Davis invited Arden Winch to write for the programme. On the face of it, Winch was an ideal candidate. As well as having written two scripts for *R3*, (one of which went out under the pseudonym Edwin Ranch), he had written in 1967 a six-part BBC2 thriller called *The Paradise Makers*, which was about a research physicist, asked by MI7 to penetrate a secretive consortium of the world's finest brains called the Independent Science Corporation. This mysterious outfit solves the government's scientific problems in return for a huge fee. Naturally, they are up to no good. Some of Winch's dialogue could have been written for Kit Pedler: 'I visualise a society in which we can programme the public as we programme a computer,' one character says. 'We supply it with the information it needs to produce the reactions we want.'

Kit Pedler was sent the script at the end of 1966 to give his view on how plausible and realistic the scientific set-up was portrayed. Kit was enthusiastic about the scripts. 'In fact,' wrote Kit, 'this particular plot is a popular fantasy of mine and I wish I had written it myself, dammit!' His comments were restricted into how plausible the Corporation was, and correct any obvious mistakes. 'One million volts out of the tube? Blimey! Super tube. Suggest 400 volts.' 'Micro miniaturisation has no meaning. Theoretical physicists would not work on this. It is an applied problem.' 'What on earth is a boosted transmitter?'

'I found myself in a scientific world I barely knew about, let alone understood,' Winch wrote as he declined the invitation to write for *Doomwatch*. 'At the moment I am not so much up to my neck in Vast Worthwhile Projects, which, as you know, rarely pay.' He wished them well and providing *Doomwatch* avoids the pitfalls which *R3* fell into 'week after week, you have something here.' Alas, he never elaborated on what those pitfalls were, but a popular complaint surrounding *R3* was how jargon heavy the dialogue could be, as would be expected from a conversation between two scientists. This was solved in the second series by ensuring a non-scientist was present to have things explained to. Since *Doomwatch* would feature a secretary and lay-members of the public, there would be people to have the plot explained to.

Another alleged failing of *R3* Andrew Osborn himself identified was that the series had been falling between two stools in that it wished to be realistic, and had conflicted with the need for strong dramatic situations, which was also addressed in the second series. Gerry Davis was an instinctive adventure writer, which could not be said for every writer or producer employed by the BBC. He could bring in the action when required. The question was, could his writers resist the temptation for lengthy desk-bound debates?

By the end of January, Jan Read and Turkish-born writer Moris Farhi had each been allocated a storyline to develop into a script – respectively, 'The Battery People' and 'The Pacifiers', about a new form of crowd control gas. Some of the writers were able to have a free hand in creating a plot based on the storylines just as long as they stuck to the theme.

In February Pedler and Davis had more synopses accepted by Terence Dudley, who liked the ideas of noise pollution in 'The Flames of Hell', computer training in 'The Logicians', genetic experiments in pest control in 'Rattus Sapiens?' and 'The Patrick Experiment', the last of these was a story inspired directly by current news events surrounding test-tube babies and was given to Harry Green to write up as 'Friday's Child'. A former schoolmaster and journalist, and an amateur archaeologist, Green had had a prolific career on radio before turning to television, writing 22 scripts for *Dr Finlay's Casebook* alone.

Don Shaw would be offered 'The Devil's Sweets', a story about drugs conditioning shopping habits. He was another former schoolmaster but now was an up-and-coming writer, who had first worked with Gerry Davis on *The First Lady* and had written a much praised *Thirty Minute Theatre* called 'A Question of Honour'. He was very excited to be writing for the series, having read Rachel Carson's *Silent Spring* earlier in the decade and been much taken by its warnings. As he himself puts it, 'I was never happier when writing about threats to our existence on Earth! It was all very adventurous in those golden years of TV. We all felt we were together on an exciting mission.'

As well as using whatever contacts they already built up for research purposes, writers would find *New Scientist* magazine an excellent source for information, and, perhaps most usefully, Dr Kit Pedler was only ever a telephone call away. After all, he was not only a scientist, but a medically trained doctor, anatomist and retinal researcher, with a smattering of cybernetics and computers. He could not be expected to know the full details of every scientific discipline under the sun, but he could find things out.

Judy Bedford: 'I have good memories of Kit Pedler. He was very involved in the science of the series and maintained a sense of reality when "creative" types came up with silly ideas. While I think he enjoyed the fun of being involved in drama production, his conversation was very much around his work at the Institute, or science in general, and the notion of ecology and environmental issues which were quite novel at the time. He was also very much still a medical doctor in the sense that he was always immediately concerned if you had symptoms of illness and wanted to know more, ask questions, suggest remedies and so on. Kit had a self-deprecating sense of humour. For example, I remember he had a sports car and made jokes about himself as a bald geriatric who bought the car while he could still manage to struggle to get in and out of it.'

Growing Frustrations

By June *Doomwatch* was under active consideration. Andrew Osborn needed to see scripts, but Dudley was not happy with the level to which he felt Pedler and Davis were writing. The only script delivered so far of which he totally approved was 'Friday's Child', and this was the one he thought should be seen as the series' yardstick. As he explained to Osborn when sending him a script to read: 'Entre nous, Pedler is brilliant in his field but doesn't understand (or chooses not to understand) the nature of the Civil Servant animal and consequently underestimates the Doomwatch opposition. The characterisation in his two direct contributions (with Gerry) needs to be much tougher-minded and a good deal more sophisticated.'

Dudley wanted the characters to be true to themselves. Pedler and Davis may have been strongly opposed to the 'mad scientist' portrayal of villainy, but in Dudley's words in *Talkback*, 'We quarrelled about over-simplification that Kit particularly wanted in the characterisation of Doomwatch's opposition. I felt that it was too tendentious – and too like propaganda, actually, to be dramatically viable ... Dr Pedler was, in my view, a great man with a mission in life, which I admired and respected. Unfortunately, he was so obsessive with the message of the series that he was convinced that all the villains should be depicted as fools or rogues, and I felt that to fall in with this view would depreciate the format. Aunt Sallies don't make for much opposition.'

The 'villains' of the piece would be people with true motivations, working under financial or political pressures to get results, unable to accept the consequences of what they were doing. Others were just selfish or greedy or plain careless. Dudley never lost sight of the fact that their job was primarily to entertain. This did not mean he did not have sympathy with the message, but he wanted to do it his way.

Dudley had already seen through certain changes to the format. He wanted a far more realistic view of dealings with the civil service but did not want an easily identifiable government department. The Ministry for National Security was created, which replaced the original idea of Doomwatch coming under the purview of the Ministry of Defence. The idea of having the same Minister or a regular civil servant to act as an 'official' protagonist and appear in a number of episodes appears to have been considered very early on indeed, but since Doomwatch would cover a wide variety of briefs, and as such liaise with different ministerial departments, this was dropped. Presumably this was also to prevent having to engage a sixth actor on a long-term contract with a minimum number of episodes.

The producer was determined to get the scripts up to scratch and told his head of department this in no uncertain terms. He alone chose which

41

scripts went into production, and his very strong views were not to be ignored. At least, not yet.

Rejections and Replacements

Not every writer commissioned could produce the type of story required, at least not to Dudley's own satisfaction. Despite rewrites, Farhi, Read and Forbes all had their scripts turned down. Forbes' was rejected at the end of April. Moris Farhi's script, now called 'Any Man's Death', was rejected in May because of concerns about characterisation and dialogue. Despite the 'amount of effort and vitality' put into the script, it did not do justice 'to the deep issues implicit in the theme'. Gerry Davis added 'Sorry!'

Jan Read's story, retitled 'How Safe Is Safe', was abandoned in July; Dudley thought the script was expensive, dull, pedestrian, and contrived. 'It's not got an honest, inevitable flow!' He did not like the characterisation of the students or the police, despite the writer's painstaking attempts to get it authenticated by students and a senior policeman.

How Pedler or Davis felt about this is not clear. Davis had certainly worked for some tough producers before, such as Innes Lloyd on *Doctor Who*, and had nurtured people's ideas to script stage only sometimes to reject them.

Judy Bedford: 'Gerry Davis wasn't very prominent in the team dynamic – I was very young at the time of the first *Doomwatch* series so not very sophisticated in understanding nuances in relationships. It always seemed to me that Gerry took a hands-off approach to the work, but I wonder how much that had to do with his relationship with Terry and what that was like. Gerry doesn't feature very much in my memories of the group surrounding *Doomwatch*. He was either not in the office (probably working with writers elsewhere), or if he was in his office he tended to stay there. Terry could be very funny and could be very witty and entertaining when he was in the mood, and we'd all sit around and enjoy the joke and his "performances", but I don't recall Gerry joining in a lot of the time.'

More storylines were accepted at the top of July, and old ones such as 'The Pacifiers' and 'The Battery People' were cast aside. The new stories were 'Hear No Evil', which was about a workforce being bugged, 'The Synthetic Candidate', concerning the creation of a perfect politician, 'Burial at Sea', deep-sea dumping of chemical waste, and 'Re-Entry Forbidden', a story featuring nuclear powered rockets. The first three of these already had writers assigned to them. Another two storylines would be needed to replace the rejected stories, although the invasion of privacy ideas from 'Check and Mate' would be given to N J Crisp, who had been sounded out earlier in the year to write for the series but was not available until September. Norman Crisp was almost an obvious choice of writer, who since co-creating *R3*, had won the 1967 Writer's Guild award for series writing. With Gerard Glaister, Crisp later invented *The Expert*, a series about a Home Office pathologist using the latest forensic techniques for solving unexplained deaths. His script for *Doomwatch* was to be entitled 'Careless Talk'.

Stalwart ITC writer and another former *Doctor Who* script editor, Dennis Spooner, was assigned 'Burial at Sea', whilst veteran and progressive BBC writer Elwyn Jones, was given 'The Synthetic Candidate'. A former journalist and TV editor of the *Radio Times*, Jones had been head of the Dramatised Documentary Unit within BBC Drama in the 1950s and early 1960s, which gave birth to *Z-Cars*, a new type of realistic and contemporary police drama series at a time when *Dixon of Dock Green* was giving a very much idealised light entertainment version of reality. He was acting head of drama before relinquishing the role to Sydney Newman in 1962, and was made the first Head of Series, before he resigned two years later, having never been happy within the Drama Group system Newman had devised. Now working freelance, he had been yet another writer for *The First Lady* and had written extensively for *Softly, Softly*, a sequel to *Z-Cars*. He had attempted a couple of scripts for *R3* but they were not considered suitable. Davis once described him as a striking and illustrious man who should have run the BBC. Jones was reformatting *Softly, Softly* during 1969 as it was going into colour and relocating it to a different part of the country. 'The Synthetic Candidate' would be dropped and a story about hormones in chicken feed was given to Jones and would go out as 'The Battery People'. Pedler was never one to waste a good title; he had used it in his 1969 essay for *The Listener* and would do so again in a lecture in 1974.

As the scripts came in, Dudley was seconded to the Plays Department to direct a *Play of the Month* production of 'The Heiress', starring Eileen Atkins and Vincent Price. Terence Dudley himself tackled the storyline which appealed to him about genetically modified rats, called 'Rattus Sapiens?' Judy Bedford: 'My sense was that Terry's first love was the theatre, but a close second would be writing. While he enjoyed being a producer I think he still loved the excitement of being directly involved in production, so he liked to direct himself occasionally. He also had a tendency to make a personal appearance in a walk-on part in his own productions whenever the opportunity arose. But I always felt he was happiest sitting in his room writing (or re-writing).'

Second Chances
Both Harry Green and Don Shaw were asked to contribute second scripts. Green was given the invasion of privacy story 'Hear No Evil' and Shaw was offered 'Re-Entry Forbidden', a tale of nuclear-powered rockets. With Green, things turned sour because of last-minute changes requested by the

director, and Terence Dudley's own confusion over the story. Green's pride was hurt – these changes conflicted with what Gerry Davis had wanted from him. He had already been commissioned to write a third story, 'The Iron Doctor'. This storyline about computerised medicine was a replacement for 'The Flames of Hell' which was pulled from the writing pool and written by Pedler and Davis as their second script, later known as 'The Red Sky'. Their original story, 'Operation Neptune', sank without trace. Green delivered his script and attended a meeting where he soon realised he was being told to make what amounted to a total revision. He withdrew from the project and left *Doomwatch* behind, entering the world of *Jude The Obscure*. By October, just as pre-production began, Pedler and Davis were planning to write 'Survival Code', an episode about an accident with a nuclear bomb which would wrap up the series.

While the series was being recorded, scripts were still being commissioned or rewritten. 'Train and De-Train' was Don Shaw's third script, and Gerry Davis rewrote 'Hear No Evil' along the lines wanted by Dudley, before rewriting N J Crisp's 'Careless Talk' (aka 'The Lord of the Humans'), though the latter was dropped. Terence Dudley also wrote one more script, originally titled 'Pollution Inc', but which became 'Spectre at the Feast'. The storylines for the first and last of these stories were accepted as late as March 1970, even as the series was being transmitted.

Anticipation
The programme had just about made it. It had taken over a year to get thirteen usable stories, with seven rejections, at least four write-offs and two major rewrites. The producer was winning his demand for what he viewed as high standards. At this point Pedler's and Davis' relationships with Terence Dudley were not as strained as they would later become. But it was clear that the project was an exciting and original one. Judy Bedford recalls 'During the making of the first series there was a sense that this was something new and exciting and the messaging was about important issues. Although I'd have to say my experience of TV production people in general is that there can be a tendency to dramatise oneself! Having said that, I think it probably was quite different to anything that had been produced before. I can certainly remember people talking about the environmental damage concerns (particularly Kit) and the Club of Rome, which had only recently been founded. There was a lot of discussion about sustainability (or lack of) among the production team and in particular I remember concerns about the need to reduce population (or at least stop increasing at the same rate). It all seemed quite new to me at the time and it certainly wasn't anything I'd heard at school or read about previously.'

On the morning of the first transmission, the *Daily Mail* printed an interview with Kit Pedler entitled 'This Dr Who for Adults is a Real

Horror.' 'Yes, you could say Dr Quist is my other self ... I'm absolutely hooked on *Doomwatch*. Writing it gave me some sort of God complex – for about five minutes. But I hope the serious message gets across through the entertainment. *Doctor Who* was strictly for children, but this is aimed at adults who are apathetic in their private nirvana of the telly, supermarkets, bingo, and all the superficial stimuli. One of my hobby horses is the loss of individualism – the abnegation of the human quality. We are becoming units instead of people. I am horrified by our impotence to stop it. I hope *Doomwatch* will show us the real dangers of hyper-civilisation.'

A second series was commissioned. They would have to do it all over again, but this time quicker.

3
Making Doomwatch

'The first thing I said to Terry Dudley when he asked me to do *Doomwatch* was "You can't seriously be thinking of doing a programme called *Doomwatch*!"' Jonathan Alwyn, director.

'The authors became used to solving the problems of how to mount a global environmental drama and make it realistic on a shoe-string budget.' Extra from Kit Pedler and Gerry Davis' publicity notes, mid 70s.

Glyn Edwards was Terence Dudley's right-hand man for the entire three years *Doomwatch* was in production. 'In the 60s and 70s, BBC TV Drama was split into three departments: Plays, Series and Serials. I worked in Series as a Production Assistant – later known as Production Manager – that was as Assistant to the Director. In the late 60s it was decided that producers should have help with the planning and costing of a series. I had already worked with Terry Dudley as his PA on *Softly, Softly* and was allocated to him on *Doomwatch* as assistant.'

BBC1 dramas were from now on, being made in colour, and a new computerised costing system was making a producer's job far more complicated. 'My job was to cost the series, episode by episode, allocate a budget to each director, organise that the facilities needed, such as studio and location filming time, were in place and keep a close watch on the final expenditure. Obviously not every episode was identical in this respect. I was also sometimes present at script meetings and casting sessions for regular artists. The role one played apart from the costing and budget responsibilities actually differed with each producer. Some producers were very hands on, others insisted on involving you in all aspects of production which Terry was to some degree, and some, I am sorry to say, were bone idle and took all of the credit and none of the blame – no names no pack drill!'

Edwards' credit of 'Assistant to Producer' was unusual in those days, where production personnel were not credited in depth at the end of a programme and seldom got a *Radio Times* credit. 'It was on the occasion of 'Tomorrow the Rat' that Terry said that, with him in the director's seat in the gallery and having written the script himself, I should act as substitute producer and therefore get a screen credit. As this was the first time this had happened in the department, we had no idea of what the credit should be, so Assistant to the Producer came about. This credit appeared each time Terry either wrote or directed an episode and eventually, I think thanks to Adele [Paul, now Winston], on most other episodes as well. Actually, it started a trend in the department when producers' assistants on other series started to ask for and get credits also!'

The Directors and Crew
The directors assigned were a mixture of staff allocated to the Series department, and freelancers. Jonathan Alwyn was freelance and booked to direct three episodes, as was staff director Paul Ciappessoni. David Proudfoot did two episodes, whilst Eric Hills, Vere Lorrimer, Frank Cox, Hugh David and Terence Dudley himself handled one each. Paul Ciappessoni had directed episodes of *Dr Finlay's Casebook*, *The Spies*, three very notable episodes of *Adam Adamant Lives!*, *Softly, Softly* and *The First Lady*. Jonathan Alwyn had worked on early instalments of *The Avengers* for ABC (including the very first episode recorded with Honor Blackman, 'Death Dispatch', although it was not the first of hers to be transmitted). 'I had been on the staff at ABC Television before that had merged with Associated Rediffusion to become Thames and then I went freelance although inevitably I worked mostly for Thames in the first few years. I then went to the BBC and did a *Dr Finlay's Casebook* up in Scotland ['Single or Return', transmitted 22 June 1969] and that led to a BBC series in London called *Detective*. One thing leads to another. I remember when I did *The Onedin Line* the only reason I got that was because I happened to be in the gents at the same time as the producer. He asked if I was by any chance free?

'The first thing I said to Terry Dudley when he asked me to do the programme was "You can't seriously be thinking of doing a programme called *Doomwatch*!" It seemed to be a fair title for people to turn round and say "Well titled!" which indeed they did but for good reasons and not for the obvious ones I was suggesting. Terence Dudley was a difficult cuss in his way. He was a bit autocratic but he got the whole thing going and believed in it as a crusading series and was very supportive.'

Eric Hills had known Terence Dudley since he had joined the BBC in the late 1950s. 'I was working in the BBC as a production assistant and Terence Dudley arrived having done the general director's course, and he came and did his first programme as a director and I was his PA. He was a great bloke, a very nice man. He used me quite lot as a director.' Hills had previously directed episodes of *Cluff* and *The First Lady* for Dudley.

Dorothea Wallace would be the costume supervisor for the entire series. She had to settle the styles for the main characters and provide an awful lot of white coats for the scientists. Likewise, the make-up for the whole of the first series was created by Elizabeth Rowell. Rowell worked for the BBC for thirty-one years, with *The Troubleshooters* being an early credit. *Doomwatch* was one of the first productions she had worked on in colour, having recently been retrained. In later years she worked on such notable successes as *Tinker Tailor Soldier Spy*, *Smiley's People*, *The Barchester Chronicles* and *The Lives and Loves of a She-Devil*, receiving three BAFTA nominations. 'On *Doomwatch*, which was a modern programme, you ring up the ladies beforehand well in advance in case there is something you have to do that is special like a hair-cut or if the director wanted something done to them and you had to find out if they're allergic to some make-up. But normally you meet people at the first read-through, certainly on a modern series. I met Kit Pedler at the read-throughs and often he would be with Gerry Davis in the gallery in the recordings.' She would also be called to provide some gruesome make-up as the series went along.

Casting the Actors
John Paul

John Paul was just two years younger than the fifty-year-old character of Dr Spencer Quist when he won the role in 1969. He came from a Suffolk family and was educated at Harrow and Cambridge. A very fit man, he played rackets every week at Harrow, where two of his five sons were being educated, and had played for the school before the war. During the Second World War he was captured in North Africa, in 1942. He spent the rest of the war in prison camps in Germany and Italy, where he developed an interest in acting. After the war he joined the Birmingham Repertory Company and slowly branched out into theatre, TV and film work. On television he was in *Emergency Ward 10*, *Dial 999* and *The Avengers*.

John Paul was best-known for his role in ATV's *Probation Officer*, for which he was still remembered by the media when he made his debut as Quist. That had been a live television production, and John Paul told director Darrol Blake of instances where actors would be sick into the fire buckets with nerves. It was a very successful series, watched by nearly thirteen million viewers in 1961. This came to an end when the actors' trade union Equity called a strike which affected ITV's drama output for nearly six months. When it was resolved in 1962, John Paul and his agent wanted to renegotiate a new fee. ATV disagreed and sacked him, replacing him with Windsor Davies. Embarrassingly, the acting trade newspaper *The Stage and Television Today* reported Paul had wanted a fee increase from £450 to £850 per episode. Davies, they reported, would be paid a mere £160. Paul's agent, Gordon Harbord, wrote to the paper to correct their account: 'John Paul was receiving £250 a week prior to the strike, not £450 as stated in your lead story. I asked for the amount to be increased to a weekly salary of £400. ATV offered him exactly the same salary as he had been receiving before the strike, but he felt that on a question of principle – the whole purpose of the strike – this was a reasonable increase, in accordance with a sliding scale worked out by the Personal Managers' Association in relation to higher salaried artists.'

John Paul was instantly snapped up by the BBC and featured in their adaption of *Swallows and Amazons*, transmitted the following year. In a 1963 interview with *The Stage*, he put his casting down to having grown a beard. 'People always said I would suffer after *Probation Officer* but I grew this beard and I've been very grateful to it for it suits all kinds of roles, from a kindly uncle in a children's serial to a psychiatrist in one play and a murderer in another, besides the role of an advertising tycoon in *The Big Eat.*' There were roles as a newspaper editor, a building society executive, and a police inspector for *Vendetta* on BBC1 in 1966. One notable production Paul made in 1964, where he portrayed Dr Bernard Gisvius, a still living survivor of a group who wished to assassinate Adolf Hitler in 1944. This was called 'The July Plot', which went out as part of *The Wednesday Play* strand on BBC1.

It may have been his appearance in an episode of *The First Lady* called 'This Hurts Me More Than It Hurts You' that brought him to the attention of Terence Dudley and Gerry Davis. He was a good company man and helped to make incoming cast feel a part of the *Doomwatch* family. It seems he was one of those personalities about whom nobody has a bad word to say.

John Paul's electrifying central performance as Quist helped to bring the programme to life, and he would be the only actor to appear in every single episode. His confidence as an actor had been dented during *Probation Officer*, where his performance was criticised. Although that had been nearly ten years previously, it took him a while to find a comfortable level at which to play Quist. Eric Hills recalled 'John Paul wasn't very good at remembering complicated or scientific things in the dialogue as I remember! It didn't trip off the tongue.' Adele Winston remembers him putting himself down at times. 'He often said I don't think I should be playing a Nobel prize winning scientist because you can't play someone more intelligent than you are!' Jean Trend thought rather differently: 'John Paul was the most lovely, lovely man, highly intelligent. His performance stands up today.'

Simon Oates

Cast to play Dr John Ridge, Simon Oates was born Arthur Charles Oates in Canning Town, London in 1932. Educated at Christ's College in Finchley, his National Service days were in the Intelligence Corps, where he became the Army's heavyweight boxing champion. He did not finish his training as an actor when he attended the Arts Educational School since he found a job at the Chesterfield Repertory Company; he made his debut under the name Titus Oates in a play called *Someone At The Door* in 1954. Jean Trend first met him during those theatre days. 'Many, many years ago between about twenty-four of us (we were called The Twenty Four) would meet and read new plays, including Terence Frisby, who we sort of set off in his career as a writer – and that's where we met. We saw each other's plays, do play readings and say "We've heard so-and-so is casting," very much like a co-operative, which I now belong to in fact, so we knew each other a long time. Simon was known as a lothario. Incredibly charismatic.'

Television work soon came, and his first performance was on the BBC in Robert Audley's play *Shadow of Heroes*. Further roles displayed his versatility as he took on the role of a Scottish nobleman for *Dr Finlay's Casebook*, a 'punchy' American crook in *No Hiding Place* and a French nobleman in *Guy de Maupassant*. He had a role as a time and motion expert in an episode of ATV's shop floor/boardroom drama *The Plane Makers*, where Oates considered he was just playing himself.

He also made a name as a director, being invited by the creator of *Dixon of Dock Green*, Ted Willis, to direct *Woman in a Dressing Gown* at the Vaudeville Theatre in London. Another West End production was a pop concert called *Surprise Beat 64*. In 1965 Oates was cast in *The Mask of Janus* as the spy boss Anthony Kelly, a role he recreated in the spin-off series *The Spies* a year later. So it was hardly surprising that, when the role of a scientist-turned-MI6-operative-turned-scientist-again was needed for *Doomwatch*, Terence Dudley would think of Oates. He had also recently been working for the BBC in *The Expert*, playing David Lynch in the episode 'Your Money or Your Life'. Lynch was an insurance man who was investigating a suspicious fatal car accident and calls in the forensic scientist Doctor Hardy, played by Marius Goring. It turns out the accident was an 'autocide'; the driver killed himself by driving into a wall due to an unhappy love affair. 'But even Dr Hardy's elaborate equipment for investigating blonde hairs and samples of make-up lost its magic powers under the glamorous gaze of Simon Oates. Funny how one mis-cast character can send the whole thing awry.'

Simon Oates was contracted on 8 October 1969 for a minimum of ten episodes and a maximum of thirteen, with an option for a second series. His 'special activity', as the contract described it, was to drive a car. The car would be a Lotus. Adele Winston remembers 'Simon said to Terry [Dudley] that John Ridge was the sort of person who would be driving a really fancy car. "I think I can ring Lotus and tell them I'm playing him," and Terry said "Go for it!" because the BBC didn't have any money. Simon very sensibly rang Lotus and said to them "I'm going to playing this part, it's going to be very big and there's going to be a lot of filming of me driving a car," and they said "Fine, which one do you want?" I got lots of lifts in it! He was a great mate and a giggle.'

Ridge was to be the most fashionably dressed of the series. Elizabeth

Rowell felt he might need a little make-up. 'Simon Oates I had never met before. I felt his nose was quite wide, and after we chatted and found that there was nothing in particular he wanted, I said, "Oh well, I think I might just shade either side of your nose. It would be better to slim it down a little." He said to me "My dear girl, I've just paid three hundred pounds for this nose." He was very nice about it. He was very trendy; the neck-scarves were very fashionable then.' Jonathan Alwyn thought that the casting was spot-on. 'I don't think the character was that wide of the mark from Simon himself really!' It was a role Oates played with relish, and he soon got on very well with both the cast and crew, particularly Robert Powell, with whom he used to play games during rehearsals.

The character of Ridge was certainly typical of the age, with other serial seducers in bright shirts on screen at the time, such as Derren Nesbitt's character in *Special Branch*, who was very Ridge-like in dress and attitude. Simon Oates was auditioned three times for the role of the ultimate masculine role model of the age, James Bond, to replace Sean Connery. When questioned about the character by *New Scientist* in 1971, Kit Pedler had to agree, saying that Ridge 'is a sub-James Bond type who wouldn't last five minutes in a laboratory'. The article went on to explain that Pedler 'contends that the programme doesn't set out to convince scientists, who make up only a tiny proportion of the audience'.

Robert Powell

Cast to play Toby Wren was Lancashire-born Robert Powell. He started a career in law but switched to drama because it had more appeal. He was starting to become noticed in television with roles in the 'Season of the Witch' edition of *The Wednesday Play*, although he was cast before viewers would see its transmission in January 1970), *The Tower of London* as the Earl of Warwick, directed by Jonathan Alwyn, *Thirty-Minute Theatre*: 'Roses, Roses, All The Way' and had also appeared in the cinema with a small role in *The Italian Job*. It was Terence Dudley who cast Powell as Toby Wren. Judy Bedford remembers 'Terry saw him perform on TV, and was so impressed. He was absolutely determined to get him to play the part and he pursued Robert quite relentlessly.' This performance was in another *Wednesday Play*, 'Bam! Pow! Zap!' by Nigel Kneale, which was a look at comic-book violence. It was a piece of casting that Gerry Davis and Kit Pedler both approved of. Powell had already gained a favourable impression of Pedler – he knew Carol Pedler (Kit's eldest daughter) socially, and at that time she herself had ambitions to become an actress.

Robert Powell only ever intended to do one series. All of his male co-stars had options for a second series, but in his contract, dated 2 October 1969, he had none. Jennifer Wilson, who played Miss Wills in the first episode, 'The Plastic Eaters', remembers Powell saying he did not want to do a second series even then. His contract promised him a minimum of ten episodes, but in the event, like Oates, he appeared in all of them. As an up-and-coming actor, he did not want to be tied down to one role for a long period of time; typecasting was a genuine fear in the profession. 'I'm not a particularly altruistic person', he later told the *Radio Times*, 'but I'm young and unattached and therefore free to oose the work I want: if I'd carried on with *Doomwatch* it would have been pure greed for money.'

The BBC had initial concerns over launching a new series without a cast-iron star name, but they went ahead, and created new stars. Gerry Davis later admitted to the *Sun* that 'actors with "appeal" were purposely chosen', but no-one could have predicted just how interested a certain section of the audience were going to be in the leads and particularly Robert Powell.

Joby Blanshard

To play the Yorkshireman Colin Bradley, Terence Dudley cast Joby Blanshard, who began his acting career with the Theatre Workshop. He made regular appearances on television and would have been known to Dudley for his roles in *Cluff* and *The First Lady*. He also appeared in a small role in an episode of *The Mask of Janus* in 1965, alongside Jennifer Daniels who would appear in 'The Red Sky' and a certain Simon Oates. He also made an appearance in the final episode of *The Plane Makers*, playing a computer expert, one whose work brought to a temporary end the career of managing director John Wilder, played by Patrick Wymark. In 1965, he also appeared in an episode of BBC2's science fiction anthology series *Out of the Unknown*, 'Stranger in the Family', which featured John Paul.

Blanshard was contracted on 2 October 1969 to appear in a minimum of nine episodes between 17 November and 2 May 1970. He was not required for any filming for the first three weeks of production, and his only time on location in the first series was for 'Hear No Evil' in Yorkshire. Blanshard was another favourite amongst the cast and crew, with Adele Winston remembering him as particularly welcoming to the guest actors. Elizabeth Rowell remembered 'Joby Blanshard was another nice man. He was so grateful to be in *Doomwatch*. He was a delightful person and played it like he was in real life.' His wife had been a distinguished folk-singer, an interest in which he shared. At the time he had two children and lived in what he described as 'three acres of wilderness' in Sussex.

Wendy Hall

Born in the Post Office at Redcar in Yorkshire, Hall was married to a television producer and had two children. Her television and theatre appearances stretched back ten years. Wendy Hall was cast as the secretary Pat Hunnisett, a role she would hardly find demanding, having initially thought she was going to be more pro-active than would eventually be the case. She would leave after one series, having at first been excited by the nature of the programme and very impressed by her few meetings with Kit Pedler. Pedler's message would find favour within the cast and crew of *Doomwatch*, and often the strongest memory they have is of that man and his warning.

A special photo call was held inside Kit Pedler's actual lab at the Institute of Ophthalmology, featuring the cast with the electron microscope. Glyn Edwards remembers the great pleasure and delight Kit Pedler had in showing them around. Terence Dudley was also assured by his visit that the traditional stereotype of scientists in white coats is not always true. Wendy Hall remembered seeing Pedler's prize project – the construction of an electronic retina, for which he was spending time at the University of Manitoba in Canada (and would miss some of the earlier episodes being recorded as a result).

Other photo calls for the cast would be made. One of these included a glamour still of Simon Oates taken at the end of October, which declared the launching of 'a new thriller series starting on Monday, 9 February 1970.' Pedler would also record a special trailer on 30 November 1969 in Studio 3 at Television Centre, one of the studio days for the first episode. This was produced by Geoff Ramsay, and Pedler was paid ten guineas for writing and recording short pieces introducing the series.

Production

Production was planned to span six months from Sunday, 2 November 1969 to Saturday, 2 May 1970; in the event, the last studio day was on 15 April. The production order of the series was dictated by the logistical needs for filming, but this did not dictate in which order the episodes would air. Apart from an obvious first and last episode, most episodes could be transmitted in any order since there was rarely direct continuity except perhaps a reference to a previous event, such as the Beeston affair or the drugged sweets from 'The Devil's Sweets' being mentioned in 'Spectre at the Feast'.

The first three weeks of a production block, in this case November, would see 'block filming' on 16mm colour stock, performed for the first three episodes that required it the most. These were 'The Plastic Eaters', 'Burial at Sea' and 'Tomorrow, the Rat' in this instance. If possible, the number of regular cast would be kept low and their dialogue minimal; they had enough to do already and it added to their fees. The filming would normally happen four weeks before the episode itself was recorded in the studio, although later in the series filming on location which needed one of the regular cast would happen on the days immediately following a studio recording. In all cases, the film editor was Alastair MacKay.

Sometimes, a director would have a long wait after filming before he was in the rehearsal room with his cast for studio recording. A canny writer like Martin Worth would try to keep the characters needed for film and those for studio separate as far as possible. A good example of this is his second series episode 'Invasion'.

Each fifty-minute episode would be made within a thirteen-day cycle, with ten days rehearsal in any premises the BBC could rent around London. The only regular set needed for *Doomwatch* was the composite set for the offices, designed by Ian Watson. This was divided into three sections: the entrance with Pat's desk and areas for Ridge and Wren, the laboratory which also housed the Doomwatch computer, built by Ted Dove Associates Ltd, who were based at Pinewood, and finally Quist's office. As planned by Pedler and Davis right from the beginning, there were three large photographs of nuclear explosions on Quist's wall. Two of the three came from the Bikini Test and the Nagasaki explosion.

After rehearsals there would be two days in the studio, the first being purely for camera rehearsals and any complicated 'inserts' that needed more time than the following evening's two-and-a-half-hour recording slot would allow. The cast involved would get extra payments for this. In those days, colour videotape recording machines were only available at certain times, and sometimes the telecine units which played back the pre-recorded film (either specially shot or stock footage) were not available until the recording session itself. 'The Plastic Eaters' was the only exception to the two days in the studio rule.

Generally, the episode would be recorded in scene order, although sometimes complicated or numerous costume changes meant that scenes had to be recorded out of sequence. Fifty minutes of drama had to be captured in two and a half hours. Retakes did happen but were to be avoided if possible. Thus, actors' fluffed lines were sometimes left in the finished programme. Editing videotape was much simpler than it had ever been before for television, but edited tapes were not reused for other shows, and so costs could mount up. The days of having to record an entire production with only a few breaks to reposition cameras, scenery or actors were long gone, but the BBC still behaved in that way. There could be a few breaks in recording, and a few run-ons (where the recording did not need to be stopped, simply paused), but the main problem was always time. The episode had to be finished that night. Traditionally, the lights in the BBC studio would go off at 10 pm exactly. Too many breaks and retakes would result in going into expensive overtime, which would have to be negotiated with everyone involved in the studio. They had, after all, been working very long days. This meant extra payments for the contracted cast and for the BBC staff. Recently, the union recognised by the BBC, the ABS, had been crippling the service with a couple of lightning strikes, and were still imposing over-time bans.

Music and Titles
For the first series only, Max Harris provided not only the theme tune but also specially recorded music for use during an episode. The amount of music (if any) per episode was down to the preference of its director. Some episodes had none whatsoever. Other music would normally be provided for transistor radios or the background to pubs, and this could come from music library labels like KPM, Conroy or Chappell. The music would be played into the studio in the manner of background sound effects (grams) or dubbed on afterwards during editing. The music used, along with the extras and actors taking part either on location or in the studio, would be written down by the director's assistant in a document called the Programme as Broadcast Sheet, and used as a record for whoever was owed fees, or owned rights.

The striking title sequence was designed by Alan Jeapes (later a BAFTA winner for *Secret Army* and designer of the *EastEnders* graphics), and it featured film from nuclear blasts from the Baker and Trinity Tests. Baker was an underwater atomic explosion performed near the Bikini Islands in the Pacific Ocean in 1946. Trinity – the first ever test of an atomic bomb – was conducted on 16 July 1945. The titles and the theme music would be played into the studio. According to second series film editing assistant Louis Robinson, matching the titles to the music was a nightmare.

Following a successful recording, the videotape would be edited a few days later. Sometimes an episode needed trimming to bring its running time down to around the required fifty minutes. The finished episode would then be played back to the Head of Series for approval. On the Wednesday after transmission the episode might come up for discussion with the Programme Review Board. This was a meeting held at 10 am for heads of all departments to discuss not only the programmes they had seen that week but also viewing figures, responses from the public and issues such as overruns in the studio. The minutes written up afterwards would give a general summary of the points discussed.

Pre-publicity
The beginning of scheduled transmissions on Mondays in February had been fixed in the previous autumn and was announced in *The Stage* in early November.

A thirty-four-page press pack was prepared. It had a rather striking cover of a mushroom cloud against a red background, and *Doomwatch* written three times in blue ink. Inside was a montage of press clippings, one of which dealt with experiments concerning jet lag and would be the basis for a second series episode. There followed a three-page excerpt from the format document about the background to the fictional Doomwatch's creation, and then the regular characters were profiled as if they were subject to a top-secret security report by Department M/JB. It examined their backgrounds and assessed their characters in interviews; the team are considered highly dangerous and need surveillance.

Next, there were notes on where the Doomwatch team were based (on the top floor of a large block of flats), and the paper-eating virus idea was mentioned. Finally, the cast and crew (down to the three major designers) were given brief biographies. Pedler and Davis liked this approach so much that in 1971 they proposed a series of articles for a national newspaper using this approach to study current real life *Doomwatch* subjects. This never went ahead.

The series was promoted by a specially commissioned *Radio Times* cover featuring a melted and twisted plane inside a briefcase, photographed by Julian Cottrell. Inside was a one-page feature written by Elizabeth Cowley, who misrepresented the very first 'Fact' (concerning Fylingdales radar station) that the article displayed in a special section to illustrate the theme of the series; it caused a letter of complaint. Dudley and Davis were interviewed about the ideas and motives behind the series, but Pedler got a mere paragraph. The *Radio Times* would be quite supportive of this new drama, giving many of the early episodes a picture spread on the Monday pages. The BBC also showed specially compiled trailers for the episodes during the evening, most notably a shot of the infant in 'Friday's Child' and, two weeks later, the eponymous rats.

Pre-credits
Each episode began with a pre-credits teaser, designed to entice and hook an audience to watch beyond the title sequence and keep any inherited viewers on board, rather than them going to all that effort of getting up, walking across to the TV set and moving a dial to find what was on either ITV or BBC2. Some of these pre-credits teasers could be short and to the point; others, quite long and involved. This practise was quite common amongst filmed ITV series with the American market in mind, but it was very rare for a BBC drama. In fact, Terence Dudley's *The Mask of Janus* in 1965 used pre-credit teasers, implying this may have been his idea.

Scheduling
A comedy series was scheduled before *Doomwatch*. Since comedy traditionally commanded a larger audience than drama (or at least that was how the BBC felt), it should have helped the new programme's tricky first few weeks. Unfortunately, *The Kenneth Williams Show* was not proving as popular as had been hoped. But once that had finished, a new series called *Up Pompeii!* starring Frankie Howerd was expected to do very well.

The series would still be in production as it started transmission. The cast and crew would soon know if they had a hit on their hands or an embarrassing failure. So, on 9 February 1970 at 9.41 pm, following the first episode of *The Kenneth Williams Show* and a thirty-second trailer for *The Laugh Parade*, that new word entered the English language: DOOMWATCH.

Series One

Series Devised by Kit Pedler and Gerry Davis
Producer: Terence Dudley
Script Editor: Gerry Davis
Assistant to Producer: Glyn Edwards
Graphics: Alan Jeapes
Theme Music and Incidentals: Max Harris

Regular Cast:
Dr Spencer Quist (John Paul)
Dr John Ridge (Simon Oates)
Toby Wren (Robert Powell)
Colin Bradley (Joby Blanshard)
Pat Hunnisett (Wendy Hall)

1.01
The Plastic Eaters

Written by Kit Pedler and Gerry Davis
Directed by Paul Ciappessoni
Designed by Ian Watson and Barry Newbery
Transmitted: Monday, 9 February 1970 at 9.41 pm Duration: 48' 10"

Cast
First Stewardess (Gracie Luck), First Captain (Tony Sibbald), First Engineer (Richardson Morgan), First Copilot (Monty Brown), Second Stewardess (Pat Wallen), The Minister (John Barron), Commissionaire (Christopher Hodge), Alice Wills (Jennifer Wilson), Jim Bennett (Michael Hawkins), Hal Symonds (Kevin Stoney), Third Stewardess (Caroline Rogers), Second Captain (John Lee), Second Copilot (Eric Corrie), Second Engineer/Navigator (Edward Dentith), Passengers (Andreas Malandrinos, Mike Lewin, Pat Beckett, Toba Laurence, Cynthia Bizeray, Peter Thompson, Michael Earl, Tony Haydon).

Also appearing
Passengers on Plane 1 (Dilys Marvin, Karl Gray, Maria Allen, Isobel Sabel, Bob E Raymond, John de Marco). Passengers on Plane 2 (Elsie Arnold, Ned Hood). Lab Assistants (Bob E Raymond, John de Marco, Bill Lodge, Brian Gidley). Computer Technicians (Karl Bohan, Ron Gregory). Girl in Lab (June Hammond).

Technical Credits
Production Assistant: Robert Checksfield. Assistant Floor Manager: Jane Southern. Director's Assistant: Jill Haworth. Floor Assistant: John Wilcox.
Film Cameraman: Eddie Best. Film Editor: Alastair MacKay.
Visual Effects: Peter Day.
Costume Supervisor: Dorothea Wallace. Make-up Supervisor: Elizabeth Rowell.
Studio Lighting: John Treays. TM2: Tommy Holmes. Vision Mixer: John Stevens.
Studio Sound: Larry Goodson. Grams Operator: Gerry Borrows.
Crew: 19.

Radio Times
A plane crashes in South America, hardly headline news, but there is something frighteningly different about this crash. The newly created Doomwatch team face their first real challenge.

The Story
'What about you, Dr Quist? What did you take this job on for then? A pew in the House of Lords? Or was it an attack of conscience?' – Ridge

A routine flight to San Pedro ends in tragedy as it crashes into the ground, a result of insulation cables melting on the flight deck. Pictures of the melted wiring have been sent to the Doomwatch team for investigation. Their computer is not working, and so Dr Quist sends out to the crash site a startled new recruit, Toby Wren, to investigate. Wren had thought he was coming in just for a job interview but is soon sitting on a plane, reading early reports from the crash site.

Quist's line of enquiry is plastic solvents. Britain's plastic waste problem is acute, and their Minister would like to be known as the one man with the foresight to solve the problem. A phone call to the Minister reveals little on current research, except a sense of alarm when Quist asks about the government laboratories at Beeston, which they have never been allowed to monitor. Ridge suggests breaking into the Minister's office, but Quist refuses to indulge in such cloak and dagger stuff until Ridge reminds him of the part his maths played in building the first atom bomb. Quist angrily agrees.

The next morning Ridge is shown into the Minister's office by the Commissionaire and is left alone until discovered by Miss Wills, the Minister's secretary. He photographs what he needs: evidence of a new plastic solvent with a *biological* mechanism called Variant 14, being developed at Beeston. This time Quist has no problem in letting Ridge to break in there. Once inside, Ridge pretends to have been at college with Jim Bennett, one of the senior staff. As Bennett goes off to check his credentials, Ridge takes a specimen of Variant 14. Exposed as an imposter, Ridge is thrown out by security, but not before he is photographed. The Minister identifies Ridge and describes Quist's methods as unorthodox but vows that nothing will interfere with the 'Dungeness test'.

Quist believes that there is a link between a stewardess on the doomed flight and the Minister's secretary, since they share the same surname. Tests on Variant 14 reveal that if released into the outside world, it would spread across the globe, devouring any plastic it could find as food. Does Beeston have all this data? Can it be controlled? Quist knows that put a scientist under political pressure, he will go ahead even if he isn't ready, and that is when mistakes are made. They send a cable to Wren, who is on a return flight, warning him not to touch his sample from the crashed plane whilst on board. It is too late. Wren has already done so, and the effects begin to show themselves. He has touched a plastic cup, which a stewardess takes back to the kitchen, wiping the gooey mess onto a plastic surface...

Summoned to explain himself to the Minister, Quist meets Symonds, the director of Beeston, and presents him with the data that they have prepared. Ridge works on Miss Wills and forces her to remember her last meeting with her cousin before she was killed. Both the Minister and Symonds refuse to accept that the plane crash was as a result of Variant 14 contamination, until word reaches them that the virus has now escaped onto Wren's flight. Ridge discovers that Miss Wills had written a cheque with a plastic pen for her cousin. The pen is in her handbag and the plastic part has melted. Finally convinced Variant 14 has leaked from his laboratory, Symonds leaves to prepare for decontamination of the plane, and Quist asks the Minister about the Dungeness test.

Wren tries to convince the pilot of the danger they are in as more plastic items dissolve, and the passengers struggle to control their panic. Soon the flight controls are affected, and the RAF are sent to escort the plane to a military airfield.

The Minister suspends Quist as director of Doomwatch for overstepping his authority in this matter. Quist watches as the Minister dictates a memo into a Dictaphone. He realises that it had been smuggled into Beeston, and finds the cassette recording which is kept inside a metal box. It is now a congealed mess. The Minister was the carrier. The plane lands successfully and crash teams smother the fuselage in foam as fires break out on the runway. The Minister regrets the incident and blames a lack of information, but Quist counters that he was fully informed. With Doomwatch's future safe for the moment, and the Minister's own position shaky, Quist leaves Whitehall.

Behind the Story
To Kit Pedler, a plastic eating virus was, in a phrase coined by atomic physicist Alvin M Weinberg, a 'technological fix' – except this one is as bad as the difficulty it attempts to deal with. It doesn't address the original problem; it just creates new ones.

Dealing with Plastic Waste
The script was written in 1968, and the matter of plastic waste disposal was something that had long been recognised as a serious concern. According to newspapers from the time, 250,000 tons of plastic waste was disposed of in 1970, with this projected to increase fivefold by 1980. The Science Research Council's Biological Sciences Committee met with representatives from major industrial companies to discuss the problem in May 1970, aware that there was no quick fix solution to the problem. Paper rots, metal rusts, but plastic remains plastic. As an artificial substance there is no natural predator for the stuff, and incinerating it releases toxic, black smoke. Discussing these barriers facing plastic disposal, Doctor Roger

Lewin, in the *New Scientist* edition dated 25 February 1971, noted '*Doomwatch* fans should note that no plans were made to cultivate bacteria with a penchant for devouring plastics ...'

On 7 June 1971, the *Daily Express* carried a report on Professor David Hughes from Cardiff University who was developing a biodegradable plastic – one that was vulnerable to bacteria in the same way as paper and wood. The paper described it as one of the most controversial ideas ever thought of to 'Keep Britain Tidy' (a popular campaign slogan to try and curb litter), an 'army of little germs gobbling up oil slicks and cast-off cans and boxes made of plastic'. Hughes stressed that though his present research was not directed at turning out test tube germs to get rid of waste, he said 'in the long term it is on'. He explained 'What we do is sink the slicks by spreading something like ash on them. In the ash we put food for the bacteria like nitrogen and phosphate. We feed them up and make them multiply and they eat the oil. There is no danger that they could overfeed and go on to attack other forms of marine life.' He knew it was a touchy subject. 'Some firms are absolutely wild. But I must stress no-one is tampering with nature.'

Professor of Chemistry, Gerald Scott of Aston University, Birmingham, was asked to comment: 'A very dangerous development ... The prospect has the sort of *Doomwatch* implications that are frankly frightening. Some distinguished men feel it is too dangerous even to contemplate.' Professor Scott had been working for several years in developing a biodegradable plastic, but this hit the buffers when his funding ran out in 1970 and he needed £50,000 to continue for another five years. He was reluctant to take his work abroad, where both the Americans and the Japanese were working in the same field. The Japanese would test market a photodegradable polystyrene foam in 1971, and a highly photosensitive ethylene carbon monoxide copolymer had been developed in the United States to be used for such things as disposable drinking cups.' Scott received a grant from the Science Council but only to develop his other work similar to the Japanese idea, which involved plastics which break down into a powder under ultra-violet light. This received notable publicity in the summer of 1970 and won praise in an editorial in the *Daily Mirror*. This process was, as New Scientist reported: 'sunlight initiated breakdown ...'

In July 1970, the *Daily Mirror* had their own Doomwatch team, consisting of Kit Pedler and two *Mirror* journalists, including their science correspondent. Pedler and Davis took the idea of combining Variant 14 feeding on the residue from biodegradable plastic in the sewers and used it to form the basis for the first of three *Doomwatch*-inspired novels: *Mutant 59: The Plastic Eater*. Scott continued for the rest of his career working on a plastic that degraded as naturally as rubber, patenting the Scott-Gilead process in 1978. He died in 2014.

Paranoia
What goes on inside top-secret government laboratories has long been a source of fascination for writers and conspiracy theorists, not to mention the general public. Here we have a leak of Variant 14. Recently, the Pirbright Laboratories in Surrey were blamed for leaking a specific strain of the foot and mouth disease in 2007. It was one of the four places in Europe licensed to experiment on the strain of the virus found in this outbreak. The official report suggested that the virus escaped from a pipe which led to a treatment plant and that workmen building on the site conveyed it to a nearby farm, where it was first detected. Ironically the virus escaped from the same location back in 1970, into an animal holding pen on the site. The cause of the leak at that time was put down to a temporary breakdown of filters which cleaned outgoing air from the compound.

Government Ombudsman
'We were set up to investigate any scientific research, public or private, which would possibly be harmful to man,' Quist reminds himself. 'In fact, the government was practically re-elected on this very issue.'

In December 1969, the *New Scientist*, anticipating the forthcoming general election, confidently predicted: 'all signs are that the quality of Britain's towns and countryside, our seas and our air, will be a major election issue during 1970, which would be highly appropriate for European Conversation Year ... When Anthony Crosland became Secretary of State for Local Government and Regional Planning a few months ago, he was asked by the Prime Minister to overhaul government machinery dealing with pollution. It is perhaps unfortunate that in the meantime public unease has grown so rapidly that [Prime Minister] Mr Wilson felt it necessary to step in last week with a Royal Commission before Mr Crosland's wider-ranging review was complete.' The Royal Commission was announced in Parliament on 11 December 1969. Pedler and Davis in their format likened the Doomwatch set-up as 'little more than the equivalent of a Royal Commission and is quickly forgotten by the public since it is clear that any information they might produce will not be forthcoming for some months or years.' It took the Commission over a year to produce their first report.

Back to the *New Scientist*: 'The ... Commission bears all the marks of a Downing Street decision to do something fast ... The problem is not, of course, so simple as giving it to the demand for one department responsible for all environmental matters. A plenipotentiary Minister of Pollution would find himself dealing with Concorde, oil at sea, DDT, automobile exhausts, pneumatic drills, skiing in the Cairngorms and London's motor-way box. The need is rather for every Ministry to include a competent team of ecologists, capable of evaluating environmental implications of routine activities and major projects alike.

'Secondly, we need to have an environmental ombudsman responsible to Parliament alone and able to draw attention to any ecological problems that are being mishandled or overlooked at departmental level. He would need a top-grade scientific staff and the advice of outside specialists and should be able to initiate long term-research and to co-ordinate action on pollution hotspots such as the *Torrey Canyon* [a tanker responsible for a devastating oil-slick along the Cornish and French coastline a few years ago.]' By the end of the series in 1972, the Doomwatch department would be seen to be doing precisely this.

The author hoped that both the Commission and Crosland's new role could combine and spearhead a 'court of appeal' for the various environmental research groups already in existence, in and outside of local and national government. 'Equally, it could be lost without voice to Whitehall's existing scientific empires struggle to retain their frontiers.'

As an Opening Episode
As an introductory episode, 'The Plastic Eaters' sets up the premise of the series and its characters in as satisfactory a manner as is possible. We learn what we need to know of Quist: his passion; his frustration with being kept at arms-length from inconvenient facts which he needs to know in order to fulfil his function and his guilt over his involvement with the creation of the atomic bomb. The death of his wife from the consequence of their research is only alluded to and not specifically stated. We learn of his Nobel prize; his popularity with the press and public, and the suspicions these generate within the scientific community. Like a bloodhound he cannot leave the trail alone once he has caught its scent. He goes ahead and ruffles more than a few feathers as if he has nothing to lose. He has makes an enemy of the Minister, who he treats less than respectfully. The script follows the original idea of how the Minister is trying to strangle the department at birth.

Production
Filming
Paul Ciappessoni directed the episode. Ridge's break-in at Beeston was filmed on Monday, 3 November in the Bishop's Stortford area, and this was the very first piece of filming for *Doomwatch*. Robert Powell filmed his brief scene during the next two days. Bishop's Stortford, where the actors caught their train home, is close to what is now Stansted Airport, which became London's third airport later that decade. The film work on this

serial, including the re-creation of a disaster team dousing the stricken plane in foam, was transferred to videotape after the recording of 'Friday's Child', also directed by Ciappessoni. That no extras names are recorded in the Programme as Broadcast sheets for the film sequences implies these firemen and ambulance drivers were the real thing, as would be the case of the lifeboatmen seen in the third episode 'Burial at Sea'.

Stock Footage

The rather melodramatic stock footage used to depict the crash, complete with test dummies strapped into their seats, came from a fifteen-minute film produced by the Federal Aviation Administration in America. Called the 'Phoenix air plane crash' in the camera script, a Douglas DC-7 was sent down a runway full of obstacles to study the resulting devastation. Instead of fuel, coloured water was placed inside the tanks to study its dispersal. This took place on 24 April 1964 near Phoenix, Arizona. The film of the fighter originated from the Royal Air Force.

Script

The original crash site for the episode was Bogotá, the capital of Colombia, but this was changed to the more attractive-sounding San Pedro.

The dialogue on the flight deck during the pre-credits sequence was largely worked out during rehearsal, as was some of the chatter between passengers. In the camera script which survives, there is very little detail written for the passenger cabin scenes except that great emphasis is made on panicking passengers and others succumbing to heat. For example, scene 45 reads: 'One of the passengers tries to wipe the window which is smeared with melting plastic. It comes off in his hands. Andreas gets up, demanding to see the Captain. The Stewardess tries unsuccessfully to stop him.' The passenger who panics is played by Andreas Malandrinos and is noted in the camera directions. This may be because the camera script which survives was prepared for the third day and simply summarised what had been recorded on the first day.

Scene 47 says: 'The heat is growing. One of the passengers is practically passing out with the heat. A Stewardess passes him a glass of water. His neighbour goes to turn on an air conditioning binnacle which softens and melts in her hand.' When Toby is sent back to join the passengers 'Wren reacts with horrified disbelief at the chaos. Another passenger has passed out with the heat and is being tended by the Stewardesses. The other passengers get up and try to help, but are shepherded back to their seats by a Stewardess.' This is different from the shot eventually taken, which is of Wren looking more annoyed than anything, by the very wet conditions in the cabin.

The script showed that in case the episode overran, the brief scene of

Christopher Hodge as the Whitehall Commissionaire showing Ridge the Minister's office was selected for cutting, as were the subsequent shots of Ridge searching inside Miss Wills' office. The file which Ridge photographs is called Beeston Project Polysolve.

Cast

The very first actress seen in *Doomwatch* is Gracie Luck, who is now the author Susan Surman. Richardson Morgan was the most experienced television actor amongst those playing the doomed flight crew, having started with a part in *The Paradise Makers* in 1967. He owed most of his early work to director Douglas Camfield. For Canadian Tony Sibbald, this was a very early television appearance and Monty Brown has no other credits.

John Barron, cast as the Minister, had only recently come to the end of a lengthy spell playing Assistant Chief Constable Gilbert in the police series *Softly, Softly* episodes, one of which Paul Ciappessoni had very recently directed. Characters from the series were being relocated from the west country to Kent and his character was not going to follow suit. He told the *Illustrated London News* in September 1969, 'I haven't done much this summer except recover from mumps. I've been in this series for two and a half years now. Of course, playing all this time gives one a sense of security, but when it's over it is not going to be easy to find work. It's a question of letting people know you're out and about again.' Frequently playing over-bearing authority figures, he had portrayed an urbane consultant in the hospital soap *Emergency Ward 10*, a role he was still remembered for, even in 1969. He had also been the Dean in BBC1's Church of England sit-com *All Gas and Gaiters*. He would return for the fourth and fifth series now he was free from *Softly, Softly*. His most famous role was as CJ, the domineering founder of Sunshine Desserts in *The Fall and Rise of Reginald Perrin*. This would not be his last *Doomwatch* appearance by far. He had worked with John Paul on *The Troubleshooters* in 1966.

John Lee, as the second pilot, makes the first of three *Doomwatch* appearances. Another familiar television face, he had played against John Paul in *The Wednesday Play* about the failed assassination attempt on Hitler, 'The July Plot', in 1964. He had also been directed by Ciappessoni in *Softly, Softly*. Eric Corrie, another of the flight crew, was more a film actor and this is his last credited role and soon afterwards retired to Lanzarote.

Kevin Stoney had worked with John Paul on the film *The Blood Beast Terror*, which took for its plot a vampire moth which can take on the form of a beautiful girl. He had been directed by Ciappessoni in *Dr Finlay's Casebook*. Edward Dentith had been a police officer opposite John Paul in

Probation Officer and in *Gideon's Way* with Joby Blanshard in a 1964 episode called 'The Fire Bug'. He had recently been directed by Ciappessoni in an episode of *The Expert*.

Michael Hawkins had played a regular character during the second series of *R3.*, and would later play a strange salesman opposite fellow cast member Jennifer Wilson in *The Brothers*. Wilson herself had only recently recorded six episodes of *Special Branch* on Thames where she played a detective-sergeant.

Studio

'The Plastic Eaters' was given a rare three days in studio TC3, two of which would be used for recording. All the passenger extras were needed on Friday, 28 November. Scenes were rehearsed and then recorded between 2.30 pm and 5.30 pm, and again after dinner from 7.30 pm and 10 pm Presumably this was for the complicated effects of the plastic melting, and perhaps for the new CSO [Colour Separation Overlay, called chroma key by the rest of the television industry], which was used to give views outside the flight deck windows.

The cabin set had to represent three different planes: the initial doomed crash and Toby Wren's two flights. To add to the impact of the melting plane, a video disc was used during the recording to slow down some of the ooze effects and add to the impact. Video discs were used by the Sports department for action replays, and Drama sometimes had to beg, borrow or steal the facility for their programmes. It could slow down or speed up action as required, something normally achieved on film. 'It looked very nice too. Like a dripping multi coloured ice cream cone', commented the *Daily Sketch*'s Gerald Garrett. Most of the rest of the country would have seen this in black-and-white and not even necessarily as a 625-line picture, but as a low definition 405-line image.

The second studio day was on a Saturday and was taken up with camera rehearsals for the following day's recording, which comprised all the non-aeroplane scenes. The extras for the two labs were booked for these days. Sunday's recording night overran beyond ten o'clock, which meant overtime payments for the cast and crew.

A photo call was held that day, although the pictures in the *Radio Times* seem to come from the earlier photo session in Dr Pedler's lab with his electron microscope. Robert Powell had also earned overtime on the second day and performed in a pre-recorded insert.

Post-Production

The episode was edited on Monday, 12 January 1970 between 4 pm and 7 pm No music was used apart from the opening and closing titles theme.

Promotion

The new series was greeted with features in the *Daily Express*, which assumed it was to be Wendy Hall's series. This certainly gave them an excuse to print some nice photographs of the actress. A couple of weeks earlier on the 30 January, the same paper had announced 'It's the *Doctor Who* team again!', noting how the BBC was joining the debate on pollution hazards with a 'fictional TV thriller series', and how Wendy Hall was 'guaranteed to brighten up any environment'. The *Daily Mirror* also imagined that she was the star of the series, envisaging a 'Perils of Pauline' situation for 'Pat Hunnisett [sic], Girl Friday to a government department team whose job is to ensure that man does not destroy civilisation with his own ingenuity'. The *Guardian* was more formal in its little mention of 'an interesting stab at a science fiction series'.

Reception

The idea of a plastic-eating virus was certainly one which people will remember as a quintessentially *Doomwatch* idea. For some it remained an outlandish concept. Raymond Williams in the *Listener* liked 'the emphasis on social responsibility in science and that suspicion of secret research which is now becoming habitual. But I remained puzzled that a virus could consume plastics'. Nancy Banks-Smith in the *Guardian* wished 'that last night's episode was a serial so that the enzyme could continue its rampage. Decomposing and liquefying television sets and telephones and typewriters and washing-up bowls. I can think of nothing plastic I possessed which I could not cheerfully live without.'

Stewart Lane writing in the *Morning Star* loved the series: 'Capably done ... with a high degree of suspense and what's perhaps more important, fairly clear implications. After all, how much do we know about what's going on at [illegible word] and other places? Indeed, isn't it possible that there could be a leak of some grisly toxic bacilli and that it could be too late before we learned about it? It makes you think. And a series which does just that is worth having around.'

Sylvia Clayton in the *Daily Telegraph* thought John Paul gave his role 'an indignant integrity'. The *Sunday Telegraph* reported that representatives from the plastics industry complained to the BBC that the programme had ruined their image.

The *Stage's* John Lawrence was left unimpressed: 'The production lacked tension throughout. I would not have thought it possible that a plane fighting to land before it crashes could be shown battling its way down without communicating any feelings of excitement or suspense whatsoever, but between them, the writers Kit Peddler [sic] and Gerry Davis, and the director Paul Ciappessoni managed it.'

James Thomas in the *Daily Express* didn't want to be made to think;

'Don't Preach Doom At Me!' thundered the headline. 'However seriously the BBC may pretend to take its message, for me it was just a new kind of romp which is probably going to be a secure successor to *Quatermass* ... *Doomwatch* tends to preach too much about the danger of man's inquiring mind. As an idea I feel it will take a lot of sustaining.'

'Doom – a winner in the horror stakes,' declared the critic T G for the *Coventry Evening Telegraph*, who managed to watch both channels that night. 'Liquid plastic drips and oozes from the walls of an airliner in flight; unearthly sounds escape the dank confines of a Victorian cellar. What devilry, you might say. The dispensers of such horror were BBC1 and Thames. They quietly threw down their gauntlets last night for a battle – a fight to decide which one could best give viewers a kind of TV rigor mortis. Their weapons were two new series – *Doomwatch* on BBC1, and *Mystery and Imagination* on Thames. Both were designed to paralyse their victims, the viewers defying them to move a muscle let alone fumble for the channel switch. But the reign of terror ended on this occasion with a mutilating defeat for Thames. Sheer professionalism and originality paid off for the BBC, while Thames struggled with a rather predictable piece of self-conscious melodrama. *Doomwatch* ... promises to be fine science fiction if 'The Plastic Eaters' ... is anything to go by ... The tale was intelligent and alarmingly plausible. John Paul fits in well as the quiet-voiced, resolute Dr Quist – a name, though, that belongs more to a children's science fiction adventure. One regrets is that some unorthodox breaking and entering by Quist's assistant were made to look a little incredible.'

This view was not shared by reader J R Parker, who wrote to the paper: 'To have described ... the series as "intelligent" and "plausible" was about as intelligent and plausible as the possibility of the existence of such a nondescript organisation within the Government's control ... I hope T G and I never have to share a television set!'

Programme Review Board
After watching the first episode, David Webster 'looked forward to seeing one day an adventure which would star a dim scientist and an efficient civil servant and an obviously able straight-forward Minister of the Crown'. A few members wondered if the casting of John Barron was unfortunate in light of his role in *Softly, Softly*. However, Head of Series Andrew Osborn expressed how quite pleased he was with the way the series was turning out, and another board member admitted that he had been hooked but that it would need time to get established – and that it would need good writers.

The World In Danger
'The Plastic Eaters' was the first of three scripts to be adapted in 1975 into

an educational book by the Longman Group ltd as part of their Longman Structural Readers range for children between 12 and 15. Edited by Gordon Walsh, the language was very clear and concise with no room for humour or irony and people explain themselves very plainly. Here's an example of Ridge telling Toby Wren the philosophy behind their department: 'Our work is very important, you know. Science has given the world many good things – but science can also be dangerous. Sometimes scientists make mistakes; they can be careless. So the government have started "Doomwatch". We're all scientists too, and we watch all the scientific work in Britain. If we're sure that the work is safe, we do nothing. But sometimes we find work that may be dangerous. And then we have to stop it.' A few moments are missing from the adaption and motivations of the characters are made clear. Variant 14 is simply called Number 14, and the initial crash is given more detail and dialogue than seen on the television. The Captain on the second infected flight goes to see Wren's sample and discovers the plastic is starting to melt around the seat. The story was illustrated with both BBC photos and artwork.

Meanwhile...
Concern is now very high over the amount of plastic waste polluting and choking our oceans and landfills. The United Nations passed a resolution to outlaw any further plastic waste entering the ocean. It is not legally binding. Recycling is only going so far, and plastic waste is more acute than ever. Shopping bags are not a thing of the past in most supermarkets, simply a nominal charge per new bag. Two-thirds' of Britain's plastic recycling goes to China and Hong Kong, according to the *Guardian* in December 2017, something the Chinese authorities are planning to reduce This is a problem that is not going to go away, until we reduce plastic usage at source.

1.02
Friday's Child

Written by Harry Green
Directed by Paul Ciappessoni
Designed by Ian Watson
Transmitted: Monday, 16 February 1970 at 9.40 pm Duration: 49' 30"

Cast
Mrs Patrick (Mary Holland), Mrs Norman (Delia Paton), Shopkeeper (John Tucker), Passer-by (Susan Lawrance), Detective-Sergeant (Bill Straiton), Dr Patrick (Alex Scott), Prosecuting Solicitor (John Graham), Defending Solicitor (Margaret John), Gwilliam (Richard Caldicot), Giles Patrick (Sam Ciappessoni).

Also appearing
Mr Norman (Ronald Nunnery), Secretary (Anne Lee), Male Magistrates (Richard Gregory, Charles Adey Grey, Herbert Aldridge), Female Magistrate (Pat Symons), Male Clerks of Court (Charles Rayford, Edward Kingsley), Men in Court (Brian Gardner, Salo Gardner, Tony Somers), Women in Court (Dolly Brennan, Pat Orr), Extras on location (Joan Shulman, Betty Bevan, David Harris).

Technical Credits
Production Assistant: Robert Checksfield. Assistant Floor Manager: Jane Southern. Director's Assistant: Maria Ellis. Floor Assistant: Alistair Clarke.
Film Cameraman: John Tiley. Sound Recordist: Bill Wild. Film Editor: Alastair MacKay.
Costume Supervisor: Dorothea Wallace. Make-up Supervisor: Elizabeth Rowell.
Visual Effects: John Friedlander.
Studio Lighting: Jimmy Purdie. TM2: Jack Shallcross. Vision Mixer: Jim Stephens.
Studio Sound: Larry Goodson. Grams Operator: Gerald Borrows.
Crew: 6.

Radio Times
Doomwatch are unwillingly drawn into a controversy which confronts Dr Quist with one of the fundamental questions of our time …

The Story
'My boy's not an untested hypothesis: he's flesh and blood! And it's his flesh now!' – Mrs Patrick

A woman called Mrs Norman follows a mother and child from their flat and tries to abduct the child from his pram, left outside a shop. Although she is stopped and caught, she calls the mother, Mrs Patrick, a thief. When the case is brought before the magistrates, it appears that Mrs Norman believes the little boy Giles has her dead son's heart, taken without consent by Dr Patrick, who had performed a heart transplant on his own son the same day Mrs Norman's baby died. Dr Patrick denies this.

Quist is not interested in the case when Wren brings it up, but allows him to attend the hearing. Wren is at first satisfied with the evidence – there would have been a lot of witnesses in the operating theatre – but the next day, Mrs Patrick turns up at the Doomwatch office, having had Toby pointed out to her at the hearing. The previous night someone had thrown a brick through her child's bedroom window. Mrs Patrick tells Quist that she feels her husband was hiding something. They had divorced a year earlier on grounds of cruelty; he worshipped his son but just saw his wife as the packaging in which he arrived. Quist is very reluctant to get involved. Dr Patrick has so far refused to answer where the heart for his son came from, but Quist is sure that the press will soon find out the name of the donor and that will settle the matter and hopefully convince the Normans that their son's heart is not in her son's body. Mrs Patrick agrees to wait but wonders if this will stop the attacks?

By Monday morning, Quist is disappointed that the 'muck-rakers' have failed, and he now feels uneasy. Doomwatch is to be involved but will only make a limited formal enquiry. Toby visits St Crispians Hospital and talks to Gwilliam, who checks the files concerning the operation and comes across the reference R.27 – Refer to Dr Patrick. Toby approaches Dr Patrick directly but is quickly brushed off. Ridge finds out that there have been more heart transplants than donors. With the Ministry of Health also not helping, he is given permission by Quist to break into Dr Patrick's lab, providing if he is discovered, he gets out: 'No unbecoming capers.'

That evening, Ridge climbs up the side of the building and enters the floor where Patrick's offices and laboratories are. He is disgusted to finds a cage of docile monkeys, and after examining a couple of files, discovers they have been decerebrated: 'Even monkeys have the rights to all of the brains they were born with.' Doctor Patrick discovers the intruder and explains that the heart inside his son's chest came from a monkey. Patrick is unimpressed with Ridge's disgust nor Quist, the self-righteous snooper. Ridge's threat to decerebrate him does make him pause. '*I'll* tell *you* what I am. I'm the father of a son. Are you? I gave my son a monkey's heart. I'd do as much for a son of yours.'

Quist reassures Mrs Patrick that her son's heart did not come from the Norman baby but declines to tell her the truth. Ridge is still angered by the experiments, but Toby views the amazing scientific breakthrough dispassionately.

RIDGE: Toby, you know that no human heart will ever be used to give a sick monkey a new lease of life. Who made Patrick Lord of Creation, with the right to cripple one beast to save another?
WREN: There's no shortage of precedent for what Patrick has done. Every cow and pig bred for the market is a pre-determined assemblage of joints – the size of an oven decides the size and shape of a beast. What's your conscience been doing since the day you were old enough to hold a knife and fork?

Quist is also impressed. 'We know that Patrick has transplanted seven monkey hearts into human patients. Moreover, he has solved the problem which lies, or rather lay, at the centre of the transplant surgery. He has evolved compounds, and an appropriate technique, in tissue culture fluids, which enable any surgeon to tailor a donor heart to the patient who receives it. He can prove that he has done so in seven cases. And all this with animal hearts. This is a major contribution to twentieth century science. But he hasn't published. Nothing that he has done is so ... so staggering as what he has not done.' He chastises Ridge for letting his feelings get in the way, and he has missed something. Ridge realises what this is – there was another door in the lab.

That night Ridge breaks in again and is met by Dr Patrick, who barks German at him. He knew Quist had smelt a rat. He shows Ridge his new experiment – an artificial womb containing an eight-month-old male human foetus conceived in vitro: a test-tube baby. Patrick sees the foetus as a homunculus, an artefact. The foetus, too, is decerebrated. No brain functions. He tells Ridge to leave the way he came in, like a thief. '*You* call me a thief?' exclaims Ridge. 'Patrick, you'll have no trouble financing your research. Your lampshades will go like a bomb, especially if you tattoo the skin.'

The next day Ridge wonders if Patrick used his own sperm to create the foetus. First adultery in a test-tube, then infanticide. Wren is still on Patrick's side.

WREN: He had to provide a habitat. A unit where it can continue to grow for ten years.
RIDGE: Till it turns into a death cell.
WREN: John, your attitude has been coloured by the circumstances of this

particular experiment. That doesn't alter the fact that this is an astounding technical breakthrough.

RIDGE: Did you ever see that picture by what's-his-name: the use of the air pump. A bird asphyxiated to demonstrate a vacuum. Toby, scientist or not … I'm with the bird, and I'd be happy to put Patrick in the air pump.

Quist takes Mrs Patrick to see the homunculus. It will be kept alive for ten years – the length of time a monkey heart will work. Quist tells him that life is sacred, and scientists should respect that. He tells Patrick to kill the foetus and publish his work. Patrick offers Quist the opportunity to end his burden. Quist replies: 'Patrick, every moral problem for the last 2000 years is implicit in the situation you've created. But it's not my job to find the answers and make decisions.' He will report to the Ministers. Mrs Patrick takes the key, but as she approaches the womb, she hesitates, and puts her hands to her face …

Behind the Story
Kit Pedler felt that 'Friday's Child' was the story closest to home. 'In that one', he told the *Radio Times* in 1970, 'we've moved into the field of producing animal hearts which cannot be rejected by human tissue. I know that may sound all right – but I can tell you there's a horrifying twist in it.' Pedler and Davis certainly allowed their imaginations to run riot. The twist was test-tube babies, but more than that: Dr Patrick, in his desire to prolong the life of his son, had moved on from just transplanting the short-lived hearts from decerebrated monkeys and was now breeding a homunculus inside an artificial womb – a brain-dead body as spare parts for his son.

Heart Transplants
The first theme to be added into the mix was the new procedure of heart transplantation, recently developed in the States. The first successful operation on a human being was carried out in Cape Town, South Africa by the pioneering surgeon Professor Christian Barnard in December 1967. The donor was Miss Denise Darvall, an accounting machine operator in a bank, who had been fatally injured in a car collision and was being kept alive on heart-lung machines. She had no chance of survival. On those grounds, her father gave consent for the donation. The recipient was a man called Louis Washansky, who had only a few weeks left to live. The procedure was successful, except it had not been anticipated that Darvall's heart was smaller than Washansky's, and there was what Barnard described 'a slight side-to-side motion of the donor heart within the enlarged peri-cardial cavity of the patient.' The only danger Washansky was in was from tissue rejection as his body's immune system rejects the

new tissue and this had to be treated with drugs borrowed from cancer research. He died eighteen days later.

A few days later, a second procedure was carried out in America. This time, on a two-and-a-half week-old baby in New York who was born with an inoperable heart defect. The team of Dr Kantrowitz searched the country for a baby born with brain lesions incompatible with life, an encephalic infant. One was found, and Dr Kantrowitz talked to the parents, who he described as 'intelligent and understanding' and they gave the necessary consent. The transplant was successful – for seven hours, and then the heart stopped beating and the recipient died. 'We consider this procedure a failure,' Kantrowitz said to the press, adding that they were 'disheartened and a little sad.' Previously, they had been experimenting on dogs.

Pedler would query the procedure in his 1979 book *The Quest For Gaia*. He does not deny that the motivation of the majority of doctors is to help to ease the patients of their symptoms, but he not only questions the cost of removing a heart from a dead man to one whose own heart is diseased, he also sees it as a demonstration of something symbolic. He saw transplants not as a method designed to extend life but merely a 'ritualized and theatrical ceremony of medico-technological power. A myth for our times.' The heart is the symbolic centre of the human being, and thus a transplant is a miracle, and miracles, he argues, reinforce belief. It wasn't until the late 1970s that Britain managed its first transplant. Although the average life expectancy after transplants was six months, as Pedler wrote at the time, some patients from those early days still live now. But for Pedler the Gaian, prevention was better than swapping one part for another, and the causation was partly the modern way in which we lived.

At the time, the procedure did not go uncriticised. Dr Barnard's operations and the accompanying publicity, *The Times* noted on 11 January 1968 the criticism from the Canadian surgeon who developed the pacemaker, J C Callaghan. He called it 'medical sensationalism at its height' and explained that Doctors needed a complete understanding of protoplasmic typing – the ability to match proteins in the heart, cell membranes, platelets and white cells in the same way as blood types are now matched before attempting a transplant. 46 operations had been performed by Barnard on dogs, Callaghan noted, and none survived. This explains why Quist is so impressed with Patrick's work.

The Press

One of the issues raised in 'Friday's Child' was the press being unable to discover the identity of the original baby heart donor. The right to privacy had been questioned by Ian Hamilton Fazey, chief feature writer of the *Liverpool Daily Post*, who spoke at a conference called *Science and the Press* in September 1969. As reported in the *Daily Mirror*, Fazey believed that publishing the identity of heart donors would help to 'banish any suspicion that less care has been taken with the socially less fortunate'. He recognised the nagging doubts of a 'vast section' of the public about the issues involved. Embarrassment for the deceased, he felt, was not justification for a case of secrecy. Others may disagree. There was to be great controversy in apartheid South Africa when it was discovered that the second transplant operation featured a white man being given the heart of a coloured. Some saw this as a vindication against perceived racial superiority of whites. The press interest in Barnard's work was so great his second patient was offered $50,000 by the American station NBC to film his operation. Barnard also had to eject a photographer who entered the operating theatre disguised as a medical student. Barnard took part in a fifty-three-minute debate on the controversy surrounding the subject, which was hosted by *Tomorrow's World* on 2 February 1968.

Test Tube Babies
In his radio discussion *Of Ombudsmen and Cybermats*, recorded in January 1969 before the storyline had been written, Pedler was asked by presenters Elizabeth Card and David Wilson that if Pedler was an ombudsman, created along the lines of *Doomwatch*, what would be his first case? 'I think we've had a lot of moral meandering around physics and its capabilities… I think perhaps the most important aspect of science now is biology and in biology in particular I think if I was this man, I would single out one particular line of research, which I must say is going on in a number of countries, simultaneously and that is the attempt to artificially fertilise human germ tissue; that is to say, to start developing foetuses in laboratory, rather than in mothers. I think the potential that this type of work, artificial growth of a person (somebody has coined the term test-tube genesis), this sort of work has so much more capability for damage and harm and degradation of us to a degree, that I think I would single out as a first task for this ombudsman.'

Gordon Rattray Taylor's *The Biological Time Bomb* was published in 1968 and evaluated current research, offering a prediction of what the future may hold for mankind. There had been more and more advances claimed in genetics, and the fertilisation of an egg outside the womb was only a matter of months away. Taylor quotes scientists who were concerned by the work. It is not that the motives are in anyway suspicious, but that no-one seems to be thinking about the issues, or wondering how the work could be perverted or corrupted – or just go wrong. How can these things be misused? Test-tube babies may be a godsend for barren couples, but what else could that knowledge be used for?

Taylor argues that 'the feeling that some kinds of knowledge are too dangerous, at least in the current state of social and intellectual development, is founded... on the belief that he [the scientist] is more likely to use new power for ill than for good. Or perhaps...that more people will misuse the new powers, or that they will be misused more often than they will be used for good.' He concludes that society will have to control the pace of research. Well-meaning and well-intentioned scientists could develop something that the less well-intentioned could create havoc with. They have to face up to their responsibilities and beware of the consequences. There wasn't long to wait.

Developments
Throughout 1969, the year of the episode's pregnancy and delivery, the IVF story kept developing. The first successful fertilisation inside a test tube was reported in November 1969. There would more news to come in 1970. On 15 February 1969 (and not Valentine's day as is often reported) research was published in *Nature* from Cambridge physiologists Dr R G Edwards, Dr B D Bavister and Dr P C Steptoe, a senior consultant in gynaecology and obstetrics at Oldham Hospital (and whose first name, perhaps not coincidentally, was Patrick). They announced the first in-vitro fertilization – IVF – and survival of human oocytes. The eventual aim was to fertilise an egg outside the womb to help women who could not conceive due to, for example, blocked fallopian tubes. For the past ten years, experiments had been conducted on animals, and a rabbit's egg had been successfully fertilised in a test tube. Now, the first human experiment was carried out. One of the difficulties was replicating the type of fluid found within a woman's reproductive tract. The *Nature* report caused a media sensation. But the moral and ethical minefield that would later engulf IVF didn't immediately occur – except in the minds of people like Kit Pedler and Gerry Davis.

The Artificial Womb
The artificial womb seen at the end of the story was an extension of the artificial placenta being developed in Britain and other parts of the world. The purpose of such a unit was to provide a way of helping prematurely born infants who are too young to cope with breathing. *The Biological Time Bomb* describes how one machine in King's College Hospital, London, kept a 26-week-old foetus alive for five hours. The design was based on heart-lung machines. The Department of Experimental Medicine at Cambridge had been developing artificial placentas by experimenting on pig embryos. Taylor wondered what would happen at the end of a working day in a lab. How many foetuses would be washed down the sink? Which ones would be chosen to live? It is a debate raging today – when does a human life begin and what are our responsibilities towards the unborn child? In 1970

Pedler argued 'If you succeed in technically getting the foetus developing you have a potential man on your hands. What do you do with it once you have no more use for it in your experiment? Do you throw it in the trash-can. Or give it a Christian burial?' The closing moments of 'Friday's Child' show Mrs Patrick faced with this very dilemma as she is invited to switch off the artificial womb which is keeping alive the decerebrated baby. We do not see the resolution.

Production
Writing the Script
'Here, hot from the press, is a very contemporary and topical story!' wrote Gerry Davis to Harry Green on 17 February 1969, enclosing a copy of the storyline he had written with Kit Pedler called 'The Patrick Experiment'. 'We thought that one up as a warning', Pedler later told the *Radio Times*. 'If the technique were perfected, a general, for instance, might be able to order 100,000 troops to be produced. The possibilities would be terrifying.' This was the eighth storyline accepted, on top of the two scripts Dudley and Pedler had already written. Harry Green had recently written a script for *The First Lady* called 'Blow Hot, Blow Cold' and was one of Terence Dudley's favourite writers. Green had turned down several other storylines but did indeed accept this one and was contracted on 26 February to deliver 'Friday's Child' – the sixth script to be commissioned. The target delivery date was 1 April. The issue of heart transplants was subject for an episode of ATV's business drama *The Power Game*, where a dying minister is needing a heart donor, and the dealings in trying to secure consent from a grieving wife. 'The Heart Market' was transmitted in March 1969.

Green was very excited by the story and sent the script (three copies of it) in on time. However, he apologised for delivering such a 'cack-handed' piece of work, thinking only a psychiatrist could explain why his mind insisted on calling Quist 'Quince!' He also feared that the script was two minutes too long (each episode had to be forty-nine minutes) and wanted discussions before it was trimmed. He noted that a recently transmitted edition of *Horizon* called 'The Unborn Patient' featured colour pictures of an advanced foetus, which the author felt was not in the least bit off-putting and ideal for a telecine insert he had written into the early draft of the episode.

With the scripts officially received on Monday, 31 March, rehearsal scripts were sent out to Green by the end of the week. Judy Hall, secretary to Gerry Davis, noted that once the planning people got around to telling them when the rehearsal dates for the episode would be, she would let him know. In June there were moves to write in Pat Hunnisett, but this did not happen. Green was paid very quickly, and a very happy production team (especially Terence Dudley, who felt it should be the series yardstick in terms of characterisation) commissioned Green a few months later to write the tenth script for the series, entitled 'Hear No Evil'.

Script

Harry Green's script contains several interesting asides. Patrick's hospital is described as a 'Victorian gothic building.' He suggests that during the trial scenes 'all that is needed is the witness box, and area near it for the Solicitor and a part of the public area where we see Mrs Patrick, Wren and Mr Norman, a choleric workman bursting with resentments.' When Ridge breaks open Patrick's filing cabinet, Green notes: 'If there's a way of forcing filing cabinet drawers without leaving marks. I hope M.I.6. knows it: I don't.'

There is a little light relief in the presence of a present. Ridge brings a Bassett hound puppy into the Doomwatch offices, which he briefly hides in a waste paper bin to surprise Wren, who has been wanting a dog. Green noted: 'I'm not bigoted about the breed of dog – anything endearing will do.' The puppy is taken into Quist's office, where a number of allusions to the pup is made. Ridge talks of an itch to scratch. Green notes: 'I'm afraid even a well-trained dog couldn't take this cue.'

Filming

There was minimal location work. Of the regulars, only Simon Oates was needed, scaling the walls to break into Patrick's laboratory. The other filmed material concerned the attempted baby-snatch outside a shop and the brick coming through the window of Baby Patrick's room, presumably at Ealing Film Studios.

Cast

Neither Joby Blanshard nor Wendy Hall were required for the episode. Delia Paton, who appeared briefly on film as Mrs Norman, (but not in the studio during the trial scenes), would later play Mina in Terence Dudley's next science fiction offering *Survivors*. She also had a small role in *The Big Pull* as a nurse.

The young child in question was the director's own boy, Sam, and the mother of the piece was the director's wife, Mary Holland. She had been famous throughout the 1960s as the angelic housewife Katie who knew what was best for her family by giving them Oxo cubes. To give the actress a different look, make-up designer Elizabeth Warren designed a new hairpiece. On the day of transmission, the newspapers focused on Mary Holland's first straight acting role since her eleven-year stint as Katie. Interviewed by the *Daily Mirror*, Mary explained how she had paused her career to look after her family and hoped one day to play Jane Eyre. She brushed aside the idea of favouritism (if not nepotism) in her casting by explaining that this was the first time her husband had ever cast her in one of his productions. Mary and her son Sam Ciappessoni got their pictures in the *Radio Times*, taken from the filming of the first scene: 'Doomwatch asks whose heart?'

Alex Scott, who plays Dr Patrick, had been directed by Paul Ciappessoni in an episode of *Vendetta* in 1966. Richard Caldicott, playing Gwilliam, was very much in demand as an actor, often playing blustering comedy admiralty types in *The Navy Lark* on radio, or on television in *The Avengers*. Margaret John had been a regular in the second series of *The First Lady*.

Studio
'Friday's Child' was the fourth episode to be recorded. It took place in Studio TC3 on Saturday, 10 January 1970, a day after the camera rehearsals, which ran into overtime. After the episode had been recorded, film was transferred to tape for 'The Plastic Eaters'.

Stock Music
Thirty-six seconds of 'Jungle Soul', a track from Chappell's Dance and Mood Music volume 6 by Jack Arel and Jean-Claude Petit, performed by the Jean-Claude Petit Orchestra, backed one of the film sequences. In a sense, it is all that survives from 'Friday's Child', which is the earliest missing *Doomwatch* episode.

Editing
The episode was edited on Monday, 12 January 1970 between 10.30 am and 1.30 pm The rest of the day was taken up with 'The Plastic Eaters'. Terence Dudley was so pleased with the script and final production that when Doomwatch was nominated for the Mullard Science Award, 'Friday's Child' was the episode he put up for nomination. 'There wasn't a hope of being placed in the documentary field', Dudley told Harry Green in 1972, 'but it was pleasant to be acknowledged'.

Press Reviews
The artificial foetus which featured towards the end of the story certainly impressed Gerard Garrett of the *Daily Sketch*, who wrote 'Highly surgical stuff for a thriller ... and the programme asked the question: it right to chop up monkeys for science? Is it ethical to breed brainless children to provide spare parts? I'm all in favour of light entertainment delivering food for thought but these were rather weighty moral problems.'

Mary Malone in the *Daily Mirror*, on the other hand, found the episode a bit too much: 'A dry scientific discussion on *Tomorrow's World* dealing with these topics is just about tolerable. But when you wrap up all the issues in a drama involving a mother and her dead child, a surgeon who has used a monkey's heart to save his own boy and is growing a brainless foetus to replace the heart in ten years' time, you have a horror film for the audiences of 2000 AD ... The agony was piled on without restraint even down to those early evening blurbs that showed a chubby infant and asked: "What is so special about this particular baby?" which sounds fine until later you found out it had a monkey's heart.' Nancy Banks Smith, writing in the *Guardian*, was more interested in seeing Katie from the Oxo commercials in a straight drama and pontificated on the jingles from adverts as nursery rhymes for our time ...

The *Press and Journal* said: 'I wasn't every enthusiastic about BBC1's new series *Doomwatch* after reading the advance publicity. It looked as if we were in for gimmicky pseudo-science fiction – a kind of BBC *Avengers*. And anyway who could believe in a team of scientists headed by a man with the extraordinary name of Spencer Quist ... I still don't feel that the Doomwatchers have piled up much credibility as a team. They seem a rootless bunch and their smart but featureless office home lacks character. Quist's two colleagues Tobias Wren and the unorthodox Dr John Ridge are, I think, based on character concepts too exotic and old fashioned in a TV world which has taken [down at heel *Public Eye* enquiry agent] Frank Marker and [government assassin with a conscience] *Callan* to its collective heart. None of this really mattered last week, however, if the script ideas are as interesting as "Friday's Child" by Harry Green.'

Programme Review Board
At their meeting on Wednesday, 18 February, it was praised as a very good episode, if a little 'harrowing'.

The Beginnings of a Reputation
The *Radio Times* notched up 'Friday's Child' as one of Pedler's prophetic storylines when they were promoting the second series in December 1970, although it slightly confused the time-line of the experiments in their reporting. A week after the transmission of 'Friday's Child', Dr Steptoe announced on the BBC that they expected to replant the egg taken from a 34-year-old woman, having fertilized it in a test tube, within six weeks' time. On Sunday, 23 February an edition of *Horizon* dealt with the subject of test tube babies. That same night, BBC Radio 4's *Ten O'Clock* programme interviewed Pedler himself on the subject and the next evening he was interviewed on BBC1's teatime news magazine series *Nationwide* the following evening. He outlined his argument that if the technique of creating babies outside of a mother's womb was perfected, a general could order up his troops in advance. His words appeared all over the world, as

the story was syndicated via the news agency UPI. *The Times* reviewed the radio broadcast and quoted from it. 'If you extend this experiment a little bit, it is a question of biological engineering ... This can only be stopped by the public making some sort of objection.' Dr Steptoe, also interviewed in the programme, said he did not have any moral qualms but understood that they needed help from public opinion. But as the Horizon programme showed, there were no shortage of women volunteers prepared to try this method of overcoming infertility.

The *Guardian* was on Pedler's side of caution. Science correspondent Anthony Tucker wrote 'Genetic engineering of a kind likely to have moral impact may still be some years away, but the uncritical enthusiasm which greeted the announcement of laboratory fertilisation should be a warning. There seem ... good grounds for suspecting that the ... experiment pegged to a "human interest" story is no more than an emotional smokescreen designed to cover the scientific desire to expand an experiment.'

Pedler told the *Hospital Times* not too long after transmission: 'I think further I don't quite know how you tell a child when it grows up that its mother was a bottle. That's an exaggeration, but something like that. The psychological effect on a child might be quite profound. I asked a number of people, especially my own four children. My daughter [Carol] is at university, and a lot of students come to the house. I get a lot of different responses. I asked them the question: "What would you feel like if you had been told you had been conceived in this way?" I wouldn't say all, but the majority of feelings were totally against it. They thought this was a complete satire on the way in which a child is normally conceived.'

Pedler, a father of four children, also felt it was like heart transplants, a total waste of money: 'The medical arguments put up for this by the people involved were nothing less than a sentimental smokescreen for what was essentially a scientific experiment. They made great play with the childless mother, which is a very bad situation. But there are children crying out to be adopted. I think the medical arguments for this ... is sentimental rubbish.'

Finally
It took another seven years and thirty failed pregnancies before Steptoe and Edwards succeeded in producing the first successful birth of a test-tube baby in 1978. Their success saw the creation of the Bourne Clinic to help the infertile. Naturally their work created a media sensation and hostility from religious and ethical groups. Steptoe died in 1988 and Edwards received the Nobel Prize in 2010. The issue of improving fertility in an over-populated world would be touched upon by *Doomwatch* in the next series.

1.03
Burial At Sea

Written by Dennis Spooner
Directed by Jonathan Alwyn
Designed by Moira Tait
Transmitted: Monday, 23 February 1970 at 9.40 pm Duration: 49' 17"

Cast
Lifeboatman (Steve Emerson), Angela Connor (Nova Sainte-Claire), Cobie Vale (Julian Barnes), Peter Hazlewood (Brian Spink), Admiral Tranton (Peter Copley), Dr Collinson (Gerald Sim), Johnny Clive (John Stone), Superintendent (Alec Ross), Nurse (Venetia Maxwell), Astley (John Horsley), The Minister (John Savident).

Also appearing
Extras on location
Toni Lee, David Seyforth, Leslie Conrad, Roger Wright, the crew of the Plymouth Lifeboat.

Extras in studio
Crawford Lyall, Wally Goodman, Freddy White, Archie Wilson, Brian Johns, Brian Scott, Geoffrey Witherick, Vic Taylor, Alec Dolman, Tony McKinnon, Peter Roy, Andree Cameron, Sheila Vivian, Sandra Satchwith, Ann Pip, Audrey Stewart, Dilys Marvin.

The BBC thanks the RNLI for their co-operation.

Technical Credits
Production Assistant: Christina Lawton. Assistant Floor Manager: Marion Wishart. Director's Assistant: Gwen Willson. Floor Assistant: John Wilcox.
Film Cameraman: Eddie Best. Sound Recordist: Bill Wild. Film Editor: Alastair MacKay.
Costume Supervisor: Dorothea Wallace. Make-up Supervisor: Elizabeth Rowell.
Studio Lighting: Jimmy Purdie. TM2: Jack Shallcross. Vision Mixer: Jim Stephens.
Studio Sound: Larry Goodson. Grams Operator: Gerry Borrows.
Crew: unknown.

Radio Times
A luxury cruiser adrift in the channel ... a lifeboat out to the rescue. What they find aboard starts a national scandal and involves Quist in another investigation.

The Story
'I'm making the point that oceans are becoming vast dustbins.' – Quist

The Plymouth Lifeboat is called out to investigate a mysterious vessel called the *Saracen*, adrift in the English Channel. Once on board they discover four young people unconscious inside a cabin. The fact that they are from a famous band called The Hoarse Chestnuts makes this front-page news. Quist is reading about it, much to Bradley's surprise. Is there anything in this for Doomwatch? A drugs overdose is the suspected cause of their coma. The story also worries Peter Hazlewood, the ADC to Sir Richard Tranton, an admiral on the verge of moving onto another job with the Transport Board to oversee the building of the Westingham Docks. It is the location of where the boat was found that disturbs Hazlewood – it must have sailed across a trench in the Channel called Hounds Deep. Tranton dismisses the concern: 'Oh, it's ridiculous. You know I might have expected something like this from one of our mono-hysterical crank societies, but from you ...'

Quist tries to speak to Dr Collinson, who is caring for the four unconscious band members at Plymouth General Hospital. At the moment he is refusing to discuss the case with a reporter, Johnny Clive, who is ushered out by the superintendent in charge of the criminal investigation. There are still two members of the boat's crew unaccounted for (their bodies will soon be washed up upon the shore), and the superintendent is waiting for the band's singer Cobie Vale – or any of the others – to recover for questioning. He has already made up his mind. When he speaks to Quist, Dr Collinson confides he doesn't know what type of drug would have produced this type of coma. Collinson rattles out a list of test results. The unusual symptoms alert Quist and he gets Pat to get Wren and Ridge to see him immediately.

Wren and Ridge arrive in Plymouth and are noticed by Clive. He follows them to their hotel and tells the uncooperative pair that Cobie Vale's band had been treasure hunting out in the Channel. Ridge sends Wren down to the boat, but not to look for drugs. He suspects Clive is on a different scent from the police. 'He's getting wind of a story all right – other than the one published,' Ridge muses. 'Some of the boys seem to have a sixth sense ...'

Tranton is troubled by the events on board the *Saracen*. He visits a man called Astley at his club, who was on a waste-dumping advisory board.

Astley can see no connection: 'Admiral. I can assure you that despite popular disbelief, not every advisory board is composed of idiots. I can assure you, also, that our task was accomplished with a high safety margin. Any other suggestion, from any quarter, would be totally irresponsible ...' Tranton agrees, but he is not so sure.

Ridge visits the hospital and speaks to the superintendent, who is following his drugs misuse line of enquiry. As Vale recovers consciousness, he does not seem to be able to move or communicate properly. Collinson tries to protect his patient from a police investigation for the moment. A girl named Angela is now well enough to speak, and she describes a cannon which they had recovered from the wreck of an eighteenth century East Indiaman. She describes what happened to her before she blacked out. 'My hands ... my hands started to shake ... uncontrollably ... The others too ... One by one ... Cobie was ... He seemed the worst ... He fainted I think ... I was ill ... terribly ill ... I couldn't focus my eyes ... I had no idea of time. I couldn't say if it was seconds, or hours, before ... before everything went black ...' She also explains that they had a party but strenuously denies they took drugs. The superintendent is disappointed. When Ridge speaks to Quist on the telephone, they discuss Hounds Deep, which is fifty miles off Start Point.

Ridge goes to look for Wren and finds him unconscious on board the *Saracen*. He had touched some green slime which he found on the recovered cannon and was putting into a sample jar, and went into convulsions. Before he collapses, he sees an image of himself, smiling from the cabin door.

The next day Quist speaks to a Minister, one he has not met before, but one well aware of Quist's reputation. Quist wants to know about deep-sea dumping sites and what was dumped at Hounds Deep. The Minister stonewalls but tries to reassure Quist that every safeguard had been taken. Quist disagrees. 'There's always an 'X' factor ...' After Quist leaves unsatisfied, the Minister calls Tranton. Quist decides to go down to Plymouth himself.

Wren is now in hospital, conscious but unable to speak. All he can do is look over at his clothes next to a cupboard. He is luckier than Cobie Vale, who dies. Quist uses a Geiger counter on the cannon, which registers, though not strongly enough to have caused the illnesses. Ridge discovers from the log that the crew had used explosives to dislodge the cannon. Wren manages to reach the cupboard and gets out a sample jar containing the slime he had collected. It takes a lot of effort and Quist praises him for it.

The Minister speaks to Tranton and Hazlewood. It seems Quist was right. Tranton explains that out of the three disposal methods, deep sea dumping was the most economic. The Minister reminds Tranton that he was given the responsibility, and it wouldn't do if this business led to a public enquiry. It may cost him his next job.

Quist confronts Tranton, Astley and Hazlewood: the dumped material at Hounds Deep was not only nuclear waste at a permitted level, but also nerve gas. 'Do you have any idea of what this stuff can do? A few gallons can wipe out a nation! When the Americans carried out a recent test, there was a wind change. They were on an isolated island – but seven thousand sheep died. Forty miles away! Even a minute case can cause ... reversal of vision – upside down, left to right. People have even seen themselves. A loss of touch. Of pain. And that's the best of it. The worst is lethal.' Astley robustly defends the committee, and Tranton is satisfied that the deaths were caused by drug misuse, especially now that illegal substances have been found aboard the boat. The idea that explosives ruptured canisters of nerve gas, causing a leak, is dismissed.

Back at Doomwatch, Bradley and Quist work out the direction the leaking poison would take. Ridge passes on this information to Johnny Clive, who visits Felm Estuary and finds the area full of dead sea birds. A mother and child, shrimping in rock pools, are brought into hospital. Wren fully recovers and is told that Quist has his ammunition now. The evidence is enough for the Minister. Quist is not apportioning blame, he explains, he just wants it put right before anyone else suffers.

Tranton leaves his office for the last time, taking one final look at the model of the docks which it is clear he will never build.

Behind the Story
Between the end of the Second World War and 1970, there had been over 100 worldwide burials at sea of chemical weapons. Sixty of them were done by the Americans. It began in 1945: twenty old merchant vessel ships containing German nerve gas shells were scuttled in the Baltic by the Allies. The rate of deterioration is unclear, and in some cases the sites are unknown. Legacy of the war would come back in the second series of *Doomwatch* to haunt 'The Islanders', but in the case of this episode, recorded in the closing weeks of the 1960s, the Cold War was still producing these terrible weapons. And they needed disposal. Greg Williams, the national spokesman for the Kentucky Environmental Coalition, an organisation that works for the safe disposal of chemical weapons, told *The Bulletin of Atomic Scientists* in 1997 that 'From the 1940s to the 1960s, the level of security and openness about the environment was less than it is now. It's still a struggle, but back then, nobody batted an eye about the environment.' Greenpeace and Friends of the Earth were just around the corner.

Britain's Doorstep

Britain was in on it too. Drums of sarin, tabun nerve gas and cyanide were dumped during the 1950s in the Atlantic Deep, situated west of the Outer Hebrides and north-east of the coast of Northern Island. *The Times* reported on 29 January 1955 that 1500 tons of radioactive waste, from its nuclear facilities at Harwell, including contaminated equipment, had been dumped, 1200 fathoms deep, south-west of Land's End in the Atlantic Ocean, well away from shipping lanes. The Atomic Energy Authority said that this was the largest amount so far dumped. The original plan had been to dump the material into disused coal mines in Gloucestershire, but local protests soon put a stop to that. The enormous weight was made up by the heavy steel and concrete containers. 'Some of the waste will be safe within a year or two,' a spokesman claimed. 'A smaller proportion will take 20 years, and a smaller proportion still may take 30 years. The effect of corrosion on the containers was calculated beforehand, and they have been constructed that those holding the more active waste will not disintegrate before their contents are harmless.' The report said that special care had been taken to select a spot where the containers could not end up washed ashore, nor salvaged and processed.

In 1960, the French created controversy when they planned to jettison their own waste into the Mediterranean Sea between Antibes and Corsica. Britain's own dumping grounds included Hurd's Deep, a deep-sea trench in the English Channel, off the Plymouth coast. The 1954 Atomic Energy Act allowed the Atomic Energy Authority to dump up to 5000 tons per year into the Deep, providing the radioactivity did not exceed 200 curies of alpha activity, a curie being the amount of radioactivity given off by one gram of radium. The waste, consisting of radioactive sludge, graphite, glass or metal, was packed into thin-walled drums which were again designed to rapidly erode, allowing the radioactivity to quickly disperse. The Atlantic Deep was allowed 1500 tons per year except there was no limit on radioactivity. These containers were expected to last for a much longer time since contained a deadlier and longer-lasting load. Pipes from the Windscale and Calder Hall plants in Cumbria sent 25,000 curies of active waste into the sea at this time, while Harwell also had a pipe, feeding into the Thames. Scotland contributed to this toxic soup with its waste from the Dounreay plant.

As early as 1960, concerns were raised as to the sustainability of disposing nuclear waste in this manner, especially considering the number of other countries wishing to join the nuclear club.

Production
Storyline
Pedler and Davis' storyline exists, and the Story Theme runs as follows:

The weapons' industry produces a large quantity of lethal material which never gets put to its proper use – killing people. It has to be disposed of. The European Nuclear Energy agency has given considerable attention to the problem and has published a detailed account of national and international agreements governing the dumping of nuclear waste.

There are now many substances other than radioactive materials which also have to be disposed of. Recently, the American military authorities decided to dump several thousands of tons of mustard gas and an unspecified nerve gas into an ocean which they do not own. This unequalled example of social irresponsibility will doubtless recur and when it does, the canisters in which the material will be dumped will eventually corrode and release their contents into our already polluted seas. But by this time, the persons responsible will probably have retired and will not be available to answer for their actions.

One of the most astonishing admissions to be found in the report of the European Nuclear Energy agency is that some of the canisters are deliberately designed to corrode rapidly.

Lethal waste is disposed of all over the United Kingdom. For example, the UKAEA have burial grounds in Cumberland and Lancashire. The Admiralty use the Firth of Forth and the Aldermaston establishment pipes hot material into the Thames. Relevant to this story, the UKAEA also use the Hounds Deep, a 69 miles long trench off Start Point, near Plymouth.

The conversion of our oceans into lethal rubbish tips is often under the control of high-ranking military or naval personnel who are commonly so devoted to the successful prosecution of the task in hand that they fail to see the obvious dangers to people and to wild life. Moreover, if a title and honourable retirement are at hand they are not going to admit responsibility for a disaster which they have initiated by a decision made many years ago.

The basic plot outline, written in June 1969, runs almost exactly as transmitted with just a few minor variations. Ridge and Wren make facetious remarks to Quist about the reports in the press of the 'drugs party to end all drugs parties.' The lead singers are called Bobby Vale and Dan Rogers, and Bobby survives to the end of the story, unlike Dan. There is no Johnny Clive, Minister nor any of the Admiralty characters other than the Admiral himself, who comes later into the story. It is stressed that the Admiral is a week away from retirement and sees Quist's investigations as a personal attack. Hounds Deep was either a misreading of Hurd's Deep or just considered to be a better sounding name. The climax takes place in the hospital when the shrimping family is brought in sick. 'This is the evidence Quist needs. He sets a trap for the Admiral, closes it, and demands that the [clean-up] operation be mounted forthwith. The Admiral reluctantly agrees, aware that the full-scale storm about to break over him will probably overshadow the achievements of a lifetime of service.'

Dennis Spooner

Dennis Spooner was commissioned on 26 June 1969 to write up the storyline 'Burial at Sea', the 13th story commissioned. The delivery date was 11 August 1969. Speaking to *Fantasy Empire* in the 1980s, Spooner recalled finding the experience of writing for *Doomwatch* a much more serious project than he was used to. Spooner was a veteran of ITC film series, some of which he created (like *The Champions* and *Department S*). He preferred a light touch and was more at home with the eccentricities of *The Avengers*, but, being such a technically able craftsman, he always delivered the goods. His episodes of *Doctor Who*, which he also script edited for over six months, nearly always contained a humorous streak, but he knew when to pull back and not let it swamp the drama. He brought the second Doctor to life, rewriting David Whitaker's very verbose interpretation of the new character, and turned him from a Sherlock Holmes into a Charlie Chaplin; he was virtually doing his old job of script editor for the programme's real one, Gerry Davis, who was having to write a brand-new story almost from scratch. Spooner was a very safe pair of hands.

Spooner reused an idea from an episode of *Department S* which he had scripted called 'A Small War of Nerves'. This too featured a character exposed to nerve gas who sees a hallucination of himself in the same room, smiling back. 'Burial at Sea's opening sequence suggests *Department S* – the investigation of a seemingly deserted boat reveals …

The script, when read cold, reads like a straightforward drama-documentary. There is some light relief with the character of Johnny Clive, who attempts to eavesdrop on a conversation in the hospital between the superintendent and Collinson, and has some comic interplay with Ridge. He recognises Ridge, and suggests that this is still very early days for the Department – 'You know, I thought your Department had had its wings clipped.' He also recognises that Toby Wren is new. Spooner has some fun with Pat Hunnisett, who is making a welcome return after a week's break.

She naturally knows all about the rock band in question, and Quist's preference for facing the engine whilst travelling in a train. 'Can't stand travelling backwards', Quist explains. 'Funny, some of our government superiors seem to make a habit of it', comments Bradley. 'Would it be too far afield to suggest that someone up there doesn't like politicians?' pondered the *Morning Star* review.

The script uses topical instances of dumping and nerve gas going wrong. 'Last September...five European countries jettisoned eleven thousand tons in the Atlantic alone' Quist tells the Minister. This occurred in 1967, and was reported a year later by the European Nuclear Energy Agency, which alarmed Pedler and Davis. The £85,000 operation was an international effort. There is also a reference to a cannister containing radioactive waste being washed upon a Lincolnshire shore, and the Americans claiming responsibility. The deaths of sheep attributed to a nerve gas leak took place in March 1968. The sheep died at an appropriately named semi-desert region called Skull Valley, 50 miles west from Salt Lake City, but fifty miles south-west from the Dugway proving ground and the Great Salt Desert. Nerve gas was being tested at Dugway, and an accidental release was presumed.

Filming
This would be the second episode to go into production, as the film effort required needed three of the regular cast in substantial scenes, meaning it had to take advantage of the pre-filming block. A week in Plymouth was scheduled from Monday, 10 November onwards. Robert Powell was needed every day except Thursday, Simon Oates for the first three days (but stayed with the unit the whole time) and John Paul was needed for just two. It seems probable that the Plymouth lifeboat crew filmed their scenes on Thursday, 13 November.

One man who remembers the filming very well is John Dare, who served as a volunteer with the Plymouth Lifeboat from 1959 until 1990. His profession was a rigger in the dockyards. 'In those days you couldn't just take out the boat when you wanted to. So [the BBC] got in touch and gave a donation, and the RNLI said to us if you are willing you can do it. I was the second coxswain at the time. Peter White was the coxswain, but his wife was having a baby and he asked me to do the job. I think we spent eight hours on this filming. You do it one way and then you do it another. We had the cameraman on our boat and then on the yacht. Then he was on another boat, taking a shot of us putting the moorings or ropes onto the cruiser so we could tow her. Next thing, he's on our boat, looking at the one we're towing. They were doing most of the filming from us. We were moored alongside the yacht, so they could get a close-up whilst talking to them. It was all dirty great big cameras! And it was a bit rough. The continuity girl, the one that takes all the times [the PA], she was sea sick, and in the end our assistant mechanic had to do the job.

'We met a few of the actors. One actor on the cruiser had a talking part, and all I had to say was "Full ahead!" I was the only one of us doing the talking! I think I had one close-up when I was giving the orders. In those days we didn't have radios – we had to shout our orders. One engineer would be on one engine and his assistant on the other. "Hold the port! Stop board engine! Full ahead on starboard engine!" and whilst working the wheels. Then Morse code came in and it was easier. When you try to shout out an order to a bloke on the wheel, and it is really rough weather, with all the noise he can't hear you.

'[The *Saracen*] was a local boat they brought out to do the job. It was a cabin cruiser, I think, that had broken down outside the break water. The chap that owned it died not long after. He used to live up in the Millbay docks, and the BBC contacted him because his was the only boat around at the time to do it, because in those days a lot of the boats used to be left out of the water in winter time and insurances would stop at the beginning of October. There were a lot of wooden boats, not much fibreglass then, and there weren't so many marinas around. He was all right because he was in Millbay docks on the inner basin. You go in and shut the gates, and the water would stay in all the time at the same level, no rise or fall. When we got inside the breakwater, it was a bit calmer. There wasn't so much water splashing around, so what they would do is get buckets of water, and when the bloke stuck his head out of the side of the cabin they flung a bucket of water over to make it look like big seas! After filming we went over to Cremyll, where they had a caravan where they put the food on. We put a mooring on the shore and they invited us along for a meal.'

Scenes were filmed inside the cruiser once it had reached the Millbay docks. Other scenes were filmed at the train station and at a local beach, where the two dead bodies from the Saracen are washed ashore. This was probably Wembury Beach as name-checked in the script. It may also have doubled for the fictitious Felm Estuary, where reporter Johnny Clive finds the dead seagulls. Over eight minutes of the episode were shot on film, not including the title sequence.

Casting

Making the first of two appearances as a Minister in *Doomwatch* was John Savident, who was frequently cast as a government official, but could easily portray a grotesque character. Peter Copley often played authority figures but always with charm, courtesy and precision, and here he is Admiral Tranton. He had appeared in 'The July Plot' edition of *The Wednesday Play* in 1964 along with John Paul and also appeared with him in the Out of the Unknown episode 'Stranger in the Family'. The sardonic

Astley was played by John Horsley, better known for his comedy roles such as the hopeless Doc Morrissey in *The Fall and Rise of Reginald Perrin*.

Gerald Sim, Richard Attenborough's brother-in-law, was also a comedy favourite in years to come, with a scene stealing performance as a vicar in both *The Fall and Rise of Reginald Perrin* and *To The Manor Born*. John Stone, playing Johnny Clive, had featured in the BBC's classic science fiction serial *Quatermass II* as Captain John Dillon and was at the time married to former film star Margaret Lockwood. Alec Ross, sometimes confused with Alex Ross, had been Shelia Hancock's first husband. He died in 1971 from cancer.

Studio
'Burial at Sea' was the second episode to be recorded and went into TC8 on 9 and 10 December 1969. The recording overran its allotted time in the studio. Max Harris provided two and a half minutes of background music for the episode.

Editing
No date is known for the editing of the programme. No recording survives of this episode.

Radio Times
The *Radio Times* continued to promote the series. This time it was a picture of Quist, Ridge and Wren inside the *Saracen*. A picture of Quist facing Tranton, Astley and Hazlewood appeared in the edition promoting the second series.

Myth Busting
In an article on *Doomwatch* in a 1988 edition of *DWB*, Gerry Davis recalled how the *Daily Mirror* printed a still from the episode alongside a story about canisters of poisons being washed up on the shores of Cornwall in 1972. Davis was confusing 'Burial at Sea' with Tigon's *Doomwatch* film, which featured a similar idea. However, on 12 December 1969, reports of mysterious drums being washed up on the Devon coast were reported. The *Press and Journal* wrote: 'They had been trawled up by fishing vessels off the South Devon Coast and dumped without the consent of the Ministry of Agriculture Fisheries and Food, who operate a scheme for the control of dumping chemical waste outside the three-mile limit of territorial waters and most of it disposed of safely in deep waters clear of fishing grounds.' The *Times* added that these drums were labelled 'caustic' and contained industrial waste. Several containers were corroded and had burst in the trawler nets. The crews were naturally concerned the effect the waste would have on fish and themselves. The stretch of coast in question

was close to one of the points where oil tankers transfer cargoes from large to smaller vessels, a controversial procedure since it was only five miles off shore. Although these events were too late for inclusion in 'Burial at Sea', Pedler and Davis would use the illegal dumping theme in the 1972 film.

Programme Review Board

The Board had some mixed views on the episode, which was watched by seven million viewers, with differing opinions on the acting. Shaun Sutton believed that the public would like the series very much. One commentator recognised how the series was not just pure entertainment, but dealt with issues now often in the news, citing a recent *Nationwide* edition that had covered the dumping of cyanide drums in the ocean. Michael Mills, from Light Entertainment, thought that this made the series more frightening than *Doctor Who*.

Press Reviews

Stewart Lane wrote in the *Morning Star*: 'As I asked myself (and I'm quite sure other viewers did the same) at this point; what was the official reason given for all those dead sea birds last year? If this series can continue to strike hard at real problems of today, and concern itself a little less with slightly unbelievable cloak and dagger activities, it will serve a useful warning and may be an educational function.'

John Dare

'I saw the episode when it went out. What I remember of it, it was good. I used to like *Doomwatch*. It was a good series. It's funny that they lost that one. The BBC got rid of a lot of good films as well when they were sorting out things. They didn't realise they lost some of the best things they did. I always keep an eye out on the old [UK] Gold to see if it comes up. I'd seen another film of that, all the off-cuts. They joined them up and sent it down to us. What happened to that I don't know, because I couldn't understand it – one of my crew was on my boat, but when we looked on the off-cut he was on the other boat! I'd like to find out who had that cut film. Somebody must have it somewhere.'

In the Public Memory...

The United States needed to dispose of nerve-gas rockets, which they had been producing only a few years before *Burial at Sea*, and these rockets were leaking. What would become one of the last dumpings occurred in 1970, but it did not happen quietly, and British journalists were quick to remember the *Doomwatch* episode. The plan was to dump 3,000 tons of nerve gas into the Atlantic Ocean, some 280 miles off the Florida coast, and at a depth of 10,000 feet. Conservationists created an uproar which delayed

Operation Dumping – but only for a short while. A Federal court judge refused to grant an order forbidding the dumping, and requested the authorities to choose a shallower zone, concerned that deep sea pressure would force open the canisters. The British Government supported the dumping, having sent out their own investigators, but their territory in Bermuda joined the outraged protests. Kit Pedler was on Radio 4's lunch time news programme *The World at One* on 7 August, discussing the issue, before appearing two weeks later on the evening equivalent, *The World Tonight*, to debate the proposition: pollution – are we making too much fuss? He reminded *Radio Times* readers of this very matter later in the year at Christmas.

Public opinion halted further deep sea dumpings by the United States Government. A study prepared by the National Academy of Sciences backed this up, and legislation was passed in 1972 to outlaw the practice. A year earlier, Icelandic, Scandinavian, British and Irish Governments put pressure to stop chemical waste dumping by the *Stella Maris*, a Dutch ship.

Hurd's Deep Now
As for Hurd's Deep, dumping stopped in 1963. Some 28,500 cannisters of British and Belgian waste had been deposited. Radiation levels are still being monitored by a plethora of agencies due its close proximity to the Channel Islands, and regulated discharges from two French locations, a reprocessing plant at La Hague and the nuclear power station at Flammanville. An investigation by German public broadcaster SWR, reported by *Spiegel Online*, suggested in that in 2013 there were still uncorroded cannisters of radioactive material within the Deep, at a point very close to the French coast. The German Green Party commented 'It's not for nothing that that dumping in the ocean has been forbidden for 20 years.'

1.04
Tomorrow, The Rat

Written and directed by Terence Dudley
Designed by John Hurst
Transmitted: Monday, 2 March 1970 at 9.40 pm Duration: 50′ 01″

Cast
Small Boy (Stephen Dudley), Joyce Chambers (Eileen Helsby), Dr Mary Bryant (Penelope Lee), Dr Hugh Preston (Robert Sansom), Fred Chambers (Ray Roberts), Ambulance Driver (Ian Elliott), Nurse (Marcelle Samett), Reporter (John Berryman), The Minister (Hamilton Dyce).

Also appearing
Extras on location
Hilde Walter, Samantha Tomlin, Philip da Costa, Lindsay Barker, Deborah Baker, Craig Maitland, Adam Richins, Catrina Munro, Sian Jones, Paul Nameer, Paschal Allen, Linda Stewart.

Extras in studio
Dilys Marvin, Michael Durham, Stella Munday, Nigel Stevens, Robert Howard, Ricky Logan, Barry Summerford, Richard Haines, Beryl Bainbridge, Harold White, Jo Hall, Gordon Styles, Connie Carling, Alastair Meldrum, Sylvia Rattray, Matthew Grey, Mary Huntingdon, Jack D'Arcy. Rats trained by John Holmes.

Technical Credits
Production Assistant: Haldane Duncan. Assistant Floor Manager: Hilda Marvin. Assistant: Adele Paul. Floor Assistant: John Wilcox.
Film Cameraman: Eddie Best. Sound Recordist: Bill Wild. Film Editor: Alastair MacKay.
Costume Supervisor: Dorothea Wallace. Make-up Supervisor: Elizabeth Rowell.
Visual Effects: Tony Oxley.
Studio Lighting: Jimmy Purdie. TM2: Jack Shallcross. Vision Mixer: Jim Stephens.
Studio Sound: Larry Goodson. Grams Operator: Martin Ridout.
Crew 6.

Radio Times
Genetic engineering can alter the shape, personality and intelligence of a

human being, even before it is born: by tampering with nature we can make Supermen. Today, we experiment on lesser animals, like … the rat.

The Story
'Embryonic Nazis on four legs!' – Quist

After a small boy is attacked in his pram by a rat, Doomwatch are called into investigate. Vulnerable people throughout London have also been attacked, but Ridge is not convinced rats are to blame; they don't go for people unless threatened. Toby Wren and Pat Hunnisett visit the Chambers family, whose son Alan has been hospitalised by a rat in their own kitchen. A previous caller to the Chambers household, Dr Mary Bryant, is currently expressing her concern to her boss, Preston, at the Ministry. A batch of cannibal rats have been released from her home, where she had been conducting approved experiments to keep down costs. Preston advises her to keep quiet and not indulge in a 'cosy sense of guilt'. Quist visits Preston to discuss the rat problem, which lies in the Cruel Poisons Act 1962 and failed attempts to sterilise the animals, then returns to Doomwatch, where a dead rat has been found to have a higher density of brain cells. He is suspicious that Preston is holding something back and that Bryant may be the key, since he remembers that she is a geneticist. He sets Ridge on to the case, describing her as 'a nice bit of homework'.

That night, as Ridge seduces a depressed Bryant in a bar, Toby and Bradley set rat traps in the Chambers' kitchen. They don't have to wait long, but discover that the rats have propped open the traps with knives and forks and taken the bait. Suddenly the rats attack, but they manage to fight them off, killing at least two of them. The rest escape, taking their dead with them. Ridge and Bryant discuss the ethics of genetic engineering. She explains her motivation in trying to remove abnormality from DNA, but Ridge is shocked – Hitler endowed people like her. He still sleeps with her, however. The next morning's papers are full of rat stories, and a stable girl finds a half-eaten horse. Ridge tells Mary he is a snooper from Doomwatch, and Preston calls her in to talk. She will be asked to resign, though her resignation will not be accepted, and then will cooperate with the media by explaining her experiment.

The Chambers read an interview with Bryant in horror, recognising her from her visit. Bryant tells Quist she doesn't understand what's happening: the rats she released were sterile and conditioned against eating human flesh. She shows Quist and Ridge the bunker where the rats live at her home and the rudimentary electronics to measure what they eat. They later examine a rat that had been trapped in the ambulance taking the Chambers' son home. Mary Bryant says it is not one of hers; it is too young and has no skin graft. Toby discovers, after cutting himself on a cage, that the rats are attracted to blood. That evening Ridge is investigating the observation room in Mary's house. Despite her protests, Ridge declares that unsterilized rats have escaped. He has been looking for weaknesses and anomalies in the concrete and steel walls; the rats have jammed the sensor pad used to monitor their feeding, levered open a sliding plate at the back of the room, chewed through the wall and escaped.

Quist confronts Preston over the cover-up and wants to go down into the sewers. Bryant goes with him, and they find a rats' lair with mice herded like cattle. Meanwhile, the rats are getting bolder and kill three children in Brentford, including the Chambers boy. Quist demands to see the Minister straight away, wanting immediate action. He reminds the Minister of how fast rats can breed: fertile in three months, six litters in a year, ten young to a litter. A pair of rats could create a colony of a hundred million in twelve months. Anticipating the Cabinet's decision, the Minister authorises the use of banned poisons, even though it may affect wildlife and farming. Amidst huge banner headlines about rats, local authorities begin to flood the sewers with rat poison. Soon, evidence of their effectiveness is apparent by the number of rat corpses in the sewers and by river banks. Quist is pleased by the figures but warns Preston that there could be a 'rat day' every month.

Guilt-struck, Mary Bryant turns down the offer of a date with Ridge when a distraught Mrs Chambers comes to see her. Chambers blames Bryant for the loss of her son and attacks her with a kitchen knife, slashing open her arm. Bryant goes to clean the wound. When Ridge arrives at the house, he is horrified to discover her half-eaten body in the rat bunker. He collapses to his knees in horror and grief.

Behind The Story

This is one of the most famous episodes of *Doomwatch* -- a frightening and gruesome story with some shocking moments (and some unintentionally amusing ones). If an ironic, modern-day programme wants to show a clip of a revered actor battling with stuffed rats safety-pinned to his trousers, they usually show Robert Powell going berserk in the kitchen whilst poor Colin Bradley doesn't quite know what to do with a frying pan. But what we really have in 'Tomorrow, the Rat' is a proper stab at the theme of genetic engineering first hinted at in 'Friday's Child'. But this time the experiment is on animals: in particular, rats. The purpose of the experiment was pest control, and there is no less a pest that people would wish to control than a rat. The *Radio Times* launching the series in 1970 declared 'Fact: in Asia there are seven rats to every Asian, in Europe one to every European.' So, what if the experiment goes wrong? And the shy, cunning rodent, rather than avoiding humans, actively seeks them out?

The War on Rats

Since the 1940s, the industry standard rodent poison was Warfarin. This was an anti-coagulant which stops blood-clots so the mouse or rat dies from internal bleeding over a ten-day period. That the rats had developed a genetic resistance was first identified in 1959 in a farm near Welshpool in Montgomeryshire. They established themselves in the next two years and started to spread out.

In 1966, the Ministry of Agriculture decided to create a three-mile wide belt around the county and use zinc phosphide to contain the resistant rats and prevent them spreading. Colonel Ralph Beaumont, chairman of the Montgomeryshire Agriculture Executive Committee wanted the Ministry to go further. He said: 'We feel that what is needed is not only containment but, as soon as possible, a great campaign of extermination promoted by the Ministry.' All it would take was one rat to jump onto a lorry in a bale of straw and end up in a city. Some success was reported in 1967, but the campaign would last for another two years, involving a thousand neighbouring Shropshire farmers to create a 300-square mile kill zone. At the beginning of 1969, the Local Government Information Office began an education campaign for councils and public alike on the dangers of the rat population.

In February 1969, when Pedler and Davis were putting together their storyline, the war on rats had reached South Lincolnshire where 25,000 of the animals were killed in just a few days with gas guns. More funds were made available and the campaign in Montgomeryshire was extended for another two years. They believed the resistant strain had been constrained in Welshpool and were now concentrating efforts in a West Midland site. The *Birmingham Post* reported that same month: 'Ministry officials believe that all the "super rats" within 1000 square miles of could be descended from the one which first acquired resistance to Warfarin.' Yet, despite positive noises about the use of a new German developed rat killer, a despondent official in Welshpool admitted defeat in April. 'Everybody has failed,' he said, 'failed miserably.' Mr Davies went on to say to the *Birmingham Post* on 30 May. 'There is no positive step the Ministry can take at present. What is needed is a new scientific breakthrough.' The article concluded: 'The council agreed that the Government should be pressed for grants to tackle the resistance problem.'

In 1970, the *Daily Mirror,* in an article titled 'Menace of the Super Mice', reported the words from a Rentokill official: 'Once the Warfarin resistant rats get into the towns no-one can stop them.' Dr Pedler was under no illusion about the rodent problem. In his capacity as the *Daily Mirror*'s chief scientific adviser, and probably drawing from his research for the storyline, he wrote about super-mice and the rat problem, concluding 'The answer is to find a new wonder killer, but everyone from the Ministry to private drug firms and local councils has so far failed … But something MUST be done. Cases of leptospirosis, a potentially fatal disease spread by rodents, nearly trebled between 1968 and 1969. In the meantime, rats and mice, which already outnumber us by two to one are increasing steadily, at a rough annual cost to the nation of £1 a rat and ten shillings a mouse.'

Genetic Engineering
Rather than do an episode about some wonder poison going wrong, Pedler and Davis' focus was on genetic engineering and how that could go awry. A single human gene had been isolated at Harvard University by a team including James Shapiro in November 1969. Shapiro abandoned his work for 'moral and ethical reasons'. He, too, had an imagination. Science correspondent Anthony Tucker, writing in the *Guardian* on 26 February 1970, had linked this event with the uncritical reaction towards the first fertilisation of a human egg and sperm outside a mother's womb. Tucker postulated that the next step in these experiments was to mature human embryos to their full term in a lab. 'Scientifically, such embryos destined for destruction after experiment would be useful to determine drug effects and to investigate cell behaviour. They might also lead to the emancipation of women from pregnancy and even to a reduction of live abnormalities.' Pick and choose your own embryo – designer children. Dr Bryant explains in the story how she is not averse to creating a 'super-man', believing that the height of irresponsibility is to knowingly conceive a disabled or an abnormal child. This is definitely Hitlerian, as Ridge points out – but he sleeps with her all the same. Later, Quist warns her that if you create a biologically perfect being, you may come face to face with God. She is willing to take that risk, and she also plans to extend her experiments to humans.

There were experiments being conducted on intelligence in rats. Peter Harper was a student working towards his PhD at Sussex University and had become disturbed by his research. He told *The Times* in July 1970 'I was doing experimental biochemistry on memory. This involved experiments on certain strains of rats which involved the transfer of memory from one animal to another by brain extract. At the moment we are working with rats but it might not always be the case and the obvious extension is to humans.' The purpose of the study was to unravel the mysteries of the central nervous system that could lead to cures for physical and mental diseases. He resigned as the implications of his research being transferred over to the human animal sank in.

Production
Script Development
The storyline was accepted under the title of 'Rattus Sapiens?' on 20

February 1969. Terence Dudley agreed to a £550 fee on 25 June 1969 to write it up into a script. Having spent six or more months criticising Pedler and Davis' writing, and having rejected at least three other scripts, it was his turn to put his money where his pen was. The same day his fee was agreed, he had sent 'Friday's Child' to Andrew Osborn, feeling that this was the only script he was comfortable in showing him.

The rat problem was being investigated by the Ministry of Agriculture's Rodent Research Department of the Ministry's Infestation Control Laboratory in Surrey. The London Pest Unit was based in Aldgate. In 'Tomorrow, the Rat', their fictional counterparts are developing long-term solutions to the rat problem – a form of genetic attack since humane poisons no longer worked. By the end of the episode, thanks to a lack of funds and carelessness, mutant rats are now roaming free in London and capable of producing several million offspring, attacking animals and vulnerable humans, such as children.

The Animals (Cruel Poisons) Act 1962 is the villain of the piece, at least so Terence Dudley's script seems to suggest. It prohibits the use of the strongest poisons on the market to be used on animals where a more humane method is available. A chemist in Coventry was prosecuted in 1967 for selling strychnine to a restaurant-owner to kill rats. After three children have died, Quist declares 'To hell with the Cruel Poisons Act!' Much earlier, Dr Mary Bryant is quoted in the newspapers and attacks the Act (which was then eight years old) as only being possible in a country that loves animals more than children. Adele Winston recalls: 'Terry certainly felt that the British cared more for animals than for children. He pointed out that the British made a fuss about the cruelty of bullfights but the Spanish didn't need an NSPCC (National Society for the Prevention of Cruelty to Children) because they didn't harm their children.'

To help the Minister justify the final attack on the mutant rats, Quist employs a number of military metaphors, and so does Dudley throughout his script. When Quist and Bryant enter the sewers, the rats do not run away but 'beat an orderly retreat'. This is war, echoing the various headlines 'War on Rats' seen during the 1960s. The metaphor, incidentally, is extended to include sex. When Ridge pounces on Mary on the sofa, he 'attacks' and she 'surrenders' ...

Since this is normally the second episode seen by those discovering *Doomwatch* for the first time (because the tapes for 'Friday's Child' and 'Burial at Sea' no longer exist), it comes as a complete and total contrast to the spartan, direct, scientific and realistic dialogue that Gerry Davis and Kit Pedler produced for 'The Plastic Eaters'. Dudley's first script is quite astonishing in its approach: violent, gory, sexy, sinister and funny. Dudley would never write again such a shocking, and hard-hitting script with a high casualty rate, and pouring grief after grief on the Chambers family.

Their son is first attacked and later killed (and two other children's deaths are reported), and Mrs Chambers attacks Bryant with a kitchen knife in a superbly acted scene. Bryant tries to comfort Mrs Chambers, perhaps wanting forgiveness, but is instantly repelled with a vicious, disgusted look. It is a powerful moment. Then, there is what is left of Dr Mary Bryant herself at the end: Dudley wrote in the script 'On the floor, near the end of the pipe from the bunker, is a female skeleton. It is partially covered with the remains of Mary's clothes.' Her death has sometimes been put down as a suicide, but clearly this was an accident. The smell of the blood she was trying to wash off brought the rats to kill their creator.

Cast

The part of Dr Mary Bryant was especially written for actress Penelope Lee, whom Dudley would cast as a lead in his next series, *The Regiment*. Bryant is described as 'thirty-two years old and no bluestocking. She is sexually very attractive, but is female rather than feminine.' Penelope Lee auditioned to be one of the very first *Doctor Who* companions, and had recently finished a series for Yorkshire Television called *The Flaxton Boys*. Hamilton Dyce and John Paul had appeared together in the 1967 *Softly, Softly* episode 'The Next Voice You Hear'. Robert Sansom had recently appeared in *The First Lady* as had Eileen Helsby, who had been previously cast by Dudley in his episode of *Softly, Softly* called 'Cause of Death' in 1968. Helsby would later appear as a regular in the first series of *Survivors*. John Berryman had also been in a *Softly, Softly* directed by Dudley, this time in 1968 as a policeman. Making her first *Doomwatch* appearance, as one of the extras booked only for the studio day itself, was Beryl Bainbridge, later to be a hugely successful and influential author. Bainbridge trained as an actress at the Liverpool Playhouse and had worked for BBC Radio in Manchester.

Filming

Dudley decided to direct this episode himself. It was the third to go into studio, and the filming began on Monday, 17 November 1969 in London. Simon Oates' one scene was shot on Tuesday, 18 November, and John Paul filmed his descent into the sewers the next day, with John Berryman as the reporter making his only contribution to the episode with dialogue not in the script. Ian Elliott and Marcelle Samett were the ambulance driver and nurse taking home young Alan Chambers, played by Philip Da Costa. Elliott and Samett had dialogue to be performed out of view, which was not used in the finished episode. Other filmed scenes included the discovery of the dead horse in a stable mews, rats emerging into a school playground and a rat inside a car, driven by Terence Dudley himself. A rat attacks Dudley's real-life son, Stephen, out of vision in the opening moments, and his wife, listed as Hilda Walter, is one of the terrorised housewives.

Studio

'Tomorrow, the Rat' went into camera rehearsals on Friday, 19 December 1970 in TC3 and was recorded the next evening.

As well as on film, the rats made appearances in the studios in cages and on the Chambers' kitchen set. Tony Oxley of the Visual Effects Workshop handled the effects required, assisted by Ian Scoones. One of the things they had to make were animatronic rats but quite where they were used in the episode, if at all, is unclear. The stuffed rats which 'attack' Wren and Bradley in the Chambers' kitchen were safety-pinned to the actors' trousers by Elizabeth Rowell during a recording break. The camera positions for the attack itself were decided during camera rehearsals.

The final scene was one Simon Oates refused to rehearse; Adele Winston remembers that 'At the end when Simon Oates is picking up Penny Lee for a date and he finds her body, he said very sensibly beforehand, "I don't want to see it, I just want to react to it," and he does, he falls to his knees in horror, it was disgusting. Simon always gave beautiful performances.' Oates certainly follows the directions in the script, which tell him to sink to his knees in grief. It is a most effective and unsettling ending to the episode. Make-up Supervisor Elizabeth Rowell had to make up the corpse. 'They presented me with a skeleton and we had to try to make it up. We bought little pieces of meat for it. Simon said to me afterwards, "That was a bit of a joke, wasn't it?" And I'm sure if I looked at it now I would cringe.'

Music

Music was a mixture of Max Harris cues and stock records, some played so quietly as to be nearly inaudible. 'All Things Bright and Beautiful' was specified in the script to be heard drifting in through the Chambers' kitchen window and came from a *Music For Pleasure* album. It was sung by the Salvation Army Sunbury Junior Singers (MFP 1188). 'Strange Galaxy' by Jack Arel and Jean-Claude Petit (or the 'bouncy tune!' according to the unidentified DJ) can be heard in the beginning of the car scene where the driver is attacked by a rat. Arel and Petit's 'Ahmedabab' *Theme* was also used, both tracks coming from *Gravure Universelle: Dance and Mood Music Vol. 6*, published by Chappell (DWM306). *Harry Howard and his Music* provided 'A Touch of Brass', written by F Berlipp, from the easy listening range Mozart Edition LP range (MELP 039).

Editing

The episode was edited on Monday, 22 December 1969. Nothing appears to have been cut.

Press Reaction

Jazz singer and the *Observer* television critic George Melly enjoyed *Doomwatch* but felt that 'there was no need to show the nympho after the rats had got at her'. He wasn't alone. According to the *Daily Express* the day after transmission, 'Angry viewers telephoned the BBC to protest at gruesome scenes in an episode about a plague of super rats … One scene was about a woman half-eaten by the rats.' The fuss was even reported in the *New York Times* in April – London: 'Of Man, Rats and the Absurd'. Adele Winston remembers the opening scene disturbed one viewer. 'I've got a solicitor friend who isn't a fool, and he said, "If that was my little boy I wouldn't never let him near a rat," and I said "Well, nobody did. The rats were there in the morning and the little boy was there in the afternoon." He swore he saw little Stephen in the same shot as rats! But if you inter-cut quickly people think they've seen things that they haven't.'

A correspondent to the *Birmingham Daily Post* found Monday's night viewing a depressing experience in general. 'Take the repulsive play on ITV … *Rumour*, at peak viewing time, sodden with drink, sex (naked men and women in bed), strip-tease, belly-dancing, blackmail, murder (twice), dead bodies in the morgue, – the lot. Then, if you switched over immediately to *Doomwatch* you saw a most revolting programme about brainy rats killing people, finishing up with a woman covered in blood eaten to death by our little furry friends. I didn't seek these programmes out. I turned on for an evening's entertainment and that is what I got. As I said to my wife as I staggered off to bed, "We'll have to sell the tele [sic]. I can't stand this sort of stuff!" How do they get away with it? It is just a monumental disregard of what people think, and personally I think they should be restrained.'

The *Listener* thought the rats seemed positively abstemious, considering their number. 'Beyond the odd nibble at a passer-by they contented themselves with one or two children and half a lady scientist. When you think how humans treat each other, this amounts practically to peaceful coexistence. The rats one saw most had a quiet, pet shop air, and seemed alarmed by the panic they aroused. "It's like a shark!" screamed Quist at one cowering specimen. Well, like a large mouse.' The reviewer reflected that a scientist could certainly turn a rat into a horrible image: 'He does it by letting it lump around with huge induced cancers or with part of its intestines clipped outside its skin. A glimpse of one of these humanitarian experiments would have been more stomach churning than the furry monsters of *Doomwatch*.' Graham Chedd in the *New Scientist* agreed. What rats underwent during a genuine laboratory experiment was horror enough.

Programme Review Board
The Board concurred with the complaints. Some of the commentators felt that the adventure had been well done, but terrifying. One thought that 'some rather nasty moments had been held on to by the camera direction too long'. Andrew Osborn agreed that the episode contained many things that the 'service could have done without', and the blame seemed to lie on the same person writing, directing and being in charge of the production. No-one had told him that he had gone too far.

Ten and a half million viewers watched the episode. *Doomwatch* was a hit.

1.05
Project Sahara

Written by N J Crisp and Gerry Davis
Directed by Jonathan Alwyn. Designed by Moira Tait
Transmitted: Monday, 9 March 1970 at 9.41 pm Duration: 53' 35"

Cast
Commander Keeping (Nigel Stock), Barker (Robert James), Computer
Technician (Margaret Pilleau), Computer Voice (Peter Hawkins), Dr Stella
Robson (Hildegard Neil), Jack Foster (Philip Brack), Old Man (Erik Chitty),
Young Man (John Linares)

Also appearing
Gary Dean, Jay Neill, Roy Hathaway, Derek Chaffer, Bill Leonard, Peter
Roy, David Felton.

Technical Credits
Production Assistants: Nick Parsons, Christina McMillan. Assistant Floor
Manager: Marion Wishart. Assistant: Gwen Willson. Floor Assistant: John
Wilcox.
Costume Supervisor: Dorothea Wallace. Make-up Supervisor: Elizabeth
Rowell.
Studio Lighting: Jimmy Purdie. TM2: Jack Shallcross. Vision Mixer:
Graham Giles.
Studio Sound: Larry Goodson. Grams Operator: Gerry Borrows.
Camera Crew: 19.

Radio Times
The time is fast approaching when a person's entire history – educational,
medical, criminal, even financial – may end up as a foot of computer tape
in some impenetrable central file. Worse still, a man's future career may
depend upon the computer's evaluation. This week the Doomwatch team
fall under the baleful eye of a newly established section.

The Story
'In calculation the computer is my superior, but in judgement it is not.' –
Quist

Inside Department XJ7 of the National Security Section, Commander
Keeping is calling up files on Doomwatch personnel, which are displayed

105

and intoned by a computer. Barker, the Minister's Parliamentary Private Secretary, explains that his mission could mean disbanding the current Doomwatch team because of their investigations into Project Sahara. The Doomwatch offices are full of potted plants as their investigation into the new top-secret defoliant Sahara progresses. Dr Stella Robson is assisting the team and is very popular. She seems to have the whole team in order, especially Ridge. Their test shows how quickly and devastatingly the defoliant spray works on vegetation. Concerned over its effect upon the soil, Stella is adamant that it must never be used as a weapon. Wren points out that all they can do is make recommendations. Quist calls Stella and Toby into his office – direct orders from the Minister: they are suspended as of now.

Stunned, Toby drowns his sorrows in a bar, and Stella leaves him when he becomes obnoxious. A man offers to joins Toby for a drink and soon they get chatting. The man is Commander Keeping. Stella returns to the Doomwatch office, where Quist explains that Toby's weakness is to hit the drink when he is faced with injustice or despair. Quist is determined to fight the suspensions and tells Ridge to find out who is behind them. He wants both of them back and invites Stella to join the Doomwatch team on a full-time basis. She agrees.

Stella is having an affair with a married man called Jack Foster, who tries to comfort her over the suspension. He is also very interested in a manila envelope marked 'Project Sahara'. Ridge discovers that Department XJ7 is a new set-up and very clever; after his discreet enquiries, he had received a telephone call from Commander Keeping at home. To Wren's horror, Keeping, the very man he had been boozing with, turns up at the office to talk to Quist. Keeping knows very little about Project Sahara and explains this is why the suspensions were recommended. He will not divulge the source of his information, and Quist refuses to budge on his stance. A little later, Wren confesses to his drinking spree – and that Keeping had been there too.

Wren hits the bottle again, in the full knowledge that if he had said one word about Project Sahara to Keeping last night, his career would be over. He passes out in Stella's bed, much to her dismay: she is expecting Jack. Keeping arrives and questions her on her background in order to regain her clearance. She relates how her father was killed in Palestine by a Jewish terrorist but that she has no hate within her, and would not offer Sahara to the Palestinians in revenge. She is shocked when Keeping asks if she has a lover, declaring that she does not. After Keeping leaves, Jack returns, having waited for the Commander to leave. He is not pleased to find the unconscious Toby but decides not to hang around whilst Stella tries to revive him. As he leaves, he takes the envelope. Stella notices.

Quist goes to see Barker to demand the source of the Commander's information, threatening to telephone the Prime Minister and resign. Quist is shown the computer room and is appalled: Wren and Stella have been tried and found guilty by a machine. Barker explains that centralising information on people is going to happen and that Government was the most logical place to start. Quist insists on seeing the information; Barker reluctantly agrees. The next morning Keeping returns to Stella's flat, asking if she has anything to add to last night's statement, and when she says she does not, he goes, much to her surprise. Quist rejects Keeping's assessment of the information, but the Commander is adamant in his decision. Meanwhile Jack hands over the Sahara documents to an old man in a bric-a-brac shop. He is prevented from leaving by a younger and much stronger man. The envelope contains blank paper – and a note from Stella, which says she hopes he never reads it, otherwise they can never meet again. The old man does not look pleased.

Quist fights a losing battle with Barker and Keeping to retain his colleagues, but a phone call for the Commander changes things. He takes Quist and Stella to a mortuary where the body of Jack is laid out. She confesses to her affair with him and learns that he had been spying on her. Keeping warns her that she will have to prove that he knew nothing about Sahara. Quist now agrees that Stella will have to be replaced but asks for the Commander to make the final judgement over Wren. It was Keeping's thirty years as a policeman that made him suspect Stella was lying, even though the computer made no mention of her affair. Quist's confidence pays off, and Wren is reinstated with a clean bill of health. Ridge is impressed, wondering if Quist used blackmail, but Quist explains that human nature reasserted itself over the machine. Human judgement must always have the last word.

Behind the Story

This episode isn't about the titular defoliant which Doomwatch is investigating; it is about the security measures in place to monitor the team. It is very much a product of its time, but the themes still resonate – privacy, and the interpretation of our seemingly eccentric, human behaviour being used against us by the state. 'We are about to create a Data-bank Society. It could be as beneficial as penicillin or as dangerous as the machine gun. We had better sit down and think about it before we are engulfed,' according to a review of the book *The Databank Society* in *The Times* in 1970.

Harvey Matusow

'Human beings of the world, unite! The computers are taking over – and from now on it's got to be them or us!' So wrote American journalist and film maker Harvey Matusow, once America's most hated man, in his book

The Beast of Business: A Record of Computer Atrocities in 1968. In the early 1960s Matusow was living in New York, editing the *New York Arts Calendar* and recovering from his imprisonment after the McCarthy show trials. He was initially one of those who had stood up, testified and named names. Then he revealed it was all a ruse, published a book about it and in later years claimed he deliberately acted as an FBI stooge and knowingly lied to destroy them from within. For this act of perjury, he was jailed. Matusow became interested in the widespread use of the computer and of its abuses. With a few friends, he formed the International Society for the Abolition of Data Processing Machines.

By 1966 he was living in London, a wildly eccentric professional clown and musician (he formed the Jews Harp Band), but he aimed for the destruction of the computer that interfered and encroached upon our lives. His book listed examples culled from the media of computer abuses. In hindsight they read pretty mildly, but his dominant theme was how the 'word' of the computer was accepted over that of a human being. A computer should know its place, he argued. 'The computer is just an over-rated adding machine' declared Matusow, echoing Quist's frustration with the Doomwatch computer in 'The Plastic Eaters'. It is excellent for problem-solving, but with poor programming (as we shall see in 'The Iron Doctor'), the resulting mistakes can cost a person money – at the very least. The computer's omnipotence was accepted by those who worked under its spell: ordinary people who refused to accept that the machine could make a mistake because 'the computer can't be wrong.' Matusow blamed the ongoing conflict in Vietnam (which Britain was struggling to avoid engaging with) on the computer analysis of the war itself. Joint Chiefs of Staff were reduced to being overpaid messenger boys. The war itself was boosting the money going into the development of computers, computers which according to Matusow were sending more men to the killing fields. Membership of the Society grew year on, year out, many of them computer specialists and IT operatives, all equipped with an anecdote or two.

If Kit Pedler hadn't read the book he would certainly have recognised the sentiment, for he knew Matusow personally during his the latter's stay in England until his departure in 1974. The premise of the story is very close to Matusow's view: 'The computer is an abdication of responsibility', he told American radio in 1972 whilst promoting an avant-garde musical performance. He wrote about the computerised pooling of information the episode portrays, and which happens today. He told *Time* in September 1969 that when the computer is involved with business or government, 'the individual is tyrannized then we make our stand'. 'Even in this country', Pedler told the *Radio Times* just before the second series aired, 'there's evidence of a lot of information stored on computer tape which should be private – and certain people we'd prefer not to may have access to these tapes'. Barker mentions the idea that if enough information is known, potential future offenders can be dealt with in advance, taking away temptation. It's a frightening concept, suggesting that patterns of behaviour, background and environment can predict someone's future criminality. The idea would be more fully explored in *By the Pricking of My Thumbs …* during the next series.

Questions in Parliament
Civil liberty campaigners and some politicians were aware of the potential misuse of the computer databank. In May 1969, Conservative MP Kenneth Baker introduced his unsuccessful Data Surveillance Bill which would introduce a code of conduct, backed up by legal sanctions for computer operators who collect and access private and personal information. He calculated that of the 120 computers (which lest it not be forgotten, were massive pieces of equipment at this time,) half of them were recording personal information. The Post Office had recently installed an £800,000 system 4-70 computer at its National Data Processing Service's north-eastern division in Leeds to calculate an efficient route for a postman on his rounds and make compiling the telephone directory less labour intensive. It was also designed to help track down TV license dodgers. Baker argued that there needed to be safeguards to ensure the accuracy of the information and allow the individual to see what they had on him, and challenge mistakes. Oddly enough, civil service resistance to this very idea became the basis of an episode called *Big Brother* of the civil service sitcom *Yes, Minister* in 1980.

The Spooks
Vetting by security is never pleasant, and there were cases in the 1960s and 1970s of it going wrong for the most trivial of reasons. Reading the *Morning Star*, a very left-wing newspaper, was seen as indicative of a type of thinking, according to Tony Benn's diaries from the time. The episode is not arguing against the need for security, only who is behind it. There is genuine espionage going on. We have no idea who the sweet old guy played by Eric Chitty represents, or to whom he is selling information. Commander Keeping is concerned that Dr Stella Robson is going to pass on secrets to the Palestinians or the Syrians in order to starve Israel into submission in revenge for her father's death, but a few well-placed bugs in the Doomwatch offices would have overheard her declare twice that the substance must never be used. 'Makes a change from finding communists under the beds', remarks Quist.

Chemical Warfare
Sahara seems to be a take on Agent Orange, recently used by the

Americans during the Vietnam War. As well as starving the enemy of food, it was designed to remove their cover. This was chemical warfare, but America had never ratified the Geneva Protocols of 1925 because military pressures needed such weapons and fought hard to reserve the right to use anti-plant agents. In response to a protest statement written by twenty-nine American scientists against the use of anti-crop agents in Vietnam, Pentagon spokesman Major General Davison is quoted as saying 'this is not chemical or biological warfare, nor is it a precedent for such. It is in actuality a relatively mild method of putting pressure on a ruthless enemy.' The argument ran that it was harmless to humans in the long term, and non-toxic; therefore it was not a chemical weapon. Chemical warfare, especially when used to kill plants in a time of war, is forbidden under the Geneva Convention. Project Sahara kills plant life almost instantaneously and reduces the soil to a sand-like powder after only a day. Let us hope it was never taken up by NATO in the end.

Production
Script Development
'Project Sahara' had a complicated route to production. It started off life as 'Check and Mate' and was one of the very first storylines compiled by Pedler and Davis in 1968. It was given to Hugh Forbes, who was commissioned on 17 December 1968, to deliver by 20 January 1969. It would be script number three. Revised versions were received on 2 April but rejected shortly afterwards. However, Forbes remained in contact and on good terms with Gerry Davis, sending him a copy of an article he wrote for *Tribune* magazine in July.

On 9 September Norman J Crisp was commissioned to write 'Careless Talk', which the contract noted was previously 'Check and Mate'. This was the fifteenth commission and was due in at the end of October, when it was renamed 'The Lord of the Humans'. Once again, it was not accepted by the production team, who rejected it in December. In return for keeping the first half of his fee, Crisp agreed to allow another writer to revise his script and to have his name removed from the credits. This letter made it clear that it was Terence Dudley who rejected the script.

Gerry Davis performed the rewrites and received extra money on top of his usual script editing fee. He was paid by the traditional half-in-advance and half-on-delivery on 28 January and 3 February. Presuming that Davis wrote the scenes in question and didn't preserve some of Crisp's material in its entirety, elements of the series format document are given active expression here, such as MI6's suspicion about people of theirs who leave and Quist's bitter fight to protect his staff, even at the sacrifice of his own job.

The script was now called 'Project Sahara'. Davis would get the credit in the *Radio Times* and on screen, but N J Crisp was still listed as 'author' in documents such as the Programme as Broadcast sheets and the first page of the camera script, although the cover sheet which lists the production personnel and schedule features Davis' name.

Director
This was Jonathan Alwyn's second episode for the series following 'Burial at Sea', having been taken off 'Hear No Evil' as it went through another acrimonious rewrite. The episode was the first not to feature any location filming.

Casting
Hildegard Neil was cast as Stella Robson and was regarded by the *Daily Mirror*'s Jack Bell as one of the faces to watch in 1969. He was pleased to see her making more appearances on screen. She had recently been seen as the 'luscious' woman in black in an episode of *Mystery and Imagination* called 'The Suicide Club', which went out on the same night as *The Plastic Eaters.* Robert James had been in Nigel Kneale's *Wednesday Play* 'Bam! Pow! Zap!' with Robert Powell. Nigel Stock had recently played Dr Watson opposite Peter Cushing's Sherlock Holmes for the BBC in 1968. He had been directed by Jonathan Alwyn for ABC's *Out of this World* anthology series, 'The Yellow Pill' in 1962. Philip Brack had also finished a long running role as Detective Inspector Jim Cook in *Softly, Softly* and his first episode had been directed by Terence Dudley.

Studio
'Project Sahara' was the fifth episode to be rehearsed and recorded, in studio TC6, on Tuesday, 20 January (when camera rehearsals overran) and Wednesday, 21 January 1970. Margaret Pilleau, playing a computer technician, pre-recorded a line. Peter Hawkins also pre-recorded his broken-up computer dialogue. Stock film from a recent horse race was shown on the TV in the bar. Photos wereused for the chroma key computer screen which displayed graphics of Quist, Ridge and Wren's faces.

Extras
The extras listed in the camera script include a name called Labro, but he does not appear in the Programme as Broadcast sheet, whereas the opposite is true for Peter Roy and David Felton. The actual extras seen in the episode comprise a male computer technician called Mr Hayles, the bar man who is either Charlie, George or Cyril, two customers, two policemen at the morgue and the photo on display on the computer when Quist comes to call. The face of 'James Kingsley' is presumably one of the extras but has a passing resemblance to Gerry Davis. There was to have been a

policeman seen at the beginning of the programme, but he was edited out.

Design
Unfortunately, time has not been kind to the computer seen in the episode, nor does its cinema style display screen, covered by curtains when not in use. One of the keyboard props is also damaged. Design like this was sometimes brought to Dr Kit Pedler's attention by his critical colleagues at the Institute of Ophthalmology, or the wrong piece of equipment in a laboratory setting.

Music
As well as some especially composed Max Harris cues, the episode featured tracks from the Mozart Edition label to be heard on Stella's radio. These were 'Sweet Violins', from *George Hermann and his Orchestra*, (MELP 09) and 'Moonlight & Love' by Kurt Becker, performed by the Jay Harman band (MELP 11). Corelli's *Concerto Grosso No. 1 in D Major,* played by the Slovak Chamber Orchestra (Supraphon SUA 10571), can be heard as Keeping confronts Stella one last time in her flat.

Editing
The episode needed some cuts to bring it down to the correct length. However, even after editing on Friday, 23 January (between 2.30 pm and 5.30 pm), the episode was still very long, running for fifty-three minutes. The first cut was to the opening scene itself. After an establishing shot of the door to the computer room guarded by a policeman, we were to have seen Barker entering the computer room from the corridor outside as he explains that his visit is not an inspection but for work. He and Keeping settle down and watch the curtains pull back from the computer display screen, and this is where the episode begins, following the establishing shot.

The opening to Scene 16 was also cut. This was where Stella speaks to Quist and tells him that she will return to university if they'll have her. Quist can't see why not. She then asks why she is supposed to be a security risk.

After Ridge tells Quist about Commander Keeping, he went on to say that the Commander is coming to visit the team this morning. The end of the scene where Wren tells Quist he had a drink was cut. This lost Wren saying 'I'm sorry. I can't swear to what I said, but I don't believe I let you down.' Quist hopes so, for his sake as well as theirs.

Scene 41 was cut in its entirety. Here, Ridge explains that by lying to security, Stella has had it and won't come back. The worst thing is that Toby may well be 'tarred with the same brush. If the computer is right about Stella then they will assume that it is right about him as well.' Quist won't accept that and admits to having made a mistake. He underrated Keeping because he detested the system. He assumed that the man was just an extension of the machine, but he's clearly not, and that is something he has to work on now.

After the next scene, where Quist challenges Keeping, we lost some material set in the Doomwatch offices where Bradley sets up another experiment and Ridge is looking for somewhere to put a soil sack. Pat warns him not to put it on her desk and has an idea where he can put it. Ridge teases her into thinking Dr Robson is coming back but tells her Toby is returning. How did he know? 'Evening classes' says Ridge, continuing a running gag. The transmitted scene picks up from Quist's entrance.

Reaction

The episode was watched by ten and a half million viewers. Kit Pedler missed this episode on transmission as that week he was in Mexico City attending the 21st International congress of Ophthalmology, and delivering a paper on a logical analysis of retinal fine structure. Kit Pedler told the Sunday newspaper the *People* on 1 March, a few weeks before the episode aired, that he hoped the story will 'destroy the complacency over the use of computers to store personal details about the way we as individuals work and live. This is a terrible invasion of privacy. People are already being hired and fired because of what some tycoon's computer says about them.' Stella Robson's fate annoyed a number of viewers who thought that two female scientists in a row making serious mistakes was pushing it a bit. George Melly took their side in his *Observer* review. He also objected to the shot of Jack Foster's corpse. 'Reaction shots are just as effective, and less stomach-churning, but one nasty image per programme seems to be a growing habit.'

Programme Review Board

The Board had some interesting observations for the episode. There was a debate as to the realism of the programme when compared to the science fiction anthology series *Out of the Unknown*. Aubrey Singer found some 'elements of hokum too strong, whereas good science fiction was always totally credible', but Michael Mills felt *Doomwatch* to be totally believable. Head of Serials Shaun Sutton thought that *Doomwatch* was different from *Out of the Unknown* because it was centred on a philosophic concept. Andrew Osborn explained that the series walked a tightrope, as it tried to deal with what scientists were doing or were starting to do. But he felt that at times the dialogue had been too strident.

There was criticism of John Paul's acting. The Controller of BBC1 expressed reservations about the calibre of John Paul, having noted how a guest star like Nigel Stock acted the others off the screen. Andrew Osborn explained how John Paul came to be chosen for the part and that the actor had 'difficulty in relaxing in a way that would allow him to give some variation to his performance'. One kinder soul felt he was not helped by the writing nor the direction.

It is perhaps fair to say that Paul's performance was more on edge than usual in this episode, particularly during his long and passionate outburst about the computer. He certainly stumbles over a few words, but then actors frequently did in those days of almost 'live' recording. It was not an episode where Quist was able to relax and display other sides to his character. Jonathan Alwyn certainly understood the criticism. 'I never felt that John had the sort of gravitas of the status of scientist that we were trying to suggest he was, and I am talking with the wisdom of hindsight looking back and I suppose the whole production looks kind of amateur compared to what we are dealing with now. It's unfair to be critical – I always thought at the time whereas as much as I liked John as a person (he couldn't have been a nicer person to work with, a good team to work with) but I just felt that John didn't have that cutting edge that character needed. Although there was a kind of goodness about him. I think the [whole episode] slightly lacked the dramatic thrust it should have had, but on the other hand it made its mark and became a talking point.'

New Horizons
A clip from 'Project Sahara' was used in a school education documentary transmitted on 23 November 1970 called *New Horizons*: 'People and Computers', which featured an interview with Kit Pedler, recorded at his home in Clapham on 27 July. This still exists in the BBC's archives.

UK Gold
Because of the advert breaks, the single 1994 repeat of this episode had some material missing. The first break lost a close-up of the TV set showing the racing and some of the initial dialogue between Wren and Stella, and a bar steward turning down the volume. The second break lost a longer sequence of Stella going into the bedroom after Wren, who lies down and mumbles some apologies for his previous bad behaviour before falling fast asleep. A shorter loss was simply Quist screwing up Keeping's written recommendation before the scene set in the shop.

And the issue of privacy, complacency, and the dominance of the computer has never been more relevant in the internet age. How much of it we willingly surrender every day on line would have appalled the very private Kit Pedler.

1.06
Re-Entry Forbidden

Written by Don Shaw
Directed by Paul Ciappessoni
Designed by Ian Watson
Transmitted: Monday, 16 March 1970 at 9.41 pm Duration: 50' 00"

Cast

Dick Larch (Michael McGovern), Carol Larch (Veronica Strong), Bill Edwards (Craig Hunter), Max Friedman (Noel Sheldon), Charles Goldsworthy (Joseph Fürst), Gus Clarke (Kevin Scott), Kramer (Grant Taylor), Johnson (John Kidd), Brown (John Boxer), TV Commentator (Dougal Fraser), BBC Man, London (James Burke), BBC Man, Houston (Michael Aspel).

Also appearing
US Air Force Colonel (Fred Gambier or Gambler), Major (John Wilder), Captains (Paul Freemont, Steve Kelley), US Navy Commander (Bob E Raymond), US Captain (Mike Saunders), US Police Constable (James Hamilton), NASA Technician (Mark Warren), British Air Force Commander (Tony Somers), Captain (John Emms), Pressmen (Ernest Fennemore, Alfred Roberts), Security Men (Freddy Clemson, Derek Shafer), Men at Tracking Station (Alastair Meldrum, Cy Wallace).

Technical Credits

Production Assistant: Robert Checksfield. Assistant Floor Manager: Jane Southern. Director's Assistant: Peggy Dowdall-Brown.
Film Editor: Alastair MacKay.
Costume Supervisor: Dorothea Wallace. Make-up Supervisor: Elizabeth Rowell.
Studio Lighting: Jimmy Purdie. TM2: Malcolm Martin. Vision Mixers: Graham Giles, Roger Sutton.
Studio Sound: Larry Goodson. Grams Operator: unknown.
Crew: 19.

Radio Times

A new, nuclear powered rocket is being tested, with the first British astronaut aboard. The smallest error could turn it into a flying nuclear bomb spreading radioactive fallout over a wide area of Europe. And an error does occur.

The Story
'He was on control when something like a major catastrophe nearly happened.' – Quist

Sunfire 1 – the first nuclear-powered rocket containing the first ever British astronaut, Dick Larch – successfully launches into orbit. Dick's wife Carol and his sponsor Dr Charles Goldsworthy watch the coverage on a TV set at Cape Kennedy, whilst the Doomwatch team follow the BBC's coverage. Quist is uninterested, even though Larch had been a student of his and for whom he had helped to write a reference. Larch makes an error when inputting re-entry coordinates. His fellow astronauts Bill Edwards and Max Friedman don't notice, and he covers up his mistake. Goldsworthy notes an increase in Larch's heart rate but tells Carol not to worry. Off course, the capsule will now splash down near the English Channel to be picked up by the British Navy. The BBC's Michael Aspel reassures viewers that the capsule is not going to burn up, as it is still in its permitted flight corridor. Quist tells Ridge that had the capsule burned up, the contamination could have spread across Britain from London to Carlisle.

The capsule is taken to Farnborough, where a representative from NASA, Gus Clarke, thanks Navy officials for their help and explains that their next job is to debrief the crew and examine the capsule to find out what caused the error. Dick Larch is reunited with his wife; their relationship is not easy. He is a jealous, suspicious man, and she is nervous around him. The debriefing begins. Was it a computer fault or human error? Goldsworthy talks to Larch in private but cannot get any admission. Wanting his man cleared, Goldsworthy approaches Quist and asks him to help, but Quist is reluctant to get involved. He can see that if Larch was responsible, the political ramifications would be enormous. Goldsworthy wants to keep Quist's involvement unofficial, but Quist refuses. Everything must be done through the proper channels. They reach a compromise: if nothing is found, nothing need be said. 'All desperately covering ourselves', observes Goldsworthy.

Quist agrees to invite Larch to the Doomwatch lab on the pretext of asking him to help with some tests. Larch is uncomfortable at the little party Quist throws for him. He is clearly perturbed by his wife talking with Ridge and Wren and has a shrewd suspicion that Quist has been approached by NASA. Colonel Kramer is also concerned, telling Goldsworthy that they don't play hunches. Are the British trying to white-wash their man? Larch agrees to the tests. He is rigged up to a machine to examine the effects of the space flight on his body. Quist is uneasy at the attempt to assess his former student, wondering how they can interrogate a man who doesn't know he's being interrogated, especially as Larch is already suspicious and defensive. Ridge can't understand how a man like

Larch, who went through every conceivable test, could have been allowed on the flight if there had been a problem. Quist points out that he had only been tested in simulation. Quist has had enough; he decides to confess to Larch and pass the problem back to the Americans. NASA's subsequent official statement attributes the problem to a malfunction on the on-board control panel of the capsule. Unofficially, Goldsworthy, Kramer and Clarke are still not so sure.

A few months later the Doomwatch team are visited by Carol Larch, who tells them that her husband is among the crew for Sunfire 2. Speaking to Wren, Carol casually mentions how her husband had made the error and blamed everybody else. As Goldsworthy watches the launch alone, Wren bursts into Quist's office, alarmed at what he has heard. Quist gently questions Carol and gets a diagnosis from Ridge: Larch is a paranoid schizophrenic. They have to get a message to the command pilot. As Sunfire 2 enters its final orbit, Quist, Ridge and Carol arrive at a tracking station and get Johnson and Brown, the duty officers, to set up a channel to NASA. Sunfire 2 is now in its final orbit. Command Pilot Edwards is in control of the equipment, putting in the course codes. Larch watches calmly, but he reacts when Friedman expresses his hope that the United States recovery craft are ready in their splashdown area. The tracking station has difficulty in sending a signal to America.

Quist is impatient; there is enough radioactive fuel on board to blanket half of Europe. Thanks to a crossed connection, Quist's warning about Larch's condition is heard by the horrified Sunfire crew, and Larch panics when Edwards tries to input the coordinates for re-entry. He misses the information – and they are out of the safe flight corridor. The capsule goes back out into space; they are unable even to abort. Carol tells Quist that he has killed them. When communications are restored, all three astronauts are sitting calmly. Edwards delivers their eulogy, aware that they are going to die. 'We have missed the corridor due to my error and my error alone. What you may have seen just now on your screen … Dick Larch is a friend of mine. We are not judged by how we die, by how we have lived …' The screen is swamped with static.

Behind the Story
Nuclear Powered Rockets
Pedler and Davis are postulating nuclear-powered rockets – or rather, capsules – and the frightening consequences of a disaster. Nuclear powered rockets had appeared in science fiction before. *Quatermass II* in 1957 predicted concerns about the radioactive fall-out they would cause if they explode on take-off. The first rocket in the story does precisely that but thankfully out in the deserts of Australia. That rockets would one day be fuelled by nuclear elements never seemed in doubt, taking us to bases

on the moon, space-stations, or perhaps, Mars …

In 1966, manned flights to Mars were being forecast for 1976, and at an eye-watering cost of £357,000,000. Mr Milton Klien was deputy manager of the Space Nuclear Propulsion office of the US Atomic Energy Commission and the US National Aeronautics and Space Administration, better known to us as NASA. He claimed that tests had shown that nuclear rockets could be used for space flight, which would be mandatory for a flight to Mars. These vehicles would have at least five engine systems, three of which were necessary to provide the velocity to escape the gravity pull of earth. A fourth would be needed to brake the flight as it approached Mars. Each engine system would be launched into orbit by conventional Saturn rocket and then assembled together in a manner already perfected by the recent Gemini missions. Had there been an accident on the launch pad, there would have been no nuclear explosion as we saw in *Quatermass II*, but radioactive material would have spread for miles …

The Apollo capsule was powered by hydrogen-based fuel cells, which produced water as a waste product which the crew could drink. It is safe to assume that the two Sunfire space flights were launched using conventional rockets, but with enough nuclear fuel on board the capsule to cause an environmental catastrophe should it burn up on re-entry and along its flight corridor across Britain. It was an experimental first step to manned flight through the solar system, taking a fraction of the previous time needed to cross space.

There were plans in the late 1950s and early 1960s for something far more dangerous, sponsored first by NASA and then by the American Air Force: the launch of massive rockets into space using controlled nuclear explosions as thrust – the nuclear pulse drive. This top-secret project was called Orion. There would be no more cramped capsules or weight issues, and not only would it have allowed rockets to escape Earth's gravity, it would have made exploration of the solar system possible. The motto of its designers, Freeman Dyson and Ted Taylor, was 'Mars by 1965, Saturn by 1970.' (This was before President Kennedy made his pledge to get a man on the moon by the end of the 1960s.) However, the signing of the nuclear test ban treaty in 1963 by the USA, the Soviet Union and the UK put an end to Orion. Although disillusioned by the cancellation, Dyson eventually came to the conclusion that there were radiation hazards associated with a ground launch. We had stepped back from further poisoning our world in order to visit another, which was incapable of supporting life anyway.

This was all top-secret and not common knowledge, unlike the Space Race; a nervous America was being overtaken by the USSR in the bid to launch first a satellite, and then a man, into orbit around the Earth. In the event, Neil Armstrong had stepped out onto the moon's surface from Apollo 11 by the time the storyline for 'Re-Entry Forbidden' was written, and more flights were planned. Britain, however, simply could not afford its own space programme.

Pedler and Rockets

Kit Pedler had a thing about rockets and silos, Gerry Davis remembered. He certainly had a thing about orbiting capsules in trouble. His first *Doctor Who* script 'The Tenth Planet' features a doomed space shot, one of the first things invented for the serial. In 1970 Pedler wrote a short story called 'Image in Capsule', which appeared in *The Sixth Ghost Book* (edited by Rosemary Timperley, first published by Barrie & Rockcliff and later by Pan). It concerns an astronaut apparently getting paranoid delusions about his flight computer aboard a capsule called the Dynasaur 9. *Mutant 59: The Plastic Eater* is topped and tailed by the sending of a capsule to Mars with a plastic-eating virus on board. Pedler and Davis would later base their third *Doomwatch*-inspired novel *The Dynostar Menace* on an attempt to move away from nuclear fission towards nuclear fusion; the titular space station is designed to utilise the power of the sun. Unfortunately, it appears that should the Dynostar be activated it would disrupt the Earth's ozone layer and create more havoc and devastation. It doesn't help that there is a murderer and saboteur on board, who does not want the project stopped. He's more than a little paranoid. In 'Re-Entry Forbidden', a psychologically disturbed astronaut under huge pressure because he's the first Briton to go into space is added to the mix. Covering up human error features in the second post *Doomwatch* novel *Brainrack*, as people in charge of power stations and air traffic control suffer from colour blindness. The idea of a potential flying nuclear bomb with an unstable human element in its crew was irresistible to the writers.

Tone

The episode is a much quieter affair than the ones already seen in the series. Whilst Larch is covering up his own behaviour, the authorities in America are trying to avoid a political scandal by blaming their British astronaut for a near-disaster. The performances are quiet and understated, and we see a different side to Quist as he becomes a man trying to conceal his unwanted job as an interrogator. Mrs Larch, married to a paranoid schizophrenic, is played with under-stated nervous tension, unsure when she is going to trigger a jealous explosion in her husband. The scene between husband and wife as they are reunited after the near fatal accident is quite lengthy, an indicator of Dick Larch's state of mind. It is quite unusual for a great deal of time to elapse between major events in a *Doomwatch* episode, but it happens here with the two space flights. The capsule's ultimate fate is not explicitly stated; the last thing we are told is that it is going back out into space. Did it just head off into the void, waiting to run out of oxygen? Communication with the crew is lost – had they drifted out of range or did they burn up? The final few moments of the episode after Edwards' farewell message were not in the camera script, but it noted that Quist is horrified by what he has done. If there was an enquiry afterwards, Quist was obviously cleared, but not in Mrs Larch's eyes.

Production
Script Development
The writer chosen for this episode was Don Shaw, who had already written 'The Devil's Sweets' back in the spring. He was commissioned to write the fourteenth script on 15 September 1969, with a delivery date for the end of November. The storyline for 'Re-Entry Forbidden' was written sometime in the late spring of 1969 and was officially accepted by Terence Dudley on 1 July. Shaw had recently written a radio play about heat shields, which put him in good stead for the story. However, he found Kit Pedler's advice less helpful this time around, although he appreciated what help he got. As well as the storyline, he was supplied with newspaper cuttings, which weren't of much assistance either. Shaw also discovered that Pedler was out of date with the 'firing sequence' at the top of the programme, so he copied it from a tape recording of the most recent Apollo launch (either Apollo 11 or 12 – the latter took off on the 14 November). 'He must be fallible sometime!' Shaw concluded.

When Shaw delivered his first draft, he estimated that it ran to length despite being a shorter script than usual. He had recently done a script for *Softly Softly* which had fewer pages but overran by five minutes. He decided to make the script less technical, even though he appreciated that the more real science in a script, the more credible the finished programme. He also wanted the story to end with laconic space dialogue (i.e. mission control speak) in the midst of death, feeling that this was the right thing to do, and end the whole thing on a note of rational thought rather than having panic stations from the crew. He suggested that the final scene, where the image of the rocket crew shrinks to a dot on a monitor screen, could tie in with the closing credits: 'Do you end titles with a dot coming up to doom … WATCH? It could be effective …'

The script did overrun; a rewrite in December saw a reduction the amount of material on film, the removal of a corridor set and the name of Buginski changed to Kramer. It was a coincidence that the current moon shot allowed Shaw to introduce some more technical dialogue.

A few seconds were added to the end of the episode, and the first time we see Mrs Larch and Charles Goldsworthy watching the monitor was pushed back to follow the opening titles.

Having enjoyed his second assignment greatly, Don Shaw was keen to write a third episode if another project fell through. Final rehearsal scripts were sent to him on the 18 December, when Judy Hall explained that Kit hadn't given an answer about the correct term for 'thrust rocket'. The episode was scheduled for a read-through on 2 February 1970.

Production

For director Paul Ciappessoni, this was to be his third and final *Doomwatch* episode. There was now going to be no film effort required, but there would be a great use of stock footage, edited together by Alastair MacKay. These featured rocket launches, splashdowns, boats and helicopters in flight and came from NASA, featured the launch and flights of Apollo 10 and Apollo 12.

Cast

The roles of the television commentators had yet to be cast by the time the camera script was prepared. Real-life broadcasters were eventually chosen: newsreader and TV host Michael Aspel was given the job of the BBC Man, Houston, and science historian James Burke appeared as BBC Man, London. Their casting 'added a touch of realism', according to Shaun Usher from the *Daily Sketch*, probably quoting directly from a press release.

Ciappessoni employed genuine American actors like Kevin Scott and Craig Hunter, whose management took out an advertisement in that week's *The Stage*, promoting their client's role as Command Pilot Bill Edwards in the episode. The Austrian born Joseph Fürst is another actor to have appeared in *The Wednesday Play* about the failed assassination attempt on Hitler. Usually cast as loud villains or former Nazis, Furst played Edward's Air Force mentor. To counteract the accents, John Kidd and John Boxer played their English parts in clear BBC standard received pronunciation. Veronica Strong was a versatile actor, having recently played a villain in *The Avengers*. She is married to writer Jeremy Burnham. One of the extras booked for the episode, Nigel Treamer, was replaced by John Emms at short notice.

After the last day of rehearsal on Monday, 9 February, 'The Plastic Eaters' was transmitted, and any cast interested in reading the reviews, would have been doing so during the first day of camera rehearsals at Television Centre.

Studio

'Re-Entry Forbidden' was the seventh episode to be recorded, which took place in studio TC1 on Wednesday, 11 February 1970, two days before the first episode of *Doctor Who*'s 'The Ambassadors of Death' was recorded, which used the same capsule set (although slightly modified and with an airlock added). The two production teams had agreed to share the cost of the set, which was jointly overseen by *Doomwatch* designer Ian Watson and *Doctor Who* designer David Myerscough-Jones. *Doomwatch* would be transmitted first, by five days.

The evening recording session lasted three hours, from 7.30 pm until 10.30 pm, which was unusually long. Following that, five minutes or so of 'control track' was recorded to play over the Sunfire cabin scenes in case they were slowed down to give the illusion of zero gravity.

Andrew Osborn would later praise Paul Ciappessoni's direction and his ability 'in getting this programme together in very adverse circumstances because of the strike/over-run situation.' There was an over-time ban on all BBC studios. This was being enforced by the Association of Broadcasting Staff who had been in dispute with the BBC over pay since October 1969 when they flexed their muscles at the BBC and organised two walk outs which disrupted the schedules for some time.

In the event, the episode did overrun on both days it was in the studio. A minor fluff made it onto the screen; when Veronica Strong, playing Carol Larch, says to her husband in their first scene that they have had 'four weeks' to find out what the fault was, Michael McGovern, playing Dick Larch, sticks to the scripted 'four days'.

Editing
The episode's editing date is unknown.

Apollo 13
Transmission on 16 March 1970 was just under a month from the launch of Apollo 13. When that flight hit serious problems, the cast and crew were recording the final episode, 'Survival Code'. It was inevitable that one of the missions would go wrong. In this case, tragedy was averted by sheer skill. When Apollo 13 splashed down in the early evening of Friday, 17 April, it was watched by an astonishing twenty-six million viewers on the BBC and by another five million on ITV.

Programme Review Board
The Board were very impressed with this episode and thought it had been very good entertainment. David Rose, Gerry Davis' favourite producer, thought that the already high viewing figures were a tribute to the idea behind the series, especially since it did not have a star in the cast. Both the Controller of BBC1, Paul Fox, and Aubrey Singer thought it was a regrettable error to allow James Burke to play himself. 'It was once again, a blurring of fact and fiction which the Service was trying to prevent.'

The UK military scenes were set at the Royal Aircraft Establishment in Farnborough, but this is not made clear in the episode, causing a member of the board to wonder why a civilian agency such as NASA had staff members wearing military uniforms (NASA staff were generally in their shirt sleeves).

'Re-Entry Forbidden' was watched by nine million viewers, down a million and a half from the previous week. The board didn't mind. *The Kenneth Williams Show*, which was not regarded as a success, was finishing and Frankie Howerd's *Comedy Playhouse* entry *Up Pompeii!* was being repeated the following week to usher in a full seven-week run of the bawdy comedy. The BBC was confident that this would give *Doomwatch* a boost, as if it needed it.

1.07
The Devil's Sweets

Written by Don Shaw
Directed by David Proudfoot
Designed by John Hurst
Transmitted: Monday, 23 March 1970 at 9.48 pm Duration: 49' 00"

Cast
Miss Cooper (Penny Dixon), Scott (William Fox), Mrs Tyler (Bay White), Jack (John Comer), Shipton (Maurice Roëves), Pegg (John Law), Miss James (Pamela Sholto), Benson (John Young), Dr Gray (Mary Loughran), Dr Green (Patrick Connell).

Also appearing
Extras in studio
Nurse (Beryl Bainbridge), Lab Technicians (Dilys Marvin, Don Vernon)

Extras on location
Marilyn Gothard, Susan Hale, Wendy Kelly, Nikki Colgan, Michael Mulcaster, Paul Harrington, Bryan John.

Technical Credits
Production Assistant: Marilyn Gold. Assistant Floor Manager: Anna Yarrow. Director's Assistant: Adele Paul. Floor Assistant: John Wilcox.
Film Cameraman: Eddie Best. Sound Recordist: John Woodiwiss. Film Editor: Alastair MacKay.
Costume Supervisor: Dorothea Wallace. Make-up Supervisor: Elizabeth Rowell.
Studio Lighting: Jimmy Purdie. TM2: Jack Shallcross. Vision Mixer: Graham Giles.
Studio Sound: Larry Goodson. Grams Operator: Gerry Borrows.
Crew: 6.

Radio Times
Attractive Pat Hunnisett, the Doomwatch secretary, takes a give-away chocolate on the way to work. What results involves Doomwatch in a desperate fight against time – to save her life.

The Story
'Anyway, what's the difference between experimenting on a few people and

124

on a thousand? Two thousand?' – Shipton

Four strangely dressed young ladies, wearing chequerboard-patterned miniskirts and silver tights, ambush two city gents with a tray of sweets, which they eagerly sample. Pat Hunnisett, late for work, is also offered some. When she arrives at the office she finds Quist grumpier than usual and Ridge a little bit too flirtatious. The team have helped cut tobacco sales by 9 per cent, but there are still anomalies to sort out. There has been a 49 per cent increase in sales in the Greater London Council area over the past fortnight. Ridge is sent out to collect random samples and discovers a shop where the sales in Farfillers Checker Board cigarettes have increased by 100 per cent, all bought by girls who work at a nearby chocolate factory. Ridge notices a Checker Board hoarding next to the factory. Quist decides to visit their advertising agency, Shiptons, run by a young man of the same name, who is concerned by news of Wren visiting Farfillers.

As Doomwatch consider how Shipton's advertising can have boosted sales so much, Pat smokes her first cigarette in five years. When Pat is questioned, she explains that she just fancied a smoke earlier and bought a packet of Checker Board. Quist asks Pat to help them in some tests with an ECG machine which Bradley is setting up in the lab. The results show her reactions to the packaging and chequerboard images to be quite normal – until she sees the pattern from the advertisement. They make the connection with the free chocolate Pat had eaten that morning. Ridge remembers the 100 per cent sales increase, and Wren goes to investigate the chocolate factory. Here, he asks about the free give aways, which surprises the manager, Pegg, as there had been no brand name on the wrapper. Pegg has tried the free chocolates and takes a Checker Board cigarette automatically when Wren offers. He reveals that his advertising agency is also Shiptons.

Quist questions Shipton over his qualifications and learns that he went to West Sussex University to study experimental psychology. Shipton thinks that the whole investigation is really in connection recently discovered links between cancer and smoking. Posing as a Ministry of Health man, Ridge visits Scott, the owner of Farfillers, and later that evening he phones Quist to tell him that he followed Scott down to a pub, where Scott met Pegg and Shipton. The next day Quist visits Dr Benson at his department at West Sussex University and notices that experiments are being carried out on pigeons' response to chequer pattern stimuli, helped by drugs. Benson is alarmed and phones Shipton, who now knows they are onto him.

More tests are carried out on a tired Pat Hunnisett, who complains of having a headache. Once she eats another free sample chocolate, the reactions are acute. The drug, secreted in the chocolate to enhance reactions to chequer pattern stimuli, clearly has a cumulative effect. Becoming frustrated at the way she is being treated, Pat demands an explanation, which Quist provides. To save time, Ridge breaks into Benson's lab and takes photos of various formulae, hoping one of them is the drug. Pat is now feeling very unwell. Alone in the Doomwatch offices, she lights up another cigarette and decides to phone for an ambulance. She barely makes it to a chair to speak into the phone before collapsing over her desk, leaving the operators to trace the call. Discovered by Bradley, Pat is taken to hospital and put into an iron lung. They realise that this new drug has reacted with the slimming tablets Pat has been taking.

Shipton goes down to the university to see Benson, who wants them to get their stories straight before Scott and Pegg arrive. Benson is horrified that the drug he supplied to his former student has been used on so many people. Shipton is also worried: he thought the drug was safe. The doctors dealing with Pat have discovered that none of the formulae Ridge photographed at Benson's lab was the right one, and Pat has to fight the illness on her own. Meanwhile, Pegg tells Scott that Shipton had promised him free advertising on one of their cigarette posters, on the strength of which he could afford to give away a few free chocolates. That's news to Scott, and Pegg isn't convinced when Shipton then asserts that the Ministry of Health is investigating the confection market in order to cover up their victimisation of the cigarette industry.

Quist and Ridge arrive. Ridge confronts Pegg and Scott; Quist deals with Benson and Shipton. Neither have any luck. Quist demonstrates to Benson what is happening to Pat: few slimming tablets in a flask are combined with a few milligrams of a phototropine drug, and ... A sickly orange foam quickly erupts and Benson makes his escape. Wren phones the university to tell Ridge that Pat is dying. This alarms Scott and Pegg, who confess all they know. Scott says that he did make a grant to the university, but in return for information on the use of packaging, not drugs. He didn't question anything as sales were so good. The next phone call tells Ridge that Pat is dead. He punches Shipton, who tries to shift blame onto the absent Benson: he had wanted to try out his drugs, and experimenting on pigeons was one thing, 'but drugs aren't meant for pigeons, are they?' Shipton claims that he asked if the drug was harmless and was assured so. But it was Shipton who doctored the chocolates. With the investigation over, Quist reveals the truth to Ridge: Pat is actually alive and recovered; her death had been a ruse to force a confession. 'You bastard,' says Ridge.

Behind the Story
This is a story about manipulation, getting someone to do something that they don't necessarily want to, but think they do. Pedler could see that society is full of conditioning processes. One of them comes from advertising.

Advertising

Informing the general public that a new product is on the marketplace is all very well and good, but the aim is to convince consumers that they not only want the product, but that they must have it. Aspiration. Desire. Even fear – for if you don't have it, you are either behind the times or unusual. Children suffer from that the most. One of the advertisers' greatest weapons is sex. Sex is used at the very top of the story: four mini-skirted young ladies, flirting and giggling with two city gents (who can't believe their luck), offering them chocolates on a plate. All this to make someone smoke a particular brand of cigarette.

Subliminal advertising is mentioned and dismissed by Quist. A market researcher called James M Vicary claimed to have boosted the sales of food and drink at a cinema screening in America in 1957 using this method, but later admitted that this itself was simply a marketing ploy. In other words, he lied. But this was not before the idea had spread, causing alarm at the idea of hidden messages being relayed by TV and cinema screens. Vance Packard's book *The Hidden Persuaders*, first published in 1957, analysed and criticised modern advertising techniques in America, playing into paranoid fears of authoritarianism and potential political manipulation.

In this day of outlawed cigarette advertising and graphic images on the packaging of the effects from smoking, it is best to remember that this episode was aired only eight years after the Royal College of Physicians first raised concerns over the health impact from cigarettes, and it wasn't until 1971 that packets carried health warnings. At this point, smoking was still socially acceptable, and passive smoking wasn't even an issue – except for non-smokers who had nowhere to escape it. There are plenty of smokers in *Doomwatch*. The American television commentator in 'Re-Entry Forbidden', for example, is puffing away whilst on screen.

Universities

The story touches upon the links between business and university departments, for whom funding from the private sector was just as important then as it is now. It shows how a business in difficulty will take any help offered to gain a competitive edge. A struggling firm helps an underfunded department in a university, which in turn gives secrets to an ambitious ad agency. For Benson, he wants the prestige gained from delivering a paper based on his research, 'The most authoritative on the subject yet!' The advertiser deceives his cigarette clients into thinking that their sales increases is a result the use of red in the packaging, as that colour allegedly appeals to women. Both the chocolate and the cigarette manufacturers are in thrall to Shipton. He has a degree in psychology. That is enough for his clients. Shipton understands the mind-set of his clients –

or victims – and uses it against them. Quist understands psychology, too, enough to turn the supposed death of Pat Hunnisett into a weapon against the stonewalling trio of businessmen. Quist might have predicted that Ridge would be the one to receive the fake news. Ridge would certainly have heard it very quickly, and Quist knew how he would react.

Drugs

The story also points out the number of unnecessary drugs and chemicals we pump into our bodies on a daily basis. As well as nicotine from the cigarettes, we see Pat on slimming tablets. According to Quist, they contain a Benzedrine (amphetamine) derivative, which was widely used as an appetite suppressant in the US. Its use in Britain was treated with alarm. In 1968, the Ministry of Health followed American concerns over slimming pills which had been linked to deaths and reports of addiction. Another form of slimming pill had recently been taken off the market when it was found to trigger pulmonary hypertension.

Informed consent

The episode's other theme is illegal experimentation. Shipton is quite happy, even proud, about having 'a few thousand' people to experiment upon. To be as fair as possible, he was sure the drug was safe – he took Benson's word for it – but that's where his ethics end. He poisoned those women. Pat Hunnisett is an unwilling guinea pig for the experiments in the Doomwatch lab, treated as a specimen by Wren, Ridge and Quist. It is only when she storms into Quist's office and demands an explanation that he treats her as a human being again. The public and Pat are the pigeons in Benson's lab.

Production
Script Development

'The Devil's Sweets' was the sixth story idea by Kit Pedler and Gerry Davis, accepted by Terence Dudley on 18 December 1968. The storyline was handed over to Don Shaw, who was commissioned to write the script, the eighth so far, on 10 March 1969. Three days later, Shaw may well have tuned into BBC2 to watch the edition of *Horizon* called 'Powers of Persuasion', which investigated the application of scientific methods in modern day advertising. Shaw delivered on time, despite having been unwell and having to attend a recording for another project.

Confirmation was sent to him on 1 April and the usual rewrites took place. Both Davis and Pedler were very pleased with the script, the latter trying to phone the writer whilst he was on holiday to tell him so. Don Shaw sent in a revised four pages of the opening, which was recorded nearly word-for-word except for two things: the appearance of a gaudily decorated float from which the chocolate girls emerge, giving passers-by sweets as they enter the mews, and the bowler-hatted gents, who manfully decline the sweets in this version. The script also went into a detailed description of the ECG machine that Pat is wired up to, including an illustration of the five-line paper read-out.

Rehearsal scripts were sent to Shaw on 8 May. Judy Hall wrote that 'production is still miles ahead, but I'll be able to let you know the dates after the summer.' With one successful script under his belt, Shaw was offered the chance to do a second one by autumn ('Re-Entry Forbidden', which was transmitted the week before 'The Devil's Sweets').

David Proudfoot

This was first of two episodes in this series of the programme directed by David Proudfoot. Adele Winston remembers him fondly. 'I worked with David Proudfoot a great deal on *Softly, Softly, First Lady*, and *Doomwatch*. Everybody liked him. He was witty, funny and a very good director. He was good at casting and at interpreting texts. Thora Hird got on with him very well. Thora was very easy and wonderful value, no trouble at all, but she didn't like the feeling that she was being pushed around. One of the directors said bitterly, "She expects to be treated like a star," and David and I said together, "But she is a star!" Series didn't have the budgets to get a star and talent like her. He was, like Terry Dudley, from the old school of weekly rep, you got that feeling.'

Cast

This was an early role for Scottish actor Maurice Roeves, who was starting to establish himself as a television face. Shipton is the closest *Doomwatch* ever had to a true villain, even dressing the part of a gangster albeit working in advertising with a science degree. Unusually for the programme, Ridge has to beat the truth out of Shipton, albeit with one punch. John Young, who plays Dr Benson, clearly needed more time rehearsing his telephone acting since he holds the receiver at an alarming distance away from his ear. He might be better remembered for his brief appearances in two Monty Python Flying Circus films: *Monty Python and The Holy Grail*, as a doomed historian and plague victim, and *The Life of Brian*, as the man who dared to say 'Jehova'. Sly looking William Fox had worked with Proudfoot on *Softly, Softly*, as had Pamela Sholto and John Law, who also appeared on *The First Lady*. This was also true of Manchester born actor John Comer, who comedy fans will recognise from the early days of *Last of the Summer Wine* where he played the café owner, Sid. Bay White appeared in an *Out of the Unknown* episode called 'Stranger in the Family' episode with John Paul and Joby Blanshard.

Filming

Filming was performed in the week beginning Monday, 12 January 1970. Robert Powell and John Law filmed a lengthy scene at a chocolate factory in Hackney owned by one Mr Salomon. Simon Oates was needed on the Tuesday and Wednesday to film his brief scenes outside a newsagent shop, driving from the university, and pursuing Scott (William Fox) in Staines. The script helpfully notes that a double could stand in for Scott. Not a particular fan of unglamorous film locations, Adele Winston does recall one nice moment from the shoot: 'I was filming somewhere with him and it was night filming and very late. He was absolutely lovely, Bill Fox. If you're away filming and an actor offers to buy you a drink, you say half a lager. It was very cold, dark and awful, and I had other things to do and got there late, and Bill Fox stood up and said, "Adele, you look as though you could do with a large brandy," and I said, "Thank you so much," and he went off to the bar, and there was a stony cold silence, and he came back with a drink, and I said, "Bill, I'm getting very filthy looks letting you buy me a very large brandy so can I tell you I'm a tailor's daughter?" He fell about, and everybody else is looking blankly, and he explained to them very sweetly "What Adele is saying is if I can wear this suit on a grotty location, I can afford to buy her a large brandy. She's quite right, I can!" He actually owned vineyards. He was very wealthy. I had clocked the fact that he was wearing expensive tweeds on a grotty location.'

Rehearsals

Don Shaw was unable to get down to the script read-through for the episode due to a bout of flu. There were a few small changes to the dialogue in places. When Ridge is discovered taking photographs in Benson's lab, he says 'We provide information – rival tobacco companies – play off – against – the other', as he photographs what he needs. He then thanks Benson and smashes the fire alarm. 'Save what you can.' A one-and-a-half-minute scene showing Ridge following Scott by car appears to have been filmed but dropped, presumably for timing reasons. As dusk falls, Ridge discreetly follows Scott along a country lane, passing a sign that reveals they are in Staines. Ridge was supposed to have mentioned he was in Staines when he later telephones Quist.

Studio

'The Devil's Sweets' was the sixth episode to enter the studio. It went into TC6 on Saturday, 31 January 1970. It too overran its allotted studio time.

Music

Max Harris was no longer quite so prevalent on Monday nights on BBC1 now that *The Kenneth Williams Show* finished the previous week. Although there was plenty of Max Harris music to be heard this week, thirty-seven seconds of 'Tam Tam' by Jean Leroi, performed by Paul Bonneau, came from the *Telecine Radio Volume 7* by Chappell.

Editing
A small cut made to the episode was Toby Wren's first scene in the Farfillers office: Miss Cooper, Scott's secretary ('forty, severe looking and efficient') is puzzled by Wren's presence, but at the mention of referring the matter to the Minister, she gets onto the intercom. This is where the scene picks up in the transmitted version. Another small scene was cut, with Bradley telling Wren how seven out of ten women now prefer Checker Board cigarettes when they couldn't tell the difference before. Wren asks why, and Bradley replies 'Ah, that's what you lot get paid for.' A one-and-a-half-minute filmed scene showing Ridge following Scott by car was dropped. As dusk falls, Ridge discreetly follows Scott along a country lane, passing a sign that says Staines. It is possible that this sequence was removed before studio, as Ridge was supposed to have mentioned he was in Staines when he telephones Quist.

Publicity
Since Pat Hunnisett was in peril this week, the tabloids sat up and took notice, using the opportunity to print another picture of Wendy Hall on their TV pages. Nine million viewers tuned in for the episode. Wendy Hall made an appearance on *Call My Bluff* on 26 March 1970, a few days after 'The Devil's Sweets' transmitted.

Easter Break
Doomwatch took a break for the Easter weekend. In its place was a film called *The Colditz Story*.

1.08
The Red Sky

Written by Kit Pedler and Gerry Davis
Directed by Jonathan Alwyn
Designed by Moira Tait
Transmitted: Monday, 6 April 1970 at 9.44 pm Duration: 50' 07"

Cast
Captain Gort (Edward Kelsey), Dana Colley (Jennifer Daniel), Bernard Colley (Aubrey Richards), Dr O'Brien (Dudley Jones), Alastair Reynolds (Paul Eddington), Mrs Knott (Sheila Raynor), Duncan (Michael Elwyn).

Also appearing
Holt (Gordon Steff), Police Constable (Derek Chafer)

Technical Credits
Production Assistant: Christina McMillan. Assistant Floor Manager: Marion Wishart. Director's Assistant: Gwen Willson. Floor Assistant: John Wilcox.
Film Cameraman: David Prosser. Sound Recordist: Bill Meakin. Film Editor: Alastair MacKay.
Costume Supervisor: Dorothea Wallace. Make-up Supervisor: Elizabeth Rowell.
Studio Lighting: Jimmy Purdie. TM2: Malcolm Martin. Vision Mixer: Fred Law.
Studio Sound: Larry Goodson. Grams Operator: Gerry Borrows.
Crew: 6.

Radio Times
Noise from roads, industry, and aircraft is one of the penalties we have to pay for modern technology. But what happens when the rising crescendo of sound becomes more than an irritant? When noise can actually kill?

The Story
'Thunder will create a resonance that will shatter glass.' – Quist

Visiting their friend Captain Tommy Gort at his converted lighthouse cottage on the Kent coast, conservationist Bernard Colley and his daughter Dana are horrified when he appears to commit suicide by jumping off a cliff. They invite Quist down, convinced that this death was no suicide or accident. Quist is on the point of nervous collapse, and his colleagues are finding him unbearable. Following a tense meeting, Quist grudgingly takes Ridge's advice and decides to take a break to visit his friend Colley. Arriving at the Colleys' cottage, Quist is pleased to see Dana and learns that the Paugan-Air Corporation are making their lives a misery with noise from their testing station. Quist has barely finished his tea when Bernard returns from Gort's lighthouse, wild-eyed and babbling about fire, fire everywhere. As he recovers he explains that before Gort died, he had seen a vision of the flames of hell and heard a noise, a terrible noise, which seemed to come from the earth. Bernard knows because he too has experienced them.

The next morning Quist can hear the intensity of the testing and decides to investigate. He joins Bernard back at the lighthouse and is amazed to see that a glass has been split cleanly in two by resonance – a phenomenon known as thunder shake. But was it caused by thunder? Following a stroll along the cliff tops, Quist returns to the lighthouse to find Bernard barely conscious and his glasses shattered. He has suffered a cerebral haemorrhage. Quist sends for Ridge and Wren, who bring sound-testing meters. Quist meets Reynolds, head of the testing station, and explains about Bernard's condition. He wants to investigate any possible link with the tests, remembering the German sound cannon during the war. Reynolds wants concrete evidence, but Quist thinks he has a case to answer and warns him that he is in a position to get permission.

Bernard Colley dies in hospital without regaining consciousness. Ridge is worried about Quist's judgement in 'investigating the wonderings of a crank' but carries out sound-level measurements with Wren at Paugan, where Reynolds is apparently co-operative. Quist returns to the lighthouse. At three o'clock, as he sets up equipment, he too falls victim to the visions and the terrible noise, which seems to come from the lighthouse tower itself. Back at the cottage, Ridge discovers that the Minister is furious with Quist for investigating hearsay stories. It is only after he accidentally offends Dana, who overhears him referring to her father as a nutcase, that he learns Quist is in bed upstairs – he has suffered some form of an attack. Ridge conspires with Dr O'Brien, the local GP, to get Quist into a retreat to recover quietly. This would get him off the hook and avoid press attention. Wren is not so sure and listens to Quist's words as he slips in and out of consciousness – 'A closed column of air … a standing wave … pressure …' Wren persuades Ridge to let them investigate further, promising to drop the case if they find nothing.

They speak to Gort's unfriendly housekeeper, who says nothing unusual ever went on at the lighthouse. Later, Wren finds her unconscious when he goes to collect Quist's equipment from the lighthouse and notices a vapour trail in the sky overhead. He returns to the cottage where Quist is putting up a fight with Dr O'Brien and Ridge.

Wren thinks he has figured it out. Still unwell, Quist works on Wren's hypothesis with Ridge while Bradley assembles data from the computer. They conspire to get Reynolds and Richard Duncan, the Minister's 'hatchet man' to Gort's cottage by 2.30 pm Ridge persuades Reynolds to attend when he reveals the name of their secret project being tested: the T9. Quist explains that what all the victims of the lighthouse had experienced were hallucinations caused by energetic waveforms, shock waves from a high-flying, hypersonic aircraft -- the top-secret rocket-propelled T9, which passes overhead at precisely the same time everyday. 'Our eyes were literally shaken into action.' The noise was amplified by the lighthouse, acting almost like a musical wind instrument. Reynolds is sceptical, but, since the next test flight is due at 3 pm, he and Duncan stay to see what happens. Quist has expected this outcome and waits outside, where Wren is monitoring the sky. The plane passes over at Mach 4. When the shock waves reach the lighthouse, the noise and light display nearly send Duncan running over the edge of the cliff, like Gort. Reynolds is stunned as he realises the truth. At great personal cost Reynolds supports Quist at an inquiry, but all that is decided is to pull down the lighthouse and fence off the cliff. 'Can't let an isolated death stand in the way of progress, can we?'

Behind the Story
'The Red Sky' is about as pure *Doomwatch* as you are likely to get. It takes a familiar concern, this time noise pollution, and then gives it a twist. Writing in *The Listener*, Raymond Williams remembered talking with Kit Pedler before and during a *Late Night Line Up* programme on the subject of noise. 'A five-man discussion of the problem of noise, in the stale public language of committees and boardrooms. No whistle there. No jet-stream to disturb public relations. Late at night and tired: a very evident and very general public mood.'

It is perhaps the closest *Doomwatch* ever got to a Nigel Kneale supernatural play -- mysterious sounds coming from the ground, people literally scared to death. A couple of years later, noise would be activating ghosts in Kneale's *The Stone Tape*, not to mention something much nastier deep down in the ground. One almost expects a supernatural presence to be unveiled at the end of 'The Red Sky', but rationalism and scientific enquiry save the day. Raymond Williams got the point of the story. 'It was convincing, I thought, because it used dramatic concentration -- literally in the tube of a lighthouse -- to emphasise what is at the very least a symptom of civilised disorder: uncontrolled and destructive noise.'

Flight Paths
Those of us who have lived close to airports, listened to the venting of

engines late at night or lived underneath the flight paths of major airports such as Heathrow can appreciate the view of Bernard Colley. Living next to a military airbase isn't much fun either. One minute all is quiet; the next minute there is the interminable shriek of a passing fighter jet. Noise can be used as a weapon – to try and end a hostage situation or for torture. The German sound cannon, mentioned twice in this episode, was never used, but the principle was sound and could have killed people quite easily.

The problem of noise was one well-known at the time. NASA was financing research into developing a new 'quiet engine', whilst Boeing, in tests with new acoustical linings and a Pratt and Whitney J-57 engine, claimed to have obtained a noise reduction of nearly forty decibels. The Boeing 747 was being developed at this time but with engines which produced 100 decibels at take-off. In 1968 legislation was passed in the United States for the 'control and abatement of aircraft noise'.

In the 1960s the British and French governments were developing the first supersonic aircraft, in a joint venture which would greatly reduce the time taken to cross the Atlantic when compared with ordinary passenger jets. But not everyone was happy. The Treasury wasn't, for a start, and whenever plans came about to scrap the project (despite the crippling cancellation costs and loss of face with a country whose support was vital to join the Common Market), Tony Benn MP fought to preserve it, despite perceiving the escalating costs and bureaucratic nightmares. This was a prime example of the white heat of technology that Prime Minister Harold Wilson envisaged: a prestige project of technological skill; the dawning of a new industrial revolution for Great Britain. Tony Benn was Minister of Technology at the time, and his constituency was Bristol South East, where parts of Concorde were being manufactured. He saw the battle as a battle for jobs. He was also critical of what he called 'the grotesque image of technology …' Speaking in March 1968 at the Motor Industry Research Association establishment at Lindsay, and quoted by the *Coventry Evening Telegraph*, Benn wondered if this was the reason so few children were taking on engineering as a career, which in turn explained why some firms had not always been competitive in their respective fields. 'Technology is all too often automatically equated with noise, pollution, danger, gadgets and the escalating cost of huge projects. It is widely spoken of as if it were a torment, devised by boffins to invade our privacy, strip us of our personality and dehumanise us by banging and belching at us. What nonsense this is. Technology means no more than the application of the human mind to the problems of contemporary life.'

Concorde first flew in 1969. After many test-runs it broke the sound barrier and created a sonic boom. Quist questions whether noise pollution is justifiable simply to cut the time of a transatlantic flight. Perhaps Pedler and Davis read a letter by Mr Williamson in the *Illustrated London News* in

November 1968: 'For each thousands of passengers who will gain a few hours in travel time, there are millions on the ground who will suffer increased and more persistent noise ... Infections and contagious diseases of past centuries have been mainly over-come; but we are now confronted with the modern curse of noise, which is seriously affecting the health of many more people ... Our technocrat planners proceed with immunity, and the victims are being presented, as usual, with *faits accomplis*. Unless protests are made now, there can be no remedy.'

Residents of the Japanese city of Itami live in the flight path of Osaka International Airport. A study reported in June 1970 suggested that providing pregnant mothers lived there in the first five months of their pregnancy, their babies will sleep through the sound of a passing jet. The scientists conducted the study to discover why some infants slept through the noise and some didn't. They believed that unborn humans received 'acoustical information' through their mothers which allowed them to adapt to overwhelming noise. 'What an example of the remarkable adaptability of the human race,' the *Coventry Evening Telegraph* reported. 'The possibility of the evolution of humans to adapt to the ever-increasing environmental noise.' A similar sentiment will be expressed by a scientist in the next episode, 'Spectre at the Feast', and Quist's response will not be sympathetic.

Production
Operation Neptune
On 28 November 1968 Gerry Davis commissioned Kit Pedler (in conjunction with himself) to write the second script for *Doomwatch*. Called 'Operation Neptune', it was due for delivery on New Year's Eve. Pedler was paid the £275 that was his half of the fee the same day and Gerry Davis got his half the day before Christmas. This was most likely to be a story about a sunken and damaged nuclear submarine near the coast of Scotland, which had over time affected the local fish, with each generation mutating until they become accustomed to the human flesh of the drowned sailors from whom they have been feeding. They attack swimmers and divers. Surviving amongst Kit Pedler's papers is a hand-written synopsis of a story called 'They Won't Bite/The Microcosm' which was clearly intended as a plot line for the first series.

It was usually Terence Dudley who decided whether an idea becomes a *Doomwatch* episode, and perhaps this one seemed a little too unlikely for him, not to mention expensive and impractical to make. *Doomwatch* did not have a budget any larger than the average fifty-minute drama which were proving costly since the introduction of colour. Instead, they abandoned whatever stage they had reached and pulled out of the pile of unused storylines one they had delivered in February 1969 called 'The Flames of

Hell'. Its project number 2245/1285, was reassigned to a new storyline they prepared to fill in the gap called 'The Iron Doctor'.

The New Script
Pedler and Davis went back to the idea of a hostile ministry trying to undermine the *Doomwatch* team. They refer back to the Beeston affair ('The Plastic Eaters') and in their adaptation of the script for *Doomwatch: The World in Danger* (see below), the civil servant described as the Minister's 'hatchett man' was originally Barker, who had been in 'Project Sahara' and mentioned in 'The Plastic Eaters'. If this was the original intention, by the time of production, Robert James, the actor who played Barker, may not have been available to reprise the role. In his place was Richard Duncan.

Cast
Michael Elwyn was cast by Jonathan Alwyn as Richard Duncan. At this point Duncan was not envisaged as a regular, but he would be brought back by the same director for his next appearance. Welsh-born actress Jennifer Daniel had worked with both Terence Dudley and Simon Oates before in *The Mask of Janus* and had appeared in an episode of *Probation Officer* in 1962, though after John Paul had left the series. Aubrey Richards and Dudley Jones had both been in *Doctor Who* stories written by Pedler and Davis and featuring the Cybermen. Paul Eddington was only a few years away from situation comedy fame in *The Good Life* and, most significantly, as Jim Hacker MP in *Yes Minister*. He had a few more years left in him to play establishment figures such as a Ministry bod in the last series of *Special Branch*.

Filming
Filming took place in the first week of February 1970, with the South Foreland Lighthouse near Deal on the Kent coast as the main location. Simon Oates was needed on Monday and Tuesday, spending the night in Deal. The only extras used in the production appeared on film. Edward Kelsey played the doomed Captain Gort, and a stuffed dummy was thrown over the sheer white cliff in this week's shock moment. Elizabeth Rowell remembers the name of the unfortunate character to this day. 'Captain Gort went over the cliff. We had to dress up a dummy, put a wig on it, and of course the coast guard were called because they thought it was a real body. I think it got stuck on a ledge and somebody called the coast guard thinking it was a real person.' Jonathan Alwyn recalls: 'We had two goes at it. We had a couple of dummies in case one of them went wrong. The first dummy we threw over got stuck half way down. We had a camera down on the beach to get the shot. The tide came in and swept the dummy out to sea and somebody spotted it in some strange way and

didn't know what we were doing, and the coast guard were called out to go to the rescue. We did get told off for not telling the coast guard what we were doing, and for wasting a lot of public money by mounting an unnecessary rescue operation for a dummy!'

Studio
On 26 January 1970, before filming took place, three special effects shots of a picture, a teapot and a clock were pre-recorded for Quist's hallucination. It would be just under a month before 'The Red Sky' went into studio TC4 on Saturday, 21 February 1970 for the eighth recording of the series. Both days in the studio overran.

The Hallucination
A forty-one-second insert was recorded between 8 pm and 9 pm on Friday, 20 February during camera rehearsals. This was for the rest of Quist's hallucinations. The shots were recorded in order, starting with Quist's hand on a blue tablecloth. The blue was replaced via the chroma key process with a shot of the table with the oscilloscope. The hand was then distorted using a 'frequency adjustment' box. Next, the shelves seen from Quist's point of view were recorded, reflected in a highly flexible mirrored surface – 'mirrorlon' – which could then be shaken to good effect. The image was to pulse to the rhythm of the 'organ pipe' sound. A cardboard vignette was placed onto camera 3 and through it the glass on the shelf was recorded, to give an image-splitting effect. Next, camera 5 zoomed into John Paul's eyes, and then mouth, as he 'sees' the flames of hell. Finally, camera 2 recorded the window, again reflected in mirrorlon to make it pulse. As flame effects were played onto a back-projection screen, the two images were mixed with a revolving lens attachment to achieve the final shot. The last shot of the last studio day was an insert of the oscilloscope reacting wildly.

Sound
The script called for a particularly important piece of sound design. Peter Neill, a boom operator on most of the first series, remembers 'the Sound Supervisor, Larry Goodson, was thinking about the sound effect for the resonating tower, which we would be recording the following week. Synthesisers were not that abundant then, and he suddenly asked, "Has anyone got access to a church organ?" I did, indeed, have access to the organ in my old school chapel (St Joseph's College, Beulah Hill, London, SE19). And having obtained permission, we went armed with a Nagra and recorded some very long deep notes from said instrument. When we got back to base, Larry decided that it still wasn't quite what he wanted and rigged a large loudspeaker at the bottom of the stairwell outside TC1 and a

microphone halfway up the stairs and played the organ notes, mixed with some feedback from the microphone. I can't remember if there was any further sound treatment, but that was the basis of the effect.'

Music
Apart from over two minutes of Max Harris' musical cues, thirty seconds of Arthur Sullivan's *Overture di Ballowas* used. Performed by the New Symphony Orchestra, it was sourced from an Ace of Clubs LP (ACL 108) and can be heard in Jennifer Daniel's first scene with Quist.

Editing
The episode was edited on Tuesday, 24 February 1970 between 10.30 am and 1.30 pm Some scenes were cut short. After examining the thunder-shake glass, Quist decides to go for a walk and wants Bernard to go back home, but he wants to see if Gort wrote anything else about 'this business'.

After Quist warns Reynolds that he is in a position to get the authority to make his own tests, he leaves the office, and Reynolds picks up the phone to make a call to the chairman in London. This led into the next scene, where Dana brings Ridge and Wren into the living room and offers to make some coffee. Ridge can see she is upset and suggests that they can stay in a hotel and not bother her further. She is about to get ready for the hospital when the phone rings, and she hesitates to answer it.

The film sequence of Holt leading Ridge and Wren towards the test bays was to continue. Ridge and Wren start to set up their equipment, and Holt glances at his watch, which shows 2.55 pm.

After Quist's hallucination, we were to have seen Ridge and Wren showing Reynolds that the noise from the test engines is within allowable limits. Reynolds believes it is the end of the matter, but it has been no trouble as 'We're using the tax payer's money, aren't we? I suppose that gives almost anyone the right to look us over.'

One final cut was in Gort's cottage. Reynolds asks Duncan how much power Quist has, and he is warned not to underestimate him. 'A strong recommendation from his department can't be ignored.' They would be obliged to act on it and suspend all test flights until the allegations were proved or disproved. Reynolds reacts in horror.

Duncan's line before Quist enters the lighthouse cottage seems to have been dubbed over an extra shot of Ridge. Some paperwork suggests that Michael Elwyn recorded an insert, but whether it was for this line or his horrified reaction to the flames is unknown.

Reaction
The Sunday before transmission, Radio 4's arts magazine *Options* reviewed *Doomwatch*, as well as featuring the film *Kes* and the National Portrait

Gallery. In his review for *The Listener*, Raymond Williams thought that the conclusion to the episode – that the authorities merely pull down the lighthouse and suspend test flights for a while – was remarkably near to the way things happen.

Programme Review Board
Monica Simms at the board praised this episode. The ratings, when discussed a week later, were pleasing for the Board. Nine-and-a half million viewers had tuned in, more than for ITV's programming at the same time. *Doomwatch* was winning its slot. *Up Pompeii!* was getting a further million viewers. This was a good showing for a Monday night.

The World in Danger
The story was the second of three to be adapted for *Doomwatch: The World in Danger*. It contains a few interesting changes, or perhaps reflects an earlier draft. Colley lives in Cornwall, not Kent; Dana Colley is unmarried and calls Quist 'Uncle Spencer', although whether this is an affectation, or an actual relationship is not made clear; Colley dies in the lighthouse; and Quist is very angry in his first meeting with Reynolds, telling him 'You're destroying our environment with your tests and your planes. He wanted to save it!' Barker arrives at the Colley cottage with Reynolds, where Dana accuses Paugan of killing her father. Barker is not nearly as supportive as Duncan was on screen, but he is the one to suspend Reynold's tests as a result of being subjected to the noise, as Reynolds did not have a change of mind when faced with the truth of the situation.

Questions in Parliament
During a debate in the House of Commons on 6 May 1970, Mr Michael McNair-Wilson, MP for East Walthamstow, was supporting a proposed bill for restricting the noise levels of, amongst other things, aircraft. There were moves afoot to add a protocol to the European Convention on Human Rights which would guarantee the right of the individual to freedom from undue noise. He gave an interesting example of how a director of the Cycle and Motor Cycle Association told him that if the Government forced them to impose 'unrealistic noise levels', they would stop manufacturing in the UK. This is the usual form of blackmail from industry. 'Do we seek noise levels which keep pace with what industry finds easily achievable or do we … consider it to be our task to say what are acceptable limits, taking into account the medical factors as we know them, the simple evidence of our ears and then what industry says is reasonable? … The truth is, like the man in the BBC *Doomwatch* programme on noise, the individual today feels that he is a peripheral nuisance whose voice is unimportant and will rapidly be drowned in the thunder of diesel lorries and high powered jet engines.'

1.09
Spectre At The Feast

Written by Terence Dudley
Directed by Eric Hills
Designed by Moira Tait
Transmitted: Monday, 13 April 1970 at 9.47 pm Duration: 49' 47"

Cast
Fielding (William Lucas), Whitehead (Richard Hurndall), Egri (George Pravda), Bau (Oscar Quitak), Laura Lindsay (Helen Downing), Royston (David Morrell), Head Waiter (Bruno Barnabe), Mrs Bonenti (Karen Ford), Negro (Roy Stewart).

Also appearing
Wine Waiter (Stewart Fell), Waiters (Peter Holmes, Brian Scott, Gabrielle Confino), Men for Conference/Diners (George Barnes, Freddie White, Verne Morgan, Freddy Wiles, Bill Lodge, Andy Devine, Reg Cranfield, Roy Hatherway, John Kimberlake), Maids/Diners (Dilys Marvin, Dolly Collins, Julia Fry, Sandra Richards, Sally West), Secretary (Ann Lee), Page (Mark Paffingham).

Technical Credits
Production Assistant: Christina McMillan. Assistant Floor Manager: Marion Wishart. Director's Assistant: Pauline Bullock-Webster. Floor Assistant: John Wilcox.
Costume Supervisor: Dorothea Wallace. Make-up Supervisor: Elizabeth Rowell.
Studio Lighting: Jimmy Purdie. TM2: Jack Shallcross. Vision Mixer: John Law.
Studio Sound: Larry Goodson. Grams Operator: Gerry Borrows.
Camera Crew: 19.

Radio Times
Quist convenes a conference of top scientists to make recommendations on the problems of pollution. Many of the delegates become victims of food poisoning. Are they being got at?

The Story
'Nobody's denying there's a pollution problem. But you don't solve the problem by crippling the economy. Because, if you do, you solve one problem by creating many more.' – Fielding

Jayson's – an exclusive hotel in London. Quist has finished dining with delegates for a conference he has called. He is being baited by an industrialist, Fielding, who is the reason the conference has been called. He is amused that Quist doesn't smoke cigars. Quist objects to the other pollutants that Fielding's firm, Newington Chemicals Ltd, are pumping into the air and rivers. That is what the conference is all about. Whitehead, Fielding's scientific adviser, is fixated by a bowl of fruit in the centre of their table. No-one else notices, but he can see cockroaches swarming all over the fruit. Panicking, he pulls a table cloth over the bowl; when it is removed, there is nothing there.

The next day, Quist discusses the hallucination with a delegate called Egri back at the Doomwatch office. There have been 500 other cases from all over Britain, and several delegates have been stricken. Ridge thinks the conference is being sabotaged by Fielding to stop the vote going against his company. However, Egri admits that he too saw something last night.

Fielding has a penthouse suite at the hotel. He is dictating to his secretary, dismissing anti-pollution measures, when Whitehead enters, having recovered from his experience. Fielding does not like his scientific adviser. They discuss Quist's general motivation: guilt over the atom bomb and the death of his wife from radiation poisoning. Egri takes Pat out to dinner at Jayson's, but after a spot of mild flirting his vision blurs, and, to his horror, he sees Pat turning into a repulsive crone. He collapses from a mild heart attack. Quist and Wren have been working late and so are there to talk to Pat about the incident.

There are yet more cases, including that of a lady who apparently saw ballerinas dancing out of a wall. The media dub the illness the Millionaires' Shakes. A note from Rogers of the British Medical Association tells Quist that the symptoms so far detected could be caused by any number of exotoxins. Pat goes through what Egri had been eating, and Quist asks her to check the same for the other victims. Royston the hotel manager is pleased to assist Pat. He already has a list of what was eaten by those who have fallen sick, as requested by the Medical Officer of Health looking for signs of food poisoning. None had been found.

Fielding, meanwhile, is disturbed to find that four of the stricken delegates were on his side. Quist visits him and is surprised that Fielding is prepared to grant the conference (which Fielding is funding) an extension. There can be no proper vote with so many of the delegates temporarily incapacitated. It isn't long before Quist and Fielding argue out their respective viewpoints on pollution.

FIELDING: D'you know how much Newington Chemicals alone spends on research?
QUIST: A quarter of a million.

FIELDING: More.

QUIST: Peanuts to what all concerns are paying to develop non-pollutant petrol.

FIELDING: And what happens when they succeed? We have to redesign the internal combustion engine. Who pays for that? D'you think the man in the street's going to pay more for his car because it doesn't spit lead and carbon monoxide.

QUIST: He's going to have to if he wants to stay alive.

FIELDING: Quite honestly, Quist, you're the most dangerous man I've ever met.

QUIST: I'm flattered.

Quist returns to the office to find that there have been more cases in the hotel and around the country. Wren is exasperated: they simply have nothing to go on. The lobster is a common factor, but other guests had eaten some with no ill effects. Jayson's keeps them alive in tanks before they are wanted. Ridge offers to go and steal one, but Quist warns him that he is on his own. Ridge agrees and decides he will need some camouflage, which he warns will be exotic and expensive. More cases are telephoned through, including a man who has crashed his car as a result. He is a waiter from Jayson's called Bonenti. Wren speaks to his wife, who works at the hotel as a maid. She tells him about her husband's hallucinations – that he saw something that terrified him, kicking away at an invisible enemy. She swears her husband ate nothing from the hotel.

Ridge's camouflage is an elegant black woman called Laura, who orders a very expensive dinner. Ridge asks for a couple of lobsters from the tank. Meanwhile, Fielding is talking with Bau, one of the delegates, and offers him a job, telling him 'I'm in the market for the best brains in Europe to clean up my mess as I make it.' Whitehead pours him a drink. Bau returns to the dining room and suffers a hallucination, giving Ridge his opportunity to steal a live lobster before leaving. Laura's home is decorated with voodoo masks, and, as she goes to take a shower, Ridge starts to feel ill. He has difficulty focusing on the masks and starts to hear drum beats. In a mirror he can see himself fighting with a warrior. He loses the battle and is about to be speared on the sofa when Laura rushes downstairs to find him fighting something that isn't there.

Bradley tells Quist that there is nothing wrong with the lobsters. But now there is a death: Bonenti. His widow confesses that he had stolen a lobster, but she lied in order to protect his job. Bradley gets more samples from Royston, who is happy to cooperate. Soon the Doomwatch lab is one giant kitchen, with Pat in charge of cooking the poor creatures. Most come from Cornwall, but some come from the river Whittle in Yorkshire. Quist is excited by the news and wants as many lobsters as Bradley can get from

Whittledale Fisheries. They may get that conference vote yet.

At the conference Fielding is telling the delegates that they must get their priorities right. Quist arrives and talks about the hallucinations and the death they have indirectly caused. The poisoned lobsters did come from the Whittledale Fisheries. They contained concentrations of phenyl siloxane, a plastic effluent from Fielding's plant. Fielding protests that they pollute at the permitted level, but Quist accuses him and Whitehead of being sheltered from the facts of life. Quist, like a detective in a room full of suspects, runs through the course of the river Whittle, noting the other polluters up and down stream. Bau and Egri catch on. Nitric acid, starch residue, naphthalene waste (or muck, as Quist calls it), inorganic salt leads from batteries ... But opposite Fielding's Newington Chemicals is a power station whose waste is warm water. All the ingredients for a high-yield reaction are in the river. The reaction creates a molecule closely resembling LSD, and it is concentrated inside the lobsters. 'Today he poisons the rich man's lobster, tomorrow it'll be the poor man's fish and chips.' Fielding leaves the room, knowing he has lost. Whitehead is left alone to consider Quist's words that there are times when men of science find it either convenient or profitable to justify the sin of omission.

Ridge is much recovered and presents Quist with his bill for the fateful evening, which shocks him. Ridge thought the business was a dead lucky coincidence, but Quist disagrees. Nemesis.

Behind the Story
'Spectre at the Feast' is about industrial pollution, which would have been familiar to most of its viewers of the time, and the debate over who pays for cleaning it up. Government was taking its first slow, lumbering steps towards taking pollution control seriously. On Monday 24 November after viewers on BBC1 watched the splashdown of the Apollo 12 mission, they may have watched an edition of *Panorama* which dealt with river pollution. The Hudson river in America appeared deceptively blue and sparkling, but it was being polluted most notably by General Electric and General Motors. That same month, a number of new power stations being planned to be built alongside the river Rhine, and the European Commission investigated the impact thermal pollution would have on the ecosystem. In December 1969, Dr Fraser Darling, vice president of the Conservation Foundation delivered six talks for the BBC's annual Reith Lectures: 'Most pollution comes from getting rid of wastes at the least possible cost. We were not prepared to pay the price of our technology, the cost of cleaning up after ourselves.' According to Darling: 'One of the American electricity generating utilities is studying a method of reusing the cooling water from power stations by piping it under agricultural land in controlled farming experiments.'

In February 1970 the Royal Commission on Environmental Pollution was brought into life by Anthony Crosland MP, the Minister for Housing and Local Government, and was headed by Sir Eric Ashby. It was designed to be a standing commission, which meant it could practically go on forever, but was wound up in 2011. It would be a year before the Commission published its first report, 'an essay on the state of the natural environment [which would] tell the public in simple terms what they need and need not worry about, and get a set of priorities established.' according to Michael Allaby in his summary of recent environmental developments *The Eco-activists*.

'This is Conservation Year' declares Fielding to Bau. The European Nature Conservation Year was launched in February 1970 and was organised by the Council of Europe. Its purpose was to draw attention to the way we affect our environment with modern industrial and technological needs. Twenty countries joined in. Over in America the first Earth Day was about to be held on 22 April. The aim for the day was to focus the nation's attention on bettering Man's environment. If nothing else, Fielding's statement gives the series its date: 1970.

Friends and Enemies in Industry
The protagonists in the story are Benjamin Fielding, chairman of Newington Chemicals Ltd, and his chief scientific adviser, Doctor Robert Whitehead, whom the script describes as an academic who has sold out to commerce. They represent the viewpoint of industry and deploy all the contemporary arguments in favour of the status quo. Pollution is a fact of economic life, and to deal with it ruthlessly involves cost. Newington Chemicals is pioneering work in silicostyrenes to replace cast-iron engines with cheaper plastic cylinder blocks, and in the process they are polluting rivers with organic silicones and the air with peroxides. They are quite happy to have the mess cleaned up afterwards, preferably at the tax-payers' expense, just as long as they don't have to put in too many expensive preventative measures first. 'We must phase the application of anti-pollution measures to the needs of the national economy' says Whitehead. 'You can't easily fool the man in the street. He knows that where there's muck there's money.' Egri, an ecologist, tells Pat that industry cannot be expected to pay for it all. Quist's biggest battle, he says, will be with the ordinary taxpayer. For Fielding, Quist is the most dangerous man he has ever met because of his own beliefs.

The arguments expressed in the episode reflected the debate in real life. The idea that cleaning up the environment would somehow harm the economy and lower the standard of living was not an uncommon one. This was a period when the economy was stagnant, and business and investors did not see Britain as a good bet. Both political parties saw economic growth as a major priority, if not the only one. Environmentalists and 'doomwatchers' were viewed as the type of people wanting to take us back to the Stone Age, rather than seeing the need to modify our lifestyles in order to have a less devastating impact upon the planet. Only through growth, and thus more tax receipts, would government be able to pay for the clean-up operation.

The chemist Whitehead has the finger of blame pointed at him throughout the story. Pedler would have regarded Fielding as a 'technological toymaker', surrendering his responsibility as a scientist for the financial rewards of industry, and Whitehead, not that very deep down, would agree. He supports the party line, but his conscience is bothering him, as Fielding cruelly points out. At the end of the final conference scene he is left alone, feeling terrible after being presented with the evidence of what their pollution has contributed to. Is it really his fault that he overlooked the warm water in the Whittle affecting his plastic effluent? Could he really have predicted the mixture of pollutants further up and down stream? Would Fielding have pressurised him into facing 'business realities'? Fielding accuses him of having a cosy sense of guilt, a favourite Dudley theme (and indeed a description already used in *Tomorrow, the Rat*). Whitehead loses all credibility when he feels that man will adapt to the pollution, learning to breathe sulphur dioxide. He is certainly presented as a lackey, even acting as a wine waiter when Fielding is bribing Bau for his vote with a good job.

Pedler's Attitude

So much of Quist's argument to Fielding could have been lifted directly from Pedler's 1979 book *The Quest For Gaia*. Fielding counters that if the oil industries were to clean up the dirty emissions from petrol, the motor engine would have to be redesigned, and the motorist would have to 'pay' for it, which he viewed from his penthouse-suite outlook as something the ordinary man would refuse to do. Quist (or rather, Pedler and Dudley) maintained that people's lifestyles would also have to change, and we would have to pay more for certain things. Pedler told Roderick Kennedy, for an article reprinted in Singapore's *The Straits Times* later that year, 'The public has got to decide whether it is going to pay twice as much for the plastic angel on top of the Christmas tree in order to have clean rivers.' Quist's other argument, as Pedler spent the seventies arguing, is don't make the mess in the first place. The financial argument was a favourite theme of Terence Dudley's, and he would return to it several times in the series.

Secrets

Pollution data on rivers was kept secret from the public, sometimes protected by law, sometimes out of habit. The only people who had a right to know what local businesses were dumping into rivers were those who lived closest to the outflow pipes. This was a cause for concern in the early 70s. Colin Ward's 1972 lecture 'A Doomwatch for Environmental Pollution' reported an investigation by the *New Scientist* into this issue. 'If a factory owner should choose to pour thousands of gallons of cyanide into a river, the maximum fine the courts can impose is £100. But if a river inspector analyses a sample of this effluent, and mentions the results to a member of the public, he can be sent to prison for three months.' The public did not have a right to know. The attitude was they would not understand the figures nor the implications, which mostly is true, but a concern all the same. The chapter on 'Waiting for a Knighthood' will demonstrate what happens when this secrecy is challenged.

Production
Script Development
The eleventh script slot was still outstanding in the production schedule. It was filled by the producer himself, based on a storyline by Pedler and Davis called 'Pollution Inc'. It was to be a studio-bound affair and retitled 'Spectre at the Feast'. The first half of Dudley's fee was paid on 20 February, just a month before rehearsals were due to begin. The storyline, along with 'Train and De-Train', was paid for on 10 March.

The plot is structured to make the 'nobbling' suspected by Ridge a real possibility. Bau, for example, sees Whitehead shortly before his collapse. What we are left with is another textbook science detective story. Like an Agatha Christie whodunnit, it is resolved with all the protagonists in a drawing room situation as Quist reels off the evidence before coming to a devastating conclusion. Dudley is drawing on 'The Red Sky' here, which had a similar conclusion. Speaking of that episode, the laboratory set up to analyse the lobsters was scripted to be identical to the one seen in that episode.

The hotel is called Jayson's. Dudley writes: 'Those who can afford to eat there know that Jayson's is among the five most exclusive hotels in Europe. If you could persuade Orson Welles to eat in London he would insist on the Jayson's.'

With Quist, Wren and now Ridge having all suffered from hallucinations during the series, Colin Bradley was probably looking nervously over his shoulder.

In-jokes
Director's assistant Adele Winston remembered 'Simon had been the heavyweight boxing champion of the Army Intelligence Corps, but Robert Powell insisted he got it wrong – he must have been the heavyweight intelligence champion of the Army Boxing Corps.' Terence Dudley slipped in a line into the script where Ridge recalled his boxing days, a nice example of fact and fiction combining. Dudley also puts in a reference to 'The Devil's Sweets'. One interesting line is when Quist says to Fielding 'No-one's suggesting you're a villain or a fool', the kind of protagonists Dudley

preferred not to be seen in *Doomwatch*.

Casting

Modern-day sensibilities may be concerned that Ridge had an unconscious fear of savages from Africa, as his hallucination was triggered by Laura's collection of voodoo masks and other native paraphernalia. Freudians will love the idea of Ridge being penetrated by the spear of a huge black man, which is ironic, since Ridge was rather hoping to do something similar to Laura. The 'shiny Negro' was played by Roy Stewart, who had been Toberman in Pedler's and Davis' 'The Tomb of the Cybermen'.

Richard Hurndall, here playing Whitehead, was often called to portray troubled souls but would end his career giving his own interpretation of the very first *Doctor Who* in 'The Five Doctors' in 1983. He had recently played a regular role in ITV's *The Power Game* as a melancholic senior civil servant. With William Lucas, the Czech actor George Pravda and Oscar Quitak, this was a very high calibre cast that Eric Hills had assembled for his first episode.

Studio

'Spectre at the Feast' was the 11th episode to go before the cameras, on 25 March 1970 in TC4. For once, a transmission date was known for the episode as it went into rehearsals. Although the day of camera rehearsals overran, the recording did not, despite the director having some rather interesting technical challenges to overcome. Rather than pre-record several inserts the day before, Hills decided to go for it on the night itself. Predictably, the cockroaches were a problem, escaping from their fruit bowl and having to be hunted down by the studio staff.

The end of the dinner date between Egri and Pat was recorded twice, first as normal, with
shots of Wendy Hall being distorted in a reflective flexible mirror, and then again with similar camera moves but with Wendy Hall wearing a 'gorgon mask'.

The most complicated scene to be recorded that evening was the one where Ridge has the hallucination of himself fighting Roy Stewart. It was recorded in short little sections, one of which was of the empty room which needed to be superimposed into a mirror during the next take. Then there were little cutaways showing the spear being plunged down upon Ridge on the sofa. The effect didn't go as smoothly as Eric Hills wanted. Hills remembered 'I had great difficulties in explaining to Simon what I wanted to do. I wanted to do something rather fancy with that, with him looking in the mirror and then seeing this bloke coming down the stairs and him fighting him, then turning and watching it. I had a blue cloth to go in the mirror, but I couldn't get him to look and turn so that I could get a recording of it to go in the mirror, which wasn't happening in real life. He had to do it twice. I couldn't get that through to him! So, I just had to cut it so he was standing there looking and cut to a shot of him with Roy. I couldn't get into it as I intended because I just couldn't get him to look into the mirror and turn twice the same.'

Following this, inserts were recorded of his imaginary self-fighting on the sofa, then the real Ridge fighting the invisible menace and a close up of Roy Stewart plunging the spear down.

Music

Max Harris provided over five minutes of his own music for the story. Ridge's hallucination was backed by thirty seconds of 'Gyil Dance' from the Keith Prowse Music library album *Native Africa Vol. 2* (KPM 1054) by Ghanaian musician Guy Warren (later known as Khofi Ghanaba). Warren used the gyil (a wooden West African instrument similar to the xylophone), two drums and a shaker for this piece, and it is disturbingly catchy.

Editing

With a long and wordy script, there may well have been edits performed to the episode, but with his experience, Terence Dudley knew instinctively how to time an episode, but this time he was not directing. The episode was edited on Tuesday, 31 March 1970 between 11 am and 5 pm

Promotion

By now the *Sun* had noticed how popular the programme was proving with the female viewers and promoted the episode by asking each of the three leads about their fan mail, with John Paul being rather coy upon the subject. The *Daily Mirror* saw it as another good opportunity to print a picture of Wendy Hall.

Programme Review Board

Andrew Osborn praised the episode as being very good at the Wednesday review. It is a great shame that we cannot see if he was right or not, as this is the third missing episode from the first series. Nine and a half million viewers tuned in.

Script Book

The script was published with the permission of the Dudley estate in 2011 among four other lost *Doomwatch* episodes in a collection called *Deadly Dangerous Tomorrow.*

1.10
Train And De-Train

Written by Don Shaw
Directed by Vere Lorrimer
Designed by Ian Watson
Transmitted: Monday, 20 April 1970 at 9:45 pm Duration: 49' 44"

Cast
Boy (Mark Sinclair), Ministry Inspector (Peter Whitaker), Guard (Ron Gregory), Mitchell (George Baker), Ellis (David Markham), Branston (Bill Wilde), Miss Sephton (Patricia Maynard), Stephens (Brian Badcoe), Miss Jones (Rosemary Turner).

Also appearing
Male Lab Workers (Reg Lloyd, Alf Costa, Bernard Jackson, Freddie Clemson), Female Lab Workers (Sylvia Rattray, Ann Lee) Female Lab Worker and Copy Typist (Lynn Howard), Security Guard (Alastair Meldrum).

Extras on location
Robert Murphy, Gordon Stiles, Donald Graves, Derek Ware-Benthar, Derek Parey, Keith Kibourne, Mark Warren, Marcia Bennett.

Technical Credits
Production Assistant: Robert Checksfield. Assistant Floor Manager: Jane Southern. Director's Assistant: Maria Ellis. Floor Assistant: John Willcox.
Film Cameraman: Eddie Best. Sound Recordist: George Cassidy. Film Editor: Alastair MacKay.
Costume Supervisor: Dorothea Wallace. Make-up Supervisor: Elizabeth Rowell.
Studio Lighting: Jimmy Purdie. TM2: Jack Shallcross. Vision Mixer: Chris Griffin.
Studio Sound: Larry Goodson. Grams Operator: Gerry Borrows.
Crew: 6.

Radio Times
There has been a mass extermination of wildlife in Somerset. Doomwatch investigate and the trail apparently leads to field trials of a new type of pesticide. At least that is the way it looks to Toby Wren ...

The Story

'I was forced into conducting tests into 3051 which I knew would be dangerous. 3051 is still dangerous despite improvements, and I will not be party to indiscriminate pollution.' – Ellis' suicide note.

Doomwatch is called in following the discovery of dead animals in an area of common land in Somerset. Ridge is handed a canister marked AC 3051, and Wren, busy on his own report, is asked to visit pesticide firms for samples of their new product. Quist is about to leave for a conference in America and tells Wren to keep an open mind. Wilfred Ellis, the chief chemist at Alminster Chemicals, arrives at work to find his parking space has now been reassigned to Branston, his junior, and discovers that his office is now lacking a telephone and carpet. Hunnisett links the AC 3051 canister with Alminster Chemicals, and Wren is surprised to learn that his former tutor from Cambridge is now its chief chemist. He remembered Ellis as being a nice man and doesn't want to upset him.

Wren goes down to Alminster Chemicals to see the managing director, a confident man called Mitchell. Outside Mitchell's office he meets Ellis, who has been summoned to see his boss. They are delighted at their reunion, and Ellis takes him back to his office – or rather what used to be his office. It is now empty, and there is a strange new secretary working there. Furious, Ellis storms back to Mitchell's office, where the director takes an almost perverse pleasure in telling the man that, at 51, he is now totally useless and is to be reassigned to a more menial job. Wren is outside listening, appalled by the way Ellis is being treated, insulted and shouted down. He bursts in at one point, but, unsure of himself in Mitchell's presence, goes back outside again to wait. When they have their meeting, Wren asks him point-blank for a sample of his new pesticide, mentioning 3051. Mitchell becomes angry that he isn't even being asked for the results of the company's own tests on the pesticides, resenting the implication that they are guilty without a chance to prove themselves innocent. With the first shipment of 3051 imminent, and with rival firms ready to usurp Alminster, he will only hand over samples once they have cornered the market.

Back at the Doomwatch lab, Wren is furious with Mitchell to the point where Ridge has to calm him down and point out that Quist might question his objectivity. Ridge explains that what happened to Ellis was de-training – a standard procedure in the States to get rid of a useless member of staff without upsetting the unions. They still need to get a sample of the pesticide, so Ridge smuggles Wren into the plant whilst posing a representative from the Export Advisory Board. Wren finds Ellis inside his lab and warns him that Mitchell is getting rid of him. The former chief chemist is calmer and more reflective today. He listens to Wren's description of the Somerset deaths but expresses confidence in their product. He leaves Wren alone long enough for him to take a sample, but Wren is caught by Branston. As Ridge is having some brandy with Mitchell, the news about Wren comes through. Mitchell calls for Ellis, leaving Wren and Ridge alone long enough to pass over the stolen sample. Ridge goes, and Mitchell accuses Wren of being a spy from another company – a thief with Ellis in his pay. They protest, but Mitchell calls Ellis' actions revenge. He is pleased when Ellis resigns. Wren can no longer contain himself, calling Mitchell a bastard, and tries to explain what a good man Ellis is. Mitchell lets Wren speak his mind but labels him an idealist. Wren agrees: 'It's a bloody nuisance, isn't it?' He intends to let everyone see Mitchell for what he is, unaware that Mitchell is recording the conversation. Wren leaves just as Branston works out that a sample of 3051 is missing.

Mitchell, now suspicious of Ridge's identity, has Miss Sephton transcribe the tape and make a copy. It is sent to Doomwatch. Ridge and Bradley wince as they listen to the playback, and Quist is contacted and asked to return. Ellis, meanwhile, hesitates over a letter he is about to post, but an impatient lady makes the decision for him and it goes into the postbox. The next morning, Mitchell receives the letter, burns it, and summons Ellis. But his secretary tells him that he is dead.

Quist confronts Wren about the tape and sacks him, though he can stay until he finds another job and will get a 'damn good reference'. They discuss Ellis' death, and Quist tells him it has nothing to do with him. Suspicious as to why Mitchell did not send the tape to where it could have done some real damage, Quist visits him. Mitchell is pleased to see Quist, and claims he holds all the cards. He tells him that their tests would interfere with production, accusing Quist of trying to take away evidence of a vendetta against Mitchell by a member of his Quist's staff. He warns him that he will use the tape if they interfere further.

Hoping to find a link between the death and the pesticide, Wren is disappointed to learn from the coroner that Ellis took his own life by swallowing a massive dose of poison and didn't die from slow absorption. Then he reads a letter that is waiting for him on his desk. Meanwhile, Quist visits Mitchell a second time, still not satisfied, and asks for his co-operation in a series of tests. Mitchell refuses and plays his hand again. Wren arrives with the letter, which is a copy of the one sent by Ellis to Mitchell, who feigns ignorance and suggests Wren forged it. But the implication of the letter is clear: Alminster Chemicals has been ruthlessly developing a pollutant pesticide, intending to release it despite its dangers. If the letter is handed to the police, it would be read out in open court at Ellis' inquest, with serious consequences for Alminster. Mitchell gives in, handing over the tape and promising official co-operation.

Unable to admit he is wrong, Quist commends Wren on his Greenland lice report, using it as an excuse to give him a second chance. Wren, fully understanding, accepts with a smile. Mitchell, on the other hand, discovers he has lost his parking space to Branston …

Behind the Story
It is perhaps not surprising that in his opening scene in the episode, Wren is compiling a report on the organochlorine content of Greenland's coastal lice. Organochlorines do not occur naturally except in very rare exceptions. Traces of DDT, the most famous organochlorine pesticide, could be found stored in the fatty tissue of marine animals living in the Baltic ocean and is also present in human fat. These pesticides stay in the environment and are spread by the weather, accumulating in animals for a long time after it is first applied. DDT had been used extensively in America from the 1940s, and by the time *Silent Spring* was published in 1962, the US Department of Agriculture was actively encouraging farmers to use it far more than was actually necessary. There was big money to be made. Critics were regarded as cranks, especially the Soil Association, who campaigned against pesticides and antibiotic use in animals. By 1969 the dangers posed by DDT were starting to become accepted. Population collapse in certain species of bird was put down to DDT thinning the egg shells to the point where they would cave under the slightest touch. Accumulated DDT was also reducing the reproductive rate of fish. In Britain, the use and development of pesticides such as dieldrin and aldrin ('those terrible organophosphorus twins', according to Gordon Rattray Taylor's *The Doomsday Book*) was regulated under a voluntary code, the Pesticides Safety Precaution Scheme. 1969's *Further Review of Certain Persistent Organochlorine Pesticides Used in Great Britain*, a report compiled under the scheme by the Advisory Committee on Pesticides and Other Toxic Chemicals, effectively stopped the issue being a political hot potato.

Legal Issues
For Doomwatch, there were few laws which they could invoke for their investigation into the Somerset deaths to make Alminster Chemicals cooperate. All Toby could do was to go in and ask for sample. *According to The Law Relating to Pollution: An Introduction* by James McLoughlin LLM, published in 1972, the Minister could have glanced at the Town and Garden Chemicals Act 1967, where he could impose requirements as to the of labelling and marketing of a product. The Agriculture (Poisonous Substances) Act 1952 protected employees against the risk of poisoning, but that was about it. Mitchell did not have to 'notify new pesticides or new use of existing pesticides to the Ministry of Agriculture, the Ministry of Health' or 'advise on precautionary measures … which should be employed when used'; he was under no duress not to 'introduce such products until agreement has been reached on the appropriate

precautionary measures' or even 'to withdraw the product from the market if recommended to do so by the government departments'. This voluntary scheme was considered a success at the time by both government and industry. In 1972 there were concerns that new legislation enforcing the code would slow down work on launching new products – precisely Mitchell's fear.

Mitchell completely ignores the voluntary code. This is about business in a desperate hurry: export or die, to quote post-war Britain. Alminster Chemicals is owned by an American outfit, Neopolomo Chicago, at a time when pesticides and the chemical industry were none too popular but still an important economic backbone to America. Alminster Chemicals has only the one viable product: AC3051. This is a company with only one chance, and Mitchell plans to succeed, exporting before the rival firms mentioned do. In 1972 it was estimated that around £1 million was being spent on developing a new product. A delay of only a few months in marketing could be expensive.

Ellis
Ellis – now here's a funny thing. We are meant to feel sorry for this man. His hesitant mode of speech is exactly as scripted and beautifully played. He conducted the field trial two years ago, complained it wasn't safe, and had recently visited Somerset and seen the results. Yet when he was told by Wren of the consequences of the test, he was surprised. He is another Whitehead, a chief scientist who sold out to business, which is now spitting him out. De-training comes from one of the sciences, psychology, rapidly being applied to the workplace – the gradual destruction of moral and self-worth in order to remove a useless member of staff without upsetting the powerful unions. Mitchell chews Ellis up and spits him out, considering him to be useless because of his age and his moral scruples over the safety of their product. Mitchell is honest, callous and crushes the man, offering him an exit by means of relocation to another division, where he can no longer be an obstruction to the company's ethos. Why did Ellis commit suicide? Was it losing his job? Guilt over the tests? Over his life's work? Or perhaps the state of his mind was unbalanced, and this was a strange sort of revenge.

Mitchell
AC 3051 is a metaphor for Mitchell: his personality pervades what we see of the firm. Like DDT it has a cumulative and corrosive effect. He doesn't engender loyalty in his staff; he works through fear and directness, hence Miss Sephton's evident delight at his own de-training at the end of the episode. She in turn obviously takes her cues from Mitchell in the way she talks to Wren and no doubt to the rest of the staff that cross into her

sanctum. Then there's Branston: smooth, smarmy, witty; a man who knows that he is on the way up and apologises insincerely when he's walking on your head. This is a totally morally bankrupt outfit, and one hopes the American Head Office did close it down.

Mitchell is a *tour de force* of characterisation and performance by George Baker, who would later play another memorable despot in *I, Claudius*, with the role of Tiberius. A ruthless managing director who wants to keep his company going by sheer force of personality, Mitchell is probably a psychotic lacking in empathy and thus has no care of the harm he does to the human spirit. It makes you wonder whether he sees the starving in (presumably) Africa as a tragedy or a commercial opportunity; probably the latter. Rude and ruthless (although he would probably call it being honest and straightforward) you almost want to boo whenever he appears on screen. He lights a cigar with a letter sent from his prime target. He praises Ridge for being someone who's certain and sure. He delights in his treatment of Ellis, possibly even recording the conversation in order to play it to his American masters. His recording of the conversation that sees Wren temporarily sacked from his job was a technique that would later bring down President Nixon, whose habit of recording all Oval Office conversations proved his knowledge of the Watergate break-ins as well as showing the American public his true personality. No wonder Quist is so circumspect in what he says to Mitchell in their two scenes together.

Script Development

Having proven to be a reliable writer for the series, Don Shaw was invited to write his third (and, as it turned out, final) script for the series whilst he was delivering rewrites for 'Re-Entry Forbidden'. 'Train and De-Train' was commissioned on 15 December 1969 with a delivery date for 12 January 1970. This was the seventeenth commission for the series. Pedler and Davis had been paid for their storyline in March. Shaw delivered his own storyline and explained to the production team that, although this story didn't have the grand technical drama of the other episodes, it was more in line with boardroom dramas like *The Power Game* and likened it to Kafka in its theme of demoralisation and the behaviour of the management at (what was then called) Altringham. There was originally a strand featuring Branston 'plotting' following Ellis' death. Hints of it are in the final scene, such as the pay-off. Shaw also asked for at least six minutes film effort for his episode. Shaw delivered early in the New Year and left a few questions for Pedler, whom he had consulted on the de-training method. He wanted to suggest sophisticated techniques but leave the big dramatic stuff, such as the business with Ellis' office, for the viewer to see. Rehearsal copies were sent to the writer on 19 February with news that Vere Lorrimer would be directing and that a read-through of the episode was scheduled for around 5 March.

The story itself takes a different path than one might expect. Ellis did not die from exposure to the pesticide accumulating within him from exposure over the years, which the story appears to hint towards. Ridge talks about chemical warfare to Branston, and for a moment one wonders whether Alminster Chemicals were secretly developing something a little more sinister than just a pesticide. But the story goes in neither of these directions. It keeps it real.

This story, as transmitted, can be seen as the first in a trilogy about business and the sciences going bad in the workplace. Something not explained in the script is just what did happen in Somerset? Mitchell claims that after the initial field trials, they worked for two years to make their one product safer. They had spent £20,000 in safety measures that year alone. If their test was two years ago, were the resulting deaths the result of a cumulative effect? The dead squirrel at the top of the programme suggests it died instantly, not gradually. It is a mystery indeed. The animals photographed by Ridge did not look as if they had been dead for long. Was this an example of spray drift, where the wind blows the pesticide over public land?

Filming
Filming took place in the last week of February 1970 in or near Harlow. Simon Oates was needed on Monday 23 and Wednesday 25.

Editing and Changes in Rehearsal
By the time the camera script was prepared, a serious problem had emerged: the script was overrunning dramatically. Many cuts were imposed, including the elimination of an entire character, Graham, the Minister's PPS, who was to have been played by Clifford Earl. Graham is covering for Quist's trip to America in order to do a personnel check. Although Ridge is suspicious of Graham and thinks he is a 'cretinous berk', he is actually quite supportive of Wren's investigation and problems at Alminster. When the blackmail tape is sent, he doesn't want to upset him further. He brings Quist back to deal with the matter before the Minister returns from his own trip, when Graham would have had to report it.

After Wren is caught stealing the sample, Ridge pulls up outside a newsagents and telephones Mitchell's office, pretending to be calling from the Ministry and wanting to speak to Wren. Miss Sephton is confused, as Mitchell is on the phone to Ministry now. Ridge quickly hangs up. Mitchell is told of this development and works out that 'Mr Ridge keeps me talking while Mr Wren sticks his hand in my pocket!' This suggests another change had been made to the script – Wren passed the sample to Ridge in the office and did not pickpocket Mitchell. A tobacconist's shop set was ordered and extras already hired to play lab workers would also to play the tobacconist (Reg Lloyd) and a customer (Lynn Howard).

The last big cut was a two-handed scene between Quist and Ridge after Wren has visited the morgue. Ridge tentatively asks Quist if he has a replacement for Wren yet and also enquires if he has read Wren's Greenland report. 'Thought it was pretty good myself. Course, once you've established a principle, it's difficult to abandon it – without loss of face.' Ridge is thinking of the good of Doomwatch, but so was Quist, which was why he sacked Wren. Bradley enters and waits while Ridge suggests Quist is going to do a deal with Mitchell to get the tape back. Quist looks up sharply. He agrees that doing that would be compromising principle. 'We can exist without Wren…but nothing exists without Doomwatch.' They have one more day before the Minister gets back.

Studio
'Train and De-Train' was the tenth episode to be recorded. This was in studio TC4 on Friday 13 and Saturday 14 March 1970. There were overtime payments for the camera rehearsal day and for 11 March, one of the rehearsal days. Robert Powell and George Baker pre-recorded a part of their confrontation to be played back in the studio the day before recording, as did Patricia Maynard and Wendy Hall for their intercom moments. The extras were only needed for the recording day.

Editing
Editing was on Monday, 16 March between 3 pm and 6 pm. The episode was watched by nine and a half million viewers.

1.11
The Battery People

Written by Elwyn Jones
Directed by David Proudfoot
Designed by Stuart Walker
Transmitted: Monday, 27 April 1970 at 9.46 pm Duration: 49' 10"

Cast
Davies (David Davies), Dai (Edward Evans), Vincent Llewellyn (Jeremy Young), Bryn (Michael Newport), Colonel Smithson (Emrys Jones), Elizabeth Llewellyn (Eliza Ward), Jones (Ray Mort), Mrs Adams (Mary Hignett), Laing (Jay Neill).

Also appearing
Extras on location
Norman Brown, Alec Pleon, Freddie Miles, George Kalder, Stenson Falke, Philip Bass-Walker, John Lord, Clive Desmond, Pat Donaghue, Johnny Watson, Bill Howes, Bryn Jones, Charles Erakine, Harold White

Extras in studio
Dilys Marvin, Don Vernon, Jan Bolitho, Johnny Watson, Alec Pleon, George Wilder, Freddie Wiles, Stenson Falke, Philip Bass-Walker

Technical Credits
Director's Assistant: Adele Paul. Production Assistant: Nick Parsons. Assistant Floor Manager: Sue Allan. Floor Assistant: John Wilcox.
Film Cameraman: David Prosser. Sound Recordist: Malcolm Webberley. Film Editor: Alastair MacKay.
Costume Supervisor: Dorothea Wallace. Make-up Supervisor: Liz Rowell.
Studio Lighting: Jimmy Purdie. TM2: Jack Shallcross. Vision Mixer: Graham Giles.
Sound Supervisor: Trevor Webster. Grams Operator: Gerald Borrows.
Crew: 19.

Radio Times
Tough ex-miners in South Wales drinking gin instead of the traditional beer, giving their wives the cold shoulder and secretly turning to cock-fighting. It all sounds wildly out of character to Dr Quist and his team who investigate despite the fact that all this is taking place in the Minister's own constituency.

The Story
'Why … That's all I want to know. The doctor says I'm perfectly healthy … Why this.' – Llewellyn

At a large fish farm somewhere in Wales, workers scoop out a fish with their bare hands and inject it with a syringe. The foreman, Vincent Llewellyn, has an altercation with Dai, a much older man, who accuses him of bullying a junior worker and taunts him for losing his bottle as well as his wife. The ensuing fight is stopped by Colonel Smithson, who fires Dai and then speaks to the apologetic Llewellyn about a Ministerial visit due the following week. He reminds his staff to put their gloves on, but after he leaves the gloves come off again.

The new Minister of National Security is the Welshman John Timothy-Davies, and his appointment does not impress the Doomwatch team. Quist wants to make a favourable impression on him at their first meeting, but it doesn't quite go that way. 'Don't give me trouble, boy', the Minister warns after an awkward meeting. Quist tells Ridge and Wren to forget their plans to make constructive suggestions for the Minister's constituency, but the research they have done has turned up unusual behaviour for ex-coalminers – taking to gin as a favourite drink, a high divorce rate and prosecutions for cockfighting – which interests Quist. He tells Ridge to go undercover and investigate.

Ridge settles into the Red Lion and meets Jones, a local journalist, and pays him for news in the valleys as part of a background feature on the new Minister. He brings up the cockfighting; that night, he witnesses one such event and is sickened. The next day, Ridge realises that he didn't see many youngsters at the fight. Jones explains that they've mostly gone, and a new factory farm employs a lot of the older miners, preferring a stable workforce. They take a look outside the gates, and Jones sticks up for the company despite its battery farming methods – it's all they've got. They return to the inn and meet Colonel Smithson, who stays there. Smithson is eager to talk about his company, Factory Farming Ltd, and explains that their standards are higher than at other farms. He invites Ridge to take a look around after lunch. Ridge visits the farm and sees the frankly gruesome and mechanical nature of the process – chickens are killed, their feathers boiled off and feet clipped before packaging. Afterwards Smithson gives Ridge a drink in his office and explains his labour policy and the economics of working in Wales which offset the extra transport costs. Meanwhile, Wren and Bradley have been wondering if an unusually high level of hormones in the chicken feed could be enough to emasculate the men, but when a background check on Colonel Smithson reveals he had worked for Eastern Command RU Section 14 from 1956-62, they discover an abandoned project: the potential destruction of bone structure in noncarnivorous organisms.

Llewellyn is lurking outside the house of his ex-wife, Liz, who sees him and calls him inside. He tries to kiss her but then suddenly breaks down, distraught. He doesn't understand. The doctor says he is a perfectly, healthy man but he cannot perform. Liz tells him to go, clearly upset. At the Red Lion Mrs Adams, the landlady, offers Ridge some fish from Smithson's farm, which interests him as he didn't see any on his tour. His curiosity grows as he hears that Smithson's fish never have any bones in them – not a single one. That night he tries to get a sample from the inn's kitchen but is nearly caught by Smithson, thinking he heard a burglar. Ridge pretends he came down for milk. Smithson talks about his boneless fish – the 'Tasteaway Trout' – but the process is a trade secret. The next day, Wren reports to Quist that the bone structure of the chicken has a low calcium content, and the idea of boneless fish is significant. Since fish bones aren't eaten, it's a logical step to stop them forming, but the only means of inhibiting bone growth are dangerous to the health of those who do the inhibiting. But does the Colonel know this?

Ridge visits Liz Llewellyn and discovers the reasons behind her divorce: her husband had lost interest in her, so she had an affair. She is keen on Ridge and quite flirtatious, but he is rather reluctant and leaves after some more questions. On the phone to Quist he is quite clearly worried that his virility is at stake after eating the chickens, but Quist reassures him that the danger lies in working with a live animal. Quist tells the Minister the results of their unofficial enquiry. Angry and appalled at the same time, Davies at first refuses to believe Quist, especially as that part of Wales is crying out for jobs. He decides that the only thing they can do is confront Colonel Smithson, and they go down to Wales together.

Smithson is shifty about the nature of his trade secret, which he learned from his time at the Glyne research station. When he refuses to handle the live fish with bare hands, the Minister agrees to an enquiry. Quist tells Llewellyn that the nature of the liquid has virtually castrated the men, and Smithson deliberately chose an older workforce in the hope that they wouldn't notice. As Smithson walks back to his office along a gantry, Llewellyn pulls him into the fish tanks. Everyone thinks he slipped, but Quist, who saw it, plays along. Smithson had swallowed some of the liquid; the chances are he will not survive, but Quist believes that might be a blessing: 'When these men find out what's happened to them, I think even the Colonel will consider it a timely exit.'

Behind the Story
Factory Farming
After the Second World War, the need to mass-produce food was urgent. Sentimentality towards animals did not go terribly far if you had lived

through rationing (which included having to eat a horrible tinned fish called Snoek). Food production became more industrialised than ever before, and thousands of chickens were shoved into tiny cages, row after row of them, force-fed and de-beaked, waiting for slaughter. Fewer staff were needed, the animals' environment could be controlled and they could be forced to grow fatter than before with drugs.

In 1964 factory farming was exposed in a book called *Animal Machines: The New Factory Farming Industry* by Soil Association member Ruth Harrison, and farm animal welfare suddenly became an issue in Britain. Harrison is credited as having inspired Britain's first farm animal welfare legislation – the 1968 Agriculture (Miscellaneous Provisions) Act. Her book prompted the Minister of Agriculture at the time, Christopher Soames, to call a press conference stating the official attitude of the Ministry towards the practice, and an enquiry was held. Although their recommendations were not adopted, a standing committee was created with Harrison as one of its members. At a symposium held in 1968 by the British Association for the Advancement of Science, Harrison stated that in the previous year, an estimated 86.8 per cent of laying birds were in battery cages. Over sixty-two million birds existed in conditions where they could not 'fly, scratch, perch or walk freely. Preening is difficult and dust bathing impossible.' wrote Michael Allaby in *The Eco-Activists*.

Hormones
The episode is not about the ethics of battery farming. Wren is looking for evidence of an abnormally high level of hormones in the chicken feed to explain the emasculation of the ex-coal miners. In his book *Our Synthetic Environment* Murray Bookchin tells of how in 1947 the use of stilbestrol pellets, designed to tenderise poultry meat, was passed by the FDA (the US Food and Drug Administration). This was a synthetically prepared drug which caused body changes identical to those produced by oestrogens (female sex hormones). A single pellet was implanted into the chicken's neck for a month or two before marketing them, so there would be no residues left over by the time the carcass reached the butchers. Male birds were emasculated, as they lost all inclination to crow or fight. However, it was all a bit of a fraud, as the chicken grew more body fat than meat, and the pellets were not always absorbed into the chicken. The use of stilbestrol was discontinued in 1959 on the recommendation of the FDA.

What we have in Colonel Smithson is an opportunist. Perhaps as a former soldier and officer at a weapons research centre, he was used to the British Army using human guinea pigs, with or without their consent. He saw potential in the farming industry for a fluid which inhibited bone growth. He knew the health risks involved and chose a workforce which would not (or was not supposed to) notice impotency. He did try to ensure that they wore gloves in the fish farm, but this was not very strictly observed, as his staff found them cumbersome to wear when handling the fish and took them off. How were they to know?

A Man's World

'Hear No Evil' will investigate how a Man is a Man by his trade. Communities that lose a central employer – whether it be a factory, mine, shipyard or steelworks – can simply die out. The young leave because they no longer feel there is a purpose to stay. We hear talk of development grants to encourage new industries, but very few would have the need to employ so many people as some of those dirty, heavy trades that built the economic backbone of Britain in the nineteenth century. In 'The Battery People' we are given a definition of what makes a Man a Man. It is his ability to have sex, a source of masculine pride. The episode, which had a cut scene that featured the issue, suggests the male fear that if you can't satisfy the wife on a regular basis, she might run off with younger, more virile stock. It is perhaps a little alarming that scriptwriter Elwyn Jones seems to imply that a wife will automatically have an affair should her man no longer perform. Still, a hundred years ago, the idea that a woman might enjoy sex was unheard of, and more sentiments of this nature from the time will be explored in the third series episode 'Without the Bomb'. Women were simply brood-mares, economic investments and housewives. Divorce for the common family was still quite a relatively recent development. The Llewellyn divorce was the first in this village (which is described as having a strong chapel tradition in a cut scene). Elwyn Jones was a Welshman himself and would have understood the mindset. It was probably only recently that Llewellyn tried to analyse why he lost his sex drive, and we see him struggling to come to terms with it. It is good that he gets his revenge on the Colonel. One can only wonder if the revelation that Llewellyn had at the end of the episode might have brought his wife back to him. He divorced her, not the other way round, and she claims to be fond of him still. There is no mention as to whether they had any children in the past.

As an aside...

Hormone treatment was being used on men gaoled for sex offences. For two years, experiments had been carried out on forty volunteer prisoners in Wormwood scrubs. They had a pellet of oestrogen implanted under their skin. The idea being the female hormone would counteract the male sexual urge. Unhappy voices in the *Birmingham Post*, dated 28 November 1968, said the experiment was fine as far as it went, but only if the deviancy was sexual, and not psychopathic. The treatment was dependent on whether prisoner on his release would continue to have his treatment

162

repeated every three months.

Script Development

The first script to have the title 'The Battery People' had been commissioned from Moris Farhi in January 1969, assigned a project number of 2249/1269 and was based on a storyline by Pedler and Davis of the same name. It may have been a story about hormones and factory-farming. Later called 'Any Man's Death', the script was rejected later in the spring.

The Synthetic Candidate

Elwyn Jones was commissioned to write 'The Synthetic Candidate' from a storyline by Pedler and Davis. Although commissioned on 18 March, no script was expected from the busy author until the beginning of August 1969. This too fell through, and the original notes of the plot are reproduced elsewhere in this book. 'The Synthetic Candidate' was about a group of extreme right-wing activists trying to get a candidate elected. With a willing accomplice, they create the perfect politician to appeal to the public by using plastic surgery to make him physically attractive. Computerised data accumulated by phrenologists was fed directly into his brain to give him answers designed to appeal to any possible kind of voter. Doomwatch discovers the fraud and exposes him by showing him up to be the racist bigot he is.

Elwyn Jones appears not to have pursued the project as there is no record of the script being either rejected or written off. 'The Synthetic Candidate' went on the pile of abandoned stories, along with 'The Pacifiers' and 'The Logicians'. No extra storyline seems to have been required, unlike the situation where 'The Flames of Hell' was replaced by a new storyline, Jones was given Farhi's storyline.

Hormones

'A little light reading for trains!' was sent to the author by Judy Hall on 17 June, but it wasn't until 2 July that Gerry Davis sent Jones some 'nauseating bumph' on 'Battery Chicken Farming – very sinister if you have that kind of mind.' On 4 July Jones was paid the first half of his fee for a fifty-minute script simply called 'Hormones'. It wasn't sure whether Jones would eventually write the script at all, but his contribution was finally confirmed in September. Jones' script was acknowledged on 1 October, and rehearsal scripts were sent out on 22 January 1970 but with no director assigned to the 4 March recording date.

In the *Radio Times* piece to launch the series, it seems an earlier version of 'The Battery People' was discussed. Terence Dudley explained the notion that 'baddies' in the series were not necessarily the scientists.

'Sometimes they're men who exploit science for their own ends. In an episode entitled "The Battery People", it's a retired army officer who, though he is within his legal rights in rearing battery hens by ultra-efficient methods, quite knowingly allows the excreta of his hens – containing artificially added hormones – to be sold commercially as manure. The men who collect the manure absorb enough of a new hormone (Actimycin S) to make them impotent. Result: a staggering divorce rate in the local village! It's frightening but – scientifically plausible.'

Filming

Given to David Proudfoot to direct, the episode needed a good amount of filming, which was performed in the week beginning 9 February. Oates filmed his scenes (which included a night shoot for the cockfight) on the 12 February and stayed for two nights. He had just finished recording 'Re-Entry Forbidden' the night before. Filming took place during a cold snap and snow can be seen on the ground for the scene outside the battery farm when Ridge and Evans visit.

It was another unglamorous, and unknown, location for Adele Winston to endure: 'It was freezing cold and snowy, horrible. No-one wants to do film locations like that. Countryside locations you only want to do during the day and in August really.' The crew also paid a visit to Ealing Film Studios to record all the scenes needing the fish tanks, as it was never a good idea to fill water tanks within the electronic TV studios. Plus, there was the need for a stunt as Emrys Jones takes a plunge at the end of the episode.

The battery farm sequence was taken from stock as Elwyn Jones expected when he reached this point in his script: 'I'm not going to attempt to write this (a) because the experts can do it better (b) because it will depend so much on what film there is available … the only thing that will emerge as really unusual in this set up which is the number of people about. These are all white-coated sort of laboratory-like but there are a lot of them, only they're all men too.'

Casting

Amongst the marvellous cast was one David Davies, playing the new Minister for National Security, who had acted alongside John Paul in a regular role for *Probation Officer*. He had played a Labour Minister for *The Avengers* in 1963. Elwyn Jones was anxious that the Minister was not played as a stereotype. He wanted to avoid an extravagant Lloyd George style. He had in mind the recently deceased Lord Hall, who had been First Lord of the Admiralty. Emrys Jones had a very long career behind him but sadly would pass away in 1972 in South Africa where he was playing Sir Winston Churchill. Jeremy Young was a popular face on television and known to fans of science fiction and fantasy thanks to notable appearances in *Doctor Who, The Avengers* and *Adam Adamant Lives!* He would have been seen by *Doomwatch* fans waiting to watch *The Red Sky* as he appeared in *Up Pompei!* Just to show the small world television can appear, he also appeared in an Elwyn Jones scripted episode of *Softly, Softly* in January as a publican in trouble. Simon Oates and the softly spoken Ray Mort had both worked together and interacted on an episode of ATV's *The Plane Makers* in 1963.

Cast as the 'buxom but sexy' Mrs Llewellyn was Eliza Ward who was more often to be seen on the stage. She had recently written a musical called *Ringa Ranga Roo*, a survey of the oldest profession in the world. Her first rare TV appearance had been on the musical hall recreation *The Good Old Days*. The script said that 'she is the type of woman whose very walk is an invitation.' Edward Evans, one of *The Grove Family*, had been a prolific actor, his small cameo as a sacked worker is not indicative of the type of role he could command, and would be seen again in *Doomwatch* in a different class altogether. Child actor Michael Newport had recently been Jim Hawkins in *Treasure Island*, and *Doomwatch* would be his last television role. This was to be Jay Neill's only credit in *Doomwatch*, although he had been an uncredited man in 'Project Sahara' and will appear in more episodes.

For some reason there were overtime payments during rehearsals for Simon Oates on 26 and 27 February. On the latter date Kit Pedler recorded an appearance on the BBC2 programme *Line Up* in Studio B at TV Centre, participating in a discussion about Desmond King-Hele's book *The End of the Twentieth Century?*

Studio
'The Battery People' was the ninth episode to be recorded and went into studio TC6. Originally scheduled for a Wednesday, 4 March recording, the episode went before the cameras on Friday the 6th, following the usual single day of camera rehearsals.

Interestingly, the scene in which the two 'journalists' Ridge and Evans talk together in the snug of the hotel (as seen on screen) is just one take with no camera cuts at all, which is not how David Proudfoot planned it originally. Perhaps the amusing chemistry between Simon Oates and Ray Mort needed them to be seen together in the intimacy of a continuous two-shot. Both days ran into overtime. Incidental music made a return this week, all by Max Harris.

Editing
It was originally planned to edit the episode on Friday, 6 March, so the new date was probably the following Monday. In the end, the editing was

quite severe. The first cut came after Ridge telephones Jones at his newspaper office to set up a meeting. Ridge is then shown around the pub by Mrs Adams, watched by Llewellyn. Interestingly, the scene in which the two 'journalists' talk (as seen on screen) is just one take with no camera cuts at all, which is not how David Proudfoot planned it originally. Perhaps the amusing chemistry between Simon Oates and Ray Mort needed them to be seen together in the intimacy of a continuous two-shot. The next cut came after the cockfight: Ridge is on the phone to Quist, who warns him against the worst kind of sentimentality – the one about animals.

We were supposed to see Ridge driving towards through the village and park beside the farm as large refrigeration vans marked 'Farming Developments Ltd' drive up and down, transporting chickens. Jones explains that the farm employs some young people, such as the men at the gates and the drivers. 'They're a randy lot from what I've heard.' We also discover it was adultery on the part of the woman in all of the divorce cases. This then led into the scene down by the gates. The scene where Wren discusses Colonel Smithson's career with Colin was much longer. When Wren wonders how many chickens Ridge has eaten, Colin suggests 'Just what he needs, quieten him down a bit. Give the birds a rest for a change.' This went straight into Ridge asking if there is anywhere else to eat, as he doesn't fancy chicken and chips. Jones tells him it'll have to be fish and chips. 'Now we've got seven fish shops.' Ridge agrees to try one of them.

Wren tells Quist that he wants one of these fish, and Ridge will have to provide one as they are not on the market yet. This led into Ridge's midnight raid on the fridge. The scene went on for much longer and ended with Smithson pointing out to Ridge that his fish product has a good deal less Strontium 7 than the milk he is drinking. After Ridge tells Quist on the phone that some of the wives have noticed their men becoming impotent, the scene continued. Quist says it is only a small percentage, based on the divorce figures, but Ridge says that won't do and he knows it. Ridge says he's better get away from here – it might be catching. This is when Quist says that he'll be meeting the Minister in the morning. He is going to demand a formal enquiry and Ridge can leave.

Transmission

The camera script announced that the episode was going to be the transmitted ninth on Monday, 13 April, but in the event 'Spectre at the Feast' was put in its place. *The Guardian* was pleased to note the author of the episode, thinking it would be 'better written than usual: Elwyn Jones (late of *Z Cars*) has turned in a script full of cockfighting and South Wales atmosphere.' Ten million viewers tuned in.

Programme Review Board
Andrew Osborn felt that this was a weak episode, even though it had been written by Elwyn Jones, and that for once it had 'not come off.' John Paul's performance was noted by others as 'improving'.

UK Gold
When cable channel UK Gold repeated this episode back in 1994, they vandalised it in order to make it more palatable for the time slot by removing most of the chicken production-line film. Worse, they removed the whole of Quist and the Minister confronting Smithson in his office, and about fifteen seconds from the end of the previous scene, where we would have seen the Minister putting on his hat and coat as he talks to Quist.

Hindsight
Not only was this an episode remembered by Gerry Davis as an example of what *Doomwatch* was all about but also Robert Powell singled out its plot during *The Cult of... Doomwatch* (broadcast on BBC Four in 2006). Carol Topolski, Kit's eldest daughter, also remembers this one as a classic case of how the fiction mirrored reality, which helped to feed the myth about Pedler. '*Doomwatch* had a reputation for being prescient, but of course my father had a very fiendish imagination. He writes that episode a year before broadcast, and something like the week before, male workers in a battery chicken farm started developing secondary female characteristics, and of course it looked as if he was capitalising on something that had just happened, but actually he imagined it sometime in advance.' Kit Pedler told the *Radio Times* in 1970 that 'This seemed a little over-speculative at the time we thought it up two and a half years ago. But just a few months before it was screened a similar incident actually occurred on a farm in Leicestershire.'

The British Medical Journal broke the case and it was in the press on Friday 13 February 1970. Pesticides and insecticides were blamed for rendering four men out of a team of five impotent and were only cured after a course of hormones. Other cases may not have come to light considering the reluctance healthy men had in coming to see their doctors. One landowner thought the impotence was down to the men working long hours. It is not the same case seen in 'The Battery People', but it highlights the dangers of using chemicals without proper protection or knowledge, something unthinkable now.

Carol concludes 'He understood what the verges were like. When scientific research was on the verge of something. He imagined what it would be like to go over that verge and into the next step.'

1.12
Hear No Evil

Written by Gerry Davis and Harry Green
Directed by Frank Cox
Designed by Tim Gleeson
Transmitted: Monday, 4 May 1970 at 9.46 pm Duration: 48' 05"

Cast
Falken (Griffith Jones), Operator (Derrick O'Connor), Cook (Peter Miles), Bill Owen (Brian Cox), Tom Reid (Michael Ripper), Mrs Lucy Reid (Tessa Shaw), Stripper (Sheila Sands), M C (Alec Pleon).

Also appearing
Security Man (Pat Gorman), Waiter (Peter Morton), Barman (Freddie White), Blue Coats and Union Meeting Extras (Ron Tingley, Paul Barton, Eddie Summers, Gordon Steff), Women (Betsy White, Rosina Stewart, Audrey Stewart, Jenny Roberts, Betty Duncan, Jean Hilton, Cathy Nielson, Dilys Marvin, Beryl Bainbridge, Pippa Reynaud, Maggie Vickers, Kay Fraser, Delia Sainsbury), Men and Union Meeting Extras (Leslie Bates, Peter Kaukus, Bill Burridge, John Demarco, Leslie Bryant, Rikki Lancing, Sonnie Willis, Barry Kennington, Don Vernon, Noel Mitchell, Jan Dolitho, David Bacon, Carl Bohan, Ian Selman), Man (Peter Ardren).

Technical Credits
Production Assistant: Nick Parsons. Assistant Floor Manager: Hardi Verdi. Director's Assistants: Georgina Hodson, Chris Whiting. Floor Assistant: John Willcox.
Film Cameraman: Eddie Best. Sound Recordist: Doug Mawson. Film Editor: Alastair MacKay.
Costume Supervisor: Dorothea Wallace. Make-up Designer: Elizabeth Rowell. Studio Lighting: Jimmy Purdie. TM2: Jack Shallcross. Vision Mixer: Chris Griffin.
Sound Supervisor: Larry Goodson. Grams Operator: Gerry Borrows.
Crew: 6.

Radio Times
How do you combat unofficial strikes? One northern firm's answer is to use the latest scientific discoveries to manipulate the lives of their employees – private as well as public. Quist is forced to fight them with their own methods.

The Story

'I can't think of a better reason for bloody revolution. I would wish to cut the throat of a man who has destroyed my privacy, and there are circumstances in which I would do just that.' – Quist

In a town on the Yorkshire Moors lies the factory of Jedder & Co Ltd, a subsidiary of Voltmixer International. In the factory's club entertainment room, a meeting concerning future redundancies begins, called by shop stewards Bill Owen and Tom Reid. The meeting is secretly being monitored from a small, windowless room by a man named Cook and his assistant, listening with headphones and recording every word. Also present is Falken, the Managing Director. They have built up a complete picture of the employees to spot potential trouble situations, personality clashes, square pegs and so on. But Falken is more interested in the shop stewards. He wants dirt on them. He wants Owen and Reid fixed.

Quist sends Bradley on a routine survey of the emanations from Fylingdales Radar Station, which is close to where Bradley comes from. On the moor he meets Cook, who is making a recording of bird song (which Bradley has just ruined with his singing). As they discuss their respective work, Cook describes himself as an industrial anthropologist. That evening, Bradley meets up with his old friend Owen at the club, noting how different it appears since his last visit. Owen tells him Jedder paid for the refurbishment not only of the club but also of the workers' houses. The equipment Bradley has been using on the moor was built by Voltmixer, and whilst the entertainment is in full swing, he demonstrates the machine on the microphone on the stage – but it also registers when pointed at a wall lamp. Suspicious, Bradley checks the lounge and finds more readings. Acting on a hunch, Bradley and Owen go to Reid's home and discover hidden microphones in the bedroom. Reid is devastated.

Bradley reports his findings to Quist, accompanied by Owen and Reid. They believe that the bugs must have been installed when the houses were redecorated after Voltmixer settled a strike the previous year. Nothing illegal has taken place because there had been no break-in. Quist tells them the disclosure would cause a countrywide frenzy. Reid and Owen both suspect the productivity deal is the reason behind this espionage – an attempt to drive a wedge between their two Unions, which intend to take action over the redundancies that the deal will cause. Quist asks them to leave the matter to him. Meanwhile, Cook and Falken discuss Reid and Owen and their motivation: it appears to be the canteen door. VIPs, manual workers and white collar staff all have their own separate doors into the canteen, and by having to use his particular door, Reid feels that he is segregated, that he is just dirt to all the 16-year-old temporary typists who use the white-collar door.

Quist gives Wren and Ridge the job of stopping Voltmixer without disrupting the economic life of the country, and reluctantly agrees to let Ridge bug Falken's office. He recalls how uneasy Owen had been in their interview. Would the recordings have revealed something, something he wanted to hide? Helped by Reid, Ridge bugs the office and listens outside the plant with Bradley. They hear mention of the celebrated Tape 47, which seems to be singled out for particular attention, and Reid agrees to find it. Ridge also wants to bug Falken's home – to give him a taste of his own medicine – and is surprised when Quist instantly agrees. 'If Falken believes that Reid's and Owen's private lives are fit subjects for espionage, then so is his. Go ahead.'

Pat has been transcribing some of the bugged conversations and mentions a lady in the case called Philana. Wren has a hunch that this is no lady. Tape 47 is taken from the office and played in the deserted club. They hear a budgerigar ... and Owen's affair with Mrs Reid in full expression. A fight breaks out between Reid and Owen; Reid is the victor. Quist urges him to put aside his personal distress and carry on with their unofficial strike. Falken had obviously planned to use the tape during the strike and produce a public split, leaving the men leaderless, demoralised and likely never to trust Owen and Reid again. Falken would have a completely free hand in his policies. Reid agrees to go ahead as planned.

Quist confronts Falken about the bugs, but the tycoon is not concerned. At first he simply blames Cook and says he will fire him. When this cuts no ice, he states that the Reid and Owen business will be assumed to be the work of private detectives. Falken is very confident that, as a public servant, Quist would do nothing to provoke industrial trouble on a national scale. Quist agrees, but still demands that the bugs are removed, the operating base dismantled and the tapes handed over. He plays his winning hand – tape recordings of Falken's home phone calls and his knowledge that Philana is a not a person, but a boat. He shows Falken an aerial photograph of the Philana carrying Voltmixer equipment, supposedly being shipped to Abu Dhabi but in reality headed for Rhodesia.

Quist claims that they have copies of every forged document in the long train from England to Angola. 'You're a sanctions breaker, Falken. And we can prove it.' Ridge eavesdrops, proud of Quist as he beats Falken down: 'Get those bugs removed. I want industrial peace in this country. I wouldn't hesitate as a man to destroy you. Your kind of corruption is deadlier than any form of chemical warfare. You destroy common decency and the dignity of man. But I won't see my country finished just to finish you ... Don't ever forget, Falken, that there's no dirtier fighter in the world than an Englishman who's been kicked in the groin. I'm a dirtier bastard than you, and there are times when I'm proud of it.'

Reid and Bradley walk on the moor, where they see Cook once more. Reid fires a shotgun over his head and frightens him away. Bradley then points out the Fylingdales Radar Station: the biggest bug of them all …

Behind the Story
Falken and Cook are violating Article 12 of the Universal Declaration of Human Rights, which states 'No-one should be subjected to arbitrary interference with his privacy, family, home or correspondence, nor to attacks on his honour or reputation. Everyone has the right to the protection of the law against such interferences or attacks.' The Trade Union movement had long been suspected of being a hotbed of open or closet Communists who took their orders directly from Moscow in much the same way as Catholics look to Rome, regarding it as a higher authority over their own national leaders. Any strike was seen by more extreme right-wingers as a Communist ploy to bring down the country. The right wing of the Labour Party also had its fears. During the Seamen's Strike of 1966 Labour Prime Minister Harold Wilson declared in Parliament, using coded language, that it was a Communist-inspired plot against his Government. The biggest fear was always that another General Strike would lead to revolution. This is why Owen was on several people's files, but, as Wren discovers, there is no blatant left-wing leaning to him. To belong to a trade union did not automatically mean you were even a Labour supporter. In the year before this episode was transmitted, the Labour Government had attempted to regulate and lessen the impact of industrial strikes with a new piece of legislation entitled In Place of Strife. At the time it was too controversial and failed. Reid and Owen are not militants, Communists nor subversives; they are simply trying to prevent redundancies. A big firm takes over a smaller one with a troubled past and wants to slash jobs. We are not supposed to take sides in the dispute as, in dramatic terms, it is the pretext behind the story.

A Man's World II
This was a country that was still largely defined by class and trade. Reid's back story is one of feeling belittled by having to go through a particular door whilst white-collar teenagers used another, making him feel like an inferior (or at least feel like he is regarded as one) because he gets his hands dirty, no matter how long he or his fellows have been there at the firm. This unionised him and gave him back the dignity that he felt had been eroded by the three-door canteen system. Reid speaks of being young in the 1930s and having suffered 'no boots or beef'. He also talks about how his father (who presumably remembered the Great Depression of the 1920s) thinks his son 'hasn't been born' because he has a car and a fridge, things his father would never have even thought possible in the

depression. Jedder & Co Ltd was the type of firm that Harold Wilson was probably thinking of when he warned that the white heat of technology would not stand for outdated working practices.

In 1970 working class men were still 'real' men, and their wives stayed at home and kept away from working men's clubs, unless they were strippers or singers. (Germaine Greer's *The Female Eunuch* wouldn't be published until later that year.) A job was a job for life, and your trade defined you, gave you a sense of identity and position within your community. It gave you dignity, a word frequently used in the episode. You belonged to a trade union, and the movement protected your rights and hopefully your job. Men settled their differences with punch-ups.

Falken's prejudice towards Owen and Reid is that they are illiterates who don't attempt to earn any more than they already do. To prove Falken's villainy, he is a sanctions buster. It was very lucky that sanction-busting was going on, otherwise Quist's superb stand-off with Falken at the end of the story would not have worked. But there were plenty of supporters of White Rhodesia in the 1960s who would have approved of Falken's actions in this case. The Monday Club, a small but influential section of businessmen and Conservative MPs, was created in 1961 to oppose the erosion of colonialism and counted White Rhodesians and South Africans amongst their supporters.

Cook

Consultant 'industrial anthropologist' Cook doesn't seem to have much concern about his methods. No doubt he sees his subjects as just specimens. He is another in the line of amoral scientists who seize the chance to put their theories into practise. Cook didn't sell his soul, like Whitehead in 'Spectre at the Feast', as he didn't really have one to begin with. There is no sign of the antagonism between Falken the boss and Cook the henchman as there is between Fielding and Whitehead, although Falken was happy to have Cook fired when he realised Quist was serious in his threats. He likes to bug birds as well – the feathered kind – with his parabolic microphone, which prefigures the budgerigar Reid's wife has in her living room as heard on Tape 47. For Cook, knowledge is power. The unnamed operator who monitors the bugging is presented as a salacious voyeur; he wants to listen in to 'Dirty Gertie' in the entertainment room for the seven minutes it takes Reid to reach home from the club.

Scripting Hell

The storyline 'Hear No Evil' was given to Harry Green, who had already penned the successful and well received 'Friday's Child'. Contracted on 12 June 1969, it was noted as the tenth script commissioned so far. It was due for delivery on 22 August and the script was acknowledged on 26 August by Judy Hall. Apparently the production team received the script enthusiastically, and Green was commissioned to write his third episode, 'The Iron Doctor', almost immediately. Green suffered a bout of illness whilst writing that episode and then had to resume work on the classic serial adaption of *Jude The Obscure*. But by October, Green had been asked for some rewrites. Things became unpleasant.

The director assigned to the project was Jonathan Alwyn, who was confused by the script and made some suggestions for amendments. Davis passed them on to Green, who agreed to do them. Then Alwyn wanted a major change to the end of the episode, which an exhausted Green made but did not like. When sending it to Davis, he wrote 'If your director wants to alter a single word in 'Friday's Child', just take my name off it. I can deal with Jesus Christ but not with the second coming. And don't think I'm joking.' The name 'Smith' and two new sets, 'Telephone Kiosk' and 'Reid's Lounge', were added.

On 23 October Terence Dudley added his thoughts to the script, apologising to Green for the 'runaround'. He explained to Green the points of confusion. Alwyn apparently felt that Falk and Co (as they were called in the script at this point) were too 'unsubtle and … profligate in setting out to "Get Reid and Owen."' Dudley thought that Falk and Co had bugged the entire works in order to gain universal vigilance and a better potential for manipulation. Gerry Davis countered that the bugging was specifically targeting the shop stewards. Dudley thought this was improbable and that it made more sense to show the horror inherent in the size of a long-standing operation, which Green had concentrated into the impact on Reid and Owen's lives. He thought the wide-scale application of the technique was a natural extension of Cook's professional interest. Dudley realised that the premise had been called into question and that other areas of the script now needed illumination, if not development. He also had his doubts about Fogdens, a private firm used first by Falk to bug his workforce and then by Quist to bug Falk. Dudley thought it would be better if the bugging was kept 'in house', performed by Ridge, and therefore 'better for the "coup de grace"'. Dudley said he went back to the original storyline and found that what he had read into the script was there. 'I could be bonkers' said Dudley. 'Could we all talk?'

Unfortunately, Green was not placated and wrote back the next day, Friday, with his version of the week's events so far, concluding that it seemed the producer, script editor and director were in fundamental disagreement about the intention of the original synopsis. He wanted an extra fee for all the work he felt he would to have to perform on the script. He regretted having to write in such formal terms and that an extraordinarily successful personal relationship in professional matters should be disrupted by a director who appeared to 'regard himself as a super-producer/editor'. Dudley wrote back on the following Monday, agreeing to the extra money, but defending Jonathan Alwyn as being genuinely confused by the script and quite opposite in nature to Green's perception of him. Dudley also explained that his reservations about the structure and the opening to the script might have contributed to the confusion. He asked for a meeting to sort it out.

Whatever happened, Green sent in a revised copy of the script on 9 November, though he noted 'It isn't a script now, it's a bundle of used nappies', and mentioned that he hoped to attend the read-through for 'Friday's Child'. 'Remember that one? — the good old days.' 'You nostalgic old thing, you!' replied Gerry Davis, writing the next day to thank him for the used nappies, 'It all looks good to me.' Green was paid an extra £100.

Copies of the rehearsal script were sent out on 17 November, the same day a very unhappy Green decided to pull out of delivering a second draft of 'The Iron Doctor'. By 22 November he had signed himself up to write an eight-part classic serial, calling it quits on *Doomwatch*.

The Changes by Gerry Davis

The final rewrite was performed by Gerry Davis which removed and added material in accordance with Dudley's views. Names were changed: Falk became Falken, possibly because a Bernie Falk was a presenter on the tea-time news magazine programme *Nationwide*. Falk was an American in the original, though we do not know if he remained so. The company was now Jedder rather than Jason, which Dudley used as the name of the hotel in his 'Spectre at the Feast'. The sanction-busting vessel was originally the *Vanessa*. Some mild language like 'arse' was cut and a strong anti-American flavour removed. ('They can put a community on the moor – but their social thinking comes out of a covered wagon.') Things were originally more formal within the Doomwatch office, with the 'Secretary' (only referred to as 'Pat' in dialogue) asking Wren or Ridge to go into Quist's office when summoned and Ridge addressing Quist as 'sir' from time to time. New scenes were added by Davis, but there was a lot left from Green's original with barely a change.

The original script began with a montage of film mixed in with newspaper headlines, depicting unofficial industrial strikes threatening the 'new Jason Productivity deal', and a white-coated technician closing down an electronics production line. The first scene between Cook and Falk was set in his office. The first scene in the Doomwatch office was cut, where Ridge is proudly showing off a consignment of bugs and asks Wren if they make him feel uneasy. Bradley has already met Cook the year before and doesn't speak to him on the moor, just watches him from a distance. When Quist meets Reid and Owen, he actually records their conversation and gets Wren to listen to it later on. Ridge, who has just bugged a meeting, finds this amusingly ironic. Quist berates him, and Ridge retreats back into formality, asking Quist to tape record his instructions. 'In spite of his high intelligence, Quist cannot see the joke because he takes his standard office equipment for granted.'

A series of film sequences, with Ridge driving through the Yorkshire Moors whilst Cook is recording more bird song, was cut. Ridge's receiving a general layout of the works from Owen in a car park was written by Green as a filmed location scene. Here, Ridge comes across as an unpleasant, unsympathetic James Bond-type. From this point Green's version of the script and the Gerry Davis' rewrite diverge quite significantly. Ridge phones Wren to tell him he wants to bug Falk's home, and Quist asks for it to be arranged with Fogden's Agency. As the strike begins with fears over the new deal, a film sequence originally saw Cook driven into the factory. A reporter asks a picket who he is. 'He's interested in birds.' 'Who isn't?' replies the reporter. The next scene was also dropped, in which Wren gives Quist Fogden's report on their bugging of Falk's country house, believing they now have proof against Falk. 'Dirt's enough in a dirty game against dirty men.' It is the tape operator, posing as a BBC reporter, who plays the recording of the adultery to a packed club lounge. Mrs Reid is present and becomes hysterical. The operator gets punched during the ensuing fight. The strike ends as planned by Falk and the implications are tremendous – even a national strike. Reid tells Bradley that his young wife has gone back to her mother's, Owen has been hospitalised, he himself is now a laughing stock and the men are demoralised. Bradley invites Reid for a walk. Reid brings a twelve-bore shotgun with him which he fires at Cook, whose backside is peppered with shot. Bradley looks at the Fylingdales spheres and says to Reid 'Dicey! But the only way we survive.'

Two new rehearsal scripts were sent out to Harry Green on 27 February 1970, with Frank Cox now booked in as director after the scripting delays had pushed the production further down the line. On 4 March Green replied that the script in its present form was not written by him and politely asked for his name to be removed from the project. It appears that he had already spoken to Terence Dudley the same day and that this was to be regarded as a formal letter. No writer's credit was given in the episode, but some documents still mention Green as the author.

Filming

Filming was performed around 17 March. Two days were spent in Yorkshire, which needed Joby Blanshard, Peter Miles and Brian Cox to film their scenes on the moor. Simon Oates was also required, as was his Lotus.

Myth Busting

For some time, a myth suggested that the working title for this episode was 'The Black Room'. This does not appear to be the case at all. The confusion arises from an instalment of *Paul Temple* called 'The Black Room', which was transmitted the night before the *Doomwatch* episode and ended up in an internal BBC listing for this story by mistake, which then became accepted as fact by early researchers. 'Hear No Evil' never went by any other title from storyline to transmission. It was just one of those things.

Cast

Derrick O'Connor and Brian Cox were relatively new to television, but Griffith Jones had been acting since before the war, a distinctive looking actor. Michael Ripper, playing the older trade unionist Reid, is better remembered for his many appearances in Hammer Horror films. His distinctive face was his fortune and he was often cast as a working-class man. He was the gruff sergeant in the original BBC *Quatermass and the Pit*. Peter Miles appeared in practically every drama series produced in the seventies. His clearest memory of making the episode was Simon Oates' aftershave, which apparently could be smelled before he arrived. Miles also remembered how nervous Griffith Jones appeared to be. Shelia Sands was commonly seen as a stripper, notably in *Monty Python Flying Circus* as a topless newsagent.

Rehearsals

The script leaves it up to Frank Cox to decide what entertainment is on stage in the working men's club. Davis/Green suggested a singer or a stripper for the first scene, and a stripper, played by Shelia Sands, is indeed credited for the episode in the *Radio Times*. There at least has to be a microphone in the second performance for Brad's detector to be tested upon. The second set suggests another singer, but stage directions mention the word 'bingo', and later dialogue implies it may even be a working men's club comedian telling 'clean dirt' compared to the 'blue boys'. There was an uncredited Master of Ceremonies, played by Variety performer Alec 'Funny Face' Pleon, who had been an extra in 'The Battery People'. Perhaps he was a rude bingo caller …

Recording

'Hear No Evil' was the 12th episode to be recorded for the series and went into studio TC1 on Saturday, 4 April 1970. Some sound pre-recording was made with Griffith Jones, Brian Cox, Tessa Shaw, Peter Miles and Simon Oates. These were for telephone calls and, in the case of Cox and Shaw, their illicit tryst. Tessa Shaw also provided the voice of a secretary out of vision. Photographs seen in the episode came from London Express. Max Harris provided two minutes of stripper music for the episode, apparently recorded with three musicians.

Editing and Transmission
The episode was edited two days later, less a month before transmission. The programme was watched by nine and a half million viewers. Once again, this is an episode missing from the archives.

Reviews
'It says volumes for *Doomwatch*,' said KAB in the *Coventry Evening Telegraph*, 'that recently a Cabinet Minister, questioned about pollution, referred to a "Doomwatch situation". This programme has really made an impact, and at various levels. The science-fiction stories are often uncannily realised in real life. It warns very vividly of the dangers that face us and our environment in an increasingly complex and scientific society. And it also manages to be good entertainment. True, the series had made great use of coincidence. One or two stories (last nights for example), strain our credulity; and we have to accept that a scientist could stride the corridors of power with such impunity and success as Dr Quist. That we do accept these things is due very much to John Paul … With this series he has joined the still-sparse ranks of television actors who can dominate a scene by their sheer presence.'

The Real Trade Unions
A suggestion for a future script came from a very unusual but telling place: 'Delegates had no doubt seen a programme on the TV called *Doomwatch*' said a speaker at the 1970 Scottish Trades Union Congress. 'A script could be written, thereby ensuring as much publicity as possible, involving the Doomwatch team investigating along with shop stewards some of the cutting oils which some employers used, which gave some of the diseases to the workers in the factories. Many of the diseases likely to be contracted were progressive diseases which passed through prolonged preliminary stages, stages which were quite likely to be ignored.'

1.13
Survival Code

Written by Kit Pedler and Gerry Davis
Directed by Hugh David
Designed by Ian Watson
Transmitted: Monday, 11 May 1970 at 9.47 pm Duration: 49' 54"

Cast
Air Commodore Parks (Donald Morley), Wing Commander (Colin Rix), Geoff Harker (Ray Brooks), Toni Harker (Stephanie Turner), Sam Billings (Tommy Godfrey), Commander Sefton (Robert Cartland), The Minister (Hamilton Dyce), Len White (Edwin Brown), Chief Supt Charles (John Dawson), First Man on Pier (David St John).

Also appearing
Wrens (Beryl Bainbridge, Carol Pedler, Marcelle Elliott, Pam Saire, Jo Hall), RAF men (Keith Norrish, Bill Strange), Man on Pier (Mick Burnett), Squadron Leader (Reg Lloyd), Police Constable (Frederick Clemson).

Technical Credits
Director's Assistant: Adele Paul. Production Assistant: Robert Checksfield. Assistant Floor Manager: Jane Southern. Floor Assistant: John Wilcox.
Film Cameraman: Eddie Best. Sound Recordist: Doug Mawson. Film Editor: Alastair MacKay.
Costume Supervisor: Dorothea Wallace. Make-up Supervisor: Elizabeth Rowell.
Studio Lighting: Jimmy Purdie. TM2: Jack Shallcross. Vision Mixer: Fred Law.
Studio Sound: Larry Goodson. Grams Operator: Gerry Borrows.
Camera Crew: 6.

Radio Times
An object drops into the sea near a South-coast pier. To Sam and Geoff, it appears to be a weather-detecting device. They start to dismantle it. What the object actually is, however, is something very, very different …

The Story
'Ever since Los Alamos he's almost been waiting for death. This one didn't land in the sea – it landed smack inside his head and it's hurting.' – Ridge

An aircraft from RAF Manston, carrying a nuclear warhead with three bombs, has crashed into the sea fifty miles off the Isle of Wight. Air Commodore Parks informs Doomwatch. As Quist says, 'It's Palomares all over again.' A sinister-looking object is seen floating off the timbers by the Byfield Regis pier. Geoff Harker and his wife Toni think it is a World War II mine, but Sam Billings, Toni's dad, scoffs at the idea. Toni does not like the object, but the men haul it out of the water and bring it into Sam's arcade machine workshop on the pier. Convinced it is a weather satellite, Sam intends to break it open for spare parts for his arcade machines. They fail to understand the significance of the radiation hazard symbol on its side as Geoff begins to strip away the plastic surround.

In the Operations Room Quist refuses to be placated by Parks' assurance that the warhead cannot have been damaged in the crash. He is concerned about any potential detonation, whether nuclear or conventional. He tries to convince the Minister that the public should be warned of the possible danger, but the Minister is satisfied with Park's assurances, especially as the warhead's marker signal has been picked up and a submersible is on its way to investigate the wreck. A little later, Parks is discussing a newspaper article about Quist with Sefton, a Navy Commander. The paper calls Quist the Man of the Year, but Parks considers him a man who encourages disloyalty within the services, a magnet for malcontents and the aggrieved. He mentions a recent incident in which a whistle-blower from Transport Command had gone to Quist with a confidential dossier on a new defoliant spray.

Geoff tries to get the machine working by giving it some electric power from a twelve-volt battery. Toni is still frightened of it, and, as a lower panel containing a numeric counter begins to move, she wakes up her dad and demands the machine be switched off. She knows what both men are thinking: it may be a bomb. Despite Sam's protestations earlier, she points out that he hasn't seen one since the end of the War, and things must have changed. The counter reaches 4700 as Sam reluctantly agrees, but he still wants to break the machine down further. Back in the Operations Room Parks is now getting tired of Quist's presence. Doomwatch will be contacted should any developments arise, but Quist insists on staying until the bombs have been accounted for. A conventional explosion still bothers him greatly because it would release the radioactive core, spreading contamination. Sefton agrees, but sees the small amount that would escape as being well within safe limits. Ridge is frustrated and impatient to return to London, pointing out to Quist that the only reason they are staying is guilt: Quist's guilt. Guilt over helping to build the first hydrogen bomb and guilt over the leukemia which claimed his wife's life after she worked on the project. Wren is shocked at Ridge's outburst. Parks is watching, too. He presses home his advantage, telling Quist he will gain nothing by waiting. Quist finally leaves.

By early evening Geoff is feeling ill and in pain but goes to the pub with

Sam. Toni stays behind to put some make-up on and turns to the same newspaper with Quist's face on the cover. She telephones the Doomwatch office and Quist answers. At first he isn't interested, but then he hears about Geoff's illness and asks her to describe their find to him. He calls Ridge and Wren back to the office and briefs them that the warhead may have split open, releasing the three bombs inside. One of them may be at the Byfield Regis pier, so he sends them to investigate. By the time Ridge and Wren arrive it is 9.30 pm, and Geoff is very ill but still alert enough to be suspicious and stop them from gaining entry. Ridge phones Quist.

By now, the Minister has been told that the bombs did indeed scatter. Two of them have been recovered but the third is still missing. In Byfield Regis, Sam and Geoff try to throw the object back into the sea by removing some planks from the pier and shoving it through, but it gets stuck in the timber frame. Quist arrives just as Geoff collapses, and Wren goes down the hole on a rope to investigate. The bomb has been damaged on its side; a conventional explosion is more than possible. Ridge gives the news to a shocked Parks, who orders a team of RAF technicians down to Byfield Regis. In the meantime Quist is to do nothing.

When Sam reveals that Geoff had got the device working, Toby goes down again to take a better look. The countdown has now reached 1500, and to his horror the control panel is broken – they can't switch it off. He backs away from the bomb as far as he can, numb with fear. Quist calculates that they have twenty-five minutes before either a conventional explosion or a full nuclear holocaust.

Pat Hunnisett wakes up from a bad dream in which she saw the deaths of Quist, Ridge and Wren. As Quist is prepared to dismantle the bomb himself, Superintendent Charles tries to evacuate everyone from the pier. Quist orders him away. He climbs down among the timbers to snip the wires between the detonators and the arming unit, using a mirror to see what he is doing because of the angle of the wedged bomb. As he is about to start, he slips and falls, breaking his arm. When he is hauled up out of the supports, Toby goes down in his place, refusing Ridge's offer of help. Seven minutes remain.

Toby carefully snips through the first two wires, sweating, every sense heightened. The jagged shell of the casing is cutting his hands to shreds. As he snips the third wire, he drops the cutters inside the bomb. Parks and his team arrive. Ninety-five seconds left. Toby retrieves the cutters and snips the fourth and final wire. The counter resets. Assuring the technicians that he's done it, he accidentally drops the cutters again. They fall into the sea. As he removes the last detonator, his relief turns to horror: there is another wire. The technician warns him not to pull it, but to follow it back to the terminal and unscrew it. As he feels his way along the wire to the detonator, staring into the mirror, a final trip motor activates.

'I think he's done it' says Quist, just as a blinding light is followed by the force of a huge explosion. The end of the pier is completely destroyed. Getting back to his feet, Quist stares out of the window.

QUIST: Non-nuclear.
RIDGE: Right. Who'll tell Toby?
PARKS: When will you people learn not to interfere?

Behind the Story
The characters in 'Survival Code' had clearly never read United States Atomic Energy Commission's 1957 book *The Effects of Nuclear Weapons*, which had been revised in 1964. 'Nuclear weapons are designed with great care to explode only when deliberately armed and fired. Nevertheless, there is always the possibility that, as a result of accidental circumstances, an explosion will take place inadvertently ... It is the high explosive component – in the trigger mechanism – which comprises the main possible hazard just as it does with conventional weapons.'

The story was based upon the Palomares incident, which occurred on 17 January 1966 (although the script says 1962 at one point). It was a mid-air collision between two US air force planes, one a KC-135 refuelling plane, the other a B-52G bomber carrying a cargo of four nuclear bombs. Seven airmen were killed. The flights were part of Operation Chrome Dome, which ensured that there were always nuclear weapons in the air ready for use. One bomb was later safely recovered from the sea, but the other three fell to earth near Palomares, a fishing village on the Spanish coast. Two of them detonated on impact in conventional, non-nuclear explosions which spread radioactive debris. This was not a one-off accident. They were rare, but they happened. In 1968 another US B-52 caught fire and was ditched off the coast of Greenland. Again, the conventional explosives were set off and contaminated the area with radioactive detritus. Three of the bombs were recovered. The remains of the fourth is rumoured to be out there still. Over forty years later Palomares is still counting the cost. 50,000 cubic metres of contaminated soil remains at the site. The Americans removed 1,300 cubic metres at the time of the incident, but it will take thousands of years before the soil is safe again. It is the most contaminated place in Europe. In 2008 the American Government withdrew the annual funding it had been supplying to Spain for monitoring the contamination and performing blood tests on the locals.

A major theme brought out in the episode is a clash between authorities. A Minister has to rely on advice, and Air Commodore Parks suggests he should relax and leave it to the experts, which in itself is not bad advice, but he refuses to countenance any possible theories or to expect the unexpected. This complacency is mainly due to his bias against Quist, whom he sees as encouraging disloyalty. Parks refers to a defoliant which a whistle- blower from the RAF revealed to Quist. (Presumably this is Project Sahara.) Quist does appear totally unreasonable in his initial scenes with Parks, though he is quite right in hindsight to be concerned about the possibility of bomb damage and radioactive leakage. Only Sefton, representing the Royal Navy, is prepared to listen to Quist and accept his point, but Parks points out that this is because his service hasn't been 'done over' by Doomwatch. Presumably this means that the business of 'Burial at Sea' didn't damage the Royal Navy's reputation.

What we see here is a lack of imagination on the part of the official mind. Quist has an imagination, possibly a morbid one, but he is right to examine the possibilities. Parks and the Minister may think that they have learned from Palomares, but they trust in the fail-safes (as Doctor Warren would have done, as we shall see in the follow-up episode 'You Killed Toby Wren') even though each incident can create a new factor. In Quist's mind, the idea of a conventional explosion irradiating the area is not an exaggerated threat. The only difference between reality and this fiction is that it happens on our door-step and the decision to cover up the crash leads to the disaster becoming worse. Davis and Pedler add in a random element with the characters of Billings and Harker, who rip into the bomb and give it electrical power, and it leaks radioactive material along the way. For all Quist knew, it could well have resulted in a full-blown nuclear incident. Quist's view as expressed by Kit Pedler was reprinted in Singapore's the *Straits Times* later that year: 'There's an attitude in the industrial military complex which says: "Do it till you're rumbled. Put in enough fail-safes for 10 years. By that time you'll be retired and no longer amenable to responsibility."'

Production
Script Development
On 15 September 1969 'Survival Code' became the sixteenth script to be commissioned for the first series, due for delivery on New Year's Eve. It seemed from the very beginning that Pedler and Davis wanted to write about an accident with a nuclear bomb. It was quite logical to end the series with a tale that brought Quist face to face with something which had haunted him and shaped his life since his days on the Manhattan Project.

The original idea that Pedler and Davis had may have been different to the one they eventually went with. According to the *Guardian* in 1973, 'There was the one about the trawler which hauled up a neat piece of nuclear hardware in its nets and almost solved the problem of the fish shortage by killing off the demand.' Around 20 September 1969, Kit and Gerry set off for the Holy Loch [a nuclear submarine base] by plane for a two-night trip at the BBC's expense, to confirm that their idea was feasible. They were sufficiently impressed to ditch the story whereupon the US Air Force wrecked a neat PR job by accidentally dropping a warhead in Texas. When the top brass went to inspect their toy, they discovered that five of the six fail-safe devices were in the unsafe position. It was either a Swedish or Danish newspaper which broke the news about the accident in Texas. Four days later Kit and Gerry emerged sleepless but triumphant with a new script for *Doomwatch*.

Another idea was a storyline called 'The Bomb'. It features a code to prevent accidental detonation, a survival code which does not appear in the finished episode. This story involves a bomb, accidentally dropped from a plane and its descent is arrested by a parachute and the roof beams of a London dance hall. Doomwatch are called in and discover that the bomb is active and ticking down to destruction. To stop the countdown a code is required. The details of the code were known only to the scientists, both of whom fell to their deaths when the bomb bay doors accidentally opened. The team have to investigate the lives of the dead scientists to crack the code.

You Exploded Toby Wren

The script had to write out Robert Powell, who was determined to not to become typecast or commit himself to another long haul. It may have been during rehearsals for 'The Battery People', with the series one month into its run, that Adele Winston recalls 'I remember Terry saying to him, "This is your choice, obviously, you've been very popular, but I'm assuming you don't want to come back for another series," and Robert said, "Yes, that's right. I don't."' The production team decided to kill him off in an explosion. By no stretch of the imagination is it impossible that, had Powell decided to stay on, Wren could have walked into the pier-head office after the explosion and brush himself down, having escaped in the nick of time. Equally, the situation could have been left as a cliff-hanger. The script would also revisit the suppressed tensions between Quist and Ridge, which only Pedler and Davis seemed to enjoy bringing to the fore.

The writers pulled out all the stops in their description of Wren disarming the device. They wanted the background noise of the sea and gulls faded down, Wren's breathing to be heard and the snip of the wire cutters amplified. They also wanted to dwell on the inner workings of the bomb once Wren starts his work: 'The actual sight of this, the core of destruction, is very important psychologically.' Pedler and Davis were given advice as to how a nuclear bomb worked. In the script, Len White takes the doomed technicians to the arcade and not Superintendent Charles. Davis was paid for his half of the script on 20 March 1970.

'Survival Code' takes place just before Easter. If we take Hastings as the location for the fictional Byfield Regis, a one megaton nuclear explosion would not have had too great an effect on London in quite the way Bradley commented to Pat: 'If it went off, we'd know about it as soon as they would. Or not know about it, as the case may be. Have some coffee.'

Cast

Tommy Godfrey was often cast as Cockney villains, a contrast to the more educated tones of Donald Morley and, making his second and final appearance as a Minister, Hamilton Dyce. Stephanie Turner would later find fame as the first female Inspector in *Juliet Bravo*, and Ray Brooks was already a familiar face, having appeared in the 1965 film *The Knack ... And How to Get it*, and was becoming a frequent guest on TV series. He had only just worked for Hugh David on *The Expert*.

Filming

Location work for director Hugh David was minimal. Thus only three of the guest cast – Ray Brooks, Tommy Godfrey and Stephanie Turner – spent a day down at Eastbourne for the one lengthy film sequence of the episode. Glyn Edwards visited the filming as part of his duties. In a later *Radio Times*. Terence Dudley remembered the filming as taking place at Hastings, and Adele Winston recollects Brighton.

Model Work

Some rare model filming was performed for the episode, featuring the destruction of the pier. The pier itself was a false perspective model with hardboard-mounted silhouettes of the buildings. A flash charge was detonated behind it for the explosion. The 'sea' was black plastic sheeting. Behind-the-scenes material of the model filming was shot for a BBC Visual Effects Department promotional reel; it can be found amongst the bonus material on the *Doctor Who* DVD release 'Inferno'.

Studio

The final episode of the series, 'Survival Code' was recorded in TC4 on Wednesday, 15 of April 1970. Despite the intensity of the piece, Robert Powell and Simon Oates did have some fun in rehearsal, adding in a few double entrendes ('I saw it first ... This thing is bigger than both of us ...') which were apparently kept in.

Carol Pedler (now Topolski), Kit's eldest daughter, was one of the Navy personnel. Carol was a great favourite with the production team. Judy Hall (now Bedford), Dudley's secretary, was the same age as Carol, and had been impressed that she had been to Woodstock a few years earlier. At the time, Carol had very much wanted to act. 'I did very little else at university first time around', Carol remembers, 'and so Dad weaselled me in! All I did was to move bits of paper around on a board in the background wearing the uniform. I had to be very cautious about talking [about] how I got in (although the name was a give-away), and, quite properly, the union rep on the cast kept pursuing me as to who was my agent, so I had to be rather circumspect. I was taking up a job some out-of-work actor could have used.'

No music featured in the story except for some unidentified stock discs for Toni's radio on the pier. The production did make use of 'grams' played into the studio of the sea, seagulls and wind for the pier scenes and of computer tapes clicking in the Operations Room.

The camera script was split into two sections. All the scenes set underneath the pier were to be recorded after the main part of the episode. After Wren's last scene was taped, the recording resumed with the final scene, in the arcade office, which required the special effect of the windows being blown in. The final shot of the evening, after the titles had been recorded, was of a slow zoom into the final countdown, which was later cut into Toby Wren's final moments.

The recording was only completed by a fifty-minute overrun beyond its allotted studio time, which did not go down too well with the BBC accountants. A week later at the Programme Review Board, Ian Atkins, Controller of Programme Services for Television, said he 'would like to draw attention to the connection between over-runs and planned breaks; in this recording there had been 22 planned breaks, which had absorbed 54 minutes; there had been 14 production retakes taking 30 minutes.'

Editing

The episode was edited on Friday, 17 April 1970. Although this is another lost episode, the last couple of minutes survive as a recap in the opening episode of the second series, and they show an atmosphere and tension that we would never see again in *Doomwatch*. Nothing except a few snippets survives from Hugh David's ten episodes for *Doctor Who*, either, but telesnaps and clips show an enormously visual and atmospheric director. Eric Hills remembers being very impressed by the episode and wished he could have directed it.

Promotion

This is how the *Daily Mirror* promoted the episode: 'The story is terrifyingly near present day possibilities. A long-range bomber, carrying the latest type of nuclear weapon, crashes in the English Channel … What happens then, you can see tonight.' The eleven and a half million viewers who tuned in saw what happened.

Reception
The Programme Review Board commended a 'fine' episode and carried on with their praise of John Paul's performance. It earned a 'teleletter' from the *Daily Mirror* on 15 May. Mrs J H from Ruislip in Middlesex wrote 'A pity that we've seen the last of the present series of *Doomwatch* on BBC-1. But what a cracking good idea that it should go out literally with a big bang. The bomb incident had me in a lather of suspense. There were times when I could hardly bear to look. Roll on the new series.'

World In Danger
'Survival Code' was adapted as 'A Bomb Is Missing', the third and final section of the book *The World In Danger*. There were some major differences. In the book, it is the Minister who is furious that Quist has been named Man of the Year by a newspaper, rather than Parks giving his rather snide analysis. Ridge argues with Quist in a car journey returning to London while Wren drives. After the explosion Quist tells Ridge that they have to stop the nuclear radiation. 'Ridge walked slowly along the pier. He looked into the sea as he walked. But Toby Wren had gone.'

Impact
He had indeed, and the programme was never the same again. The death of Toby Wren garnered the highest number of letters the *Radio Times* had ever received on one subject. The BBC itself received 130 letters about his 'apparent' death. It was the character's shock demise that cemented the series' reputation in people's memories. Robert Powell was surprised by the reaction and the volume of mail it generated to the *Radio Times*. 'I didn't realise people took it that seriously: there really were tear-stained letters.' Judy Hall wrote the replies to these letters and Powell signed them all.

Jonathan Alwyn regretted his departure. 'He was a popular character. My daughter was heartbroken when he went. She was very obsessed with Toby Wren. She was only about twelve.' Both Kit Pedler and Simon Oates were to find that disgruntled viewers would occasionally remind them of their roles in the death of Toby Wren for many years afterwards. Wren's appeal amongst women was huge. His fan mail amounted to several thousand letters (along with proposals of marriage and invitations to strange parties). 'I suppose Toby – an enigmatic person with no girl-friends – attracted the more romantic female viewer.' He told readers of the *Sun* midway through the series' run that he spent hours every night trying to answer the mail and promised that everyone would get a reply.

Departures
Robert Powell doesn't mind admitting that he owes the rest of his career to

Doomwatch. Following a BBC classic serial called *Sentimental Education*, he went on to play the lead in Harry Green's adaptation of *Jude the Obscure*, in which the *Daily Express* described his performance as excellent. His heart-throb status stuck with him for a few more years. In 1972, just as the last series of *Doomwatch* finished, the *Daily Express* interviewed him at the Dorchester Hotel, where he played the game and spoke of his yearnings for romance. His new film *Asylum* was mentioned in passing by reporter Katharine Hadley. Powell went on from success to success, playing Jesus Christ and Richard Hannay, the latter both on film and in a successful ITV series during the late 1980s.

Another departure was Wendy Hall. With such a disappointing role to play, she decided not to accept the offer of a second series. Just imagine the scenario had Pat Hunnisett gone down to the pier with Toby and refused to leave him alone. A year after she left the programme, the *Daily Mirror* told its readers how, after she left the part, she worked temporarily as secretary to a 'real-life group of scientists equally worried about Doomwatch-type problems. Meanwhile, Wendy is looking forward to returning to the environment of TV.' One of her next jobs, however, was on the stage, playing opposite Simon Oates' John Steed in the short-lived stage play transfer of *The Avengers* in 1971.

Fall Out

The next series had to address the fallout from the Byfield bomb in more ways than one, and Powell featured on the cover of the *Radio Times*, even though his character only appeared in the brief recap of the closing minutes of 'Survival Code'. Viewers would have to relive the agony one last time in December.

4

Reaction To The First Series

'Doomwatch must surely be the most significant fiction series on TV for many years.' Anonymous reader, *Daily Mirror.*

There was little doubt at the BBC that *Doomwatch* had been a runaway success. John Paul, Simon Oates and especially Robert Powell had become household names. Within its first month, and despite its late time slot, it had reached ten and a half million viewers. Gerry Davis remembered the flood of book and film offers that he and Kit Pedler both received.

Letters of praise were received by the BBC, the *Radio Times* and even the daily newspapers. '*Doomwatch* must surely be the most significant fiction series on TV for many years', wrote R F from Devon to the *Daily Mirror* in April. 'It is so taut and credible that it has me on the edge of my seat from start to finish. Spine chilling, topical and first-class entertainment.' Also in April, *Daily Mirror* TV reviewer Matthew Coady pointed *Doomwatch* fans towards BBC2's Heritage series, which discussed population control and the scarcity of fresh air. 'The villains – sulphur dioxide and the rest – invisible but they chilled me. Dr Quist! Dr Ridge! Doomwatchers! HELP!' Children, staying up well past their bed time, preferred this adult fare to what was being given to them at a more civilised hour, or so the head of children's programmes for Thames Television told the *Daily Express* when he announced a new wedge of programming for the summer (which included classic children's tele-fantasy show *Ace of Wands*). In a letter to the *Radio Times*, a Mrs Marshall wrote 'At last the scientist is shown in a better light – as an intelligent, hard-working, understanding, broad-minded, sociable and, above all, humane person, diametrically opposite to the administrator.'

Simon Oates was very proud of *Doomwatch*'s success. This particularly applied to Pedler's message, which he agreed with and found influenced his own outlook in life. He told the *Radio Times* in 1972 that when he started *Doomwatch*, 'I had no idea of the problems of pollution. I didn't know quite what was going on. But if you do thirteen 50-minute programmes, each one of which is devoted to some aspect of ecological disaster, then you have to become more aware of the problems as they are; you realise more and more – and I've said this before – that in about fifty years it's going to be too late unless something's done about it immediately. [*Doomwatch*] is an opportunity to make a meaningful statement, to push home a point, to tackle the pressure groups … It's up to newspapers, the magazines and programmes like *Doomwatch*.'

The title of the show began to slip into the language of 1970. Any situation which contained a technological hazard or a polluting side-effect became a 'Doomwatch' situation. The media were suddenly noticing how many of the episode's themes were being mirrored in real life and were happy to cast Kit Pedler in the role of some kind of visionary, a prophet of doom. People were asking: could it really happen? The *Daily Mirror* snapped him up as their own personal Doomwatch-style adviser and began an irregular series of articles from July. Dissolving stockings, giant hogweeds, concerns over nitrate levels in the water supply and the deaths of plants in a garden ... The issues were hardly as exciting or extraordinary as those presented on the programme, but something had started.

In April 1970 Kit Pedler spoke at a science fiction convention called *Eastercon*, held in the rather run-down venue of the Royal Hotel in London, about the need for a real Doomwatch. He would soon be lecturing before audiences of a different type and putting forward this message. Indeed, it wasn't long before the need for a real-life Doomwatch became a regular call by public and politicians alike. April also saw the *Daily Mirror*'s inside page reporting that Labour MP Ray Fletcher and a group of colleagues were planning a Doomwatch committee within Parliament. 'The idea is to discuss regularly with scientists, technologists, architects and planners what sort of dangers future holds [sic] and to get Ministers to act on their warnings. One of those said to be interested is biologist Dr Kit Pedler.'

The issue of the environment had not been invented virtually overnight, but *Doomwatch* made it topical. Following the shock election result which brought the Conservatives to power in June (one thing Doomwatch did not see coming), they created the Department of the Environment, which merged the former Ministries of Housing and Local Government, Transport and Public Building and Works, headed by Peter Walker as its Secretary of State. Pedler and Davis were invited by Walker and the Labour Shadow Minister, John Silkin, to give briefings on how an actual Doomwatch team would work and what disciplines it would need.

How could there not be a second series ...

Part Two

The Battle For Doomwatch

1

Certain Internal Stresses

'Oh dear, another one. Story approved, as you know contracts exchanged.
Now Terence Dudley doesn't want the story, though Gerry Davis likes it.'
– Robin Lowe, Tony Williamson's agent.

When the *Radio Times* promoted the second series with a montage cover featuring the last few minutes of Toby Wren's life and Quist and Ridge at loggerheads, it could well have been about the falling-out Kit Pedler and Gerry Davis had with Terence Dudley. In a colourful two-page spread reflecting on the impact of the first series, it was now Kit Pedler who dominated the article instead of Davis and Dudley, highlighting the 'success' rate of *Doomwatch*'s uncanny sense of prediction.

Each of the three protagonists had their approach to the series summed up quite well. Kit Pedler explained that as a scientist he was deeply concerned about the dangers of uncontrolled scientific growth. Gerry Davis declared their intention to discomfort, shock and provoke. Terence Dudley, however, said that he believed in the characters as much as he did in his friends. These views should have dovetailed and produced another winning series. But the tensions that had developed during the production of the first series now snapped over the direction the programme was going to take.

By the end of 1970 Gerry Davis had asked to be moved on to another programme, Kit Pedler had asked for his scientific adviser's credit to be removed from an episode and Head of Series Andrew Osborn had to tell Terence Dudley to stop spending any more money on scripts. By the time the fifth episode was transmitted, Osborn himself admitted that he thought that the series might be showing signs of having suffered from 'certain internal stresses'.

In the end, Dudley's will prevailed. His mission statement is to be found within a preview of the new series printed in the *Evening News* in December 1970. Attributed to a BBC spokesman, the following quotation sounds suspiciously like it's been lifted from promotional material prepared and written by Dudley himself: 'It can be claimed quite justly that *Doomwatch* not only gave a word to the language but also helped draw attention to the ecological hazards which threaten the human race. The programme will continue to do this through its prime function, which is to entertain.'

The message was clear. *Doomwatch* was an entertainment programme, not a vehicle for Pedler's propaganda.

Immediate Needs
The second series was agreed in March and announced in the *Radio Times* during April. Filming was scheduled to begin at the end of June, barely two and a half months after 'Survival Code' had been recorded. Concerns at the BBC had to be met: having apparently gone too far with 'Tomorrow, the Rat', the gore would need to be toned down where possible; having real-life presenters playing themselves, as seen in 'Re-Entry Forbidden', was also not to happen again. Later, Terence Dudley phased out any reference to the Ministry for National Security, hoping that the public would draw parallels with the soon-to-be-created Department of the Environment instead. Besides questions of tone, a new character needed to be drawn up to replace Toby Wren. The criticism of sexism also needed to be addressed, so what better way than to introduce a second new character – this time a female scientist? Again, this was promised within the *Radio Times*. Gerry Davis (and presumably Kit Pedler) devised the characters of Geoff Hardcastle (called Jeep in early storylines) and Dr Fay Chantry as well as the new secretary, Barbara Mason.

The Cast Old and New
John Paul, Simon Oates and Joby Blanshard had their options taken up and new contracts were signed in April. John Paul was contracted on 28 April whilst Simon Oates and Joby Blanshard were given theirs the next day. Blanshard was offered a minimum of nine episodes to run from 27 June to 20 February 1971 and Oates, a minimum of ten.

Cast to play the role of Geoff Hardcastle was 31-year-old actor John Nolan. He had worked extensively in the theatre with a couple of years in both the Royal Court Company and then the Royal Shakespeare Company. He did several small roles for independent television productions such as *The Prisoner* and *Strange Report* before coming to the attention of the BBC, when he was cast as the title role in 1970's six-part serialisation of *Daniel Derondaon* BBC2. Allegedly, John Nolan had difficulty finding substance in the part of Hardcastle, and as late as 'Flight Into Yesterday' (recorded twelfth) he discussed the matter with Darrol Blake. He was contracted on 29 April 1970, the same day as Simon Oates and Joby Blanshard.

Doctor Fay Chantry was given to established actress Jean Trend. She had been acting for some time and had made many television appearances, most notably in ITV's *Emergency Ward 10*, which some of the press previews remembered her from. It had been live television, but Trend was unfazed. 'As I come from theatre I could cope. You were just dragged by your collar onto the next set. You certainly had to have your wits about you because you came out from one scene and you had to get your brain in gear to get rid of that last scene and get ready to go on for the next scene.' She had also been a member of the BBC's Radio Repertory Company and had a regular role in the Radio 2 soap opera *Waggoner's Walk*. She had recently taken time off from what was proving to be a successful career to have her second child. By 1970 she was determined to get back to work. One of the people she contacted was Terence Dudley. 'I [had] just had my son Piers and sat there fidgeting, wanting to get back to work, so I just wrote to Terry saying "Have you got anything?" and days later came the offer of the role! I had worked with him before on *Cluff*. I'd done a couple of things for him and then …' Jean's contract was issued on 8 May 1970, and a second one followed in September.

In common with many of the cast, Dr Kit Pedler made an enormous impression on her: 'I was a very big fan of the man. He cared so desperately about the planet and the carelessness by society of using natural resources. We sometimes thought he was a witch! All those things he foresaw and wrote about – and when that episode went out – lo and behold that very subject was headline news. Such a modest man too but once you got him on the environment he buzzed with energy and enthusiasm.' It was decided to hold back the introduction of Fay until the fourth episode, probably in order to give the new boy a chance to settle in with the viewers.

Finally, Barbara Mason was given to actress Vivien Sherrard, who had been acting for ten years when she won the role. Having performed in rep with Darrol Blake's wife, Anne Cunningham. Vivien Sherrard is now Vivien S Smith and emigrated to America to live with her husband shortly after *Doomwatch* finished in 1972. 'Getting the job was akin to winning the lottery considering that 90% of Equity members are unemployed at any given time, regardless of talent or training. Having a connection of some kind, and the higher up the better, is the thing. I had none. I started the three-year course at the Central School aged 16 in September 1957, the same year that Judi Dench and Vanessa Redgrave left. Lynn Redgrave and Julie Christie were in the year below me. For the record, in those days students at Central were given no training whatsoever in acting before a camera. Our only nod to television was to visit a rehearsal at a TV studio. My first job was at the Buxton Playhouse in Derbyshire. Thereafter I joined many repertory companies all over the country, usually but not always cast in younger leading lady parts. I played Amy Spettigue in *Charley's Aunt* on a three-month tour and understudied Sian Phillips and June Ritchie in the West End, taking over from the latter for a week towards the end of the run of George Bernard Shaw's *Too True to be Good*. On television, I played small parts in *Comedy Playhouse, Call Oxbridge 2000, Callan*, and *Justice* which starred Margaret Lockwood. I think my biggest and best role on TV before *Doomwatch* was in Pinter's *The Birthday Party* directed by

Christopher Morahan.

'Memories of those times consist of looking at Edward Woodward's back while he was sitting in a chair; Margaret Lockwood ignoring my existence; Julie Christie playing a schoolgirl while I played a maid; and Christopher Morahan directing me with his eyes closed as he was wont to do with everybody.

'Having played my heart out in the provinces, and becoming thoroughly disillusioned with my agent, I decided to plough through the *Radio Times* and write to every producer and director listed there. Terry Dudley responded and invited me to an interview. The details of what happened next are unfortunately a total blank. But I do remember telling my father "I got the job!"' She signed her first contract on 8 May 1970.

New and old Storylines

Not wanting to see good ideas go to waste, three storylines that had been developed for the first series but never made it to the screen were brought to life in the shape of 'The Pacifiers', 'The Iron Doctor' and 'The Logicians'. Dennis Spooner was given 'The Logicians', the first commission, on 2 April 1970. Pedler and Davis then got to work on seven brand-new storylines. These were called 'Darwin's Killers', 'Lonely the House', 'A Condition of the Mind', 'Massacre of the Innocents', 'Death of a Sagittarian', 'A Will to Die' and 'Inventor's Moon'.

In March 1970, Pedler told the *People* the basis of 'Condition of the Mind', which came from his psychiatrist wife, Una: 'She has been very useful on a story we are doing about the use of mentally disordered people as human guinea pigs – being shut up in rooms and given psychiatric tests lasting for days. It is research gone sick.' The issue of informed consent in a psychiatric ward will be raised in the third series episode 'Hair Trigger'.

Terence Dudley did not like some of these stories and he rejected 'Death of a Sagittarian' and 'A Will to Die'. His problem was that he felt they were veering away from the original intention of *Doomwatch* and too far towards *Doctor Who* in terms of plot and character. Pedler and Davis were pushing the possibilities of their 'What if?' scenarios into what Dudley considered to be unacceptable territory, Dudley wanted more realism. He never saw *Doomwatch* as pure science fiction. He also wanted to tone down the adventure/spy element which raised eyebrows among Pedler's contemporaries, an attitude shared by some of the writers as we shall see.

According to a memo written by Dudley at the beginning of July, Davis had agreed with his criticisms of the rejected storylines but went ahead and found writers for them anyway, promising drastic reconstruction of the contentious plots. Since time was of the essence, it was on that understanding that Dudley signed the commissioning contracts for the stories.

In April 'Lonely the House' was given to Martin Worth, 'Death of a Sagittarian' to Bill Barron, 'Darwin's Killers' to Dennis Spooner and 'Condition of the Mind' to John Wiles. In May, 'The Iron Doctor' was given to Brian Hayles, and John Gould was allotted 'A Will to Die'. 'The Massacre of the Innocents' was given to Roger Parkes around this time and 'The Pacifiers' to David Fisher. There are gaps in our knowledge of other commissions, the type that can only be discovered by chance.

The authors were each very experienced script writers and story editors, some having worked on previous Terence Dudley series, or for Gerry Davis on his programmes. The first series was still transmitting. They should have known what was expected from them, and not be phased by the surprisingly short space of time they were given, which was virtually non-existent. Most of them had only been given a fortnight to turn over a script, some even less than that, for example, John Wiles. He had taken over from Verity Lambert as producer on *Doctor Who*, and had left after nine months, disillusioned with the job and wanting to return to freelance writing. His final few weeks on the programme overlapped with Gerry Davis' first few. They next worked together on a failed script for *The First Lady* in 1969. Wiles had written to Gerry expressing his admiration for 'The Plastic Eaters' back in February. He was officially commissioned on 24 April and seems to have delivered three copies of the script the next day, implying that either he had been working on it for a while before or the month is wrong in his covering letter. In an earlier letter, dated simply 'Wednesday', he says 'When later I am blamed for having *Doomwatch* taken off the air, I hope it will be remembered that I had about 8 days for my first script and about [?] for my second – but I don't suppose it will. This is not meant personally. I've greatly enjoyed working with you and hope we can do it again some day under less harrowing circumstances!'

Dudley's Judgement

As the scripts arrived, only three met with Dudley's approval, and he wasn't prepared to compromise. He and Gerry Davis fought their corners, and Martin Worth was one of those who saw both sides of it. He witnessed the gradual deterioration of the relationship between producer and script editor as he worked on his own script. Neither Davis nor Dudley liked direct confrontation, preferring a war of memos which Judy Hall, caught in the middle, had to write down and pass on. Worth remembers: 'Gerry Davis' office was next door to the producer's office. They couldn't stand each other. I used to go up into the lift to see them and I had to walk past Terence's office to go into Gerry's office, and he always had his door open. "Oh, just a minute, Martin," so I had to pop in there to see him and Gerry knew this was happening because he could hear us talking next door.' And then Martin would hear the other side of the latest argument from Gerry. He saw this as a clash of personalities, but it was more than that. It was a clash of styles.

In May, Dudley was stung by the usual jibe of wooden characterisation that often gets thrown at Series department productions, but this time it came from an article by Graham Chedd in the *New Scientist* which greeted the end of the first series. Chedd was actually one of the programme's more constructive critics and applauded the series intention and subject matter, but did not like the presentation of the scientists: 'To accept fiction of any sort one has to begin to believe in the humanity of its characters and the scientists in *Doomwatch* have as much humanity as you would find in a month of Sunday supplements. *Doomwatch* studiously avoids the stereotype of omniscience and austerity which is the delight of devotees of old movies, yet replaces it with another stereotype which is certainly trendier but just as incredible. This is all the more regrettable because of the great opportunity to break down the few barriers between science and the lay public ...' The programme's serious message would be lost because 'the serious scientific content may be assessed on the same level as its cardboard characters and dismissed as enjoyable nonsense. The ironic remedy is that the series can best do service to science by improving its dramatic qualities.'

Chedd's argument was one of the reasons why productions from the Plays and Serials departments of the Drama Group were highly regarded both at the BBC and by the more high-brow commentators in the media in terms of quality and characterisation than the Series, although ITV was currently demonstrating how popular series could be with *Callan* and *Special Branch*. These were transmitted opposite the BBC's prestigious and controversial *The Wednesday Play* and beat it in the ratings so badly, it was moved to another time slot and renamed *Play for Today*. When production on the second series of *Doomwatch* was wrapping up, an article in *New Scientist* reported that Dudley 'was conscious of the cardboard characterisation of which some critics have complained, [and] wants to emphasise human reactions to catastrophe a bit more and develop conflict among his characters.' He may well have read some of the criticism directed at the first series in the Programme Review Boards in which one member wished to see a thick scientist and an intelligent minister for a change.

Director Eric Hills' thoughts were that 'Kit Pedler was more into the science of it. My feeling was behind him, not that I knew him personally, that his was [sic] the ideas of the future and so on, but Terry was more interested in the relationships, the play and the drama. He wasn't very interested in science. So there was a bit of tension there. Terry was very good at getting annoyed with people. It was a pity as with *Doomwatch* there were strong possibilities, like with *Survivors*. I worked on those. Again, he didn't see the possibilities.'

On top of all this, Dudley's wife was in hospital and he was under a lot of strain. He asked Andrew Osborn to arbitrate on the quality of the material delivered by Gerry Davis. Osborn sided with Dudley. So what was to be done? They needed a temporary script editor who could get the scripts in shape for the rapidly approaching filming dates. They called back in Martin Worth, who had script edited the BBC2 historical drama series *The Borderers*.

Martin Worth – Script Editor

Martin Worth remembered the circumstances which led to his being asked to take over the script editing. 'I knew Andrew Osborn quite well. He was a great character, a very entertaining character. He asked me to come in and see him, and I wondered why, and he just told me that they were looking for a script editor. I had worked with Terence Dudley before. I was briefed on the series then and I was asked if I would be interested and I jumped at the chance. Terry did think the scripts were getting too much like *Doctor Who*. Andrew told me that there had been five scripts or something that Gerry had commissioned which were absolute rubbish. Andrew said to me, "There was only one script out of all these that we liked, and that was yours. Therefore you're the ideal person to sort those two out!" There were only five or six scripts and they were terrible. Andrew didn't like it, Terry didn't like it. Gerry Davis had fallen out of favour with Andrew Osborn. That's why I was called in really. Andrew wanted a spy in there. Andrew asked whether I would rewrite one and at the same time become story editor on the series.'

Martin Worth was booked for two months from 7 May to 1 July to provide six workable scripts. He commissioned Patrick Alexander, Louis Marks and Robert Holmes and continued to work with Dennis Spooner and John Gould on their stories. Towards the end of his stint, he also briefed Tony Williamson on the series. Andrew Osborn signed the commissioning slips in place of Terence Dudley for Louis Marks' and Robert Holmes' episodes. Alexander's story 'Public Enemy' took as its starting point Ibsen's *An Enemy of the People*. He may have also invited Granada's controversial and prolific crime writer Robin Chapman to pitch ideas.

There would be no more storylines required from Pedler or Davis. Martin Worth made it clear to both of them where he stood. 'Kit Pedler through Gerry Davis was pretty arrogant about the whole thing, and Andrew Osborn as Head of Series wasn't having that and they both knew that I was a spy for Andrew. I made it quite clear that I was engaged for this job by Andrew Osborn. I remember saying that to both of them the first time I met them. In other words, if Andrew wanted to know how things were going, he was going to ask me. But I didn't see much of Kit. He didn't have an office in the building.'

The day after Worth officially started, Gerry Davis wrote to David Fisher, rejecting his very quickly written script 'The Pacifiers'. 'The consensus of opinion is that it doesn't come off. The sense of conflict, excitement and climax ... is simply not there. "*Doomwatch*" is a special type of scientific thriller and is extremely hard to write for', he explained. 'The action must be highly inventive and charged with edgy confrontation, and at the same time be entirely viable. We do not feel that this has been achieved in your version of 'The Pacifiers'. I'm sorry. I had hoped to be able to use it but ... not this time.'

Worth was not afraid to reject scripts. He recalled in a 1989 interview for *Time Screen* that an idea which Dennis Spooner had been given to develop – 'Darwin's Killers' – involved a Minister being given implants in his brain. Despite considering it absurd fantasy, Worth accepted the implicit theme of political manipulation from a right-wing group. He is actually misremembering another attempt at 'The Synthetic Candidate' rather than Spooner's storyline which was another attempt to do a story about a sunken nuclear submarine. This apparently formed the basis of 'Diplomatic Incident', which Spooner's daughter remembers it to be another version of 'Darwin's Killers'. As the submarine involved was Russian sunk in British waters, that makes sense of the title. It also was rejected.

It appears that John Gould's script 'A Will To Die', about a scientist trying to beat an incurable disease by becoming a brain inside a box, was also dropped and he was commissioned by Worth to write a new version of the idea on 1 July called 'The Head'. Another script casualty during Worth's time was one that he himself had been going to write. The storyline of 'Inventor's Moon' had been acceptable to Terence Dudley, and Worth was commissioned on 21 May. However, after conducting some research, Worth found that the story was both tendentious and out of date, and it was quickly abandoned.

In his short tenure, Worth got the first three scripts ready for filming and worked on Louis Marks' and Roger Parkes' stories. Roger Parkes' fee wasn't sorted out until June.

What was Gerry Davis doing during these two months? He was probably on leave, licking his wounds. On 26 May Andrew Osborn authorised payment for the first four storylines, the writers sharing £500 between them. On a similar memo of 1 June which authorised payment to Gerry Davis, there is a comment written in red ink: 'They're off their heads – I've spoke.' This was presumably written by Brian Head, the Senior Personnel Assistant. Davis and Pedler wanted to be paid for their other three storylines because the producer had now signed the commissioning contracts with the relevant writers, even though he had initially rejected two of those storylines. On 1 July Dudley accepted that he had done this because Gerry Davis had agreed to changes. In the end, Dudley felt that only 'Inventor's Moon' qualified for payment. Andrew Osborn suggested that the situation with Gerry Davis needn't get any worse and agreed to the payment, having learned a valuable lesson for the future. Dudley wrote to the Assistant Head of Copyright, saying: 'For the rest, any contributor who qualifies for payment and is contracted by you must be engaged by this office and not by Gerry Davis as was the case referred to me by you today.' Osborn agreed. What this refers to is a mystery.

Pedler's fate

At the beginning of July, Dudley decided that Pedler would now simply be the programme's adviser on the scientific content of every script and an 'originator of themes or areas of technology'. He was still to be a sounding board and would be paid for any vetting of scripts. A formal agreement was drawn up on 16 September to be retrospectively applied from the beginning of July to the end of January 1971. He would be asked to discuss possible themes for episodes, be available for consultation with writers or BBC staff working on the series and attend rehearsals or recordings if required by the producer. As per the original deal with the BBC, he was still to be credited on screen with Gerry Davis as one of the programme's creators and in the *Radio Times* as its scientific adviser. But how much Terence Dudley actually intended to use him is unknown. Jean Trend certainly remembers meeting Kit during some (but not many) of the rehearsals, as he made an enormous impression on her. Darrol Blake, for instance, never met him when he was directing 'No Room for Error'. Pedler was certainly sent scripts to vet, as we will see with 'Public Enemy'. Pedler was kept at arm's length.

Davis returned to the script editor's chair at the beginning of July just as block filming began for the second series. The episodes were 'The Iron Doctor', 'The Logicians' and 'Invasion' (as 'Lonely the House' was now called). They had far more filming allocated than any previous episode. 'The Human Time Bomb' by Louis Marks, 'No Room for Error' (formerly 'Massacre of the Innocents') and Gerry Davis' own story, 'The Web of Fear', would be next before the cameras before a two-week break in production, scheduled to allow for some more extensive filming. In his first two weeks back, Davis had a writing team consisting of Tony Williamson, Eddie Boyd, Keith Dewhurst, and David Whitaker. Robin Chapman, Robert Holmes and John Gould were around and would see their work made. None of Davis' new writers would see their work made. He did try to interest Harry Green with 'Condition of the Mind', but the writer was still bruised from his earlier experiences.

The Misguided Missile

Edward Boyd had created and written a surreal detective series called *The Corridor People* and had tried a couple of times to write for the science fiction series *Out of the Unknown*. His first attempt was a black comedy with scientific overtones called *Sex Change* before abandoning that in favour of a supernatural horror called *The Put On*, which did not get made either. Boyd was commissioned to write 'The Misguided Missile' (the 20th commissioned script so far) on 13 July with a target delivery date of 15 October. It appears he never delivered the script and by December agreed that his first half-fee of £312.10s.would be recovered from his next BBC commission.

Green, Green Fields

Tony Williamson also did not deliver. Williamson had acted as story consultant and writer for *Adam Adamant Lives!* and *Counterstrike* and had written episodes for *The Avengers, The Mask of Janus, The Spies, Dr Finlay's Casebook* and *The Revenue Men*. He could write quickly and to the style of any programme. When first approached to do a *Doomwatch* during the first series but he had been too busy, but his agent Robin Lowe contacted Terence Dudley towards the end of June when Williamson became free. Dudley, away in Yorkshire, was keen to use him and suggested telephoning Martin Worth. He was also interested in another of Lowe's clients, David Chantler, who provided an episode of *The Mask of Janus* for Dudley and *R3*. *Green, Green Fields* was commissioned as script number eight on the same day as Eddie Boyd. It was needed by the end of the month. Williamson met with Dudley and Davis to discuss the idea of a fertiliser which proved dangerous when combined with an insecticide and how to prevent the wholesale use of such a product which, on its own, was harmless. He found at their first meeting there had been a reversal of view about the story he wanted to tell and so insisted, due to the shortness of time, that he would write just the storyline as a guide, even though Dudley was happy for him to go ahead and write the full script on the basis of their discussions.

Dudley disliked the storyline as soon as he read it and told the writer so at another meeting. Doomwatch analysed a substance found on a golf ball far too early in the story for Dudley, who felt it was contrived and that there was insufficient evidence to lead *Doomwatch* to their conclusions. He didn't like the character of Parker, the man behind the project, who Williamson claimed was motivated by malice and self-motivation. Dudley suspected that he was a 'villain'. He also disliked the method used to isolate the cause and the way Quist was characterised in relation to 'abnormal behaviour' in Ridge. Dudley described the situation as the most contrived he had ever read, but it was based on a true incident: one of Williamson's friends had swallowed fertiliser via a golf ball (!) whilst on a golfing holiday and collapsed into a coma.

After the meeting Williamson discussed the matter with Davis and decided to produce a second outline and another possible idea. He was encouraged to carry on scripting, and this was acceptable to Dudley, who was satisfied with the changes discussed. He started from scratch, wrote up a new storyline and started the script. A week later Gerry asked him to stop and outlined some new objections from the producer based on the revised storyline. Dudley thought the new approach to Parker, who was now to be ignorant of the situation, made him a fool. Ridge and Dr Chantry were to spot golf balls at the beginning of Act Two amidst grass that had been affected by either insecticide or fertiliser, and the next logical step would be for them to analyse them. Dudley felt that this was the end of the story – his niece or nephew would see that. But it was to be the start of the conflict with the manufacturers, Williamson explained. He had put the analysis towards the end of the story, not the start, on the grounds of previous objections. Dudley also disliked the 'debasing of the Whitehall element', doubting that Parker could intercede at Ministry level and get Ridge suspended. With all this in mind, he rejected the story.

Williamson was aggrieved to be turned down on the basis of a storyline before a script had been read and withdrew from the project. 'Because of the attitude adopted on this story, and the fact that whenever points were agreed with Gerry they appeared to raise objections with you, I felt there was little point in continuing', Williamson wrote on 7 August. 'Throughout our meetings, Gerry Davis has been helpful and constructive. Our mistake was perhaps attempting to meet urgent deadlines by assuming that I was a sufficiently experienced writer to avoid "childish" attitudes and contrived situations. It is, in fact, the simplest thing of all to say that plot points in an outline are contrived. The very nature of an outline makes this inevitable.' Robin Lowe wrote to Dudley explaining that, in his experience, no BBC contract is ever exchanged until a story has been approved. In addition, there had been an unusually long delay in receiving their contract.

Dudley wrote back on 11 August and agreed that he had given a verbal go-ahead on the basis of their first discussions, but that he had rejected a revised storyline which hadn't been asked for. He then wrote to Williamson and disputed the purpose of a storyline (they had different views on this). He also reiterated that Ridge and Fay were acting out of character when they found that licking a golf ball was a possible way of ingesting chemical substances. 'As scientists they should pursue this angle until it proved a positive or a negative line of enquiry. They do not.' He pointed out examples of descriptions used for Parker which he felt made him a fool or a villain. After all this, it was decided to let Williamson keep his first half-fee in view of the work he had done on the storylines.

One interesting detail which came from the correspondence between Williamson and Dudley was how the writer had had no scientific advice offered to him whatsoever. Williamson wrote: 'I was hoping to get some assistance from your department with scientific advice and material, but at our last meeting you indicated that I should already have done this myself. I must confess that I am a writer, not a scientist, and the difficulties of obtaining confidential scientific material from an industry being accused of producing cancer agents and chemicals causing genetic damage are considerable.'

Dudley would eventually find *Doomwatch* a researcher who would provide writers with material relevant to their stories. Anna Kaliski had been with the BBC since the 1960s and trained with Glyn Edwards on the BBC Radio Studio Management course. There were limits to what she was allowed to do. Eric Hills remembered 'Her job was to do with the technicalities of the script. She started to make comments on the content of the stories, which wasn't directly her job, and Terry got very cross with her because that was his job, and he had demarcation very clear.' Any story query went to the producer and any scientific query went to Kaliski. This uncredited work is known to have been carried out for Robert Holmes's rabies scare story. He was recommended to Dudley and Worth on the strength of a rejected script for the *Play for Today*, and he was initially welcomed by Gerry Davis.

Home-Made Bomb Story

A highly individualistic writer, Keith Dewhurst had written episodes of *Z Cars*, *Softly, Softly*, *Thirty-Minute Theatre* and other television plays. Dewhurst was commissioned to write a script simply called 'Home-Made Bomb Story' (script number twenty-one) on 20 July 1970. 'Gerry Davis and I knew each other for a good while. We liked each other and were on more or less the same side in what I call "the theatre wars" – taste, appreciation, objectives. My vague recollection would be that he was encouraged by people whose provenance was the Drama Documentary Department [which made *Z Cars*] and its maestro Elwyn Jones. By 1970, Elwyn had lost the battle and his department disbanded, its ideals ignored. Except that they continued through people like David Rose, who actually ran the BBC drama at Pebble Mill, and then Film 4, and Joan Clark, Elwyn's original researcher, who was for twenty years script editor on its police series, from *Softly, Softly* to *Juliet Bravo*. Gerry had a lot of charm and a serious mind and he knew his onions script wise, but I don't think he had the grit of someone like Joan Clark. Ruthless people probably took advantage of him.

'I was commissioned to write this script from a basic idea by Kit Pedler, who had realised it was possible for someone who knew how to make a small nuclear bomb in a suburban garage. I had lunch with Kit and Gerry to discuss ideas and met them again, I think, when I delivered. I can't remember if they suggested bits of rewrites but I assume they did. I have a very strong recollection of Kit's intensity. I think that it was after I delivered a final script that Terence Dudley took over.'

The script was delivered on 7 August and Davis invited him to discuss it a week later. By October Ben Travers, Assistant Head of Copyright, wrote to Dewhurst's agent Elspeth Cochrane and said that the story had been rejected and no further payment was owing.

Dewhurst: 'What Dudley proposed was to reject the script, not pay its acceptance fee and start again with new people. He would have his own chums, so to speak, whom he had used on other shows. You will find, I think, that there were other writers and scripts involved, as well as me and mine, and eventually other agents, as well as mine. Writers worked in all good faith to a brief but when they delivered were told that the brief had changed, and that they would not be paid for acceptance. They and their agents objected strongly ... I think that David Attenborough, whom I knew somewhat at the time, got involved.' Attenborough, best known now for his nature documentaries, had been Controller of BBC2 and since 1969 had been Director of Programmes for both channels, responsible for budgets amongst other things. 'The argument went upwards until it reached him whereupon he ruled that everyone must be paid out, which we were, although of course, the scripts were not used. David Attenborough would have been very open to the original premise of *Doomwatch*, but to what extent other parts of the bureaucracy sympathised I do not know, and I mean people both above and below him. Certainly, not many of them would have had an equal grasp of its scientific issues.'

Elspeth Cochrane wrote back to the BBC. Her letter does not survive, but the BBC's response does. After consulting with Dudley and Davis, Travers explained that 'the producer felt that a major part of the script was devoted to a debate concerning the ethics in developing nuclear devices and it could only be acceptable if the writer rethought his idea as a story.' There were objections to the characterisation of Quist and to a small part of the script that echoed the content of 'You Killed Toby Wren' the episode Dudley will write to launch the new series and will be recorded seventh. These points were made to the writer, who in their view failed to put them into his revisions, and 'as he was unwilling to make alterations we considered necessary we were obliged to notify you that the work was not acceptable for television.' In the event, Dewhurst was paid a further quarter of his fee.

For Dewhurst, the conflict between Dudley and Davis reflected the struggling transition from the slightly genteel drawing-room dramas of the past to a more socially aware and gritty representation of reality, instigated by John Osborne's watershed stage play *Look Back in Anger*. 'Terence Dudley was probably a bit snobbish towards Gerry. I don't think his tastes were very deep. He would knock you out a thriller on budget, if you know what I mean. He was a BBC type. Andrew Osborn was another. So were John Elliot [*Mogul, The Andromeda Breakthrough*] and Gerry Glaister [*Colditz*]. Elliot was pragmatic (I worked with him on *Fall of Eagles*), but the others did not really like this new post-1956 *Look Back In Anger* drama, which both me and Gerry Davis would seem to them to represent.'

How The Other Half Dies
David Whitaker had been writing at the BBC since the 1950s, and was *Doctor Who*'s first story editor and, again, another writer with whom Gerry Davis had worked with during his stint on the programme. As a BBC staff member, Whitaker had to gain clearance to write 'How the Other Half Dies'. The reason given for his contribution was 'his unique knowledge of world hunger which is the theme for the script'. This was requested on 23 July, and he was offered a fee of £625 in the middle of August. What became of this story is unrecorded.

Into August and Beyond
Louis Marks was commissioned on 11 August for a second contribution, 'Desert Island' (script no25), which transmitted as 'The Islanders' as the eighth story recorded, to be followed by Robin Chapman's 'Evil Inherited', now retitled 'By The Pricking of My Thumbs ...'

Elwyn Jones was commissioned to write 'Dangerous Cargo', also on 11 August (script no 26). A then-current *Doctor Who* writer, Malcolm Hulke, with whom Gerry Davis had again worked during his time on the programme, wrote 'Your Body Will Never Forgive' (no 27), commissioned on 27 August and apparently delivered the next day. When that didn't work out, Hulke was commissioned for 'Covered All Over' (no 30) on 11 September, and he delivered in October. They may both have been the same script recommissioned in the same manner that befell Dennis Spooner and John Gould. Hulke was only paid the first half of his fee for both commissions.

Brian Hayles was commissioned to write a second story, 'St Anthony's Harvest' (no 28), about ergot poisoning (also known as Saint Anthony's Fire), on 7 September. He sent in his rewrites mid-October, but the script had to be cancelled in November because the theme clashed with an episode of *Dr Finlay's Casebook*. As Hayles' agent Harvey Unna pointed out to Gerry Davis, the script was not unacceptable, and the clash was not his fault. Payment was gently requested for the second half of the fee.

With Robert Holmes' 'The Inquest' to be the tenth story scheduled, on 23 October, to be recorded in November, there were still three more slots to fill. Eight days earlier Terence Dudley had commissioned Martin Worth to write the 31st commissioned script for the second series. This was 'Jet Rag', which would be recorded twelfth and renamed 'Flight Into Yesterday'. Gerry Davis' signature is not on the contract. Possibly, Dudley already had in mind the last two stories to be made, but there was still one more commission to come from Gerry Davis – or at least with his signature on the contract. This was to be Robin Chapman's second script, and it was called 'The Drug Story'. Script number thirty-two, it was commissioned on 3 November and due for delivery on 16 November. It was only halted on 20 November just as he was beginning the rewrite stage. This was the day after Andrew Osborn decided that more than enough money had been spent on scripts for the series. Thirty-two commissions were enough. What was there had to be made to work. Chapman still got paid simply because Dudley had not been able to get him on the phone the previous day to tell him to stop.

On 9 December the regular cast were booked for the three studio sessions that would wrap up the series in January. 'Public Enemy' by Patrick Alexander would be the first of these, then 'Flight Into Yesterday' and finally John Gould's 'In the Dark'. Gould's script was a new version of 'A Will To Die', as 'The Head' was never delivered. He was not commissioned, just paid his second half fee for him to perform the rewrite.

Precisely when Gerry Davis asked to be moved on is unclear, but he did. Robert Holmes once claimed in an interview that it was his script that caused the split, and in hindsight, and as we will see later in the book, there is just cause for this story to be the straw which broke the camel's back. It was almost a complete rejection of *Doomwatch* as both Pedler and Davis envisaged. But the future looked good for Davis. *Doomwatch* book and movie deals were underway, and he was already writing his first novel: *The Death of Plastic* with Kit Pedler. Davis did not receive a script editor's credit on 'You Killed Toby Wren' nor the last four stories in production. Martin Worth is only credited on 'The Human Time Bomb' having requested that he was not to be given further credits in case it damaged his chances of being offered other work. Davis worked out the rest of his BBC contract as script editor on the police series *Softly, Softly*. He was still at the BBC in August 1971 when he worked with veteran script writer Rex Tucker on a script about P G Wodehouse, to be produced by Gerald Savory.

Final Comments
We don't know the full story behind the thirty-two scripts. As we have seen, some were never delivered and some had to be cancelled through no

fault of the writers or the production team. Others were rejected out of hand by Terence Dudley and Andrew Osborn, leaving behind a lot of upset writers and agents. But Dudley's preferences did appear to lie with the stories Martin Worth had either prepared or instigated, and it is possible that Davis was trying to block stories like 'The Inquest' and 'Public Enemy' in favour of those more in line with his and Kit's original idea. Significantly, the best script of the series, according to Dudley and Osborn, was 'Public Enemy', the most down-to-earth story of the series. It was not a view shared by Pedler.

Adele Winston has her own view on the matter: 'Kit Pedler was smashing and so was Gerry Davis. They had a lot of trouble with Terry. I worked with Terry for a long time and I think anyone would tell you that he was a quarrelsome man. He couldn't work with anybody or know anybody for very long without deciding there was something awful the matter with them. He had meningitis as a kid and he use to blame it on that. He could be the world's greatest friend, but he did pick fights.'

2
Production Of The Series

'I got it into my head that it was a semi-documentary series, so you wanted
to make it as realistic as possible.' Darrol Blake, director

When choosing his directors, Dudley invited Jonathan Alwyn, Eric Hills
and David Proudfoot to come back. Dudley would direct his own episode
again. Of the newcomers, Lennie Mayne had directed *The First Lady*, *The
Borderers*, *Brett* and *The Troubleshooters*, and would be responsible for three
episodes towards the end of the production block. Another first timer was
Joan Kemp-Welch. She had done a lot of work for ITV and had recently
made a film for them called *Skyscrapers*, putting her in good stead for the
second of her two *Doomwatch* episodes, 'The Human Time Bomb', a story
of claustrophobia and panic amidst high-rise accommodation.

A significant new arrival to the series, and new to directing drama
itself, was Darrol Blake. 'Around 1963 or 64 when I was a jobbing designer,
I had to fill in for someone. There was a series called *Moonstrike*, which was
about the SOE (Special Operations Executive) dropping agents into France
during the war, and the episode happened to be directed by Terry Dudley.
We got on fine. All I can remember is a night shoot in an airfield in
Bedfordshire or somewhere and we laughed and laughed and laughed.
The first assistant was a marvellous man called David Proudfoot. I'd done
three years in Arts and Features, spending three years making films, and I
thought "Now is the time to get into drama." At this point, Terry had just
had a tremendous success with the first series of *Doomwatch*. So I wrote to
him and said, "If you're going round again, I'd love to come and direct
something for you." Back came a note saying, "Been watching your career
with interest, nothing for you at the moment but keep in touch." I kid you
not, about a fortnight later I saw him in the bar, and he said, "Oh, thank
God I've seen you! I've got something for you." And that was *Doomwatch* –
my first drama series.'

There would be new costume and make-up supervisors in the form of
Mary Husband and Pat Hughes, whilst designing the episodes would be
Ian Watson, Jeremy Davies, Graham Oakley, Colin Shaw, Stanley Morris,
Tim Gleeson, Christine Ruscoe and John Hurst. Colin Shaw had designed
the Pedler and Davis *Doctor Who* story 'The Moonbase', and he once visited
Pedler's home to find that he had no furniture, so they all had to sit on the
floor. Oakley would later find fame as an author and illustrator of *The
Church Mice*: a series of children's books about mice who lived inside a

church organ.

The production block was scheduled to run from 27 June 1970 to 20 February 1971. In the event, recording was completed in January. Once again there would be a block of filming at the top of the production for three to four weeks. Then, six episodes would be recorded, one every fortnight, with some additional filming slotted in. After a two-week break for some more advance filming, four more episodes were taped, this time every ten days. December saw no studio work, which is presumably when the final block of filming occurred, before January saw the final three episodes taped, again one every ten days.

For the first series, rehearsals had been conducted in any large space available in London, such as halls belonging to the Territorial Army. In May 1970 the BBC's custom-built rehearsal block, soon to be affectionately known as the 'Acton Hilton', was opened. In its canteen would mingle actors and personnel from all manner of productions in rehearsal; it led to many a happy memory from those working in what was seen to be a golden age of television. Jean Trend recalls the period with affection: 'All the rehearsal time at the Acton Hilton – we were so lucky. I had the best of times. I was 36, so I'm astounded at myself as I look and see all these people that one was working with! We did bond as a company, and what was so good was that we were a nice company and welcoming to the guests. When you were a regular it was nice to see new people.'

Music
This time around Max Harris' music was confined strictly to the opening and closing titles. Any music, if needed, would now come from the library music collections of KPM, Chappell or the BBC's own collection of discs and tapes. However, it was an optional extra in those days to use music. Whereas Eric Hills would use a copious amount of dramatic mood music for 'The Web of Fear', he used hardly any on 'By The Pricking of My Thumbs ...', and even that was simply heard in the background of a café scene. Joan Kemp-Welch's episodes were also music free.

Darrol Blake used music sparingly. 'I had come from Arts Features, and you didn't soup it up with music. Occasionally you cut a sequence to music, which is what I did with the cows in 'No Room for Error'. I got it into my head that it was a semi-documentary series, so you wanted to make it as realistic as possible. So highlighting or mickey-mousing with music was not on, but in addition to that I don't think we had dubs in those days. You either put the music on in the studio or in the edit, and that was very, very crude compared to a normal sort of dub. But ... one of my bugbears, and it took me years to sort it out ... was the mix between sequences shot on film and all the stuff shot on video. Film was edited to an inch of its life and dubbed with effects and music, and then you cut to

210

the studio and there is this terrible let down, so I did my best (other than with that jokey sequence with the cows) not [to] soup it up with music or effects, so there wasn't quite [such] a lurch when you cut between the two, not to mention the picture quality. In those days it was a 16mm inserts cut into a videotape production.'

Promotion
The second series began transmission on 14 December 1970 at 9.50 pm. Each week, the *Radio Times* gave the programme good promotion. The listing was accompanied by a photograph from the episode and a fake newspaper report which highlighted the menace or an incident the *Doomwatch* team would be facing. Each episode listing featured an extract from the dialogue. A rather subtle change to the closing credits was the introduction of a caption slide listing the week's 'Guest Stars', if they were deemed so, which appeared after the roll call of the regular cast and other actors.

After the New Year, the programme went out at the earlier time of 9.20 pm, usually after the news. On BBC2, *Horizon*, the BBC's science documentary series, would run in opposition. This prompted Controller of BBC1 Paul Fox to ask his fellows at the Programme Review Board if the clash caused them any anxieties. Andrew Osborn wasn't terribly concerned. He felt that the contrast between fact and fiction was strong enough. However, John Culshaw, Head of Music Productions for Television, grumbled that the episode of *Doomwatch* one particular week had been 'so incredible' that he wished he had watched *Horizon* instead.

This series had two breaks in transmission, the second of which would have a strong influence on the third series by what was being shown on BBC2.

Series Two

Producer: Terence Dudley
Script Editor: Gerry Davis (Episodes 2, 3, 4, 5, 6, and 12)
Script Editor: Martin Worth (Episode 9)
Scientific Adviser: Dr C M H Pedler
Assistant to Producer: Glyn Edwards
Graphics: Alan Jeapes
Theme Music: Max Harris

Regular Cast:
Dr Spencer Quist (John Paul)
Dr John Ridge (Simon Oates)
Geoff Hardcastle (John Nolan)
Dr Fay Chantry (Jean Trend)
Colin Bradley (Joby Blanshard)
Barbara Mason (Vivien Sherrard)

2.01
You Killed Toby Wren

Written and Directed by Terence Dudley
Designed by Graham Oakley
Transmitted: Monday, 14 December 1970 at 9.51 pm Duration: 51′ 03″

Cast
Sam Billings (Tommy Godfrey), Dr Judith Lennox (Shirley Dixon), Professor Eric Hayland (Graham Leaman), Dr Warren (Robert Gillespie), Barmaid (Margie Young), Dr Anne Tarrant (Elizabeth Weaver). Guest Stars: Minister (John Barron), Permanent Secretary (MacDonald Hobley), Air Commodore Parks (Donald Morley), Chairman of Tribunal (Edward Underdown).

In 'Survival Code' reprise
Toby Wren (Robert Powell), Len White (Edwin Brown), First Man on Pier (David St John), Man on Pier (Mick Burnett).

Also appearing
Man in Laboratory (Steve Peters), Tribunal Member (Michael Mulcaster), Sefton (Robert Cartland). Extras: Bella Emberg, Albert Cranston, Elfrica Cranston, Harry Douglas, Margo Boht, Mary Masters, Florence Allsworth, Domini Turner, Barry Ashton, Leslie Montague, Reg Turner, Walter Turner, Kedd Senton, Beryl Bainbridge, Ian Elliot, Anne Lee, Pat Symons.

Technical Credits
Director's Assistant: Adele Paul. Production Assistant: Vivienne Cozens.
Assistant Floor Manager: Derek Nelson. Floor Assistant: Nicholas Wood.
Costume Supervisor: Mary Husband. Make-up Supervisor: Pat Hughes.
Studio Lighting: Dave Sydenham. TM2: Lance Wood. Vision Mixer: Fred Law.
Sound Supervisor: John Holmes. Grams Operator: Gerry Borrows.
Crew: 6.

Radio Times
'I'd say Dr Quist's is cooked: in fact, I'd say it is positively overdone!'

The Story
'You haven't got an honest feeling in your body. You're an emotional hypocrite! You're a self-indulgent bloody murderer ... And what's more, you're finished, bust, kaput!' – Ridge

213

Toby Wren is barely a minute away from disarming the nuclear warhead lodged in the timber frame beneath Byfield Regis pier. As the RAF's bomb disposal arrive and tell him to come up, Wren relaxes – he's managed it. But then he discovers another wire and can only try to unscrew it at the terminal with his sweaty fingers. The explosion is seen by Quist, Ridge and Air Commodore Parks, who asks 'When will you people learn not to interfere?'

The Minister tells his Permanent Secretary that Quist is responsible for the deaths of three people. A Tribunal of Inquiry is to be set up. Meanwhile, Colin Bradley meets the new secretary, Barbara Mason, and she is kept busy answering phone calls from Geoff Hardcastle, who wants to speak to Dr Quist. The Minister is also busy, talking to Air Commodore Parks, who describes his dislike of Quist's behaviour throughout the incident but would rather that the inquiry decide whether Quist was right to attempt to disarm the bomb. The Minister is intrigued by Parks' account of Ridge's attitude in the Operations Room towards Quist.

Ridge, meanwhile, meets Barbara; his rather trendy appearance confuses her. Colin tells him that Pat will soon be out of hospital and that Quist has gone down to see Toby's parents. Ridge thinks that is particularly ironic as he has something he wants him to see – a large photographic enlargement of Toby. A little later, Quist returns with his arm bandaged up in a sling. He stops in his tracks at the sight of Toby's picture and looks at Ridge, who is sipping coffee. He goes into his office, followed by Barbara as she receives yet another call from Geoff. Initially sharp and abrasive, he tells Barbara to advertise the vacant situation in various publications and only softens when she asks him if he would like a cup of coffee. Ridge is disgusted at the haste in searching for a replacement for Toby. Quist rushes back in, wanting to speak to this Geoff Hardcastle, a biologist working in extra-uterine conception. He had resigned from a research establishment in Norfolk last week, and Quist seems to think he might be looking for a job. Ridge goads Quist, who walks away and stands in his office, stunned. Ridge goes to The Feathers, the pub over the road, to get 'quietly stoned'. He meets Geoff Hardcastle there, who explains that he is not looking for a job but wants to stop his professor's experiments with animal-human hybrids – including a human-headed chicken – before he is crucified by the press for them.

Quist goes to see Harry, the Minister's Permanent Secretary, and wants to resign. Harry does his best to persuade him not to. He advises Quist to stop feeling sorry for himself and go and see a psychiatrist. 'It's a friendly warning – prove them wrong.' Ridge returns to the Doomwatch office with Geoff, who gets to see Quist. Ridge is sent to see the Minister. He misunderstands the meeting – he thinks he is being offered Quist's job. But the Minister is merely sounding out his interest in the possibility of Quist's departure. Doomwatch is something that even the Americans are interested in, and this may lead to a certain political advantage. Meanwhile, Quist tells Geoff that he is being squeamish over his work and should at least finish stay in the job to finish his PhD. He doesn't see the need for Doomwatch to get involved. Ridge, disgusted by the work, is furious when he finds out and loses his temper with Quist, cutting off a threat and throwing aside a chair. Quist sacks him. when Ridge accuses him of being responsible for Toby's death, Quist shouts at him to get out. Ridge does so – 'With pleasure!' Bradley tries to calm matters down with Quist and tells him the tribunal wants to see him on Thursday. Later, Quist goes to his appointment and is surprised that the psychiatrist he has been sent to see is a woman: Dr Anne Tarrant. He explains his background before she asks him if he'd like to talk about the bomb. Quist pauses before answering. 'Which one?'

Ridge has arranged with Geoff to get a look round the lab by contacting Judith Lennox, Professor Hayland's assistant. He travels down to Norwich, takes her out for dinner, gains her confidence and, in typical Ridge fashion, sleeps with her. When he visits Hayland's lab and the Professor describes his work, the atmosphere turns unpleasant as Judith realises why Ridge is really there. She explains that Hayland isn't creating monstrosities for fun. He is on the way to discovering the problem of immune rejection and has made it possible for sterile women to host their eggs in another uterus. Ridge sees some of the experiments: a chicken with two tiny, malformed human heads and a monkey with a human scalp. Disgusted, he tries to attack the Professor and breaks the jaw of another scientist who tries to intervene. Judith is the disgusted one now. Ridge knew what he would see when he came here yet he is shocked. She calls him a hypocrite and an ape. He makes her sick. No matter how much Doomwatch try to interfere, the experiment will be completed. She herself has been implanted with animal cells – fertilised in the usual way. She is pregnant with a man-animal hybrid; if they had met three months earlier, Ridge might have been its father.

Sam Billings is up before the tribunal, headed by an erudite and polite chairman, and cross-questioned by a nuclear physicist, Dr Warren. Air Commodore Parks is next to be called and wastes no time in concluding that Quist was unbalanced, pointing out Ridge's accusation of overcompensation for his part in the Manhattan Project. Quist discusses this with Anne and remembers the way the scientists tried to stop it from being dropped upon a city. He also recalls his wife's slow death and her last words to him: 'Start again, put it right.' This discussion is helping him formulate his belief in why he tackled the Byfield bomb. At the end of the day, the Minister is convinced that Quist's goose is cooked – 'Positively overdone!'

Ridge returns to London to face the tribunal and quickly cottons on that Warren believes Quist should have left the bomb to the experts and that a nuclear explosion had never been a possibility. He strongly defends Quist, calling him a morally courageous man without whom there would be no Doomwatch. Before Quist goes in, gloomy at the thought of Ridge's evidence after their recent confrontation, Anne Tarrant wishes him luck, repeating the last words of his late wife, and agrees to see him again – but this time not in a professional capacity. Soon Quist is locking swords with Dr Warren over the wisdom of his actions. Warren, like Parks, believes in the fool proof nature of the bomb's design, but Quist skilfully traps him into being unable to define what would constitute a safe dose of radiation if Wren had not dismantled the detonators. Quist wins the tribunal's clearance, and the Minister congratulates him with a forced degree of jolliness.

Back at the Doomwatch office, Quist stops Ridge from clearing out his desk and offers his hand in thanks. Ridge accepts. He takes down Toby's picture and puts it in his drawer.

Behind the Story
It is hardly surprising that one of the most famous and talked-about episodes from Doomwatch's first series had to be tackled head-on at the start of the second. There was no way it could just be business as usual without addressing the fallout from 'Survival Code', although a different fallout from the type Doctor Quist had been trying to prevent. The tensions between Quist and Ridge had to be brought to a head in the episode and dealt with, but it is a pity that the simmering character clashes throughout the first series would never be experienced again in such sharp relief. 'You Killed Toby Wren' is the first story where the needs of the characters dictate the plot rather than allowing them to react naturally to any given situation. By the end of the episode all is well, and the series can continue as before – almost. Because of the chaotic nature of the script commissioning process, it was not possible to string out the tension and lead up to an inquiry later in the series in the way that, for example, the 1990s police series *Between the Lines* serialised an impending inquiry over many episodes, showing the pressures on the protagonists while they worked on each week's case.

As well as dealing with the death of Toby Wren, the episode also had to introduce two new characters: Geoffrey Hardcastle, the Toby Wren substitute, and Barbara Mason, Pat Hunnisett's replacement. It also reacquaints us with the surviving regulars in ascending order of importance – first Bradley, then Ridge and finally Quist. Terence Dudley also wanted to sow the seeds for his vision of *Doomwatch* now that he had (by the time of recording) been rid of his turbulent priest and archbishop in the form of Kit Pedler and Gerry Davis. It also gave Dudley a chance to introduce yet another new Minister, albeit one played by an actor who had already appeared in the series in a similar role. (For more on this, see later in the book.)

This Minister wants to get rid of Quist but sees the value of Doomwatch. This new Minister's Permanent Secretary and adviser, known only as 'Harry', is a warm, positive man as opposed to the favoured Pedler and Davis slimy type seen in 'Project Sahara'. This is in contrast to the return of Air Commodore Parks, who is definitely sticking the knife into the man he so despised in 'Survival Code'. In his testimony he does not mention that the bomb had been tampered with, nor that when his unit arrived they would have had no chance to deactivate it in the thirty seconds or so remaining. Parks and his complacency are clear in this episode. The two unnamed bomb disposal experts Parks sent in were already dead men.

Yet again Terence Dudley takes up the theme of negative emotions, especially guilt, as a source of self-indulgence. We first heard it in 'Tomorrow, the Rat', then 'Spectre at the Feast' (described as 'a cosy sense of guilt' on both occasions) and here it is again. In those two episodes it is either a senior civil servant or a businessman accusing a scientist of indulging in guilt, but here it is Quist who bears the brunt as he comes to terms with Toby's death. This follows on from 'Survival Code', in which Ridge accused Quist of satisfying his own need for self-recrimination over the Manhattan Project. After Ridge has had his own morbid indulgences sharply exposed at the experimental lab, he understands the driving emotions behind Quist's actions a little better and realises that he was right to try and defuse the bomb at all costs. Even Geoff Hardcastle, barely introduced, doesn't escape: Quist suggests that his squeamishness over the work at the Norfolk labs is indulgence. A very clear parallel is drawn between Ridge and Quist when you consider that in the Dudley written third series opener 'Fire and Brimstone' (and also mentioned by Wren almost jokingly in 'Friday's Child'), Ridge claims to have killed three men in the service of the State to protect millions during his time in MI6; Quist is made to see that the three lives lost at Byfield Regis indirectly but potentially saved three million.

The Manhattan Project
At last we hear Quist talk a little more about what he contributed towards the Manhattan Project, but it is enough. The horror the scientists felt at Los Alamos at what they had achieved is fact. The scientists, like Quist, saw the Bomb as a deterrent. The initial Trinity test blast was enough to make them realise the implications. They had made it, but it wouldn't be their decision to use it. It was a time of total war. Germany had only surrendered after

being reduced to rubble, mile by mile, street by street, and the Japanese soldier had an even greater dose of tenacity. The taking of a single island could result in massive casualties. Anne Tarrant's assertion that the Bomb saved more lives than it took is certainly one that was held by many at the time, and for those who remembered the war, including Terence Dudley, the argument was seen in those terms. Saving American lives was what mattered to President Truman. There was even a financial argument. $2 billion had been spent on the project. In his book *The Bomb: A History of Hell on Earth*, Gerard J DeGroot points out that if the Bomb was not used by the end of the conflict, 'critics would argue that Los Alamos had simply been a refuge for liberal intellectuals keen to escape the war. Furthermore, every parent of every GI soldier, or airman killed after the Trinity Test would argue that his or her son had died in vain.' At the time, no-one saw the difference between this and 20,000 tons of TNT. Conventional raids on Dresden and Tokyo 'rivalled anything that an atom bomb promised to achieve'. Tarrant believes that the Bomb will never be used again. That is very sweet of her.

The Biology
The sub-plot of the animal-human hybrid is simply there to show Ridge indulging his own sense of morbidity. Ever since 'Friday's Child', the chemist has displayed a queasiness over extreme biology. His own lack of judgement displayed in that story also comes to the fore here, though this is hardly surprising because he is grieving over Toby's death. He also made his own feelings on genetic engineering quite plain in 'Tomorrow, the Rat'. Judith Lennox is very, very different to Mary Bryant, and he doesn't realise until it is too late that she has become an experiment herself. Unsurprisingly, it completely stuns him to learn that she is utterly willing to give birth to a something part human, part animal.

One wonders just how we are meant to experience the hybrid sub-plot. The way it has been written and directed suggests that long-term viewers were meant to be reminded of 'Friday's Child', which had been a highly successful. The unfortunately less-than-chilling shots of a chicken with two tiny human heads and a bald monkey are possibly supposed to make us feel the same way as the eight-month-old foetus in an artificial womb did nearly a year before.

New Scientist reckoned that it was Henry Harris' research into hybrid cells that inspired the science fact-fiction of this episode, but his work on such things was seen as a step towards curing diseases at a genetic level. 'Cells of individuals or foetuses affected with a genetic disease could be grown outside the body, hybridised with chicken cells and, after having rapidly lost all except the complementing chicken gene, they would be re-implanted into the diseased individual where they might be gradually replace the affected original cells.' It could even regenerate an entire organ. Are we as viewers meant to think it is worthwhile in pure research terms if it helps the problem of infertility, or is this research meant to be seen as an indulgence in an overpopulated world?

Dudley presents Professor Hayland neither as a Frankenstein nor a Nazi-esque scientist but as a sweet little old man. Perhaps Dudley is pointing the finger at Pedler, whose moral message is seen in terms of black and white and whose antagonists, in Dudley's eyes, are fools and villains. Hayland would not have been written as sympathetically in the first series. And in another triumph for Women's Lib, Dr Judith Lennox is strong and dedicated to her work to the point where she is three months pregnant by it. In a delicious scene she twists the knife into Ridge's metaphorical guts and gets no comeuppance from it. Mary Bryant's revenge?

Production
Script Development
Precisely when Terence Dudley wrote the script is unknown. It may have been at any point during the spring or early summer of 1970. He agreed to his £600 fee for writing the episode, originally called 'He Killed Toby Wren', on 4 September 1970, but that was when rehearsals began. The memo was sent to Gerry Davis, but whether all Davis did was just look at the script is anyone's guess, considering he does not get his usual script-editing credit at the end of the episode (but he does in the camera script). All the details of Quist's family background came from the original format document and the subsequently embellished publicity notes for the first series. The details of the Manhattan Project scientists came from history. The political and international themes expressed here would be developed by Martin Worth for his mid-series episode 'Flight Into Yesterday'.

The two-headed chicken was in the script, but the bald monkey was not. Dudley's first idea was to have a dog whose front legs were human arms and hands. Doctor Warren was not named in the script; he was just written as 'Scientist'.

Casting
Edward Underdown and Robert Gillespie would make appearances as semi-regular characters in the third series of *Survivors* in 1977. Underdown had just recently appeared as Spike Milligan's side kick in his comedy series *Oh In Colour*. Macdonald Hobley was a writer and a presenter as well as an actor. Robert Cartland is listed in the PasB sheets as making an appearance in the story, but he isn't credited on screen. Tommy Godfrey and Donald Morley return from *Survival Code*, six months after it had been taped, and, of course, John Barron makes his second barn-storming

appearance in the series. Graham Leaman was disabled and genuinely needed the crutches seen in the episode. He was a friend of Terence Dudley, who liked to use him whenever possible. He would later play Ridge's dying father in 'Cause of Death'. Elizabeth Weaver was cast as Dr Anne Tarrant in what could be seen as her audition for the third series. One notable appearance she had made for the BBC was in a 1962 four-part serial, *The Monsters*, where she played newly-wed Felicity Brent, honeymooning by the banks of Loch Ness.

Studio
'You Killed Toby Wren' was the seventh episode in production order. It was taped in TC4 on Friday, 16 October 1970 between 7.30 pm and 10 pm, and came after a two week break for those in the cast who weren't required for 'The Islanders' location filming. The episode was shot entirely in the studio except for a 3' 55" extract taken from the closing minutes of 'Survival Code'. For its inclusion, Pedler and Davis were offered a once-for-all fee of £22 on 21 October, which was approved six days later.

Music
There were a few tracks of drum beats used in the episode, but their source is unknown, as is the piano playing away in the background of the scenes set inside the Feathers pub and the restaurant.

Editing
The editing was done on Monday, 19 October between 10.30 am and 1.30 pm at TVR, 9/11 Windmill Street, London W1. Nothing appears to have been cut from the programme.

Performances
John Paul puts in a strong performance, whether it's losing his temper, giving long and reflective stares into the distance as a drum tolls in the background (a motif that will be repeated with Ridge when the implication of his overreaction sinks in), quietly and authoritatively standing up to the tribunal or dissolving into tears. Simon Oates' performance in this episode is equally outstanding. Interviewed in 1992 by Anthony Brown for *TV Zone* magazine, Oates explained how he was able to use his own feelings about Robert Powell's departure and visualise how he would have felt about him being blown up. The action of throwing the chair across the room was ad-libbed. He received a lot of mail from viewers blaming him for the death of Toby Wren, but quite a few enquired as to what became of the large picture of Wren that he used to prick Quist's conscience. 'I'm afraid there's only one copy of the picture', he told readers of the *Radio Times*, 'and as he's a mate of mine, I'm hanging on to it!'

Vivien Sherrard pulls off some comic moments rather nicely in her first appearance as Barbara Mason, especially in her first scene with Quist. Vivien S Smith recalls: 'The reasons why the cast would have adrenalin pumping on studio days included the fact that we knew that retakes cost time and money, and should be avoided if possible. So it was with alarm that I received the news that my very first scene with Quist had to be done all over again! Thankfully, I was quickly assured that it was something technical that had gone wrong. Still, I had to summon up the necessary mood, and try to do exactly what I had just done. It was slightly nerve-wracking, but happily it went just as well the second time around.'

The viewers wouldn't see Barbara again until the fourth episode. Terence Dudley wrote to the actor a few days after the studio session as it became clear she wasn't going to be needed for 'The Inquest' in a few month's time: 'First, profound and grateful thanks for that really super performance as Barbara. As profound an apology for your not being included in No 10. That this is through no fault of mine is quite apparent in the fact you are currently my favourite actress. Do not agonize!!! There will be goodies to come and, even if I fail you, that performance can do you nothing but tremendous good.'

Vivien S Smith: 'I've watched the entire second series recently and said out loud "Where's Barbara Mason? She must be on holiday." It is a surprise to me that I am missing from so many of the episodes. I do recall being disappointed but not desperately so when not included in an episode, but also recall this happening only now and then, not so many times in a row. Naturally I wished my part had been bigger in series two.

'As a director Terry was calm, letting the actors interpret their characters as they saw fit, and intervening as little as possible. In other words, he was an actor's director. Frank [Vivien's husband] and I watched *All Creatures Great and Small* later in the 1970's, and you could always tell which episodes Terry had directed, and better still written, because they were noticeably "tighter", and all in all superior to others. Once when he and I were having a drink by ourselves, baring our souls to a certain extent, he talked about the intense 24/7 pressure of his work on *Doomwatch*. I liked him very much, and of course was forever grateful that he trusted me with the gift of Barbara.'

Reaction

With expectations high and a nice gaudy *Radio Times* cover promoting *Doomwatch*'s return, ten and a half million viewers tuned in on Monday night to see the start of the new series. Nancy Banks-Smith, writing in the *Guardian* two days later on 16 December, appeared to be pleased to see *Doomwatch* back but described the writing as punchy yet pedestrian, the plot neat and gaudy. She noticed how at least six of the characters sported either broken limbs, jaws, hands, or were pregnant, on crutches or got blown up. However, she was never quite sure where fact ended and fiction began, and the grafting of inspired guesswork onto scientific reality was 'so neat ... The production does it proud and as thrillers go, it goes with a bang. It aims to be and is primarily entertainment, and considering the subject matter, how's that for horror?'

An anonymous reviewer writing the following Saturday for the *Evening Express* called 'Watchdog' had feared that 'Toby's death might have "killed" the series, but I was proved wrong. The two newcomers look like fitting in well and John Nolan seems a natural successor for Toby. *Doomwatch* has a lot to live up to after the last series, but it has started off on the right note. I hope the standard will be kept up.' Frances Horsborough, writing in the *Press and Journal*, wasn't terribly keen on Barbara Mason, and thought the episode 'exploded into life' as accusations of guilt for Toby's death were flung at Quist. She thought that it had been a mistake to have two plots running in the episode, wishing it had focused more on the inquest since 'to probe a lot deeper into the psyche of Dr Quist himself ... I wanted to know a lot more about the motives of the gentle, crippled scientist who had created the hybrid monsters.' It remained to be seen 'whether John Nolan ... will be able to develop a character solid enough to register effectively in competition with the commanding personas of Ridge and Quist.' The review was head-lined 'Toby Wren meets his Doom-Twice'.

Programme Review Board
The Programme Review Board also gave it the thumbs-up, especially Andrew Osborn, who felt that if the events of 'Survival Code' had to be revisited, then this episode did it remarkably well. There were more comments of approval for John Paul's 'improving' performance, leaving it to Shaun Sutton to remind them that he had grown in confidence during the last series.

2.02
Invasion

Written by Martin Worth
Directed by Jonathan Alwyn
Designed by Jeremy Davies
Transmitted: Monday, 21 December 1970 at 9.53 pm Duration: 49' 06"

Cast
Soldier (Simon Cain), Dr Wilson (Barrie Cookson), Reggie (Leslie Meadows), Dave (David Lincoln), Joe Bates (Victor Platt), Sandy Larch (Arthur Brough), Sergeant Harris (Anthony Sagar), Tom Hedley (Peter Welch), Mrs Smith (Sheila Raynor), Sergeant (Bill Straiton), Mrs Hunter (Joyce Windsor), Child – Wendy Hunter (Kim Butcher), Major Sims (Geoffrey Palmer), Duncan (Michael Elwyn).

Also appearing:
Extras on location: John Price, John Avison, Paul Morrell, Johnny Stewart, Elizabeth Blyth, Bernard Atha, Ted Carroll, Paul Bryant, Vince Ingham, Ernie Tomasso, Anna Gybern, Katie Mariott, Maureen Fitzpatrick, Irene Owen, Poppy Lane, Ken Hastwell, Adam Kurakin, Dennis Mawn, Paul Simon, Michael Facer, Michael Atha, Denis Huckerby, Silvo Podkrajsek, Paul Reed, Jean Tomasso, Gayle Mitchell, Joan Hall, Sylvia Stoker, Christine Buckley, Josephine Antoss.

Extras in studio: Peter Roy, Albert Cranston, Wally Goodman, Peter Morton, Robin Burne, Crawford Lyall, Iris Fry, Margot Boht, Archie Wilson, Bert Sims, Ron Hickey, Paul Barton, Roy Pearce, Maureen Bell, Jean Craig.

The BBC thanks the 7 Field Squadron, Royal Engineers for their co-operation.

Technical Credits
Production Assistant: Christina McMillan. Assistant Floor Manager: Michael McDermott. Director's Assistant: Gwen Willson. Floor Assistant: Donald Ross. Film Cameraman: John Baker. Film Sound Recordist: Doug Mawson. Film Editor: Martin Winterton.
Costume Supervisor: Mary Husband. Make-up Supervisor: Pat Hughes.
Studio Lighting: Jimmy Purdie. TM2: Reg Hutchings. Vision Mixer: Jim Stephens.
Sound Supervisor: John Holmes. Grams Operator: Gerry Borrows.
Crew: 19.

Radio Times
Doomwatch man held. Dr John Ridge, 38, a member of the controversial Doomwatch team was held for 24 hours today by a 'mystery' Army unit in a remote Yorkshire village. 'Are you saying that anything that comes up out of the ground in this place is shot?'

The Story
'There's only one thing wrong with that place: that it exists.' – Quist

On a wet day in Yorkshire, Geoff Hardcastle and Ridge send two young potholers – brothers Dave and Reggie – into an underground river system in a cave to collect nitrate samples. Ridge stays in the Jeep whilst Geoff waits for the lads to return. But they don't. Back at their base in the Devonshire Hotel, the Doomwatch team wait for news as a rescue party, headed by the local policeman Sergeant Harris and farmer Tom Hedley, returns unsuccessful. The caves are now awash with rainwater. Geoff studies a map of the area and notices a fault line – possibly another cave mouth that the lads could emerge from – close to a big house.

The house, Wensdale Grange, appears to be occupied by the army. Surrounded by a high wall and barbed wire, it is patrolled by unfriendly soldiers – in Wellington boots. Nevertheless, Ridge and Hardcastle approach the entrance checkpoint to explain their purpose, but they are rebuffed until Major Sims, who has been reading a report on the missing boys, calls them to his office – but only after they take off their shoes. Sims asks Ridge if this is a pretext to gain entry into a top security establishment and they hear gunfire, which Sims dismisses as a pot shot at a rabbit. Back at the hotel, Ridge telephones Duncan, the Minister's Parliamentary Private Secretary, who tells them to stay away from the Grange. Elderly local Sandy Larch tells Geoff the history of the house and its reputation. Taken over during the war as a research centre, it was suddenly closed down. Deaths occurred, and no-one was allowed to see the bodies. The Grange is haunted by ghosts, dressed head to foot in silver …

Geoff is convinced that the boys are inside the house, held prisoner. Ridge decides to break in that night but is promptly captured. Quist is now called in to see Duncan, who is cross about the incident but tells him the story. A germ-warfare virus was being developed for defensive purposes, and five years ago it escaped into the house, which is now totally sealed off. Any animals in the grounds are shot and their carcasses examined for any trace of the virus. Soon Quist, Geoff and Ridge examine the precautions of the Grange with Major Sims and Doctor Wilson, their chief scientist. They assure him the boys have not turned up. Quist wants to see inside the house to be on the safe side. Wearing protective overalls and respirators they explore the inside of the house, thick in dust and cobwebs.

Geoff notices an uncorked bottle of wine, but its significance does not register until later.

The boys turn up outside their grandmother's shop and claim they got lost in the caves, only emerging this morning on Hedley's lands. Geoff finds Reggie and gets him to swear they hadn't been inside the house. The village folk are more amused than angry. Ridge asks their grandmother at her shop if she thinks they are telling the truth, and as he leaves he notices some diamond-shaped glass objects a little girl had been playing with. Later, Quist agrees that the security precautions are as tight as they can be, but Geoff is bothered by the bottle he saw: the remaining wine inside should have had a fungus on it by now. They go straight back to the Grange and find a loose flagstone in the cellar leading to the caves, and Ridge sees a broken chandelier – the origin of those diamond-shaped pieces of glass. A pair of flintlock pistols are also missing from a display on the wall.

The boys had indeed been inside the house, and they are out for the evening, hoping to sell the pistols to an antiques dealer. Quist tells Sergeant Harris the situation. The vaccine is on its way but what chances have the boys got? Very little, as they are soon found in a field, dying, if not dead already. Sims' men are now slaughtering cattle in the field where the boys first emerged. The townsfolk gather for the vaccinations, but the situation has worsened. Quist quietly tells them that the village has to be evacuated and all livestock destroyed. Sandy Larch realises this also means his beloved pet dog. Quist is unable to comfort Bates the landlord or tell him if they will ever be able to return home. Coach after coach arrives to take the 650 inhabitants of the village away. A special army unit moves in and wastes no time in sterilising the village with sprays and shooting animals. When the last of the coaches leaves the perimeter of the village, a sign is placed in the middle of the road: EXTREME DANGER KEEP OUT.

Behind the Story

During the Second World War, British stately homes were requisitioned as places for the wounded to recover or were otherwise used to aid the war effort. These places were usually out of the way from cities and industrial centres, which were more likely to be the targets of air raids. For Wensdale Grange to become a centre for biological weapons research is no surprise then.

Anthrax Island

Quist mentions Anthrax Island. The laboratories at Porton Down experimented with anthrax as a potential biological weapon during the Second World War, and the Scottish island of Gruinard, uninhabited except for sheep and rabbits, was used as their test site. A diseased carcass was washed up on Scottish shores in 1943, but that is the only 'leak' from the place that we know about. Anthrax Island came back to haunt the UK Government in 1981, when persons unknown removed earth from the island and placed buckets of contaminated soil close to Porton Down. Another quantity was sent to the Conservative Party Conference in the same year; this did not contain spores, although the soil was similar. Newspapers and TV and radio stations received statements from a group calling themselves Operation Dark Harvest, demanding action to be taken over the island. Anthrax Island remained out-of-bounds until it was declared safe in 1990.

The episode conveys a sense of community. For a whole population of 650 to be uprooted in the space of an evening must have been a traumatic experience for them all. It happened in real life, although not as quickly. In 1943 the Wiltshire village of Imber was requisitioned by the military for use as a training ground, its inhabitants evicted in forty-seven days. Their homes were to be used in practice manoeuvres by American soldiers before the Allied invasion of France. The villagers saw it as their patriotic duty to give up their community; they also thought that they would be back inside six months. Today the village is still in the hands of the Army. The church is still in use as a graveyard and for services at least once a year. The first person to be buried there after the evacuation was the village blacksmith, who died from a broken heart. By coincidence (or perhaps not), the church and woods were used as a location for *Survivors*, also produced by Terence Dudley, in a 1977 episode called 'Sparks'.

Quist's attitude

Quist is astonishing in this episode. He spends some of the episode angry that Wensdale Grange and its problem exist in the first place, insisting on inspecting their safeguards, their records and the house itself. He admits that their precautions are as tight as they can be, but by sheer chance their procedures have been breached via a hitherto unknown well, which leads down to the honeycomb of underground caves and tunnels beneath. Quist can't possibly be responsible for the sheer chance that leads to the tragedy. But the guilt he may feel manifests itself almost as hostility to the villagers – he is helpless. He cannot look Tom Hedley in the eye when he hears of the slaughter of his cattle; in an almost sarcastic tone, he repeats to the landlord of the Devonshire Hotel the mantra that the army or the government might repeat to an outraged citizen. He is probably rehearsing what Duncan will say to him.

Official stonewalling, first from Major Sims and then Duncan, contributes to the disaster. No-one in the village knew the cancer in their midst, just vague rumours and tales dismissed by those of a more rational bent. Ridge would not, as Quist points out, have gone breaking and entering had he received greater co-operation and had his request taken more seriously. Complacency again rears its ugly head in the Armed Services; Byfield Regis had been bad enough.

Production
Scripting Development
'Lonely the House' was one of the few acceptable storylines that Kit Pedler and Gerry Davis wrote for the second series that made it to script then screen. It was given over to Martin Worth to write up on 14 April and needed on 1 May. It was the fourth script commissioned for the series. In an interview for *Time Screen* magazine by Andrew Pixley in 1991, Worth recalled that the initial idea was that the village had been used by the army for germ warfare experiments, and, after they moved out, they left behind something hazardous in the water supply. The villagers return to their homes only to discover that there was an appalling toxin left over from some experiment.

A set piece for the episode had to be an evacuation at the end. Interviewed for this book, Martin Worth recalled 'I said to Gerry, "Look, this is what would happen in real life. We've got to have the villagers evacuated and we've got to have soldiers in there doing it." I didn't want to proceed too much until I knew they had co-operation from the army. If they hadn't, they couldn't have had actors dressed up, except for the speaking parts. But we needed real soldiers going door to door.'

Filming
Jonathan Alwyn would direct this episode. The location of Grassington was suggested by Terence Dudley, who had used the place for an episode of *Cluff*. Army co-operation came in the form of a squadron from the Royal Engineers. The filming in Yorkshire seems to have started on Monday, 29 June and carried on until Friday. Terence Dudley stayed with the shoot for the first two days, and Simon Oates did not start filming until 30 June, with some overtime required on 3 July. A portion of the budget seems to have been charged to the project number for 'The Iron Doctor'.

The Invasion of Grassington
Martin Worth feels that the title of 'Invasion' was perhaps an apt one, considering what happened to the locals when the BBC turned up. Jonathan Alwyn remembers 'It was quite a moment when the army arrived. We had to do that at six o'clock in the morning. We couldn't close every shop in the place. We recruited half the town to be 'evacuated' in the coaches anyway. They were all very co- operative. It was good fun to do as well. I enjoyed doing this the most.' On the day the Army invaded, local news programme *Look North* came down and filmed a report.

Former resident Elizabeth Roe remembers 'At the time I was running my own business (mobile hairdressing), so I had to work around the filming. The closure of parts of the village caused a lot of confusion. I at the time (late teens) felt Simon Oates was the "bees knees", a real hunk – so did a lot of the local girls! Myself and my mother, Dorothy Haigh, lived at 30 Main Street, which at that time was about halfway between the Square and the Town Hall. We were told (not asked) to stay indoors whilst the filming of the tanks coming down Main Street took place. I remember peeping out of the window at them. I do remember feeling that the town had gone to sleep; people didn't want to talk about the filming. I have a faint memory of *Girl on a Motorbike* with Diana Dors, and an episode of *Cluff* had been filmed here, but to the majority of people it was a new thing. I also remember the local fruit shop owner (now deceased) had a letter published in the *Craven Herald* saying, "It is wrong the way the film company and the army have taken over the village!"'

The Caves and House

Height's Cave was the location used for the cave mouth. This was west of Grassington and owned by Bell Bank Farm on Malham Moor. The interior of the cave was Stumps Cross Caverns, between Grassington and Pately Bridge. Jonathan Alwyn: 'It was a tourist attraction, and they kept it clear for us for a couple of hours whilst we went in and shot in the cave. John Nolan discovered he didn't particularly enjoy pot-holing during his filming. The story of two missing potholers may have been a distressing subject for the locals of Grassington: In 1967, barely three miles away at the Mossdale Caverns, six young potholers were drowned. The caves are sealed off to this day.

The main street in nearby Hebden was used for when the policeman discovers the dying teenagers after they had found the antique shop was closed. The only bit of film in the episode that wasn't specially shot came from the BBC library. This was a brief clip of a fairground.

The lonely house itself, Wensdale Grange, is in reality Scale House on the Grassington Road near Rylstone. Local resident Mark Cooper describes it as 'somewhat dour and imposing, with three towers surrounded by woodland, on the road from Skipton to Grassington. Although the outbuildings and servants' wing were redeveloped as separate residences in the last ten years, the main part of the house still retains its original features and layout and is likely to be immediately recognisable.' Another local, Paddy Dorrington, remembers 'The house is quite eerie and in trees, but I remember seeing the floodlights there when they were filming.'

Despite the gloomy weather, it was a memorable shoot for the director. 'I made a lot of friends up there, and myself and the family went up there several times for holidays. It opened up a whole corner of England I hadn't known before. So I have happy memories of that particular episode, despite the weather. The irony was the weather was absolutely terrible, but, on the day I had to drive back to London, the clouds all cleared and it was the first really glorious day of summer.'

Rehearsals
None of the guest cast used on location were needed for the studio recording. Playing the Sergeant was Bill Straiton, who had also appeared briefly in 'Friday's Child' as a policeman. Sheila Raynor, here playing Mrs Smith, had also previously appeared in the first series, in 'The Red Sky' as Mrs Knott. Michael Elwyn returned for his second *Doomwatch*, to play a part which was described in the script simply as the Minister's PPS. Playing Sandy Larch was Arthur Brough. He was but one of three future regulars from the BBC's famous comedy *Are You Being Served?* to make an appearance in the second series. Geoffrey Palmer was a few years away from being claimed as the property of the BBC's light entertainment department. He had recently played a politician killed by an artificial virus in *Doctor Who and the Silurians*. Anthony Sagar was frequently cast as policemen and made regular appearances in the *Carry On* films. Victor Platt passed away in 2017 at the grand age of 96, having long since retired from the business and concentrating on sculpting under his real name William Elphick.

Studio
'Invasion' was the third production of the series and was recorded in TC1 on Tuesday, 25 August 1970. The camera rehearsals the day before ran into overtime, but the actual recording did not. The schedule was slightly more complicated than usual because of some time-consuming costume changes. The first two scenes recorded were those of Quist, Wilson, Ridge, Geoff and a soldier exploring the interior of the house in their protective garb. Ridge and Geoff were supposed to call out for Reggie and Dave, but this was dropped. The rest of the episode was recorded in scene order.

Music
Jonathan Alwyn used a great deal of orchestral library music for the episode, giving it a distinctly melodramatic feel. Rather handily, the LP number and band track used were recorded on the camera script. Six tracks came from two Hudson De Wolfe LPs, composed by Spencer Nakin and performed by the International Studio Orchestra. From *Fairies and Witches* (DW 3120). 'A Sail on the Lake' was used after the titles, 'The Witch in Her Cave' was used for our first glimpse of Wensdale Grange.

From *Mood Impressions* (DW 3048), 'Lurking Death' backed Ridge's break into the Grange while 'Spellbound' was used during the first search inside the house and part of the second. 'Murderer Walks Thro' The Night' was also used for the second search. 'Expectation' was used when Ridge finds the chandelier pieces.

One other track – version 'b' of 'Looks Like Trouble' – was composed by Syd Dale and came from *Tension and Suspense* (KPM 1018). This played over the shots of the dying Reggie and Dave.

Editing

The editing was done on Thursday, 27 August and saw only one small scene removed. This was Scene 18, set inside the shop. Mrs Hunter tells Sergeant Harris that she does not want to talk to the press. They should be making themselves useful on the moor digging, she says. Although her grandsons have been without food for two days, when they return she'll give them such a good belting they'll wish they stayed in the caves. The next scene was of the elderly man, Bert, watching a 'soldier' being dropped off outside the pub – actually Ridge. The next scene was of the elderly man, Bert, watching a 'soldier' being dropped off outside the pub – actually Ridge.

Reaction

The episode received the highest ratings the programme would ever achieve – thirteen and a half million viewers. The *Evening Times* liked it. Its reviewer thought *Doomwatch* always had a strong plot and wondered if you could call the team 'Quistlings' without being offensive.

Programme Review Board

As usual, the Board tried to find some reason why so many people would want to watch the programme. This time they thought it was a strong inheritance from *Steptoe and Son*, which got over twenty million viewers. However, the episode was criticised by one member of the Board for being slightly overplayed and inaccurate in its scientific detail. Andrew Osborn noted this, although precisely what the error was is unrecorded. The episode is very light in scientific detail.

UK Gold Butchery

This was another episode that UK Gold trimmed upon its only transmission, although not as severely as 'The Battery People'. They cut out a small film sequence where Ridge and Geoff are escorted through the check-point and told to take off their boots, which, after a little protest, they do. A film sequence of Quist about to put on his protective headgear outside of the Grange was also removed.

And ...

In early March 2018, the residents of Salisbury in Wiltshire were alarmed to see homes and businesses sealed off because a suspected nerve gas agent had been used in an alleged assassination attempt on a Russian father and his visiting daughter ... At time of writing, these places were still sealed off, and areas cordoned. Life goes on.

As for Scale House, near Grassington: to the locals it is still known as the *Doomwatch* House.

2.03
The Islanders

Written by Louis Marks
Directed by Jonathan Alwyn
Designed by Stanley Morris
Transmitted: Monday, 4 January 1971 at 9.20 pm Duration: 49′ 25″

Cast
Thomas (George A Cooper), Inspector (Charles Rea), Joan (Shelagh Fraser), Alice (Geraldine Sherman), Mullery (Geoffrey Chater), Dr Somerville (Robert Sansom), Busby (George Waring), Miss Marshall (Rachel Treadgold), Islanders (Geoffrey Davion, Ian Mackenzie, Guy Grahame). Guest Star: Isaac (David Buck).

Also appearing: Nurses (Linda Oxer, Jill Goldston).

Islanders on location and in studio (Iris Fry, Betty Cameron, Jane Elliot, Betty Goulding, Rosemary Banks, Bella Emberg, Joe Santo, Charles Saynor, Denis Harward, Reg Cranfield, Alex Hood, Michael Lomax, John Scott Martin), Islanders on location only (Barry Munford, H M Soar, George Waddington, Claud Phillips, Eric Woodcock, Fuzz Groves, David Badcock, Alex Morton, Steve Kirby, Alan Crisp, Jane Elliot, Jean Morton, Jimmy Mac, Steve Ismay, Barry Kennington, Anthony Buckthorne, Willy Bowman, Bill Matthews, Leslie Bates, Maureen Nelson, Leslie Weeks), Islanders in studio only (Anthony Powell, Peter Jolly, Rodney Cardiff, Eric Kent, Steve Kelly, Lee Warren, Derek Glyn Percy).

Technical Credits
Production Assistant: Christina McMillan. Assistant Floor Manager: Alistair Clarke. Director's Assistant: Gwen Willson. Floor Assistant: Nicholas Wood.
Film Cameraman: Bill Matthews. Film Sound Recordists: Bill Wild, Alan Cooper. Film Editor: Christopher Rowlands.
Costume Supervisor: Mary Husband. Make-up Supervisor: Pat Hughes.
Studio Lighting: Dave Sydenham. TM2: Peter Booth. Vision Mixer: John Gorman.
Studio Sound: John Holmes. Grams Operator: Gerry Borrows.
Crew: 19.

Radio Times
Islanders flee. The 200 inhabitants of the tiny Pacific Island of St Simon are to be evacuated. The British Government believes that this mini-protectorate is in grave danger following recent earth tremors. A Royal Navy frigate is now steaming towards the island to bring people home ... 'You say if we go back our lives will be shortened. What if we stay here? Isn't it the same? The air you breathe here ... the food you eat ... all the chemicals ... I don't know much but aren't there poisons here too? Don't you die younger because of them?'

The Story
'We leave behind us an England of low wages and high prices, one law for the rich, another for the poor. A land of smoking factories, prisons, workhouses, and mines where children slaved ten hours a day.' – Inscription in Prentice Family Bible

Ridge is taking fingerprints inside a Nissen hut with a group of nervous and reluctant folk. Their leader, Thomas Prentice, thinks they are being treated like criminals, and a riot breaks out. Tom's son Isaac runs to a phone box and calls Quist. By the time Quist arrives, the police are already there, and Thomas is still aggressive and offended that his son appears to be on their side. Quist explains to the assembly that they had simply been running some tests. These people are islanders from a Pacific colony called St Simons, who had been living a virtually Victorian agrarian existence until earth tremors made the British government evacuate them to England. They feel lost, ignored and confused by modern living, and their community is being broken up. Isaac, for instance, is looking for a job, something that distresses his fiancée Alice.

Quist goes to see the civil servant in charge of the business, Mullery, who tells him that it is up to the islanders to decide what they want as they are not prisoners. Isaac goes for an interview with Busby, manager of a firm that mass-produces cakes. Busby thinks Isaac would be good for his company's publicity but decides to pay him the lowest wage possible. When Isaac returns he sees his father being taken away in an ambulance. He had a fever and just collapsed. Dr Somerville tells Quist about the number of influenza infections the islanders have been suffering from. They don't have the same resistance as the rest of the population because of their isolation. Isaac's mother sees it differently. Back home, life had meaning for Thomas, and he felt guilty about his people coming to England. 'What if the whole thing was just a trick?' Alice's mother also falls ill, and Quist recalls that Ridge had a cold when he did the tests.

Isaac is settling into the routine and monotonous production-line work when Busby calls him to his office, pleased with his progress. During their meeting, Isaac is allowed to take a phone call – his father is dying. Thomas' last words to him are to go home. After the funeral, Joan Prentice is angry. If they stay in this country, they will all die. They should never have left their homes.

Quist demands answers from Mullery, who explains the islanders were not as self-sufficient as they like to maintain. St Simons has also gained some strategic importance now that China has entered the nuclear arms race. It's only a matter of time before an approach is made by the US to build a base there. Quist tells him that they have a clear-cut moral issue on their hands, and sooner or later they are going to have to face it.

Isaac becomes more and more disillusioned with his mechanical work and with the noise and the chaos of London. Busby has heard about the stories of infection and is concerned over possible contamination of the cakes. Isaac storms out. He goes to see Quist at Doomwatch, where Somerville has learned that the recent deaths were helped by hepatic failure – failure of the liver – and all it needed was a dose of flu to finish them off.

Mullery tells Quist a survey team is being sent to St Simons, and Quist decides to go with them. He takes Isaac as he needs someone who knows exactly how they lived, fished and cooked. The island is rugged and beautiful, and the survey team arrive by boat in a sandy bay. Isaac shows Quist his home, its walls propped up by planks of wood. Isaac gets some fish for Quist to analyse, much to his surprise. What can fish tell him about an earth tremor? Quist soon finds something. Back in London, the results are ready. Organic mercury had been leaking from a shipwreck of 1915. It got into the fish, into the sea-birds and into the islanders. Isaac is shaken.

The islanders are being allowed to vote whether to stay or go home. Quist is appalled. At the meeting he tells them of the dangers back home, but if they stay, the government will do all it can to help. Joan says there is no choice. If they stay, with all the chemicals, pollution and noise, they will die. 'They judged us and found us wanting' remarks Quist to Ridge as the islanders vote to return. Ridge is not surprised. Isaac has left Quist a present – their family Bible. Quist reads Ridge an inscription in the front, a description of their ideals and motivations written by the first Prentice to live on St Simons. Ridge isn't impressed; such ideals have become polluted in the last hundred years. 'Everywhere except St Simons' replies Quist. Ridge shows him the front page of a newspaper: China has started long-range-missile tests in the South Pacific ...

Behind the Story
Another displaced and broken up community this week. 'The Islanders' was correctly identified by a correspondent to the *Radio Times* as being based on an incident involving the island Tristan da Cunha, a remote

British territory in the South Atlantic. In fact, it wasn't so much based on the incident, it was almost a straight forward dramatization, with a spot of mercury poisoning thrown in. This episode was the continuation of a new trend in *Doomwatch* story-telling which had began with 'Invasion', which was to reduce the scientific detail and replace it with either social commentary or discussion about pollution in general. There would also be a greater emphasis on the plight of the guest cast. But the mercury poisoning subplot gave the press one more chance to call Kit Pedler prophetic as a similar scare occurred a few months before transmission.

Tristan da Cunha
The real-life island was not actually settled until 1810, some 304 years after it was first discovered by the man after whom it is named. It was not a great success as a colony, and by 1857 nearly two-thirds of the population wanted to leave. During the Second World War it became a secret naval station, monitoring U-boat and German shipping activity. For the first time, the island was introduced to modern concepts, including money. The inhabitants lived by catching and marketing crawfish, but interestingly, a mechanised fish-canning scheme had been started in the 1950s.

Volcanic tremors began in August 1961 followed by the formation of an active fissure which emitted sulphur into the air. Fishermen reported floating rocks in the sea. The islanders were evacuated in stages to England during November, having vetoed settling in South Africa due to its apartheid laws. The islanders were heart-broken to leave their home. They ended up in a hutted army camp at Merstham in Surrey to begin acclimatizing to a new and busier way of life. For example, the children needed to be taught road accident prevention skills, and then there was the question of how they were going to survive financially. The islanders were under great public interest, and journalists watched their arrival in the country as if they were visitors from another world. 'The islanders were subdued,' reported *The Times* in November, 'clearly not in the mood to rush anything. The men wore creased suits and cloth caps, the older women were in shawls and ankle length skirts.' Employment officers began to offer unskilled jobs for those willing to try. One girl found work as a seed analyst for a seed-merchants just down the road from the camp, and they had high hopes for her. Better than a cake factory.

Problems quickly developed. What was described as a mild epidemic hit them almost as soon they arrived, and they had little resistance to our bugs, especially among the elderly. The first islander to die that November was a man named Johnny Green. He was followed by an 84 year-old matriarchal figure called Mrs Annie Swain. She had been suffering from pneumonia. A second lady, aged 66, died from bronchitis a few days later. The camp's sick bay was soon filled out with islanders suffering from colds and chest complaints. They simply could not cope with the cold climate. They were soon moved to brick-built houses at Calshot, near Southampton. There had been talk of sending them to the Shetlands, an environment similar to home, but with a far worse climate.

A delegation of islanders went to see the Parliamentary Under-Secretary of State at the Colonial Office, Nigel Fisher, who allowed a party of them to accompany a survey team that was being sent to the islands to investigate the feasibility of a permanent return. To quote from the report in *The Times*: 'they hate the British winter and dislike the way of life in Britain.' They were determined to go back even if it meant returning to the subsistence economy they had left behind fifteen years before. 'When we are living in this country,' said Mr Repetto told *The Times*, 'we cannot say we have a home of our own, but if we go back to Tristan we shall have homes of our own, and no one can drive us out. My people get much sickness here because the climate does not agree with them. It will be awful this winter getting out to work in snow and ice and we pray every night that we may go back.' In December 1962, the islanders voted whether to remain in Britain, or take their chances back home. By a majority of 148 to five the refugees voted to go home.

Experimental Samples
The islanders felt that they were being continually pestered by journalists and medical research teams, and this is where 'The Islanders' begins, with a rather unsympathetic Ridge getting turned over by a very angry mob of islanders. The team are very keen at the prospect of studying the islanders genetics, and Quist is not happy at being told to stop by Mullery, the latest civil servant to cross his path. The real-life islanders are still the studies of genetic tests. In 2003 a report appeared in the *European Journal of Human Genetics* by a team of researchers from the University of Witwatersrand in South Africa, who noted thus: 'The uniqueness of the Tristan genealogy covering a period of almost 200 years presented us with an ideal opportunity of testing the accuracy of written records with information stored in DNA.'

St Simons
The story deals with two different attitudes as expressed through the father and son of the Prentice family. Isaac wants to embrace the new world and all its challenges, being initially very impressed with a machine making 'home-baked' teacakes. His father feels he has no more purpose and does not want to be a cog in a soulless machine. Idyllically, he saw the life they led as a place where everyone had something to contribute. In their new environment, they're insignificant. He likes to be a big fish in a small pond, but, as the story unfolds, it proves to be a small pond in a

small world. Their community was set up to escape the horrors of industrialised Britain, but it cannot avoid world wars. One can almost see what many a community went through during the inexorable grind of the Industrial Revolution.

Mullery dismissively describes the islanders as wanting to get away from it all, missing the point that this is how they were brought up. Unlike the real-life islanders, the ones from St Simons are described as not being as self-sufficient as they believe, having exhausted their soil and depleted their fish stocks. The islanders are portrayed as 'dull' in the old-fashioned sense of the word – simple and uncomplicated. They all have weather-beaten, tanned faces and must be quite strong. We are supposed to be looking at early Victorian villagers. There's no sparkle to them, no idiosyncrasies. Busby's character is a marvellous contrast, complaining about production down on home-baked tea cakes – home-baked in a production line? Fantastic. He could almost be what they were getting away from in the first place; a very Dickensian task master.

From an island (if hardly paradise) to the throbbing heart of London. We see the noise of the factory starting to get to Isaac, but with the death of his father it is hardly surprising he starts to react and become aggressive with his new, frankly meaningless life. The contrast of the two lives are shown by our visit to the island, with its beautiful scenery and gentle lilting stock music contrasting with the harsh sounds of traffic in London.

Global Politics

Was the evacuation of St Simons a pretext to allow the Australians to build their base, defending themselves from the Chinese? That would have been an interesting twist. It has happened to other island communities, their homes turned into nuclear test islands. Isaac Prentice may well be the last of his line to act as leader of St Simons. The inhabitants of Tristan da Cunha had a lucky escape. Shortly after they were evacuated, the Air Ministry announced it was seeking new refuelling bases around their global territories since political developments in their former middle eastern and Indian territories has denied the Royal Air Force suitable sites. 'Although the Air Ministry said yesterday that there are no plans to build an airfield on the recently evacuated Tristan da Cunha, it could be made usable if the volcano became quiescent.'

Production
Story Development

'Desert Island' was the second script written by Louis Marks for the series and was commissioned on 11 August as episode twenty-five. Gerry Davis' name is on the commissioning slip, as is his signature, so it is likely he had a hand in its development. It was to be delivered by the end of August and was thrown into production straight away. On 7 October, having written two episodes for the programme, Louis Marks wrote to the Head of Scripts, Robin Wade, offering to contribute to other BBC series, which indeed he would do quite prolifically and successfully.

Filming

The episode had a large number of scenes set on location, and once again Jonathan Alwyn would direct. Since John Paul was needed for a lot of these scenes, the filming took place during the two-week gap between 'The Web of Fear' and 'You Killed Toby Wren'.

For Jonathan Alwyn, the biggest challenge was finding an island on which to film. 'The problem was that it was obviously meant to be loosely based on Tristan da Cunha. I first of all went to Alderney [in the Channel Islands], and there were various reasons why we couldn't shoot it there. The huge problem was trying to find anywhere where one could find absolute silence to make it really believable that there wasn't another soul alive on the place. Alderney, although very beautiful (and I had further acquaintance with it later in life when I was doing *Bergerac*), didn't work. So Terry or someone said, "Well, why not try the Scilly Islands," and we ended up shooting on the island of Bryher. But even there, would you believe, we arrived to film, and it was so quiet you could hear someone using a tractor on another island! And because of the fact we were filming there, a weather monitoring aircraft decided it would buzz round and have a look. We were still trying to get peace and quiet. We pretty much got it but it still looked very English on a remote island.'

John Paul filmed his scenes at the army camp and the cemetery on 28 and 29 September. Other filming took place in the streets around Liverpool Street Station and in a cake factory. This was the old Lyons factory in Hammersmith. Jonathan Alwyn was pleased. 'It fascinated me because in those days we had a luxury called a Fullers Cake, a very nice and tasty cake, and on this conveyor belt, the same cakes came down the conveyor belt, and the bottom bits split. The left hand lot went to Fullers and the right hand lot went to Lyons Corner House. You suddenly realised that this luxury cake was equally available in Lyons Corner House.'

The regular cast required were booked for the studio recording on 25 September 1970, but some changes were made. Alterations to the script meant that Vivien Sherrard was no longer required and Joby Blanshard now appeared in one scene. John Nolan wasn't needed, either.

Rehearsals

Arguably, 'The Islanders' contained a very impressive cast. George A Cooper played the main islander Thomas Prentice, an actor seldom out of work, and always with the same impressive and forceful accent. Villains or officious managerial types, he later played the long-running character of a care-taker in the children's drama Grange Hill. His screen wife was played by Shelagh Fraser, who would play a similar role in the *Doomwatch* movie of 1972. She had been in a 1969 episode of *The First Lady*. Isaac Prentice was played by David Buck, who already had an impressive list of television credits behind him. Geoffrey Chater is practically the go-to actor for fussy and fey civil servants, and was about to play a very dangerous one as the assassin *Callan*'s superior, Bishop. Busby's secretary Miss Marshall was played by Rachel Treadgold and she has few other credits to her name, which includes as a walk-on later in the series. Robert Sansom as Dr Somerville had been seen in 'Tomorrow, the Rat', playing Preston.

Rehearsal and Studio
By the time the camera script was prepared, the episode had a new title: 'The Land of the Lotus Eaters'. Ridge lost a line when he first sees Quist after the riot, saying he is sorry he had to be dragged down here. 'The Islanders' was the eighth production of the series and was recorded in TC3 on Tuesday, 27 October 1970. To go with the location filming, two short pieces of stock film were seen in the episode.

Music
Once again, Jonathan Alwyn went to town with music library tracks, some more melodramatic than others. Two came from *Dramatic Background* (KPM 1055): 'Disquiet' by David Lindup, which opens the episode, and Neil Richardson's 'Guide Path', for when Isaac leaves the hut.

Five nautical tracks from *Theme Suites II – Viewpoints in Orchestral Dynamics* (KPM 1040) were used, all composed by Johnny Pearson. 'Battle at Sea' was used for the islanders storming into the hut at the top of the episode (and, incidentally, also features in the *Monty Python's Flying Circus* 'Black Eagle sketch'). 'Night Watch' backed the experiments on the island. 'Prelude at Sea' can be heard on the island and also at the end of the episode, during the overlaid shots of the island as Quist reads the inscription from the Prentice family Bible. 'Tragic War Zone' backed (very quietly) the riot in the hut. Finally, 'Under Full Sail' backed the boat's approach to the island's shore.

Just one track came from a third LP: Syd Dale's 'Drama Trailer' from *Scene Setters, Fanfares and Punctuations* (KPM 1057). This can be heard when the islanders go to confront Quist and Isaac after the funeral.

Editing
Videotape editing was done on Thursday, 29 October between 12 pm and 4 pm. There were a few small cuts. When Isaac talks to Quist and Somerville, he was to have expanded on his ambitions. He plans to live in London

eventually and take evening classes. 'I want to study and get a better job.' With phones, trains and buses he can still see his parents. Quist is thinking that Isaac is probably trying to convince himself. The scene resumes with Quist wishing him luck. Scene 16 was also cut. This short sequence shows Somerville trying to get to the door of an army hut, surrounded by worried islanders, one of whom wants to know why twenty of their number aren't getting any better. Somerville wants to get to the hospital and find out for himself.

Mercury Poisoning

Before the episode was to be transmitted, the American Food and Drug Administration (FDA) issued a recall of 12.5 million cans of canned tuna. A chemistry professor in New York, Harold Egan, tested the contents of fifty cans for methyl mercury and found levels far above US food safety limits. FDA Commissioner Charles C Edwards declared that the fish were absolutely safe to eat, but nevertheless ordered them to be withdrawn from the market. 'Time and again since Rachel Carson's alarm,' read the editorial in the *Guardian* two days before Christmas 1970, 'mankind has caught itself out ... America still uses nearly as much DDT as ever. There are fly-papers being sold which appear to make people ill. And now there is mercurial fungicide. It is pollution with a purpose, but it is pollution all the same.' Britain's Minister of Agriculture, Jim Prior, did not ban the sale of tuna fish. 'We shall be getting on with this – this Doomwatch if you like to call it that', he said in a press conference. The editorial continued 'His plan [is] to keep a permanent watch on the levels of mercury and other dangerous substances in all foods.' The article added 'Most governments and most people have a tendency to look the other way when a scientist shows them something nasty is in a tin. A general doomwatch will be a safeguard.'

Kit Pedler was invited to have his say on the tuna poisoning on Radio 4's *The World at One* on 17 December 1970. By 10 January 1971 the *Guardian*'s science correspondent Gerald Leach said that the scare, 'with a suitably chilling curtain line straight out of a *Doomwatch* script, looks as if it was no more than a giant red herring'. The levels of mercury in the fish were apparently 'perfectly normal levels of mercury compounds which they had picked up from natural levels of mercury in sea water'. So, carry on dumping?

Promotion

The *Sun* seized on the coincidence when they promoted the episode with a small interview with David Buck. '"It all seemed perfectly safe, because we were dealing with a past disaster," he says in a tone of voice which says he still can't believe it. "But, shortly after we finished all this business about the tuna started to come up."'

Programme Review Board
Ten and a half million viewers tuned in on 4 January 1971, two weeks after the previous episode. The Board once again thought it had been helped by *Steptoe and Son*, which is undeniably true but still rather patronising. When the Board met on Wednesday, 6 January 1971, John Grist, Head of Current Affairs Groups for Television, thought that the scientists in the series always appeared such 'ghastly prigs' and infallible as well. Andrew Osborn assured him that in some episodes they would be shown to be fallible.

This was Jonathan Alwyn's last episode. He would later direct instalments of such series as *Brett, The Rivals of Sherlock Holmes, Callan, Public Eye, The Onedin Line, Enemy at the Door, When the Boat Comes In* and *Juliet Bravo*, which he also produced along with *Bergerac* and *By the Sword Divided*.

The Cold War Still Hurts...
When 'The Islanders' was transmitted, the population of Diego Garcia in the Indian Ocean were being forced to leave by the British government to leave to make way for a United State military base. The island group had been bought by the United Kingdom government in 1965. To favour the US/UK mutual defence strategy, the government agreed to allow the US government to build a base on the tiny island until 2016. The UK in return received a discount on their order for Polaris missiles. The small but sizeable population were intimidated into leaving. There was little, if any, compensation. The case is still in litigation. Most were repopulated in the British colony of Mauritius, but a few thousand were settled in Crawley, just outside Gatwick. In 2010, the UK declared the area around the island a protected area, which Mauritius disputes. In June 2017 the United Nations voted in favour of taking the case to the International Court of Justice.

2.04
No Room For Error

Written by Roger Parkes
Directed by Darrol Blake
Designed by Graham Oakley
Transmitted: Monday, 11 January 1971 at 9.22 pm
Duration: 48' 58"

Cast
Dr Ian Phelps (Anthony Sharp), Senior House Officer (Anthony Ainley), Professor Lewin (Angus MacKay), Minister's PPS (Michael Culver), Elliott (Norman Scace), Hilda (Freda Dowie), Gillian Blake (Sheila Grant). Guest Star: Nigel Waring (John Wood).

Also appearing
Extras in Studio: Beryl Bainbridge, Lionel Sansby, Gordon Steff, Paul Barton, Donald Groves. Julia Hand, Gilly Flower, Juliette James, Carl Bohun, Ian Elliott, Charles Rayford, Julie Lauder, Sandra Green.

Technical Credits
Director's Assistant: Adele Paul. Production Assistant: Landon Revitt.
Assistant Floor Manager: Alistair Clarke. Floor Assistant: Don Ross.
Film Cameraman: Terry Hunt. Sound Recordist: John Woodiwiss. Film Editor: Christopher Rowlands.
Costume Supervisor: Mary Husband. Make-up Supervisor: Pat Hughes.
Studio Lighting: Eric Monk. TM2: Graham Southcott. Vision Mixer: Shirley Conrad.
Studio Sound: John Holmes. Grams Operator: Gerry Borrows.

Radio Times
Children in death drug row. The government Doomwatch department are to investigate allegations that children have died after taking the new 'wonder-drug' Stellamycin. The spokesman for the manufacturers British Associated ...

'We could be on the verge of an epidemic, and absolutely no effective drugs to fight it with.'

The Story
'The space age! A shortage of vaccine and no proper cure for a thing like

typhoid.'
– Senior House Officer

A typhoid epidemic is attacking children. It is totally resistant to antibiotics except for one, Stellamycin, which has been developed by British Associated Pharmaceuticals, run by Professor Lewin. He is visited by Dr Ian Phelps, the Medical Officer for Health, who wants to know why this new wonder drug has been delayed. Lewin tells Phelps that the last thing he heard, it had been sent to Doomwatch by the Ministry of Health. Quist is welcoming the new candidate to the team, Dr Fay Chantry. He explains to her that a lot of the time they behave like civil service police, fighting bureaucracy and red tape.

Fay gets a call from her former boss, Lewin, explaining that Doomwatch seem to be delaying Stellamycin's release. Jumping in, Fay tells Quist that she will have to join Doomwatch, if only to stop the rot, and explains why. Quist discovers that the delay is at the Ministry end. He sends an embarrassed Fay back to BAP to get things moving since she helped pioneer the drug. Fay tells Lewin that they have the all clear but he is still aggrieved that she left in the first place. The reason for her departure was Nigel Waring, Lewin's colleague, who arrives and shows her around the recently built extensions.

Meanwhile, four more cases of typhoid in children are discovered. Quist hurries the Minister's PPS to clear the drug in order to fight the new outbreak, promising that Doomwatch will take full responsibility. At BAP, one of Lewin's research team, Hilda, wonders if Fay wants to come back. Lewin hopes so and gets Waring to take her to the station. During the car journey Waring tells her that he got a divorce and custody of his child and suggests dinner. He and Fay had once had a relationship after both of their marriages collapsed. Waring confesses he still loves her and Fay is interested. He tries to talk her out of Doomwatch; they're weirdo snoopers, not proper scientists. Meanwhile, Ridge is on television discussing Stellamycin, assuring the viewers that it is safe to take.

The next day Lewin and Waring prematurely celebrate the idea that Fay may be returning to BAP. But as Fay discusses things with Waring, Lewin comes in – they're having trouble with Stellamycin. The first case, Doreen Taylor, has died. Phelps blames the drug and withdraws it from use despite Fay and Waring's protests. Quist is also keen to investigate and puts Ridge onto the case. It's an all or nothing reaction – extreme side effects or none at all. Quist concludes that the cases that reacted must have previously been exposed to a low prophylactic dose of Stellamycin. Another typhoid case is reported: Waring's own daughter. He believes that only Stellamycin can save her, but Phelps won't permit it.

Ridge talks to Lewin. Following Quists line, he explains it has to be something to do with the children, but Lewin counters that they couldn't have been exposed to the drug – all their field trials and tests were scrupulously controlled. But, as Ridge points out, all the reaction cases are children in the same area as BAP. Phelps tells Ridge about the problems with cheap veal from abroad, where there is no restriction on feeding drugs to livestock. Some are given almost the full spectrum of antibiotics, and the young can develop a multi-resistant bug inside them. Phelps would be as pleased as anyone if Stellamycin could be vindicated.

Fay agrees to treat Waring's daughter herself, but refuses to be pressurised by him. Unfortunately, Waring's daughter reacts to Stellamycin, too. All these children went to the same school. Despite an initial furious outburst, the school's Head Master, Mr Elliot, agrees to help find out how the antibiotic came to be in the school's food. BAP run the tests without result, much to Waring's frustration. Hilda tries to be positive and help, remembering a feed trial with Stellamycin that they carried out on pigs at a farm. Then, the missing piece of the jigsaw – Blake's Farm, where the school gets their milk, is the same farm BAP uses for its trials there too. But there is one problem – Stellamycin couldn't have been fed to the herd by mistake because it kills adult cows.

Ridge takes Fay to the farm, which is computerised and fully automated. Gillian Blake shows them around. She tells them that she tests BAP antibiotics on the pigs and chickens and monitors the responses. In the milking shed, Ridge spots a cylinder marked BAP X-80-S. Blake explains that mastitis – a disease of the udder – can spread violently through a herd via milking tubes. As a preventative measure Blake used an antibiotic that had worked wonders on pigs and put a few scoops in the cows' udder wash at milking time from last autumn for a few weeks. X-80-S. Stellamycin. Introduced into the school's milk in minute quantities, it only caused reactions in those children treated with the drug when stricken by typhoid. Waring faces up to the fact that this was his entire fault. He left the half-empty drum at Blake's when they abandoned tests after a breakthrough. Realising that he is responsible for Doreen Taylor's death and his own daughter's possibly fatal reaction, he takes his anger, self-recrimination and bitterness out on Fay.

Quist is surprised that Fay is upset. After all, she vindicated the drug and even found a modified dose for the side cases with side effects. Ridge points out the fact of her emotional ties with Waring. Quist knew about Waring. Her affair with him was the one doubt in her security clearance, and he sent her down to BAP to wipe the slate clean. 'Take the vow?' asks Fay as she enters. 'Take it or leave it, Dr Chantry' replies Quist. 'This isn't just a job. This is Doomwatch.'

Behind the Story

Fourth episode into the new series and *Doomwatch* is beginning to feel very different indeed. And it was noticed. 'No Room for Error' deals with the wonder drug Stellamycin, and for once the scientists are making something safe and useful. The typhoid outbreak is blamed on veal, but we don't find out its precise source. It's no science fiction bug. There's no science fiction. It could almost have been an episode of *General Hospital*. There is even a romance between Nigel Waring, the developer of the wonder drug, and Dr Fay Chantry, who ends up treating his sick child. The heart begins to sink when the story switches to the inside of a car, and a long scene follows containing personal histories. Then they go to the pub for another heart to heart ... However, the origins of the story came from a much grimmer event.

Anti-biotics

In *The Quest For Gaia* Kit Pedler argued that we should restrict antibiotic use to strictly life-saving emergencies, such as after operations (which he himself readily admits had saved his life). As early as the 1950s it was realised that children were being vaccinated and given these drugs so often that they were developing very little natural resistance, especially with hygiene pushed to very strict levels. The over-use of antibiotics has become a very real issue of our times, but antibiotics did revolutionise lives. Once-fatal illnesses have now just become unpleasant periods in our lives. The first sulphonamide drug was developed in the late 1930s, but it rapidly became clear that penicillin and other antibiotics were capable of being resisted by ever-evolving bacteria. And this is what we see in this episode – a totally resistant strain of typhoid, and only the wonder drug Stellamycin can kill it.

Antibiotics also helped to revolutionise the livestock business, producing healthier animals and helping to fatten them up. Both the farming and the pharmaceutical industries are resistant to a reduction in their use, especially in America, but the European Union banned their use as growth promoters in 2003. Early concerns were raised in the 1960s both in America and Canada, as noted in Murray Bookchin's *Our Synthetic Environment*. Residues could be detected in foodstuffs even after cooking. As in this episode, antibiotics were used to treat udder infections in cattle, which increased the propagation of resistant strains of Staphylococcus aureus, which can lead to fatal cases of pneumonia.

Tees-side Tragedy

In December 1967, a gastroenteritis epidemic swept through maternity hospitals in Tees-side. By the end of the year, ten babies were dead. They would not be the last. The children had either not yet acquired a natural immunity to the bacteria or were too weak to fight it off, because they were either premature or had other conditions. Worse, the bug proved to be resistant to eight of the eleven available antibiotics. The killer organism was Eschercichia coli 0128. Researchers wondered if this was an example of transferable antibiotic resistance, where resistance is passed on genetically from one bacteria to another? This had been first identified at Tokyo University in 1961. Scientists were studying bacillary dysentery which was developing resistance to streptoycin, tetracyclines and sulphonamides. Shortly after the Tees-side incident, there was a serious outbreak in Lancashire. Twenty children died in maternity hospitals in Bootle. Parliament was given a report on the affair a few years later, and suspected that the drug resistance started on a farm where antibiotics were being given to animals.

Warnings

In August 1968, Dr Payne, director of the Public Health Laboratory in Portsmouth, warned during a symposium on factory farming that drug resistance acquired by bacteria through the use and misuse of antibiotics constituted a 'potential serious hazard to health.' He feared that should chloramphenicol [the best antibiotic used against septicaemia salmonella, typhoid and para-typhoid] be put into poultry feeds, resistant strains could nullify its effectiveness. The government had been given powers to regulate antibiotic use on farms in 1968 and a year later, the Swann committee, which had earlier raised this issue in 1965, recommended they should be banned.

When Pedler and Davis prepared their storyline in April 1970, this issue was being raised again in Parliament which proposed as an amendment to the Medicines Act that a register should be created of chemical substances which may not be used at sub-therapeutic levels in animal feeding stuffs. Later in 1970, at the Trades Union Congress annual conference, Agricultural Workers' delegate Ted Parry warned his fellow delegates of the dangers of more and more chemicals being used in farming. On 9 September the *Daily Mirror* reported the context and his words thus: 'Calves pumped full of antibiotics to make them bigger more quickly ... then rejected by breeders because they do not produce good stock. "I believe this problem associated with chemical farming requires urgent attention. We are drifting into an ever-widening sea of uncertainty which may easily create disaster or even destruction for future generations of mankind."'

A View of Doomwatch

Doomwatch itself has developed an elevated opinion of itself. Quist uses metaphors about taking the vow and has become very keen on probing into the private life of his staff in the interests of security, something which the 'Project Sahara' Quist would have baulked at. Maybe he learned from that unfortunate incident. Was the query on Fay's security clearance flagged up by the computer? He gives the Minister's PPS a hard time as well, walking out with a comedy 'D'oh!' before slamming a door out of shot at the end the scene. We also get to see the view the medical industry has of Doomwatch, with Waring under no illusion of what he feels towards them.

Sexism

For a programme that was attracting criticism of how it represented female scientists, women are treated as a very strange species this week. Miss Blake is portrayed as a careless and ignorant farmer's daughter (posh too), and women in general seem to be portrayed as professional until their hormones run away with themselves at the sight of a handsome man. 'It was her sex that cost her her job,' said Llewellyn, reminding Hilda that Fay left the laboratories because of her relationship with Waring. Quist is surprised Fay is upset that her investigation cost her another relationship, but after Waring's extraordinary outburst of self-pity rather than gratitude, she is well shot of him.

Farming

The farm we see here is very automated. Fay does not even recognise the collection of silos as a farm. The machines mix the feed and deliver it as required to the caged animals. Ridge is not as queasy about the battery hens as he was in the previous series, but this time he wasn't watching their slaughter.

Production
'The Massacre of the Innocents'

As can be seen, Fay is already working for Doomwatch, and once again the story involves the University of West Sussex, last seen in 'The Devil's Sweets'. The title comes from the Biblical story of King Herod killing the first born. Pedler and Davis' background notes and storyline survives, and there are few significant differences. Fay Chantry is already a member of the Doomwatch team but is disillusioned by the tedious nature of the paperwork and misses the laboratory bench. She wants to return to her old medical laboratory where she had worked on a PhD thesis with Professor Lewin at a field testing station. Nigel Waring was not a love interest, and the local farm was owned by Bob Stillman. The paratyphoid epidemic breaks out when she is down there and she is joined by Dr Ridge and Jeep. The wonder drug Stellamycin reacts to certain patients in the manner seen in the episode. Stillman's used

Stellamycin to eliminate cattle fever, and he noticed that treated cattle produced a significantly higher meat per carcase ratio. He continued to add it to the cattle feed in what the storyline described as 'a very natural move'. Stillman and Waring bitterly argue over who was to blame. Should Waring had warned him of the dangers to begin with? The source of the infected meat is rapidly found. Fay returns to Doomwatch invigorated by the investigation.

Scripting Development
Roger Parkes was a regular BBC writer and script editor and was aware of *Doomwatch* from its inception. Indeed, it was Parkes who suggested to Jan Read that he should try to write for it, even though Read's script was ultimately rejected. So it should come as no surprise that Parkes would be an author Davis, Dudley or Martin Worth should try out in a moment of stress for the series. Parkes' first TV script was for *The Prisoner* in 1967, but he had been story-editing a strand of thriller serials for BBC2 since 1965. Coming from an agricultural and scientific background, Parkes was ideal to write about the use of antibiotics in farms and its impact if misapplied. His wife Tessa was a science teacher and his brother a psychiatrist. His scientific interest inspired him to write for other programmes such as *Survivors* and *Blake's 7*. As he told Kevin P Marshall in 1995 for his book on *Survivors*, 'I certainly took it all very seriously and I think this appealed to Terry Dudley, who was a deeply serious man himself. I remember that he and I used to have some quite deep discussions.'

Being a BBC employee, Parkes was given an internal commission for 'The Massacre of the Innocents' and terms were settled on 17 June. It was decided this was an ideal story to introduce Dr Fay Chantry and once again, Geoff Hardcastle would be absent, although the rest of the team were present, albeit briefly in the case of Barbara Mason and Colin Bradley.

Darrol Blake
'Terry offered the script to David Cunliffe, who turned it down. [This was over staffing issues]. A year or so later, I turned something down and he picked it up. There's a sort of symmetry to these things. It was *The Lotus Eaters*, which was created by a friend of mind, Michael Bird. It was all pretty embarrassing but I had committed myself to Terry to do the third series of *Doomwatch*. So, reluctantly, I had to say no to *The Lotus Eaters*, and Cunliffe picked it up.'

Filming
Filming was conducted on Thursday 27 and Friday 28 August, with only

Simon Oates, Jean Trend and Sheila Grant needed. The farm was near Shrewsbury, and Jean Trend took her children with her for a short holiday afterwards. Interestingly, the farm in the episode is called Blake's Farm. The director believes it was probably a coincidence.

Darrol Blake recalls Simon Oates: 'Simon Oates was one of the joys of *Doomwatch*, a great lark. He had to lean against filing cabinets and sit down and put his feet up on something because he was so tall. Getting two-shots was quite difficult. John Paul was quite tall, about six-foot-one, but not as tall as Simon. Simon must have been six-foot-three or four. He was so jokey all the time. Never any stress, he was laid back all the time. He had an eye for the ladies, of course, and they had an eye for him, that's for sure. I remember the very first thing he said to me on filming: "Which side do you want the bruise?" I said, "What?" And he said, "Well, he's been in a street fight, it says in scene one – if you've read it!" I suspect he said that! If you have a cast of ten or twenty people in your cast, you have ten or twenty types of flirting to do! Different languages, different allusions, different meanings of the same word as you talk to the cast, and then there is the crew. You learn that when you see someone come towards you, you know which one to switch on. That's part of the job as it were. So you know if Simon is bearing down on you it's going to be sensible and specific questions but always dressed up in an amusing way.'

Judy Bedford: 'He wore a dog collar as a fashion statement – literally the collar intended for a canine, not a religious item.' And if you want to see it on screen, there it is in this episode, worn by Oates to win a bet with the director.'

One more Simon Oates story, from Adele Winston this time: 'When the poor actor at the read-through pronounced X-80-S as X-ATS, Simon and I solemnly saluted each other and cracked up. So they had to say it differently.'

Casting

The episode's guest star was John Wood as Nigel Waring. He had started out at the Royal Shakespeare Company and The Old Vic. Darrol Blake recalls 'I'd worked with him in a musical that Ned Sherrin had produced, and he was already a respectable actor and went onto great stuff after that. He'd just done something in the theatre and needed the money, I remember. Jean Trend was very disappointed. She wanted a movie star, a big chap with a chest or something playing opposite her, so she was a bit put off that it was only John Wood!' Trend, however remembers enjoying working with Wood. Blake: 'Tony was a writer, a director and an adaptor, a very clever man and a good friend. He came up to me when we were doing this and said, "Um, who do I have to thank for this part?" So I said, 'Well, me!' He said, "Oh, um, because it's the first time I've appeared in a

BBC drama for eight years. They think I can only do light entertainment."' Vivien S Smith remembers: 'John Wood was a stickler about his work as revealed by an intense conversation I witnessed him having with the director during the rehearsal period, wanting to get it right.'

'Our daughters used to play together so that was the initial connection. He later was in *The Regiment* for me, and in a stage play,' says Blake. 'His wife, Margaret Wedlake, was in *The Venturers* in 1974, which was about a merchant bank. I made Margaret Geoffrey Keen's secretary. She had a character name, but Geoffrey insisted on calling her Doris because he couldn't remember any name but his wife's name!'

Another notable actor was Anthony Ainley, who would later find fame playing the Master during the 1980s run of *Doctor Who*. At this point in his career, Ainley was starting to establish himself as a television face and would later feature in *Spyder's Web*, a series about a secret government organisation, and have regular roles in the historical dramas *The Pallisers*, *Upstairs, Downstairs* and *Nicholas Nickleby*.

This was an early role for Michael Culver, playing this week's civil servant. He would later play a sympathetic German officer in *Secret Army* for two series.

Studio Recording

'No Room for Error' was the fifth episode to go into production and was recorded in TC6 on Tuesday, 15 September 1970. The silent scene where Barbara Mason applies a plaster to Ridge's forehead (and then kisses it) was not in the script, but a black eye was. The titles were supposed to play over his scene with Quist in the office instead of the shot of the closed door. Simon Oates changed his line which ended the scene before he travels to the farm. Waring accuses Ridge of being illogical. In the original script he replies 'That's what they said about the Curies. And what happened? Radium.' In the scene as transmitted, Oates substitutes Columbus and America.

Darrol Blake: 'After it was all over, Terence Dudley said he was very pleased and he was amazed at how smooth the studio operation was. I looked at him and said, "I don't know why you're surprised. I spent my life in a TV studio operation! It's the one thing I can do with my eyes closed." It was practically live in those days. We used to camera rehearse for a day and a half and then tape it all in two and a half hours.'

Music

Fay Chantry and Nigel Waring spend their evening out accompanied by the strains of *Sweet and Moody*, an album released by Ember (ERL 3340). The first side is given over to the Mark Wirtz Orchestra, and Wirtz's 'Sunday Night' can be heard in the pub. The second side of the album is devoted to the John Barry Orchestra, whose 'Troubadour' accompanies their meal in the restaurant. The fairground music to which Blake cut the scene in the cow shed was from *Famous Overtures and Marches* played by the Mammoth Gavioli Fair Organ on the Ace of Clubs label (ACL 1257).

Editing

The episode was edited on Thursday, 17 September 1970 between 3 pm and 6 pm. Darrol Blake: 'My wife, Anne Cunningham, had twins at the beginning of August, and I knew my wife had worked with John Wood years before, so she came in to see a screening of the episode of when it was all cut together. When we came out into reception, there was Huw Wheldon, who was director of television or whatever at the time. "Hello, Darrol, hello hello hello. Can I give you a lift?" So we got driven home in the limo with Huw, and I remember saying to Huw, "We've just had twins!" in a very enthusiastic way. "Oh, oh, well I don't engage with children until they can have a conversation."'

Fay's Introduction

By the time she came to record her character's debut episode, Jean Trend had already recorded three episodes. So the approach needed for this one would be different. She had to uninvent the character and create relationships from scratch.

Looking back on his episode, Darrol Blake thinks he failed in giving Jean proper direction for the episode. 'It was deeply embarrassing, looking at the show now. Something Terry Dudley said to me struck home after all those years. I don't remember which recording it was, but he said to me, "Darrol, it's not good enough to hire very good actors and leave them alone. Everybody needs direction." And I think it's pretty obvious in that episode that everyone else is firing on all cylinders and Jean looks lost and alone in the middle. There isn't enough personality, not enough attack. Forty years later I can see my mistake. I should have bolstered her a lot more.' However, Adele Winston, who also worked in that episode, thought that the scene in the restaurant between Fay and Nigel was very powerful.

It is a very clever performance. Fay Chantry is stiff, formal and cautious with the Doomwatch team, opens up with her old colleagues at BAP and then becomes a no-nonsense professional when treating Waring's daughter for typhoid. Fay is in nearly every scene, and, as the implications of working for Doomwatch sink in, the episode ends with a slow zoom-in as she stares straight into the camera. The look on her face says it all. It is a debut that not even Geoff Hardcastle was given (or, for that matter, any future character).

Transmission
'Strong ITV opposition' was the reason the BBC decided that *Doomwatch* had an audience of nine million this week. When Jean Trend's first episode was transmitted she was in rehearsal for her penultimate one, 'Flight Into Yesterday'. 'There was a postal strike for most of my episodes going out. So there was no fan mail to give me any feedback. Locally, in Brighton and Kemptown where we were living, I was known by all the shopkeepers, but I was mainly recognised for the odd commercial I did. Very unsatisfactory!'

Reviews
The introduction of Jean Trend was given a lot of publicity by the papers on the day of transmission, when the cast and Darrol Blake were rehearsing 'Flight Into Yesterday'. However, the backlash against *Doomwatch* was beginning. The reviews for the episode were a mixture of kind and cruel. Guess which ones Jean Trend saw first, and she received little sympathy from the producer when she needed a shoulder to cry on. Richard Last, writing in the *Daily Telegraph*, felt that the episode seemed to be less about typhoid and antibiotics than 'a middle-aged romance between two rather dreary newcomers ... They appeared to have escaped from the limbo from which *Compact* now takes its rest rather than have any connection with a scientific laboratory.' Virginia Ironside in the *Daily Mail* had it in for John Wood, who 'was squawking and squeaking like an actress who got bad notices on her first night. Every bit of drama was squeezed out of the character's temperamental and unreasonable personality rather than the situation itself – a story, incidentally, that could have produced enough drama on its own.' She also thought that Quist was flapping about like an old hen under the pretence of efficiency.

The *Daily Express* was kinder, especially to the actress, whom they very politely addressed. 'Miss Trend appeared at times on colour TV to have green hair. But there was nothing green about her performance. She has lost nothing of her punch – yet whether this series will put her talents to the best use is not easy to say ... With the addition of some glamour to these unique investigators, the Trend which is going to hold on to the audience is obvious.'

Programme Review Board
One member of the Board criticised John Wood's overacting which he felt spoiled what could have been a very good episode. Andrew Osborn thought these things 'were always a matter of taste'.

2.05
By The Pricking Of My Thumbs ...

Written by Robin Chapman
Directed by Eric Hills
Designed by Tim Gleeson
Transmitted: Monday, 18 January 1971 at 9.21 pm Duration: 49' 28"

Cast
Jenkins (Martin Howells), Stephen Franklin (Barry Stokes), MacPherson (David Janson), Painton (Robert Yetzes), Ensor (Olaf Pooley), Botting (Colin Jeavons), Avery (David Jarrett), Judy Franklin (Sally Thomsett), Woman Shopper (Julie May), Ground Hostess (Paula Smith), Airport Policeman (Patrick Milner). Guest Stars: Oscar Franklin (Bernard Hepton), Mary Franklin (Patsy Byrne).

Also appearing
Extras in Studio: Cafe Users (Leslie Montague, David Doherty, Garry O'Brien).

Extras on Film: Ground Hostess (Joanna Robbins), PCs (Jay Neill, Tommy Hayes), Driver (Jack Silk), Airport Passengers (Una Billings, Natalya Lindley, Charles Shaw-Heskith, Linzi Scott, Tina Simmons, Stantza Scourta, Gregory Scott, Derek Glyn-Percy, David Kempton), School Children (Brent Oldfield, Phillip Parker, Stephen Follett, June Liversidge, Catherine Enere, David Kempton).

Technical Credits
Production Assistant: Clive Halls. Assistant Floor Manager: Michael McDermott. Director's Assistant: Jean Davis. Floor Assistant: Nicholas Wood.
Film Cameraman: Max Samett. Sound Recordist: Stan Nightingale. Film Editor: Christopher Rowlands.
Costume Supervisor: Mary Husband. Make-up Supervisor: Pat Hughes.
Studio Lighting: Dave Sydenham. TM2: Lance Wood. Vision Mixer: John Coxman.
Studio Sound: John Holmes. Grams Operator: Gerry Borrows.
Crew: 6.

Radio Times
Scientist sacked my son. A 16 year old boy has been expelled from his

comprehensive school because, says his father, he has an obscure genetic defect. The boy's father, journalist Oscar Franklin, claims that Stephen's expulsion follows tests conducted at ... 'It's ironic, really, that images as beautiful as these should come from the blood of violent men.'

The Story
'To be told that you're different, you're marked, it's ineradicable because it's in your blood – how dare anyone say that to another.' – Quist

A prank in a school chemistry lab leaves one boy, Painton, covered in shards of broken glass as a test tube explodes in his face. The Headmaster of Dale Heath Grammar School, Botting, tells the three he thinks are responsible, Stephen Franklin, Macpherson and Jenkins, that Paignton may lose the sight in one eye. At Doomwatch, Fay is helping Professor Ensor in his work on genetics, investigating the extra Y chromosome which he believes predisposes one to criminal behaviour. Quist is not happy with this work, having only the previous day read an article in *The Lancet* that casts doubt upon the theory. Ensor believes his work will refute that view. He is doing a survey of inmates at the Berwick Institute of Juvenile Criminality, using the children at Botting's school as controls for comparison. At the school, Botting discusses the prank with Ensor, with whom the name Stephen Franklin rings a bell. He looks at some notes. Franklin was an adopted boy and very tall, even for his age. Botting is surprised he remembers Franklin. 'My job is recording abnormality' replies Ensor.

Journalist Oscar Franklin, Stephen's adopted father, is furious that his boy will not tell Botting who was really responsible for the prank; Stephen had in fact tried to stop Jenkins from setting it up. The next day, he is expelled; the others merely get an essay, the title of which suggests that Stephen has bad blood. Also present at the expulsion, and making Stephen feel uncomfortable, was Ensor. Ridge is another one suspicious of the professor's work. The DNA samples Fay is working on supposedly come from violent prisoners at Parkhurst and Broadmoor. Ridge tells her that they were taken from children under the age of twelve. Fay is shocked but tries to justify testing Ensor's theory. Oscar, meanwhile, gets nowhere with Botting, who is convinced that Stephen is a danger. Stephen reads some articles that his father wrote on the subject of the extra Y chromosome. They describe the typical XYY male – above average height, oversexed and violent. He is appalled.

Fay challenges Ensor on his theory that everyone should be screened for the extra Y abnormality at birth, especially males, and asks if he had begun to put his convictions into practice at Dale Heath Grammar School. He doesn't answer her question but admits he feels that those detected should be given supervision. She does not value less the work they have done, but Fay is angry that Ensor deceived her deliberately. He says it is not a matter of deceit but of scientific research. Oscar Franklin goes to see Doomwatch. Quist clearly has no sympathy with the journalist for his over-simplification of scientific views. Franklin even tries blackmail in his desperation. After he leaves, Ridge tells Quist about the row between Fay and Ensor over the school samples. Ensor had assured Quist that the work was purely theoretical, but Franklin's son is XYY and 17, so how does Ensor know about him? Quist asks Ridge to take his enquiries into the school.

Stephen runs away and takes a radio and his passport with him. The mother is worried that the extra Y chromosome is making him ill. Ridge discovers the truth about the prank from the other boys involved, Jenkins and MacPherson. Although Franklin had nothing to do with it, Botting had already made up his mind, even when MacPherson tried to set the record straight. Meanwhile, Geoff goes to see the Franklins and tells them about Ensor. Their other adopted child, a daughter called Judy, comes in with a sore thumb. Oscar suddenly realises the significance of the missing radio: Stephen used to listen to air-traffic control on VHF. Geoff and the family set off for Gatwick.

Ensor has been doing more blood tests and is moving up the school. Quist is surveying Ensor's studies. 'A series of hypothesis about unhypothetical people and the statistics all implying a norm.' Ten years ago Ensor was working at the Isleton Care Centre and this is where he first encountered Stephen Franklin. Ridge wonders if Quist is more concerned about being lied to by Ensor rather than Stephen's plight, and this brings Quist up pretty sharp. Fay has lost faith in Ensor's work, and that explains that the theory was only backed up by evidence from places where violent people end up – institutions or prisons. The headmaster had acted as if the theory was already proven.

At Gatwick, Stephen tries to book tickets for the Guernsey but panics when he hears his name on a public address system. Geoff and the family search the airport. They eventually find him on a runway in the path of an aircraft on its descent, determined to kill himself. He shouts he is too tall, that he could have stopped the prank but didn't because he isn't normal. After Geoff's desperate entreaties, Stephen throws himself aside at the last possible moment. Geoff reunites him with his family. The next day, Quist tears into Botting and Ensor at the school. Even though Botting has agreed to let Stephen rejoin the school, Quist wonders if his self-confidence can be restored as easily. He turns witheringly on Ensor: 'We may yet be proved by you, Ensor, amongst others, that we may be the sum total of our chemical components, but until that bleak day dawns I suggest we treat ourselves and our children as responsible – even moral – beings.' Ensor stares out of the window, lost for words.

Behind the Story

The episode examines how a flawed scientific premise is accepted as fact, acted upon in 'good faith' before it has been proven, and then destroys lives. It is the tyranny of the expert.

The XYY Theory

Once, the causes of criminality were looked for in the shape of people's skulls or the composition of their brains. In the nineteenth century, when murder became an art form, your background, your class and your ethnicity pointed to your predilection for crime. In the mid twentieth century the focus turned to blood, particularly inherited genes. Were criminals made that way? The discovery of the XYY abnormal chromosomal variety in some criminal types led a number of cytogenetisists to believe that it might indeed be the case. During the 1960s, studies were made of incarcerated criminals in institutions.

In late 1965 *Nature* published a survey conducted by cytogeneticist Patricia Jacobs at a special security hospital in Scotland, titled *Aggressive Behaviour, Mental Sub-Normality and the XYY Male*. America followed up with their own studies, and soon the press were lapping up the idea of a new way of labelling a violent male: the XYY criminal. They were usually tall, at one time covered in acne, possessed a high IQ and were very violent and dangerous. Mass-murderer Richard Speck was identified by biochemist Mary Telfer as an XYY man, but he was not. It wasn't long before cracks appeared in the theory. In 1968 the *Journal of Medical Genetics* reviewed the evidence and concluded that the studies were influenced by the institutions in which their examples were found. In May 1969 Mary Telfer (who the previous year had published the first US reports of these tall, institutionalised XYY men), decided that their behaviour might not be so different from normal XY criminals.

It was too late. The idea had set in. In 1970, surveys of the chromosomal make up of African-American males between the ages of 8 and 18, conducted by the National Institute of Mental Health Centre for Studies of Crime and Delinquency, were stopped by a law suit from the American Civil Liberties Union, who queried the lack of informed consent. One of those who spoke out against the tests was Jonathan R Beckwith, a Harvard-graduated biologist who helped isolate the first gene from a chromosome in 1969 (see the chapter on Geoff Hardcastle). For those who think that an episode of this nature was a waste of time because the science had been discredited, think again. Harvard Medical School voted to screen new-born babies for the 'abnormality' in 1975, despite there being no basis for such an abnormality to be a harmful condition. 'Even today', wrote Beckwith in his 2002 book *Making Genes, Making Waves*, 'the majority of students in my genetics classes know the XYY story and most believe that the link between the extra Y chromosome is scientifically established.'

The Press
Oscar Franklin is a man who has been hoist with his own petard. Quist views him as a 'gross simplifier of matters scientific ... to the point of misinformation'. Kit Pedler once made a formal complaint to the Press Council over an article in the *Daily Express* which he felt was an irresponsible distortion of the announcement that a biologically active virus had been synthesised at Stanford University in 1967. He lost his case. The editor of the paper defended the 'Life Created in a Test Tube' headline by explaining that it had been written for the benefit of 'lay people'. This is the same defence that Oscar Franklin gives. It was Franklin's articles in 1965 that helped to popularise the XYY stereotype. 'It was the correct view at the time' is how Franklin tries to justify his work. Quist lays into him with as much ferocity, perhaps more, than he does with Ensor at the end of the episode. He only helps Franklin when he realises it is a stick with which to beat Ensor, whom he also cannot stand – nor his theories. Ridge is quite right: Quist wasn't really thinking of the boy. But Quist has never claimed to be perfect.

In some ways the episode is quite sinister, with its revelations that Ensor is 'working his way up the school' like a creeping menace and Stephen's discovery of what might be bad blood inside him, making him feel like he is a ticking human time bomb. Anyone missing the 'horror shot' from earlier episodes would have been pleased to see the bloodied face of Paignton at the end of the pre-credits teaser. It is decidedly unpleasant, and the screaming particularly effective. This should not come as any surprise to followers of the recent work of Robin Chapman.

Production
Robin Chapman had been writing and producing a run of quirky crime thrillers for Granada during the 1960s. In 1965, he created *The Man in Room 17*, where two civil service sleuths practically isolate themselves from the rest of society and investigate and manipulate crime or espionage detection from their office. So isolated were the sleuths, played by Richard Vernon and Michael Aldridge, that they were rehearsed, written for (by Chapman) and directed separately from the main cast. This ran for two series, with Aldridge replaced by Denham Elliot for the second. The premise was resurrected for a spin-off series called *The Fellowes*, where Vernon and Aldridge's characters now look into the causes and remedies for crime from their university offices, and again, separate from a case which they are either involved with, or commenting on. This lead to another spin off, *Spindoe*, where we follow the attempts of a crime boss to

recapture his empire after a spell in jail thanks to the Fellowes. Chapman's next series for Granada, which he wrote in Tuscany, was *Big Breadwinner Hog*, another tale of gangland battles for supremacy. 'Hard, ironic and violent,' Chapman described it at the time. The first episode, shown in April 1969, ended with a jar of acid being thrown over the face of a rival, revenge for an earlier beating. The scene looks tame even at the time, the acting suggests the horror. The uproar this incident generated was felt. The Independent Television Authority expressed regret for the scenes and for a nervous moment it looked as if the series would be pulled, but transmission continued as planned.

Chapman's next work was a W Somerset Maughan dramatization for the BBC, and another crime serial for the newly created London Weekend Television. He was likely to have been approached by Martin Worth, who had worked for Granada in the recent past on a series called *Mr Rose*. The subject of crime detection was absolutely right for Chapman, and he simply had to open the episode with an acidic substance blowing up in someone's face … This time we see the result in glorious close up, not have it implied.

Script Development

'Evil Inherited' was commissioned from Robin Chapman on 13 July by Gerry Davis. It was the 19th episode commissioned and was due for delivery by 1 September. The script arrived a week later than expected where it was instantly snapped up for production, being accepted three weeks later. (Incidentally, to show the interest in the subject at the time, it may be worth noting that Kenneth Royce's thriller *The XYY Man* was published in 1970. The first of seven novels in a series, it concerned the exploits of a tall but non-violent thief, who was used by the security services whilst being hunted by the police at the same time.) The script wanted it to take place during a rainy couple of days. When Fay is taking the test Ensor has prepared for the children to fill in, it was supposed to be raining hard outside.

Casting

Olaf Pooley had only a year earlier nearly destroyed the world in the name of cheap energy in a *Doctor Who* story called 'Inferno'. Bernard Hepton was one of those seldom unemployed actors. He recently played the famous murderer Crippen in a *Detective* play in 1968 called 'Crime of Passion', and in the future would go on to play a war-time resistance leader in *Secret Army*. Seldom mentioned is that for a time he was a BBC drama producer who looked after the soaps such as *Compact* or the town hall shenanigans of *Swizzlewick*, before moving to the Plays department until he returned to acting. His screen adopted daughter in the episode was played by Sally

Thomsett whose youthful looks allowed her to be employed to play school-aged parts as she was not restricted by the by-laws imposed on the employment of children. Only a few years earlier, she played a child witness to a spectacular airfield hijacking in ITV's *The Gold Robbers*. David Janson, like Sally Thomsett, would soon be swallowed up by the world of light entertainment and appear in a string of situation comedies. Martin Howells had made his television debut in *The First Lady*, which also featured John Paul, and went on to appear regularly in the first series of *The Lotus Eaters*. Robert Yetzes played the unfortunate Painton and doesn't appear to act on television again. The few credits he did have seemed to depend on his plump stature, such as 'Fat boy' in a *Pickwick Papers* adaption, and the *Thirty Minute Theatre* play 'Is That Your Body, Boy?' in 1970. As for the boy who was too tall, Barry Stokes would make an appearance in one of the final episodes of Terence Dudley's *Survivors*. He currently lives in Canada.

Filming

This was Eric Hill's second directing assignment for the series. The night-time scenes filmed in and around Gatwick Airport only featured John Nolan from the regular cast. The script is different in places to what was filmed. The tannoy announcer was to have said 'If Stephen Franklin of Grantdale Gardens, Merstham is in the airport building, will he report to the information desk immediately, please', slightly fuller than the programme's version. The first of these announcements was scripted to be heard by Stephen as he was moving slowly through the passenger concourse. Simon Oates did his brief filming outside a London school on Monday, 19 October.

Studio

'By The Pricking of My Thumbs ...' was the ninth episode in production and was recorded in TC4 on Friday, 6 November 1970. The cinefilm being watched by Professor Ensor and Doctor Fay Chantry in the first scene after the titles came from a series of short films called *Mitosis in Endosperm of Haemanthus Katherinae* by Doctor Andrew Bajer of the University of Oregon, who collaborated with Dr Robert D Allen of Princeton University in 1965. The full 8mm film lasts for four minutes and fifteen seconds.

Music

The music in the background to the café scene was 'Cause I'm a Man' from *Electric Banana* with Tilsley Orchestra on the Hudson De Wolfe label (DW 3040). (The eponymous Electric Banana were in fact the British rock and roll group The Pretty Things, who recorded several albums of library music using the pseudonym.)

Editing

The episode was edited on Sunday, 8 November 1970 between 1.30 pm and 7.30 pm.

The first cut was after Ridge invites Jenkins and MacPherson for a cup of tea in the café. Jenkins refuses at first, asking if Ridge is from the press. He tells him that the joke was Franklin's idea and Botting backs them. As he tries to leave, Ridge grabs him and warns him not to shrug him off. It is not a free country, especially not for Stephen Franklin.

The second cut scene (which may have been dropped before recording) was back in the Doomwatch offices after Stephen tries to book tickets for Guernsey. (The ticket girl was supposed to tell him that the flight would be leaving in two hours time.) Quist thinks Geoff is on a wild goose chase. 'I like wild geese' says Ridge, and leaves. Fay wonders what makes Ensor and others like him so determined to link criminality to the extra Y chromosome. Quist thinks that when someone holds a theory long enough, it becomes a fact to them whatever the contrary evidence. Fay agrees, but thinks Ensor may be right about Stephen. Quist says that for all they know, the extra Y chromosome may be the mark of genius. Who tested Da Vinci? Today's assumed genetic set back may be tomorrow's advantage. Fay finds Quist cold for being more affected by Ensor's deception rather than Stephen's case. But he claims he has keeps a clear head in order to remain unaffected by the world's general stupidity. He doesn't hate people, but he has tried to love them and failed. 'I'm not blaming them. So now I talk of "truth" instead, as if it were … immutable.' We then leave Quist to his 'private pain'.

Transmission

Earlier that night on BBC, the second of a ten part documentary series called *Crime and the Criminal* was shown, with contributions from crime experts and the criminal.

Press Review

'Who can resist the persuasive power of *Doomwatch*?' wrote the *Coventry Evening Telegraph* the day after transmission. 'Is it morbid curiosity or a genuine concern about events that could become reality? This time genetics came under the microscope in an absorbing tale about a scientist who believed that the extra chromosome in men pre-disposed violence. A nice example here of an attempt to pigeon-hole people, but attitudes in general were slightly suspect. It was hard to swallow that a headmaster should expel a boy partly on the basis of one man's theory. And the boy's spectacular suicide attempt at Gatwick Airport really was more in keeping with fiction.'

Programme Review Board

The only reaction to the episode from the Board came from Andrew Osborn, who feared that the series had suffered from 'certain internal stresses'. The viewing figures were high at ten and a half million. Once again, the Board insisted that, good though it was, it must have been helped by the Association Football that followed. This, incidentally, began with the edited highlights of Leeds United versus Rotherham United.

2.06
The Iron Doctor

Written by Brian Hayles
Directed by Joan Kemp-Welch
Designed by Ian Watson
Transmitted: Monday, 25 January 1971 at 9.24 pm Duration: 49' 29"

Cast
Sister Trewin (Amanda Walker), Eric Godfrey (Keith Grenville), Duty Nurse (Gloria Connell), Mr Faber (Frederick Schiller), George (Harold Bennett), Mr Kemp (Frank Littlewood), Mr Tearson (Raymond Young), Second Nurse (Jeannie James), Doctor (Paul Nemeer), Visitors/Attendants (Michael Ely, Clive Rodgers), Visitor (Joyce Freeman). Guest Stars: Dr Barnett Whittaker (James Maxwell), Dr Carson (Barry Foster).

Also appearing: Patients (Walter Swash, Rex Rashley, Bert Sims), Visitor (Gregory Scott).

Technical Credits
Production Assistant: Ann Faggetter. Assistant Floor Managers: Derek Nelson, Mike McDermott. Director's Assistant: Pauline Bullock-Webster. Floor Assistant: John Wilcox.
Film Cameraman: Kenneth Westbury. Sound Recordist: Malcolm Campbell. Film Editor: Sheila S Tomlinson.
Costume Supervisor: Mary Husband. Make-up Supervisor: Pat Hughes.
Studio Lighting: Jimmy Purdie. TM2: Jack Shallcross. Vision Mixer: Rachel Blayney.
Studio Sound: John Holmes. Grams Operator: Gerry Borrows.
Crew: 6.
Videotape Editor: Ronald Sangster.
Scientific Adviser: Dr Michael Moles.

Radio Times
Patients in Britain's newest hospital ward are being cared for by a computer. At the new Intensive Care Unit at Parkway Hospital, the regular round of doctors and nurses has been largely replaced by an electronic watchdog that constantly monitors the health of the patients, diagnoses any change in their condition and then prescribes treatment. 'A great step forward' is how the hospital's governors describe the new ... 'Without this machine I could not exist. But I'm sentimental and I would prefer to hold hands with a human being.'

The Story

'Behind every machine there's a man. If the machine failed, it's my failure. It's man who's ultimately responsible.' – Whittaker

Quist is one of a few visitors being shown around the geriatric ward at Parkway Hospital by Doctor Whittaker. The patients are connected to a computer which monitors their life signs, records activity to videotape and supplies treatment where necessary. It has been keeping them alive much longer than their condition would normally allow. The adjacent computer room houses 'the iron doctor'. However, one of their patients, excited to have recently become a grandfather, dies. Quist commiserates with another doctor, Carson, who goes to see Whittaker and tells him that the computer deliberately cut off treatment to George, the deceased man. Theirs is an old argument. Whittaker has total faith in the project, but Carson is angry and deeply suspicious of the machine. Whittaker doesn't want to listen, even though this is the second time such a thing has happened.

Carson brings his concerns to Doomwatch. The survival chances of the patients are assessed, and the advice is given by the computer to a human panel. Quist asks if this advice is being acted upon without question. Carson doesn't know, but the computer-controlled treatment for George stopped. Carson is riled that Quist doesn't take this very seriously and storms out. Carson's allegations are put to the Doomwatch team by Quist, who wants to find out who is responsible for the programming. He sends Fay to Parkway, where she is shown around by Carson and Sister Trewin. Godfrey, another convert to machine medicine, explains the workings of the computer to her. The dead man had a survival index of minus nine with an accompanying recommendation of DAT. Carson explains that DAT means Discontinue Active Treatment, a secret part of the project. Whittaker confronts Fay, but once her credentials are verified he is willing to discuss the pilot scheme with her. He dismisses Carson's concerns as emotionally prejudiced, as although he is a good doctor, he has a highly charged imagination. Fay requests the data plots for the two deaths, but Whittaker refuses to be hounded. Then, a third patient dies. At the bedside, Carson hisses to Whittaker that the computer is dangerous and must be stopped. The machine, its video camera recording everything, seems to register his words …

Fay tells Quist that Carson may have a case but she isn't sure. If Carson is right, and the remaining four patients are listed DAT, they're dead. Quist is startled. The machine has to be programmed, after all, and it's Whittaker who programmes it. A tired Whittaker decides to suspend Carson, whose state of mind he believes is detrimental to his patients.

Sister Trewin sympathises with Carson but won't help him steal a computer record tape for Doomwatch to analyse. He secretly tries to remove a circuit board and is electrocuted. Geoff speaks to Mr Tearson, the man who designed the machine, and listens to his vision of a national medical grid of shared diagnostic terminals. The machine was originally a war games computer, suitably adapted for its current purpose. It has its own defence mechanism as a safeguard against patients tampering, and it can evolve and extend itself. Posing as a man from the National Research Council, Ridge questions Godfrey about the machine – whether it could kill anyone by mistake.

The X-rays of Carson's head shows that a fragment of skull has been driven into his brain, and Whittaker is preparing to operate. Feeling guilty over his accident, Sister Trewin brings Doomwatch the computer tape they need. The analysis shows that the patient whose details are on the tape died because the computer withdrew treatment. Even though the committee had overridden the computer's recommendation of DAT, nothing was programmed in to remove it. The machine acted on its own recommendation because nobody told it not to. A study of the tape also shows the argument between Carson and Whittaker. Thanks to its highly sophisticated defence mechanism and capacity to evolve, the machine has registered Carson as a hazard to itself and will not allow him to survive after the operation. They rush to Parkway, hoping to erase the machine's record of Carson.

Arriving just after the operation has successfully been completed, Quist tells Whittaker what they have discovered, but he refuses to listen. Without the computer to monitor him and treat accordingly, Carson will die. Whittaker takes Quist to see Carson whilst Geoff and Ridge go to the computer room. As they are trying to convince Godfrey what needs to be done, the computer withdraws treatment from Carson. His heart stops. In the light of this, Godfrey finally gives in to Ridge and Geoff and inserts a new memory block, making Carson a fresh patient as far as the computer is concerned. Whittaker is fruitlessly massaging Carson's heart when the machine comes back on line, and Carson's life is saved. When Godfrey explains to Whittaker why the computer started up again, and what they had to do to achieve it, Whittaker begins to understand at last. But he does not accept that the machine killed the patients, because a machine cannot be responsible in itself. It was the man behind the machine. Himself.

Behind the Story

In *The Beast of Business: A Record of Computer Atrocities*, Harvey Matusow describes being sent an example of the computerisation of the John Hopkins Medical Centre in Baltimore, USA. A 'distinguished British diagnostician' was invited to look around the wards where each patient was given a data sheet on which every detail of age, sex, pulse, temperature, blood count and symptoms was entered, and the computer did the rest. They examined random data sheets and 'the dull infallibility' grew. The diagnostician asked what happened when their young student doctors left and entered a small town or village hospital where there were no computers. What happened to their patients then? 'Oh', he was told, 'they die, doctor. They die.' What this anecdote implies, if it was correct, is that the expertise of the human doctor was being displaced by the machine.

In 'Project Sahara', the issue was in allowing a computer to recommend someone's security risk status; here it is more fundamental – whether it allowed a person to live or die. Whittaker defends the pilot scheme as simply an experiment, with a human panel being given the last say. But the problem is that what if the word of the computer goes unchallenged because it are supposed to be faster, quicker and more logical than us? What gives this episode a more delicious sci-fi twist is that the machine can think, take action and defend itself. This was in the period where computers were regarded with suspicion. Could they develop their own independent intelligence and act for themselves to the detriment of humanity? Would robots stalk the land and remove all these walking, talking, irrational, illogical fleshy things whom they were built to serve and whose lives they made easier? No, of course they can't, unless you tell them to. The computer in 'The Iron Doctor' had the ability to 'think logically', and no-one had told it not to act on its own recommendations of Discontinue Active Treatment.

The Technocrats
Mr Tearing, the man who designed the 20-90 computer in the story, envisages a time when all doctors surgeries and hospitals are linked to a central computer where symptoms and diagnoses and recommended treatments can be dialled up. The idea of a network of linked computers was not a new one. Kit Pedler's first *Doctor Who* story 'The War Machines' in 1965 had something similar. And this was long before the internet. In recent years the governments of the United Kingdom have found centralised databases a very difficult and unpopular idea and near enough impossible to set up and implement on time and on budget. Tearing is also to have told Hardcastle about the development of face-recognition software for defence purposes. The advent of CCTV cameras in the United Kingdom has made this type of idea a more practical concern. Doctor Whittaker is the leader of the project, which presumably has ministerial backing, judging by the dialogue at the end of the story. He is a technocrat and fully believes in the advance of machine-governed medicine. The computer is keeping patients alive much longer than they would have

been before. Any concerns from Doctor Carson are dismissed – rather irrationally – as wanting to push medicine back to the level of the village witch doctor. Real-life Doomwatchers at the time, and those to come in the next few years, would be accused of wanting to push mankind back to the Stone Age, as if they were some kind of technological luddites compared to the enlightened politicians who believed in growth, a strong economy and solutions provided by labour saving devices. The 'synthetic' versus the 'natural'.

Production
The Storyline
'The Iron Doctor' featured dehumanised medicine, a concept Kit Pedler first used in *Doctor Who* in the creation of the Cybermen. In his second credited script, 'The Moonbase' in 1966, medical units of the year 2070 featured machines that treated patients in a manner very similar to this episode. The Doctor thought his assistant Polly, who came from 1966, would be quite impressed, but she points out that the one thing that the machines cannot be, is nice to the patients in the way a nurse can. Pedler had been hospitalised in 1966 and while recovering from surgery, contracted peritonitis, the pain which he once described as the worst night of his life. It was only the sympathy of a nurse that pulled him through. The horrors of the ward is reflected in 'The Moonbase', as unconscious patients are kidnapped by the Cybermen. Kit Pedler's final contribution to *Doctor Who* was in the shape of ideas for 'The Invasion' in 1968 (written up into eight episodes by Derrick Sherwin), which has the Doctor extraordinarily anti-computer. 'Shut up, you stupid machine!' he shouts at an automated telephone answering service. 'I hate computers and won't be dictated to by them', he later tells one of its advocates. In 1969, Pedler and Davis were writing a stage-play about a computer and a murder. It never went into production as theatre was a medium Pedler did not care for very much.

The storyline was number seven and had an alternative title in 'Deus ex Machina'. It replaced 'The Flames of Hell' which Pedler and Davis took for themselves to turn into 'The Red Sky'. The original 9 page storyline and theme was typed up on 10 April 1969. The setting was a showpiece clinic rather than a geriatric ward. The plot featured a racial element, echoing the debate stirred up by MP Enoch Powell who had delivered the famous 'Rivers of Blood' speech in 1968 where he attacked immigration policy. As well as facing criticism, he also received support. The concerned doctor in the original idea was Dr Sardar Khan, and his superior, Dr Barmet Wilkinson despises Commonwealth doctors. The computer was called Hippocrates and kills Khan when it identifies him as a threat. Ridge infiltrates the hospital as a patient needing a gall-stone removed. Ridge assembles the necessary data and avoids a similar fate to Khan, but on the day of the operation he is given an injection which sends him to sleep. It becomes a race against time for the Doomwatch team to save his life as the operation is being monitored by the computer. This is where the storyline finishes.

Scripting Development

The storyline was given to Harry Green and was commissioned on 22 August 1969. He was working on the script in September when he fell ill and wrote to Gerry Davis explaining that he was in a very 'dicey state'. He offered to plug on, despite his 'melted mind', but did suggest 'Bear with me.' Davis didn't mind waiting and replied 'Perhaps the subject inspired the illness! ... Get well mate ... We need you.' The script was received on 3 October. Green confessed that it wasn't so much a script as a symptom. Then the unpleasantness surrounding rewrites to 'Hear No Evil' occurred. It didn't get better with 'The Iron Doctor'.

On 17 November Green wrote to Davis after their second conference on the script. What was being suggested was not merely a major rewrite, but a new play. Green found himself unable to do the work needed. 'When I was commissioned to write the script that you have, I was given a free hand with the synopsis. I do not know what you feel your contractual obligations are; I myself do not propose to press a point of view – it's a matter for you.' Then, on 22 November 1969, Green bailed out, having signed up for an eight-part classic serial. He thought it was for the best; a clearing of the air. He was paid off for his script on the 27 May 1970. In July, Davis tried to interest Green to write for the second series and sent him some material on 'Human Guinea Pigs', which was a second attempt on the abandoned storyline 'Condition of the Mind', but it did not interest the author.

Brian Hayles

Gerry Davis' first major work on *Doctor Who* was rewriting a version of 1966's 'The Celestial Toymaker', which was Brian Hayles' first successful pitch to the programme after several failed story ideas. They also worked together on a historical story later the same year called 'The Smugglers'. Hayles may, on first glance, appear to be the ideal author for this episode, having spent a great part of 1967's *Doctor Who* serial 'The Ice Warriors' having characters clash over a computer's judgement. While Hayles' next computer in *Doctor Who* was in 'The Seeds of Death', a monotonous narrator of events that didn't make any mistakes or have a nervous breakdown. 'The Iron Doctor' makes a point of the computer returning queries and asking for clarifications when faced with a problem, not melt itself down.

For *Doomwatch*, Hayles' script was the ninth commission for the second series, and 'The Iron Doctor' was rebooted on the 5 May with a target delivery just three days later, meaning Hayles had been given the go ahead much earlier, as this was the period of turmoil between Dudley and Davis. Whether Martin Worth had any input into the shaping or rewriting of the story is unknown. Hayles was paid his full fee at the end of the month. Rehearsal scripts were sent to him on 17 June, and Joan Kemp-Welch was booked in to direct. The read-through for rehearsals and studio recording was on 23 or 24 July.

Production
It was straight into production, presumably as it one of the few scripts ready along with 'The Logicians' and 'Invasion'. Filming seems to have occurred after the lengthy shoot for 'Invasion'. Joby Blanshard was required on 8 July for the interior car shots. He was made available for five nights just for this. Jean Trend performed her first work for *Doomwatch* this week, doing an interior shot for the brain operation sequence later in the story and a quick scene on location with Amanda Walker. John Nolan and Raymond Young filmed inside a computer lab.

Another Scientific Advisor
The story was unique in that a second scientific adviser was credited in the *Radio Times* billing: Dr Michael Moles. It is probable that he gave advice on the surgery scenes although Kit Pedler himself had performed operations on cancer patients in the 1950s. Moles had a career in anaesthesia and spent five years with the Royal Army Medical Corps, where he developed interests in trauma, mass casualty management, anti-terrorism, chemical and biological warfare agents and humanitarian aid. It was this that led him to co-found WADEM, the World Association for Disaster and Emergency Medicine, in 1976.

Rehearsals
Since the series was not recorded in broadcast order, Vivien Sherrard, John Nolan and Jean Trend were thrown into the deep end with 'The Iron Doctor', which would go out as the sixth episode. They had to create their characters from scratch. Jean Trend remembers: 'I had no help, advice or words of wisdom from anybody, directors, producer or writers. I got the script for the first one, I think, and I don't remember having any discussions with make- up or wardrobe as to how Fay would appear. We did go shopping for clothes, I remember, and a hairpiece was decided on to give my short cut some "body".' Vivien S Smith remembered: 'I never met Kit Pedler or Gerry Davis, probably because they were on their way out by the time I became involved with the series.'

Casting

The second future cast member of *Are You Being Served?* Can be seen in the episode, Harold Bennett, playing the first patient to die. Barry Foster would go on to play the title role in Thames' smash hit series *Van der Valk*, and would recreate the role several times over the next couple of decades. James Maxwell would go onto play King Henry VII in *Shadow in the Tower*, a role he had played a few years before. Joan Kemp-Welch would direct one of these. Gloria Connell worked with Kemp-Welch in *ITV Playhouse* 'Remember the Germans' in 1969, and will play a small role in 'The Human Time Bomb', later in the series.

Studio

'The Iron Doctor' was the first episode of the new series of *Doomwatch* to go into the studio, which in this case was TC6, on Monday, 3 August 1970. A very complicated recording was planned, and, hardly surprisingly, it overran. The reason was the amount of costume changes needed, especially for Barry Foster being prepared for his operation. The recording began with Scene 38, where Carson is watched by Whittaker, Fay, a Sister and a nurse. The recording then proceeded up to the end titles – but even then not entirely in order.

After a recording break, it was onto Scene 16 between Fay and Quist in his office followed by cross-cuts as she speaks to Whittaker on the phone following Carson's accident. Next, the episode was recorded up to and including another phone call sequence, this time between Fay and Sister Trewin. Then it was back to the opening of the episode, up to Carson's accident. After a shot of Carson on the floor, a dummy was placed before the computer and an explosion set off.

Two more shots set in the wards with Carson before the operation were recorded next and that was the end of the evening. As well as the need for costume and make up changes, there was a lot of resetting (for example, bed-screens put into place and other equipment moved around in the wards).

One small film insert that was dropped before recording was to have been the last shot of all. As Whittaker makes his statement that it is man and not machine who is ultimately responsible, we were to see a shot of the computer room and then film of a 'computer wheel' as Whittaker speaks his final words.

Editing

The editing was done on Thursday, 6 August 1970. The amount of editing required would earn videotape editor Ronald Sangster an on-screen credit, a rarity in those days.

Programme Review Board
The Programme Review Board gave the episode a thumbs-up, although there was a comment that the last five minutes were rather weak.

UK Gold
UK Gold cut out a good four minutes from the episode (or perhaps the tape, recovered from Canada, had already been cut there). This was a film montage of the rather gruesome operation (sawing through bone ...) and of the Doomwatch team driving to the hospital.

2.07
Flight Into Yesterday

Written by Martin Worth
Directed by Darrol Blake
Designed by Christine Ruscoe
Transmitted: Monday, 1 February 1971 at 9.27 pm
Duration: 47' 27"

Cast
Duncan (Michael Elwyn), PM's Secretary (John Quarmby), Thompson (Desmond Llewelyn), Air Hostesses (Mary Loughran, Penny Service) Reporters (Bill Bailey, Steve Preston).
Guest Stars: The Minister (John Barron), Ainslie (Robert Urquhart).

Also appearing
Ann Gary Lee, Jay Neill, Reg Turner, Kedd Senton, Steve Patterson, Ted Matthews, Violet Lee Own, Gilly Flower, Beryl Bainbridge, Rachel Treadgold, Daryl Sirr, Michael Mulcaster, Ian Elliot, Leslie Montagu, Denis Marlow, Bernard Barnsley, Willie Bowman, Richard Sheeky, Benny Shulman, Donald Groves, Fred Bourne, Dilys Marvin, Pat Simmons, Wendy Johnson, Anne Down, Joyce Lee Crossley, Tracy Vernon, Ernest Blythe.

Technical Credits
Director's Assistant: Adele Paul. Production Assistant: Vivienne Cozens.
Assistant Floor Manager: Sue Allan. Floor Assistant: Nicholas Wood.
Costume Supervisor: Juanita Waterson. Make-up Supervisor: Pat Hughes.
Film Editor: Christopher Rowlands.
Studio Lighting: Eric Monk. TM2: Graham Southcott. Vision Mixer: Fred Law.
Sound Supervisor: John Holmes. Grams Operator: Gerry Borrows.
Crew: 6.

Radio Times
Doomwatch chief flies back. Dr Spencer Quist, 50 year old head of the government's Doomwatch department, had 'no comment' when he flew back to London Airport last night. Dr Quist was ordered back by the Prime Minister before addressing the major Ecological Conference in Los Angeles this week where Americans … An aide said: 'Dr Quist is very tired. He will be reporting to 10 Downing Street … 'Is the Minister aware of recent

271

tests conducted by industry and the Ministry of Defence into the physical and mental dislocation likely to be brought on by rapid long-distance flights across different time zones ...?'

The Story
'Doomwatch will never stand a chance whilst that man is in charge.' – Ridge

Quist arrives late for an urgent meeting with the Prime Minister, unsteady on his feet, confused, slurring his speech and looking exhausted. He blames the driver for getting them lost on the way from the airport. He asks to be briefed on the meeting, leaving the Minister in no doubt what is wrong with the man. 'He's drunk! Dr Quist is drunk ...'

The rest of the Doomwatch team are shocked by the news. They question Barbara, who had gone to the conference in Los Angeles with him. She tells them Quist had spent most of the flight home talking to Jim Ainslie, who had looked after them during the trip. Miss Wills, the Minister's secretary, calls the Doomwatch office to makes an appointment for Ridge to see the Minister, adding that Duncan would like a chat first at his Pall Mall club. Fay goes to see Quist at his flat. He is in a state of hyperactivity, telling her how inefficient a host Ainslie had been. He is also puzzled over why he had been called back from America at such short notice only to have the meeting adjourned as soon as he arrived at Whitehall. He is shocked when Fay tells him they thought he was drunk. She suggests they run some tests.

Duncan tells Ridge that Quist is still under suspicion since the Byfield bomb. He makes people in the Government nervous. Behind the scenes at the Los Angeles conference, there are plans for an American Doomwatch, which was why Quist was to address them. To whom does Quist owe his first loyalty? The tax payer or science or mankind? Barbara is being tested for the effects of jet lag by Colin when Quist turns up. He learns about Ridge's meeting. Could this be about his job? Fay encourages him to take the same tests as Barbara. That way at least they'll be able to prove it was jet lag and not drunkenness that was responsible for his state. He tries the tests and doesn't do particularly well, his score on a par with Barbara's, and he loses patience. Fay points out that if he had just arrived for a business conference in this condition, someone might have been able to get the better of him if they exploited it.

Next morning, the Minister is underwhelmed by the jet lag theory, ascribing it more to the pressures Quist finds himself under because of leading Doomwatch. He maintains that only last month he himself flew out to Tokyo on negotiations and nobody thought he was drunk. Quist is to be given sick leave for two weeks, and Ridge will go to the conference instead. The Government are concerned that Quist's speech might be politically indelicate, so Ridge can take his place and present a more palatable version to the Americans, telling them that Doomwatch is an arm of the State with no anti-government stance or real power to interfere. The Minister warns Ridge that this is not an opportunity to be missed and reminds him that he was once in this position before, during the Byfield bomb inquest.

Ridge later returns to the Ministry with a speech written for the conference. The Minister approves, finding the speech diplomatic and informative. To his surprise, it was written by Quist, who had obviously changed his mind if he had indeed originally wanted to a swipe at governments. Ridge suggests that the Minister fly out to Los Angeles and deliver the speech himself; Ridge and Fay will accompany him and provide any scientific back-up needed. Despite the concerns of Duncan and Miss Wills, the Minister decides to take on what he realises is a challenge: to prove that he can cope with the gruelling schedule better than the 'unstable' Quist; otherwise, he would have to exonerate him. Bradley is also appalled by Ridge's plan, but Ridge says Quist needs him because he fights dirty. They hear a tape recording of the Minister's Tokyo press conference: he sounds tired and confused. Barbara remembers the pressures that the Minister was under at the time and agrees that if the Minister is affected by the flight, it won't be for the first time.

Fay goes to see the Minister's people, including Thompson, the press secretary, and Duncan agrees with her report on Quist but is too loyal to criticise the Minister's judgement. Quist is tipped off by Bradley and returns to the office to warn Ridge that he is responsible for the success of the Minister's mission.

On the plane the Minister meets Ainslie, who just happens to be on the flight and does a good job of flattering the Minister. Duncan is suspicious of the man when his name appears on a security check of other passengers. Asking Quist what he thought of him, he realises he must have been the one who tipped off Whitehall about Quist's speech, which they had been told would be overly critical. They investigate further and find he is a public relations man, hired by American industrialists to stop an American Doomwatch and possibly finish off their own. Quist realises that Ainslie had used techniques to disorientate him, such as taking him to the wrong hotel and waking him up in the middle of the night.

During the flight Ainslie works hard on the Minister, persuading him to change the speech to suggest that Doomwatch is not as strong as it appears, pointing out how he would get a standing ovation. He tries to get him to view Doomwatch as a way of absorbing public guilt over enjoying and using things that are harmful. Despite Fay's advice, the Minister eats heavily, drinks alcohol and does not rest. He begins to rewrite the speech.

Ridge, watching from a few rows back has twigged onto Ainslie but does nothing. London tries to warn the Minister when they stop off at New York, where Ainslie has organised a lunch in honour of his visit, tiring him further.

On the next leg of the flight, Thompson and Miss Wills virtually force Ainslie to go back to his own seat and leave the Minister in peace, but his work is done. By the time they reach the hotel in Los Angeles, the Minister is tired, excitable and confused. He refuses to admit he has been got at by Ainslie and wants him at his side. The press surround him, hurling hostile questions about Doomwatch, organised by Ainslie. Fay tries to calm him down but it is too late – the Minister has a heart attack and collapses. Ridge, however, has been acclimatising himself to Los Angeles time since they left London and is refreshed, ready to give the speech as he intended all along.

Back in the Doomwatch office, Quist is berating Ridge for cottoning onto a phoney like Ainslie but doing nothing about it. Ridge counters that Doomwatch doesn't stand a chance while someone like the Minister is in charge. Quist believes the opposite: their Minister is the only man capable of simultaneously keeping the department running whilst fending off their enemies. 'You're stark, raving mad!' Ridge tells him. 'I know' agrees Quist. 'In this job it's the essential qualification.'

Behind The Story
Project Pegasus

'Testing time-zone fatigue in jet travel.' This story appeared in *The Times* in November 1969, written by Arthur Reed, Air Correspondent. It reported an inquiry by Syntex Pharmaceuticals called 'Project Pegasus', which would involve fourteen medical volunteers flying from London to San Francisco at the cost of £15,000. 'Time-zone fatigue has in the past, it is thought, caused officers to give incorrect orders, politicians to make wrong decisions, and at least one quite sober industrialist to seem drunk at a board meeting.'

The former medical director of British Overseas Aircraft Corporation, Dr Kenneth Bergin, wrote to *The Times* on 20 October about the difficulty of adjusting to time-zone changes. Between London and San Francisco there is an eight-hour difference, as there is eastbound between London and Hong Kong. Our bodies can only adapt slowly due to the rapid time changes. 'The business executive who leaves London at midday gets to New York five hours later to find it is still midday and thinks he can thereby do more work in his day. He does not always realise that he loses in efficiency what he saves in time.' The *Guardian*, who also reported on the press conference, wondered about the Prime Minister, Harold Wilson, preparing for an important visit to the President in Washington. Upon arrival, he would immediately engage in hours of frank and fearless talks, but would he be in a fit state to do so? 'His biological clock could be disturbed.'

And there, basically, you have the plot of 'Flight Into Yesterday'. The results for 'Project Pegasus' were expected to be ready before Concorde was pressed into regular service, whose speed of 1,300 miles per hour was expected to intensify the time-zone change. The *Daily Telegraph*'s article upon the subject had a picture of a lady volunteer attached to the same sort of monitoring equipment that Barbara Mason would be seen using in the episode. It should also by now come as no surprise that Martin Worth visited the project in Maidenhead, Berkshire, during his research into the writing for the episode, where he met Dr George Christie, the medical director of Syntex Pharmaceuticals.

The idea had been flying around *Doomwatch* for a while. The *Telegraph* article was amongst a gaggle of press cuttings in the publicity material for the first series. *New Scientist* summarised the findings of the project in 1971 during an interview with Terence Dudley when the episode transmitted. 'Pilots suffered least and extrovert go-getters more than solid company men. It's also better not to travel alone but with a colleague of roughly approximate status to give you psychological support.'

The Politics
Ainslie, the manipulative public relations man, seems practised in using the effects of time-zone changes brought on by a long haul transatlantic flight, amplifying them with other disorientating techniques. With the Minister, he seeds the idea of publicly (and by implication irrevocably) presenting Doomwatch as essentially powerless, clipping its wings and placating influential industrialists in America and perhaps Britain too. The Minister even starts to believe these are his own ideas, not Ainslie's. 'You Killed Toby Wren' had laid down the roots for an American version of Doomwatch, which is at the centre of this episode's politics. American industrialists do not want a Doomwatch 'prying into the research laboratories of the country', and with good reason. DDT was in the process of being banned, and environmental issues, such as the impact of noise from Concorde in New York, were becoming headline news.

President Richard Nixon had used his first State of the Nation speech to talk about the right for every American to breathe clean air and drink clean water. He signed the National Environmental Policy Act on New Year's Day 1970, which was designed to 'create and maintain conditions under which man and nature can exist in productive harmony'. All Federal projects had to take into account their environmental impact. Earth Day was 'celebrated' on 22 April the same year. At the same time, according to Michael Allaby, the Administration was sabotaging efforts to put more money into improving the sewage works of the country. Big business is very slow to react to the dangers or a side effect of a product. Far better – and cheaper – to discredit the critic.

Production
Script Development
'Jet Rag' was commissioned as Episode 31 on 15 October 1970, the day before Worth's 'Inventor's Moon' story was officially abandoned. It would be directed by Darrol Blake.

Casting
Robert Urquhart, who puts in a mesmeric performance as the manipulative PR man Ainslie, had been a cast member in ATV's series *The Plane Makers* where he played a test pilot affectionately nick-named Aunty. As well as the return of John Barron, the episode saw Jennifer Wilson reprise her role as Miss Wills from 'The Plastic Eaters'. 'I remember having trouble with her husband [Brian Peck], who actually played a lead in one of my third series episodes,' remembers Darrol Blake. 'He said, "She's a star and they're not treating her well." I'm the same with my wife, of course, who is an actress. She hadn't had the chances she deserved, etc, and I could understand his reaction.'

For what would be the first of two episodes in a row, Michael Elwyn returned as Duncan. Desmond Llewelyn, Q in the James Bond films, appears as Thompson, the government press officer. Mary Loughran had been Dr Gray in 'The Devil's Sweets'.

Rehearsals
The read-through was held on 11 January 1971. Darrol Blake: 'I remember Simon Oates in the rehearsal rooms saying, "What am I doing?" So I said, "Well, you go to sleep," and he said, "Yeah, yeah, and I wake up about … here." "Yes, that's OK, Simon." "Do you want me to wake up pretty or wake up ugly?" "Oh, wake up ugly!"'

Studio
'Flight Into Yesterday' was the twelfth episode in production for the series. It was videotaped in studio TC8 on 19 January 1971. The shot of the empty lounge had Jean Trend superimposed using chroma key, which was also used to make the American hotel much larger than it was and with views out of its windows.

Stock Footage
A lot of stock film was used for the episode, a montage of which was cut together by Chris Rowlands, with material on both 16mm and 35mm. The

35mm *Britain Welcomes King Hussein* was supplied by COI and *Airport Now* came from World Background. BSIS and Pathé provided the 16mm silent film inserts. Apparently some specially shot film was used for the episode, but whether this was BBC stock or not is hard to identify.

One of the pieces of film was supposedly of a computer print out, which was to be played on the Doomwatch computer when Quist tells Geoff to investigate Wyatt Morley, but this isn't seen clearly.

Stock Music

Music used in the episode started with 'With Sword and Lance' by Hermann Starke from *World Military Marches* (Supraphon SUA 54739), which backed the 10 Downing Street opening. The Eric Rogers Chorale and Orchestra provided the traditional song 'America The Beautiful' from *America Sings*, a Decca LP (LK 4589), which can be heard during the first stopover. 'Summer Flight' by James Clarke came from *Open Air* (KPM 1060) and can be heard when the passengers board the plane after their stop-over. Finally, the simply barn-storming rock and roll that haunts the Minister's stressful confusion in Los Angeles was courtesy of *Even More Electric Banana* on the Hudson De Wolfe label (DW 3123), with the instrumental version of their song 'Eagle's Son'.

Editing

The episode was edited on Wednesday, 20 January 1971 between 11.45 a.m and 6.45 pm.

Transmission

The episode was due to be transmitted a week earlier than it was. Presumably the break after the second episode was the reason for it being pushed back. This is the only camera script for the second series to have a planned transmission date written on it.

Reception

Hobb's Choice in the *Evening Standard* had this to say about the well-promoted episode: '*Doomwatch*'s obsession with choosing topical – not to say telepathetic – subjects seems to be cramping its style. Tonight's far-seeing scientific saga probes the disorientation dangers caused by flying through different time zones: Dr Quist goes into a flap after a long distance trip on an aeroplane.'

Richard Last, reviewing the episode in the *Daily Telegraph*, thought it stuck out like a sore thumb. After reviewing an edition of Horizon concerning nuclear stalemate, he thought that reality was more frightening than *Doomwatch*'s fiction. He wrote 'The real *Doomwatch* – or the unreal one – was way off course last night with an adventure which didn't even pretend to adhere to the series format ... It was more like a bad *Avengers* than a genuine *Doomwatch*. The only redeeming feature was a major part for that excellent actor, John Barron, who is not seen so regularly on the screen as he used to be.'

TG writing in the *Coventry Evening Telegraph* wasn't impressed either. 'The thin line of credibility was stretched to the limit by BBC1's *Doomwatch* prophets last night. It wasn't so much the basic story idea as the events within the framework which couldn't be believed. Using the *Doomwatch* formula, writer Martin Worth took a piece of generally known fact and illustrated the possible consequences it could eventually lead to. His mistake lay in splashing too much colour – making the issue over-fictitious. In doing so, that thin line became one of the thinnest *Doomwatch* has trodden so far. Worth worked on the fact that travellers become confused when flying long distances into different time-zones. Good enough. He then theorised that certain characters, experienced in the art of being mean, could play on this disorientation and brain-wash a person if they stood to gain. Ye-es, but ... And in the story a government minister, no less, was practically brain-washed by – a public relations man. Positively not on.

'But there's more. That this PR chap was really a former MI6 agent employed to stop a Doomwatch department being set up in America. More far-fetched than a 14 hour trip to Los Angeles. Considering the amount of highly-charged invention, the drama was set on an incredibly short fuse. It also got side-tracked occasionally. Chats between the Minister and John Ridge, with references about going far in the eternal power game didn't fit in all that well with the story. And Ridge's offhandeness with his ministerial boss gets more unbelievable with every episode. But this episode wasn't one that merited complete rejection by any means. Even if it did amuse unintentionally, there was the seed of an interesting debatable theory. And good to see the bombastic minister get taken for a ride as it was. Anyone who's anti-Quist deserves it.'

On the 5 February edition of the same paper, an anonymous letter writer wrote: 'We saw last week in *Doomwatch* the spectacle of a diplomat and a scientist being confused and unable to act in a reasonable manner after having been transported across the world time zones in a manner made possible by modern aircraft. We all treat these things as a bit of fairly harmless science fiction and that is all they really are, but in view of the recent Rolls-Royce debacle one begins to wonder! A year or two ago great play was made of the Rolls-Royce officials who it was stated, were literally commuting back and forth across the Atlantic in order to clinch the RB-211 deal. Now it is said that this was a thoroughly bad deal. I suggest that if we are to salvage something out of the Lockheed contract, it might be a good idea to invite them over here and usher them quickly into the conference room with some very astute accountants.'

2.08
The Web Of Fear

Written by Gerry Davis
Directed by Eric Hills
Designed by Jeremy Davies
Transmitted: Monday, 8 February 1971 at 9.21 pm Duration: 49' 31"

Cast
Minister (John Savident), Duncan (Michael Elwyn), Patterson (Desmond Cullum-Jones), Dr Seaton (Walter Horsbrugh), Jenson (John Lee), Griffiths (Glyn Owen), Janine (Stephanie Bidmead), Dr George (Anthony Newlands).

Also appearing
Nurse (Anne Lee), Ambulance Man (Paul Nemeer).
The BBC acknowledges the co-operation of the Wellcome Museum of Medical Science

Technical Credits
Production Assistant: Vivienne Cozens. Assistant Floor Manager: Michael McDermott. Director's Assistant: Gwen Willson. Floor Assistant: Donald Ross. Film Cameraman: Bill Matthews. Sound Recordist: Derek Medus. Film Editor: Christopher Rowlands.
Costume Supervisor: Mary Hubbard. Make-up Supervisor: Pat Hughes.
Studio Lighting: Eric Monk. TM2: Graham Southcott. Vision Mixer: Dave Makes.
Sound Supervisor: Larry Goodson. Grams Operator: Gerry Borrows.
Crew: 19.

Radio Times
Scillies in quarantine. The Scilly Isles have been 'sealed-off' following an outbreak of Yellow Fever on one of the islands. The Chief Medical Officer for the Scillies said today 'We aim to keep this emergency quarantine as ... Be careful! ... these spiders are infected. Don't let either spider or web come into contact with your skin ... Be very, very careful!'

The Story
'What has happened must be fully recorded and published. Griffith was not alone in the field. The next man-made virus may be completely unstoppable.' – Quist.

The Minister of Health is holidaying on an island off the Cornish coast at a health farm. As he dictates notes to Duncan concerning the danger of flooding in the Thames Valley, another man in their sauna collapses. His shivering fit is diagnosed as yellow fever.

The health farm, owned by a Scandinavian called Jenson, is now isolated, and the Minister is less than happy about this turn of events. Though he knows he has to follow the edicts of his own department, he still complains to Duncan, only stopping when Duncan interrupts to brush a spider from his clothes.

That the Minister of Health has been quarantined causes great amusement for the Doomwatch team with the exception of Quist, who needs an urgent decision on the flooding issue. To force the Minister's hand, he decides to travel to the island on the pretext of helping with the outbreak, taking Fay with him. At the RAF base on the Cornish mainland, a very angry scientist, Griffiths, is denied permission to go over to the island. He refuses to divulge the reason for his urgency and the nature of his work. Before he leaves with his wife Janine, Quist and Fay arrive. It is not a happy reunion. As Quist later tells Fay, Griffiths is a brilliant biologist who spent fifteen years of his life working on a genetic theory. When he eventually presented his findings at a conference, they were demolished in a couple of hours by three scientists, including Quist, because of two tiny, fatal flaws.

By the time Quist and Fay reach the island health farm, two more cases of yellow fever have broken out. Jenson is upset by the news that the apple orchards will have to be sprayed, since the crop is not yet ready for picking, and his health-conscious clients will not be happy at the use of an insecticide. Dr George, from the Faculty of Tropical Medicine, tells Quist that he has a slight doubt as to the nature of the virus. Although the patients exhibit all the symptoms of yellow fever, the virus has a slightly uncharacteristic cell structure. Fay invites Quist to go on a mosquito-hunting mission with her to try and track down its source.

The Griffiths break quarantine and reach the island by boat. They set up camp in a disused tin mine as Griffiths reflects on all his wasted years of hard work, years which have cost him and Janine the chance to raise a family. He is currently developing a biological way to kill insect pests, experimenting with a technique of viral infection on the codling moth, whose maggots eat the apples on the farm. He is anxious to check on the progress of his specimens before spraying destroyed them, hence his urgency to reach the island. The tin mine appears to be full of their husks, and Griffiths decides to explore the workings underground to see if there are unsprayed specimens down there. Janine agrees to look overground. Just before she sets off, she notices a blue spider.

At the health farm, Dr George believes that spraying and immunisations will take care of the outbreak. Fay hopes he is right, but she too is bothered by the pictures of the virus in case it is an unknown strain that just looks like yellow fever. There is another new patient: Duncan. Although he is starting to become delirious, he is very sure that he hasn't been bitten by a mosquito. Ridge arrives and tells Quist about a woman he seems to have startled in the grounds. From her description, Quist realises that it must have been Janine Griffiths and tells Ridge to find her again. Meanwhile, Griffiths has explored a tunnel in the mine workings, brushing through spiders' webs to reach a large, partially water-filled shaft which leads to the surface. He starts to climb the ladder but feels weak and dizzy and slips back down.

As another case of yellow fever comes to light, the Minister is concerned for Duncan. He is very weak but will survive. Quist talks to a fraught and overworked Jenson, who faces ruin if his insurance will not cover the outbreak. One client is already dead, weakened by the health farm's near-starvation diet. The conversation turns to Griffiths, who has been treating the orchards for three years; last year the moth population was considerably reduced and this year would have seen a maggot-free crop. When Quist hears of his virus preparation, which only attacks the codling moth and nothing else, he begins to wonder. Investigation shows that the infected moths have taken on a bluey hue. Even though they are the only species affected, if they pass the virus on to another species it might trigger off a latent virus in the new host, a virus which could be deadly to man.

Ridge finds Janine and brings her to the health farm. She is worried about her husband, and, when questioned, describes seeing blue spiders unaffected by the virus in the mine and the orchard. Ridge is sent to find Griffiths but is warned to be very careful. He goes into the mine, armed with gloves and a feather duster to collect web samples, and soon finds a very weak Griffiths, infected by the webs. The way they came in is blocked suddenly by a tunnel collapse, and the sea levels in the shaft are rising. There is an upward ventilation tunnel they can use, but Griffiths passes out and Ridge has to drag him very slowly along the tunnel, inching his way under the hanging webs. When they reach the health farm, tests show that the webs are indeed crawling with infectious diseases.

Unexpectedly, Griffiths dies of the virus. Fay and Dr Quist break the news to Janine, who can only manage to say that his life had been wasted. Quist tries to offer some comfort: the measure of the man is not that he failed, but that he so nearly brought it off. Twice. Quist tells the Minister that this line of work is essential but there are no controls or safeguards. The incident must not be forgotten; its details must be recorded and published. The new disease will be named Griffiths' virus, in his memory. 'He gave us all a warning' reflects Quist. 'There have been worse epitaphs, you know.'

Behind the Story
It was well known by this time that pesticides were only useful as long as

their victim had no resistance to them. In the case of farmer-versus-pest, if acres of habitat are to be supplanted with just one crop, it will encourage a population explosion of whichever insect feeds on that crop the most. The answer is biodiversity: you grow another crop which encourages the natural predator of whatever is eating your first crop. It is probably a coincidence, but Jenson, the anti-pesticide owner of the health farm, very nearly shares his surname with Dr Soren Jensen, a Swedish research worker at Stockholm University who in the late 1960s discovered unusual levels of polychlorinated biphenyls (PCBs) in two hundred pike taken from different parts of Sweden. As well as being found in paints and varnishes, PCBs can be used to extend the life or enhance the performance of pesticides. Jensen also turned his attention to levels of DDT in creatures living in the Baltic.

Myxomatosis is mentioned by the Minister, and this refers to the virus which was deliberately introduced into the rabbit population of Australia in 1950. Professor Frank Fenner and two other colleagues who worked on the virus actually injected themselves with the myxoma virus in order to show it was not harmful to humans. When the rabbits eventually developed a resistance to the virus, Fenner described it as 'an evolutionary change'.

Characters

Griffith is a most fascinating character. He is a passionate, dedicated and committed, an angry scientist desperate to prove himself. His problem is that he makes mistakes. After fifteen years of work, his theory was demolished at a conference in three hours. His wife doesn't want to see him fail a second time and endure the same humiliation. Griffiths does not blame himself for the rejection of his ideas. He blames Quist and the other scrutineers who saw the two tiny flaws that demolished his whole elegant theory. His wife could see it objectively. As she puts it, his work failed him, not the other way round. And this time, he makes an error once again, possibly one he could not have foreseen. As he says in the episode, he would love to have studied spiders if he had ever had the time. He did not realise what could happen if his virus-infected moths were ingested by another insect, triggering a new latent virus. This time his mistake kills people – including himself.

It had an impact on his wife Janine, as we see. The Stockholm debacle ended fifteen years of research, and it cost her a family. Another few years and she is a widow, who considers his life – and, it is hinted, her own – a waste. Their scenes in the tin mine might seem to be padding, but they are essential for understanding the sheer motivational driving force behind a scientist wanting to achieve something and its impact on those close to them. It's not greed in this case, or the thirst for recognition, but the desire to succeed.

Script Development

With Gerry Davis writing this script, 'authentic' *Doomwatch* is back: the detective element is here and adventure has returned. Gerry Davis liked claustrophobic environments in which to play out his dramas owing to an incident when he was a boy, crawling inside a small, dark tunnel. This allows Ridge to get trapped inside the abandoned tin workings and its ventilator shafts with a dying scientist, surrounded by lethal blue spiders and their cobwebs. There is no record remaining of when Gerry Davis was commissioned to write the script. What we do know is that there was a dispute over fees in September because the BBC had reached the limit that they could pay him outside his script editor's salary.

The Institute for Tropical Medicine, from which Doctor George is drawn, is a real organisation based in Antwerp. Gerry Davis received help with tropical diseases from the Wellcome Museum of Medical Science in London, who were credited in the episode.

Casting

Evidently no one seemed worthy of a guest star billing this week, despite the quality of the cast. Michael Elwyn and John Savident return to the series, as does John Lee, who plays the second of his three characters for *Doomwatch*, this time as the hapless Jansen. Glyn Owen was familiar to viewers for his long drawn and haunted face, which seemed to be designed to scowl. He has guest starred in practically every series going. He often held regular roles, most notably in the first series of the family saga *The Brothers*, and then much later, as Jack Rolfe in *Howards' Way*. Stephanie Bidmead was a versatile actress, often cast to play troubled or villainous women, whereas here she is troubled and sympathetic. She died in 1974, aged only 45. The man who collapses in the sauna, Patterson, was Desmond Cullum-Jones, who was also one of the non-speaking members of *Dad's Army*. Ironically, Cullum-Jones had been booked to appear as a museum attendant in a 1968 *Doctor Who* story but was paid off and never used after a rewrite. He would have only been seen briefly in a film sequence. The story title was 'The Web of Fear' ...

Filming

This was Eric Hills' second episode for the series. A small amount of filming took place near Swanage in Dorset. John Paul and Simon Oates appeared briefly on film, which was shot on Tuesday, 8 September 1970. The sauna scenes were also filmed and featuring the return of John Savident and Michael Elwyn, who recalled 'acting his guts out' for the later scenes where he had contracted the disease.

Studio

'The Web of Fear' was the sixth episode in production and was recorded in TC1 on Friday, 25 September 1970. Anthony Newlands as Dr George pre-recorded his out-of-vision lines to Ridge in the tunnel the day before during the camera rehearsals, which overran. Originally, Ridge was to have entered the web-strewn tunnels with a pocket aerosol spray. 'Sorry about this blue eyes!' he says to his victims.

Music

Unfortunately, no record appears to survive of the copious amounts of stock music in the episode. However, Pierre Gabaye's 'Suspense' is used to back the scene when Griffith first enters the tunnels. It is commercially available on the Chappell CD *Science Fiction* (CHAP213).

Editing

Editing was done on Monday, 29 September between 10.30 am and 5.30 pm. More post production followed on Tuesday, 30 September.

The scene where Quist gets to see the Minister in the Health Farm was shortened before taping. After Dr George is taken to see the rest of the farm, the Minister said that he wouldn't like to have had any money invested in this place, even though it is a good one. Here, he pats his waist line, saying 'I felt marvellous until this happened.' Whereas on screen the Minister gives a comedy scowl as he realises Quist wants to talk about the flood menace, in the script he agrees that Quist has a convincing case, but not just now. Quist says that in his opinion there is an 80 per cent probability of massive flooding on the next spring tides which could easily flood various underground lines, and it needs stringent anti-flood precautions now. There was more material at the end of the scene. The Minister says he can hardly operate his department efficiently from Bawden Island. Quist replies that he has a brief from the Ministry of National Security and will need the necessary clearances, and the Minister agrees to contact his Minister this afternoon. Quist wonders if this will sound like a personal request. The Minister says it is. 'Well, get busy then.'

Scene 13 was heavily cut. Set in the Doomwatch office, it began with Barbara bringing in coffee and biscuits as Colin and Geoff are working on the flood problem. As Colin discusses 1953 flood levels, he holds his hand out for a drink and Barbara asks when his last slave left. Bradley asks for the mosquito reports from the microscopy unit and Geoff claps his hands, saying 'Bring it then. Chop. Chop!' He asks Colin if the last one, Pat, was as cheeky. 'Not to start with. They get that way. It's having John Ridge around...' Barbara brings in the reports and the scene carries on as transmitted.

Scene 15 is cut at the top and bottom. Ridge has just arrived on Bowden

Island and is nursing his arm, which he explains to a sceptical Fay is sore because he has extremely sensitive skin. Quist is on the phone to 'Jeff '. Ridge asks if Jenson caters for 'our slightly unbalanced brethren', and twitches to emphasise his meaning. Quist doesn't think that anyone who submits themselves to a 'diet of wheat germ and dried nuts can be said to be in his right mind'. The scene carried on until Ridge leaves, unable to think of a riposte to Fay's 'Good question!' after he wonders why he always seems to end up following women. Quist asks Fay if she has seen Jenson this morning. She looks at his timetable. 'Ladies, poetry in motion exercise...'

Scene 30 was shortened for recording. Ridge returns from the tunnel to talk to Griffiths about getting out of the mine workings. Originally, Griffiths wonders if he has got yellow fever, but Ridge tactfully tells him it is something like that and warns him not to touch any spiders or their webs.

Several scenes do appear to have been dropped before recording. Quist is pacing up and down the entrance to the mine, which Fay and Janine are waiting by. Ridge has been gone for twenty minutes. Quist wants to go in as he can't stand waiting. In the episode, he sends Fay off with the samples to the mainland and stays with Janine. In the main tunnel set, Dr George and the nurse have put Griffiths onto a stretcher, and Ridge is sitting down by the entrance to the ventilator tunnel, drinking from a flask of brandy. He stands up but his legs give way; he staggers and holds onto the tunnel walls. Dr George says they will come back for him, but Ridge is alarmed and follows them, holding onto the wall as he goes. The next scene began with Jenson talking to the Minister. Jenson has warned his clients not to touch the spiders. 'I'm not sure they need the warning – as far as the women are concerned.' Quist then says that they have an electron microscope at the Penzance

Research Division of Newington Chemicals, and that Dr Chantry has gone over by helicopter with the specimens. He clearly hasn't noticed that she is behind him bandaging Ridge's hands! The next scene is as transmitted with Janine sitting by her husband in the bedroom. Newington Chemicals, of course, is a reference to 'Spectre at the Feast'.

Reception

Although they are never mentioned in the episode, the *Radio Times* splashed 'Scillies in Quarantine' over the picture accompanying the episode's billing. This led to an amusing letter a few weeks later from R Phillips, Clerk of the Council on the Isles of Scilly, who wrote that just in case anyone thought that the fake newspaper headline was real, 'the residents of the Isles of Scilly are enjoying the ruddiest of health, and that the only yellow fever affecting them is the golden harvest of flowers'.

Another correspondent, R Rogers, was getting confused with the geography of the programme. He recognised the Scilly Isles as the location used in 'The Islanders', yet here they were filming for the Scilly Isles in somewhere that looked nothing like them. Terence Dudley was impressed and pointed out that a bit of Scotland had also been shot near Swanage.

Less kind was the television reviewer for *Plays and Players* magazine, who thought that the programme, 'with its chunks of Scientific Journal, its heavy breathing and its God What Comes Next style of acting, seems to have nudged its way into the hearts of most housewives. *Doomwatch*'s awfulness is quite disarming and it deserves to survive, blue spiders and all, until it begins to behave as though it feels it deserves to survive.'

2.09
In The Dark

Written by John Gould
Directed by Lennie Mayne
Designed by John Hurst
Transmitted: Monday, 15 February 1971 at 9.20 pm Duration: 49' 50"

Cast
Receptionist (Jane Dore), Andrew Seton (Simon Lack), Journalist (David Purcell), Naval Officer (Michael Ellison), Dr Jackson (Joseph Greig). Guest Stars: Lyon McArthur (Patrick Troughton), Flora Seton (Alethea Charlton).

Also appearing
Extras in Studio: Board Technicians (Jon Santo, Paul Johnson), Nurses (Carrie Lambert, Jo Hall), Journalists (John Wilder, Ricky King, Victor Munt, Gerry Alexander, Johnny Watson, Jo Hall).

The extras on film are unknown.

Technical Credits
Production Assistant: Anna Yarrow. Assistant Floor Manager: Derek Nelson. Director's Assistant: Norma Flint. Floor Assistant: John Norton.
Film Cameraman: Nat Crosby. Film Editor: Christopher Rowlands. Sound Recordist: not credited.
Costume Supervisor: Roger Rees. Make-up Supervisor: Pat Hughes.
Studio Lighting: Eric Monk. TM2: Graham Southcott. Vision Mixer: Clive Doig.
Senior Cameraman: Paul Kay. Studio Sound: John Holmes.
Crew: 9.

Radio Times
The death of 19 year old Alex O'Mullin was caused by mustard gas escaping from an English merchant ship, sunk in the Irish Sea during World War 1. Older inhabitants of Ballymunna, a tiny fishing village on the Cork coast, remember hearing of a ship-wreck as children and a pathologist last night confirmed ... 'Have you considered the implications once this gets out? Look what happened when they started heart transplants before they were ready!'

NB: This *Radio* Times entry used dialogue that doesn't appear in the finished episode nor is it in the camera script.

The Story
'I defeated an incurable disease by not trying to cure it. I ignored it ... My body could no longer cope, so I replaced my body with machines that could.' – Lyon McArthur

A swimmer just off the coast of Cork is killed by a leak from mustard gas. Ridge's job is to investigate known dumping sites nearby. There was one ship, the *Woodstock*, that sank before it reached its destination in 1946. The ship's commander was Lyon McArthur, an old friend of Quist, and Ridge can't seem to get hold of him at his own company. A letter from Quist yields nothing. This is because his son-in-law, Andrew Seton, intercepts the letter and refuses any contact. Flora, the daughter of McArthur, wants the meeting to go ahead, but Andrew is concerned. He tells her that not only are they keeping her father alive, they are conducting a scientific experiment which must be controlled.

McArthur holds a press conference in London to dispel rumours of his death. He tells the assembled journalists that he has been ill for some time but seems uncomfortable at Ridge's questions about the sinking of the *Woodstock*. After the conference, he tries to help Ridge pinpoint the wreck with a map, explaining that his recent illness has affected his memory. A subsequent dive fails to show any evidence of the scuttled ship. When Ridge then hears a tape recording of McArthur's voice, he realises it is not the man he met. The man is revealed to be McArthur's cousin, sent by Andrew Seaton and Flora to reassure investors. However, Flora has had enough and has invited Quist up to see her father. Andrew is appalled. 'It's my responsibility to keep your father alive.' Flora tells him that he is no longer just keeping him alive – 'You're preventing him from dying.'

The real Lyon McArthur is encased in an iron lung and other machinery, with only his head showing. Through an observation window, Dr Jackson is monitoring him. Jackson tells Flora of a communication experiment he and McArthur have just completed, in which McArthur triggered the supply of an ecstatic drug from Jackson by merely forming the correct thought pattern. Ridge and Fay have made their way to McArthur's Scottish island home ahead of Quist receiving his invitation. When they are refused entry, Ridge suggests a diversion and gets Fay to build and light a bonfire whilst he breaks in. This leads to Fay being caught by shotgun-wielding men, and Ridge sets off a burglar alarm. Andrew Seton decides to leave disciplinary measures to Quist and is not impressed with Ridge's accusations of withholding information from a governmental department.

When Quist arrives, he visits the laboratory outside McArthur's bedroom with Ridge and Fay. Seton tells them the diagnosis: chronic ascending myelitis. He should be dead, but the machines are keeping him alive. McArthur calls for Quist and explains to him what has been done. A combination of both myelitis and Wilson's disease can't be treated, so McArthur has built this machine to keep him alive. One day he will just be a brain in a box. A heart machine circulates the oxygenated blood through the brain, and soon they will use artificial blood. That would scrap half of the machines. McArthur sees himself as simply brain; pure and uncluttered. He wants to separate himself from animal instinct and emotion until his existence is defined only by thought. He is not mad, he tells Quist. He sees himself as perfect Man – because he is only brain.

Fay wonders if people would choose death rather than this. Seton sees no why McArthur could not go on forever. He reminds them that McArthur is his father-in-law. As well as providing general benefit to mankind, they are saving a life. Flora later tells Quist how grateful she was when Jackson and Seton worked on saving her father's life. Her mother had died very young. But she doesn't think that he is truly human any more. She wants Quist to make him change his mind. A little later, Ridge is finally having his discussion with McArthur about the *Woodstock*. Seton tells Quist about the thought pattern experiment, designed to allow McArthur very simple communication once the myelitis reaches his skull. Fay is bothered. 'How will you know when he is screaming?' Seton dismisses the idea; McArthur will have nothing to fear any more, not even the prospect of death. Quist sees it differently: 'He may learn to fear perpetual life.'

Ridge tries to get Quist to return to London. Whatever ethical mess Seton and the McArthurs have made for themselves is nothing to do with Doomwatch, and he thinks Quist is once again taking the world's problems upon his shoulders. Quist chooses to stay, telling Ridge to go and find the sunken ship.

McArthur and Quist debate the nature of choice and how the body shapes the brain's stored experiences. McArthur has only a few weeks of speech left, and Quist reminds him that eventually he will become totally alone, in the dark, so utterly divorced from the real world that communication will be meaningless to him. Flora tells her husband that she wants it finished. He has kept her father alive longer than previously thought possible, but now is the time to end it. After his discussion with Quist, McArthur has decided it would be better to end it, too. 'It has been worthwhile up to now, hasn't it, Flora?' he asks his daughter. 'Oh, yes, father! It added two years to your life.' He suggests she should do it now, whilst Quist is still with them, but she is shocked by the suddenness. 'It would be better quickly, without saying', McArthur tells her. 'I wouldn't be able to see.'

A little later, Flora is watching the printout of her father's heartbeat. Jackson, Quist and Fay look on. Seton ask her if she is sure about what she is doing, and she replies that it is not their decision, it is her father's. Suddenly, she turns off all the switches. The heart monitor flatlines.

Behind the Story
This was the last episode to be recorded, and in many ways would have been a good closing episode for the series. The subject matter is about death and the time to die. It has an interesting set of observations on Quist, as Ridge tries to free him from a moral dilemma, and it closes with another friend of Quist's dying, but this time it is a mercy killing.

Transplanting Heads
Lyon McArthur tried to make a virtue from his terminal illness, to see if he could cheat death and became just a brain in a box. Pure, unmitigated thought. But his daughter did not want him to endure the unimaginable suffering of when he could no longer speak, hear or sense. The idea of keeping a head, or at least the brain, alive is a staple of science fiction. In the 1950s Russian scientist Vladimir Demikhov created a world sensation by transplanting the head of a dog onto a second one, resulting in a two-headed dog. This inspired Dr Robert J White of the Cleveland Metropolitan General Hospital to attempt head transplants in monkeys. At first they removed a monkey's brain from its skull and kept it alive with artificial circulation for seven hours. Alive, in this case, meant there was electrical activity recorded, and that it was consuming oxygen and expelling carbon dioxide. By the time three Wisconsin surgeons had experimented with the brains of fifteen dogs, there were questions asked about the ethics of such experiments. The surgeons had considered the possibility that the brains may experience pain so applied anaesthetic to the back of exposed neck tissue. By 1966 the Cleveland team had removed entire heads and discovered that individual nerve cells in the brain were still alive. The pupils of the eyes contracted when a light was shone on them. But were the brains conscious? No-one knew. Dr White believed that by the 1990s, such techniques that they had developed would have made it possible to keep a human head alive. He did not consider such a thing himself because of the social implications, and, no doubt, the fact it would have been illegal.

Man becoming machine
The machine in which McArthur is slowly being enveloped is akin to the more modern version of a Cyberman in *Doctor Who*, with a human brain in an otherwise mechanical shell, rather than the surgically altered creatures Pedler and Davis envisaged in the 1960s. McArthur wants to become a thinking machine divorced from the outside world, which makes his own thoughts quite useless to anyone other than himself. But to be fair to the man, he had little choice. This is what his life was going to be like, and he was rationalising it, putting a positive spin on his awful condition. This is self-induced dehumanising medicine brought about by choice. McArthur's

lungs have been replaced by machines and the plan was to synthesise an artificial form of blood. He would no longer be able to communicate except through brain waves. Could he have gone on forever? The brain itself would have aged and withered. Would cells have continued to be replaced? If you want a Cyberman origin story for the original *Doctor Who* series, here it is. No wonder Terence Dudley felt this story was veering too much towards *Doctor Who* territory, despite the message of the piece.

Production
Scripting Development
The son of a distinguished WWII Naval Officer, Rear Admiral Gerard Muirhead-Gould, John Muirhead-Gould was only in his thirties when he wrote this episode, yet he already had an amazing track record at the BBC. According to his obituary in *The Stage*, written by Simon Masters, Gould began writing for the BBC in 1965 when he was taken under Elwyn Jones' wing in the early days of *Z Cars*, for which he acted briefly as a script editor. In 1965 he created and wrote for the highly praised and downbeat spy series *The Mask of Janus*, which Terence Dudley produced, and then contributed scripts to a wide variety of programmes such as *The Troubleshooters, The Revenue Men* and *Vendetta*. According to Masters, Gould was always happiest when working in the thriller or spy genres to 'explore his own view of human frailty and the morality – or lack of it – in government action and within personal relationships. He used his scripts to venture into the deepest aspects of human behaviour, always with an insight and originality that was startling. More than anything else, he dealt in ideas of total universality, relevance and importance, and in a way which was both compulsive and entertaining – an achievement rare in television series writing.'

'In The Dark' was the final version of Pedler and Davis' 'The Will to Die'. Gould was commissioned to write the first script by Gerry Davis and he acknowledged receipt of the script on May 29, but this was apparently rejected as Terence Dudley felt the script veered too much towards *Doctor Who* territory. Gould was sympathetic and did not like the approach taken by Davis and Pedler, feeling their sense of adventure and levity was misplaced for such a serious series. Gould was commissioned to write a second script called 'The Head' by Martin Worth in July 1. This was apparently never delivered, and so the second half of his fee for this script was paid to Gould for him to rewrite 'A Will To Die' when there was still one script needed to complete the series – and fast. Gould was sent the final rehearsal script on 13 January.

Gerry Davis did appear to have a hand in the editing the final version of the script and introduced the comic 'How?' 'How!' interplay between Ridge and Fay Chantry as they discuss how to break into the McArthur house. This annoyed Gould since he had used a quote from Macbeth: 'Hew me down a dough' for Fay as a put down 'even if no one realizes it's a put down' complained Gould to Dudley. Ridge replied, 'I say, a moving grove, Malcolm.' Slightly later in the script, the stage directions for the moment when Fay is caught by the game keepers of the McArthur estate read thus: 'She smiles, pleased with herself, then bethinks herself of Birnam Wood (private joke: the most demanding stage direction I've ever seen for an actor was "Her aunt looks at her as though to say that the police of today aren't what they used to be."'

Gould claimed some of the scenes were among the most difficult he had ever written, as it required such dense dialogue. 'It reads like a radio play,' Gould commented to Terence Dudley. The script seemed dramatic to him but thought that Gerry Davis was 'somewhat scared by it. It also contains a guide to most of the world's religions, excluding communism.'

One slight snip in the dialogue was Dr Quist telling Barbara Mason how to spell McArthur's first name, Lyon, and not Lionel as has been previously reported. Sorry about that.

Clash of styles

Having had effectively three editors, the script shows it in places. The first twenty or so minutes are almost a knock-about comedy at times as we see John Ridge sparring with a very snooty receptionist, his bamboozling of the press conference and his antics outside of the McArthur residence with a very confused Fay Chantry. Once inside the house, the atmosphere becomes more sombre and reflective, with very lengthy scenes between Quist and McArthur debating philosophy. It is almost inevitable that McArthur will die, so the ending should not be a surprise to any viewer. The episode also evokes previous *Doomwatch* episodes: the opening mustard gas leak is reminiscent of 'Burial at Sea', and when Ridge tries to persuade Quist to leave Scotland, he uses the imagery of Quist walking along the shattered planks of a seaside pier. 'The Iron Doctor' was also concerned with life extended beyond its natural limit.

The script helpfully describes which day is which. For example, when Flora speaks to her father, it is 'Day 12'. There is also a reference to the 'Dudley Committee', an in-joke on the producer's name.

Casting

The role of Flora Seaton was written by John Gould especially for Aletha Charlton, who like Stephanie Bidmead, would also die very young. Gould suggested Mark MacDignam or Michael Machiannor for the role of McArthur, which went to character actor Patrick Troughton. Mayne would direct Troughton as the Doctor in 1972 in the tenth anniversary story 'The Three Doctors'. Jean Trend had 'murdered' Troughton in an episode of Z Cars some years earlier, in which he played her husband released from jail.

David Purcell could be described as a member of the Lennie Mayne repertory company, here earning his first recorded credit. Playing the snooty receptionist is Jane Dore, who was also a dancer, who will be seen as an extra in 'The Inquest', which had been recorded earlier in the month.

Originally, Vivien Sherrard was not going to appear in the episode when the cast were booked for their three January 1971 studio appearances. John Nolan was also to have appeared on location and is noted as such in the PasB sheets.

Filming
Lennie Mayne had already directed 'The Inquest' and 'Public Enemy' (although both came later in order of transmission). Location shooting probably took place in December 1970. Dorset was going to have to stand in for Scotland with filming at Encombe House near the coast. This privately owned stately home was worth £25 million in 2008.

Studio
'In the Dark' was the thirteenth and final production to be made for the second series. It was recorded in TC3 on Friday, 29 January 1971. Troughton's scenes as McArthur's cousin were recorded first. This gave Troughton a chance to don his make-up before lying within a plywood box for a couple of hours. His son Michael recalled in his recent biography of his father that he was unable to scratch his nose unless he asked a lady from the make-up department to do it for him,.

Music
Two pieces of library music were used. A track by Robert Cornford came from *Dramatic and Horror* on the Studio G label (LPSG 1008). From *Television Fillers* by Frank Rothman (Hudson DW3061) came 'Dramatic & Mystery No. 57', a pedal timpani piece.

Editing
The editing was done on Saturday, 30 January and Monday, 1 February 1971. Part of the first office scene was trimmed. Quist has been dictating to Barbara, and, as she leaves the office, Ridge comes in. The next cut came after the receptionist suggests Ridge writes a letter. He politely asks for a piece of paper and an envelope, saying 'It'll save a stamp.' The press conference lost the opening question from a journalist, played by David Purcell, who identifies himself as Howard from the Financial Times and asks 'McArthur' about the rumours that he is dead. After 'McArthur' tells Ridge he will speak to him after the conference, Ridge sits down as the other guests look at him with distaste and Howard
asks another question. At the beginning and the end of the real McArthur's

first scene, he was supposed to be dictating his next radio programme. Barbara loses her last line of the episode when she tells Dr Quist that he will need a boat to reach McArthur's island. The end of the encounter between Ridge and Seton is cut. After Seton tells Ridge to return to London later today, he leaves the room and locks the door. 'Hello, turn up for the book' says Ridge. 'You can say that again' replies Fay in French. Towards the end of the episode, Ridge finds the sunken vessel using a sonic depth-counter in the company of the commander and the frogman from before. This thirty-second film sequence came before Flora's first scene with her father.

Reaction

'And what have the other channels lined up for our delight and digestion?' asked the *Evening Express* that Monday. 'BBC1 gives us another edition of *Doomwatch*, about which no one should complain. Compelling drama, this stuff, and tonight a look at two different situations – gas dumped in the sea and a man being kept alive mechanically.' '*Doomwatch* came up with its best story in weeks,' claimed the *Press and Journal*. 'It was a particularly macabre and mind-bending tale about an eminent scientist kept alive by machines, who wanted to live on, immortal, in mind alone. Sensible down-to-earth Dr Quist talked him out of it, of course. But there were a lot of shudders around the fireplace as my slice of the viewing public tried to imagine the extraordinary idea of existence perpetuated without sight or sound or physical sensation. A mind living on like some turtle which had discarded its shell. Patrick Troughton, seen recently as the Duke of Norfolk in *The Six Wives of Henry VIII*, lent tremendous conviction to the tale with his quiet, low-key portrayal of the stricken scientist.'

The episode struck a chord with Mary Malone writing in the *Daily Mirror*. She was fascinated by the idea of a brain in a box, which she had dreamt about as a child. 'At last, the disembodied brain has got itself on the box, and mercifully, ordered its own destruction. But I can't believe there is no end to the experiment. As a fantasy theme it will be revived time and again. *Doomwatch* (BBC1) brought it to life last night with a tale involving a great scientist, a millionaire, suffering from an incurable disease of the body who had found a way to keep going without all those aches and pains the flesh is heir to. But a few humble yet well-chosen words from an old friend Dr Quist and The Brain quickly decided to shuffle off. It's a dream that has always fascinated us. One of avoiding mortal cares and worries, to live in cloud cuckoo land where thinking nice thoughts – or brilliant thoughts or poetic thoughts or wise thoughts, take your choice, is all. It's a dream that has always fascinated us.'

2.10
The Human Time Bomb

Written by Louis Marks
Directed by Joan Kemp-Welch
Designed by Colin Shaw
Transmitted: Monday, 22 February 1971 at 9.20 pm Duration: 49' 38"

Cast
Hetherington (Talfryn Thomas), Mrs Hetherington (Joan Phillips), Man in Flat (Tom Collister), Donovan (Ray Armstrong), Cavendish (John Quayle), Laurence (Laurence Bulaitis), Baby (Dina Othman), Stephen (Nadime Othman), Mrs Frank (Ursula Hirst), Inspector Drew (Philip Bond), Police Woman (Gloria Connell), Grant (Patrick Godfrey), Scobie (Roddy McMillan), Sir Billy Langly (Kevin Brennan), Mrs Scobie (Doreen Andrew), Drunks (Eric Kent, Trevor Lawrence, Steve Peterson, David Wilde)

Also appearing
Extras on location: Stan Hollingsworth, Kumar Datta, Matilda Mensah, Jay Neil, Jules Walter, Pam Hollyer, Steven Ismay, Emmett Hennessy, Harry Davis, Elaine Williams, Frank Bennett, Stanley Simmons, Royston Rowe (an unspecified '9 children' are also listed)

Extras in studio: Waiter: Ray Marions.
Pam Hollyer, Elaine Williams, Jay Neil, Jules Walter, Harry Davis,

Technical Credits
Production Assistant: Ann Faggetter. Assistant Floor Manager: Derek Nelson. Director's Assistant: Pauline Bullock-Webster. Floor Assistant: Donald Wood.
Film Cameraman: Eddie Best. Sound Recordist: Derek Medus. Film Editor: Christopher Rowlands.
Costume Supervisor: Mary Hubbard. Make-up Supervisor: Pat Hughes.
Studio Lighting: Jimmy Purdie. TM2: Jack Shallcross. Vision Mixer: Christopher Griffin.
Studio Sound: John Holmes. Grams Operator: unknown.
Camera Crew: 19.

Radio Times
A new look for housing? A new age demands a new architecture – this was the call by property millionaire Sir Billy Langly last night. Speaking at an

annual dinner last night ... 'In the year 2000 there will be over eighty million people living in this country. They'll want cars and places to park them. They'll want clothing and feeding and educating ... to say nothing of housing.'

The Story
'The whole thing's so horrible, so frightening, I just want to get away.' – Fay

Living close to the top of an ugly block of flats, on the twentieth floor, is a Mr Hetherington. A small and nervous man, he kisses his wife goodbye and goes to the crowded lift, where his greetings are ignored. Emerging onto a London street, he panics and is knocked down by a car and killed. Fay Chantry witnesses the accident and has to comfort the shocked widow, whose children are aggressive and start to hit the police inspector who comes to take a statement. They think he is hurting her. Fay has been living at this tower block – the Amblethorpe project – to compile a report on the living standards there. Quist is annoyed that there hasn't been any contact for a couple of days. Ridge thinks she is upset because her daughter has been ill whilst staying with Fay's mother for a few weeks.

Fay is not having a good time. She is wolf-whistled by a neighbour and has been having problems with the electrics. The caretaker, Donovan, is in her flat to repair them when Mr Grant from the council planning department arrives to speak to her. She comments on the small size of the flat, which makes her feel oppressed and claustrophobic even though she has been granted a 'Family B2' unit. Fay is edgy and jumps when Donovan drops a spanner. Grant is defensive and refutes claims that any shortcuts have been taken in the design of the development. Donovan accidentally smashes the picture frame which holds a photo of Fay's daughter, and she is distraught. The next day, Fay wants to see plans of the building, and Mr Grant takes her to see Scobie in the council records department. Scobie, a highly aggressive man, agrees that Langly's development company doesn't give a damn about standards and wants to rake in profits. His recommendations are always ignored. As Scobie becomes more and more agitated, Grant suggests that he has been drinking, which provokes a physical assault. Fay and Grant leave whilst Scobie vandalises his workplace. Later, Ridge finds Fay back at the flat. She tells him that she won't be finishing her report. She has had enough of the many frustrations of living in the tower block and has also been receiving obscene phone calls. She wants to leave.

Quist meets Langly, the developer, for drinks and dinner. Langly believes that by the year 2000, the population of the country will have reached eighty million and one of the problems will be housing. He thinks his project is a step in the right direction. If everyone had their own dream house, Langly argues, the economy would collapse. He believes people will be happy to accept what's given to them without question. People make their family numbers fit their car, and they will do the same with housing, which is why elderly relatives are sent off to a home. Quist thinks that places like Amblethorpe will leave the country full of apathetic, conditioned and dehumanised zombies. Langly then turns the conversation to Fay, who he believes is prejudiced and causing a lot of trouble. He tells Quist that Doomwatch will be a laughing stock if she puts any of her findings into her report.

A neighbour, Mrs Frank, calls on Fay. She mentions that during the last thunderstorm, the noise was deafening and the building shook. Quist visits and remarks on Mrs Frank, who Fay thinks is just lonely. He hears an example of an obscene phone call. Fay says she doesn't want to end up in a mental hospital like Scobie, who has been committed since the incident with Mr Grant. She remembers Hetherington and believes that he was murdered. He worked in the assessor's office of Langly's corporation. She wants to convince Quist, and they go to speak to Mrs Hetherington, who rapidly becomes upset when she confirms that her husband had been frightened. 'He kept saying 'they'd get him.' This is witnessed by her young children, one of whom is playing with a hammer.

Quist visits Inspector Drew and explains the situation rather uncomfortably. Drew is defensive; he believes Hetherington may have committed suicide. Quist leaves, humiliated, and in silence drives off with Fay, who takes him back to the estate. As he gets out of the car, a group of children push him to the ground. Most of them scatter when Fay sounds the horn, but one of the Hetherington children, unseen by Quist, moves in with a hammer to attack him. Fay drives at them at top speed and Quist sees the child, pulling them both out of the way. He doesn't realise what has happened and is furious with her. He tells Ridge on the phone that Fay is leaving tomorrow. He will have to write the report himself.

Fay, meanwhile, has had her flat plunged into darkness again and is feeling more and more oppressed. She tries to get someone to repair her electrics, locks herself out and is harassed by offensive drunk men jeering at her. She finds Donovan and pleads with him to fix the lights. Inside her flat, once he has replaced the fuse, she is suddenly afraid of him.

Driving home, Quist is speaking his thoughts into a Dictaphone. He makes a comparison between people living in boxes and chickens in a battery farm. He goes on, noting that rather than becoming docile, the chickens tear each other to pieces if their beaks are not removed. Realising what he has just said, he turns back hurriedly. At the flat, he finds Fay threatening the confused Donovan with a hammer. He comforts her and tells her that the sooner he takes her away the better.

The next day, Quist has a meeting with Cavendish, a Government official. Quist thinks that putting people into a numbered box robs them of their identity, creating insecurity and fear. Hetherington suffered from a similar condition. Fay felt totally isolated and stress induced a breakdown. Quist will put all this in his report, but he thinks it needs more than that. He suggests setting up a Royal Commission: The Roots of Violence in Modern Society.

Behind the Story
The Need for Housing
In 1967 the *British Medical Journal* printed a paper called 'Families in Flats' by D M Fanning. It studied two groups of people in the armed forces in Germany. One group lived in an estate of houses similar to the layout of a local authority estate, and the others lived in blocks of flats three or four storeys high. Respiratory illnesses were higher in the flat dwellers, as were instances of neurosis. Lack of communication between families living in the flats was more prevalent than those in houses. Play areas were underused, with mothers reluctant to let their children out of sight – 'A further indication that people tend to be less active and more confined when they live in a flat.' In addition, the housewives were bored and lonely.

The Ambleforth complex Fay is living in is dehumanised and hostile. No individualistic touches, all moulded from the same pattern. Units are numbered, not named. There are belligerent and defensive bureaucrats on the point of nervous breakdowns and a lack of privacy (the overworked caretaker-repairman can just let himself in with a master key). Little community spirit exists (you can't just force a community to start, they have to evolve). Fay feels that the design of the building was tested to see the limits of what a human being can tolerate.

High-rise flats were seen as the solution to the slums left over from the nineteenth century. Slum clearances were first achieved by the various bombing sprees of the 1940s. Architects in the 1930s had visions of modernistic architecture to replace the ramshackle mishmash of decaying buildings that cluttered our cities. Some even welcomed the prospect of aerial bombings flattening our cities, allowing them to rebuild in the new style (though it should be noted that they didn't actually want people to die in order for them to achieve their vision). It might be strange for people to want to bulldoze quaint timber-framed cottages, medieval churches and such, but once these type of buildings were emblems of a diseased, poverty stricken past. The future was cleaner, brighter, shinier – and mainly sculpted from concrete.

With an increasing population, and without destroying the middle classes' idyllic green belt, building upwards seemed to be the answer. Prefabricated buildings were a quick-fix solution to replace the bombed-out housing stock, but the need was for something permanent. And it would be cheaper to build if was standardised. Architects did their best to make the living experience pleasant and had visions of life being lived amongst the clouds, but these 1950s blocks of flats soon became nightmarish icons of an urban experiment that had failed: broken down lifts, gangs of bored youths roaming the corridors and stairwells, isolated and forgotten people. A new symbol of poverty.

The Money Man
Langly represents the type of millionaire who thinks he has the answers to everyone else's problems. In 1971 the population was around fifty-five million. The eighty million projection was based on the population rise from 1951, which would have reached the estimated number if it had continued at the same rate. However, the population growth levelled out in the 1970s before rising at a slower rate in the 1980s. It was under sixty million in 2001. Langly's solution is to put people in compact urban units, neatly tidying them away. His alternative vision is of nightmare and chaos. Quist is quite right: Langly sees those people who want something different as eccentrics.

Langly-style developments have thankfully not housed the extra population. Flats have sprung up in converted warehouses, factories, churches, anything big enough for a bed. The decline of industry and manufacturing left a vacuum in which housing development took over. But as Langly feared, or rather pretended to care about, the green belt has been encroached upon, new towns have been planned and suburbs have expanded further and further out into the countryside, the rich man's playground.

Dehumanisation
'The other day I saw a man knocked down by a car,' Kit Pedler told a syndicated journalist in 1967. 'It was a terrible thing. He lay by the pavement just as a rush-hour crowd was streaming into King's Cross Underground. The people in the crowd merely gave a cursory glance at the man, then swept by in a mass down the steps.' Pedler felt this was a symptom of life in a heavily urbanised setting, a dehumanising effect. He suspected there were forces conditioning people to accept this intolerable environment: 'The blonde girl pushing a pram through the supermarket – she is a cardboard character careful never to get involved in anything outside the set way of her life, living to the programmed procedure in the pattern of the image makers.'

'What we need to fight against, and what I feel so strongly about, is today's mindless technology; the kind of thinking that puts up high rise flats and high density housing and only as an afterthought considers the human beings they are going to put inside, so that people are like rats in a cage and behave accordingly,' he told the *Birmingham Post* in March 1971. That these places were little more than battery farms for people was a concern for him. Pedler was lucky. He and his family of five lived in a large house in a leafy suburb in Clapham, but only a few minutes walk from the congested hell of central London.

Production
Scripting Development
The episode was designed to showcase the newest member of the team, Dr Fay Chantry, and as such only John Paul and Simon Oates would appear alongside her. This was Louis Marks' first script for *Doomwatch*. He was commissioned on 28 May 1970 to write 'The Dove of Peace' which was the fifteenth commission. It was needed by 12 June. Andrew Osborn signed the contract as acting-producer, with Martin Worth as script editor. 'I knew Louis very well', Worth remembers, 'and I brought him in immediately. He was working for independent television. I met him quite independently and asked him if he would write for the series. He came up with some good ideas.'

Casting
Once again, no one was considered a guest star. Talfryn Thomas was a distinctive face on the television, often playing shifty grotesques or comedy figures, rather than the sympathetic and fearful figure we see here. He will later work for Terence Dudley on *Survivors* as an equally doomed, and rather unsympathetic figure in its first series. He had recently worked for Kemp-Welch on *Menace*. Philip Bond usually played rather well-bred characters and had just finished a stint as a solicitor in ITV's *The Main Chance*, so playing Inspector Drew made a change for him. He will soon play a leading role in *The Onedin Line*. John Qualye gets to play a sympathetic civil servant, which makes a change for the series so far. Joan Phillips appears to have given up acting after playing the traumatised Mrs Hetherington. Gloria Connell, playing a policewoman, had recently been seen in 'The Iron Doctor' as a nurse.

Filming
Directed by Joan Kemp-Welch, the filming was performed in August at either Winterton Point or its twin, Gelston Point in Tower Hamlets in East London. The original 24 storey high flats were built in 1968, constructed from concrete and light steel and lightweight exterior panels. There were only four towers built to this system. There were problems with this form. The lightweight nature of the walls lead to complaints about a lack of privacy. Gelston Point was demolished in the 1990s and Winterton House,

as it is now known, has been completely redeveloped. There are websites devoted to the reconstruction of Winterton House with pictures of the original. Winterton Point was redeveloped in 1990s. In 1968, a tower block in nearby Newham suffered a partial collapse following a gas explosion, killing three people and injuring many more. People suspected there had been a design flaw since the explosion caused flats on one side of the building to collapse like dominos …

John Paul filmed his scenes on Monday 17 and Wednesday 19. Jean Trend was needed on location. 'I do recall trying to start the car and being frustrated at it not starting first off and giving a rather weepy gasp. Turned out to be perfect for the situation.'

Studio
'The Human Time Bomb' was the fourth story in production for the second series and was recorded in TC6 on Friday, 4 September 1970. Because of the presence of very young children in the studio, all of their scenes were pre-recorded in the morning between 11.15 am and 11.45 am.

Uniquely, this episode sees the 'fourth wall' of Quist's office; upon it, a picture taken from a Palaeolithic cave painting in Niaux in France, probably to illustrate how far housing had come in a few thousand years.

There would be no music used this week except for the usual opening and closing theme.

Editing
The editing was done on Wednesday, 9 September.

Ratings
Fifteen per cent of the population watched this episode. Twice that number was watching the series *Man at the Top* over on ITV. 2.8 per cent were watching BBC2.

Audience Research Report
The episode was subject to an audience research report based on thirty-nine completed questionnaires. The following report was compiled on 2 April 1971.

> Viewers were asked to rate the broadcast on four dimensions defined by pairs of adjectives or descriptive phrases but because the sample is small, these replies will not be published in details. It would seem, however, that this edition of *Doomwatch* was generally regarded as gripping and entertaining, scored high on credibility, and moved at a good pace.

As was remarked 'we all know this is fiction but unfortunately yesterday's fiction is often today's fact' and, certainly, this study of the tensions that could develop in those living in towering blocks of flats seemed uncomfortably near reality, in several opinions. It was a programme that highlighted one of today's social problems, and proved both entertaining and thought provoking, it seemed – '*Doomwatch* always leaves me with something to think about such as "can that really happen?". In most cases the answer is "yes" so if there isn't a real Doomwatch, there ought to be'.

According to a few, the plot was weak and the treatment of the high-rise neurosis theme unconvincing ('displayed little scientific knowledge. There was not much attempt to explain in detail the cause of the illness'), they could not believe in the characters, others claimed, or this particular programme did not measure up to others in the series.

Usually, however, the small sample audience had enjoyed the episode and, although occasional viewers were unimpressed by the acting, most evidently felt that it had reached a high standard, particularly on the part of the 'regulars'. The production, too, was regarded as entirely satisfactory.

37 of the 39 viewers in the sample saw all the programme – the other two switched off before the end.

2.11
The Inquest

Written by Robert Holmes
Directed by Lennie Mayne
Designed by Graham Oakley
Transmitted: Monday, 1 March 1971 at 9.26 pm Duration: 49' 32"

Cast
Dr Fane (Frederick Treves), Dog Owner (Laurie Webb), Philips (David Spurling), Mary Lincoln (Judith Furse), Pritchard (Frederick Hall), Marge (Jean Marlow), McAlister (Robert Cawdron), Harry (Garry Smith), Coroner (Edward Evans), Policeman (George Giles), Mr Duffy (Bill Hayden).

Also appearing
Mrs Duffy (Dilys Marvin), Reporters/Customers in Bar (Gordon Styles, Barry Ashton, Kedd Senton Steve Peters).
Extras in bar and court: Ann Garry Lee, Christine Cole, Jane Dore, Tania Parker.
Extras in court only: Brian Gidley, Bob Turner, George Hancock, Pamela Bale, Celia Hunting, Bella Emberg, Wendy Johnson, Margot Boht, Ajit Chauan, Mohammed Shamsi, Ian Ainsley, George Day, Eileen Matthews, Elizabeth McKewan.

Technical Credits
Director's Assistant: Norma Flint. Assistant Floor Manager: Derek Nelson. Production Assistant: Vivienne Cozens. Floor Assistant: Nicholas Wood. Costume Supervisor: Mary Hubbard. Make-up Supervisor: Pat Hughes. Studio Lighting: John Treays. TM2: Arthur Relph. Vision Mixer: Graham Giles.
Sound Supervisor: John Holmes. Grams Operator: Gerry Borrows.
Crew: 19.

Radio Times
Every dog within a five-mile radius of Silby must be destroyed. This was the shock recommendation of Doomwatch scientist Colin Bradley at the noisy inquest into the death of Marion Duffy the local schoolgirl who died from rabies at the weekend. 'How long is it since anyone in this country died of rabies? A 10-year-old child is dead and they don't even know how she got it!'

The Story

'People just don't understand. They have no conception of what it would be like in this country if rabies really got a hold.' – McAlister

Visiting Dr Henry Fane at the Tyrel-Clark laboratories in Suffolk, Geoff Hardcastle learns that it has been the victim of a campaign of violence by animal lovers. As if to prove the point, a shot rings out, and Geoff is hit in the shoulder.

We next see him in hospital, eyes closed and very still. Quist tactlessly gives Bradley the news and sends him down to Suffolk to take Geoff's place at an inquest. A little girl has died after contracting rabies. One theory is that it was a bite from a fly which gave the girl the infection; because the Tyrel-Clark laboratories breed tsetse flies, the Ministry of Agriculture had called in Doomwatch to investigate. Bradley first goes to see a recovered and cheerful Geoff in hospital and then visits Fane, who thinks he should investigate the mentality of the woman who is leading the campaign against him – Mary Lincoln. The Silby Arms is to hold the inquest the next day. Bradley grabs a bite to eat and speaks to the representative from the Ministry, McAlister, about the case.

Local feeling over the muzzling of dogs is running high, but McAlister is in no doubt that the rabies came from an infected dog. He warns Bradley of a journalist called Philips, who later tries to pump Bradley for information. Philips eventually gives up, but not before saying that fly-killer sprays have sold out in the local area.

Pritchard, the landlord, is doing good business the next day. His son brings Miss Lincoln a glass of water before the inquest begins. The Coroner opens the case into the death of Marion Jean Duffy of Silby and warns the assembled crowd that though feelings may be running high, he will only deal with facts. McAlister is called to the witness stand who explains that no rabid dog has been found in a five-mile radius. Miss Lincoln asks why he believes the carrier to be a dog. McAlister agrees that in theory it might be something else, but it is extremely unlikely. She produces a Petri dish containing a tsetse fly. The flies were all over the village last week. Fane can no longer contain himself and accuses her of using this tragic death in her campaign against the laboratories.

Bradley is called up to give evidence regarding Miss Lincoln's theory. Bradley, giving the combined view from Doomwatch, explains that Fane's researches are directed towards producing a fruit fly with a low fertility pattern, and he is trying to do the same with tsetse flies using biological material from fruit flies. The implication from Lincoln is that he has created a mutant virus, hosted in the tsetse fly, which escaped and infected Marion. The sigma virus found in fruit flies is of the same family as rabies, but it would be an astronomically high set of odds for it to randomly evolve into a transmittable rabies-like virus. Miss Lincoln does not give up, but the Coroner has had enough. He asks Bradley what he thinks the cause of death is. Bradley thinks it came from a dog and in his view every dog in the area should be destroyed. An uproar ensues.

Geoff discharges himself, and he and Quist join Bradley in the bar while the inquest is adjourned for a short while. After ribbing Bradley for the fuss he has caused, Geoff notices Dr Fane's choice of drink, which is not available in the UK. It is poured from a bottle kept under the bar. The inquest resumes with news that a rabid dog has been found at Silby Hall, where Miss Lincoln lives and keeps kennels. She identifies it as one of her stray dogs, one that Marion and the Pritchards' son Harry (who, Geoff notices, has bite marks on his hand) would come to see. She thinks it was a dog freed from the laboratories. Fane can't believe what he is hearing. Her theory has been dismissed and now she thinks he keeps a stock of rabid dogs! But it is true that there had been a raid which released some of the experimental subject animals. It had been reported to the police.

Quist and Geoff follow Harry to ask him about his bite marks. They also believe he knows where the rabid dogs are – Geoff saw him stealing food for them. Harry runs off after punching Geoff's injured shoulder. They have to find Harry and get him to hospital immediately, and Geoff remembers a ruined barn where he might be keeping the dogs.

The Coroner has some more data: the date that the dogs were released was a week before Lincoln found the stray, the same day that the girl was admitted to hospital. In the ruins Quist and Geoff find Harry, who covers them with a rifle. The dogs are there too, rabid and very ill. It was Harry who shot Geoff. He didn't want Fane to kill the dogs in his experiments, and he doesn't want them to die now. They persuade Harry to let them have the gun and he is rushed off to hospital.

Quist tells the inquest that the dogs did indeed come from the laboratories. Fane, under oath, has to admit he got them from a private source: Pritchard. The landlord explains that he thought it was for important work. He didn't want to do it. Quist says they must have been smuggled into the country by the same source from which Pritchard got Fane's drink. A picture of the first rabid dog shows that it had cropped ears, a practice not yet banned on the Continent. The Coroner turns to Pritchard, concluding 'The death of this little girl is a direct consequence of your greed for money and your criminal disregard for the laws of this country. But no doubt you will suffer other consequences.'

As Pritchard stands down, the villagers are clearly not happy with him, and he stops to look at the dead girl's parents. The verdict is death by misadventure. After the inquest, Quist tells Fane that Miss Lincoln was right about one thing – he runs a sloppy lab. Pritchard is left to explain Harry's condition to his wife.

Behind the Story

Animals and children are not having a good series so far. The two are combined for this episode. In an unusual twist for *Doomwatch*, the poor young girl did die from rabies, a known disease. The question was how did she get it?

Rabies

Rabies is a virus that attacks the central nervous system of the victim. It is without exception, as the episode stated, fatal. It is a horrible way to die. Rabies is thankfully non-existent in the UK, due in part to the six-month quarantine procedures which used to be in place for animals entering the country. The sea also provided an effective border. It didn't stop the entrance of the bubonic plague, admittedly, but dogs were harder to smuggle in unnoticed. The British government announced an indefinite ban on the importation of domestic pets after two incidents, one in 1969 and another in 1970. This led, in April 1970, to the setting up of a committee of enquiry which reported to Ministers in May 1971. By way of comparison, France had 512 cases of rabies in 1970, and in 1971 the figure rose to 883. Not of all those were dogs; some were foxes. The figures would continue to rise in the next couple of years. The threat of the disease crossing the Channel was very real at the time.

Animals in laboratories

If you wished to protest against vivisection, then belonging to the Royal Society for the Prevention of Cruelty of Animals (RSPCA), as Mary Lincoln did, was futile. It was an extremely conservative organisation which was basically about stray dogs and cats. It was run at that time by 'retired army officers' and 'women in big hats', to quote Richard Ryder (later to be chairman of the RSPCA in the late 1970s). However, new members joined with a view of reforming the society and turning it into a campaigning organisation, determined to make its presence felt in animal rights amongst the farming community. In late 1972 newly-elected council member and reformist Richard Ryder helped to create an advisory committee on animal experimentation. It was to be chaired by none other than Dr Kit Pedler. Had the character of Miss Lincoln existed in reality, she too would have supported the reformists. It wasn't until the *People* published an exposé in 1976 about beagles being forced to smoke cigarettes that public opinion turned against unnecessary cruelty inflicted upon animals for the sake of our safety. Called for a quote at the time was Pedler. He understood well the conflict scientists faced when it came to animal experimentation. At first he supported the practice, but over time he changed his mind as he found the number of experiments conducted on animals were for trivial reasons.

Another change in emphasis

Doomwatch as a programme or as a fictional department is not against animal experimentation, as 'Train and De-Train' demonstrated. But the Doomwatch team seem to be suffering from an imagination shortfall this week. The very process Bradley dismisses as impossible – the accidental mutation of a virus injected from fruit fly into tsetse fly, creating a rabies-like disease – is remarkably similar to the events of 'The Web of Fear', where a virus used to kill off codling moths mutates into a killer within the gut of a spider. This week, however, it would only be possible by 'postulating a combination of the most freakish circumstances' according to Bradley, who dismisses the chances. This may have been the reason Gerry Davis allegedly disliked the script enough to walk out from the series, as Robert Holmes once related in an interview. It could be argued that they are keeping the episode plausible by showing that not every death or illness has an unusual cause. Bad practice at the laboratories, blind hatred of their activities, and greed – those are the causations here, as Fay might say if she were not on sick leave this week. (Ridge is away too.)

Although this episode is rather static, with some very long and dry speeches, it is tightly plotted as an unfolding courtroom drama which twists and turns its way to reveal the true nature of the outbreak. The animal lovers who oppose the laboratories inadvertently brought this on themselves. The laboratories, presumably either to save money or to avoid red tape, break the law. It is almost a precursor to *28 Days Later*, with rabies instead of the virus known as 'Rage'. Then again, the two aren't dissimilar. Nearly ten years after 'The Inquest', rabies featured in a three-part BBC thriller called *The Mad Death*, which was a little bit more exciting, and Bradley's suggestion of shooting every dog in a certain area was taken up by the army. One of the best rabies scare episode of any programme was the 1977 *Survivors* episode 'Mad Dog', written by Don Shaw, in which the effects of rabies turn a philosopher into a savage animal.

What happened next?

Once again, a community is thrown into turmoil. What did become of the Silby Arms? Were Pritchard and his family cold-shouldered and forced to sell up and move? He was probably jailed for smuggling in a diseased animal, possibly even tried for manslaughter. Did his son survive? As for Dr Fane, it's hard to imagine him remaining at the laboratories for much longer. As for As Miss Lincoln, she is convinced that her theory is fact before seeing it dismissed by the Coroner at the hearing, eventually finding out she had unknowingly housed the rabid dog herself.

Production
Scripting Development
Robert Holmes was invited to write for *The Wednesday Play* by its script editor, Anna Scott, shortly after his third *Doctor Who* script, 'Spearhead From Space', had been transmitted in January 1970. She had wanted a treatment along with a few key scenes, but Holmes was one of those writers who absolutely hated the whole process of storylines and scene breakdowns. He just wanted to write the whole thing and not think about a particular scene until he got to it. Scott allowed him to do so, and on 24 February 1970, Holmes was commissioned to write what he considered to be his 'first bit of real writing for ten years', called simply 'Organochlorine Farm'. The themes: 'A chemical fertilizer causes the death of a child. The businessman owner of the firm hushes up the incident in the interests of sales to farmers and buys off the few people who might have ruined him.' By the time he delivered it on 15 May, it had been given the title of 'The Brilliant New Testament'. Unfortunately, producer Graeme MacDonald and Anna Scott did not like the play as written, but rather than just send it back unloved, they thought it was perfect material for Gerry Davis at *Doomwatch* and forwarded it to him on 21 May.

Seven days later Robert Holmes was commissioned by Martin Worth to provide an untitled script to be delivered by 12 June. The commission was countersigned by Andrew Osborn. On 22 July Gerry Davis thanked Anna Scott for sending the script and said that Bob Holmes was 'doing a *Doomwatch*' for them. 'You were right on the button with this writer.' There is no suggestion that the episode is based upon the rejected play. How much work Davis did on the episode is unknown. Although his name is in the camera script as script editor, he did not receive an on-screen credit. The research into the story ideas was conducted by Anna Kaliski.

No filming was allocated to the episode, which would be the first for Lennie Mayne to direct. The episode would only feature John Paul, John Nolan and Joby Blanshard from the regulars. Vivien Sherrard was disappointed to miss another episode. Miss Lincoln was originally called Miss Hulls.

Casting
That no guest star status was awarded to Judith Furse is ridiculous, especially since the acting honours for this episode must go to her. A veteran actress who died only three years after making this episode, Furse was frequently cast because of her size either as a butch lesbian or a comedy battle-axe stereotype. Here she demonstrates her abilities as a

sensitive actress. Edward Evans had a brief role as a fish farmer in 'The Battery People' and is here playing the coroner in a very smooth and commanding manner and succeeds in preventing his rather long speeches from becoming dull or uninteresting. Frederick Treves would play Colonel Cranleigh-Osborne in the final series of *The Regiment*, produced by Terence Dudley, who would also cast him very much against type as a space pirate in his only directed *Doctor Who* serial, 'Meglos'. His character name was Brotadac, an anagram of 'bad actor'. Robert Cawdron had appeared as Det Insp Cherry in *Dixon of Dock Green* and Sgt Le Duc in *The Saint*. He appeared as Taltalian, a villainous scientist in *Doctor Who*. Frederick Hall was good for rustic parts, and Laurie Webb, who had been part of the *Hancock's Half Hour* television company, and George Giles were both regularly employed by director Lennie Mayne.

Studio
'The Inquest' was the tenth episode in production and was videotaped in an unknown studio on Tuesday, 17 November 1970. The dog handler and animals came from Ellis Pet Stores. The actor who played Mr Duffy is not mentioned in the camera script, the *Radio Times* or the Programme as Broadcast sheets, but he does get his name in the closing titles.

Music
Played almost imperceptibly in the background during some of the bar scenes were 'Nothin' Doin'' and 'Supper by Candlelight' from *Bar Piano* by Tony Ross and Bill McGuffie (KPM 1030), as was 'Deontology', composed by Gino Peguri and played by the Franco Chiari Jazz Quartet, from the Mozart Edition label (MELP 05). From the Impress range came an untitled percussion piece by Ivor Slaney (IA385), used over Geoff 's prone body after the titles.

Editing
Editing was done on Thursday, 19 November 1970 between 7.30 pm and 9.30 pm. There were a few edits. One cut was after Bradley's recommendation for every dog in a five-mile radius to be destroyed. Miss Lincoln was to have been heard shouting during the uproar that it was monstrous, and he was a barbarian. Philips, the journalist, is writing 'Boy oh boy! Grist to the mill!' Bradley begins to retort 'If it's barbaric to regard human life as more important than animal life –', but Miss Lincoln interrupts 'I was forced out of the scientific profession by men like you!' The dog owner shouts 'You try it! You try touching my dog!' All the time, the Coroner is calling for silence. Another tiny cut was of McAlister on the phone in the hallway, thanking the caller. The next cut came just before Quist and Hardcastle investigate the disused farm buildings; the Coroner

works out a timeline for the girl's contraction of rabies by establishing the length of time that the rabid dog was loose.

Programme Review Board

The Board's only comment on the episode was that John Paul was still getting better – a year since his performance in 'Project Sahara' was criticised. However, Shaun Sutton told the panel about the confidence issues the actor had experienced since *Probation Officer*.

A Break in Transmission

After this episode came a week's holiday for *Doomwatch*. In its place, BBC1 had spent £50,000 on the rights to show the recording of the fight between Joe Frazier and Cassius Clay, which was taking place in the early hours of the morning in New York. The *Evening Express* took the cancellation philosophically: 'To whet our appetites, Harry Carpenter reports from New York tonight on the build up and the atmosphere. It means missing *Doomwatch* for one week but that's just excusable in the circumstances.' The recorded fight was shown the following night. There had been a fear that it could be over in the first round, making it a very expensive couple of minutes, but the 'Fight of the Century' between the two rivals went to the full fifteen rounds.

BBC2 offered some more cultural refinement in the form of *Horizon*'s 'Due To a Lack of Interest, Tomorrow Has Been Cancelled', which looked at predictions of ecological disaster. The Programme Review Board displayed signs of things to come: Robert Reid felt that the show had 'over-killed' the subject; others were tired of the whole 'Eco-doom' theme for a programme. Next morning, the *Daily Mail* gave *Horizon* very short shrift and would have their words quoted back at them in the opening episode of the next series.

2.12
The Logicians

Written by Dennis Spooner
Directed by David Proudfoot
Designed by Graham Oakley
Transmitted: Monday, 15 March 1971 at 9.22 pm Duration: 47′ 40″

Cast
Priestland (Noel Johnson), Kelsey (Michael Gover), Mrs Grantz (Irène Prador), Handyman (Stanley Lebor), CID Sergeant (George Selway), Withers (John Kelland), Colin Tredget (Peter Duncan), Richard Whetlor (Robert Barry Jnr), David Wagstaffe (Stuart Knee), Malcolm Priestland (Robin Davies)

Also appearing
Extras on film and in studio: Thomas McCabe, Freddie Wilson, John Gugolka, Gary O'Brien

Extras in studio only: David Docherty, Keith Dewhurst, Robert Bartlett, Kedd Senton, Reg Turner, Crawford Lyall

Technical Credits
Director's Assistant: Adele Paul. Production Assistant: Vivienne Cozens. Assistant Floor Managers: Alistair Clarke, Amanda Abrahall. Floor Assistants: Donald Ross, Ian Pleeth.
Film Cameraman: John Baker. Sound Recordist: Doug Mawson. Film Editor: Sheila S Tomlinson.
Costume Supervisor: Mary Husband. Make-up Supervisor: Pat Hughes.
Studio Lighting: Jimmy Purdie. TM2: Graham Southcott. Vision Mixer: Christopher Griffin.
Studio Sound: John Holmes. Grams Operator: Gerry Borrows.
Crew: 6.

Radio Times
Break-in mystery. Industrial spies are blamed for the mystery break-in at Beresford Chemicals. Hampshire police have no clues as to how thieves broke through a sophisticated, electronic security system, to steal vital papers. Papers which, Managing Director Jack Priestland says, 'could be invaluable to competitors, particularly …' 'Logic, in a child, is in many ways superior to that of an adult.'

The Story
'It's all the fault of that school. They're not educated there, they're programmed. And they love it. Little tin gods ... tomorrow's elite.' – Priestland

With a plan of a building, knowledge of its security arrangements and the location of a safe, a ventilation shaft and a security alarm, a group of three young teenagers are planning a raid. 'Tomorrow's the big day!'

David Wagstaffe, Colin Tredget and Malcolm Priestland are part of a group of students from Elsdene, a private boarding school, who are visiting a pharmaceutical company called Beresfords, managed by Malcolm's father. The group are warned by their teacher not to be patronising or supercilious. In Priestland senior's office, a handyman painting the skirting board is watched by Ridge as he waits for Fay, who seems to be a big hit with Priestland. Doomwatch are there to monitor the development of a powerful new antibiotic, K-27.

The children are being shown around by Kelsey, a senior chemist. With the aid of a diversion, Wagstaffe is secreted into a ventilation shaft. He remains there until night-time; he then emerges and opens the safe in Priestland's office. First he uses a chair to switch off the safe's alarm and then a small machine to crack its combination. He returns to his hiding place. Back at the school, Malcolm and the boys plan to take Wagstaffe out unnoticed as part of the second group due to visit the company.

At Beresfords the next day, Ridge and Geoff find Priestland senior and Kelsey talking to a CID sergeant. The file containing the K-27 formula is missing from the safe. Ridge is a little bemused to be questioned by the sergeant who wants some information on Doomwatch's involvement with the drug tests. Kelsey wants to go as he is going to be busy with the second tour, but Priestland tells him that he telephoned the school and cancelled the trip. Ridge notices chair-leg marks on the skirting board. He starts to have suspicions about who could have committed the robbery.

He and Geoff visit Elsdene and wander around. They witness a class in action, all performed with the aid of computers. It is an exercise in logic: how to find a new source of energy for a stalled boat and get it out of a danger zone. The class are encouraged to think using a flow chart of logical possibilities inscribed on a blackboard.

Back at Doomwatch, Ridge tries to express his concerns to Quist. Geoff thinks that the classroom looked more like a space shuttle. Quist isn't surprised as Professor Grantz, the Headmaster who founded the school, helped to pioneer that form of teaching. Quist quite approves of logic machines. In his opinion, clear thinking is just what the country needs. Grantz was 'a great educationalist in the human sense'. After he died, his widow took over the running of the school. But it was the inhumanities that bothered Ridge, who gets heated: a well-planned crime would seem as amoral as an exercise in logic to any pupil from the school. Quist takes the challenge silently.

At the school, Wagstaffe's absence has gone unnoticed due to the informality of the place. The boys decide that they don't need the file for the next stage of their plan. Wagstaffe, having spent a second night in the ventilation tunnel, returns to the office and telephones the school. Malcolm answers the phone and tells him he'll bring some food in.

Quist visits Mrs Grantz and quizzes her about the teaching methods created by her husband. She knows that there is a lack of traditional discipline here. The children are afforded the same sort of liberty as a university student, which impresses most visitors. Quist is getting worried by Mrs Grantz's answers and lack of understanding of the dangers of 'education by computer tape' now that her husband is not supervising. She also tells him that the school is always in financial crisis. They are not subsidised because their methods are considered too unorthodox, and the boys know this. She offers to show Quist around and put his fears to rest.

Malcolm sneaks in food for Wagstaffe when he visits his father's office. When Ridge arrives to discuss the theft with Priestland, Malcolm recognises him from the school. Ridge denies having gone there, but, after Malcolm leaves, even Priestland seems to have his suspicions those 'little horrors' might be behind the robbery. But he won't admit it. He is explaining the reasons for sending his son to Elsdene as a demand on tape arrives. It gives instructions for how Priestland can get the formula back. Money is to be thrown out of a railway carriage at a predetermined signal from a receiver, also enclosed in the package. The demand is for £25,000, and Priestland is prepared to pay it as he dares not risk involving the police.

On the train, Geoff Hardcastle fits a tracker into the briefcase full of cash. No-one has told Priestland about the device, which is being monitored by Colin Bradley back in the Doomwatch lab. Quist tells Fay he thinks the scheme is the safest way for the thieves to collect their money, which could be jettisoned anywhere between London and Portsmouth. It's been logically thought out. And they'll soon find out if the boys are doing it. Ridge is down at the school to see which of the 350 pupils are missing. They all are. It is a holiday.

Geoff throws the case out of the window when the boys transmit the signal. They recover it, find the tracker, put the money into another bag and leave. Later, they treat the money to make it untraceable, and all that remains now is for their anonymous, rich, dead woman to make her donation through a fake solicitor to the school. Wagstaffe finally escapes from the company building, leaving the files behind.

Quist and Ridge confront Priestland. He knew his son was behind the robbery but wanted to protect him. What he didn't know was that his son was going to frame him, covering his tracks by planting the bugged bag in Priestland's own back garden. In order to clear himself he has to report Malcolm to the police. He looks on the bright side: as Malcolm is a minor, the school will have to take responsibility. 'At least he can take care of himself,' laughs Priestland. 'He'll do well in business!' Quist and Ridge exchange glances.

Behind the Story

It is hardly surprising that this episode, recorded second and buried towards the end of the series, was a Kit Pedler and Gerry Davis storyline. This story is another take on one of Pedler's favourite themes: dehumanisation by an over-reliance on technology.

In 1962, the *Coventry Evening Telegraph*'s Langston Gray wrote an article about 'Teaching by machine ... the mechanical schoolmaster is about to start work. The electronic teacher is coming to our aid at a time when school teachers are finding it almost impossible to cope with over-big classes ... The NAVY, the Army, the RAF and a number of big industrial firms wish to incorporate machine teaching in their training programmes ...' Earlier in the year, a small group of educators and industrialists had formed the Association for Teaching Machines and Programmed Learning. The description of a teaching machine, and a child's interactivity with the machine does not sound terribly sinister neither does the reward system for a correct answer – which in the case for infants, might be a marble. These days, employees can take training courses at home and on their laptops in, for example, health and safety. What was Pedler and Davis concerned with, and practically every other science fiction series which dealt with computers and super-educated children?

Logic

1960s Britain wanted to be a technocracy and looked towards the next generation. Education had been reformed and extended during this period. It was almost inevitable that computers would be used in the classroom. As Priestland points out, they were living in a technocracy. He felt his son would benefit from a computer-based education that would give him an advantage in life, to see through problems and reach the solution. A first class-mind for business. Doctor Quist approves of the school at first. He believes that youth, without the emotional distractions of adulthood, can absorb a lot of symbolic training. The ability to think straight and appraise any situation, uncluttered by emotional bias, is what the modern world needs, he declares. 'The day of the half-educated amateur ... is finished. At least, I hope it all is.'

In 1968, teaching machines were used in another *Doctor Who* story, 'The Krotons', by Robert Holmes. Here, they trained students to increase their mental power in order to power a spaceship. 'Speed learning' of facts and figures was highlighted in an episode of *The Prisoner* in which the teacher is revealed to be a computer, 'The General' of the title. Being over twenty years since the indoctrination of an entire generation by fascist governments and similar goings on in the communist states of the USSR and China, it shouldn't be much of a surprise that education in the 1960s was seen as a potential for perversion and indoctrination in the west. Children could be used as a political tool: one of the most sinister aspects of Orwell's 1984 were the children who denounced their parents.

Yet the problem addressed in 'The Logicians' is not a concern over political indoctrination, but morality – the boys simply forget their sense of right and wrong. The school needed money; they got the money. Simple as that. Once Malcolm Priestland and his ilk had left school and entered commerce, who knows what methods he would have justified as logical, if immoral? When their plan is uncovered, they do not suddenly reconnect with their emotions, Priestland works out a method of shifting the blame onto his dad.

Pedler and Davis had tackled logic in *Doctor Who*'s 'The Tomb of the Cybermen' as a basis for a power-hungry brotherhood that wanted to use the cold, emotionless (and logical) power of the Cybermen to rule a weak Earth. Pedler also provided ideas for 'The Wheel in Space' which introduced a new companion, Zoe Herriot, whose reliance on logic, facts and figures, and a natural arrogance and assumption of her superiority, coupled with a lack of empathy made people uneasy around her, especially when facing a catastrophe. The difference between Zoe and the Brotherhood of Logicians is that she is a teenager.

Production
Script Development
'The Logicians' was the second of four Pedler and Davis storylines accepted on 18 December 1968 by Terence Dudley. Had it been given to any previous author, it was clearly one of the casualties. It was finally given to Dennis Spooner as the first script commissioned for the new series, on 2 April 1970. 'The Logicians' is possibly the closest Doomwatch comes to having its own comedy episode. With John Ridge as the gooseberry of the Priestland/Chantry 'romance' and a foil for the CID inspector, making wisecracks at the expense of Geoff Hardcastle and knocking the desk twice for some unfathomable reason in Quist's office, he provides more than ample light relief. Once he starts calling Fay Chantry 'Mother' on the phone, you can see Dennis Spooner is channelling his ITC instincts where humour and adventure went hand in hand. The script identifies Elsdene School as being in Surrey, and the *Radio Times* places Beresford's in Hampshire.

Filming

David Proudfoot directed the episode, and filming was done after 'Invasion' and 'The Iron Doctor'. Simon Oates filmed his scenes on the 21 July with John Nolan at a Grade 2 listed mansion in Otterhaw Park, Chersey, Surrey. The opening shots of the Mansion were on its south side, including the mirror pond, while the north side was seen for the comings and goings of the bus and Ridge.

Casting

The young cast is notable for some of its future stars. Robin Davies as Malcolm Priestland had played Carrot in *Catweazle*, with his hair suitably dyed, and would later star with Wendy Craig in the sitcom *And Mother Makes Three*. He died of lung cancer in 2010, having had a successful career as an actor, writer and director. Peter Duncan, playing Malcolm's accomplice Colin Tredget, would go on to appear in several episodes of *Survivors* (as would Michael Gover) and become a *Blue Peter* presenter. Noel Johnson should have been accorded guest-star status. He was famous for his radio role as Dick Barton, and practically lived on television. He had brushed with computers before in the two BBC *Andromeda* serials of the early sixties. Irène Pradnor came from Germany and usually played roles in her natural accent.

Studio

'The Logicians' was the second story to be recorded. This was in TC5 on Wednesday, 14 August 1970. No music was used.

Promotion

The episode was promoted in the *Daily Sketch*. After summarising the plot it told its readers 'Be sure Quist (John Paul) and his boffin sleuths will survive some crises of conscience before the end.' Philip Purser reviewed the episode in the *Sunday Telegraph* on 21 March, writing 'Last week's episode set up an even more arbitrary villain: logic ... The wholesome moral of the tale was that by producing children with over-developed logical faculties but no extra moral restraints we'd end up with a dangerous elite. The only snag is that nowhere that I could see was logic involved, and certainly not in the classroom problem that the boys were shown tackling. Behind the gadgetry of computer and closed-circuit TV, there was – nothing.'

Audience Research Report

This episode is the second for which reports survive. It was estimated that 18.8 per cent of the population of the UK watched the episode, compared to 3.1 per cent for BBC2 and 14.7 per cent for ITV (which was showing *The Misfit*, starring Ronald Fraser). Twenty per cent of the viewing panel tuned into *Doomwatch* and were asked to choose one of five scale positions between

'Gripping' and 'Didn't hold attention'. The results showed that most viewers were held by the story. Likewise, most found it entertaining and quick moving, but it scored lower on the believability side:

> The majority of reporting viewers had evidently enjoyed this story, which held their attention to the end, leaving food for thought and the feeling that 'this could come true'. As one of the more enthusiastic remarked; 'This programme always seems so real to me; that kind of teaching could possibly produce boys with minds like computers and no real sense of right or wrong'. But for a good many its appeal was generally moderate. This was not one of the best episodes in the series, in their opinion; it lacked 'the holding power of previous ones' and was 'not very exciting'; above all it was 'much less likely than most of the others'. Verdicts as to its improbability ranged from 'rather far-fetched'; 'the only story I could not quite believe could ever happen' to isolated objections that it was 'very unrealistic' and 'ridiculously incredible'.

> Acting and production were generally considered satisfactory, quite a number, in addition to commending the Doomwatch team, praising the performances of the young actors playing the schoolboys, who, it was said, for instance, come over as 'real characters'. There was some criticism, on the other hand, on the grounds that the children appeared 'stilted' and lacking in conviction, a few finding the acting generally not very convincing...

> Asked for their opinion on the series, the majority of those reporting were appreciative. According to some, admittedly, the stories varied in credibility and holding-power. But generally, they agreed that the series had been an interesting and entertaining one, and many had enjoyed all or most of the episodes heard, finding them compelling and thought-provoking and 'splendid entertainment value'. Their topicality was a special feature it was said, and also the fact that they 'touch on things the layman never gives a second thought to', and 'make people realise how progress can get out of hand'.

> Less often there was support for the view that this series had 'never quite made the standard of the previous one' and had lost 'some of its earlier impetus and appeal'. Isolated viewers were inclined to dismiss it as far-fetched rubbish.

2.13
Public Enemy

Written by Patrick Alexander
Directed by Lennie Mayne
Designed by Graham Oakley
Transmitted: Monday, 22 March 1971 at 9.22 pm Duration: 49' 49"

Cast
Jimmy Brookes (John Trayhorn), Jimmy Walsh (Terry Bale), Mrs Freeman (Rhoda Lewis), Mrs Jones (Barbara Bolton), Donovan (Norman Florence), Dr Barton (Roy Purcell), Secretary (Francis Pidgeon), Duncan (Michael Elwyn), Nicholls (Bill Weston). Guest Stars: Arnold Payne (Derek Benfield), Lewis (Trevor Bannister), Gerald Marlowe (Glyn Houston).

Also appearing
Town Clerk (Frank Lester), Union Members (Bob Babania, Derek Deadman), Mr Mannering (Leslie Montague), Councillors (Michael Mulcaster, Jim Tyson), Lady Russell (Bonnie Seimon), Mrs Rudyard (Rita Tobin), Guild Member (Coralai Wilson), Mr Formby (Roy Hathaway).

Extras on film: Sam Mansaray, Lucita Lijertwood.
The BBC wishes to thank the Foundry Division of the Zenith Carburettor Company

Technical Credit
Production Assistants: Christina McMillan, Anna Yarrow. Assistant Floor Manager: Derek Nelson. Director's Assistant: Norma Flint. Floor Assistant: Nicholas Wood.
Film Cameraman: Nat Crosby. Film Editor: Christopher Rowlands. Sound Recordist: not credited.
Costumes: Mary Husband, Juanita Waterson. Make-up Supervisor: Pat Hughes.
Studio Lighting: Eric Monk. TM2: Graham Southcott. Vision Mixer: Rachel Blatney.
Sound Supervisor: John Holmes. Grams Operator: Gerry Borrows.
Senior Cameraman: Paul Kay.
Crew: 9.

Radio Times
Doomwatch probes metals firm. An urgent investigation into pollution,

described by a local alderman as 'revolting, dangerous and now deadly' is being made by the government's Doomwatch team. A ministry spokesman said last night 'Dr Spencer Quist and his assistants will examine all processes and disposal systems at Carlingham Alloys ...' 'At the rate we're going ... at the rate we're polluting ... over-crowding ... chemicals ... noise ... we've got thirty years. Thirty years of slow, dirty dying.'

The Story
'But someone has to pay!' – Quist

A young boy called Jimmy Brookes borrows a ladder so he can get his football from a factory roof. He ends up having to be carried back to the ground when he is seen staggering along the roof, choking and gasping for breath. He dies.

Doomwatch are called in to investigate by the angry Alderman of Carlingham, Arnold Payne, who believes that their town is being slowly poisoned by Carlingham Alloys, a firm his father founded and which was later bought out by International Metalloids. The death rate from pulmonary disease is well above the national average in Carlingham. Payne tells Fay of other incidents he believes Carlingham Alloys is responsible for, such as the trees in the park which lost all their leaves in one night. Ridge has been looking into background to the firm: they are a respectable outfit that make omnistahl, a special alloy. Most of the profits from omnistahl are being used to fund the development of a new secret product that could replace carbon fibre.

The managing director is a man called Marlowe, and the scientific brains is the young Anthony Lewis. Geoff remembers Lewis from Durham – the mad metallurgist, obsessional about his work. Ridge looks into Lewis' background, just in case there is a file on him.

Lewis is told of the boy's death by Marlowe. Although shocked, Lewis hopes nothing will hold up his work. Fay talks to some of the locals, who are suspicious about the factory and the smuts it used to produce. According to Barton, the town's Medical Officer of Health, the smuts were caused by the factory's heavy oil heating, which was soon altered. By the time Quist and Geoff visit the factory, the cause of death has been found. The boy's football broke open a pipe and he breathed in a lungful of poisonous beryllium fumes. The gas is part of the process for developing their new, secret alloy: superstahl. Lewis says that they are very close to completion and the Americans are in direct competition. Lewis takes Doomwatch on a tour of the noisy industrial factory floor explaining the processes before them. When the boy broke the chimney pipe, the whole system was shut down in three minutes flat.

A workman, Harry Nicholls, is within the girders supporting the roof in another section of the factory where molten metal is poured into crucibles and then into moulds. Geoff spots that the Nicholls is in trouble before he falls to his death. Marlowe is stunned at the news. Supported by Joe Donovan from the Works Committee, Quist suggests checking and tightening up safety procedures, much to the disgust of an appalled Lewis, who resents any delay that might affect his work. As far as he is concerned, the boy's death was an accident caused by trespassing, and Harry Nicholls died in a fall which could have happened anywhere. Lewis insists that they already take reasonable precautions. Quist counters that his suggestions are reasonable.

Back at the Doomwatch office, Quist and Geoff have an argument about Lewis' attitude. Geoff accuses Quist of sounding like a heavy father and can understand why Lewis is in a hurry. He thinks that whenever Britain has a new invention, it is taken over and developed by America, which then sells it back to be manufactured under license.

News comes from the hospital: Nicholls' lungs were full of beryllium when he fell, but how? Geoff traces the man's activity throughout his last day, but it is Lewis who realises that he had been breathing in a heavy dose of fumes that had become trapped in the apex of the roof. Quist tells Lewis and Marlowe that the fumes will build up in their workers in time. Lewis argues once again with Quist over safety levels, fearing the extra costs and delays will go down badly with head office. Marlowe tells him to leave head office to him, and Lewis storms out. Marlowe apologises and assures Quist that head office will accept his recommendations. They don't.

The news is soon broken to a council meeting discussing recent events (from which Payne is making great capital) that the factory is going to be closed down. They are just one of International Metalloids' subsidiaries, and rather than spending money on the safety precautions recommended by Doomwatch, the parent company is moving production of superstahl to their new Leicester plant. It will mean the death of the town: the workers will have to move if they want to keep their jobs.

Duncan brings gentle governmental pressure on Quist to reconsider his report, and now Payne, whose livelihood depends on the workers renting his houses and their wives using his supermarkets and dry-cleaners, tries to get Fay to change her mind too. Even the once-supportive Joe Donovan and his union are now furious with Doomwatch. Quist is beginning to 'feel like a public enemy' but stands firm. He is invited to address a private meeting with Carlingham Alloys and the town council. As he says to Geoff and Fay, they are up for judgement.

At the meeting Fay tells the hostile audience that the factory needn't shut down altogether; it would only be for a few weeks to fix things. But the argument rages over who pays. Is it the town through its rates, the factory itself or the Government? During the angry objections, Quist loses patience. He packs up to leave and Payne protests, which causes Quist to lose his temper. 'But someone has to pay!' he bellows.

'Now, we all want a clean, healthy world to live in, don't we? We're all against pollution in any form? But only when the cost of fighting it is borne by someone else. When our own pocket's hit – a shilling on the rates, six weeks on the dole, a capital investment which makes a company merely viable – then no thanks, let's forget it. Well, I'm warning you: forget it and you're dead. Not just this community, but the whole of industrial civilisation. The way we're carrying on, the way we're polluting – over-crowding, chemicals, noise – we've got thirty years. Thirty years of dirty, slow, dirty dying. Or else it's thirty years for us to clear up the mess. That's the choice. That's your only choice. Pay up or pack up.'

He singles out Payne; Donovan; Marlowe and Lewis. 'Not only you, or you, or you, but every single one of us. Every living one of us. All of us.'

And there, he is looking at us.

Behind the Story

'Public Enemy' is the next turning point of the *Doomwatch* saga – where shock-horror fantasy and warnings over technological and scientific hazards are replaced with more realistic and mundane everyday menaces and nuisances. In this case, industrial side-effects. Although the episode is more factory-floor drama rather than fantastical imagining, it is not dissimilar to 'Train and De-Train' from the previous series.

At the time it was commissioned, during Martin Worth's tenure as script editor, Kit Pedler had become the official *Doomwatch*-style advisor to the *Daily Mirror*. The first 'shock horror' exposé in the edition of 22 June was the case of the melting nylon. It seemed obvious that whatever was causing nylon in two different parts of the country to develop melted patches was airborne and acidic in nature. Several local industrial factories with chimneys were fingered as culprits. Scientist Kenneth Daniell of the Environmental Sciences Group at the Greater London Council, who assisted the investigation, wrote 'I have an uneasy feeling that this is a concentrated sample of what is going on fairly generally ... I think that the smuts are too small to be dangerous to health but it is nevertheless wrong that we have to live with little drops of acid in the air.' One solution to the problems of industrial pollution was to be build higher chimneys and allow the wind to carry it away. The problem was it ended up in northern Europe, and the issue of acid rain killing forests in Scandinavia became a very hot potato in the early 1980s.

Although this episode is more of a traditional drama in nature, it tries in places to suggest that the issues at heart are more sinister. Quist and Geoff exchange knowing glances when the town's Medical Officer makes a throwaway comment about some process they don't know about. 'What are you making down there? Poison gas?' Quist later asks. 'Smuts?' repeats

Fay Chantry in a close-up. It is just simple pollution brought back down to earth by rainfall – acid rain, as we later called it. It is not some by-product of a careless, greedy or immoral scientist. There is no sinister, secret process endangering the lives of unsuspecting workers and their families. It isn't germ or chemical warfare. Instead, the programme shows the typical growing awareness of the time that if you work in heavy industry, reasonable precautions are not always enough to prevent long-term illness or death. Quist goes out of his way to dig into the firm, perhaps unfairly, because of the angry and rude resistance from Lewis, but even he cannot find much to fault.

Positive Business
Carlingham Alloys is a responsible employer – it has excellent relations with the unions, a good record in health and safety and the managing director, Mr Marlowe, does not respond to either death in his plant as if it was someone else's fault. Problems that can be placed at his works' door are dealt with. This is no asbestos story. (The fact that asbestos was known to cause cancer after long-term exposure was allegedly covered up.) There is also a little foreshadowing of 'Waiting For a Knighthood' in Professor Lewis' argument over lead in petrol. At the time, it was known to be harmful in exhaust emissions but considered safe enough. What constitutes a safe and permitted dose of anything is tackled in 'Spectre at the Feast' and 'You Killed Toby Wren'.

The question of who pays to clean up the environment was one that Terence Dudley went into at length in 'Spectre at the Feast' and would do so again. It explores the consequences not just for our pocket but for our jobs and lifestyles as well. It can't all be left to governments. Quist in 'High Mountain' knows that only governments can protect the environment and repair the quality of our lives if they so choose. A telling scene in this episode is Duncan's visit to Quist. He gently tries to persuade Quist to downplay the long- term health hazards in order to protect the town's economy. What is wrong with a little dirt as long as we are earning a living?

Local politics
Politicians in the series are usually of the Whitehall variety. Here, in Alderman Payne, we see local politics and a seasoned player of the game. He starts off in emotional high dudgeon over the death of a boy, but by the end of the episode we see him for what he truly is: a grubby opportunist with a huge chip on his shoulder over the factory his father started and lost; a man who has done well out of the town – a landlord and a businessman – and who now sees how his way of life will be eroded if the object of his resentment is removed. (It is also implied that he is not a very

good landlord, either.)

Enemy of the People
It is a fascinating episode in that the previous series finale saw Quist nominated as Man of the Year by a national newspaper, but now he feels like he is a public enemy. This brings us to the second influence of the episode: literature, and in particular an 1882 play by Ibsen called *An Enemy of the People*. Terence Dudley held this piece in high regard for its conflicts of ideas, opinions and emotions. It shares some similar elements to 'Public Enemy'. In a Norwegian coastal town, a doctor is trying to draw attention to the dangers of pollution from the town's tannery business, which could make people visiting the new public baths ill. The locals ignore his warnings as it would affect their industry and thus their economy. During a public meeting, he too is made to feel like an enemy of the people.

Production
Script Development
Patrick Alexander was a BBC producer and writer. He had been in charge of the unsuccessful science-fiction programme *Counterstrike*. 'Public Enemy' was considered to be the best script of the series so far by both Terence Dudley and Andrew Osborn, who declared that 'it was what the series was all about'. Unfortunately, when it was shown to Kit Pedler, he declared it 'jejune and scientifically unsound'. He asked for his name as scientific advisor to be removed. Dudley was astounded. Pedler's credit was duly removed from both the *Radio Times* listing and from the closing titles.

Precisely what Pedler found to be so offensive in the writing is unclear as his letter does not appear to have survived. It could be that without Gerry Davis in the office, he was feeling as powerless as he did by the time his presence on *Doctor Who* was only tolerated when they needed another Cyberman story. 'Public Enemy' was about as far from the original intention of *Doomwatch* as it was possible to go, even though the arguments were perfectly in tune with his own thinking. Pedler believed that we would have to pay more money to buy things that were environmentally damaging in order to pay for the eventual clean-up.

Filming
It was the second story given to Lennie Mayne to direct. Unlike his first *Doomwatch* to be recorded, 'The Inquest', this one would have extensive location filming, which took place in and around the Foundry Division of the Zenith Carburettor Company plant in at Honeypot Lane in Stanmore, Middlesex, long since closed down. This was presumably done in December 1970. Not all of the location material was filmed. A series of

photographs intercut with studio material of John Nolan writing in a notebook was used to show him questioning the staff at the factory.

Casting
Charles Morgan was to have played Marlowe but was replaced by Glyn Houston. The character's first name is given as 'Harry' in the programme, but both the end credits and the *Radio Times* bill him as 'Gerald Marlowe'. Roy Purcell would work with Lennie Mayne in the future, in particular on *Brett* and in *Doctor Who*. Derek Benfield will return to *Doomwatch*, and in a few years time, will represent the worker who enters into management during the entire run of *The Brothers*. The third and final member of the regular *Are You Being Served?* cast to appear in the series was guest star Trevor Bannister as Anthony Lewis. Derek Deadman is listed in the camera script as being one of the extras, but is not in the PasB sheets. Deadman was later to give an interesting performance as a Sontaran in the *Doctor Who* story 'The Invasion of Time', but is much better known from his appearances in the ITV sitcom *Never The Twain*. Francis Pidgeon was Lennie Mayne's wife and she frequently appears in his productions, usually in tiny roles.

Studio
'Public Enemy' was the eleventh story to be recorded for the second series. It was videotaped in an unknown studio on Friday, 8 January 1971. The still photograph sequence was recorded after the main episode.

Music
The only bit of stock music was heard over the photo montage where Geoff traces Nicholls' last day. 'Exclusive Blend' by Keith Mansfield comes from the KPM album *The Big Beat* (KPM 1044).

Editing
The episode was edited on Monday, 11 January 1971 between 1.30 p.m and 4.30 pm. The only cut made to the episode was at the beginning of the scene between Arnold Payne and Fay. Barbara explains to Payne that the Minister's PPS is with Dr Quist at the moment and invites him to sit down, but instead he crosses over to Ridge's desk and looks at the posters.

Programme Review Board
The Board praised a 'very good episode', and Paul Fox, Controller of BBC1, thought that the series had ended strongly.

Press Reviews
'Dust to dust, ashes to ashes … Will our destruction be pollution, our

epitaphs inscribed ironically by that graveside text?' pondered the *Coventry Evening Telegraph*. '*Doomwatch* laid its message right on the line last night, bowing out of its present run with shock warnings that Doomsday is 30 years away … Potent stuff indeed, and performed with an unshakable conviction you can only credit. Again, *Doomwatch* achieved its purpose in generating concern, carefully blending slight, if fanciful, fiction with cold, hard fact. The point, as always, was made with all the impact of a coffin nail being driven home. It was a pity that last night's episode had some of its thunder stolen by *Horizon* on BBC2 a couple of weeks ago. Patrick Alexander's story did, however, look at the human attitudes to the problem -- of some people who want to do something about it and others who can't be bothered… *Doomwatch*, we are told, is returning, but after Quist's gloomy remarks shouldn't it have been the end?'

Post-Pedler
Towards the end of July 1971, Terence Dudley defended the episode and its science content to the BBC's Head of Copyright. This was in the form of a discussion concerning the Kit Pedler situation and the reaction the episode had generated when aired. 'Public Enemy' had stimulated more viewer appreciation than any other, he said, in particular from men in industry, such as Richard Tulley, Senior consultant of G M Buckle and Partners, consultants in Mechanical and Electrical Services; David Johnson, secretary to Sir Alexander Gibb & Partners, Architects; Dr Frank Taylor, President of the Institute of Heating & Ventilation Engineers. Even the Duke of Edinburgh's Wildlife Fund had been in touch, and their letter was forwarded on to David Attenborough. The science content had been praised as well.

Archive Holdings
Perhaps because of this reaction, 'Public Enemy' is the only episode from the second series to survive in its original form of a 625-line videotape copy. The other twelve were wiped, although black-and white-film recordings survived as potential exports to those countries that did not transmit their programmes in colour or at such a high definition. The other episodes also exist as colour recordings in the 525-line NTSC format.

3

Reaction To The Second Series

'The "scientists" it portrays bear not the slightest resemblance to any I have ever known.' Graham Chedd, *New Scientist*

By the time the second series had finished broadcasting in March 1971, the programme was achieving an average audience figure of nine and a half million viewers, although there had been a dip in the figures midway through the run after the very good highs it achieved over the Christmas and New Year period. As *New Scientist* observed in February 1971, '... the huge following the series has built up among the young is not put down to the trendiness of Dr Ridge's gear. Letters, while they include many from girls obviously hooked on one or the other of the characters (the late Toby Wren led the field), do show that the concern demonstrated by the stories is shared and welcomed. This concern is also to be found in an older group of people uninvolved in science. The rest of the mail is made up of requests for source material and the occasional GP worried lest his patients get the wrong idea. Complaints of inaccuracy, says Dudley, usually spring from mishearing or misunderstanding the dialogue.'

As far as the press seemed to be concerned, Kit Pedler was *Doomwatch*. No matter who thought up the idea for that week's script, or who actually wrote it, or indeed if there had been other advisers whom Dudley had asked for help, Kit Pedler would get the credit. However, the number of 'hits' the series scored by sheer coincidence was much lower this time. Apart from the incident of the mercury-tainted fish, which the *Radio Times* gleefully pointed out as being evidence of the prophet of doom striking another victory, there hadn't been any typhoid epidemics or two-headed chickens or jet-lagged ministers collapsing in American hotels.

Pedler and Davis tried to interest newspapers on a series of six articles each written around a major environmental theme. Each 2000 word article was to be divided into two parts; the first half was to have been written in the form of a "Top Secret" report for the Cabinet, in the manner of their original press pack. Each 'report' would have been labelled: 'File no 24/004/D1978 Top Secret. Eyes: Min of Envir. Cabinet Office, Min of D.' They wanted to describe the plight of a community or group of individuals subjected to an environmental hazard or disaster and contain all the information which failed to reach the newspapers or other media. The example Pedler and Davis gave was the plight of one Mrs Benson who had frequently complained to her local GP about the condition of her youngest son, Timothy, which he considers to be frivolous ... This would have lead into the second section giving the factual background in 1971 of the material in the fiction of the 1978 report. In the case of Mrs Benson, it was the relationship between atmospheric organic lead and mental deficiency in childhood. Other subjects planned were the storage of radioactive materials, chemical dumping at sea by ships of other nations, the wreck of a one-million-ton tanker at the mouth of the Thames, the increasing reliance on machine control of weapons systems, and over-population of Great Britain.

Scientists' view of Doomwatch

Pedler was regularly on the radio or television promoting *Doomwatch* (or perhaps talking about tuna fish contaminated by mercury). His family would poke good-natured fun at the variety of topics their medically-trained ophthalmologist father would be called into discuss on both television and radio, and it raised eyebrows amongst some of his colleagues past and present. 'They call me Doctor Doom at the laboratory where I work,' Pedler told Michael Jeffries for a syndicated article. 'I get a terrible clobbering if one of the TV sets are not quite accurate.' But it was more fundamental than that. Some felt he was beginning to get big-headed and talking outside of his area of expertise – a populariser and a simplifier – although his family puts some of these views down to simple jealousy. His stance on animal experimentation was also criticised when he went public on the matter.

The *Radio Times* article promoting the second series compared episodes from the first series with events in the real world, and this infuriated one reader, Dr Robin Brightwell, a producer for Further Education on BBC Radio. Although he shared Pedler's fears about the genuine danger of uncontrolled scientific growth, 'articles of this type undoubtedly lead to fear, as well as condemnation of science and technology, so they must present information in a responsible way. Important parts of your article are irresponsible and ambiguous.' After going through some of the article and the episodes to which they related, he concluded 'I agree *Doomwatch* could inform viewers of real dangers, but it must not be used as an excuse to magnify and distort those dangers. Nor, and this is worse, must those distorted dangers be used as an excuse to blow *Doomwatch*'s own trumpet.'

Pedler defended the ideas of the programme and its research, questioning how Brightwell could be sure that techniques such as those seen in 'Friday's Child' could not be developed. 'Does he think it wrong to put out a story about a nuclear weapon armed by accidental release and impact when a precisely similar event occurred in Texas some years ago?' He reminded Brightwell that they were producing dramas not documentaries.

Pedler also used the same argument in *New Scientist* a month later in March 1971. He was interviewed by Graham Chedd, who first had his own say on what he thought of the programme, which had not changed since he looked at the first series. 'By the usual light entertainment standards, the series is indifferent; the characters are straight comic-cuts, the acting and direction are not exactly inspired, and it descends too readily to the melodramatic. More seriously, the "scientists" it portrays bear not the slightest resemblance to any I have ever known, and it often seems to blur dangerously the line between fact and fiction – between real or at least plausible situations, extended a bit to make a dramatic point, and quite unwarranted extrapolations of present research. Recently, the programmes have not been quite so culpable on this last point, but the first of the present series pointed up the danger graphically, with a scientist growing hen-human hybrid creatures in his lab—a foolish, even mischievous, leap from the research on hybrid cells going on at Oxford.

'With all that said, the fact remains that *Doomwatch* has undoubtedly got more about science and its concomitant dangers across to more people (some twelve million watch each programme) than a host of earnest, learned documentaries.' Pedler agreed with these points but countered with the argument that he wasn't the programme's producer and often disagreed with the production committee's decisions. It was the closest he had come to criticising Terence Dudley in public up to now.

Pedler's time as a 'boffin' at Judd Street may have been coming to an end, but Pedler had found his new calling. Following his Eastercon lecture in April 1970 concerning the need for a real Doomwatch, he carried on in this vein, and was now, one year later, actively campaigning for such a department to exist. Initially encouraging noises came from the newly elected Conservative Government, who created the Department of the Environment and gave Pedler and Davis the chance to meet Peter Silkin MP and his opposite number in the Labour Party. Pedler told the *Guardian* in early 1971 that his dream was to have the entire world's pollution data at the team's fingertips, stored on a computer. He saw the first of his Doomwatch-inspired novels as being a good source of funds, although he hinted at having rich friends with guilty consciences (probably Teddy Goldsmith, who was launching *The Ecologist* at this time, though there were others).

Overseas Transmission

Vivien S Smith started to receive fan mail from Canada, which is how she was aware the episodes were being shown. This news came much to Terence Dudley's surprise. Episodes from the first and second series were transmitted in Canada over the summer of 1971. This was a country which had seen its own ecological awakening in recent times. *Doomwatch* was shown on Saturday nights on CBKRT-MT and started on 2 July with 'Tomorrow, the Rat'. Bruce Peacock, writing in the *Leader-Post*, gave it a good build-up: 'It deals with the real villains of our modern world, the forces of ecological disruption that could eventually destroy the planet itself.'

Kaspars Dzeguze hated it. Writing in the *Globe and Mail* on 5 July, he thought the episode was 'clearly another in the series of wildly inaccurate forecasts of things to come. And how original is the ecology angle now?' Canada does not appear to have broadcast all of the available episodes. It went into the second series with 'Invasion' on 9 July. It is thanks to Canada that colour copies of the rest of the second series as well as 'Tomorrow, the Rat' and 'Train and De-Train' survive to this day. Other countries would transmit the second series over the next few years. Australia started with 'You Killed Toby Wren' in 1972, as did Singapore.

The Press Backlash
The television critics were also starting to become negative. By 'No Room for Error', Richard Last, writing in the *Daily Telegraph*, felt that the series was losing some of its original compulsion. 'The writing is less assured, the characters have become a little tired. The original purpose of the series seems to escape from the script's grasp.' The *Daily Mail*'s Virginia Ironside, commenting on the same episode, felt that the *Doomwatch* team reminded her of neurotic housewives. In its edition dated 4 March, *The Stage* seemed frustrated by the direction of the programme: 'The one good idea BBC series have shown recently and which they could justifiably say indicates a fallacy about characterisation being the dominating factor in series is *Doomwatch*. Here, one would have thought, the BBC was back where it belongs, originating a series which dramatised important, disturbing, interesting or controversial issues, tackling the kind of series that ITV would not think commercial enough. *Doomwatch*, despite some very mediocre acting, halting direction and too often weakly edited scripts, is not a failure. But it is an irritating programme, irritating because it could be so dramatic (so documentary dramatic) and could make a real impact on a public tired of policemen, spies and doctors. It is difficult to think of a similar series where plots and thoughts alone could dominate.'

Towards the end of the series, Philip Purser in the *Sunday Telegraph* was also feeling dismayed. 'When is *Doomwatch* (BBC1) supposed to be taking place? According to the first series it can't have been much earlier because in the original episode supersonic transports were in airline service. Since then they seem to have been slyly winching the whole thing back to the present day. One recent episode about life in tower block flats could have come out of anything from *Softly, Softly* downwards. I used to wonder why I was so irritated by this series, and now begin to see why. It was ridiculously over-praised when it first appeared. Because of the real concern which has sprung up lately about the rape of our natural resources, people went out of their way to discover salutary warnings in these crude fables. It was even suggested that life should emulate art and we ought to set up a real Doomwatch organisation to monitor the excess of science and industry ... This is what really dismays. There's a place on television for imaginative fiction, for plays that make use of the shiny new apparatus of the world, for the concrete expression of new ideas, and visions and forebodings. Indeed, you could say there is a crying need for such things. Alas, it seems to be the one department of TV that deserves all those generalisations about triviality.'

The BBC
The Programme Review Board was commenting on the series less and less and were beginning to compare it with *Doctor Who*, which, in its current incarnation, was attracting complaints and concern over its level of scares and violence. One particular story set inside a state prison, 'The Mind of Evil', had been compared with *Doomwatch*. Some members were not too sure which was the more frightening of the two series. As has been seen, Andrew Osborn was aware of how the behind-the-scenes stresses were sometimes showing in the writing. The BBC may have been forgiven in letting the series finish quietly with Quist's apocalyptic warning to the audience at the end of 'Public Enemy'.

At the end of the Audience Research Report on 'The Logicians', the interviewees were asked for their thoughts of the series as a whole. There was an opinion amongst some that the second series was not up to the standard of the first, and it had lost some of its 'earlier impetus and appeal'. The majority, however, were appreciative of the series and found that although the stories varied in credibility and holding power, the series had been an interesting and an entertaining one. Words like 'compelling', 'thought-provoking' and 'splendid entertainment value' were used. The topicality of some episodes delighted many, and others liked the way some issues were raised which weren't generally given a second thought. The series could 'make people realize how progress can get out of hand'. The report ended by asking whether viewers would like another series, to which 2 per cent said definitely not, 22 per cent said not particularly, but 76 per cent said YES, VERY MUCH.

And so did the BBC.

Part Three
Ecological Overkill

1
New Order

'There is even a danger that familiarity with the theme has spawned its contempt. The third series will challenge this contempt.' Terence Dudley, third series publicity material.

'This is what *Doomwatch* is all about', Andrew Osborn told Terence Dudley after watching 'Public Enemy'. The BBC's Head of Series decided to offer the Controller of BBC1 a third series, and, since the viewing figures were still very good, and the reaction was on the whole positive, another run was duly ordered.

There was no shortage of ideas; Terence Dudley had run through them with *New Scientist* in February 1971: 'Treatment of laboratory animals by students, transportation of nerve gas, nuclear engineering, massive river pollution (of the Rhine), sewage disposal at Lake Constance, booming anti-pollution business in the United States, the use of dolphins to aid navies, race and IQ, the production of quick results to satisfy fund-providers, mining the continental shelf, etc.' As usual with *Doomwatch*, it wasn't going to be plain sailing. The producer would this time fall out permanently with Kit Pedler -- and it would become a very public affair. Out of a planned series of thirteen episodes, only eleven would air.

Departures
During the rehearsals for 'Flight Into Yesterday' Simon Oates told Terence Dudley that he did not want to appear in a third series. Oates was dissatisfied with the direction that the series had been taking, not to mention the noticeable watering down of his character. It was felt that the regular characters were being relegated in favour of the guest cast. 'No wonder Simon Oates eventually became disenchanted with the enterprise: the juiciest parts too often went to visiting artistes,' reflects Vivien S Smith. Darrol Blake remembers that 'Simon used to say early on, "All I get to do is lean against the filing cabinet drinking coffee."' The producer persuaded Oates to do four episodes. This was necessary because Dudley was axing Geoff Hardcastle and Dr Fay Chantry.

Jean Trend was not given any explanation as to why her character was dropped. Understandably, this upset her, and she wondered whether it was because her performance had been less than satisfactory. At the wrap party for the second series, held at John Paul's home, Terence Dudley avoided her as best he could, and she didn't understand why until a letter came through the post announcing that the next series would not feature Dr Fay Chantry. Vivien S Smith sympathises: 'I keep asking myself whether a face to face meeting prior to the letter would have helped to soften the blow. Doubtful, but if the same thing had happened to me, I might have requested an interview to try to find out the reason why. I sympathize with Jean because clearly it is something that is hard to recover from and can never be easily forgotten.'

As a former actor himself, Dudley knew too well how it felt to be rejected, and, as has been noted earlier, he did not like confrontations. With no explanation forthcoming, the actress was badly hurt and her confidence dented. Jean went back to working in the theatre before taking a break from acting altogether, but she remained close friends with Simon Oates and Gerry Davis. She resumed her acting career in the mid-1990s after a spell working for a charity and has recently made a large number of television appearances.

So why was a character like Fay Chantry dropped? Terence Dudley was the sort of producer whose instinct was to alter the course of a programme from series to series. Having already changed the direction of *Doomwatch* during the second series, Dudley intended to develop it further in the third. He felt that Quist's character needed softening. Quist was starting a relationship with Dr Anne Tarrant in the second series, and this was just the tool with which to do it. If Dudley had been seeing possibilities in Elizabeth Weaver's Doctor Tarrant in 'You Killed Toby Wren', there would have been no room for Fay, a Pedler and Davis creation.

If Jean Trend was told by letter, then John Nolan probably found out that way too, although in an interview for *SFX* conducted by Charles Norton, he implied it was a mutual decision reached with Dudley. He did not get to appear in the film, unlike Jean. Leaving *Doomwatch* certainly did John Nolan's career no harm. Soon after, he appeared at the Harrogate Theatre as Ernest in D H Lawrence's play *A Collier's Friday Night*, giving a performance *The Stage* described as 'fine and sensitive', and in 1973 he starred in Granada Television's seven-part adaptation of *Shabby Tiger* by Howard Spring.

Vivien Sherrard

Colin Bradley and Barbara Mason were to be retained; Dudley planned to greatly expand Vivien Sherrard's role within the series. Vivien had greatly enjoyed her experience in the series, despite the lack of screen time. 'I was thrilled to be a running character (one of only two females to boot), and would have been very foolish to leave without another job to go to. Obviously the theatre cannot match the exposure TV gives an actor as illustrated by fan letters received from abroad, and a bus conductor who said to me sotto voce, "It is *Doomwatch*, isn't it?"'

She also got on well with her male co-stars and has strong memories of Simon Oates. 'How could I ever forget him? As he remarked, playing John Ridge was easy because he was playing himself. He was most definitely a ladies' man, and quite precocious at times. I remember being in his car *en route* to a club where he was wont to play pool. This may have been a sort of date, but if so it was our first and last. He must have realized that neither Barbara Mason nor Vivien Sherrard were about to become mere notches on his belt. It was he who coined the nickname "Bristols" for me, and he and John Paul got hold of a TV camera once and trained it on said "Bristols" so if anyone was looking there they were on a large monitor for all to gape at. Charming! But I did not react in an outraged fashion, and we all had a good laugh. Nowadays Simon would probably be sued for sexual harassment.

'He had a great sense of humour, but could also show annoyance. Once when he was about to do a scene at a camera rehearsal he handed me his cigar and told me to keep it for him until he'd finished. Since it was soggy and revolting, I put it on a ledge of one of the cameras. Simon was not happy about what I did, and asked me if I knew how much these cameras cost. Did he really imagine the camera would suddenly burst into flames?

'John Paul was terrific, admirable as an actor and as a person. He really must have been the main reason for the success of *Doomwatch*. All these years later I still enjoy his performance enormously. He gave a huge party for the entire cast and crew at his home in Aylesbury. It was a terrific evening with rather too much alcohol available. What could have been a horrible tragedy occurred at the end of it. Stupidly three of us, two of the crew and me, decided to drive back to London. The man driving failed to make a sharp right turn while we were still on the property, and we ended up in a ditch. The girl sitting next to me in the back hurt her head or neck (no seatbelts). Obviously we stayed the night after that. The driver came to me later to beg me not to give the police any details. No questions were ever asked, luckily for him. The fear must have been that the accident would be reported because one of the passengers was injured.'

The Experts
Rather than just have one scientific advisor, Terence Dudley threw the door open for others to contribute. It seemed to have worked well in the latter stages of the second series, and it would do so again. In the event, twenty-four scientists from various disciplines would offer ideas, advice and criticism. The only scientist not to provide ideas was Dr Kit Pedler himself. The BBC made an offer through his agent on 19 March, asking him to contribute storylines, but Pedler turned it down. He would only work on *Doomwatch* if the current producer was removed, something Andrew Osborn was disinclined to do. So that was it, and Pedler broke off

connections. However, as the originators (as they were now to be credited) of the *Doomwatch* format, Pedler and Davis would be paid £65 per episode.

Terence Dudley rehired Anna Kaliski as 'script consultant'. As he explained in the writers' guide, 'She is available to research in depth before storylines are agreed and will thereafter supply chapter and verse when required.' She would accompany writers on their research trips, as she did with Martin Worth to Imperial College, or send them material which sometimes completely changed their script, as in the case of 'High Mountain'.

Terence Dudley asked the scientists what gave them nightmares. The answers included the testing of atomic weapons, the development of chemical weapons, the increasing use of persistent pesticides, experimental psycho-surgery, the hijacking of plutonium, the world population problem and the poisoning of the world's oceans and rivers. By August there were few ideas left. One involved the penetration of the Earth's crust – if oil was tapped, it would be enormous in quantities and unstemmable to the point of 100 per cent pollution of the oceans of the planet. A second idea concerned the controversial ideas of Arthur Jensen, Hans Jurgen Kysenck and others, which sought to prove that black people were both mentally and physiologically inferior to whites. Dudley was also prepared to move the series into more social themes, with a look at censorship and geriatric care.

Among the twenty-four scientific advisors consulted were Dr Frank Barnaby, Dr David Bellamy, Dr L J Bruce-Chwatt, Professor Derek Bryce-Smith, Dr George Christie, Dr Alex Comfort, Dr Gordon Conway, Dr Hugh Evans, Dr Nicholas Flemming, Dr William Grey Walter, Dr Thomas Lambo, Dr K Loucas, Dr Graham Nickless, Dr M H Pappworth, Professor Jack Pepys, Dr Cicely Saunders, Dr Tom Tinsley, Eric Johnson and Dr Hal Thirlaway.

As ever, Dudley was keen to emphasise that *Doomwatch* was not science fiction. 'The stories are fiction, the science and technology within the stories are fact.' He made this point to his writers: their fiction must always deal with fact.

Format and Scripting

After the scripting chaos of the second series, Terence Dudley decided that, in view of the ample amount of time he had to prepare the scripts needed, he would make do without a new script editor. It is unclear what was going on this time. Considering how quickly a second series had been ordered, quite the opposite was happening now. The first couple of scripts were commissioned in May 1971, the rest from August onwards. Contracts for the cast were signed at the end of September, and the production schedule fitted neatly within the first half of 1972, with a transmission planned for June. (The *Radio Times* told one group of Ridge-obsessed fans that the programme would be back early 1972 and then, after another enquiry, June.) Historically, a strike has been blamed for setting back actual production, but no-one now can recall the reasons for such a long delay. It may simply have been splitting the production costs over two tax years. Production teams are frequently warned that they cannot transfer any savings made from one tax year into another. Had they wanted another January launch for the series, production would have had to begin in July 1971, and thus script commissioning would have taken place much earlier. The delivery dates for Martin Worth's two stories, commissioned in May, do not reflect this. The delay may also have simply been to avoid the difficulties encountered with the second series.

Terence Dudley decided that he would once again write the opening episode, to establish the new format and introduce Commander Neil Stafford, a former Naval Intelligence Officer now working for Special Branch. At first, Stafford would be the Minister's watchdog inside Doomwatch, but he would later become a willing convert to the team. He would replace Ridge, who would be written out in the same episode but would make sporadic appearances throughout the series. Dudley also wanted to establish the relationship between Quist and Doctor Anne Tarrant. At this stage in the proceedings, they would be seen to be living together 'without the benefit of clergy', as Dudley described it to Darrol Blake. The Minister would now become a regular, christened 'Sir George Holroyd'. Dudley would claim to have created the character himself, although he inserted 'George' into a name Pedler and Davis had already come up with. Duncan would make a couple of return appearances, this time with the first name of 'Anthony' added. Once again the writers were warned that the Ministry must remain anonymous.

Doomwatch would be given new premises, a new semi-permanent regular secretary in the shape of Susan Proud and a new sense of acceptance by the State. Although not expressed as such, the Doomwatch computer was no longer part of the set up, and Quist's new office no longer had the photos of mushroom clouds.

The first four episodes were to be shared out between Terence Dudley and Martin Worth to help settle the new format, explain what had happened to Ridge and deal with the fallout. After that, the episodes were generally self-contained except for episodes where Ridge would return, building upon his new character development. The other writers were a mixture of old and new. Initially, Dudley tried to bring Harry Green and Don Shaw back into the fold. Whilst Green was initially interested and started some thoughts on an episode about population, he pulled out. Don Shaw was just too busy. Robert Holmes was also invited a little late in the day, when Dudley thought he was nearly fully commissioned. One outstanding slot was reserved for Martin Worth, who wanted to do a third episode, but Holmes was encouraged just in case one of the scripts proved to be a dud. Whilst this did not happen, Holmes would shortly write two episodes of *The Regiment* for Dudley. Louis Marks, John Gould and Roger Parkes were also invited to return.

The newcomers were Stuart Douglass, Roy Russell, Ian Curteis and Wolf Rilla. Stuart Douglass had written episodes of *Sergeant Cork* in 1966 and had just done an episode of *The Regiment* which had been directed by Darrol Blake. Roy Russell was another writer who had worked on *The First Lady* and had also written for *The Borderers*, script-edited by Martin Worth. Ian Curteis had recently penned biographical dramas for the BBC on the lives of Beethoven and Alexander Fleming. Wolf Rilla was a German-born writer, director, composer and producer who had worked in television since the 1950s. He had directed an episode of *The Avengers* in 1966 which had seen the sudden replacement of Elizabeth Shepherd with Diana Rigg in the role of Emma Peel. The writers were sent the new series format, which contained a lot from Pedler and Davis original. Curteis' was the first of these to be commissioned, for a film-heavy episode about the flooding of London.

With the scripts more grounded into reality and the style of writing more traditional, the series felt safer than ever before, with fewer plausible yet fantastical elements that would make the viewer sit up and wonder 'Could it happen?' Thriller elements were still encouraged, with foreign spies and manhunts, but the plots tended to veer more towards crime drama, with kidnapped children, a family held to hostage, break-ins, heists and ransom demands. There would also be quieter, more thoughtful episodes with fewer thrills; more philosophy and discussion of the issues. Death would now be a rare occurrence in an episode. Humour was also in short supply with the absence of Ridge; when he did turn up, with a few exceptions, he didn't find much to laugh about. The pre-credit teasers were now getting longer and longer, and, in most cases, quite wordy.

The last script to be commissioned was 'Deadly Dangerous Tomorrow', when the series was already in production. Only thirteen scripts were commissioned, and they were all going to be used – at first.

2
Production Of The Series

'I was very doubtful of the idea. I didn't even like the name. I could imagine what the critics would say if they found it boring – that it would be doom to watch ...' Simon Oates in the *Birmingham Post*

The regular cast were contracted in September for a six-month run between 1 January and 23 June 1972. John Barron was contracted on 16 September, John Paul on 21 September and both Joby Blanshard and Elizabeth Weaver were signed up on 30 September. Having been cast by the producer for 'You Killed Toby Wren', Elizabeth Weaver did not suffer the indignity that befell various actors in *Survivors*, when a one-off character from one series was brought back as a regular for the next, but re-cast. Weaver was booked for eleven episodes but in the end would appear in only nine of them. Vivien Sherrard was signed up on 12 October and, finally, John Bown was contracted to play Commander Neil Stafford on 11 November.

Bown had been appearing on television since the late 1950s and had been in films such as *Dr Who and the Daleks* and *Quatermass and the Pit*. He had directed a film a few years earlier called *Monique*, a study of bisexuality, in which he cast his wife. When it was released in the States, it was paired alongside the less tastefully titled *Hot Pants Holiday*. Maria O' Brien wasn't contracted for the lesser role of Susan Proud until 11 February 1972. She was cast by Terence Dudley. As a television actress she was no stranger to small parts at this point and had recently been seen in *The Goodies* as a housewife to Tim Brooke-Taylor's camp soap-powder advertising man. Her first appearance, in 'The Killer Dolphins', was recorded only a few days later and was a last minute addition to the episode.

In the nine months between series, Oates first appeared on stage at the Birmingham's Alexandra theatre in Garson Kanin's 1946 play *Born Yesterday*, where he played a journalist who crosses the path of an American war-rime racketeer, and in the course of educating the mobster's dumb blonde girl friend, exposes the racket. While in town, he was interviewed for the *Birmingham Post* by Judith Cook, a fan of the series who had recently written articles on the series praising its moral stance. He remembered his initial reaction to *Doomwatch*: 'I was very doubtful of the idea. I didn't even like the name. I could imagine what the critics would say if they found it boring – that it would be doom to watch ... Of course, it has become such an accepted word you are always finding it in the papers, even in the House of Commons. When I saw the scripts for the first series, though, I became enthusiastic because they were so good. I don't go away and swot up large amounts of scientific stuff, though I do alter lines if I feel I am given words to say that Ridge wouldn't have said.' The article intriguingly mentioned that Oates did not say if he would return to the programme.

The next time he returned to Birmingham it was June, and at the Birmingham Theatre where he appeared as John Steed in *The Avengers*, a comedy stage play version of the cancelled television series by Brian Clemens and Terence Feely. In the cast, he was reunited with Wendy Hall. The play was a very technical piece, requiring lots of special effects and trick props. Oates told the *Post*: 'If you started thinking of all the things that could go wrong – you'd give the whole thing up.' He was also continuing with a secondary career as a stand-up cabaret comic, the cockney Charlie Bennett, something *The Stage* remarked on in 1970 as being a surprise, but 'what he was doing was a pretty solid half hour of comedy and song'. He deliberately played some of the East End of London's toughest pubs and appeared as a compère for a package show topped by the Rolling Stones. He even recorded a single. 'When actors say how dreadful such-and-such a television role was for them, I say they should try a Welsh Sunday lunchtime drinking club; it's just you and them. After that, nothing is so bad.'

John Paul also enjoyed a return to the theatre, but this time in an eighteenth century marriage-game comedy *The Clandestine Marriage*, playing Mr Sterling, a hearty money-mad merchant, eager to sell off his shrewish daughter to a foppish member of the aristocracy.

Directors and crew
Dudley hired familiar hands to direct the episode, giving Darrol Blake four episodes to do – one a month. It was the end of a particularly busy time for the director. 'He said, "We're doing another round, would you like to come and do some?" And I said, "Yeah, yeah," because I was so newly freelance. I had to go freelance to get from Arts and Features into Drama series at Television Centre in order to do that first one for Terry, so I went freelance just as the twins were born. So I accepted anything that was put under my nose! It was two years solid work, overlapping productions like *Paul Temple*, *The Onedin Line*, and *The Regiment*. In my diary it says (to take one day): lunch 12.30 with Terry, whilst doing two other shows. At one point I was doing three shows at once. I had an office on the fifth floor in Television Centre, where the drama series were, and production teams would queue up at the door to talk to me. Once, I was in the studio for *The Shadow in the Tower* and couldn't go on

location with *The Onedin Line*.' One episode of *The Shadow in the Tower*, 'The Man Who Never Was', featured Joby Blanshard in a role.

Lennie Mayne and Eric Hills returned to the series. Newcomers Quentin Lawrence and Pennant Roberts were each given a pair of episodes. Lawrence had been directing for some time both on television and in the cinema. One notable credit was *The Trollenberg Terror*, which he directed once for the BBC and once as a later film adaptation. He was a director who had worked on a lot of filmed series such as *Gideon's Way* and *Danger Man*, so it was hardly surprising that he would be offered two very film-heavy episodes. Pennant Roberts began his television career in Cardiff with ITV before moving over to BBC Wales and then to London in 1969. He joined the Drama Series department as a production manager and then became an in-house director. *Doomwatch* was his first London credit. He would work for Terence Dudley again on *The Regiment* and *Survivors*.

Costumes were provided by Shelia Beers, except for 'High Mountain' where her assistant Ken Trew took charge. Vivien had the chance to once again go shopping. 'I remember a costume designer accompanied me to [London fashion store] Jaeger to select a number of outfits. That was some outing! The BBC bought me the purple jacket and skirt, and a matching blouse made for me in a fabulous Liberty print; the short-sleeved trouser suit and matching scarf; a wonderful black and white belted winter coat; and probably some other items; but the listed ones I loved most. Possibly against the rules, but the wardrobe department sold me all these things bar the coat, for considerably less than their retail value. They offered, I did not ask, but we were all guilty, if it was an infraction. Joby Blanshard thought I was far too well-dressed for the role of Barbara Mason, but my daughter Hope tells me that it is commonplace for women who want to move up in a company to dress at least two places above their station. Also, a good friend of mine who was secretary to the London head of Bally Shoes dressed to the nines every day. Barbara definitely did not want to let Quist down.'

Make-up was originally to be provided by Penny Norton for the entire series, but she fell ill halfway through and was replaced once more by Elizabeth Rowell. Graham Oakley once again had the largest share of the design work. Jeremy Davis designed Darrol Blake's episodes and Oliver Bayldon and Ray London were given the remainder. As before, music would come from library LP tracks. Terence Dudley's secretary Judy Hall had left *Doomwatch* to begin her training as a script editor (a duty she would perform on Dudley's next project, *The Regiment*). She was back in time for the fallout from 'Sex and Violence'. Her replacement was first Alison Fife and then Tina Michaelides.

Production

With the exception of 'Without the Bomb', every episode had some filming attached to it, even if it was just a couple of inserts, such as in 'Cause of Death'. But on the whole, the series had far more film effort now than it had ever had before. 'Fire and Brimstone', 'Say Knife, Fat Man', 'Waiting for a Knighthood', 'Sex and Violence', 'The Killer Dolphins', 'Hair Trigger' and especially 'Flood' had plenty of location material. Three weeks of block filming began in January for 'Fire and Brimstone', 'The Killer Dolphins' and 'Hair Trigger'. 'Say Knife, Fat Man' was swapped from third in production order to fourth. Production turnaround was very tight with just eight days rehearsal for the two studio days. There was a break for some more block filming on 'High Mountain' to be done midway through the run.

Transmission for the series was fixed when the camera script for 'Fire and Brimstone' was compiled, and the fourth transmitted episode was originally going to be 'Without the Bomb' until 'Waiting for a Knighthood' was taped at the end of the block and had to go in before 'Deadly Dangerous Tomorrow' which was fixed by the time of recording as number seven. 'Sex and Violence' had been due to be number five, and may have been pushed back in the schedules when concerns were first raised.

Some of the episodes were recorded in TC1. Darrol Blake explains 'The medium-sized studios were where these dramas were done, and they were booked up. The bigger studio wasn't always booked up and you were told you could have TC1, but you could only use two-thirds of it. It was a question of trying to light these things. There wasn't the staff or the manpower to man a studio that big all the time. So you did a TC3-sized production in TC1. So you had plenty of stacking room and storage space.'

Vivien S Smith remembers the studio days well. 'The atmosphere during a studio rehearsal was invariably quietly intense, naturally even more so during the taping. There was one occasion – at a rehearsal, if memory serves – when John Paul simply could not remember his lines, and had to go over and over a particular scene with John Barron. This was very frustrating for John Paul, but surely understandable given the size of his part. I was always both nervous and exhilarated on a recording day, never ever bored.'

Cancellation

In the autumn of 1971, the BBC announced it was implementing budget cuts for its next financial year, and drama was hit. Four episodes of BBC2's new drama *The Lotus Eaters* were pulled from the schedules, and other series being launched for 1972 such as *The Brothers*, and the first series of *The Regiment*, went out with fewer episodes than the standard thirteen model. This explains why Wolf Rilla's 'The Devil's Demolition', later called 'I Never Promised You a Rose Garden', was pulled. The decision was presumably taken before Martin Worth was commissioned to write 'Deadly Dangerous Tomorrow', which in any case needed to highlight Ridge. There was to have been a 13th studio recording session at the end of June, according to the casts' contracts, but in the end the series wrapped up after the 12th.

Radio Times

The *Radio Times* gave *Doomwatch* another front cover. This time it just featured Ridge, holding the phials of anthrax in his hand (which gave readers no uncertainty as to the nature of the plot). The feature within was more about environmental issues than the series, with some specially posed photos of Elizabeth Weaver and Simon Oates. It was titled 'Does Quist Give a Damn?' and interviewed John Paul and Elizabeth Weaver whilst there were on location for 'High Mountain'. The interviewer seemed surprised that John Paul didn't share Dr Quist's crusading zeal in real life. Paul said he was glad to be living in Aylesbury, outside London and away from the noise, smog and rush, but, having been brought up in a business family, he thought it 'only natural that people should make use of all the resources available to earn money, so long as you stay within the law'. As he saw it – as indeed did the scripts for that very day he was filming – the Government is the one to control the pollution. Elizabeth Weaver, however, did not hold back on her own views on the environment, with a particular dislike for the car.

Each week that the magazine ran a photograph from the episode, a torn-out dictionary definition of that week's scientific concern was placed on top. Once again, a quote was used from the episode to go with the cast list.

In the Real World

Terence Dudley wrote in the publicity notes for the third series that the press regarded the first series as prophetic. 'It was not! Neither was the subject matter coincidental with news coverage in the papers. The series had been prepared and mounted from factual material gathered from Science Journals, papers and lectures by scientists profoundly concerned with the future of mankind.' *Doomwatch* was seen as a prophetic series. But in the case of the third series, with a June transmission date for stories written and conceived from a year before, would the fiction keep up with fact or simply reflect what was happening? This was something Dudley was all too aware of during the year and a half building up to transmission. During the six months of production, several significant events happened.

The Ecologist printed their landmark edition 'A Blueprint for Survival' (later to be a book) in January 1972. Though criticised by some, it was endorsed by scientists looking for answers to the pollution and population debates, and it saw economic growth as the problem. Britain's Conservative Minister for the Environment, Peter Walker, did not think that a national Doomwatch committee as recommended should be set up to prevent mankind from destroying itself. Questioned by the press on 15 January, Walker commended them for their concern 'but disagreed with the suggestion that economic growth should be stopped and that we should go back to what Mr Walker called "primitive living". He said that without economic growth he would be unable to find the resources to clear slums, improve public transport, restore derelict land and clean the air and the rivers.' Even as Walker spoke, canisters of cyanide were being washed ashore along the coast of Cornwall from two separate freighters. This debate was touched upon in the pages of *New Scientist* later that March. An editorial spoke for the need of 5 per cent growth, and a letter quickly arrived to criticise the view, stating 'It is deplorable that such naivety should appear as the editorial opinion of *New Scientist*.'

Early Spring, and the Royal Commission on Environmental Pollution issued its second report, 'Three Issues in Industrial Pollution'. It called for an early warning system for the introduction of new products which could cause pollution. The issue 'was not being given adequate priority by the Government' said the report, continuing 'While it would not be reasonable to regard substances as guilty until proved innocent, it is reasonable to regard them as under suspicion.' Firms were legally permitted to keep the composition of pollutants a secret on grounds of commercial sensitivity – the usual excuse. It urged the Government to act sooner; the current plan was to wait until 1975 before the new system of local government would begin to operate 'new comprehensive control of waste disposal'.

Some local councils were already acting. The *Daily Express* reported how Norfolk County Council's Countryside Committee were setting up their own vigilante Doomwatch to keep an eye on pollution and waste disposal. A similar group in Warwickshire exposed illegal sodium cyanide dumping to the press. Illegal dumping had vexed the *Daily Mirror*, who campaigned successfully to have the law strengthened. Also in March, the Club of Rome published a report called *Limits to Growth*. This was based on the findings of a group of systems scientists from the Massachusetts Institute of Technology. It showed the contradiction between unlimited consumption and finite resources.

Just as the third series launched, the Stockholm United Nations Conference on the Human Environment was held in early June. It was attended by 112 nations, including China. However, with international politics so polarised in the 1970s, this event, which had been planned for three years, was boycotted by the Soviet bloc because of the exclusion of East Germany. By now, the British Government took its part in the conference very seriously.

On Television

There had been no shortage of television programmes on the subject, either. The first ever current affairs programme on the environment was launched on Wednesday, 17 May. Called *Down To Earth*, it had been announced the month before inside the pages of the *Daily Express*, which declared 'It will deal with subjects affecting the environment from slum clearances and motorways to plastic milk bottles, oil on the beaches and dangers to wild life.' The producer, John Percival, wanted to show how the environment 'affected all of us – in our jobs, in our homes and our leisure time'. One edition in June concerned a new road built in Snowdonia National Park just to film a Milk Tray advert, and a 'nasty' tale about jars of pickled song birds and the Home Office's 'hypocrisy on the subject.' Percival was delighted that this particular item generated 600 letters to the Royal Society for the Protection of Birds. The programme featured Kit Pedler, and his involvement was quite unique. As the *Daily Mirror* commented during the ten-week run on 21 June, 'He is supplying ideas for those sardonic take offs of TV commercials ... There's another batch tonight between items ranging from river pollution to Environment Minister Peter Walker discussing the recent Stockholm conference on the problems of Spaceship Earth.' The *Observer* review on 11 June by Mary Holland noted Pedler's piece, saying 'The bonus was some real wit in the acidly correct parodies of commercials to be seen on the rival channel. The best was a seductively photographed send up of Coca Cola's peace and love commercial, done to a background of a clattering rubble of empty coke cans.' Tellingly, she preferred it to that week's *Doomwatch*.

Holland's review came during the period of the Stockholm Conference, and there were a number of programmes devoted to the subject. She described it as 'ecological overkill' – the issues of the environment seemed to be dominating the schedules. Holland's problem was that what these programmes usually lacked was any 'concrete analysis of who pollutes and plunders the natural resources and why'. Thames Television examined *Limits of Growth,* and *Something to Say* – a debate following the main programme – featured former Labour Minister Tony Crosland, who was accused of watching a serious documentary on the environment with his eyes closed. BBC2 had an edition of *Man Alive* which focused on how an oil multinational was affecting the lives of the people of Aberdeen in their quest for an oil strike.

Could Doomwatch still hold its own amongst all of this? The press publicity material for the third series said 'During the two years the word "doomwatch" has been added to the language and is in constant use: doomwatching has become fashionable. There is even a danger that familiarity with the theme has spawned its contempt. The third series will challenge this contempt.' The programme still intended to entertain, as Dudley had always said, 'with cautionary tales'.

Ill Wind

There was also another ill wind blowing for the programme. Whilst production had been in full swing, Kit Pedler and Gerry Davis wrote a letter of complaint to Terence Dudley. The correspondence does not appear to survive, but the producer sent the letter to John Henderson, Assistant Head of Copyright, with a list of points explaining the reasons behind the lessening of their involvement in the writing of the series and their final departure. He felt that the writers were in search of a quotation for a press release. Henderson agreed, and sent a short and pithy reply back to the authors, pointing out some contradictions in their statement, and that was that. This was in April. Pedler and Davis appeared to be preparing for the third series and feared the worse for what was going to go out under the *Doomwatch* banner. They may well have wanted to draw attention to their forthcoming film, considering it authentic *Doomwatch*. Whatever the reasons, and they are lost to history, the fears of the BBC appeared to have been justified. When 'Fire and Brimstone' went out on Monday, 5 June 1972, the newspapers a few days later were not just of reviews, but of Pedler's reaction.

3
The Feature Film

'I wish we could put it on general release tomorrow.' Kit Pedler in the
Daily Mirror

Whilst the third series was being written, Tigon British Film Productions were gearing up production to make the movie *Doomwatch*. The story was written by Kit Pedler and Gerry Davis, but the screenplay was by Clive Exton, who would later work with Terence Dudley on *Survivors*. The story took its ideas from 'Burial at Sea', 'The Battery People' and 'The Islanders'. The film is regularly repeated on television, and, for a lot of people, it is their only exposure to the series. They could be forgiven for thinking *Doomwatch* was a horror series rather than what it was. The film can be seen as a re-imagining of the television format, with Doomwatch inhabiting much larger premises, more staff (including one whose job appears to be taking Doctor Quist's coat when he enters the room).

The starring parts went to Ian Bannen, as new wonder boy Dr Del Shaw, and Judy Geeson, who played Victoria Brown, the worried schoolmistress of a Cornish island which had recently recovered from an oil spill. Shaw discovers that a horrific disfigurement has manifested itself amongst some of the islanders. They blame themselves, attributing it to centuries of inbreeding. Shaw investigates the local fish supply and finds irregularities. It turns out that drums containing a chemical growth hormone have broken open under the sea, affecting the islanders who eat the most fish. To save money, the canisters had been illegally dumped in a prohibited area previously used by the Royal Navy to dispose of low-level radioactive waste. The islanders fear the break up of their community and fiercely resist Shaw's investigations, but to no avail. The film ends in a downbeat manner as they have no choice but to evacuate.

Production
Peter Sasdy, the film's Hungarian-born director, had recently made *Countess Dracula* and *Hands of the Ripper* for Hammer Films and would soon direct Nigel Kneale's *The Stone Tape* for BBC1. However, *Doomwatch* was still going to perform its primary function: to warn of the consequences of technological hazard. Sasdy certainly thought so. He told *Photoplay Film Monthly* 'I hope that in this film I have made a personal statement combined with entertainment. My main function, as a director, is to entertain. I feel I can look in the mirror in the morning and say "Pete, you tried."' He aimed

for a documentary style but kept it exciting at the same time. Filming was performed in November on location in the Cornish village of Polkerris and around the Cornish coast. Filming finished 4 December 1971 at Pinewood Studios.

The film did not go down well with some of the regular cast, who were asked to make little more than cameos in favour of Bannen, Gleeson and George Sanders (who committed suicide shortly after the film was completed). John Paul, Simon Oates, Joby Blanshard and Jean Trend were the only regulars asked to appear in the film. Oates later recollected that he only agreed when they upped the original fee, feeling that his part was now being given to Bannen. It was probably no coincidence that the *Avengers* stage play had folded at the end of September. The involvement of the TV cast allegedly came simply through the insistence of Kit Pedler and Gerry Davis. 'I was a very close friend of Gerry's for some years' remembers Jean. 'He always said to me "You have been seen on the Metro-Goldwyn-Mayer [MGM] cinema screen!" because he had taken over the film of *Doomwatch* and was trying to drum up an American version.'

Kit Pedler was very happy with the film, being allowed more of a hands-on approach than he was on the television series. He was frequently on set, advising on how a 'fish' autopsy would be performed, for example, and would be the focus for a lot of the film's pre- publicity. One day he took some of his family down to the set, as his son Mark recalled. 'Dear old Dad, he was vainglorious. He was showing off: he was with us kids, and he wanted to look his best. He had the script in his hand, and they were rehearsing some scene. We were on some kind of a gantry, overlooking the scene, and Dad shouted down to the director "Oh, can we change that word from such-a-beam to such-a-beam?" He wanted to demonstrate that he was part of the ongoing thing, but I thought "You silly old fool!"'

'Drums of Death'
Just for a moment or two, Kit Pedler began to wonder if he did indeed have powers of prophecy. In the New Year, one month after production had finished, an environmental catastrophe threatened the same stretch of coastline that they had filmed on. The film-makers seized upon this piece of enormous serendipity or coincidence. 'A chilling story from today's headlines!' boasted their publicity material. In December 1971 the Spanish freighter *Germania* was shipwrecked near the Channel Islands. A couple of weeks later, 'Drums of Death' (as the *Daily Mirror* put it) began to be washed up on the Cornish shore. The Navy and government scientists from Porton Down ('Nothing sinister in that' stressed a government spokesman!) began a search along 100 miles of coastline to find them. By 17 January, 90 out of 900 drums had been located. However, over the next few days the number of drums estimated to have been lost had risen to 2,000 and then 3,000. The

orange canisters contained tolylene di-isocyanate, forty-five gallons in each. It gives off a highly irritating vapour and is potentially explosive. The ethyl acetate drums were white, and, if the liquid makes contact, is harmful to the skin.

This was Cornwall's biggest disaster since the *Torrey Canyon* oil slick of 1967. If this wasn't enough, it emerged a few days after the alert that a second cargo of toxic chemicals was heading towards the holiday beaches. Two days before the *Germania* sank with its cargo of cyanide, a shipment was washed off the deck of a Somalian-registered vessel during a gale somewhere off Land's End on 19 December. This load contained dimethylamine, an ammonia-like substance. Lloyds of London, who insure freighters such as these, termed the new menace 'flashpoint zero'. In other words, potentially lethal. The two cargos were mingling together, and no-one knew until a Cornish fire chief had a talk over a cup of tea with a Ministry chemist. Under-secretary of State for the Department of the Environment, Eldon Griffiths, told a press conference 'It is highly unsatisfactory that ships containing toxic materials can sink and that there is no mechanism by which Governments of countries whose shores might be polluted can be notified. Other shipping nations will now be consulted.' More seriously, the Ministry of Agriculture and Fisheries warned fishermen to throw back any drum caught in their nets and jettison their catch too.

Kit Pedler told *Titbits* magazine in 1972 'When we read of the incident we were absolutely shattered. For one moment we began to believe there must be a little devil sitting on our shoulders.' He told the *Daily Mirror* 'I wish we could put it on general release tomorrow.'

The disaster got Pedler thinking about how the government should respond to such crisis, and an idea Gerry Davis would later expand and try to turn into a future television format called *Worldforce*. In hand-written form, Pedler outlined his thinking. 'As technology expands, the number of new and poisonous materials one increasing in direct proportion. These materials have to be transported either by air, land or sea and since all transport is fallible, the one certainly is the case of accidental release. Recent events in Cornwall have emphasized the potential dangers involved and have shown very clearly that there is no organisation equipped and trained to deal with these materials in time. Days elapsed before any effective action was taken and then only a recovery operation was seen by the medial to be in operation, one of the ministers involved visited the area and was reported to have said "I came looking for a disaster and couldn't find it." This type of continued complacency does nothing to help a situation which is rapidly growing more dangerous. It was purely chance that protected the Cornish people from exposure to the lethal materials. That no one died reflects credit on no one at all. Although it is clear that dumping in the ocean is a matter for international political agreement, that is in no argument for failure to act on a national basis. I believe that there is a case for a National Disaster Force and that this should be set up as soon as possible.' He would also lecture on the issue.

By chance or by design, the *Doomwatch* film was going to be released at the same time as the third series went to air. It was generally given good, if not terribly enthusiastic, reviews in the papers. *Film Time* reviewed the movie on 22 April 1972 at 16.00 on Radio 4. It was introduced by John Bentley and written by Lyn Fairhurst. It was first shown on BBC1 ten years later as the late film on 14 May 1982 at 22.50. A second movie, based on *Mutant 59: The Plastic Eater* was abandoned after the *Doomwatch* film initially failed to secure a release in America (though it later appeared there in 1976 under the title *Island of the Ghouls* and saw service on a triple bill with *Grave of the Vampire* and *Garden of the Dead*).

Main Cast
Dr Del Shaw (Ian Bannen), Victoria Brown (Judy Geeson), Dr Quist (John Paul), Dr Ridge (Simon Oates), The Admiral (George Sanders), Hartwell (Percy Herbert), Sir Henry Layton (Geoffrey Keen), Vicar (Joseph O'Connor), Mrs Straker (Shelagh Fraser), Dr Fay Chantry (Jean Trend), Ferry Skipper (George Woodbridge), Mrs Murray (Rita Davies), Brian Murray (Brian Anthony), Bob Gillette (James Cosmo), Tom Straker (Michael Brennan), Brewer (Norman Bird), Miss Johnson (Constance Chapman)

Technical Credits
Directed by Peter Sasdy. Produced by Tony Tenser.
Director of Photography: Kenneth Talbot.
Production Manager: Jack Causey. Art Director: Colin Grimes. Editor: Keith Palmer. Assistant Editor: Eddy Joseph. Location Manager: Jim Brennan. Assistant Director: Derek Whitehurst.
Sound Recordist: Ron Barron. Sound Editor: Michael Hopkins. Dubbing Mixer: Ken Barker. Sound Re-recording Mixers: Graham V Hartsone, Otto Snel.
Camera Operator: Ron Maasz. Focus Puller: Ronald Anscombe.
Continuity: Doreen Soan.
Hairdressing Supervisor: Ann McFadyen. Wardrobe Master: John Hilling. Construction Manager: Ken Softley. Make-up Supervisor: Tom Smith.
Scientific Advisor: Dr Kit Pedler.
Music composed and conducted by John Scott.

A Tigon British Film Production

Registered March 1972. Duration: 91' 55" Certificate: A

Series Three

Producer: Terence Dudley
Assistant to Producer: Glyn Edwards
Script Consultant: Anna Kaliski
Graphics: Alan Jeapes
Theme Music: Max Harris
Series originated by Kit Pedler and Gerry Davis

Regular Cast
Dr Spencer Quist (John Paul)
Dr John Ridge (Simon Oates)
Sir George Holroyd (John Barron)
Dr Anne Tarrant (Elizabeth Weaver)
Commander Neil Stafford (John Bown)
Colin Bradley (Joby Blanshard)
Barbara Mason (Vivien Sherrard)

3.01
Fire And Brimstone

Written and Directed by Terence Dudley
Designed by Graham Oakley
Transmitted: Monday, 5 June 1972 at 9.21 pm Duration: 52' 34"

Cast
Duncan (Michael Elwyn), Dr Richard Poole (Henry Knowles), Julie (Caroline Rogers), Reporter (John Berryman), Bystanders (Marcelle Samett, Julia Hand), Police Sergeant (John Drake), Police Constables (Jonathan Pryce, David Waterman), Prison Officer Clarke (Eric Longworth), Prisoner Warren (Talfryn Thomas), Radio Operator (Clifford Cox), Chemist (Frank Singuineau).

Also appearing
Prison Governor (Michael Mulcaster), Newspaper Men (Mike Urry, Peter Holmes, Peter Cassilles), Detective Constables (Eric Kent, Derek Tobias, Richard Lawrence, John Hine), Police Constable (Vic Taylor), Male Civil Servant (Steward Myers), Female Civil Servant (Margaret Pilleau), Woman Police Constables (Sarah McDonald, Iona Macrae), Prison Officer (Sonnie Willis).

Extras on location
Alan Thomas, Charles Shaw-Hesketh, Ron Tingley, Bill Gosling, Walter Goodman, John Cannon, Cy Town, David Ballen, Thora MacDonald, Margaret McKechnie, Vi Delma, Lionel Wheeler, Kevin Moran, Brian Nolan, Jill Goldstone, Leslie Ann Robinson, Anthony Buckthorpe, Reg Cranfield, Vera Hill, Berry Richardson, Leslie Bates, Ian Elliot, Patrick Milner, Geoff Witherick, John Scott Martin, Ursula Grenville, Peggy Scrimshaw, Kevin Moran.

Technical Credits
Production Assistant: Christina McMillan. Assistant Floor Manager: Derek Nelson. Director's Assistant: Jean Kerr. Floor Assistant: Timothy Wood.
Film Cameraman: Fred Hamilton. Sound Recordist: Bob Roberts. Film Editor: Alastair MacKay.
Costume Supervisor: Sheila Beers. Make-up Supervisor: Penny Norton.
Studio Lighting: John Dixon. TM2: Richard Ashman. Vision Mixer: Jim Stephens.
Studio Sound: Chick Anthony. Grams Operator: Gordon Phillipson. Crew: 1.

The Story

'By these three was the third part of men killed, by the fire, and by the smoke, and by the brimstone ...' – Ridge.

Dr Richard Poole is delighted to receive a surprise visitor to the Microbiological Research Station at Porton Down: Dr John Ridge. Ridge wants to know what the most dangerous microbe held at Porton Down is. Poole suggests anthrax; they have some, fresh in from the States. Poole leaves his assistant Julie in charge, who then goes to fetch a cup of tea for Ridge. Alone, Ridge begins to help himself to six phials of anthrax. After a brief stop at the Doomwatch office, Ridge takes packages all over London – a post office, the docks and London Airport, quoting from the Bible to himself. Sir George Holroyd speaks to Quist on the phone at Anne Tarrant's cottage and demands to know what Ridge was doing at Porton Down. He assumed it was some Doomwatch operation. After the call, the Minister tells Commander Stafford from Special Branch that he is satisfied that Quist knows nothing about the theft.

Ridge visits Quist and Anne and quite calmly tells him that he intends to hold the Government to ransom. He doesn't want to involve Quist. The anthrax is 'on its way', but he won't say where. Quist calls him mad. Ridge leaves to hand himself in to the police, and tells Anne to look after Quist.

Stafford questions Barbara, who remembers typing a label for Ridge: an address for a school. Stafford then questions Ridge himself in a police cell. They know each other from Ridge's days in the secret services and the dislike is mutual and hostile. Ridge's scheme will 'mature on Monday', he says. 'Ever seen a case of anthrax?' asks Stafford, 'it's nasty.' Ridge agrees. 'But it's quicker than chronic bronchitis ... and diseases of the liver ... and the kidneys ... and the gut. D'you know what I've learned in the time I've been with Doomwatch? We've got a generation in which to grow up. My generation! Your generation! During our life time ... that's if we get to three score year and ten ... we've got to get rid of warheads buzzing about up there round the clock and in submarines ... also cruising round the clock. During our lifetime we've got to control population ... to control ionizing radiation. We've got to cleanse the rivers and the seas, we've got to unclog the air and we've got to have made a bloody good start by the time we're dead or homo sapiens has had it: men perish from the earth. We've got to start washing underneath the arms and stop sweeping muck underneath the carpet. We've got to plant more trees than we cut down. We've got to recycle the Earth's resources ... even our excrement and urine. We've got to abolish the petrol engine or pay more for it. We've got to pay more for everything. Our money or our life!' Stafford dismisses it as rhetoric.

Ridge's ultimatum is received by the Minister on Monday morning.

Ridge wants six lectures published in newspapers around the world, paid for by the Government in return for one phial of anthrax for each publication. The subjects are disarmament, population, industrial effluent, the internal combustion engine, noise and recycling development. The Minister considers Ridge's scheme very ingeniously planned and costed, but quite out of the question.

Quist and Anne go to see Ridge in Brixton and to try to get him to reconsider. Ridge refuses to believe that they have achieved anything in three years of Doomwatch. He starts to gets angry as he refers to the Tobacco Bill, which was dismissed in Parliament, and the complacency shown in a *Daily Mail* television review towards pollution. Ridge is prepared to kill millions to save the rest of the world's population in the same way he killed three men to protect the State.

As a disturbed Quist drives away from Brixton, Barbara remembers the address she typed. A school in Wandsworth is sealed off and searched by men in protective gear, who find an envelope. The envelope, addressed to Rachel Carson, contains no anthrax, just a message in a bottle from Ridge congratulating them. Stafford wants a free hand with him. Anne protests that Ridge is suffering from classic paranoia but, as yet, with 'no personality disorganisation'. It wouldn't take much to push him to schizophrenia and a complete withdrawal from the world. She tells the reluctant Minister to agree to Ridge's demands, and tells him her plan.

The newspapers are brought to Ridge with the lectures printed as per his demands. All except *Pravda* have cooperated, which Ridge reveals he requested as a test: he knew the Russians would refuse. However, he wants to go out and pick up a newspaper himself to make sure they aren't dummies for his benefit. The hundred and eighty newsagents within a mile radius of the prison are going to have special copies planted. Ridge is escorted to one of his choice and is satisfied. He tells Stafford that he sent one of the phials to a Mafia millionaire in Rome and gives the address. The Minister is pleased, but Quist is worried about what will happen to Ridge when he realises that he has been duped. Duncan tells them that the one sent to the United Nations has been recovered, addressed to a fictitious secretary.

When Ridge has given all the locations but one, he gets a convict, Warren, to lift a copy of *The Times* from the Governor's office. He finds he has been conned and angrily tells Stafford so. Stafford comes up with a new plan to let Ridge escape but discovers that the man has bitten through a vein in his wrist and is passing out. Stafford struggles to save his life. He thinks the last phial is in the Doomwatch office as Ridge said it was 'under his nose'. They soon work out that it is in Barbara's deodorant. She has left work early to visit her mother and is on the tube train in a hot and bothered state. She uses the deodorant on her hands.

By the time she reaches Ealing Broadway, the police have caught up with her, but the deodorant is harmless. She'd picked up a refill at a chemist in Holborn. The anthrax is in a pile of rubbish at the back of the shop. Stafford thanks Quist for his help. The Minister tells Duncan that nothing like this must happen again; it is time 'to wield the shears ... to clip the Doomwatch wings'. Quist and Anne visit Ridge in hospital. He is in a catatonic stupor, and, as Quist tells him that they will do all they can for him, Ridge can just about whisper his goodbyes.

Behind the Story

There is no scientific mystery to solve in the story this week; it is simply a police case with a lot of broad-ranging environmental or ecological statements thrown in. It is a job for *Special Branch*, dealing with a mad scientist while Doomwatch looks on. This will happen again in the series. However, it catches the mood of the time of its writing (1971) in that the issues were not being taken seriously enough by government.

Terence Dudley, that denier of prophecy, uncannily predicts a future event. John Ridge is the Unabomber! But twenty years early. The Unabomber was the nickname for Dr Theodore 'Ted' Kaczynski, was former assistant professor of mathematics. In 1971 he retired to an isolated area in the United States where he wanted to be self-sufficient and became a recluse. He saw the wilderness around him being eaten up by new developments and started a one-man terrorist campaign, sending letter bombs to universities (hence his nickname). For nearly twenty years he waged his private war on those he blamed for technological disasters. He killed at least three people. He tried to bomb an airliner, which then made him a target for the FBI. He offered to stop his campaign providing a newspaper such as the *Washington Post* published his 35,000-word essay entitled 'Industrial Society and Its Future', which they did. Depending on your point of view, it was either lunatic ramblings or a coherent and well thought-out manifesto. It proved to be his undoing – his style was recognised by his estranged brother.

Ridge's motivation is like Kaczynski's: to wake up the world to its doom and force governments to act against further technological disaster. The plethora of Biblical references in the script doesn't make for too hard a decoding session. The story title comes from the Book of Revelation, as do Ridge's voice-overs at the beginning. He had often showed signs of a religious side, from as early as 'Friday's Child'. The script makes reference to Ridge's seeming obsession with six in terms of the number of anthrax phials, lectures and the newspapers they are to be published in on consecutive days, equating them with the six days it took God to create the world, according to the Bible. However, there is another possible connection, not specifically mentioned. Six phials, six lectures, six newspapers: 6-6-6 is the infamous number of the Beast, also found in the Book of Revelation, who had the power to rain down fire and destruction on the Earth.

The feeling of it being too late to save the world was not uncommon amongst environmentalists at the time. The television review Ridge quotes from was from the 1971 *Horizon* documentary 'Due to Lack of Interest, Tomorrow Has Been Cancelled'. Here, predictions of ecological disaster made by certain scientists were investigated, such as those of Professor Paul Ehrlich of Stanford University. He will get a name check in a later episode. The actual *Daily Mail* review quoted is as follows: 'I'm sorry, but no-one will convince me that the human species is destroying itself. We have been mutating successfully for twenty million years. If we survive a ten million year drought – which we did – we will survive anything.' A slight pre-echo of this stance can be heard in Dudley's 'Spectre at the Feast', where Doctor Whitehead wonders if we might evolve to breathe sulphur dioxide. Ridge sends the decoy anthrax to Rachel Carson. She is, of course, the author of *Silent Spring*.

After filming but before studio, the *Daily Express*, a paper slow to notice Doomwatch-type affairs, decided to wade in. The 19 January edition introduced their plan: 'Hardly a day goes by without some new wave of pollution – of the mind, of the body, or of the land – flooding across our country. Are we powerless to turn the tide? The *Daily Express* gives its answer in a massive, campaigning counter-attack. Today we turn on the spoilers of the environment.' Chapman Pincher, billed as 'The Man Who Knows Even Before MPs' – and who had an ear in the intelligence services – wrote a powerful argument demanding legislation with teeth 'to force industrialists and local authorities to spend more on pollution abatement'. He identified one of the problems as the public's reluctance to spend more money. 'An increase in the price of coal to prevent mine washings fouling rivers or a rise in the rates to pay for a better sewage works is usually resisted.' His third point on why inaction is the cause of the day is the industrialists' argument that anti- pollution restrictions will cause unemployment when they are put out of business. At the end of *Public Enemy* Quist warns the people of Carlingham – and us, the audience – that we have only thirty years left of slow, dirty dying. Ridge was not there to hear it, but he was probably told about it. And it must have sunk in. Ridge displays faith in the power of legislation, which the Minister, who sympathises with Ridge, envisages taking ten years. Once again, the issue is about who pays.

Production
Script Development
When Terence Dudley wrote the script, he probably envisaged Ridge's exit

as a shocker on the lines of Toby Wren's death. He received permission to write the opener on 4 May 1971 'because of his particular involvement with and knowledge of the series ... providing necessary continuity, the writing out of one of the main characters, establishment of a replacement and restatement of the theme of the series.' This was approved by Andrew Osborn, and the fee was agreed on 7 July. This memo was sent to Martin Worth, but he would not play a part in script editing the programme. This 'pilot' script would be sent out to prospective writers along with the format document.

Filming

Terence Dudley would direct the episode. The bulk of the film work was done in the first week of January 1972 in Greater London, with one of the locations being the London Transport Depot in Ruislip. Apparently some night filming took place at a house belonging to a rich Saudi prince in the Jersey Road in Osterley (although film cameraman Fred Hamilton may have been misremembering another episode). For the first time, Vivien Sherrard went out on location.

Casting

The episode made heavy use of the new regulars and the guest star appearance of Simon Oates, there are few other characters of any note. On location playing a reporter once again was John Berryman, the same role in which he was last seen in 'Tomorrow, the Rat'. Marcelle Sammett had also been in that episode as a nurse and Julie Hand was an extra in 'No Room for Error'. Jonathan Pryce makes an early acting appearance as a policeman, and Talfryn Thomas had been an unfortunate fatality in 'The Human Time Bomb'. Caroline Rogers had been a stewardess who survived 'The Plastic Eaters' and been a secretary in one of the last *Softly, Softly* episodes to feature John Barron. The unfortunate Poole was played by Richard Knowles who had been a regular in *The First Lady*. Frank Singuineau, playing the chemist on location, was born in Trinidad in 1913, and like Pryce was only needed on film.

Studio

'Fire and Brimstone' was the first episode to be recorded. This was in an unknown studio on Tuesday, 8 February 1972. The old Doomwatch office set was used for the episode, and the laboratory seen briefly was the new set but shot in close-up. After the recording, Simon Oates would not be needed again until May.

Stock Music

Classical music was the order of the day. Seventeen seconds from 'The

Execution of Stepan Razin', composed by Shostakovich and performed by the Slovak Philharmonic Chorus and Orchestra (Supraphon SUAST 50958), was played in the background for one scene. Eighteen seconds of Stravinsky's 'Fire Bird Suite' was used, performed by L'Orchestra de la Suisse Romande on the Decca Eclipse label (ECM 508). Over four minutes was taken from Vaughan Williams' 'Symphony No 5' and his 'Fantasia on a Theme' by Thomas Tallis, played by the Sinfonia of London on EMI (HMV ASD 2698). A similar length was used from Bartok's 'The Miraculous Mandarin' suite, performed by the London Symphony Orchestra (Decca SXL 6111).

Editing
The episode was edited on Thursday, 10 February 1972 between 1.30 pm and 5.30 pm. The episode was transmitted from videotape. Terence Dudley told Martin Worth in a letter that the episode 'came out a treat'.

Promotion
Transmission had been fixed as far back as the episode's recording, and its promotion gave away the plot quite happily. The *Radio Times* asked on the front cover 'Will Ridge destroy the world?', and then wondered if he had anthrax on their caption of him accompanying the billing. The *Sun* previewed the episode in dramatic terms as 'Six Phials That Hold the World to Ransom!' 'Fans of Dr Ridge should not worry too much however, if his behaviour seems to indicate an automatic exit from the series. For there must surely be a scientific explanation for such uncharacteristic carryings-on.' The *Daily Mirror* explained the ransom plot and quoted Simon Oates as saying 'It's all possible … Just half a drop of a certain anthrax virus in a reservoir is enough to kill a city.' The *Guardian* suspected that the return of *Doomwatch* might be more comforting than ITV's opposition, *Man at the Top*'s opening episode 'You'll Never Understand Women'.

Reaction
Next morning came the reviews. Peter Black in the *Daily Mail*, having reviewed a programme exploring the Club of Rome's report on the *Limits to Growth*, declared that 'Fire and Brimstone' set a deplorably superficial tone for the new series … The huge moral question of why the virus was being made was lost sight of in the fast and implausible pace of the story, the actors never seemed to have time to think about what they were saying.' The *Daily Telegraph* a week later called it 'frenzied nonsense'. The *Coventry Evening Telegraph* said: 'This was not one of the best episodes in a normally compelling series … It could have been tense, the search for the deadly phials: but, from the beginning, the episode lacked credibility, real

drama and surprise. At times, the action even seemed amateurish. The *Doomwatch* team can do better. On past performances we can be certain that they will.'

Programme Review Board

Six million people, 13% of the available audience, watched the opening episode, a figure that the Board were satisfied with, even though 20% were watching ITV instead. The Controller of BBC1 commended the episode to his colleagues, but no-one commented on what they may have read in their newspapers that same Wednesday morning.

Pedler and Davis

The *Guardian* reported 'The two writers who created the BBC TV series *Doomwatch* about the dangers of modern science yesterday announced the latest programme as a travesty of their original concept, and said they were severing all connection with the BBC. Dr Kit Pedler, one time head of the anatomy department at the London University Institute of Ophthalmology, and his co-writer, Mr Gerry Davis, thought up *Doomwatch* two years ago, and wrote the outlines and some of the scripts of the first series. The idea, Dr Pedler said last night, was to raise the environment issue in a serious way with drama based soundly on scientific reality. Dr Pedler and Mr Davis objected to Monday's episode, 'Fire and Brimstone', written by Terence Dudley, the programme's producer. Dr Pedler called it "absolutely awful – a mad scientist going amuck yet again" … "Just a spy thriller," Dr Pedler and Mr Davis said.' In the *Daily Express*, Pedler added 'This was a travesty of the programme's intention to reflect the dangers of science based on realistic scientific ideas. Instead the BBC reverted to a 1930s style mad scientist epic. It is no more than horizontal toothpaste.'

The BBC 'spokesman' who answered calls from reporters stated that it was the writers themselves who had veered away from the programme's original format and that they had cut their connection with it over a year ago. The papers reported that Pedler and Davis were going to write to the BBC asking for their names to be removed from the *Radio Times* as 'originators' of the programme, and from 'Say Knife, Fat Man' onwards this happens. Mary Holland, writing for The *Observer*, decided in light of Kit Pedler's denunciation of the series not to bother writing her review lamenting the trivialising of a series 'which was originally so exciting and intelligent'.

Precisely how these comments from Pedler and Davis were transmitted to the press is unclear. It may have been on a review programme, but not on BBC radio, for Pedler would discuss both the movie and the TV series on Radio 4's *Scan*, recorded on 14 June and transmitted the following day.

Radio Times
Readers of the *Radio Times* had their say, especially in light of the criticism from Pedler. '"Fire and Brimstone" was not only poor value even as a thriller, but coming under the same title and publicity build-up as the original programmes can only encourage viewers to believe that concern for the environment is just the latest fad of hysterical scientists instead of a matter of potential popular interest for every member of the human race', wrote E Marshall from Eastbourne. 'Why has the BBC chosen to adopt this cheap, sensationalist format, when the series was perfectly successful at the outset? I am sure that the vast majority of *Doomwatch* fans cannot tolerate another 12 programmes of the quality displayed in the opening episode.' This was from M Dennerly of Denton in Lancashire.

However, Terence Dudley, who answered some of the criticism, was pleased to see one reader got the point he was trying to make, as Miss J Curry from Ilford wrote 'The story was of a man, Dr John Ridge, usually carefree and very confident, who obviously cared about the insanity of a world killing itself. After years of talking to people who just did not care or were indifferent, he became so frustrated that he was driven into drastic action, hoping to draw the attention of 'governments and people alike to what they were doing to their children and grand-children's future. I think the story was good, the acting excellent – especially by Simon Oates as Dr Ridge – and I am sure it made its point with a lot more impact than any documentary could have done. Will Simon Oates ever return to Doomwatch?' Dudley wrote 'I think Miss Curry says it all. Her reception of "Fire and Brimstone" was what was hoped for. Perhaps I may point out to Mr Dennerly and Mr Marshall that Dr Pedler and Mr Davis wrote the first and the last stories of the first series. The first, "The Plastic Eaters", was about a plastic-eating virus that doesn't exist: it was a will-the-infected-plane-land-in time suspense plot. The last, "Survival Code", was about an atomic bomb washed up on Hastings pier and was a will-the-bomb-go-off suspense plot. "Fire and Brimstone" was quite in key with these. The rest of the series will confirm the intention of the original format. I think, too, that it is important to remember that the programme's prime intention is to entertain.'

On the bright side *New Scientist*, previewing television in their issue dated 15 June, pointed out that 'the "mad scientist" ethos (about which P & D are complaining) is no stranger to BBC. Tonight's film is *The Quatermass Experiment*, based on Nigel Kneale's tv serial which, says the Beeb, "thrilled and frightened audiences in the early '50s."'

Audience Research Report
The panel for the audience research report compiled for the episode wasn't terribly impressed either. The Reaction Profile recorded that 73 per cent

thought that the episode was entertaining, but 23 per cent, boring. The plot rated 67:33. This would be one of the lowest figures of the series.

'Although widespread pleasure was expressed at the return of a favourite series, it was clear that, for a sizeable number, this particular episode failed to come up to expectation. The main cause of disappointment was apparently a far-fetched and over-dramatized story that struck several "more like a common-or-garden thriller on the 'mad scientist theme' than the fictional but realistic treatment of serious current problems" which they had come to expect from *Doomwatch*. The complaint was not so much that the actions of John Ridge in holding the world to ransom with phials of deadly anthrax was quite out of keeping with his character as built-up from the beginning of the series (which could have been a result of his illness) but that no real attempt was made to explain the events or make them seem more realistic, with the result that the episode was totally lacking in that "it could happen here" feeling which had made the previous series as riveting. "Not a patch on the last series": "first Toby was blown up and now John has gone off his head: are you trying to kill off all the best characters?": "I was so looking forward to this, but what a let-down!" were typical comments from this group, several of whom felt that *Doomwatch* had completely drifted away from the original concept of the series.

'Nevertheless, a substantial number of reporting viewers were clearly delighted with an enjoyable and exciting opening episode which kept them on the edge of their seats. The topical theme of concern at Man's pollution of his environment was in the *Doomwatch* tradition: the suspense was well maintained, especially in the tube-train sequence, when it was thought that Barbara might be carrying one of the deadly phials, and, in their opinion, the series had got off to a good start.

'There was a little criticism of "over-acting", especially from Simon Oates, but several reporting listeners felt the part he was called upon to portray this week was so exaggerated as to be almost impossible to play in a natural or realistic way. Most, in fact, thought him very good – "giving, in the circumstances, a commendably convincing impression of desperation" – and John Barron (the Minister) being singled out for special mention. It was occasionally said that the dialogue was inaudible at times, while the use of music during Ridge's "outbursts" was "rather corny", in the opinion of one or two, but most considered the production entirely satisfactory, and there was a special word of praise for the camera work.'

The much-needed explanation was only three weeks away in an episode that was being rehearsed as the episode was transmitted. Quite how the cast reacted to this reception is not remembered, but it couldn't have been pleasant.

The camera script was published in the now out of print collection of missing *Doomwatch* stories *Deadly Dangerous Tomorrow* in 2014 with permission from the Dudley estate.

3.02
High Mountain

Written by Martin Worth
Directed by Lennie Mayne
Designed by Graham Oakley
Transmitted: Monday, 12 June 1972 at 9.21 pm Duration: 49' 22"

Cast
Ian Drummond (Ronald Hines), Cowley (John Scott), Alexander
Drummond (Moultrie Kelsall), Barman (Kedd Senton), Mrs Bell (Betty
Cardno), Manservant (Ian Elliott), Gillie (David Grahame).

Also appearing
Secretary (Frances Pidgeon), Steward (Ian Munro), People in Bar (Ian
Elliott, Dilys Marvin, Stuart Anderson, Joe Santo).

Technical Credits
Director's Assistant: Norma Flint. Production Assistant: Vivienne Cozens.
Assistant Floor Manager: Liz Mace. Floor Assistant: Mike Thorne.
Film Cameraman: Fred Hamilton. Sound Recordist: Basil Harris. Film
Editor: Alistair MacKay.
Costume Supervisor: Ken Trew. Make-up Supervisor: Elizabeth Rowell.
Studio Lighting: Ralph Walton. TM2: Bob Warman. Vision Mixer: Jean
Ellis.
Sound Supervisor: John Lloyd. Grams Operator: Gerry Borrows.
Senior Cameraman: Rod Taylor.
Crew: 3.

Radio Times
'Every man has his price, and from what I've heard lately, Dr Quist will
come cheaper than most.'

The Story
'Damn Quist! Are we to be ruled by these men?' – Ian Drummond

Ian Drummond, managing director of the Drummond Group, is about to
launch a range of aerosol paints just as Doomwatch is about to come out
against isocyanates. Drummond doesn't think Quist will be much of a
problem for long, as he knows of the anthrax incident. After lunch with
Anne Tarrant, he invites her to bring Quist to Scotland and meet his father,

who used to run the company. There might be a job in it for Quist if what he has heard is correct. Quist hands in his resignation to the Minister, who refuses to accept it, at least until Quist finds a job worth leaving it for. He is concerned about keeping the anthrax business quiet and not add fuel to the rumours by Quist leaving. Geoff Hardcastle and Dr Fay Chantry are to be removed, and Stafford will join Doomwatch as a watchdog. When Quist finds Anne in the pub waiting for him, Stafford is there with a notebook from Ridge, which he finds fascinating. Quist feels tired, and Anne suggests a weekend in Scotland. Quist doesn't fancy being fattened up by some international tycoon, but Anne assures him that he'll like Drummond senior. She treated his wife when she fell ill. Quist agrees to go, simply to avoid Stafford.

Quist and Anne travel by plane to the highlands, where they are met by Alex Drummond with his Range Rover as his chauffeur is ill. On the journey back to the house, Alex comments on the beautiful scenery and how it is worth protecting. 'Your promised land, Dr Quist. What a lot of it could still be like – even now. Three hundred acres of uncontaminated countryside. Not a pylon, not a power station, not even a main road. And bang in the middle of a so-called development area too. If that can survive, there's hope for us all.' He firmly believes organisation is the way to get things done.

Over drinks Quist meets Ian, who asks if he would like to be head of a Doomwatch funded by the Drummond Group with no strings attached and all recommendations followed. He explains that to be on the anti-pollution bandwagon is good for business. 'Pollution is the bogey of the 1970s. A poisoned planet, famine, no room to move, the end of all life – it used to be the bomb, today it's the pollution. There's a growing swell of public opinion on your side, Quist. When supersonic aircraft can be cut from the sky, in America of all places, and when men with pitch forks can get an aerodrome shifted. We're going to have to be responsible to sell in the eighties.'

Alex advises Quist to take only half the money on offer. The rest would come from rival competitors, universities, even government grants. Everyone would be keen to get Quist's stamp of approval. Alex supports the idea because of the damage his firm has done to the environment and to people's health. His wife had undergone a breakdown the previous year; he blames himself for concentrating too much on the business. And he doesn't trust Ian's motives. Going for a walk, Anne tries to persuade Quist that this is the next step for him but he is sure only governments can make the changes necessary to clean up the muck. On their return, Quist phones London and wants to speak to Bradley, who has been doing some work that may be useful. Ian tells him an old friend of his is here: Stafford. The next day, Stafford tries to convince Quist that he is not here to spy on him and that he may be useful in the decision he might be taking. Ian's friends have been questioning Stafford about Quist's 'availability'.

Bradley's report is into the harmful effects of isocyanates in the aerosol sprays the Drummond group are producing. This is a test to see if Ian Drummond is sincere and will follow through with his promises.

In the end, Drummond says that he will simply pull the aerosol paints. Stafford intervenes, knowing that the true game is simply to re-brand the product if necessary. Ian calls him a bastard as his plan is exposed, but Stafford explains his own position: he now works for Dr Quist. Alex urges Quist to consider the Doomwatch offer and that, as he owns 40 per cent of the shares in the Drummond Group, he himself will declare their new product dangerous. Quist agrees to think about it. Ian thinks this is professional suicide.

The Minister is anxious to see Quist. The French press have been reporting in guarded terms the Ridge-anthrax affair. Quist is not terribly concerned but is amazed by headlines in the evening papers: the Drummond Group has indeed declared the aerosol paints dangerous. Alex plans to oust his son from the company at a shareholders' meeting on Friday and give the funds to Quist for Doomwatch. Ian will fight this and have Alex removed instead.

Stafford persuades the Minister that Alex will win and Quist will leave the Government for business, confirming the suspicion that there has been some kind of cover-up. Stafford then tells Quist the reverse: Alex hasn't a chance in hell in winning. Quist realises that this is an opportunity to force the Minister's hand that he may never get again. The Minister sees Quist before the shareholders' meeting and welcomes him in while Anne and Stafford wait for him in the pub. When Quist joins them, he is slightly bemused: new facilities and funding are to be provided for Doomwatch. It is all thanks to Stafford, who leaked the story to the French. Stafford explains Ridge's protest and activity had triggered something within himself.

As for Alex, he returns to his Scottish home a broken man; once there, all he can do is gaze up at a portrait of his wife.

Behind The Story

This script can be seen as developing the themes Terence Dudley first touched upon in 'Spectre at the Feast', in which the managing director and his tame chief scientist buy up scientific experts to clean up the mess they have made. In 'High Mountain' we see a powerful company trying to buy up Quist himself, who has lost his confidence and sees the writing on the wall, and use him as an advertising gimmick. The story naturally follows on from 'Fire and Brimstone', showing that the fallout from the Ridge's actions has initially played directly into the hands of the Minister. But by the end of the story, the Minister has no choice but to prevent an international scandal by making Doomwatch twice as big and powerful.

Generational Business

We see two types of businessmen here: the young pragmatist and the older man, full of regrets, who believes in values of a bygone age that probably never existed. Old Alex Drummond is an aesthete who sees art, heritage and the unspoilt landscape as the same thing and who thinks of himself as a patron for the arts. He shares his paintings with galleries, but is always pleased to get them back. He prevents a road from being built through his estates in order to have something unsullied to look at. He achieved this, he tells Quist, by using his money, influence and blackmail. 'The whole weight of the Drummond group. That's the way to get things done, Quist.' His need for beauty is a side effect of the ugly guilt he suffers over his wife and her mental breakdown, which he had not seen coming as he was so involved in building up his empire. He only saw the physical pollution of his company when he returned to a beauty spot of some significance in his life. He even shut down the plant responsible, but the cottage dwellers who worked there no longer live amongst the beauty he restored. He sees the appointment of Quist as the recruitment of an ally in his cause to be of some good to the world – now that he is of no use to the company. He objects to and fights the plans of his son, who is probably just the younger version of himself: utterly committed to profit. Did Alex really believe the shareholders would put other people's interests before their own?

Ian is the 'realist', a cunning operator who just sees Doomwatch as a way of selling more aerosol paint. He doesn't have an aesthetic. He prefers his London skyscraper to the Scottish mansion house, which is hardly surprising. His ethics are those of a businessman. He is exploiting a public fear (in this case, pollution) in much the same way as resistant car manufacturers finally twigged that safety could be made into a selling point. In the 1950s the idea and expense of seat belts were an anathema to some manufacturers, even though cars had dashboards with sharp, metallic lines which cut through people even in low-impact collisions. The theory went that compensation pay outs were cheaper than a wholesale redesign of the feature. Ian Drummond simply wants to relaunch an existing product with a new brand name.

Health and Safety

At the heart of the episode is a simple health-and-safety-in-the-workplace story, but we don't get to see the impact on the workers this time, and we only hear second-hand accounts from Anne Tarrant about the consequences of the pollution on Alex's estate. That Quist 'dramatically' asks for a health warning to be placed on aerosol cans sounds quite lame forty years on, but health warnings had only been recently introduced on tobacco products (as referred to in the script for 'Fire and Brimstone and mentioned under the entry for 'The Devil's Sweets'). Various businesses were worried about the impact on sales such warnings would have, but the real issue is of course informing the public of potential dangers to their health. We all now know that the inhalation of aerosol sprays is dangerous; look at the 'craze' of glue-sniffing and solvent abuse that haunted parent's minds in the seventies and eighties. The products were not banned, but education and warnings issued. This episode shows how far we have come, and it is a surprise that it was ever an issue. We still use aerosols, but without the chemical discovered to be harming the ozone layer.

Production
Script Development
'The High Mountain' was commissioned from Martin Worth on 4 May 1972, to be delivered by 30 July. Terence Dudley was very happy with it. The health hazard was originally to be from enzymes used in detergents. The script makes Mrs Bell the focus of the sub-plot; her aprons have to be kept bright and white, and as a result she has developed an allergic reaction in the form of eczema. Her husband, now a chauffeur, was ill because of exposure to dust in the factories. Bradley's report was therefore full of different examples of health hazards from those in the transmitted version.

IAN: Don't worry. I doubt if Mr Bradley is going to say anything worth revealing. No scientist yet has come up with proof that enzyme detergents are harmful to consumers.
BRADLEY: There's some proof they've been harmful to workers who make them, sir.
IAN: So nowadays everyone handling them wears overalls, gloves, goggles, even respirators.
QUIST: But how many of your workers had to lose their health before you recognised the danger?
BRADLEY: (Consulting his report.) 'Of 115 men engaged in enzyme preparations for the Drummond product "Vanish", 45 were found to have become sensitised, resulting, in some cases, in irreversible lung disease.'

It was probably the advisor working on the episode, Dr Jack Pepys, who suggested the substitution of isocyanates; he had conducted research into allergic reactions to enzymes, his area of expertise. Dudley wrote to Worth on 11 February 1972, telling him that director

Lennie Mayne had been asking for a sight of the script, and Dudley did not want him to see the out-of-date version. Anna Kaliski had gathered together material on isocynates [sic].

The next day, Kaliski herself wrote to Worth, hoping that he would be delighted at the close parallels with the enzyme story so that the swap-over would be quite simple. 'Also, I think this is a (famous last words) sort of *Doomwatch* scoop! Dr Pepys of the Brompton hospital is going to write a very strong report on the hazards of these both industrially and domestically for a periodical called *Clinical Allergy* – and this will appear at the end of June!' She also enclosed press cuttings related to the drums on the Cornish coast, some of which contained isocyanates.

The rewrite shortened the script quite considerably in various places, eliminating a speaking board member from the first scene and a couple of sets from the studio recording, one of which was the music room in Alex's house. This change of set removed a great deal of dialogue from Alex, who saw himself as a soloist in charge of a large orchestra (he would play the violin to recordings of concertos without the principle soloist) and applied this metaphor to Quist and Doomwatch.

ALEX: Do you play the piano, Dr Quist?
QUIST: (Surprised.) No.
ALEX: A pity. You could have accompanied me on the fiddle. We'd have made something good – together. (He picks up a violin.) The violin is strangely ineffectual on its own. (He goes to record playing equipment.) Which is why I have records here of violin concertos and sonatas where the solo part has been left out. (He puts on a record.) So I can play a great work like the Brahms with one of the finest orchestras in the world. That is what you need to be effective, Quist. A full scale professional orchestra to back you. You cannot do it on your own.

By the time Lennie Mayne got to see the script, the episode needed a new ending scene. In the original Alex comes back home, defeated, and finds that his record player is broken. He picks up the violin to play unaccompanied. In the new version he returns home defeated and demoralised, and Mrs Bell works out what has happened. Either Mayne or Dudley added Alex entering the drawing room to look at the portrait of his wife, a scene which Martin Worth objected to quite strongly. He also objected to having Alex's car, a Rolls Royce, replaced by a 'splendid Range Rover', which defeated the point Worth was trying to make about Alex's preference for older, more reliable values.

Casting

Guest star Moultrie Kelsall had played a regular character, Deputy Director George Fratton, in the first series of *R3*. Versatile actor Ronald Hines had recently emerged from a sit-com called *Not In front of the Children*, and would later portray William Cecil, England's spy-master in *Elizabeth R*. John Scott, playing Cowley was an extra in 'The Islanders'. Scott had also played a regular role in *Probation Officer* alongside John Paul. This was an episode unusually light in extras and walk-ons. This was Ian Elliott's third appearance: he had been the ambulance driver in 'Tomorrow, the Rat', had a walk-on part in 'No Room for Error' and would later be seen in 'Flood'. Lennie Mayne's wife, Frances Pidgeon, gets an uncredited role as the voice on the intercom for both the Minister's and Ian Drummond's secretaries. She had previously played a secretary in 'Public Enemy'. Kedd Senton was really Kenneth Seddington and had featured as an extra in other Lennie Mayne and Darrol Blake episodes. He is best known as a stuntman for Benny Hill. Betty Cardno was one of the jurors in the classic *Hancock's Half Hour* episode 'Twelve Angry Men'.

Filming

The filming in Scotland was done during the break in production in the first week of April 1972. John Paul and Elizabeth Weaver were needed for three days, with some of the filming taking place near Callander in the Trossachs, Perthshire. Here, the pair were interviewed by the *Radio Times*. Only veteran actor Moultrie Kelsall, playing Alex Drummond, was needed in addition.

Studio

'High Mountain' was the eighth story in production. It was videotaped on 2 May 1972 in TC6. This would be the last episode to feature the original outer office set.

Stock Music

The pub scenes were backed by the London Studio Group on a 1967 Hudson De Wolfe LP called *Bossalena* (DW 3058), from which came the title track, composed by Earl Ward, as well as three numbers by Keith Papworth: 'Singing Surf', 'Swaying Palms' and 'Pink Flamingos'. Hudson De Wolfe also provided Adrian Bonsel's 'Early in the Morning' from *Music for Wind Quartet* (DW 2967) and Jack Trombey's 'Pastorale Flute' from *Pastoral Music* (DW 3188). Also used were two Chappell discs: *Classical Idiom Vol 2* (Small Group) (CIS 5012) for 'Pastures Green' by David Snell and *Pastoral Music Vol 1* (CIS 5018) for 'By the Riverside' by Roger Roger.

Editing
The episode was edited on Thursday, 4 May 1972 between 2.30 pm and 11.30 pm.

Programme Review Board
The episode itself was greeted warmly by Shaun Sutton, but the ratings had fallen to five and a half million. The Reaction Index measured by the BBC for the episode was an improvement on last week's episode, with a ratio of 80:20 for entertaining/boring.

Reception
Richard Last in the *Daily Telegraph* praised the episode, calling Martin Worth's script 'considerably better than the blurb suggested and vastly better than last week's frenzied nonsense which so properly upset Dr Pedler'. He thought the episode was 'credible' and that 'it offered valid opportunities for moral argument, like private ownership of vast estates being balanced against the benevolent use of that ownership.' As a 'grateful do-it-your-selfer', he hoped that the alleged dangers of polyurethane paint was fictional. He ended his review by praising the sterling performance of Moultrie Kelsall.

Both rehearsal and camera scripts were published in the now out of print anthology *Deadly Dangerous Tomorrow* with the blessing of Martin Worth.

3.03
Say Knife, Fat Man

Written by Martin Worth
Directed by Eric Hills
Designed by Graham Oakley
Transmitted: Monday, 19 June 1972 at 9.22 pm Duration: 49′ 05″

Cast
Susan (Maria O' Brien), Chief Superintendent Mallory (Geoffrey Palmer), Professor Holman (Hugh Cross), Rafael (Peter Halliday), Carlos (Anthony Andrews), Michael (Paul Seed), Sarah (Elisabeth Sladen), David (Adrian Wright), Ian (Hugh Ross), Lawson (Alan Hockey), Eddie (Peter King), Williams (Sean Lynch), Harry (Leslie Schofield).

Also appearing
Extras on location and in studio: Denis Marlow, Louisa Carol, Chris Hodge, David Wilde, Tony West, Michele Lisiard.

Extras in studio only: Terry Leigh, Frank Menzies, Natalie Andon, David Ianson, David Pelton, Reg Turner.

Technical Credits
Director's Assistant: Adele Paul. Production Assistant: Sheila Atha. Assistant Floor Manager: Derek Nelson. Floor Assistant: Timothy Woods.
Film Cameraman: Fred Hamilton. Sound Recordist: Basil Harris. Film Editor: Alastair MacKay.
Sound Supervisor: Chick Anthony. Grams Operator: Gordon Phillips.
Special Effects: Jim Ward.
Costume Supervisor: Sheila Beers. Costume Assistant: Ken Trew. Make-up Supervisor: Penny Norton.
Studio Lighting: John Dixon. TM2: Dickie Ashman. Vision Mixer: Rhoda Carrs.
Prop Buyer: Peter Sproles.
Crew: 3.

Radio Times
Student power reaches a new high in Doomwatch. 'A kid held a knife to my throat when I was six years old. Even at that age I knew he wasn't going to kill me; but I knew he could. That's enough. A state of war exists.'

The Story

'Any competent nuclear physicist can design a workable A-Bomb. Ask Quist. The technology's not beyond the powers of most countries either. It's the plutonium that's hard to come by.' – Sir George Holroyd

A group of young people fake a motorbike accident to hijack a van containing a consignment of plutonium. One of the drivers is drugged and left behind; the other is forced at gunpoint by a man called Carlos to drive the now-empty van to Wales. In the morning the driver is coshed outside his van and left in a ditch. Meanwhile, the plutonium arrives at its new destination and is unloaded by two of the hijackers, Sarah and Ian.

As the Doomwatch team explore their new facilities, Stafford comes to tell Quist about the heist, and soon they are discussing the matter with the Minister. There was more than enough plutonium in the unusually large consignment to make a nuclear bomb. At the new offices Colin is telling Barbara, now Quist's PA, and the new secretary, Susan Proud, about the dangers if the plutonium slabs were to make contact with each other. They would generate heat, and, whilst there would be no nuclear explosion, the release of energy would contaminate the area. Ian arrives at the office and leaves an envelope on Susan's desk before quickly leaving. Stafford opens it. He is soon visiting a South American embassy official called Rafael, who has read about the hijack in the papers. Rafael wonders if Stafford is going to visit all the other 'irresponsible countries' not trusted to generate their own nuclear power in case they build weapons from the plutonium. The package for Stafford contained a photo of Rafael with a well-known gangster figure called George Talbot, but the picture has clearly been doctored.

Stafford knew it was a fake but wonders why the photo had been made. Chief Superintendent Mallory from Scotland Yard is in charge of the case. He thinks that the whole heist has been made to look as if organised crime was behind it, and the van's route was designed to put them on a false trail to suggest that the plutonium's final destination would be a port, from where it could be smuggled out. However, he believes it is still in the country and that whoever is behind the heist plans to build a nuclear bomb.

Stafford reports this to the Minister, who is horrified, but he is incredulous as to whom Mallory thinks is behind the theft: students. The bike used in the fake accident had borne the insignia of Stainfield University Football Club. There had recently been some trouble at this University, and the police had gone in, in strength. The man in charge of its physics lab, Professor Holman, had worked on the Manhattan Project with Quist. Mallory asks Quist to go down and talk to him. Barbara is not very convinced by Mallory's arguments and questions her boss on the subject, but Quist is convinced by the evidence behind Mallory's reasoning. He intends to go down there and wants Barbara to go with him in her new role as his PA.

The students have now got the plutonium into the University laboratory. Michael, their leader, begins the slow and dangerous job of machining the plutonium inside a sealed glove-box. Carlos thinks they are missing a trick by not selling the plutonium. He knows how to contact George Talbot, the gangster they have been setting up. No-one is interested, so Carlos decides to act independently, reasoning that they don't need all of the plutonium to make their bomb. Quist, Stafford and Barbara arrive at the university. Quist goes off to see Holman and is noticed by Sarah, and Stafford spots Talbot's white Mercedes parked outside. Stafford is himself spotted by Ian, as is Barbara, whom he recognises from the Doomwatch offices. As Barbara idly looks over a noticeboard, attempting to blend in with the students, Ian points her out to Sarah, who approaches her to find out more. She invites Barbara to an Action for Peace meeting taking place that evening. The pair go for a coffee together and arrange to meet later.

Carlos makes contact with the occupier of the Mercedes, Williams, who works for Talbot. They drive to meet up with Harry, another of Talbot's employees. The Mercedes is left conspicuously outside a hotel while they talk in a second, unremarkable car to avoid detection by the police. At the University, Michael is not concerned by the arrival of Doomwatch, nor is he as suspicious of Carlos as Sarah and the others are. That night, as they continue working, they are startled when Barbara turns up, asking for Sarah. As Quist tries to persuade Holman of the situation with his students, the group tell Barbara their motivation. Michael remembers having a knife held to his throat as a boy; he knew that he wasn't going to die, but the threat was there. He sees that threat as being expressed by all authority throughout society – from parents to policemen, magistrates to Ministers. They all wield power because, in one form or another, they have the knife. The bomb the students are building will be their own knife.

Carlos bargains with Williams over the price for the plutonium and is driven back to the University to fetch the spare slabs. Soon, Michael and Sarah discover the furtive theft and Barbara persuades them to call the police. Carlos is being driven back to London rather unwillingly, and Williams becomes suspicious of the plutonium. He is convinced it is just lead. He stops the car beside a reservoir and demands Carlos get the real stuff, but in his carelessness he allows the two slabs to make contact. They begin to smoulder.

Mallory and Quist arrive at the lab and wonder if Carlos knows what to do if the plutonium gets hot. 'As long as he doesn't put it into a bucket of water' Quist remarks. Williams and Harry have thrown the plutonium out of the car, and Carlos, scared it will explode, picks it up with his jacket and slides down the bank to the reservoir. He throws it into the water. There is a brilliant blue flash; he is killed. Back at the Doomwatch offices, Stafford tells Quist and Barbara that the two gangsters are in hospital, probably dying, and that it is going to cost thousands to decontaminate the reservoir. He still doesn't think much of students. Barbara asks Stafford which was worse – that plutonium fell into the hands of morons or that students were making an atomic bomb. In her view, a third option is the worst: that the students were building their bomb because they felt they needed to.

Behind The Story
If Kit Pedler thought 'Fire and Brimstone' was an episode of *Softly, Softly* rather than *Doomwatch*, what did he make of this one? Actually, he might have liked it, since it was a theme he had suggested for the second series, although Gerry Davis may have had issues with Doomwatch's periphery to the plot. For the second time this series, a theft of a killer substance has connections with the Doomwatch offices and the police search the offices for an envelope, just as they had two episodes ago. Quist is simply called in to advise the police on the recovery of the plutonium whilst Stafford follows a few hunches and visits an embassy, a job Quist might have done in an earlier series. The students themselves seem to know of Stafford's involvement with Doomwatch, since they send him the doctored photo in order to draw incorrect conclusions. Quist is a commentator on events, agreeing with Mallory's conclusions, calming down Barbara (who has finally been given a voice) and confronting Holman.

The story deals with a straightforward theft and how the students begin to construct their bomb. They have everything they need; all they have to do is machine down the plutonium. That is plain enough in terms of narrative, but what makes the story different from other nuclear bomb blackmail plots is the motivation. The 'Fat Man' of the title refers to the codename of the atomic device dropped on Nagasaki in 1945. The 'Knife' is having the power to threaten, even if the threat is not carried through.

For Michael, the bespectacled young student physicist, the knife is for the Young. It has been erroneously reported in the past that their motivation was ecological, but it wasn't. We were still at a time of student radicalism where the generation gap was wide enough to be unbridgeable in terms of attitude. Michael just wants to show the judge, the copper, the State, that the young can bite back. Michael equates the nuclear bomb to the knife held to his throat when he was a young boy. The bomb is their knife to authority's throat – a deterrent and a threat. A recent sit-in at the University had turned into a nasty conflict with the police, which had presumably enough to provoke the students into the plutonium heist. The script does not go into precisely what they were going to do with the bomb once they had finished it. It is only when the students realise that it is now in the wrong hands – or might be in the wrong hands – that they give up. But they had made their point.

Advisor
Dr Frank Barnaby, one of the advisers for the episode, wrote of his fear of nuclear proliferation in an edition of *New Scientist*, for which he was the defence consultant, dated 24 June 1971. He had trained as a nuclear physicist and worked at the Atomic Weapons Research Establishment at Aldermaston in the 1950s. He helped to organise the Pugwash Conferences on Science and World Affairs to reduce the danger of armed conflict and threats to global security. He was soon to become Director of the Stockholm International Peace Research Institute for ten years. For him, the most serious danger of the widespread use of 'breeder' reactors (ones which eventually produce more fuel than they were originally fed) was the preferred fuel of plutonium-239 and the difficulty of safeguarding not only power stations but also the additional industrial process involved in separating the plutonium from the spent fuel. In addition its bulk transportation within and between countries makes it more difficult to stop proliferation between countries. The South American embassy man, Rafael, points out that his country is not allowed nuclear power by the North Americans in case they develop their own defence. His country wants to be one of the 'big boys' too, on the world stage, and presumably shake themselves free from the commercial dominance of the US in their lives. The script mentions other countries who might have benefited from a plutonium heist. Israel, for example, wanted the Bomb, and would eventually get it, and fight very hard to prevent their neighbours from acquiring it.

Production
Scripting Development
'Sound and Fury' was commissioned on 4 May 1971. This was the second script Martin Worth would write for the new series, and he was commissioned for 'High Mountain' at the same time. It was due to be delivered at the end of August. He was given the brief to produce a story of plutonium theft and provided with scientific material to write his original script from.

Perhaps the formation of the story was helped by an article printed in the *Daily Mirror* on 16 September, which practically predicted the plot of the episode, save for the involvement of students. Titled 'Down Doomsday Road' Arthur Smith writes: 'On a lonely road, the lorry driver stops to help a prostrate figure lying in the gutter. As he jumps down from the cab he is over-powered by a gang. They bundle him into a car and his lorry is driven away. It's not a rare scene in these days of lorry hijackings. But this could be the start of something much bigger – if it was the theft of enough plutonium to hold a city, or even a nation, to ransom …

'It is a problem the world's atomic leaders, meeting this week in Geneva for the Fourth International Atoms for Peace conference, are not discussing openly. In the marble corridors of the Palais des Nations, they are privately expressing anxiety … With many trucking firms in the US owned by known Mafia leaders, American delegates admit that they are scared – especially as serious short-comings in security arrangements have already been revealed.' As the Minister himself says in the episode, 'A big time criminal organisation with plutonium to flog in their possession wouldn't just sell it. They'd use it to protection for their own activities. That alone could have grave social consequences in some parts of the world. And if on top of that it means another Fat Man is going to rear its ugly head in the hands of some tinpot dictator …'

It appears he delivered the script in October and was paid the second half of his fee on the 22nd. Anna Kaliski and Worth then went to have the script vetted at Imperial College in London, where seems they were advised by Dr Hugh D Evans of the Nuclear Technology Laboratories, Department of Chemical Engineering and Chemical Technology.

Massive rewrites were in order due to 'technological developments and new information'. The rewrite was sent in on 14 November. Enough changes (estimated at 50 per cent of the script) had been made to warrant an extra one-off fee for Worth, which was duly granted on 19 November. Again he was paid in two instalments, with the second forthcoming in January. Such was the amount of work he put in, he wasn't sure if he was as keen to write a third script, this time on the subject of DDT, as he had been, at least not until after Christmas.

Camera Script
By the time Eric Hills turned 'Say Knife, Fat Man' into a camera script, a few minor changes had been made. Chief Superintendent Marriott became Mallory, and references to the Black Mountains and the research centre at Harwell were removed. This was probably because the filming was not going to be performed outside the Greater London area. A couple of cutaway scenes were absorbed into the scenes either side of them. Some of the attitudes were softened. 'What did you get out of that bird?' becomes 'Well, did you get anything out of her?'

Barbara Mason – whose strident defence of the students and youth in particular was a theme in the episode – lost a lovely line during her argument with Quist on whether students were responsible for the theft: 'Television pundits moralising on Youth, and a storm in a teacup trial before an unctuous judge still waiting for Churchill to be summoned to the Palace!' She also suggests Quist is a copper's nark when his previous working relationship with Holman is revealed. Quist doesn't want to see students pillorised either: 'Now I can't bear to see another university exposed to all that hypocriticak attitudinising you were hinting at either.'

Casting

With the need for young actors, this episode featured early appearances for Anthony Andrews (playing Carlos), who later starred in *Brideshead Revisited*, and future *Doctor Who* companion Elizabeth Sladen (playing a character named Sarah, and not for the last time in her career). Sladen later recalled how she thought she got the part because she went to her interview with Eric Hills, carrying the *Guardian*. She certainly didn't get it for her driving skills needed at the top of the episode, as she had a few nervous moments reversing the car with an equally nervous sound recordist hiding out of shot.

Playing Michael was Paul Seed, who later went into television directing, most notably the first two instalments of Michael Dobb's Francis Urquhart trilogy, *House of Cards* and *To Play The King*, in the 1990s. Peter Halliday, playing Rafael, is well known to genre fans as the angry young scientist Flemming in the two *Andromeda* serials of the early 1960s and for a number of roles in *Doctor Who*. Geoffrey Palmer playing Mallory was last seen in Martin Worth's second series episode 'Invasion'.

It must have been confusing to have two actors with very similar names in the cast – Hugh Cross, playing Professor Holman, and Hugh Ross, playing one of his students, who has since gone on to have a good solid career within the business. Leslie Schofield was another 'television face', either thug or hero, you most certainly did not cross his characters.

Filming

More of this episode was shot on film than was usual. Moor Park Golf Club in Rickmansworth, Hertfordshire was used and a hospital in West Ealing stood in for the university interiors as well as the usual exteriors. Visual Effects Designer Jim Ward was on hand to provide the 'fizzing' plutonium and the explosion in the reservoir at the end of the episode. In one scene, Carlos is asked how Wales is and his original reply was 'mountainous'. This was replaced by 'wet', suggesting the weather faced by the crew on the location shoot, and the lack of mountains … Some of the cast such as Leslie Schofield and his two henchmen were only needed on location, while others were only needed in the studio.

Vivien Sherrard was once again required to film on location but although this was one of her favourite episodes thanks to her large involvement with the story for once, she did not enjoy working with the director, Eric Hills: 'He is memorable for being the one person connected with *Doomwatch* that I felt at odds with. These days I can only speculate as to the reason for this because the details have evaporated. Maybe it was just a clash of personalities. I suppose one reason for my failure to recall most of the directors is that I rarely had a lot to do with them, and that goes for many of the excellent guest stars too.'

Studio
'Say Knife, Fat Man' was the fourth episode to be recorded. This was in TC1 on Friday, 10 March 1972. The new Doomwatch set of outer office, laboratory and Quist's office are finally unveiled to the viewer, although part of the lab had been seen in close-up during 'Fire and Brimstone'. The idea of having a lift entrance to the outer office was not thought of when the script was written, and parts of the script had to be altered to accommodate this.

Stock Music
Over ten minutes of music was used for the story, all sourced from library music LPs as usual. The wide selection included three tracks composed by Max Harris called 'Dark Alley', 'The Account' and 'The Arrangement' from the Standard Music Library (ESL 108). The Southern Library of Recorded Music provided 'Foxes' Folly' by Arsène Souffriau on *Dramatic, Titles, Fanfares/Dramatic, Disaster, Mystery* (MQLP 5) and 'Air Power' by Sidney Sager (MQLP 11). Boosey and Hawkes provided 'The Raid' by Dennis Farnon, performed by the New Concert Orchestra, from the 1969 LP *Dramatic Impressions/Big Band Sound* (SBH 3009). 'Four Crime Bridges No 3' and 'Dark Dockside' by Martin Böttcher came from a Harmonic LP (CBL 640). 'Histeriso Background','Tension Background' and 'A Study in Dramatic Overlay' by Don Banks came from the Conroy label (BM 067). Finally, the KPM label provided a Trevor Duncan piece called 'Maniac Pursuit', familiar to *Quatermass* viewers (KPM 016), and 'III Omen' by David Lindup, from *Dramatic Background* (KPM 1055).

Editing
Editing was performed at TV1 between 10.30 am and 3.30 pm on 13 March.

Reaction
The viewing figures increased to six and a half million viewers this week, but the criticisms continued with the first letter to *New Scientist* sniffing with disapproval at the heist. Mary Malone in the *Daily Mirror* also gave the episode a good kicking. 'They said it, not me. A secretary ... made this somewhat prophetic remark which I could have told her after last week's episode, never mind this one. "We are going to get lumbered," she said, "with every pseudo-scientific problem that other departments cannot find time for." Because I warn you something nasty and probably far-fetched is

going to creep up and grab you by the ankles.' After looking at the plot, she concluded 'What on earth had all this to do with reality? Dr Quist was asking a similar question: "Do the police think organised crime is moving into the nuclear field?" Let me tell you, doctor, it is if those writers can get away with it. They have tapped and exhausted one natural source of material, now they are onto another. It will be nuclear cops and robbers until we are sick of that, too. From there what's left but social work or science fiction. It is not a Dr Quist they are going to need, but another *Dr Who.'*

Audience Research Report

The Report was largely positive with the Reaction Profile Index 85:15 when it came to entertaining/boring. It was the most favourably received episode so far.

> 'This episode had a very interesting theme, in fact, quite a "stinger", as appreciative viewers said, in its slant on the most dreaded of pollution problem (radioactivity from nuclear fission), and also proved a "valid and sympathetic comment on student unrest and activities". It was added many times, that the story-line and characters had been believable, and the situations dramatically telling, especially in the final scenes – "so realistic as to be horrifying in its possibilities". The following observations from those reporting most favourably: "As always, this *Doomwatch* story came close to possibility and was really gripping … Quite right what Barbara Mason said – that we should all think why students should feel the need to make an atom bomb … An unusual story of rebellious students against authority and law. A reminder that help and understanding young people today really need."

> 'However, the behaviour of the characters … seemed less plausible to a minority, apparently, while the plot was described as moulded too much in the style of "any everyday thriller" – "why turn *Doomwatch* into another whodunnit series?" was the chief point of grievance here, various viewers complaining of signs, in this new series, that the "old type *Doomwatch*, with much more emphasis on the science aspect and/or dangerous vested interests was a thing of the past. Despite such criticism, however, only a handful supplying evidence found the story downright boring."

> 'The performance was nearly always the subject of praise and

apart from the "regulars" of *Doomwatch*, viewers paid especially favourable attention to the way the parts of the students were acted, one of the viewers remarking that, both in hijacking of the plutonium containers and in later scenes, "the urgency was there, and the determination of these young people very well portrayed."

'Viewers were specifically asked which, if any, of the regular characters in Doomwatch they found most interesting, and it was clear from their answers that Dr Spencer Quist is thought of by most as the central figure, and excellently portrayed by John Paul. Colin Bradley, Dr Quist's new scientific aide, is also, it appears, arousing some quite keen interest, and several viewers remarked that they hoped that Joby Blanshard ... would have plenty of opportunities to expand this characterisation. For the rest, it seems that the Minister ... is regarded as another indispensable figure in these stories, and, moreover, the absence (just at the moment) of Simon Oates' Dr John Ridge was noted, and hopes for his reappearance in the series voiced. Vivien Sherrard made Barbara Mason stand out, it was said, as a decorative, but also intelligent, foil to the men.'

Campus
This episode triggered something in Martin Worth who was later commissioned by Andrew Osborn in March 1973 to research a series based on life in a modern university campus. Peter Graham Scott was a possible producer for the project. Disliking the proposed central characters, Osborn rejected it in November. He explained he was leaving his job as Head of Series next June, and had already put into motion a further ten months of productions, and therefore did not want to overload his replacement, the current Head of Serials Ronnie Marsh.

Kit Pedler
Dr Pedler became a vocal critic of the nuclear power in the mid to late seventies, and frequently highlighted the problems of plutonium falling into the wrong hands. Following a similar project by a university student in America, a national newspaper commissioned Pedler to see if he too could build a nuclear bomb, using currently published research papers. He could indeed. All he needed was plutonium and the high-explosive, and he was away. The idea was that this diabolical knowledge, as he described it, was already in the public domain, and that the most determined of people could find plutonium on the black market. Shockingly, reports

from America suggested that the 'off cuts' of plutonium, once shaved and shaped, as shown in 'Say Knife, Fat Man', sometimes went unaccounted for. No one knew what happened to the missing pieces. Pedler also campaigned against the expansion of facilities in Windscale, and contributed to a public enquiry on the matter.

The script was published in the out of print anthology book *Deadly Dangerous Tomorrow*.

3.04
Waiting For A Knighthood

Written by Terence Dudley
Directed by Pennant Roberts
Designed by Ray London
Transmitted: Monday, 26th June 1972 at 9.22 pm Duration: 48' 00"

Cast
The Reverend Frank Simpson (Anthony Oliver), Mrs Simpson (Margaret John), Richard Massingham (Frederick Jaeger), Peggy Massingham (Ann Firbank), Stephen Massingham (Stephen Dudley), Josie (Julie Neubert), Joan Sylvester (Glen Walford), Detective Chief Inspector Logan (Don McKillop), Mrs Duncan-Foster (Noelle Middleton), Norman Sylvester (Bruce Purchase), Mike (Anthony Edwards).

Also appearing
Manservant (Richard Atherton), Detective Sergeant (Leslie Weekes), Cartwright (David Melbourne), Minister's Secretary (Sarah Gardener), Lab Technicians (Anne Lee, David Ianson).

Extras on location: Haydn Wood, Reg Turner, Stuart Barry, Barbara Bermel, Sue Crosland, Dilys Marvin, Maureen Neill, Christine Cole, Dina Martyn, Natalya Lindley, Sally Sinclair, Carole Brett, Gilly Flower, Nichola Sterne, Nelly Griffiths, Tanya Parker, Beryl Bainbridge, Olwen Jones, Geraint Jones, Charles Adey-Gray, Michael Parkes, Jay McGrath, George Ballantyne, David J Grahame.

Technical Credits
Director's Assistant: Adele Paul. Production Assistant: Landon Revitt. Assistant Floor Manager: Marion Wishart. Floor Assistant: Mike Thorne.
Film Cameraman: John McGlashan. Sound Recordist: Jack Curtis. Film Editor: Alastair MacKay.
Costume Supervisor: Sheila Beers. Make-up Supervisor: Elizabeth Rowell. Studio Lighting: Ralph Walton. TM2: Bob Warran. Vision Mixer: Rhoda Carrs.
Sound: John Lloyd. Grams Operator: Gerry Borrows. Props: Peter Sporle. Crew: 1.

Radio Times
Industrialist Massingham meets the Minister. 'What we have isn't ours to despoil and pillage. We hold it in trust … not just for our children but for future generations of mankind.'

The Story
'Industry spends millions on research. There is no health hazard. This whole situation has come about because the press has blown up irresponsible statements from cranks and malcontents.' – Richard Massingham

Anne Tarrant is at church and watches her local vicar become delirious and collapse during his sermon.

A few weeks later his wife, Joan Simpson, tells Anne and Quist that he had been suffering from lead poisoning but no-one knows how he got it. Quist sends Bradley and Barbara over to the Simpson residence near Shepperton to find out. A laboratory assistant overhears this and it isn't long before the Minister is questioning Stafford, worried that Doomwatch will get embroiled in the whole issue of lead in petrol, a political hot potato that he does not want his department to get involved with as there are enough bodies investigating already. Bradley soon discovers that the vicar had been stripping down engine parts in his garage by soaking them in petrol. It was this exposure that had made him ill, and the effect is cumulative. As Quist says to Anne, how do they know that lead poisoning isn't affecting other people's behaviour around the country?

Meanwhile, the Minister has dinner with the family of Richard Massingham, who is in the oil and petrol industry. Massingham is concerned by panic legislation in the United States over smog in Los Angeles and doesn't want something similar to happen in Britain, especially after the case of the vicar. Holroyd feels that concessions and subsidies are not the answer, but improving the product is. But to improve the product costs money, argues Massingham. Is the government prepared to announce a raise in the price of petrol just before a general election?

Anne visits a much improved Ridge in his mental hospital. During the course of the conversation, Ridge's passion for high performance cars arises, and he admits to tinkering with them in the garage underneath his mews flat. This sets Anne thinking. Bradley and Stafford visit the garage and discover he has been welding. They are interrupted by Mrs Sylvester, who looks after the flat whenever Ridge is away on behalf of his landlady. She is shocked to discover Ridge has been ill. Stafford and Quist explain to the Minister that they think Ridge was affected by lead poisoning when he went berserk. Even the Minister is surprised that this isn't happening all over the place. It might not be the petrol or exhaust fumes in this case, but welding, using red lead and performed in a confined space.

Colin discusses the matter with Barbara, who is reading the paper. Now that they think they've identified the cause, the cure is quite simple, but Ridge won't be able to return to Doomwatch. Quist has had enough of the matter of lead in petrol. Warning Bradley to keep off the subject, he sends Stafford to see if he can get Ridge released. Barbara comes across a story in the paper about a child who has been kidnapped. It is the Massinghams son, Stephen. Mrs Massingham remembers a woman making a great fuss of Stephen at a shareholders' meeting.

Chief Inspector Logan quizzes the over-friendly woman, Mrs Duncan-Foster, and her driver, Norman Sylvester. Norman is afraid to tell the police that he thinks his wife, Mrs Duncan-Foster's maid, did the snatch. She is the same woman who looks after Ridge's flat, and Sylvester goes to see Ridge in hospital to tell him his suspicions. Stafford overhears. It seems that the Sylvesters lost a young son to lead poisoning, and Mrs Norman blames Massingham. Stafford visits Norman Sylvester house to find out what might have killed the boy and learns that he used to play with lead soldiers. Stephen has indeed been taken somewhere by Mrs Sylvester. And she has brought toys for him to play with: lead soldiers.

Richard Massingham tries to convince Holroyd to make an announcement that lead in petrol is safe, which the Minister realises is his way of saying he did not kill the Sylvester child. He can't do it, but instead tells Massingham of the theory that the Sylvester child was a victim of pica – an appetite for something non-edible. The boy might have discovered that flakes of old lead-based paint taste sweet. Bradley and Barbara discuss the matter. Bradley thinks it is a smoke screen to cover the real issue: the lead from old toy soldiers is avoidable, but what about that which pollutes the air for everyone? Take the lead out of the petrol and people like Barbara might not be able to afford a car; she would become an outraged 'moral midget', in Bradley's words.

Ridge is being discharged, which Stafford hopes was on his recommendation. He also suggests getting rid of a lab assistant who is another spy for the Minister. Stafford drives Ridge home to his flat, feeling that a member of Doomwatch ought to do it. Ridge thanks him. Inside his flat he finds Mrs Sylvester and the child, playing with the toy soldiers.

Some time later, as Quist and Anne relax one evening, Quist sees an article about the oil industry voluntarily reducing the maximum amount of lead in petrol by 25 per cent, with a consequent increase in price of tuppence per gallon. But the figures are deceitful. A study conducted a couple of years earlier showed the average amount of lead already to be 45 per cent less than the maximum allowable. 'Even though they make a twenty-five per cent reduction, they can still chuck in up to three-quarters of a gram more than they're doing at the moment' says Quist. 'I call that a really adventurous step towards improving the environment.'

Behind the Story

The argument in this episode has been won, but it took a long time to achieve. Lead in petrol has been phased out in nearly all countries around the world. Back in the early 1970s it was a political 'hot potato', as the Minister describes it. The episode gives you a good potted history of lead in petrol and its ubiquity in our environment. Lead, already known to be poisonous, was first introduced as an anti-knocking agent in motor cars in the 1930s, when there were a million cars already on the road. But, as Bradley points out, a million new cars are added every year. Geoffrey Lean, writing in the *Daily Telegraph* on 29 July 2011, described it as 'the greatest experiment in mass poisoning ever undertaken'. Other countries had taken steps to ban it, why not Britain? Before lead became a public issue, it was carbon monoxide that concerned environmentalists and medical fraternity. Kit Pedler did an experiment to see how much carbon monoxide a body absorbs in a busy city for the *Daily Mirror* in October 1970. There were choking smogs in Los Angeles and New York, and in Tokyo, the most air polluted city on the planet at the time, 'the traffic fumes are so thick that policemen on point duty are relieved every ten minutes to clear their lungs with pure oxygen.' The *Daily Mirror* article stated that car manufacturers were experimenting with ways of cutting the amount of CO gas expelled from cars but warned that 'the only immediate remedy would make cars more expensive and slower and petrol would be up to 6d [sixpence] a gallon dearer.' The Medical Research Council at the time were studying the effects of CO. Could a driver's 'apparently irrational behaviour', causing accidents, be due to CO intoxication? Or could it be something else …?

The fight Against Lead

In the late 1960s, Derek Bryce-Smith, Professor of Organic Chemistry at Reading University, became concerned with the amount of lead in the atmosphere and how it could affect our behaviour. He decided to go public but found it 'a very lonely battle for a very long time … A lot of my colleagues looked at me sideways, because many chemists are in debt to the oil industry, which provides them with money for research.' Smith wrote letters to the *Guardian* in 1970 attacking the use of lead in petrol, then published in *Chemistry in Britain* the following year, and the debate went public. Another critic, Professor Jean Piccard, warned that lead poisoning of plankton in the upper layers of the oceans might reduce the oxygen content of the atmosphere. Writing in *The Times* the following February, Sir Robert Robinson dismissed the worry: 'Neither our "Prophets of Doom" nor the legislators who are so easily frightened by them are particularly fond of arithmetic.' In his opinion, the lead in the air would be so diluted as to have a negligible effect. Sir Robert was a consultant for Shell.

Bryce-Smith published again in 1971, this time in *Biology*. He now levelled the charge that lead in petrol, breathed in as a vapour from car exhausts, might be responsible for a 'significant proportion of mental illness'. He believed that one in twenty city-living children had more lead in their bodies than the highest safety levels suggested, echoed by Quist's example of children playing in the dust of city streets. Smith looked at data from admissions to mental hospitals between 1964 and 1968 and found that the number of children being treated for mental disorders had rocketed by 100 per cent for girls under ten and 60 per cent for boys. The average rate for all ages was 11 per cent. Jon Tinker, writing in *New Scientist* (27 May 1971), suggested that 'Environmentally, we sometimes lack a sense of balance. World production of lead is 3000 kilotons a year, and of mercury only 9 kilotons. To get as close to the danger levels for mercury as we now are for lead we should have to eat nothing but tuna fish for months on end. Yet mercury carrying fish are banned in more countries than have restricted lead in petrol.'

The Government were aware of the issue, as a debate in the House of Lords in 1971 shows, but proposed to take little action. 'We probably get more lead in the atmosphere from the coal burnt in our grates and our factories than we do from lead exhaust in petrol; but there may be some need to reduce the lot' admitted Lord Mowbray according to *Hansard* in March 1971.

Derek Bryce-Smith appeared on the third programme of BBC2's Monday series *Controversy*, in which scientists with controversial views gave a lecture and were then faced by a panel of scientists who held the opposite opinion. Of all of the contentious issues in the series, this was the only one which could be described as sane. (Other debates recorded before an audience at the Royal Institution included Professor Hans Eynsneck's views of race and intelligence and Dr Edward Teller on the industrial uses for the H-Bomb, in which he also stated that a scientist owes it to his or her country to work for its defence and should be held in high esteem. Kit Pedler spoke in opposition during this edition.) Bryce-Smith's contribution went out at the end of August 1971. One of his opponents was a representative from Associated Octel, the company that put lead into petrol, who did not attack the idea that to remove lead from petrol would remove 50 per cent of lead from our air. Instead, he made a joke about how tetraethyl lead was his company's only product.

Business View
Richard Massingham is the oil man and probably has control of the petrol

refineries as well as pumping up the black stuff in the first place. Massingham (whilst polluting his dining room with cigars) reasonably points out that the incidents of lead poisoning in the episode are caused by misuses or accidents. 'Must we legislate for idiots?' But, as Quist asks twice in the episode, how do we know that more of this isn't happening thanks to cases being misdiagnosed? Massingham accepts that we have the right to clean air but argues that no-one is simply dropping down dead in the streets. He doesn't mind the odd spot of conjunctivitis or bronchitis but objects to panic legislation (which our Government at the time was resisting) and the 'ill-informed and irresponsible pressure groups' that seemed to be winning the argument in America. Perhaps he was thinking of President Nixon's 1971 proposal to tax lead in petrol and sulphur dioxide emissions because of the smog in Los Angeles, a problem considered by British politicians to be unique to America. The kidnapping of Massingham's child leads him to hate even more those 'malcontents' who dare to demand clean air and despise the muck his industry produces, regardless of whether we are dependent on it or could learn to live without it. By the episode's conclusion, he has not changed his mind, learned from the experience or had an epiphany like Reynolds in 'The Red Sky' or Whittaker in 'The Iron Doctor'. Why should he? It was simply another deranged woman trying to replace her boy with the son of someone she blames for her bereavement. Sounds a bit like 'Friday's Child'.

Production
Scripting Development
Terence Dudley was given staff clearance to write the untitled episode on 10 August 1971. The reasons for the internal commission were stated as 'his specialised knowledge of the series and the subject of the script in particular, coupled with the fact that the script is a sequel to one already received and accepted from this author, and the fact that he created three of the leading characters in the new series'.

With the issue quite new in the public eye, it is not known when Dudley decided to devote an episode to the subject. Derek Bryce-Smith brought to him the story of a parson who had been admitted to hospital after he started to behave oddly. Like the Reverend Simpson in the episode, he too had been a vintage motoring enthusiast and had been stripping down parts of a 1920 'bull-nose' Morris and degreasing them in bowls of petrol. He was suffering from organo-lead poisoning. It also provided Dudley with a reasonable explanation for John Ridge's behavioural change to keep him in the programme. He also consulted Lord Kennet, and a Dr K Loucas, both of whom are credited as owning the episode's copyright on the PasB sheets.

Dr Loucas was a consultant psychiatrist at Broadmoor from where he took early retirement in 1991 over allegations of breaching terms of mental health legislation as reported in the *Independent* in 1992). Presumably he advised on Ridge's condition. Lord Kennet was born Wayland Young and was a reluctant peer who only took his seat in the Lords in order to prop up the Labour Party in the 1960s. He entered the Ministry of Housing and Local Government in 1966, working most notably as Chairman of the Preservation Policy Group. In opposition in the early 1970s, he was Chairman of the Advisory Committee on Oil Pollution of the Sea. A glance at the debates to which he contributed show virtually any *Doomwatch* subject going, from the use of nuclear weapons to censorship, aircraft noise to pollution.

The same cannot be said for the Government. Terence Dudley and Glyn Edwards went to visit the Department of the Environment for their views on lead in petrol. They spoke to Eldon Griffiths, the Under-Secretary of State, who told them that there was no danger from lead in petrol to the public and explained the standard argument of the cost to the driver if it was banned. The Government's line was expressed by Lord Mowbray and Stourton during a House of Lords debate on lead on 24 March 1971 when he said 'The amount of extra lead we get from pollution by exhaust gases is comparatively very small. I accept that we should be better without it, but if we do without it we have to use a lower compression engines. These factors bring other problems in their wake. It's a matter of economics and sense.' Glyn Edwards remembers Terence Dudley coming away from the meeting not at all happy with what they had heard.

Pennant Roberts recalled in *The Cult of ... Doomwatch* documentary that the Government were rather keen for the programme to drop the subject. No doubt Associated Octel told Terence Dudley the same thing when he went to visit them in November, scribbling notes on the back of a copy of Roger Parkes' 'Without the Bomb' by accident. In 1972 the company began developing lead traps for cars, under license from America.

Lead in the News
In December 1971, Dr Robert Stephens, senior lecturer in chemistry at Birmingham University told local BBC radio that deposits of lead in city street dust could prove to be a serious danger to children, especially to those living within heavily congested areas, and Birmingham's spaghetti junctions are infamous. 'For 20 years vehicles have been pouring lead into the cities. Much of this would be washed away by rain but not in sheltered places. Children's behaviour is unhygienic. They could be taking in lead from city dirt.' MP for Edgbaston Mrs Jill Knight was campaigning for a Government sponsored national screening of children for lead poisoning. Dr Stephens pointed out that a thimbleful of high-grade petrol contained more than six times the safe daily exposure level of poisonous lead for an adult.

Avonmouth

Not trusting the government's assurance of safety shouldn't be regarded merely as cynicism. In early 1972 workers at the Imperial Smelting Corporation at Avonmouth near Bristol were discovered to have been poisoned by inhaling lead dust, and the plant was closed in March just as a public enquiry was launched. Concerns had been raised as early as 1968, but it took an unrelated death to have the matter taken seriously. Only in February had Peter Walker stood up in Parliament and assured the House that there was no evidence health was being affected by the base metal pollution of the atmosphere by a Rio Tinto-Zinc smelter at the plant. This was based on a monitoring programme carried out by RTZ itself. However, two scientists from Bristol University who had been on a RTZ committee had been conducting their own survey. They started to publish results that showed the area was far more polluted than ever suspected, an inconvenient truth for the Corporation and for Bristol's movers and shakers on its Council. Stafford refers to Avonmouth obliquely, but the audience of the day would have understood the reference.

Coincidence

Coincidence is stretched to near-breaking point in the script. Dr Anne Tarrant watches the Reverend Simpson collapse during a sermon and learns that this is through lead poisoning, which the Doomwatch team discover is also behind Ridge's breakdown. The vicar's tale is seen in the newspapers by the still-grieving Mrs Sylvester, whose employer is Dr Ridge's landlady, and she takes the kidnapped Massingham child to his flat. Massingham is a friend of the Minister whose department is obliquely investigating lead poisoning.

Director

Why this script was held back to the end of the now-shortened production block is unknown. It might have been because Terence Dudley had hoped to direct it himself or perhaps to gain topicality. It could have been due to Simon Oates' availability, as he recorded his final three episodes together. In the event, the episode was given to Pennant Roberts to direct. The rehearsals and studio dates coincided with the launch of the new series and the controversy that we have seen.

Filming

The filming was performed around London. The scenes of the police searching for the kidnapped boy were shot in Notting Hill. John Ridge's mews flat was 45 Cranley Mews in Chelsea, SW7. Elizabeth Weaver filmed her one interior church scene on Monday, 15 May. Joining her was Margaret John whose only line from her first scene – 'Oh, Frank!' – was cut.

Casting

The producer's son Stephen makes a reappearance as Stephen Massingham. A notable cast member was Frederick Jaeger, who was Terence Dudley's best man at his wedding. Pennant Roberts cast Julie Neubert for the small role of the maid; she would later appear in three episodes of the first series of *Survivors*, playing the unfortunate Wendy. Margaret John had a small role in 'Friday's Child' as a barrister. Welsh born Anthony Oliver appears to have left acting after this role, making only the rarest of appearances on screen. Bruce Purchase would work again with Pennant Roberts in *Doctor Who* as a half robotic space pirate. Don McKillop had recently been a villain in *Doctor Who* where he was killed by a living stone gargoyle from a church. Ann Firbank had played the wife of John Wilder in *The Plane Makers* standing in for Barbara Murray when she was not available, and she would work again with Terence Dudley on the family saga *Flesh and Blood* in 1980. Glen Walford worked mainly in the theatre as a director, where she still is today, enjoying a six decade long career.

Studio

'Waiting for a Knighthood' was twelfth to go into studio, the final episode of the third series and the final episode of *Doomwatch*. It was recorded on Tuesday, 13 June 1972 in TC1. The script was careful to disguise the location where Mrs Sylvester was holding Stephen, describing it as 'unidentified'. This set was only needed in the morning between 11 am and midday; all of Stephen Dudley's scenes had to be recorded in advance of the evening session because of his young age.

Stock Music

Very little music was heard this week with 'Street Beat' composed by Kenny Graham from an early KPM album (KPM 21). Quist was listening to Mozart's *Prague Symphony no 38 in D*, played by the Royal Philharmonic Orchestra (Philips SBL 5226), and the episode ended with Franco Chiari's Jazz Quartet playing 'Cool Blues' by Daniele and Mellier from the Mozart Edition range (MELP 15). This track frequently pops up in comedies and dramas such as ATV's *The Power Game* to back party scenes.

Editing

The episode was edited at TVR on Thursday, 15 June 1972 between 2.30 pm and 11.30 pm.

Viewing Figures

The episode was watched by only five million viewers, which was 10 per cent of the available audience. ITV's *Man at the Top* got 24 per cent. *Doomwatch* now entered that most dreaded of categories of all on the

Programme Review Board's weekly agenda – disappointing viewing figures.

Audience Research Report
The reaction profile was lower than 'Say Knife, Fat Man' at 82:18, but this still made it the fourth most popular episode of the series. However, the rating for the plot was low, although not as low as the first episode.

> 'For the majority of viewers this had been quite an entertaining episode in the present *Doomwatch* series, containing a certain amount of "food for thought". Based on the topical theme of pollution, this ingenious tale – conveying the strong effects of lead poisoning on people – was thought to have been all too credible. However, the story had been of moderate appeal only to a sizeable minority with, here and there, complaints that it was "rather weak" when compared with episodes in the previous series. And, in the opinion of one viewer (a) to bring back Ridge, and (b) to announce that Quist was married to Dr Tarrant. In fact, according to one or two, *Doomwatch* no longer seemed to say anything realistic to say. "This highly improbable plot fell short of the standards previously set". Nevertheless, as indicated by the figures above, there was general agreement that a worthwhile subject had proved both interesting and enlightening.

> 'Marked enthusiasm was registered for first-class acting from the entire cast, the excellence of which it was claimed, "never varied". Any adverse criticism was certainly isolated, one or two asserting that the cast was sometimes guilty of "overacting", adding, however, that they may have been "hampered by a weak script" and were "doing the best they could considering the poor material".

> 'Replying to a specific question as to which of the regular characters in *Doomwatch* were found most interesting. Dr Quist far and away headed the list as being most consistently good and completely believable. He is followed in popularity by Dr John Ridge, and quite a number of viewers expressed their pleasure at his return to the series, and hoped there would be a permanent place for him in the future. The Minister, closely followed by Commander Neil Stafford, were next in line, with Dr Anne Tarrant, who "seems to bring the rest down to earth", and Barbara Mason, of whom it is said "appears to have more to her than at first meets the eye" at the lower end of the scale.

The young boy Mike was the favourite of a few, whilst there were several in the sample who thought all the characters were convincing and any one as being more interesting than the rest. About half-a-dozen viewers in the entire sample were quite unimpressed with any of the characters so far in the present series, claiming that they seemed to be "just a group of ordinary civil servants who had no go". For most, they have become very real people.'

As usual, a wide cross section of views were represented, with some thinking the entertaining story gave food for thought whilst others complained it still wasn't as good as before or even as good as previous episodes in the series. On the other hand, viewers did express delight at the return of John Ridge and had positive things to say about the rest of the cast. Stephen Dudley also seemed to have won a few hearts. John Paul came out on top, as always. 'He was the most consistently good and completely believable' was the verdict of the 'Waiting for a Knighthood' panel (some of whom thought the episode was simply designed to reveal his marriage to Dr Tarrant). His name still caused confusion for a few people, who thought he was 'Quest' or 'Twist'.

Radio Times
In an edition where readers criticised Terence Dudley's initial defence of 'Fire and Brimstone', there were also a few who had something positive to say about the new series. Seventeen-year-old Robin Haselgrove wrote 'I bet that after watching 'Waiting for a Knighthood' ... the critics of *Doomwatch* are still smarting from the smack in the eye. Terence Dudley's script and production were a stroke of brilliance, accounting for Ridge's madness and incorporating him perhaps in a later series. It also begins to serialise *Doomwatch*, which is what the first series should have done. Congratulations to the whole *Doomwatch* team. I hope the remainder of the episodes are just as well written, acted, and realistic as the first three.'

2014
Lead poisoning is not a thing of the past. Residents of Flint, Michigan in the United States switched to extracting drinking water from the Flint river in 2014. Lead levels were detected in one home seven times higher than the national acceptable limit. The unacceptable state of drinking water caused President Obama to declare a state of emergency. The water was simply not safe for drinking or cooking. The long terms effects on the children who drank the water remains to be seen. The current American administration wishes to roll back many environmental regulations ...

Sex And Violence

Written by Stuart Douglass
Directed by Darrol Blake
Designed by Jeremy Davies
Untransmitted. Duration: 52'

Cast
Mrs Catchpole (June Brown), Arthur Ballantyne (Nicholas Selby), Lord Purvis (Donald Eccles), Steven Granger (Bernard Horsfall), Mrs Hastings (Angela Crow), Mrs Angela Cressy (Noel Dyson), Professor Fairbairn (Brian Wilde), The Reverend Garrison (Llewellyn Rees), Dick Burns (Christopher Chittell), Demonstrator (Queenie Watts), Young Man (Sebastian Graham-Jones), Stewards (Richard Vanstone, John Hood, Paul Nemeer).

Known Technical Credits
Film Cameraman: Fred Hamilton. Sound Recordist: Basil Harris. Film Editor: Anthony MacKay.
Studio Lighting: John Dixon. Studio Sound: Chick Anthony.

The Story
'Politicians have been doing it for years. Whenever there is a moral issue to be legislated upon they pander to our fear and guilt instead of alleviating it. Indeed, to be a successful politician, you must play upon it. "Sex killer escapes" – that's a fairly average newspaper headline at the time of a million unemployed. In times of economic crisis it is much better to talk about the moral disintegration of society rather than the economic one.' – Ballantyne

Mrs Catchpole calls to order a meeting of housewives in a hall somewhere in London and launches into a tirade against the permissive society and its advocates. She introduces their speaker for the day, whom she describes as a good man fighting for decency. His name is Arthur Ballantyne. Meanwhile, Dr Quist is baffled to be asked by the Minister to 'analyse the significance or otherwise of trends towards the corruption of youth through permissive attitudes expressed in the arts, medicine and literature towards sex and violence'. The Minister describes it as 'moral pollution', but Quist realises that this is simply a way for the Government to push aside the issue of obscenity when there is no political advantage to be gained.

A subcommittee chaired by Lord Purvis on obscenity and pornography has been set up to explore the issue, which the Government hopes will be a foregone conclusion. As a psychiatrist, Anne has been invited to join and is introduced to the other members, which include the Reverend Garrison; Professor Fairbairn, a sociologist; Mrs Cressy, a clean-up campaigner; Steven Granger, an educationist; and pop singer Dick Burns. Their job is to recommend whether a change in the law is necessary.

After one meeting, Dick Burns is stopped by Mrs Catchpole, who organised the housewives' meeting, under the pretence for asking for his autograph, but she then urges him to vote for a change in the law. Catchpole later hosts a demonstration outside the Princess Theatre of the supposedly obscene play *Do It*, which Anne goes to see as part of her research. She is jostled by the protesters, one of whom gets angry that Anne, mother of a 6-year-old daughter, should want to go and see the play. When Anne refuses to listen to her any further, there is a scuffle and she is struck on the head. Recovering, she does not want to press charges against the woman but instead find out why she acted so violently. Quist sets Stafford on to it, who is reluctant, seeing it as a job for the police. In any case, he thinks the play is obscene and should be banned.

Back at the committee, Mrs Cressy is reeling off a list of sexual themes from American cinema shown in private British cinema clubs, but Fairbairn dismisses them as exploitation films or 'skin flicks'. Cressy suggests they might corrupt the people who see them; Granger strongly disagrees. Lord Purvis decides they should view some of this material and suggests a trip to the Scotland Yard's blue film library. Burns is delighted. After they have watched one of these films, he treats it with derision. Meanwhile, Anne visits the woman who attacked her, Mrs Hastings. She is beside herself with remorse for the assault and agrees to help Anne with her research for the committee. Her husband had deserted her, and she was lonely and having problems with her son. She joined a group called Housewife, organised by Mrs Catchpole, liking their clean-up campaign. She had been brought up to feel that sex is dirty and felt her core values were being attacked by the obscene play. These values are defended by Cressy and Garrison; Granger dismisses them as ideals, whereas the committee needs to deal with facts. He says that they are living in an age of change; previously held absolutes are shifting, and children growing up in the modern world now need certainty in themselves, in their identity and their independence. Fairbairn agrees; a human being needs as broad a range of experience possible from which to build strong, decent values.

Barbara Mason shows Quist and Bradley a huge wad of reports from the Purvis committee. Bradley isn't keen on feeding them all into the computer and feels that the ministerial brief is asking it to make a judgement on morality. Quist is curious about Housewife and wonders who funds their campaigns. Stafford tells him it is a man called Ballantyne, who we see being kicked out of public meetings after taking to the stage to demand an end to obscenity. Observed by Quist, the committee is listening to Anne's report on Mrs Hastings' and her parents' attitudes towards sex. She explains that Freud had determined that sexuality and procreation are not the same thing. Wilhelm Reich's theory is that if you repress sexual instinct or 'biological energy', you produce a stunted person, which is how she regards Mrs Hastings. She has read so many violent headlines about drugs, depravity, obscenity, filth and disease that they have, ironically, driven her commit her first violent act. Anne feels very strongly that if the committee recommends a change in the law without acknowledging that people like Mrs Hastings need therapy to come to terms with their sexuality, the problem will be perpetuated.

Stafford has an amusing meeting with Mrs Catchpole, who rants on about decency and how government needs a strong man at the helm. She only pauses in her tirade to find out what he wants to ask her. Now, the members of the committee turn to the subject of violence. There is more accord on this subject and less emotion. Garrison wants to see less violence and Mrs Cressy is keen for a proper study of the effects of television and film violence upon the impressionable mind. They watch a film of a genuine execution in Nigeria that was shown on television in December 1971. The film should never have been shown, says Mrs Cressy, but Dick Burns is horrified, not by the spectacle but by the act itself. He wants to stop what he saw from ever having happened. This positive reaction fascinates Granger.

One evening Quist is reading Wilhelm Reich's *Function of the Orgasm*, which claims that a man who has his sexual urges repressed early in life will grow up to be ashamed, and that shame will make him easily dominated. He is wondering why Doomwatch has been forced to become involved in the whole affair; an item on the television news gives him his answer. The report is about Arthur Ballantyne interrupting a party conference by demanding to know what is going to be done about the permissive society.

Quist goes to see Ballantyne, who lives in a large, inherited country estate. He is politically ambitious, has extreme right-wing views and has stood for Parliament six times. Ballantyne is funding the groups Housewife and the Campaign for Clean Literature. He is also paying for their members' defence when their actions find them in court. Quist calls both groups violent, as he does Mrs Catchpole, who he describes as 'involving innocent people in a savage campaign to clean up the arts'. Ballantyne admits proudly that he is a political opportunist seeking election. He has realised that there is a fear of freedom, particularly about sex, so putting a 'legal lid on all our guilty pots' will prove popular and aid his political manoeuvring. He argues that we have been deprived of our sexual instincts since birth and that we want someone to do our thinking for us. He knows he is seen as a joke, but his time will come. He is simply exploiting attitudes and fears in the same way that advertisers, journalists and other politicians already do. It is a world we have created, and he is going to take advantage of it.

The committee is concluded as Cressy and Garrison seek to dissociate themselves from the increasingly violent campaign groups, but Granger points out that they will still be seen as being on the same side. The committee's final recommendation is no change to the law, by four votes to two. At Doomwatch, Bradley brings Quist the report of the computer's judgement. Quist is reading a book on the rise of Hitler and how the masses voted for their own subjugation to let someone else do the thinking for them. Ten years before he came to power, Hitler was seen as a silly little man who people made jokes about. The computer report says 'no change'. Quist holds up the book. 'No change.'

Behind The Story

If you remember the Sixties, then you weren't there. This is an opinion often expressed by those who were lucky enough (and well-off enough) to have experienced at a young age the sea change in attitudes towards life that swept through parts of London and eventually the country. The supposedly liberalising effect of the contraceptive pill, the discovery of hallucinogenic drugs, new trends in music and the rejection of established values started to make the older generations – those traditionally in control – start to worry about the future of the society to which they were accustomed. Sex was suddenly in the public domain. The Lord Chamberlain's office was abolished, allowing the theatre to put on whatever they liked without fear of censorship from the State. Television and cinema found that they were able to push the envelope of what was considered shocking and indecent in their exploration of social conditions. To some it was liberation; to others it was corruption and no better than pornography. For them, this tide had to be reversed, and counter-attacks came from the church and the nobility.

Two Christian evangelists, Peter Hill and his wife Janet, did not like the Britain they returned to in 1970 after four years as missionaries in India. They felt the need for a public protest against the permissive society, to try to reverse it and restore what they saw as moral standards based upon the teachings of Christianity. With notable figures such as Lord Longford and the playwright, journalist, thinker and recent convert to Christianity, Malcolm Muggeridge, they organised the National Festival of Light to show that the 'silent majority' would not let this immorality sweep across the country unchallenged. For them, it wasn't just indecent; it was harmful and would lead to criminal or deviant behaviour.

Lord Longford

Following a visit to the nude revue *Oh! Calcutta!*, which he thought was obscene, Lord Longford started his own self-funded Parliamentary committee of inquiry in 1971 into pornography. This fifty-two-man committee featured not only Muggeridge but also pop singer Cliff Richard, and they investigated pornography as thoroughly as might be considered possible. He debated with sociologists and scientists, and, after taking committee members to see live sex shows in Denmark (where liberalisation had recently come into effect), he earned the derogatory nickname 'Lord Porn'. At times, Longford saw his work as a battle between the forces of light and darkness. But he was no crank, and he had a lot of support. His report was eventually published in September 1972. Sex and violence on television was a concern for one Mrs Mary Whitehouse, the scourge of the BBC and, in particular, its socially aware Director-General, Sir Hugh Carleton Greene. Her one-woman campaign to restore 'standards' became an action group called the National Viewers And Listeners Association. Its mission was to 'clean up' television. Again, Mrs Whitehouse had a strong Christian faith and a very strong sense of patriotism. In a speech entitled Promoting Violence, made at the Royal College of Nursing in the UK Professional Conference in April 1970, she criticised the television news services for broadcasting explicit images from the Vietnam war which she felt desensitised the viewer and harmed the (in her opinion) justified war effort. She also thought it was an excuse to allow greater realism of violent imagery in fictional programmes to match what was going on in the real world.

Bernard Dixon, writing in *New Scientist* at the time the Longford committee was due to report, stated 'let's be clear that such judgements, and the crusade that follows, are entirely personal, and not based on any unambiguous scientific data whatever about adverse consequences of exposure to pornographic material. Despite extensive investigation, there is not a jot of hard evidence to support the allegations and suspicions of such ill effects.' It could be argued, as the episode hints, that exploitative pornography is a symptom rather than a cause.

A report was published in 1970 by the Television Research Committee from Leicester University called 'Television and Delinquency'. It addressed the concerns of those who felt that scenes of violence and law-breaking would encourage youngsters to copy what they saw. No link was found between the two, except in a tiny amount of cases amongst the pathologically ill. The report argued that if there was a connection, why wasn't it universal? It also pointed out how there were enough programmes condemning violence and law breaking.

Wilhelm Reich

Wilhelm Reich was a student of Freud. *The Function of the Orgasm* discusses, as does Granger, the sexual nature of a child, even from infancy. Reich makes no distinction between healthy and unhealthy sexuality, and discusses how destructive repression can be. Without adequate release, the personality becomes tense. He later developed controversial views on what he called 'orgone energy': literally, the energy of the universe expressed through sex and released by orgasm, which could be collected and stored in boxes. The authorities in America investigated the claims that these boxes – accumulators – could cure cancer, and, after he violated an injunction for inter-state sales of them, they were burned along with many of his books.

Production
Script Development

Stuart Douglass was commissioned on 11 August 1971 to write 'Sex and Violence'. He delivered it by October and handed in rewrites on 23 November along with three casting suggestions, one of which, Bernard Horsfall, was picked up. For the part of Ballantyne, Douglass urged Terence Dudley to see actor Bill Ward, whose limp would be perfect for the character, and for the pop star, either Paul Jones or Peter Moore. Although the script was accepted and paid for, Darrol Blake remembered 'Terry was nervous about the subject and Andrew Osborn, when he read the script, couldn't get past page one with the words "penis" and "vagina"!' Despite their reservations, the script was passed onto to Blake to direct, which delighted him: 'I had done a really cracking script by Stuart Douglass in *The Regiment* series, the best one I did, and this too I thought was an excellent script. The whole thing was a parallel of the Longford committee.'

Casting

Blake assembled what he considered to be a very strong cast. Nicholas Selby had appeared in his episode of *Shadow of the Tower*, and Blake would go on to direct June Brown in a very unusual Christmas edition of ITV's *Crown Court* and later in her most famous role as Dot Cotton in *EastEnders*. Noel Dyson also had a soap opera heritage, being among the original cast of *Coronation Street*, but declined to remain in the programme indefinitely and was the first character to be killed off, albeit off screen. Angela Crow was another *Coronation Street* cast member, who this time had clocked up over a hundred episodes as Doreen Lostock in the early 1960s. Brian Wilde would find fame for his sitcom appearances in *Porridge* and *Last of the Summer Wine*, but at this point he was a much-in-demand character actor who in 1971 had played a very memorable role in *Elizabeth R* as the sinister Richard Topcliffe, Queen Elizabeth's hunter and torturer of Catholics. He played against John Paul in Granada's *The Man in Room 17* episode called 'A Minor Operation' in 1965. Bernard Horsfall often played powerful and imposing figures of authority or learning, as did Donald Eccles. Queenie Watts was your go to actor playing brash and confident Londoners, and ran her own pubs when she wasn't acting.

Filming
Three days filming were done at the beginning of March 1972, with the first day spent partly at the Richmond Theatre, which played host to *Do It*. Although the names of the extras used on location are currently unknown, the two little girls sitting in their push chair at the very top of the programme are Darrol Blake's own twin daughters. The Skyline Hotel near Heathrow airport was the venue for the fake pornography film needed for the committee's entertainment, after Blake was unable to source extracts from Wardour Street Film Distributors (who were apparently disgusted that the BBC would actually want to screen that sort of thing). The material, filmed by Fred Hamilton, was tame to say the least, but it was not an experience the cameraman particularly enjoyed. The National Trust property of Polesden Lacey and its grounds, near Dorking, Surrey, acted as Ballantyne's country sprawl.

Studio Recording
'Sex and Violence' was the sixth episode to be recorded, in TC1 on Tuesday, 21 March 1972. From the studio recording, an insert survives featuring members of the committee watching the execution footage. This lengthy real-life extract came from the documentary series *24 Hours* and is generally blamed for the fate which befell 'Sex and Violence'. However, it had been shown on television twice before Blake selected it. The only music for the episode is to be heard over the pornography film.

Blake had two more episodes to direct before taking a month's holiday in France, having not stopped working for nearly two years.

Banned
The BBC were unsure about the episode. As Darrol Blake recalls, 'They were very nervous about it because of the Longford commission about moral pollution and all the rest of it. It was due to go out a week or ten days before Longford published his report. I think the overriding reason was that they were frightened of Mary Whitehouse, who was depicted in it, played by Noel Dyson.' The episode may have been pulled from transmission just after 'Deadly Dangerous Tomorrow' was recorded, as that was planned even then, to be the seventh transmitted episode. When

the *Daily Express* reported Pedler's reaction to 'Fire and Brimstone', they mentioned that a forthcoming episode was going to be upon the subject of censorship. Whenever the decision was made, it was made at very short notice.

Darrol Blake: 'The BBC issued a press release saying *Doomwatch* would be one less this time due to a substandard production. Stuart Douglass was incensed and rushed to Television Centre and said that this is absolutely ridiculous, what is going on? It was fortunate that we had in the gallery [during recording] a friend of Stewart's, Keith Waterhouse, who had a weekly column in the *Daily Mirror*. So, this got into his column that the BBC was frightened off! The BBC then put out a second release which said that the current series of *Doomwatch* was going to be one less than projected because, far from being a substandard production, it was a very good production, but they didn't feel that the subject could be dealt with adequately in fifty minutes. So all this went on without me knowing anything about it.'

Judy Hall remembers that the reasons were certainly political. The 'silent majority' had won – and didn't even know it. The episode was apparently going to be transmitted fifth, on Monday, 3 July 1972, and would have been the first of Darrol Blake's four episodes to go out. Returning from his holiday in France, he had a look through the *Radio Times* and was surprised to see another episode in its place. He telephoned Terence Dudley to find out what was going on. 'Terry said to me, "Ah, what made me think I had told you?"'

Blake soon learned about the reasons, and it was up to Judy Hall, now doing early work with Terence Dudley on his next project, *The Regiment*, to apologise in writing for not telling Blake the news. This was on 20 July, and she assured him that the episode had not been pulled because it was substandard. Six days later, she told him that there had been a management decision to wipe the episode in case it was 'put to air in error'. It was to be given a month's stay of execution in case Blake or anyone he selected wished to view it. However, the episode does survive in all of its 625-line glory, plus the brief insert of reaction shots.

This wasn't the only time John Bown would be involved in a banned episode from a programme's final series: he played an interviewer in the last-ever *Secret Army*, 'What Did You Do in the War, Daddy?', which was never shown, allegedly because of its anti-Russian sentiment.

The episode is available to watch on the Network DVD, released in 2016.

3.05
Without The Bomb

Written by Roger Parkes
Directed by Darrol Blake
Designed by Jeremy Davies
Transmitted: Monday, 3 July 1972 at 9.22 pm Duration: 47' 54"

Cast

Dr James Fulton (Brian Peck), Mrs Joan Fulton (Antonia Pemberton), Lady Holroyd (Katherine Kath), Clive Hughes (Kenneth Benda), Roger Halls (John Gregg), Harry Brooke (Charles Hodgson), Amanda Fulton (Sally Anne Marlowe), Reporter (Kenneth Gardiner), Lady Reporter (Marcelle Samett), Television Reporter (Michael Montgomery), Young Couple (Penny Dixon, Trevor T Dixon).

Also appearing
Board Members (John Moore, Michael Crane, Ned Hood, Jim Tyson), Reporters (Bud Castlemain, David Melbourne, Frank Lester, Freddie Clemson, Jason James, Brian Craven, Richard Sheekey, Cy Wallace, Fran Pomeroy), Lab Assistants (David Ianson, David Pelton, Anne Lee), Chairman's Wife (Joyce Freeman), Minister's Secretary (Iona McRae), Representative (Billy Snuffer).

Technical Credits

Production Assistant: Jackie Willows. Assistant Floor Manager: Anna Yarrow. Director's Assistant: Philippa Clauson. Floor Assistant: Michael Throne.
Film Editor: Alastair MacKay.
Costume supervisor: Sheila Beers. Make-up Assistant: Liz Rowell.
Studio Lighting: Ralph Walton. TM2: Bob Warman. Vision Mixer: John Barclay.
Studio Sound: John Lloyd. Grams Operator: Gerry Borrows.
Crew: 1.

Radio Times

A problem for Bradley: the go/stop lipstick. 'Free will is an illusion. We must manipulate man's behaviour on the pretext of ensuring his survival.'

The Story

'Can't you see all I want is an alternative to mass annihilation? A way of doing it without the bomb?' – Fulton

James Fulton is an angst ridden Catholic man. His wife suggests he should put his trust in God, but he has a mission in life to save the world, which will surely send him into the fires of hell, and anyone else who follows his path.

The cause for his anxiety is an aphrodisiac-contraceptive called Joyne, and he invented it. His pharmaceutical company is waiting to launch it, but to sell it over the counter needs political approval. At the moment, they are working out their sales pitch, and how to make a product morally acceptable. Brooke, the advertising man, believes sex does not need selling, only moral acceptance. Therefore the new contraceptive could be marketed to help couples who have had problems with their sex lives. A wise authority figure in a white coat could explain about the true value of sex in society: 'Its catalytic value in marriage, its role in health and normality, its potential for enhancing the quality of life.' Fulton thinks it is too prim. They should be selling the product for what it is – a license to have fun.

The Chairman, Clive Hughes, lobbies the Minister at his home and discusses the new birth control that can be applied like a lipstick. Holroyd's French wife, Janette is intrigued. The aphrodisiac element has been designed to work only on women because, apparently, men don't need stimulus. Men are in a state of arousal very easily. The drug has been cleared by the Medicines Committee but only as a prescribed treatment.

The Minister can foresee the political fallout if it is available for all, especially the young who will enjoy it the most. He asks Quist for a complete evaluation of Joyne; he knows that population control is a major hobby horse for Quist, and 'When the Puritan lobby start screaming, I want to know the answers.' Quist asks the Minister whether he is a puritan or a permissive, but then decides he is a politician.

Quist discusses Joyne with Anne at home later that night. What Fulton has done is to isolate a couple of pheromones, scent signals, which affect hormones and can influence libido in a woman and control fertility. Anne is all for sex to be seen as fun and not shameful. She works at a Marital Aid Clinic and sees a lot of people who are ill because of repressed sexual impulses. She agrees to field test Joyne at the clinic and gives a sample to a silent young couple who are anxious about their sex life.

Quist meets Fulton and praises him for his work on Joyne. He learns that the aphrodisiac aspect was necessary because the pure contraceptive removed all sexual desire on the woman's part. Fulton is a Catholic and is concerned about exploding population numbers, which he hopes Joyne will help prevent from increasing further. He hates the aphrodisiac aspect but argues passionately that there must be voluntary acceptance of birth control. Quist is suspicious of the strength of his outburst.

Bradley thinks the whole idea of Joyne is disgusting, much to Barbara's amusement. 'Well, wait till you've got a growing family. Wait till you come down in the morning and trip over some long-haired lout half-naked and drugged out of his senses ... some stranger who used to call you Dad.' Bradley is actually talking about a neighbour's son. Barbara claims she has been using Joyne, and it has made her give up smoking. Suddenly, her sense of smell has become very much more important now ...

Quist hands over some preliminary findings to the Minister, who isn't happy about the small amount of data concerning the effects of Joyne on young people. As news of Joyne reaches the media, Fulton faces tough questioning from reporters. He states that his work could have a big impact on the future of mankind and on the question of morality. A female reporter tells him: 'There are those who'll see you in a different light. I'm sure you'll realise that. People who'll compare you with the Marquis de Sade and the pornography merchants. Respectable, quiet-living people. Like parents. Mums and Dads with teenage children. Are you a parent, Dr Fulton? Do you understand what this stuff you've invented will mean to them? Do you have a family?'

Fulton has an adopted family, including a girl called Mandy who tells him that night what her teacher, Sister Mary, said about Joyne: 'a death blow to love.' 'I tell them one thing,' Fulton remarks to his wife, 'the schools tell them another ...'

The Minister faces equally tough questioning on the television by interviewer Roger Halls. The programme begins with an emotive slide show illustrating pollution, which is directly attributed to the three billion living on our planet. The Fultons are watching the programme as the Minister explains that the controversial addition to Joyne and its implications need to be studied, and Doomwatch's conclusions will form the basis of whatever action is necessary for the public good.

Bradley is concerned about the effect Joyne would have on young people. Anne thinks that innocence stands a chance once sex is accepted as a natural, wholesome aspect of human behaviour. Bradley replies frostily that doesn't mean that the likes of him – squares – are ready for the forthcoming sexual utopia. In bed, the Fultons are discussing if the aphrodisiac part of Joyne is essential or if it is as tyrannical as other short cuts to population control: legislation for compulsory sterilisation, political dictatorship, child permits ... His wife doesn't share his concerns; there is a choice involved with using Joyne.

Stafford reports to the Minister on Fulton's background. Voluntarily sterilised after two children, adopted four, two of them coloured. Fulton is clearly a man of considerable social conscience. Lady Holroyd suspects her husband is prejudiced against Joyne. She feels he regards sex as an embarrassment and has always directed his energies towards political ambition instead. He points out that he would not let prejudice interfere with his decision making. Although he is not a sexually driven man, his 'embarrassment' is not always dormant, and he kisses her hand. Stafford's view of Joyne is that it will destroy the traditional roles in marriage, particularly that of the woman as home maker. Barbara challenges this. She thinks he simply does not like the fact that it may give the woman the advantage, the power to be the seducer and not the seduced. To prove her point she corners the flustered Stafford with a Joyne lipstick, bringing it closer and closer to her lips ... but is interrupted by the arrival of Fulton, who has come to see Quist.

Quist has discovered that the aphrodisiac element does not, in fact, need to be strong to the point of actual stimulation. It could have been modified. Fulton disagrees. To do so would have taken another five or six years. Besides, he argues, they must have voluntary acceptance of contraception. Incentives. He loses his patience. 'Oh, for heaven's sake! Maybe if Teller and the rest of you on the Manhattan Project had been more positive in your morality, we wouldn't have had the Bomb. Or is that your solution to the population menace, Dr Quist? You sit there condemning a mild hormone stimulant as ... as a violation of man's essential humanity ... talking as though I was some sort of fiendish crank. Can't you see all I want is an alternative to mass annihilation? A way of doing it *without* the Bomb?'

Quist wonders to Anne whether he could cover up his findings and allow Joyne to go onto the market, but Anne warns him not to. He meets with the Minister, and seems to be about to hand over the report until he learns that Stafford has already revealed the findings, thanks to a 'quite by chance' encounter. Despite the briefcase he carries, Quist tells him that he hasn't brought the report, blaming a computer failure that means Joyne will have to be analysed again – in case the excitant is necessary after all. But the Minister is still happy. As Quist points out, the Government is off the hook.

The Minister goes on television and addresses the nation: 'So you will see that, in a country like Britain with its fine traditions of church and family, it must clearly be in the national interest to withhold a drug of this nature until such time as it can be refined ...'

Fulton is disappointed and crushed by the decision. 'Can't they see that unless they encourage every possible means of voluntary birth restraint now, before much longer they'll be forced to the other methods? Forced to dictate family size, to legislate for compulsory sterilizations, to euthanize for the old and handicapped. No. All they can see is that Joyne is a slight political embarrassment. Morally offensive. So they kill it – bury it away in a swamp of platitudes and distortions.' The only other way the population problem will ever be cured is by the way Quist helped make possible – the Bomb. Quist, too, is despondent. Bradley tells him that the Indians are interested in buying Joyne in its current form, and a political cartoonist has suggested it might reverse the direction of immigration. As he looks at pollution statistics on his desk, Quist thinks Fulton may be right: it's already all too late.

Behind The Story

Had 'Without the Bomb' been Episode 4 and 'Sex and Violence' Episode 5, as was originally planned, they would have formed an interesting investigation into the effects of repressed sexual attitudes which can turn towards violence (and one such expression is seen in next week's 'Hair Trigger'). Here, Roger Parkes' episode presents two themes. The first is the fear of sexually emancipating young women and what effect it might have on the family (something which concerned critics during the biological researches of the 1960s). Had this episode been made some years earlier, it would simply have been about the pill.

The second theme is that of the population explosion. The expressions 'population bomb' and 'population explosion' were coined in 1954 by businessman and population control activist Hugh Everett Moore in his pamphlet *The Population Bomb!* But the roots of the issue and its consequences for the environment go back to just after the Second World War. The population of Europe had increased by eleven million people between 1936 and 1946. In 1948 *Our Plundered Planet* by Fairfield Osborn and *Road to Survival* by William Vogt were published.

There were concerns that population pressures would lead to wars over resources and that there would be famine, plagues and social unrest. Vogt argued that the European countries were becoming less and less self-sufficient, depending instead on imports from the Americas, Africa and other places, which wrecked their environments by the plundering of their natural resources. Osborn feared that there would be an increase in war by the time the population reached three billion in the middle of the twenty-first century. It was seven billion in 2011. In 1967 brothers William and Paul Paddock wrote *Famine 1975! America's Decision: Who Will Survive?*, which envisaged that those least fit to survive in Egypt, India and Haiti would be allowed to starve in order to save the stronger ones.

Things got even blunter in 1968 with the most famous of these books. Bearing the same title as Moore's pamphlet, *The Population Bomb*, by husband and wife team Paul and Anne Ehrlich, predicted hundreds of millions of deaths from famine by the 1980s. They questioned the 'new orthodoxy' that technological fixes would save the day. Paul Ehrlich was a famous doomwatcher in his time. The book, credited solely to him, pulls no punches. It is a very emotive read and seems to be preaching to the wealthy, stirring up fears of a peasants' revolt. The have-nots will take from the haves. He founded the Zero Population Growth movement in the same year as the book's publication. In the West, the population explosion concerned governments who feared that overcrowded countries would turn to Communism, conservative thinkers in America thought too many poor people would become a burden on the tax payer, and environmentalists, as we have seen, worried about the world's finite resources. So what was the answer? Birth control.

Birth Controls

Terrified by the predictions of overcrowding by either 1980 or 2000, population control groups sprung up everywhere. The National Council of Great Britain called for free family planning advice at its annual conference in 1971. 'England is now the third most crowded country in the world' said Mrs Enid Evans, a family planning clinic worker. She might have watched 'The Human Time Bomb', for she appears to be quoting Langly: 'If it continues, how can everyone be housed, fed, educated and have their health cared for? I'm sorry this sounds like *Doomwatch*. But having successfully interfered with death, we must interfere with birth' (*Daily Mirror*, 14 October 1971). The Family Planning Association feared that compulsory birth control would be imposed within a few generations (*The Times*, 24 July 1971). The script addresses these issues, particularly in the Roger Halls section, with its series of statements derived from *The Population Bomb*.

The oral contraceptive pill for women was seen as a major step in the right direction for controlling the world population instead of the more draconian interventions from governments such as enforced sterilisations or a legal limit to the number of children. India was seen as a 'living showcase of the need for population control', in the words of Elaine Tyler May in her 2010 book *America and the Pill*, and was a setting for a conference of medical experts to discuss the issue in 1965. The pill was the answer to world hunger and poverty, one American delegate declared. Naturally, it had its opponents. The Catholic church rejected it immediately; conservatives like Joseph McCarthy thought that birth control was a Communist plot to weaken the country and spread immorality; some saw the pill as a 'potential tool of racist social engineers'; the Black Power movement urged black women not to take it as it promoted genocide. And those who did take it did it not to control the world's population, but their own fertility. For some reason, they still wanted children of their own...

Syntex

One of the major producers and developers of the pill was Syntex Pharmaceuticals Limited, whom we have met before with their experiments into jet lag. In 1969 a rumour began circulating that the company was developing a contraceptive with an aphrodisiac quality. Stewart Brand of *Whole Earth Catalog,* an American counterculture publication which specialised in promoting self-sustainability, wrote to Dr Carl Djerassi at the Syntex Research Centre in California, asking him to comment on the rumour. Brand stated his belief that the public needed a double-function pill and quoted from *The Population Bomb* about the oncoming world famine and how America should lead the way as the world's biggest consumer. 'World famine versus heavy governmental controls over sex behaviour is not a pleasant choice ... Perhaps the Combination Pill could be called Make Love Not War.' Djerassi wrote back that, yes, they were working on an aphrodisiac, and how such a combination would 'indeed be a large pill for the FDA and the medical profession to swallow even if has the favourable social effects you attribute to it'.

In Britain, Dr George Christie, an adviser on the episode, wrote in the *New Scientist* of January 1971 that he doubted there would be any more research into new oral contraceptives unless there was a radical rethinking of the attitudes of government regulatory bodies, the medical fraternity and the general public over the trustworthiness of the industry and of their product. He too quotes the received idea that the population in Britain would be sixty million by 1980. '[The government] must realize that the population problem is rapidly heading for a national emergency, and that if it is allowed to remain unchecked by the lack of introduction of new means of fertility control, the future of Britain and its economic viability are both in doubt.' He was basically asking for money to be pumped into their research.

The idea that humans did indeed have pheromones had only recently been investigated. Dr Martha McClintock of Harvard University wrote in *Nature* of how the menstrual cycles of women students in a hall of residence synchronised in much the same way as that of mice in the same cage. Pheremonal communication appeared to be at the bottom of it. Scientists began to wonder if there was a subliminal language of odours between humans, exciting fear, hostility and sexual attraction but which was being deliberately suppressed – by ourselves. Dr Alex Comfort, another adviser for the episode, wrote about this in the *New Scientist* issue dated 25 February 1971.

Attitudes to Joyne

So the idea behind Joyne is to have a contraceptive, applied like lipstick, which would reward the woman for being infertile by making her want sex with the man of her choice, giving her the initiative. Sex, as Tarrant observes, would get back to its function of pair bonding, the reinforcement of love and just plain fun. She believes the repression of the sexual urge to be a major cause of the psychosis which she sees in her surgery every day, as well as the problems in the marital aid clinic. She points the finger of blame at religion for making sex sinful and a source of shame. Except this is in Britain, and although the Catholic Church did not have a grip on the morals of the country any more, the puritans did. Sex was still seen, publicly at least, as purely for the procreation of children at best and disgusting at worst. The idea of it being fun was simply not accepted in public, and certainly not by women. Hence the Minister's fears of the puritan lobby, and we see Colin Bradley's chapel-inspired attitude of disgust at what the young get up to. For him, sex outside marriage equals disease, which suggests he remembers his National Service days. Stafford's dislike of a woman choosing her own partner (this script was written in 1971, and the Women's Lib movement – the whole idea of women's rights – was still very new and frightening to the old social order) is contrasted with Barbara Mason's feeling of emancipation as a challenge to traditional behaviours.

Catholics

For once in a subject of this type, the Catholics don't come in for a right old bashing. Fulton is a Catholic but, it seems, a lapsed one. He still has a religious faith, and his children are educated at a Catholic school, but he and his wife are prepared for their children to adopt different points of view, that they will make up their own minds. He regards original sin as a myth but wonders whether original sin was not sex but knowledge. His wife is also a progressive believer. The guilt and abhorrence over the aphrodisiac and permissiveness consumes Fulton, but he sees the greater goal of liberating mankind from sexual sin in order to control population growth. He is aware of the Catholic feeling from his daughter's teacher, Sister Mary John, who says that Joyne will take away love from the world, which is an interesting observation from someone who has chosen to be celibate. He does not want a tyrannical solution imposed upon the problem. Ehrlich had suggested an extreme solution in *The Population Bomb*: temporary sterilants in water supplies and food. Fulton hoped that Joyne would prevent unwanted births (unwanted by whom?) and reduce population in a more humane manner than dropping a nuclear bomb, which he accuses Quist, quite unjustly, for wanting.

The instinct to have children is nowhere to be addressed in the episode, or the reasons for children in the economic sense. One view is that children provide support when the parents are too old or ill to work. Even in Britain, the more children you had in the pre- antibiotic age the better: providing they survived, they could be made to work from an early age either at home or outside, especially in a city where there was more work to be had. The poor breed like rabbits and the wealthy don't like it. The idea of selling a contraceptive-aphrodisiac over the counter at a chemists is a politically troublesome. We see the Minister wrestling with the issue and his relief when he can sweep it away again. He did not want to face the battle with the puritan lobby. India – 'the land of the Karma Sutra', as Quist drily notes – is keen on the idea; in real life, the problems with the contraceptive pill proved to be getting it to people in remote areas and the lack of medical personnel required to provide prescriptions and examinations. In the end, it became one of the countries most resistant to the pill.

Production
Scripting Development
Terence Dudley wanted one of the thirteen planned episodes of the third series to tackle the topical issue of the population explosion within the First and Third Worlds and its burden on resources. Two writers selected to tackle the issue of the Western attitude towards sex were Harry Green and Roger Parkes. Green was working on a population story with some background literature and a recording of an interview with Dr Alex Comfort for research. Comfort was not that far away from the launch of his famous *The Joy of Sex* and had six months earlier published an article in *New Scientist* on pheromones and their relation to human behaviour. Meanwhile, Parkes was trying to come up with a storyline which explored the theme in a way different from Green. On 10 August 1971 he had met with Dudley for lunch to discuss the issue of overpopulation. Parkes was surprised by some of Dudley's assertions and wrote to him the next day with some counter-arguments. Dudley wrote a short reply, dated 13 August: 'What you're saying is that this small island (that gave birth to the Industrial Revolution), must set an example. Fair enough! And that's what we're working on. If this one founders (by which I mean the writer) then over to you. In the meantime, don't count on it and if you've got another idea ...'

'Without the Bomb' became commission number nine on 13 September 1971, with a delivery date for 30 October. The first scene breakdown submitted by Parkes was delivered on 22 September 1971 and was called 'Instead of the Bomb'. The story was written to have no filming needed. The covering note says 'This story anticipates the development of an olfactory contraceptive derived from organic pheromones.' Parkes notes that on its own such a contraceptive would contain a built-in revulsion factor which would be modified with a hormone stimulant, a sex excitant, and how it would be unacceptable unless society revised its attitude towards sex with its associations with sin, guilt and shame. 'Since the theme is sex, it seems appropriate that the story of public and political reaction to the pheromone contraceptive should be combined with the crystallisation of the Quist-Tarrant love affair.' In the breakdown, Anne is spelt without the 'e' at the end.

Original Story

The pre-title sequence features a boy and a girl who have reached the 'coffee in my flat stage'. He is nervous and shy. She takes out a lipstick and applies it to his lips (yes, his lips), and soon his inhibitions fall away. After the titles, a documentary film about the population explosion is shown to the Minister, with 'horrific footage of the masses of Calcutta ... contrasted with visual excesses of Californian high life'. Quist explains how each American child is fifty times more of a burden on the environment than each Indian child. To set an example, Quist is going to have a vasectomy. Later, Ann objects to this as ludicrous egotism, but the real objection is that she may wish to marry him and have a child together. A TV commercial advertises 'F-U-N' for young people and married couples. This is being shown to various executives of the drug and cosmetic company manufacturing it. Its research scientist, Jack Fulton, is appalled by the permissive tone of the advertisement because it focuses entirely on the wrong aspects. He clashes with McNabb, the advertising manager, and takes his complaint to Quist, whom he wants on board as an independent adviser. He does not want F-U-N promoted as an aphrodisiac.

The news of F-U-N leaks, and the Minister, anticipating bad reactions in the press, sets up an inquiry which will include Quist. With the press determined to sensationalise F-U-N as a contraceptive aphrodisiac, the company holds a press conference. The Minister gets legal advice on finding ways of objecting to F-U-N. Quist approves of it, but Ann strongly disagrees. The committee, which Ann is also invited to join, examines the behavioural response of students to F-U-N. The Chairman speculates on the social response to F-U-N and believes abuse of the product by bachelors will become rare. A TV debate features Mrs Houghton, the wife of a bishop on the committee, who predicts mass orgies, rape and rampant VD, contrasting with the remarks of the scientists in the previous scene. She also predicts cancer, deformed babies and psychotic disorders. The committee's research disputes this reaction, although Ann questions Fulton's methodology in his own research.

Anne's dispute with Quist is intense enough to question the whole basis of their love, and 'Both are letting emotion tinge their normal scientific detachment for once.' Similarly, the Minister's own sexual hang-ups are clouding his objectivity. Another TV panel consisting of representatives from Women's Lib, an educationist, a police commissioner and McNabb also displays 'emotionalism' in the views from both sides of the argument. This leads into the Minister remarking on how the youth favour F-U-N, and no matter what the committee decides, it won't influence the final decision, especially if the US State Department take a vote. Later, he is given a file containing smear material to be used on Fulton, just in case. The Establishment will oppose F-U-N. Back at the committee, the Bishop is more supportive of F-U-N than his wife. In bed the next morning, he substitutes her normal lipstick with F-U-N, and the inevitable occurs.

Quist is rewatching the population film; he feels that F-U-N is an ideal form of voluntary contraception but is 'likely to be banned or driven onto the prescription- only black market simply because society is still conditioned to the ancient Judaeo-Christian ethic that non-procreative sex is sinful!'

Duncan is also in favour of F-U-N and is prepared to betray an intimate confidence in order to force the Minister's hand. (Parkes speculates on whether the confidence might be a kinky side to the Minister.) In any case, the committee comes out in favour of F-U-N. Ann is still not convinced, despite an impassioned appeal by Quist. On TV the Minister explains why F-U-N is not going to be sanctioned after all, not until a more comprehensive research programme is carried out. Watching this is a contrite Ann, bitter at the political decision and coming round to Quist's view. They might make up with a sniff of the 'now illicit F-U-N' (suggests Parkes) whilst, on TV, Fulton explains that the Indian Government is interested in F-U-N, 'and if this doesn't reverse the tide of immigration, I don't know what will ...'

Second Version
When sending it to script consultant Anna Kaliski, Parkes emphasised that the outline was a starting point for discussion and that he had done no real work on the characters, nor was he terribly happy with the ending. He was confident that the two opposing attitudes of Quist and Ann could be achieved without 'either of them seeming permissive or priggish'. Scribbling in the margins of the breakdown, Terence Dudley objected to the opening scene, pointing out that Quist has no children and is at least 50 years old, and rejected the vasectomy idea. 'A Bishop?' queries Dudley about the morning bedroom scene. He also put a cross against the idea that the Minister has a kinky secret. The committee was rejected probably because it was too similar to the one 'Sex and Violence' would be using.

Working fast, a revised scene breakdown was submitted by Parkes on 27 September. In the meantime he sought advice from Dr Christie, 'who was very chuffed with the whole project'. The changes to the storyline introduce the Minister's wife and take a look at his lack of sexual activity. A subplot features an ambitious chief assistant to Fulton called Bland, and they would clash. (Parkes later felt this was too much for the already overcrowded plot.) The new breakdown begins with an advert for F-U-N.

Ann Tarrant is now pro-F-U-N. Bradley represents old fashioned values whilst Barbara is keen to get hold of the stuff. Scene 8 is a montage of some visuals of F-U-N 'turning 'em on'. This includes lab tests and even Stafford sniffing the lipstick. Scene 12 sees the Chairman fetching Fulton for the press conference forced on them by Bland, who has leaked the details. Fulton's forceful wife is introduced much later in the script. Here, she is decidedly against F-U-N, fearing that their daughter will catch VD parasites. The dilemma of Fulton is expressed as 'Survival expediency versus a healthy social environment.' Parkes sees this as the pivotal scene. Fulton's 13-year-old daughter comes home, 'tickled pink by the news of her daddy's super F-U-N invention'.

The Minister's wife, Lady Holroyd, telephones the Chairman with a favour to ask (against which Dudley put a firm 'No'). This is followed by the Minister on the phone to an Establishment figure, and we become aware that he can block F-U-N. This is before Stafford comes in with a file on Fulton. Fulton himself appears on a panel programme where he is attacked for encouraging permissiveness. The Minister is also alarmed when his wife tries F-U-N and is turned on. This carries on into another scene – the aftermath. The Minister does not approve of her 'experiment' (and neither did Dudley). Fulton's wife has been following the controversy and adds to the pressure. In his last scene, Fulton says that the Indian High Commission want to speak to him about F-U-N, but he wants to stay in Britain and refine the product, for that is where the most urgency is. The story ends in Quist's office, with Bradley smug over the Minister's decision and Quist agreeing with Fulton that it is too late.

More Changes
Parkes met with Dudley the following Monday, 4 October to discuss the story further, before meeting Dr Comfort and then going away to write the script. He was given a copy of Martin Worth's 'The High Mountain' to read. Parkes sent in the finished script on 6 November from Malta, where he was living for a few months. In his covering letter he thought his draft went over by six minutes and asked for Anna Kaliski to check up on a couple of minor facts. Dudley had wanted a reference to the ATV watchdog inserted (presumably about the advert for F-U-N), which he had been unable to do, and a couple of 'digs' at papists were ready to be removed if required. Parkes had written for just the one TV interviewer and wondered if the budget could stretch to two since there were 'an awful lot of TV shows'.

This draft did not contain Roger Halls but, according to the list of characters on the top page attached to a later draft, there was a Mrs Halls and an Astel Raymond as part of the speaking cast. The non-speaking parts required the Reverend Blatchford and three others, and 'Members of a TV Discussion Panel'. The sets list did not include the Fulton's bedroom but did mention a bedroom interior for a 'montage sequence only', in the script's single film scene. Terence Dudley's new secretary, Alison Fife, wrote back to say that the script had arrived safely and the producer would be writing a full response soon.

Terence Dudley's notes were sent on 19 November. He regarded the script as 'super' and had been waiting for responses from Doctors Comfort and Christie. His comments were enclosed with that of Anna Kaliski, with whom he had only one disagreement: that of spending programme money on 'mounting suggestions – population montages'. He did not want references to the writer Malcolm Muggeridge or the controversial right-wing MP, Enoch Powell. 'The old firm is too closely associated with the Whitehouse lobby and we don't want to acknowledge that this even exists.' A later point saw the replacing of the expression 'Powellite' with 'authoritarian'. Dudley wanted the Quist and Tarrant relationship affectionate but not overt, realising that, once aired, there would be questions asked about their relationship. He also did not want the girl in the marriage guidance clinic to get turned on too quickly by a sniff of F-U-N. His advisers pointed out that the reaction would be too quick anyway. Another suggestion was seeing some of the TV interviews in Fulton's room to set the scene in context.

Dudley's biggest concern was dealing with the sexual attitudes of the Minister and his wife. He objected to the Minister's line 'And risk having you strip off between the entrée and the roast?' as it was not characteristic of the Minister and should be written more obliquely. In the event, the line became 'And risk having you lose your Gallic detachment?' Scene 17, which dealt with the Minister's sex life, received the most criticism. Dudley wanted the scene to be less explicit and make Sir George frigid rather than kinky. 'The point of the scene is to say that the Minister is prejudged and a puritan and therefore the 'panacea' is in danger of suppression.' The wife should hint with phrases like 'lack of interest … your drive is canalised in your career.' Dudley suggested that Parkes forget the original idea of the wife getting turned on and that she has instead accepted her role as wife to a Cabinet Minister – a marriage in the French tradition – without violent regret. She hopes that the Minister won't 'thumbs-down BOND for the wrong reason'. This last bit suggests that BOND is the new name for F-U-N.

On 23 November Parkes wrote back, pleased at the response and wanting to carry out the revisions himself in Malta. He thought the script 'might make our point fairly strong for us'. A new Minister-wife scene was sent on the 27th. Parkes was more worried about Fulton's inconsistency in attitude, which Dudley felt was best left in the hands of the actor and director to sort out. Dudley was also planning to bring the story forward in the transmission schedule to number four, to be recorded on April 21 1972 with rehearsals starting ten days earlier.

Director

By the beginning of 1972 Darrol Blake was on board as director. It would be his third episode this series. A revised script was sent to Parkes on 24 March, with some minor changes made by Dudley. These included a new, more commercial name for the aphrodisiac contraceptive which Darrol Blake had decided upon; 'I named it JOYNE – and Terry Dudley said, "Oh yes, with an 'e' at the end!"'

By the time the camera script was prepared there had been some minor swapping around of scenes, the usual deletion of a few lines and toning down of the sexual medical language. But, more notably, there was the addition of three new pages: Stafford is given his second scene in the story, this time with Barbara; Fulton gets an extra paragraph after watching the Ministerial broadcast, and Quist is no longer present as Bradley and Anne argue over the merits of Joyne.

The final scene between Quist and Bradley gains some extra dialogue, ending the episode on the more downbeat note of the revised scene breakdown. In the rehearsal script, Bradley enters the office sheepishly because he isn't sure of how Quist feels about the row with Anne. He talks about India wanting Joyne and Quist comments it is the land of the Karma Sutra. The new dialogue contains a spot of foreshadowing of the already recorded 'The Killer Dolphins'.

Filming

Although there was no film as such in the episode, the montage to illustrate problems caused by population, over which Roger Halls narrates sentiments from prophets of doom, was a telecine insert. This lasted over a minute and a half. As scripted, the montage was cut into two sections separated by the first part of Halls' interview with the Minister. Originally, the narration was to be delivered by either Halls or a commentator. In the event, Halls did it all.

Casting

Casting proved problematic for Darrol Blake: 'I couldn't cast the part of the leading man [Fulton]. It was turned down by quite a few people, including an Irish actor who said he didn't want to be associated with such filth!' Brian Peck, often cast as an angst ridden character, was married to Jennifer Wilson. Katherine Kath was very striking and married to the film director Jack Clayton. She played a memorable role in *The Prisoner* episode 'A,B and C' as a French socialite. Kenneth Benda had reached the age of 70 in 1972. One scene wonder Brookes was played by Charles Hodgson who will later work for Blake on *The Venturers* in 1974. John Gregg had worked with Blake on *Paul Temple* in 1971. This was Marcelle Sammet's third appearance on *Doomwatch*, having made appearances in 'Tomorrow, the Rat' and 'Fire and Brimstone'. Penny Dixon had been Miss Cooper in 'The Devil's Sweets'.

Studio
'Without the Bomb' was the seventh episode recorded for the series. It was videotaped in TC1 on Friday, 21 April 1972.

Stock Music
Fantasia on a Theme by Thomas Tallis, composed by Vaughan Williams and performed by the London Philharmonic Orchestra, was released on the Lyrita label (SCRS 41). The Modern Jazz Quartet's interpretation of Adagio movement from *Concierto de Aranjuez* by Joaquim Rodrigo was from their album Space (Apple SAPCOR 10) Finally, The *Electric Banana* returned once again to represent what the kids listen to with 'It'll Never Be Me' from *Even More Electric Banana* (Hudson De Wolfe DW/LP 3123).

Editing
Without the Bomb was edited on Monday, 24 April between 9 am and 6 pm

Programme Review Board
The episode went out to only five million viewers. The Board criticised the casting of Brian Peck as Fulton and Andrew Osborn agreed that he had not been a good choice. Desmond Wilcox (co-editor and presenter of *Man Alive* and later Head of General Features) thought that the scene between Fulton and his daughter seemed to be 'entirely phoney'; another member felt that, although the dialogue was good, the scientist had not been a credible character.

Reaction
In the *Daily Mirror* of 4 June 1972, Mary Malone dismissed the episode in comparison to a *World In Action* documentary that concerned the misery of living next to the country's largest cement factory, which went out on the same night on ITV: '"Come on, Jim, don't be maudlin", chided the scientist's wife. "All you're guilty of is trying to save the world." And there is the problem in a nut shell. Some folk can't help playing Atlas. Quist and his team … carry the burdens of collective conscience with all the airs of people who are martyrs to lumbago. It's the good, large generalised moan that keeps them going. You've only to say to a *Doomwatch* fan "How are things today" to be pinned against the wall for an hour while the woes drown you. It satisfies him: it crushes you. The *Doomwatch* canvas is broad

and long. On its loom the tapestry will never finish. As they struggle to cope with the advantages and disadvantages of a spiced contraceptive with built in libido as an incentive to population control Dr Quist threw in a couple of beautiful come-ons. "But what", he asks, "about the recent Concorde atmosphere pollution figures? And the death of plankton in the Med?" What indeed? With the tidal wave on its way, world starvation round the corner, and the planet about to go bang, who cares about the little irritations in life?'

Audience Reaction
The audience reaction index gave this episode the lowest of the ten scores known for the series. In the Entertaining/Boring stakes, it rated 68:32, whilst the plot (Excellent/Poor) was given 67:33, a score it shared with 'Fire and Brimstone'.

Radio Times
'Three cheers for *Doomwatch*. After early lifeless, toothless, programmes, *Doomwatch* has returned with a real bite. One can only wish that all ministers, doctors, and teachers could have seen 'Without the Bomb'. *Doomwatch* has started once again to give a believable if fictional view of our future – or perhaps lack of future.' – B A Crompton of Birmingham.

3.06
Hair Trigger

Written by Brian Hayles
Directed by Quentin Lawrence
Designed by Oliver Bayldon
Transmitted: Monday, 10 July 1972 at 9.22 pm Duration: 45′ 22″

Cast
Dr McEwan (Barry Jackson), Beavis (Michael Hawkins), Professor Hetherington (Morris Perry), Robbie (Damon Sanders), Miss Abrahams (Pamela Saire), Susan (Maria O'Brien), Police Inspector (Victor Platt), Emily (Gillian Lewis), Policeman (Dan Caulfield), Children (Steven Jones, Philip Jones, Helen Jones).

Also appearing
Male Nurse (Derek Chafer), Female Nurse (Maude Cane), Waiters (Raymond George, Herbert Aldridge), Members of Royal Society (Peter Evans, Bill Gosling, Maurice Quick, John Moore, Sydney Woolf, Ned Hood, Juba Kennerly, Alan Cope), Radio voice (Terry Wogan). Police extras: unknown.

Technical Credits
Production Assistant: Robert Checksfield. Assistant PA: Peter Novis. Floor Assistant: Timothy Wood. Assistant Floor Manager: Brian Roberts. Director's Assistant: Norma Flint.
Film Cameraman: Fred Hamilton. Sound Recordist: Bob Roberts. Film Editor: Alastair MacKay.
Costume Supervisor: Sheila Beers. Costume Assistant: Ken Trew. Make-up Supervisor: Penny Norton. Make-up Assistant: Sue Miles.
Studio Lighting: John Dixon. TM2: Dickie (Richard) Ashman. Vision Mixer: Chris Griffin.
Studio Sound: Chick Anthony. Grams Operator: Gerry Borrows.
Senior Cameraman: Doug Routledge.
Crew: 1.

Radio Times
Whose finger on the trigger? 'Man isn't born him. For him ... the dreadful has already happened. He has to live with the nightmare, or rise above it. And natural evolution is too slow.'

The Story

'It was like growing a tree of knowledge in my head, only the fruits were for you.' – Beavis

Weatheroak Hall is a government-owned Maximum Security Medical Research Unit. For the past year it has been fulfilling a government brief to treating violent psychopaths in a cost-effective manner. Dr Anne Tarrant is there to observe some new techniques in treating patients with acute depression, such as Miss Abrahams, by the use of electrodes which induce a state of pleasure. The sensation is, apparently, 'better than sex'. Another experiment involves a man called Beavis. The moment he experiences an induced psychotic and violent rage, he is suddenly becalmed. Professor Hetherington and Dr McEwan proudly tell Anne that he is radio-controlled.

The whole set up bothers Anne deeply as it doesn't treat the cause of patient's condition, and she tells Quist about her concerns. For him, it is 'simply an extension of Delgado's classic experiment – stopping the charging bull'. Quist suspects the root of Anne's worry is the conflict between her approach to psychiatry and that of Hetherington and McEwan. Sir George Holroyd is also interested in the work being done at the Unit and is suspicious of Anne's visit. Quist gets to meet Hetherington at a lunchtime symposium at the Royal Society on the subject of violence and the psychopath. Hetherington thinks that Freudian analysis has had its day, and he has fantasises about controlling violent patients by computer with a network of satellites covering the world.

Anne returns to the Unit and questions Dr McEwan, who defends the project. They can put more people back into society with their techniques than Anne would be able to at Broadmoor. But Anne wonders if they are curing them or just controlling them. She meets Beavis, who remembers her from the demonstration. He is pleased with his treatment and agrees to talk to her about it the following day. That night, McEwan warns Beavis that Anne will want to speak to him about the reasons that put him into the unit in the first place. Beavis has to control his anger. He doesn't want to recall the past, but agrees that Anne must be persuaded that their work is right and his treatment a success. The next day, Anne and McEwan argue over the process. McEwan shows that a computer monitors Beavis' brain waves, and if a violent urge is detected as a wave of expectancy, a signal is automatically sent to the receiver in Beavis' head to calm him down. Anne is concerned that the computer is taking over from the brain's natural inhibitor to violence. But for Beavis, the only alternative is a lifetime's incarceration in an expensive institution. He is a multiple murderer.

Anne wants to talk to Beavis away from the observation room, saying it is just an extension of McEwans' mechanised experiment. It is agreed. Beavis and Tarrant walk through the grounds of Weatheroak Hall where he describes recurring dreams and gets angry at the mention of his mother and his wife. Beavis attacks Anne, threatening to kill her. She defends herself, but in the process she knocks herself out on a bench. Beavis' receiver is dislodged; wires emerge from his ear. In a panic, he turns and runs. McEwan is troubled by the readings. He goes out to look for them and finds the unconscious Anne. Quist is alerted to the escape and Anne's plight by an unsympathetic Stafford. Quist is angry with Hetherington and McEwan but Anne blames herself for panicking. In the fields, Beavis tears the receiver away from his head. He discovers an isolated farmhouse. Inside, he finds a shotgun and holds the housewife, Emily, prisoner.

McEwan reveals that Beavis murdered his own family with a gun. He defends his project, seeing the computer as a way to free the upper brain from its primitive responsibilities, giving it truly creative freedom. McEwan had told Beavis this, and now Beavis has run away because he feels he has failed. Emily has given Beavis food and drink and asks him to go, but when her three children arrive home from school, she panics and warns one of them to run. Beavis holds the other two hostage. He begins to crack, confusing Emily for his wife. The police soon have the farmhouse surrounded, and McEwan goes in to talk to him, aware that he could be killed. Beavis releases the family and hands over to McEwan a piece of paper. Although he broke the cycle and did not harm the family, he does not want to go back to the Unit. He commits suicide with the shotgun, shooting himself through the heart to leave his brain intact. The note is his will, donating his brain to McEwan for research. To discover what went wrong.

Behind The Story

Following on from the analysis of the role of sex in society in 'Without the Bomb' and the degrading, trivialising and deceitful nature of pornography in 'Sex and Violence', here Dr Anne Tarrant takes a look at violence and this week's fear is psychosurgery. The issue of how to deal with hard-core psychotic murderers, and whether it is possible to rehabilitate them, was not a new one by any means. Using implants and computer control was a popular idea in the air at this time, and the concerns are expressed here by Dr Anne Tarrant: that they're fitting killers with a safety valve, rather than dealing with the original trigger. *A Clockwork Orange* had been released in the cinema not so long before this episode. Also, Hayles, or perhaps Anna Kaliski, may have read the 1971 book *Beyond Freedom and Dignity* by the American behavioural psychologist B F Skinner. McEwans' plea that man isn't born free echoes Skinner's idea that man is not an autonomous, individual being and that there is no divide between the mind and the body (it's one and the same, and thus there is no soul). Behaviour is created from the society or environment in which we live, and what we would define as crime is generated by the reaction to the social environment around us, its influences and so forth, and conventional punishments are therefore useless because they are based on a false premise. Punishment is ineffective in controlling behaviour if there is no free will – the option to choose your behaviour. He advocates a 'technology of behaviour', although 'Hair Trigger' may not have been what he had in mind. Or perhaps it was?

The experiment Quist refers to was by Dr José Manuel Rodriguez Delgado, who was a professor of physiology at Yale University. In 1963, he had a 'stimoceiver' implanted in the brain of a bull, and Delgado stopped it in full charge at the press of a button; he believed the electrical stimulus caused the bull to lose its aggression. In the episode we see some of the effects Delgado claimed as a result of the stimulation of the implant – elation, as in the case of the Miss Abrahams, and a cut-off, in Beavis. The computer that 'controls' Beavis is a fictionalisation of an experiment Delgado carried out on chimpanzees. Here, when the computer recognised a particular brain signal called a spindle, the stimoceiver sent a signal into the brain and caused a reaction. After a few hours, the chimp's brain was producing fewer spindles. We are no longer safe within our own thoughts. Delgado was hailed by *The New York Times* in 1970 as the 'impassioned prophet of a new pyschocivilized society'. This is the brave new world of Dr McEwan. Two researchers at Harvard Medical School, Frank Ervin and Vernon Mark, suggested that 'psychosurgery might quell the violent tendencies of blacks rioting in inner cities'. That did it. A psychiatrist called Peter Breggin described Delgado and others in this field as trying to create 'a society in which everyone who deviates from the norm … will be … surgically mutilated', with Delgado singled out as 'the great apologist for technologic totalitarianism'. Delgado would leave the USA in 1974 and return to his native Spain, his controversial work soon forgotten.

Perhaps it is a no better way of dealing with violent patients than lobotomies, which had been the preferred answer since the 1930s. A few weeks after the episode transmitted, *Horizon* showed 'The Surgery of Violence', a documentary on lobotomies. The programme was widely reviewed, and, for some viewers, the sight of a man having his head shaved in readiness for the knives about to go in was enough for them to switch off. It went out on the same night as the *Doomwatch* episode 'Flood', and when it was discussed by the Programme Review Board, Monica Sims commented that she would rather contemplate the destruction of millions of Londoners than the realism of the destruction of one man. A recent discussion on the subject had been recorded by the BBC at the Royal Institution. Opposition to lobotomies ruled the day.

The full implications of implants are not investigated in 'Hair Trigger'. Whose finger on the trigger? Perhaps this influenced Terence Dudley to pursue the Delgado experiment line in a less implausible storyline. But this is a *Doomwatch* story reacting to what has gone before rather than looking to the future and asking what if …? If murderers can be given implants, one day so can less serious criminals, your common-or-garden thief, for example. Then your anti-social teenager, and so on. Like tagging and DNA databases, it could get round to everyone. Just as Ervin and Mark fantasised over. Brain implants are still being investigated today to see if they can help Parkinson's disease and other illnesses.

Production
Story Development
Brian Hayles was invited to write his third script for *Doomwatch* in July and came in to see Terence Dudley on 3 August 1971. The result was 'Hair Trigger', the twelfth commission for the series, on 15 September. It wasn't due until the end of November. When Hayles did deliver, he changed the title to 'The Dreadful Has Already Happened …' but this was not acted upon.

The advisers on the episode were Dr Loucas from Broadmoor (who, as we saw in 'Waiting for a Knighthood', left there over alleged consent issues) and Dr William Grey Walter of Bristol University. This fascinating man specialised in studies of the brain. He discovered how flickering light can induce an epileptic fit, (which is the trigger for Beavis in the experiment at the top of the programme). The *New Scientist* of 29 March 1973 described how a company was developing strobe lighting as a form of riot control. Called a Photic Driver, the idea was that it would trigger fits in the protesters. Walter warned that if someone suffers a fit once, they are likely to again in later life. In the late 1940s he created some of the earliest light-seeking robots, called 'tortoises', perhaps an inspiration for Pedler and Davis' Cybermats in *Doctor Who*. At the time of the script, he was trying to recover from a serious head injury he had sustained in a motorcycling accident. He never quite recovered from the injury and died a few years later.

Director
'Hair Trigger' was thrown immediately into production. The director, Quentin Lawrence, was given this episode rather than the equally location-heavy 'Say Knife, Fat Man', which he was originally down to do. The filming took up the second week of production. The locations for the

Hall and the farm are currently unknown.

Casting

One of the most memorable aspects of this very strong episode of *Doomwatch* is Michael Hawkins' wonderful portrayal of Beavis. From his full and furious murderous outbursts or trying to control himself in the siege at the end to his considering if he is free to see Dr Tarrant another day, attempting a degree of dignity, it a sheer bravura performance. Hawkins had previously appeared in 'The Plastic Eaters'. Barry Jackson had been a successful stuntman and acrobat before becoming a full time actor. Never a leading man, Jackson was a familiar face on television. The same is true for Morris Perry who had recently played a regular role as a civil servant overlord in *Special Branch* for Thames. Victor Platt had played the sympathetic barman in 'Invasion'. Pamela Saire had been a Wren in 'Survival Code', and Gillian Lewis had been *Mr Rose's* secretary and side-kick in his first series.

Studio

'Hair Trigger' was the third episode to be recorded. It was videotaped in an unknown studio on Tuesday, 29 February 1972. In the only instance amongst surviving episodes, the end tag of the closing theme music is grafted onto the opening theme (and the edit can plainly be heard). The extra music accompanies captions of the episode's title and writer's credit, superimposed over a woodland painting. In a little directorial flourish, the painting is revealed to be a record sleeve from which Anne slips an LP to put on the record player at home (and it is the genuine sleeve of the album we then hear).

With her one off-screen line, this is Maria O' Brien's only surviving episode of *Doomwatch*. She is the voice on the phone telling the Minister that Dr Quist is on the line. Whether this is meant to be Susan or a Ministry switchboard operator is unclear. Maude Cane, who plays a female nurse, also pre-recorded her intercom line.

Stock Music

The sombre music at the top of the episode is not known. The same 'stab', used twice, comes from right at the end of 'Violent Pay Off' by Reg Tilsely from the Hudson De Wolfe album *Theme and Variation* – Tilsley Orchestral No 8 (DW/LP 3174). The two pieces of classical music are the 'Adagio Moderato and Adagio Cantabile' from Haydn's *String Quartet in D Major No. 5*, 'The Lark', played by the Smetana Quartet from an HMV album (ASB 2644). Rather appropriately, 'Storm in a Teacup' by *The Fortunes* is heard on the radio (Capitol Records CL 15707). Also heard on the radio is popular BBC DJ Terry Wogan.

Editing
The episode was edited on Wednesday, 2 March 1972 between 9 am and 1 pm.

Audience reaction
Nearly 10 per cent of the available audience watched the episode, compared to nearly 23 per cent for ITV. The excellent/boring index recorded a ratio of 79:21, making it the seventh most enjoyed story of the series. The plot achieved 74:26.

The audience research report: 'This week's "frightening" story about experiments to control a psychopath was sometimes considered to be an improvement over recent Doomwatch episodes – "stronger" dramatically, and with more "action". It was said to be thought-provoking in that it "could possibly be happening" now or in the near future. In fact the majority of the sample found it quite strongly appealing. Michael Hawkins was said to have given a very convincing portrayal of the patient. However, there was also some definite adverse criticism of the episode. Several viewers said it was such a distressing or "morbid" subject that they could not enjoy the play, while others thought it far-fetched and implausible. Some also complained that there was too much "scientific" discussion, which slowed the story down and was difficult to understand. General adverse criticism of the present *Doomwatch* series was also in evidence. Quite a number of viewers appeared to feel that there had been a deterioration of dramatic standards, or that the "original concept" of Doomwatch had been overlaid. It was suggested that the excitement had largely vanished, together with the "humanity and humour" now that Quist's team had become so "bureaucratised" and had lost much unpredictable, attractive and amusing personnel as John Ridge or the still-lamented Toby Wren. It now seemed pompous, moralistic, stilted and thoroughly depressing in thematic material: 'the script is trying to teach and comment rather than entertain.

'… Dr Quist (sometimes known to the viewers as "Quest" or "Twist") was odds-on favourite. It was partly because he seemed more real and complex than most other characters (the actor John Paul was sometimes credited here) and partly because viewers admired the independence of mind and notion, sincerity, idealism and calmness under stress he personified: it was "reassuring to think there may be such men around". Also, a handful appeared to derive satisfaction from identifying him with some kind of "typical scientist" image. Finally, it was observed that there would be no *Doomwatch* without him.

'Other characters had nothing like the same number of supporters among the sample audience. However, one of the two secondary leaders this week was Quist's wife Dr Tarrant – a "caring" character, it was said, who as a psychologist brought some interesting themes into the series, and who had played an important part in this week's episode. The other was the Minister, whose principal attraction would appear to be that he was a typical John Barron character superbly interpreted by John Barron. Next came John Ridge – not present this week -who was appreciated mainly for the way he always seemed to "liven things up" when he appeared, injecting both excitement and humour. Then there was the security man Neil Stafford: a bit of an enigma, it was said, initially unsympathetic but perhaps with "hidden depths", and according to one viewer "the handsomest man on television". The "feminine element" introduced by Barbara Mason (another character with "potential" it was suggested) was also welcomed by a few viewers, as was the quiet competence and intelligence of the neglected "backroom boy" Colin Bradley.'

3.07
Deadly Dangerous Tomorrow

Written by Martin Worth
Directed by Darrol Blake
Designed by Jeremy Davies
Transmitted: Monday, 17 July 1972 at 9.20 pm Duration: 48' 30"

Cast
Duncan (Michael Elwyn), Senator Connell (Cec Linder), His Excellency (Renu Setna), Hanif Khan (Madhav Sharma), Susan (Maria O'Brien), Miss Brandon (Lorna Lewis), Reporters (Bill Ward, Marc Zuber, John Wyman), Indian Woman (Mrs Rahat Shamsi), Indian Family (Ahmed Nagi, Talib, Farhat Shamsi).

Also appearing
Londoners/Police/Ambulance (Murray Noble, Frank Lester, Richard Smith, Bill Strange), Ernest (George Boon), Nurse (Jean St Louis), Reporters (Richard Smith, Jean St Louis, Michael Potter, Chris Edwards, Crawford Lyall, Murray Noble, Terry Leigh, Frank Lester, Ronald Gregory, Doris Kitts, Tracey Vernon, Fran Pomeroy, Dana Michie), Lab Assistants (Ann Garry Lee, David Ianson, David Pelton).

Technical Credits
Production Assistant: unknown. Assistant Floor Manager: Anna Yarrow. Director's Assistant: Philippa Clauson. Floor Assistant: Michael Throne.
Film Cameraman: Fred Hamilton. Sound Recordist: Malcolm Campbell. Film Editor: Alastair MacKay.
Costume Supervisor: Sheila Beers. Make-up Supervisor: Elizabeth Rowell.
Studio Lighting: Ralph Walton. TM2: Bob Warman. Vision Mixer: Chris Griffin.
Studio Sound: John Lloyd. Grams Operator: Gerry Borrows.

Radio Times
'A bunch of Indians squatting in a tent in St James' Park ... one of them with malaria? What's it all about?'

The Story
'A third of the world's population has a standard of living not known to man since the Garden of Eden. And the others ... the millions of others, would like some of it.' – Quist

As Duncan crosses St James' Park *en route* to Whitehall, he spots a tent amongst some bushes. Inside is a family of very sick Indians, staring back at him.

The children have malnutrition. The Minister wants to be kept informed of the incident as he briefs Quist upon the visit to Britain by the American Senator Connell. News reaches them of the discovery of a dead baby, found in the bushes behind the tent, and one of the children dies. At the hospital Stafford is assisted in his enquiries by a Westernised Pakistani called Hanif Khan. The mother cannot speak English and Hanif is trying to identify her language and dialect. Quist doesn't think it matters where they come from. The symbolism of their location is enough – a stone's throw from the seat of government.

Senator Connell's visit is to whip up support for a global ban on DDT. Quist wonders if there is a connection. Connell is comfortably based at the Hilton hotel and hopes for good coverage from the media. Duncan isn't too sure in light of events. Nothing is better than spraying DDT in combating malaria, argues Quist to Connell, who protests that mosquitoes are developing a resistance. Quist points out that this is only true in some areas; in the meantime, many will die unless crops are sprayed. Quist agrees DDT must be banned, but the way to do it is not by telling the developing world what is good for them, when really it is good for the West.

Doomwatch soon discover who is behind the stunt: John Ridge, as he returns to the office in search of Quist, although he won't admit to it. He is dedicated to letting India and other places have DDT, having seen at first hand the problems out there. Those countries are now able to manufacture it for themselves, which is bad news for the American companies that have been supplying them. A worldwide ban of DDT would allow those same companies to sell them new pesticides and keep the profits coming in. Ridge believes Connell is a stooge for the industry, sent on a mission disguised as ecological concern: 'A world ban on DDT is just what the American pesticide industry wants. Countries like India are setting up factories of their own nowadays to save them buying from America. And that's bad for Wall Street. But if they can be made to use more selective insecticides, which are still only largely obtainable from the States … If you knew the size of the profits to be had from pesticides, you'd know they can outweigh a conscience any time. Unscrupulous? To make it *look* respectable, they hire a Senator to tour the Capitals of Europe and persuade lofty, dedicated innocents like our own Doctor Quist to safeguard their profits in the name of world ecology.' Stafford takes Ridge away for questioning. Ridge is now disillusioned with Doomwatch, but Stafford wonders if he has taken up the cause of innocents and martyrs because he thinks he is one himself.

The press give Connell a rough ride, and he feels angry and humiliated when the dead Indian child is mentioned. The television news will not show an interview he pre-recorded in the US and will only agree to him appearing live on air. Unwilling to face the debate, Connell accuses his detractors of hysteria and resumes his tour of European cities. Stafford tells the Minister that Ridge cannot be charged with anything. Ridge has a statement he wishes to be publicised, but that will not incriminate him either. Both the Minister and Stafford are on Ridge's side at heart.

At Doomwatch Khan is trying to chat up Barbara Mason – and failing. Bradley is horrified at the idea of a whole Westernised Asian nation acting like Khan, much to Stafford's surprise. Bradley explains: 'When one of those low flying aircraft comes out of the hills, like some weird thing from another world, to spray an Indian wheat field, it's not just DDT that gets in their eyes – it's the American way of life. The fairyland over the ocean where water comes out of taps. As long as they go on equating progress with western technology, the most they'll ever be is a reach-me-down version of what we are now. The West will see to it they never get ahead of us. The logical extension of what Ridge is doing is not just more DDT, but more of everything the West can dump on them – till one day they'll find they have all the same problems we have without solving any of their own.'

Stafford's plan is for Ridge to spend the weekend in the country with Quist and Anne to see if they can persuade him not to issue his statement. The Minister leans on Quist to agree. Stafford tells Quist: 'Ridge just wants a cause. Never mind what it is. The last one sent him round the bend, so he's back using people to hit back with. An un-horsed crusader always feels a fool. It's not DDT or world famine on Ridge's mind. It's a shining white charger and a fine new banner to fly from his lance head. And you wouldn't be listening so closely to that bit of rhetoric if you didn't feel I could very well be right.'

Khan discovers where the Indian family come from, and a furious Ridge, who wanted to keep their origin a mystery to preserve media interest, calls him an 'arse-licking nit'. Quist sees the row and is shocked. He warns Ridge that the way he is going, he will have them all aspiring to be like Khan. The rest will be driven off the land by the factory farming and industrialisation. Ridge is discomforted by that. He spends the weekend as planned, on the agreement that if Quist can't dissuade him from his course of action, he will drive him down to the TV studios himself.

Quist and Anne's retreat is an isolated cottage, without even running hot water. Anne points out Ernest, a local man who is digging up some rough ground in the cottage's garden. He won't use the Rotavator Ridge suggests to him, even though there is one in the shed (rather too coincidentally, in Ridge's eyes). Ernest won't touch it. He enjoys digging. In the same way, Quist and Anne argue that these developing countries understand their native ecology better than the West. The scale of technology should be smaller: self-sufficiency as opposed to industrial combines. Quist confides that Ridge shook people of their complacency. It was worth it.

In Whitehall, the Minister meets the representative of the country from which the family originated. His Excellency rejects any question of aid in return for a ban on DDT. He knows if they don't ban it, their own exports would be embargoed. They will ban DDT themselves – but want nothing in return. They have their own techniques and expertise. He surprises the Minister by telling him the Government should leave them alone. They want nothing: 'Nothing. Not even advisers. Not even fellowships allowing our bright young men to study in the bastion of western technology, and then return to ruin their homeland with ideas which, because they're western, they now think our synonymous with progress. We wanted to ban DDT years ago, but we had the malaria problem. Now our own scientists, most of whom have never left the country, have found a way to alter the genes of mosquitoes so they grow an extra leg instead of a mouth. I'm sure your Doomwatch would be very shocked by that. What do we want? Your traffic exhausts? Your supersonic aircraft? Your sewage? Leave us alone, Minister, and in fifty years, the way things look over here, you'll come to us for aid.'

With everything set to blow over, no charges are brought against Ridge, who declines help from Quist in looking for a job. Meanwhile, the survivors of the Indian family are given a tour of the sights of London, surrounded by symbols of the former Empire.

Behind the Story

Doomwatch in pro-pesticide shock horror? It begins to look that way, but the view here is not so much pro-DDT but against the almost blanket use which had harmed America so much, causing books like *Silent Spring* to be written and the growing call in the country to ban or restrict its use. As Quist points out, India used it selectively. It is essential in fighting malaria. Before DDT, malaria was controlled by destroying breeding grounds of the mosquito and managing the habitat. DDT proved so effective that the World Health Organisation predicted malaria would be eradicated within a decade. India saw 100 million cases in 1952 reduced to a mere 60,000 by 1962. By the mid-1970s, those numbers were back into their millions. The mosquitoes had developed a resistance to organochlorine and dieldrin pesticides. The irony was that, because DDT proved so effective, research into combating malaria was halted by the governments of the countries which had it and they were left with hardly any scientific expertise to combat the resurgence. India had the third largest scientific manpower in the world in the 1970s. Their former Malaria Institute had been renamed as the National Institute of Communicable Diseases. They had to start from scratch.

For some environmentalists of the late 1960s and early 1970s, India was their favourite target. It was one of the most densely populated and impoverished nations in the world. *The Population Bomb* begins with the authors explaining that although they understood the problem intellectually, they didn't understand emotionally until 'one stinking hot night in Delhi'. Both Stafford and the Minister have had experience of India, as they relate in the episode, which is why they are sympathetic to Ridge's aims if not his means. India is no stranger to famines. Famine was once seen as the result of population explosions; it is now seen as a symptom of political instability, civil wars, etc. In other words, bad management. To eliminate this menace the Green Revolution was launched. The idea was the make the country self-sufficient in grain supplies by use of high-yield seeds, fertilisers and pesticides. Ridge mentions wheat in Pakistan, but it was wheat in India that was the success story.

This was something of a time bomb in itself. Ehlrich was dismissive: 'India couldn't possibly feed two hundred million more people by 1980 … Hundreds of millions of people will starve to death in spite of any crash programs.' Ridge wants India to have the technology that the West has if it will help feed their populations. By 1974 India had succeeded. But at a future price to the environment.

The real theme of the episode is how the West tries to manipulate the so-called underdeveloped countries into following the interests of the West, either economically, politically or socially, and keep them in their place. Let us leave them alone, argues the script. Connell represents the wealthy Western city dweller who thinks he knows what is best for the world. We don't know if he is in the hands of the pesticide or the agricultural lobby in America that wants to keep down competition from India and make more money from their farmers. Ridge thinks so; Quist, at the end of the episode, does not.

Connell knows that banning DDT in India will affect their Green Revolution, and the reporters side with Ridge about mechanising the subcontinent. Indeed, various companies set up plants to manufacture pesticides, ostensibly to support the Green Revolution (mentioned by Bradley) in making India self-sufficient in technology as well as agriculture, but it would be easy to exploit a developing country which had no suitable laws or regulations. 'Drawn by low cost labour, new markets and lower operation costs, corporations have little incentive to address environmental and human risks once they are entrenched.' (The International Campaign for Justice in Bhopal website, bhopal.net) In 1984 the world's worst industrial disaster occurred at Union Carbide in Bhopal: a gas leak which affected over 60,000 people.

So what is the alternative? Intermediate technology is the answer that the script suggests, although it had yet to have a name (and is now called appropriate technology). Workshops, not factories; rotavators, not combine harvesters; things an ordinary man could afford, not the things so expensive only the big time farmers could have them. The term was coined by radical economist and philosopher Ernst Schumacher, and it had its own expression in Britain in the 1970s with the alternative technology movement. The organisation Schumacher formed in 1973, now called Practical Action, has had full-scale regional programmes in Nepal, Bangladesh, the Sudan and Latin American countries. Is this another way of the West telling the Rest what's good for them? You decide.

Production
Scripting Development
This was the last script to be commissioned for the third series, on 17 February 1972 and was needed by the end of March. Robert Homes declined the chance to write an episode exploring views on the Third world and DDT, so Terence Dudley offered this difficult subject to Martin Worth, who was keen to do a third script. But he hit problems with 'Say Knife, Fat Man' and didn't want to tackle another story until the New Year. This was fine for Dudley, and Worth was sent material on DDT in November. Worth found the subject didactic and feared that his script was, too. Dudley certainly found that the script contained too many long speeches for Bradley and Anne, and Quist didn't have enough to say. Darrol Blake remembers this being a common problem. 'Every now and then you'd have a giant speech, which I called undigested research material, and the poor actor had to make that sound like human speech. Some actors were better at it than others, some writers were better at it than others! I certainly didn't get that with Stuart Douglass, but that was an endemic problem with that series.'

One change that was requested but not acted upon was the opening itself: Dudley didn't want a civil servant to blunder across the malaria victims in the tent, probably because of how implausible it would be for him to peer inside, but Worth simply couldn't think of a viable replacement that would provide the contrast he wanted. He delivered the rewritten script on 9 April 1972.

Advisors
Anne Tarrant speaks of an American friend of hers who had witnessed

how close an understanding Philipino farmers had of their local ecology, hundreds of women and children crawling amongst growing cucumbers and individually wrapping each one to protect it from pests. This actually came from a conversation Martin Worth had with a friend of his. The advisers for the episode were Professor Leonard Bruce-Chwatt, a leading expert on malaria from the London School of Tropical Medicine; Dr Thomas Lambo, soon to be Deputy Director-General of the World Health Organisation, who was well- known for encouraging the acceptance of medical treatments by the people of his native Nigeria; and Dr Gordon Conway of Imperial College, who, according to Imperial College's website, worked in Malaysia in the 1960s on pest management programmes and sustainable agriculture.

Cuts:
There were a few changes between rehearsal and camera script, such as the relocation of a scene between Ridge and Stafford from a police station interview room set in the studio to a back of a car stuck in a traffic jam on film and the substitution of Duncan for an anonymous civil servant in the opening sequence. The country cottage Quist and Anne take Ridge too was originally in Cornwall.

When Connell and Quist discuss the Indian family discovered in the park:
QUIST: It's not just the joke that's sick.
CONNELL: Some bunch of leftists, I guess, trying to cause discontent. We've had our share of this in the States. A guy in flames on the pavement, and what the hell difference did it make to Vietnam anyway?

Stafford was less than sympathetic about the Indians when he speaks to Ridge. 'Some coon lingo? Why can't these people learn English?'

Ridge and Bradley argued over the merits of pesticides longer. Bradley warns him: 'There'll be even less to eat if these chlorinated hydrocarbon pesticides go on being used. DDT is not the only one you know. There …
RIDGE: That's just another of your fashionable ecologist's bogeys.
BRADLEY: As long as the doses always have to be increased –
RIDGE: Connell's not concerned with that anyway.

When Anne tells Ridge about her American friend and his experiences with Philipino farmers and their children …
QUIST: I expect the American thought they ought to have been at High School anyway.
RIDGE: Perhaps they should. Until they have proper education –
ANNE: Education can wait.

RIDGE: So the West can keep ahead as usual?
ANNE: I mean, not send them to school till they're 16 at least. An adult can learn more in a year than a child can in five. So it's far more economic to let children work in the field as they're accustomed to and not send them to school till they're old enough to learn quickly. The money saved on teachers can be spent on other necessities.

And later in the same scene:
QUIST: There are always strings attached to aid.
ANNE: All aid ever does is make them more and more dependent on us. The countries which really are now beginning to prosper are the ones who've said no to aid. Instead of getting what they're given, they work for what they need.
RIDGE: I admit their farmers often know much more about the ecology of their own bits of land than any Western 'expert'. I saw one man going about his crops, spraying a leaf here, a stalk there, sometimes with one pesticide, sometimes another. Sometimes leaving whole areas out. He seemed to know intuitively what he was doing.
QUIST: He knows his land; we don't.

Filming
The script was given to Darrol Blake to direct, and this would be his fourth and final episode of the third series. Filming took place in London and Surrey during the first week of May. Blake decided to do something a little special with the opening sequence. The plan was to shoot long shots of St James' Park and various memorials to imperialism for the top of the programme. Darrol Blake: 'My [director's assistant] at the time, Philippa Clauson, had a relative in the Guards or the Household Cavalry. We were going to film the Changing of the Guard from the Victoria Memorial to set the mood of Empire. I said, "Wouldn't it be great that when they turn up, they are playing 'Rule Britannia'?" She said, "Leave it with me ..." We were filming and had the camera on the Memorial in front of Buckingham Palace, and as the band reached the railings they changed from 'South Pacific' into 'Rule Britannia'! It was absolutely miraculous! I added in one or two shots of St James' Park and then cut to Elstead Common for the close ups of the tent and so forth because we couldn't put a tripod down in a Royal Park. We could take shots from outside of the park, but you weren't allowed in with a unit and certainly not a tent.'

Elstead Common was used because it was near the location of the cottage scene with Ridge and the rotavator. This was filmed on 4 May, the day before the director's birthday. Darrol Blake: 'I remember we were going out on location in a limousine. You never know what transport the BBC are going to send for you to take you out to location; it might be an old bus or a limo, it's really very funny! Anyway, there's this limo with a lambs' wool rug in the back, and we were going to location in the one about the Indians, out to a common in Surrey for the tent scene and various other things. And as were driving along Simon looked at me and said, "Better than working, innit?" I remember on that location we had a cottage, and I had a cherry picker and I did a very, very, high shot of this cottage.'

Casting
The small cast assembled was quite notable. Cec Linder played the Senator. He is perhaps best remembered by science fiction fans as being in the Rudolph Cartier BBC production of *Quatermass and the Pit*, playing the Canadian Dr Rooney. He was also one of the actors to play Felix in a James Bond film. Madhav Sharma was a regular face on television at this time. He had recently played a con man, taking advantage of people's embarrassment at appearing prejudiced in *Public Eye*. The following year, he would be a regular on the short- lived *Moonbase 3* and would also appear in *Doctor Who*'s 'Frontier in Space', playing a political prisoner on the moon. Lorna Lewis plays the Senator's secretary. She would play the regular character of Pet in *Survivors*, from the second series onwards, after writing to producer Terence Dudley for a job and enclosing a silver spoon. Renu Setna, appearing here as His Excellency, would often be called upon in the 1970s and 1980s when a sympathetic Asian character was required.

Music
The Scots Guards may have been the uncredited extras for the episode as it is their music which is listed in the PasB listing for the episode and it does not come from LPs. They played extracts from 'Rule Britannia', 'Now Your Days of Philandering Are Over' from Mozart's *The Marriage of Figaro* and another unidentified extract from the same opera. This was the only music for the episode.

Studio
'Deadly Dangerous Tomorrow' was the tenth episode to be recorded for the series. It was videotaped in TC1 on Tuesday, 23 May 1972.

Editing
Editing was performed on 25 May 1972 between 2:30 pm and 11 pm.

Reviews
New Scientist thought that the episode made 'a fair job of airing the differences between rich and poor countries' approaches to environmental problems', but for the *Daily Telegraph*'s Richard Last, the return of Ridge

was the worst television news of the week. 'He bounded into Doomwatch like a wild-eyed stage villain, truculent as ever and still clearly mad as a hatter. Even without him I no longer give the series much chance of credibility. It spends its time being impossibly melodramatic or making its characters talk like hand-outs – sometimes both.' Simon Oates had been in the *Daily Express* some ten days earlier when he was romantically linked with actress Dorothy Squires, who had been married to Roger Moore.

Audience Reaction

'Deadly Dangerous Tomorrow' did not go down too well with the audience research panel, either. On the Entertaining/Boring ratio it scored 72:23. Compared to the other known figures, this makes it the second most unpopular episode of the series, after 'Without the Bomb'. Clearly, episodes with debates about population problems weren't well received by those who responded.

The script was published in the out of print anthology book which took for its title *Deadly Dangerous Tomorrow*.

3.08
Enquiry

Written by John Gould
Directed by Pennant Roberts
Designed by Raymond London
Transmitted: Monday, 24 July 1972 at 9.28 pm Duration: 49′ 33″

Cast
Michael Clark (Jack Tweddle), Susan Lewis (Ann Curthoys), Dr Evans (Michael Forrest), Dr Margary Becker (Margaret Ashcroft), Colonel Jones (Barrie Cookson), Stephen Grigg (Michael Keating), Mr Clark (James Ottaway), Dr O'Dell (Eddie Doyle), Tractor Driver (Malcolm Johns)

Also appearing
Extras on location:Jay Neill, Alastair Meldrum, Michael Reynell, Adrian Reynolds, Leslie Weekes.

Extras in studio: Joe Santo Dilys Marvin, Terry Francis, Maureen Neill, Roger Marston, James Matthews.

Technical Credits
Director's Assistant: Adele Paul. Production Assistant: Robert Checksfield. Assistant Floor Manager: Hilda Marvin. Floor Assistant: Mike Thorne.
Film Cameraman: Fred Hamilton. Sound Recordist: Basil Harris. Film Editor: Alastair MacKay.
Costume Supervisor: Sheila Beers. Costume Assistant: Ken Trew. Make-up Supervisor: Elizabeth Rowell. Make-up Assistant: Judy Courtney.
Props: Peter Sporle.
Studio Lighting: Ralph Walton. TM2: Bob Warman. Vision Mixer: Rhoda Carrs.
Sound Supervisor: John Lloyd. Grams Operator: Gerry Borrows.
Crew: 1.

Radio Times
'The toxic particles are released in the form of an aerosol … It makes it possible to defeat an enemy army without inflicting any casualties on them or on the civilian population.'

The Story
'War's immoral anyway. Why divide it up? You can shoot someone, but

435

not gas them; blow their heads off, not poison them; fry them alive, but not frighten them into submission. What kind of sense is that?' – Susan Lewis

In a village street, a young man is terrified by the sight of a tractor and its driver. He is a lab assistant at nearby Longside Camp and is taken back there, straitjacketed, in an ambulance. The army camp doctor, Evans, is convinced that the man, Michael Clark, has suffered a severe nervous breakdown and has him heavily sedated. Quist and Anne are not convinced. The camp is developing a new form drug called lobotomin, which can induce passivity or, in its strongest form, abject terror. It makes it possible to defeat an enemy army without inflicting any casualties on them or the civilian population. Dr O'Dell and Dr Becker demonstrate their technique on guinea pigs. Anne points out that Clark is showing precisely the same symptoms as the terrified guinea pigs that have been administered with the stronger form of lobotomin. Becker says it is impossible for Clark to have been exposed, even accidentally, to the drug.

Anne examines Clark once the sedation wears off. He is so frightened that he collapses into a catatonic stupor. Colonel Jones, the camp's commander, grudgingly concedes it is possible that the young man took the drug deliberately, but is appalled by the idea that someone might have poisoned him with it. Soon, Stafford, Bradley and Barbara Mason arrive to form part of the enquiry, ordered by the Minister, who is suspicious of the similarities between Clark's illness and the effects of lobotomin. First to give evidence is Susan Lewis, one of Clark's fellow lab assistants, and she is hostile towards their questions, especially when Stafford probes into Clark's private life. Lewis tells them that she has no problem with the work they are doing. After all, despite the Geneva Protocols governing chemical and biological warfare, CS gas is freely employed, and she believes it saves lives. And napalm is being used in Vietnam. Bradley is shown the security precautions taken in storing and accessing the drug, and he realises that Clark cannot have removed any without someone else countersigning. And Clark's access had been withdrawn a month earlier, when he went off-shift.

Later, Quist is concerned that no-one is giving them any information that brings Clark's character to life. Stephen Grigg is the next witness. He too is shocked at the idea of someone deliberately taking lobotomin. He remembers that Clark used to moan about the drug, but no more than that. Stafford wants to know why Clark was taken off a three month shift just before he had his last weekend leave. Colonel Jones explains that anyone could apply to be relieved before the end of their rota. They never enquire why, so they don't know the reason for his taking leave. He had certainly seen Dr Evans beforehand as a matter of routine. At Quist's behest, Anne visits Clark's parents in Exeter. She meets Mr Clark, a widower, whose wife recently died from a brain tumour after a three-year illness. This surprises Anne – it is not in Clark's file.

Quist gets angry with Dr Evans' evidence, unable to decide if he is simply incompetent or deliberately obstructive. Evans sticks to the likelihood that Clark has had a nervous breakdown but agrees that there were none of the expected indications before Clark went on leave. Then, he too has to admit that Clark may have taken a dose of lobotomin. Colonel Jones explains that, at the time, it appeared to be the most fitting explanation, but it seemed impossible. Now, thanks to Doomwatch's investigations, they know that is not the case. As Quist wonders what could have made Clark so emotional and confused to do such a thing, Anne reports the news of his mother's death. Evans and Jones are almost relieved. But she had died three weeks before Clark self-administered the drug. Why delay? And anyway, after the death, Clark had seemed relieved that his mother was no longer suffering. Susan Lewis is recalled for questioning. She finally admits she helped Clark obtain the lobotomin. The cancer had ravaged his mother's brain to the point where she had no control over her mind or bodily functions. He had planned to use the lobotomin to kill her and put her out of her misery.

Meanwhile, Clark is muttering to himself. Anne examines him; he is deaf and blind. But not physically – he has become so afraid of all around him that he has simply switched off his senses. Jones reveals that Clark was under observation by Grigg, in reality working for internal security as part of standard procedure, but his reports indicate nothing about Clark forcefully objecting to lobotomin, only his views on other members of staff. Grigg didn't know about Clark's mother, and nothing he ever said was enough to make Grigg think he would take a dose of 'that stuff'. Meanwhile, Mr Clark arrives at the camp with a letter his son had sent him. It seems that Clark had linked his mother's condition with what may happen when lobotomin is used. As a protest to bring the matter to public attention, he took the drug instead of merely landing himself in prison by going to the underground or foreign press. Colonel Jones interprets the letter in his own way: the boy was confused and disturbed; that's the end of the matter. It could have been a lot worse for him had he gone to the press.

Anne tells the father what has happened to his boy. He might get better when the drug has worn off, but they don't know what damage has been done. Mr Clark wishes he knew what was going on inside his head. We get a glimpse of some strange, transcendental journey. Mr Clark says that if this is what it does to people, he thinks they ought to stop making it. The Doomwatch team set out for London. Stafford and Quist have a report to write, and the expression on their faces tells us all we need to know about what they think of lobotomin.

Behind the Story

That this script was written by the author of 'In the Dark', John Gould, would be quite surprising if you did not already know. Whereas, say, the emotional intensity and pessimism of Louis Marks' scripts makes them unmistakable, and a fluidity in dialogue distinguishes Martin Worth's stories, there are no real Gould-isms that stand out. 'In the Dark' was funny, reflective and sombre in its style. 'Enquiry' is a detective story; what made a laboratory assistant in a military chemical warfare research lab, develop the same symptoms as a potential victim of the nerve gas they were developing? There are cover- ups, false trails, obstreperous witnesses and tragedy, all the way up to the dénouement.

This season's theme is rapidly becoming the manipulation of mankind for its own good, whether it's sticking diodes in the brain of violent offenders, banning DDT with a carrot-and-stick approach or giving a contraceptive aphrodisiac properties to reduce the population. Now we have a new, nice nerve gas, one that makes you so frightened you make yourself blind and deaf.

With a title like 'Enquiry' one could be forgiven for expecting a retread of 'The Inquest', which, once the episode got going, became just that and rarely ventured outside of the inn within which it was set. Thankfully, 'Enquiry' is set within a military camp, but there isn't too much desk action to make this a post-watershed version of *Crown Court*. What makes a change from the usual *Doomwatch* fare is how the team descend upon the army camp *en-masse*, leaving only Susan back in London. Unlike other scripts this series, there are no long speeches and no information dumps. The dialogue is very terse and to the point.

Zeitgeist

As soon as the Allies occupied the conquered German territories after the Second World War was won, the Americans and Russians began to collect Nazi scientists for their knowledge. The Americans had Operation Paperclip, which famously brought the science of the V2 rocket project to land a man on the moon. They also discovered stock piles of chemical weapons, banned under the Geneva convention, but the research continued, and the Americans wanted to continue the research, convinced that the Russians would do the same in their preparations for the next World War ... Work on chemical and biological weapons was enough in the 1960s to bring concerned scientists together under the British Society for Social Responsibility in Science. They too believed that the scientist could no longer be passive and simply allow the politicians or the military make decisions. Chemical weapons would be their first and very controversial cause.

The subject matter for the episode is not so much whether these type of weapons should be developed or not, but of the impact it has on the people carrying out the research. Susan Lewis gives a pragmatic account of her attitude towards chemical warfare but rather forgets that its ban is more to protect civilians, theoretically anyway, than soldiers. Even the Colonel of the base is not terribly keen on using these weapons. So whilst those questioned were mildly bothered by their work, only Michael Clark saw the horror of the slow, lingering death his mother was enduring and equated it with lobotomin.

The Vietnam War was raging. Napalm and Agent Orange was deployed and the former is mentioned in 'Enquiry', as is CS gas, which was notorious as a way of dealing with angry students in the various flashpoints of 1968 and nearly became a plot line for the first series in 'The Pacifiers'. In 1970 the British Government did not see CS gas as being covered by the Geneva Protocols of 1925. It was being used in Northern Ireland as crowd control and would have become politically impossible to justify if its use in war was banned. Would lobotomin have been used for civilian disturbances? We are never told. Lobotomin tries not to kill, but frighten; it makes a population temporarily docile and unable to resist invasion, but they have also developed a version that produces terror. It is not a biological weapon as such. A real life Lobotomin was indeed one of the dreams of research. To make an army incapable of fighting.

Production
Script Development
John Gould was commissioned to write the script on 23 September 1971, when it was known as 'The Mind Boggles'. John Gould was clearly on Terence Dudley's side when it came to his fall out with Gerry Davis and Kit Pedler. When in July 1971 he was invited to write his second script for the series, he needed reassurances from the producer that the '*Doctor Who* concept', as it was called,' was entirely Kit and Gerry's' which had been 'the prime cause of the squabbles' in 1970. He felt that they had compromised too much with the Cowboy/Adventure school of drama. 'The inevitable levity is a total error.' Dudley replied with his assurances and hoped that Pedler's conversion to ecology has not made him a bore yet.

Gould was interested in exploring the 'dark side of Doomwatch's moral and philosophical dilemma.' He suggested a programme about cancer as a starting point. He delivered 'The Mind Boggles' late in the middle of November, and his rewrites were acknowledged on 17 March 1972. Gould felt that the episode needed only Quist, Stafford and Tarrant to carry the plot. He also wanted to be ambiguous with the precise motivation behind the man taking his own drug: 'You can never be absolutely certain why a person has done something.' The title was changed to become the more sensible 'Enquiry' when it was handed over to Pennant Roberts to direct – his first London-based drama for the BBC.

Casting
Barrie Cookson, here playing Colonel Jones, had previously appeared as Dr Wilson in 'Invasion', dealing with another defensive weapon. Michael Keating, as Griggs, was an actor Pennant Roberts would cast again in 1977 in an edition of *Doctor Who*, and the pair would also work together later that same year on *Blake's 7*, in which Keating was the only actor to appear in all fifty-two episodes. Tractor driver Malcolm Johns will be seen again, in an uncredited role, in 'The Killer Dolphins'. Michael Forrest had been in a John Gould scripted episode of *The Spies* with Simon Oates. Margaret Castleton was a regular in the ITV solicitor drama *The Main Chance*. Ann Curthoys would become a regular in *The Tomorrow People* in 1975.

Filming
Filming began on Monday, 24 April 1972 during rehearsals for 'High Mountain'. This was one of the few occasions when the entire regular cast were on location together, even though they say nothing and are just being driven about in a car.

As well as the normal filming, a dream-like montage sequence was used for our glimpse inside Clark's head. Terence Dudley was pleased with the final result and told Gould on 20 June that the episode looked 'super' and 'I know you'll approve of the intra-pyscho bit which has terrific impact.' One viewer commenting on the former *doomwatch.org* website remembers it looked like one of the *Top of the Pops* psychedelic light effects, but ended with a bird swooping down at the camera.

Studio
'Enquiry' was the ninth episode to be recorded. It was videotaped in TC1 on Friday, 12 May 1972. No music was used in the episode except for the titles. Guinea pigs were needed in the studio and had to react on cue to Dr Becker, both backing away from her finger and not reacting at all. The camera script allowed time for a retake if the scene didn't work first time. A lobby set outside the Colonel's door was added to the script.

Editing
It was edited on Monday, 15 May 1972.

Audience reaction
'Enquiry' was fifth in the Entertaining/Boring stakes, with a ratio of 82:16 in favour. The plot scored 79:21, making it the fourth most rated of the series.

Aftermath

When Kit Pedler made public his views on the new series of *Doomwatch*, Gould wrote to Dudley to offer his sympathies and support, something he was delighted to read. 'My Dearest John – What a nice letter and how welcome. Kit, to say the least, has been, is being, highly unprofessional but who's to know that. Internecine squabbles make good copy. I can't hit back – hence a letter such as yours is doubly welcome. One's peers are all that matter in the long run.'

Gould's later work included *The Donati Conspiracy*, a three part conspiracy thriller about life under a harsh regime in Britain, and episodes of *Spy Trap* and *State of Emergency*, the last of which he also created. All three programmes were script edited by Simon Masters, who had the sad duty of writing Gould's obituary for *The Stage* in 1974. John Muirhead-Gould died aged only 36, leaving behind a wife and a baby daughter.

3.09
Flood

Written by Ian Curteis
Directed by Quentin Lawrence
Designed by Oliver Bayldon
Transmitted: Monday, 31 July 1972 at 9.25 pm Duration: 49' 49"

Cast
Dr Ridley (Derek Benfield), Lieutenant-Commander Morrison (Patrick Jordan), Dr Ericson (Wensley Pithey), Critchley (Raymond Mason), Assistant (David Landon), General (Robert Raglan), GLC Man (Robert James), Ministry of Defence Man (Michael Lees), Lieutenant (Steve Kelly), BBC Reporter (Tim Nicholls), BBC Disc Jockey (Keith Skues)

Also appearing
Marine Guard (Peter Roy), Naval Officer in NATO Basement (Ian Munro), Naval Officer in NATO Ops Room (Peter Whittaker), Wrens (Barbara Burmel, Jean Sadgrove), Marines (Brian Nolan, Alan Lenoire, Ron Tingley, Alan Thomas), Sailor/Messenger (Steve Ismay), Sailors (Kevin Moran, Roy Pierce)

Extras on location only: Bill Burridge, Richard Lawrence, Brychan Powell, Bill Prentiss, Leslie Bates, Jay Neill, Ian Elliott, Kerry Sartain, Cy Town, David Billa, Dennis Plenty, David Waterman, David Melbourne, Margaret Pilleau

Technical Credits
Director's Assistant: Jill Rodger. Assistant Floor Manager: Brian Roberts. Production Assistant: Robert Checksfield. Assistant PA: Peter Novis. Floor Assistant: Michael Throne.
Film Cameraman: Fred Hamilton. Sound Recordist: Basil Harris. Film Editor: Alastair MacKay.
Costumes: Sheila Beers. Make-up Designer: Elizabeth Rowell.
Studio Lighting: John Dixon. TM2: Dickie Ashman. Vision Mixer: Rhoda Carrs.
Sound Supervisor: Chick Anthony. Grams: Gerry Borrows.
Props: Peter Sporle. Senior Cameraman: Doug Routledge.
Crew: 1.

Radio Times

Come the tide, come the tide? 'One more inch! A mere inch and we would have had a full-scale disaster in the very heart of London.'

The Story

'I must go, there's another meeting. An emergency committee in case there's a third wave – Operation Gopherwood ... What Noah's Ark was made of.' – Quist

As Colin Bradley is driving Dr Quist along the banks of the Thames, a late evening radio programme is interrupted to give a flood warning. Quist is disturbed. This is the second night in a row. In the London Flood Room, Critchley and Ericson, the chief engineer, are also disturbed: surge warnings from Southend disobey just about every natural law in the book. Quist telephones Stafford from the Flood Room, asking him to get in touch with the Admiralty for sea conditions near Greenland, something which Stafford thinks might be classified, but he will try. The surge is now twenty-five minutes from London Bridge. The North Sea is as calm as a millpond, so why the high tidal surge? The worst case scenario would be if the tide becomes one foot higher than the defences. A full-scale disaster would ensue, with normal life in London becoming impossible for days, even weeks in some areas.

Thankfully, the surge stops within an inch of a foot. This inch horrifies the Minister, who asks for Quist's report. Quist doesn't believe the flooding's cause is man-made, and certainly not from a nuclear explosion, as that would have been detected. The Minister implies that the incident might be one of a series, and Quist becomes suspicious. The Minister wants the cause discovered by midday – and backed up with evidence to take to the Cabinet. After Quist leaves, the Minister makes a call to NATO Headquarters in Paris. At Doomwatch, Barbara is taking down data relayed by the Flood Room while Dr Ridley, a government seismologist, works with Bradley in the Doomwatch lab. The focus of their attention is the Barents Sea, where considerable seismic activity has been recorded over the past couple of days. NATO also have a presence in the area, conducting routine exercises.

Quist joins the Minister at the Flood room, where an emergency committee is discussing what to do in the event of a third and higher surge that night. The Minister won't be drawn into why he fears a third event might be possible. Ericson points out what is at risk from the flood: a population of one million, two hundred thousand; fifteen power stations, four major sewage works; forty-six miles of underground and seventy stations, some of which are already out of action. After the Minister leaves with Quist, the representative from the GLC confides to a high-ranking

Army official that he thinks the Minister knows far more than he is letting on. Walking back to his car, the Minister tells Quist that he needs proof of a cause in two hours. Noting Quist's appearance after staying up through the night, he also wryly points out that a shave is always good for morale. Back at Doomwatch, Quist still isn't convinced that the moving of the sea bed is the result of nuclear activity, which would be prohibited since the Test Ban Treaty and SALT (Strategic Arms Limitation Talks). But it transpires that General Gunnerson of NATO has arrived in London, spotted when he attended a Cabinet meeting. Stafford offers to go to Eastern Fleet HQ and find out what they know. Bradley is sent to investigate the NATO exercises, using a plane loaned from the American Air Force on the pretext of 'urgent scientific research'.

Stafford is able to enter the NATO base quite easily but has to convince Lieutenant-Commander Morrison of his former rank and status by answering a series of questions which only a true Naval Officer would able to (such as the correct pronunciation of C-in-C – which is 'sink'.) Some kind of large and important operation is definitely happening. Whilst waiting to see someone in authority, Stafford loses patience and enters the Ops Room, where he asks a few questions before the alarm is raised and he is arrested. Bradley, flying over the Barents Sea, reports by radio on what he can see of the NATO exercises. He spots the presence of Russians. This is enough for Quist, along with all the data provided by Ericson and Ridley.

After the Minister tells off Quist for Stafford's arrest, he listens to an angry tirade about the stupidity of nuclear testing on the sea bed, practically on their doorstep. 'It's unbelievable, the ultimate lunacy! Right here, within a few hundred miles of Europe's coastline, nuclear devices are being exploded under the sea floor! And it seems with the full fore-knowledge of NATO! About the one ray of hope in a world going mad was the Test Ban Treaty! And the SALT talks! The one area of progress, the one definite sign that we had become so frightened of what we were doing, we were prepared to compromise with our worst enemies to achieve something! If it weren't for the Treaty, there's little doubt we wouldn't have survived 'til now, do you realise that, with the increasing level of fallout from nuclear tests, year by year!' The tests had caused a blow out, giving rise to a tsunami which surfaced as it entered the shallows of the North Sea, reaching the Thames Estuary twenty hours later as a ten-foot wave when it coincided with the normal high tide. The Minister, not impressed by Quist's 'school boy bombast' admits that he knew about the tests and had been fighting tooth and nail to prevent them. But he can say no more. He telephones the Prime Minister for a meeting, and, as he waits, asks Quist if he, in his place, would have resigned and taken the news to the press. Quist confirms that he would have. 'Sometimes, Quist, your sheer naïveté has me breathless.'

The Minister hopes their case is watertight; they had been assured that there was no possibility of any surface disturbance from an explosion of that depth. They are too late to stop the third test, and there are three more to come. After meeting the Prime Minister, Quist goes to see Stafford at the NATO Eastern Fleet HQ. They cannot talk openly, but Stafford drops hints about the Aleutian Islands, disguising it as holiday destination small-talk. Back in London, the GLC man, the Army official and others on the Flood Committee are appalled at how little they can do by way of prevention. Even the evacuation points may not be safe anymore. And the weather is worsening.

There are seven hours left before the wave hits London. Quist tells the Minister of another problem – all the fish that have been killed by the blast. Even the ones that survived may be contaminated and will not be fit to eat. A cover story is prepared concerning the leakage of toxic chemicals dumped on the sea bed. The freak weather will have broken open their containers. Quist asks about the trawler men and the tens of thousands who depend on fish for their living.

However, the weather conditions change so markedly that the only areas affected will be the low-lying parts of Kent and Essex, where some flooding has already occurred. The next day, Quist works out the background to the whole near-disaster. The US had insisted on going ahead with their secret tests on the Aleutian Islands, and the Russians would only continue arms limitation talks if they could test some of their new warheads too. A miscalculation pushed the Russian tests from the relative safety of Barents Sea onto the continental shelf, where there are certain unpredictable elements like turbidity currents. Quist suddenly feels tired and compares himself to King Canute, who, as the Minister reminds him, drowned …

Behind the Story

'Flood' is the closest *Doomwatch* ever comes to becoming a documentary-drama, with its electrifying tension as the threat of the flood gets worse and worse and very little anyone can do about it. The script is resplendent in detail, although the considerable research performed for it is not forced into the dialogue. Thus, it should come as no surprise that this lost episode was well-regarded at the time and is one John Barron remembered fondly. We get descriptions of how those parts of London most likely to be affected would be evacuated and the problems the army would face in mobilising its forces in time (with a reference to commitments in Northern Ireland, where the British troops were most active). An extra line was written into the script where Ericson thinks that even the soldiers at Buckingham Palace would have to be drafted in: 'They'll have to change the guard some other time.'

Bomb Tests

The underlying cause of the flood is a series of secret nuclear bomb tests performed by the Russians as compensation for an American test the year before. The trade-off was in order to safeguard the Strategic Arms Limitation Talks (SALT) that were going on at this time. Quist refers to how radioactive fallout had been slowly poisoning the world until overground testing had been halted. The Partial Test Ban Treaty had come into effect in 1963 and was signed by the US, the USSR and Britain. However, it did not prevent underground testing. In April 1971 Dr Frank Barnaby (an adviser during this series) wrote in *New Scientist* on the subject and explained that it was time to complete the test ban. He wrote that, on average, there had been one nuclear test per week over the previous two years. Swedish authorities had detected large underground explosions, and leakages of radioactivity had occurred.

The character of Dr Ridley was based upon Dr Hal Thirlaway, who headed a group at Blacknest, a house just outside (but connected to) the Atomic Weapons Research Establishment at Aldermaston in Berkshire. For over forty years it specialised in forensic seismology, researching techniques to distinguish the seismic signals generated by underground nuclear explosions from those generated by earthquakes. Remarkably, the work at Blacknest was not secret and the group could share their research, even with the Russians. On the rehearsal script which survives for the episode, Dr Thirlaway's phone number was scribbled into the margin as a reminder to check on certain technical pronunciations. 1972 was the year Thirlaway would be awarded the Gold Medal of the Royal Astronomical Society for his work on seismology. The character was originally called Dr Tadley. Tadley is the nearest town to Aldermaston.

Floods

So what of the flood menace itself, exacerbated by the shifting sea bed? The episode postulated the combination of the wave generated by the tests with a normal high tide and, later, with another event – strong gale-force winds blowing south. There had been deadly floods before in London, such as those in 1928 which left thousands homeless. However, as the Minister remembers, the most recent calamity had occurred late in February 1953, when a lethal combination of high spring tide and severe wind storm had caused a storm tide, overwhelming flood defences in England and Holland. 2,000 people in the Netherlands and 307 people in England were killed. East Anglia was very badly affected and the banks of the Thames within Central London came very close to overflowing. The events triggered the creation of the London Thames Barrier. In the script, the representative from the Greater London Council (GLC) thinks the barrier would be finished by 1978, then six years away. The site in

Woolwich had been chosen by 1971; work eventually began in 1974 and was finished by 1982.

In the meantime, London was at risk. The London Flood Warning Room came into being in 1967 at Room 480, Horseferry Road, Westminster. It was run by the Ministry of Agriculture and the GLC in conjunction with the National East Coast Storm Tide Warning Service. The Ministry's chief engineer was Eric Johnson. In the script, the man in charge is called Ericson. The script accurately details the activity in the Flood Room if a tidal surge was heading down from the North Sea to threaten London. Any possible surge would first be spotted in the Shetland Islands. Once the water reaches a certain level at Southend, a telex is sent instructing Scotland Yard to use the early warning system. The receiving officer would then smash the glass protecting a switch that would bring to life all eighty-five sirens. These were World War II sirens, brought back into use for this purpose in 1970 (although they were not tested until 1972). The signal consisted of three 30-second blasts, separated by 15 second intervals. They used the 'all clear' flat note rather than the more alarming air-raid siren, which many residents would remember only too well.

Four hours before flooding was due to occur, an alert would be issued to the police and local authorities, and, if the situation got worse, a two-hour warning would put the rescue squads on standby. The plan was for the authorities to identify those people who could either not hear the warnings or could not easily evacuate from the most vulnerable places (basement flats, for example) because of age or disability. At one hour, the final warning is given, accompanied by full instructions on Radio 1 and Radio London, to which listeners would be asked to retune. The BBC and ITV would have warning captions transmitted over their programmes. Since 1967 there had been six alerts.

In October 1971 there was the possibility of a flood, when the highest tide for several years was predicted. Eric Johnson was only too aware of Londoners becoming complacent or suspecting that they were 'crying wolf' if they issued unnecessary warnings. However, on 6 October, the four tidal gauges in the Flood Room, situated underneath a painting of a raging sea, registered that the tide was eighteen inches below prediction at Southend and four feet below the top of the embankment walls in Central London.

On 5 June 1972 the House of Commons debated the Thames Barrier and Flood Prevention Bill. Mr David James, MP for North Dorset suggested that what they had been debating so far could make a good script for a film. Mr Peter Mills replied 'The House will know that there is an increasing danger of the Thames overflowing its banks and flooding substantial parts of Inner London. We have had some serious warnings from my Honourable Friend, the Member for Dorset, North who talked about *Doomwatch*. After what he said, I think he may well be asked to write a script for it. The cost of such a disaster as the Thames overflowing in terms of loss of life, damage to property and disruption to the everyday life of the capital would be incalculable.' He was too late. It had already been written.

Production
Script Development
Ian Curteis started his career as an actor, then a director (working on such programmes as *Z Cars*) and finally became a full-time writer. In the late 1970s Curteis would dramatise events from recent history such as *Philby, Burgess and Maclean* in 1977, *Suez 1956* in 1979 and *Churchill and the Generals* in 1981. He was commissioned to write 'Flood' on 18 May 1971.

This very early script made great play of Quist's suspicions over Stafford's commitment to Doomwatch, which may or may not have been played out in the finished episode, due to go out ninth. As part of his research he visited the London Flood Room, watched rehearsals for a flood and received the expert advice from Dr Hal Thirlaway. As always, the script would be checked by the experts before delivery.

In the episode's two emergency meetings at the London Flood Room, the seven attendees (not including the Minister and Ericson) are given in the rehearsal script as The Commissioner of London Police (Uniform), The Commander-in-Chief London General Staff, a General (Uniform), a Permanent Under-Secretary to the Ministry of Defence (the Minister calls him Mr Adams), Movements Manager of London Transport, Operations Manager of the Post Office, London Division, Director of Administration of the GLC (the Minister calls him Mr Halliday) and the Secretary of the London Joint Hospital Board. This is an authentic list of officials who would be present at such a time.

When Ian Curteis wrote his script, one location was already decided. This was one of two huge scaled models of the Thames Estuary built by the Thames Estuary Development Co Ltd in 1969. Housed in a warehouse in London's Surrey Docks in Rotherhithe, it reproduced an area of 500 square miles to a scale of 1/1000. London's third airport was going to be built at Maplin Sands (although Stansted was eventually chosen). The developers wanted to construct a deep water port and needed to study the effects of land reclamation, channel dredging and the flooding characteristics of the area. Both models cost £200,000. By 1972 TEDCO had become the Maplin Development Company. The project was abandoned in 1974.

Casting
Most of the cast were needed only on location. Returning faces included Robert James as the GLC Man, who had previously played Barker in

'Project Sahara', and Derek Benfield as Dr Ridley, who had been Alderman Payne in 'Public Enemy'. The BBC radio announcer heard in the episode was the genuine article – Tim Nicholls. Wesley Pithey had starred in the original black and white series of *Special Branch* as Detective Superintendent Eden, who was close to retirement.

Filming
This was director Quentin Lawrence's second and final *Doomwatch*. The script was already set to feature a great deal of film work, but even more took place than had first been planned. There was considerable redistribution of studio and location material. All of the scenes set in the London Flood Room were now to be filmed.

Car interior sequences were pushed back into the studio, presumably to remove the need for Joby Blanshard on location. Vivien Sherrard was originally taking notes in the Flood Room with Critchley, but eventually the filmed scene was intercut with her taking them via telephone in the studio. Other changes included removing a helicopter interior set – all of Bradley's observations over the Barents Sea are instead relayed by his voice, out of vision and via radio, to the Doomwatch lab. Some stock film showing the effects of flooding was crossed out, as was an establishing shot of Bradley in a plane, but a small amount was still used. The flood warning at the top of the programme was originally going to be seen relayed by both a police car and a boat on the Thames.

Very few changes were made to the script. Quist originally did not know the off-screen character of Dr Rogers from the National Physics Lab personally, but in the camera script they are on first-name terms. A reference to Blacknest was replaced with Aldermaston.

Studio
'Flood' was the fourth episode to be recorded. This was in TC6 on Friday, 31 March 1972. The camera script did not detail dialogue from the lengthier film sequences set in the Flood Room, simply giving a summary and the last few lines spoken. The first two studio scenes recorded were those in Quist's car and the Minister's car, set against back projection screens. The episode was then taped more or less in order, with a large number of inserts recorded at the end of scenes to allow difficult-to-achieve camera angles of various characters poring over maps and pointing to sections on them.

Stock Music
The only music in the episode was to be heard coming from radios. 'Together in the Night' by David Howman was from the Studio G album *Beat Group* (LPSG 1001), and *Music for a Young Generation* provided 'Lazy

Evening Blues' by Alan Parker and Alan Hawkshaw, a very soporific piece from the KPM archive (KPM 1086).

Editing

The episode was edited on Thursday, 4 April 1972 between 11.30 pm and 9.30 pm at TVR.

Audience Reaction

Under 13 per cent of the audience watched the episode, half of ITV's figure, though with an audience reaction index of 86:14 it was the most successful episode of the series. The plot also scored highly at 81:19, and 90 per cent thought the episode was easy to follow. These figures were derived from a sample of 120 viewers out of a potential 200.

'This had been a particularly satisfying edition, in the opinion of a number of reporting viewers, with a credible and thought-provoking theme and a gripping plot that contained more action and suspense than some recent plays in this series; indeed, it had been "more like the earlier *Doomwatch* we used to enjoy" or if "still not the old *Doomwatch*, coming close". The threat to London by flooding provided "a horrifying real situation" since it was known that London was vulnerable to exceptionally high tides – "the implications were very disturbing".

"It was of more immediate interest than some of the earlier episodes in this series. Some of London flood warning details etc were fascinating." "The plot was first class and could, in fact, be true to life: made me think what would happen if there were flood warnings of a like nature." "One of the most realistic of the present series – absolutely fascinating throughout."

'Both acting and production ("of the usual high standard") had captured the atmosphere of realism and tension, it was said.

'Other reporting viewers found certain aspects rather unconvincing ("This was a bit far-fetched – you would not expect a Government to allow such a situation to develop" ...) and parts rather flat, the ending particularly disappointing a few. The pot seemed to be in the style of an old-fashioned thriller and the acting rather melodramatic to a small number of the most disappointed – "the sort of thing you expect in a boys' comic". However, only a small minority were seriously discontented.

'John Paul was roundly praised: "John Paul really seems to be the part. A man trying to do his job and hamstrung at every side with red tape" said one comment. "I like his voice and his cool natural movement and expression" said another. But a few thought that John Barron stole the show. He was admired as a "forceful, competent" man, played with "great aplomb"'. Stafford was getting some interest too – "very deep and unpredictable". Colin Bradley's sense of humour was appreciated, but the absence of John Ridge, who had brought colour to the series, was still being felt.'

Programme Review Board
The Board gave the episode the thumbs-up. Two of the board felt that the series was very much back to its old form, but it was too late. Two days before the episode was transmitted, the *Daily Mirror* reported that there were no plans for a fourth series.

Surrey Docks
The Surrey Docks site was demolished and levelled and remained derelict for over a decade, save for a City farm. In 1976 the site played host to a festival organised by alternative technology enthusiasts who erected a wind operated turbine. Kit Pedler was one of the participants, having wholeheartedly embraced a lifestyle which tried to have a low impact as possible and practical, on the environment in terms of waste and resources. In 1980, the site was up for development. Pedler, together with entrepreneur Nigel Tuersley and architect Tom Hancock devised the Earthlife centre, the centrepiece being a huge glass pyramid conference centre. The site would embrace recycling, wind and solar power. Despite popular support and having the financial backing in place, the traditional view on the GLC and the local council preferred traditional jobmakers, factories and offices. The winning bid eventually went bankrupt after two years of doing nothing.

With the kind permission of Ian Curteis, the script was published in the out of print anthology book *Deadly Dangerous Tomorrow*.

3.10
Cause Of Death

Written by Louis Marks
Directed by Lennie Mayne
Designed by Graham Oakley
Transmitted: Monday, 7 August 1972 at 9.20 pm Duration: 49' 27"

Cast
Edna (Jennifer Wilson), Dr Cordell (John Lee), Phillip (Nicholas Courtney), Wilfred Ridge (Graham Leaman), First Sister (Margaret Ford), Second Sister (Patsy Trench), Susan (Maria O'Brien), Laboratory Assistant (Ann Garry Lee).

Also appearing
Nurse (Anita Waterton), Mrs Wheeler (Florence Allsworth).

Technical Credits
Director's Assistant: Norma Flint. Production Assistant: Vivienne Cozens.
Assistant Floor Manager: Trina Cornwell.
Film Cameraman: Peter Hamilton. Film Editor: Alastair MacKay.
Costume Supervisor: Sheila Beers. Make-up Supervisor: Elizabeth Rowell.
Studio Lighting: Ralph Walton. TM2: Dickie Higham. Vision Mixers: Shirley Conrad, Bob Haines. Sound Supervisor: John Lloyd.
Senior Cameraman: Doug Routeledge.
Crew: 1.

Radio Times
Disagreement about death for Ridge and his father. 'Maybe we're creating just the world we deserve. And if it finally destroys us or drives us mad, that'll be what we deserve too.'

The Story
'People like me don't talk about our parents. We keep them hidden like some dark family secret. And yet our parents are possibly the most important factor in our lives.' – Ridge

Dr Cordell prevents a nurse from giving an unprescribed injection to Mrs Wheeler, an elderly and unconscious patient, even though it might save her life. Angrily, the nurse returns to her station and is patronised by Cordell. This is her last day at the Cordell Clinic, and he suggests she finds another job which is less taxing for her. Mrs Wheeler dies, and as Cordell fills in her death certificate he hesitates over the section marked 'Cause of Death'.

Quist is waiting to hear from Ridge concerning a university job in Manchester he has lined up for him. Stafford is more concerned about Quist's cold and suggests he takes a few days off, but Quist is preparing next year's estimates for a Cabinet meeting the following week. Agreeing to go on sick leave, Quist is surprised to find that Barbara is meeting Ridge for dinner that night. 'Yet something in him makes him feel he's got to fight all the world's battles single handed. Everything becomes a one man crusade.' He asks her to pass on a message.

Ridge is currently visiting his sister Edna and her unfriendly husband Phillip. Their relationship is cool because he hasn't contacted them for six months, and their father, Wilfred, is very ill. He is a patient at the Cordell Clinic, as Edna knows Cordell from her nursing days. Edna tells him that after their father dies there would be no more need for pretence; they will not have to see each other again. Ridge is shocked that his father is so close to death and even more shocked when he learns that his father has written a letter to Cordell, asking to die with dignity by having his treatment withdrawn when his condition becomes intolerable. He does not want to be a burden.

Visiting his father, Ridge is suspicious of Cordell. Who is he to decide when the time comes? Edna understands her father's wish and is angry at Ridge's attitude. He hasn't been the one caring for Wilfred, who is suffering from arteriosclerosis and will need more help as he loses the use of his limbs and constant supervision and care to avoid bed sores. Wilfred wants to be spared months of endless suffering and misery. 'No one pretends that the problems of old age and dying are easy. Certainly not me. I see too much of it. But any person has a right to be spared months of endless suffering and misery. Perhaps if you think it over for a few days. In the meantime, I can assure you at the moment he's getting the best possible medical attention and no effort will be spared to give him every comfort.' Ridge's frail father is delighted to see him, but Edna's face expresses a lifetime of exclusion and bitterness.

The Minister tells Stafford that elements of the Government want to phase out Doomwatch. Preservation of the environment isn't the pioneering concept it was three years ago. 'The argument will be that Doomwatch, if you like, it's been too successful. It's become a part of government thinking at all levels. We should be grateful, they'll say, after all that's what we've been fighting for for years. In reality of course they mean they no longer want a watchdog sniffing around their feet when they can all keep their own houses in order perfectly well.' The Minister wants no heroic gestures from Doomwatch that might give the opposition anything to bite on, and since Quist is out of the office for a week it might help matters.

Back at their house, Ridge argues with Edna and Phillip that what Cordell is doing is morally indefensible, not to say illegal. But Phillip has no time for Ridge and his 'Doomwatch nonsense'; he'd broken his promise and forgotten to come back for Wilfred's birthday. Phillip and Edna had even had to post a card – supposedly from Ridge – themselves, so that Wilfred shouldn't feel neglected by his favourite child. Ridge storms out, leaving Edna worried at what he might do. Ridge takes his anger out on Barbara, who has ignored his cancellation of their dinner date and has come to see him at his flat. Ridge isn't interested in the Manchester job, or in Doomwatch, or in anything it stands for. He is finished. He brings up the subject of parents, reminiscing about his childhood in a close community. 'It wasn't always like that. I remember the part of London I came from ... south of the river. We knew who everybody's parents were. Grandparents too. They lived in the same streets, the same houses. When one of them was taken ill or died the whole district knew about it. Before the war and the bombing and before they pulled down the terraces and put up the tower blocks. It was a way of life. My father's way of life, something I "educated" myself into despising.' Explaining his father's situation, he doesn't know whether or not to report Cordell to the Ministry of Health. Barbara tells him that Anne has done some research into the psychiatric care of the elderly, and maybe she could help.

When Ridge visits Anne at Doomwatch, he is aggressive with Stafford, telling him what he and Quist can do with their job. Barbara placates Stafford, pointing out that Ridge's father is dying. Anne tells Ridge what she knows of Cordell: he has a good reputation, his clinic is a luxury hotel compared to some – and he advocates voluntary euthanasia for the elderly and chronically sick. She refuses to hand over some confidential reports from his clinic, whose outlook she understands. It is not murder. 'Lots of pain-killing drugs shorten life if they're given in excess. Does that mean if a doctor steps up the dose to help a patient in great pain and so brings his death nearer by a few weeks he's a murderer? If he is then half the doctor's in the country are murderers.'

ANNE: The result is that many more of them die from long, painful, degenerative illnesses. They need an enormous amount of care and nursing and long before they die they've become little more than vegetables. Vegetables. The strain on the Health Service is colossal and it's going to get much greater.
RIDGE: So the answer is to kill them off because we can't afford to keep them alive?
ANNE: No, it's not.
RIDGE: Then what is the answer?

ANNE: I don't know … I really don't know!

As she becomes more vocal and passionate, Ridge backs off apologetically. She goes to take a phone call; when she returns, both Ridge and her briefcase have gone. Cordell and his clinic's methods are exposed in the press, and the Minister is gloomy. He is morally committed to Doomwatch's survival though it won't be easy now it is treading on Ministry of Health territory. Stafford defends Ridge as much as he can; Quist and Anne think he has used his own father as a selfish crusade – he is finished for good now. But then Anne gets a phone call from Mary Kendrick, the nurse from the Cordell Clinic, who wants to meet her.

When Cordell tells Edna that her father's condition is worsening, she thinks it is best that Ridge is there, just in case there are questions later. Wilfred has contracted pneumonia and could die in a matter of hours. In view of the press exposé, he now has to be treated, even though it is against his stated wishes. Edna is coldly furious with her brother. They see their father, unconscious in an oxygen tent. He is being cared for very efficiently and is responding. 'Another triumph for medicine' mutters Cordell.

Ridge stays with his father for the night, and he talks to Cordell about the geriatric wards he had visited and the horrors he saw. 'More than shocked. Nauseated. I've seen some hospital wards where the beds are so close together that there's isn't even room for a bedside table or a place to put a few belongings. Fifty men in one ward with one nurse and one auxiliary to look after them. They lie there in their own wet and filth, their faces like so many death masks, hopeless. One old man was crying for a nurse for half an hour before anyone came to see to him. And when she did she cursed him and told him off as if he was a naughty child. Worse, like a dog, because people don't treat children like that.' Ridge blames the lack of a family to support the elderly, so he intends to care for his father from home, learning what to do.

Stafford arrives, and Ridge confesses he stole the papers, not to gain leverage against Cornell but to try and find the best care home for his father. None were any use. Stafford explains that they thought he had been the one who had taken the story to the press, but it was Nurse Kendrick, impatient with the lack of action after resigning from the Clinic six months beforehand. The university post is still open for Ridge, who asks if Stafford came all this way to tell him that. It isn't: Cordell is to have certain charges brought against him; Doomwatch has become involved. 'There's nothing Doomwatch can do about this problem' says Ridge firmly. 'Nothing.'

Cordell enters and tells Ridge that his father has died from heart failure. There was nothing they could do. Ridge's head bows. He goes to the ward and stares at his father's dead body. Slowly, he crosses to the bed.

Behind the Story
Not for the first time this series, this is a story that does not involve
Doomwatch directly. There is no reason for the department to get
involved, as the Minister points out (and thus safe to give Quist a week off
with the flu), just like in 'Deadly Dangerous Tomorrow' and 'Sex and
Violence'. The backstage political skulduggery is simply there for Ridge to
apparently rock the boat once again. The Minister is fighting, again, for
Doomwatch's survival, trying to prevent a government think-tank from
doing what he himself wanted to do back in 'High Mountain'. Doomwatch
is now firmly an arm of the State, and the Minister declares that its aims
are now a part of government thinking. It does give the series a feeling of
development, but it is no longer just about the frights of science and
imbalances of technology. To people like the Minister, however, the
environment is what you can immediately see – a polluted river that
interferes with the fishing, a plastic bag on the side of a quaint country
road, the chimneys and power masts that interrupt the horizon of some
stretch of moor or coastline and spoil the picnic.

Death with Dignity
Louis Marks gives us the type of episode we have come to expect from
him: one of social issues, with every last drop of emotion wrung from the
situation, leaving the viewer wondering if it's worth carrying on with life.
It is the opposite of Brian Hayles' 'The Iron Doctor' in that the elderly and
the infirm are not kept alive longer than expected by the 'care' of
machines, but allowed an end. Cordell allows his patients to die with
dignity and by their own choice, a debate still raging today: the right to
end your own life. Traditionally, doctors are supposed to prolong our
existence in accordance with their Hippocratic oath. In Great Britain there
is no right to end one's life naturally when it could be prevented. The
Suicide Act 1961 still applies. The obvious fear is whether other people
should choose to end it for us. No religious argument is offered in the
script, which makes a refreshing change from how this subject is often
dealt with.

In February 1972 a case in Milwaukee captured the imagination. A
childless widow of 77, Gertrude Raasch, had already undergone two
operations, including an amputation of part of her left leg, and faced a
third procedure which may have extended her life by a few months. By
this point, she was depressed and would not talk, so the hospital went to
court to gain consent. The judge decided that she was not going to give
consent and that she should be allowed to 'depart in God's peace.' The
case was reported in the *New Scientist*.

Louis Marks is not writing about euthanasia, simply withdrawing treatment when there is no further hope of a full recovery. As far as one reader of the *Radio Times* was concerned, this episode was a warning against euthanasia and saw it as an attack on withholding treatment to allow for death. What is not established in the episode is whether Cordell declines to treat all those in his care when it looks like they are on the verge of death, despite having the medicines to revive them, or those he has previously discussed it with, as in the case of Ridge's father. When the press take interest in the leaked report on his clinic, he suddenly has to give all his patients treatment. This hints that his policy is universal but with informed consent at the heart of it. He is not a secret serial killer of the Harold Shipman stamp, an Angel of Death or a ward-stalking killer. Cordell is presented as acting benignly, even if he seems somewhat over-enthusiastic.

The script presents the issue but draws no conclusions. Anne Tarrant does not have an answer to the problems in geriatric care, but she has a force of passion that takes even Ridge by surprise. Ridge lays the blame on the offspring for not looking after their parents in their dotage, with himself as guilty as anyone, but overlooks the fact that his sister has been the primary care giver for some time.

The episode shows us the fate that most of us could face as a geriatric with a family unable or unwilling to cope. We see the strain on Ridge's sister's family, who cared for an elderly relative. We only hear from Ridge's father (unnamed in the script) from second-hand sources, in that did not want to be a further burden to his family when his degenerative illness was first diagnosed. With a larger budget, we may have seen the treatment of the elderly in care wards as depicted by Ridge in his last scene with Cordell. It is almost Victorian in its description.

By the 1950s most of the elderly died in hospitals, rather than at home as their parents would have done on the whole, especially in the pre-NHS days. The adviser for the episode was Dr Cicely Saunders (later made a Dame), who had been involved with the care of terminal patients since 1948. In 1967 she founded St Christopher's Hospice, which became a pioneer in palliative medicine and the care for those who were ending their days in terrible pain. She is seen as the founder of the modern hospice movement, someone who recognised that it wasn't just painkillers the dying needed, but emotional, social and – if they required it – spiritual support.

Production
Script Development

The script, originally entitled 'Birds of Prey', was commissioned on 13 September 1971 and was paid for by 12 April the following year. Louis Marks explained a personal reason for writing the script when he answered a couple of letters sent to the *Radio Times* in wake of the episode: 'My wife is a voluntary worker at a home for elderly infirm, and it is because of what I have seen at close quarters — apart from my own family experiences — that I wanted to try and place this whole question in a much broader context than the purely medical one in which it is usually discussed. This is why I gave Ridge the last word in condemning Dr Cordell's 'solution' of withdrawing medical treatment. I know many old sick people wish to be left to die. Sometimes this is because of illness or pain. Just as often it is also prompted by family rejection. This was part of the point of my play. When life becomes meaningless and purposeless death seems a desirable solution ... It is, of course, part of a larger problem – as I hinted in the play. In our streamlined, computerised world with the collapse of community life and the disintegration of the large, multi-generation family there is less and less room for the old and dying.

'So those unfortunates who linger on into their late 70s and 80s are constituting more and more of a headache. Vast economic resources will be needed to meet the social problem. I feel that all of us – doctors included – must be committed to life and must face up to the consequences of that commitment. If we aren't we shall have to face the far more terrifying consequences of a world in which technology continues to erode humanity rather than being its servant. This is the message of *Doomwatch*, and my play was meant as another comment on this theme.'

Filming
Lennie Mayne directed this, his last, episode for the series, and there were only a few small film sequences needed: those of Ridge driving along a motorway and then walking towards his sister's house.

Casting
Playing Ridge's sister Edna was Jennifer Wilson, who had appeared twice before as Miss Wills, the Minister's secretary. Cast in the role of her husband Phillip was Nicholas Courtney, who was still making regular appearances as Brigadier Lethbridge-Stewart in *Doctor Who* (and would in later years become good friends with Gerry Davis). Ridge's father was played by Graham Leaman, previously seen as Professor Hayland in 'You Killed Toby Wren'. John Lee made his third appearance in the series, this time as Dr Cordell, having had parts in 'The Plastic Eaters' and 'The Web of Fear'. Patsy Trench will have a small part in 1973s *Moonbase 3* but left acting a few years later.

Finally getting something to say (and gaining a credit both on screen and in the *Radio Times*) was Anne Garry Lee, who had been one of the Doomwatch laboratory assistants in other episodes of the third series as well as other uncredited roles in the previous two. She is the daughter of actor Bernard Lee and the mother of Johnny Lee Miller. Susan, played by Maria O'Brien, made her final studio recording this week.

Vivien Sherrard
For Vivien Sherrard, now Vivien S Smith, the episode and the rehearsal period has a far more personal resonance: 'My future husband Frank and I met on May 27 through a mutual friend, and we became engaged 5 days later on June 1st! Yes, it was a whirlwind romance, but Frank was irresistible, a unique combination of handsome looks, delightful personality, brains, Yankee ingenuity, and goodness through and through. Frank met several members of the cast and was allowed to watch camera rehearsals, sit in the Green room, visit me in my dressing room, and even sit in on the taping courtesy of the director Lennie Mayne. He said to Frank and me, "I hear you're going to do something silly!" Lennie was so relaxed and charming that he made everything seem fun and easy. He used to unexpectedly perform a dance move, seemingly out of sheer exuberance! Directors such as he always extract the best from their actors. I was distressed when I learned that he had drowned back in the 70's.

'Simon got on well with Frank, and my last little story is his funny remark when I said something he considered silly when the three of us were walking down a corridor together. He said to me, "Keep taking the tablets!" In studio rehearsal for my long scene with Simon I inadvertently hit my head on a microphone that was dangling just above me. Simon found this hilarious, and fell about to such an extent that he effectively eradicated any chance of my remembering how we played the scene! Why do minor incidents such as these stand out like photographs? '

Studio
'Cause of Death' was eleventh episode in studio production order. It was videotaped in TC3 on 2 June 1972. Simon Oates found this episode very difficult as it coincided with his own father dying. He did not feel that he could record his reactions to Wilfred Ridge's death unless it was taped at the very end of shooting, which it duly was.

Stock Music
The only music heard in the episode came courtesy of Phillip's and Edna's noisy children, who were playing 'Alexander' from *Even More Electric Banana* (Hudson De Wolfe DW/LP 3123).

Editing
The episode was edited on 5 June 1972 between 9 am and 1 pm.

Reaction

Unfortunately, the reaction indices were not recorded for this episode, and the only comments came from two readers in the *Radio Times*, who came away with different points of view. Mrs J I Anderson from Radcliffe on Trent wrote 'Surely the people responsible for this series must realise that there is a world of difference between the action of euthanasia and the passive withholding of medical treatment, without which old people are allowed to die with peace and dignity, often having suffered coronary thrombosis, or being left inarticulate and/or crippled following a stroke ... Contrary to what the programme suggested, many doctors do respect the wishes of these old people and allow them a merciful end to their suffering.' Dr S L Henderson Smith from Huddersfield thought 'John Ridge's exaggerated horror at the suggestion is typical of the attitude of many who fail to appreciate that dying, like everything else, should be a voluntary matter. Instead of that, society clings to its primitive and irrational attitude that birth may be controlled and living modified according to desires and resources, but that you must on no account die until you have exhausted all and every artificial means medicine has invented to keep you ticking over to the last gasp. It is a pity the impression remained that the doctor was culpable. His only crime was mercy.' Louis Marks responded to the letters with his motives for writing the episode.

3.11
The Killer Dolphins

Written by Roy Russell
Directed by Darrol Blake
Designed by Jeremy Davies
Transmitted: Monday, 14 August 1972 at 9.21 pm Duration: 49' 24"

Cast
Professor Fillippo Balbo (Angelo Infanti), Guila (Rita Giovannini), Paola Maria Totti (Viviane Ventura), Bill Manzaro (Richardson Morgan), Cavalli (Bruno Barnabe), Commodore Aylwood (Frank Duncan), Assistants (Mario Zoppellini, Richard Barker).

Also appearing
Extras in Studio
Special Branch Man in Minister's Office, Man in Club and Man at Palazzo (Jim Delany), PPS in Minister's Office, Man in Club and Man at Palazzo (Terry Sartain), Secretary in Minister's Office and Woman at Palazzo (Iona McCrae), Barman in Club and Barman at Palazzo (Ray Marioni), Steward in Club and Steward at Palazzo (Antonio de Maggio), Man in Club and Man at Palazzo (Kedd Senton), Men in Club (Frank Howes, Malcolm Johns), Women at Palazzo (Jean St Louis, Molly Davenport, Marie Anderson), Man (Achmed) at Palazzo (Roy Kanaris), Lab Workers and Men at Palazzo (David Pelton, David Ianson), Possible [sic] Minister's Secretary and Contessa at Palazzo (Mabel Ethrington).

Extras on location: John Bunn, Gladis Hill, Margy Young.

Technical Credits
Production Assistant: Jackie Willows. Assistant Floor Manager: Pauline Smithson. Director's Assistant: Philippa Clauson. Floor Assistant: Timothy Ward.
Film Cameraman: Fred Hamilton. Sound Recordist: Bob Roberts. Film Editor: Alastair MacKay.
Costume Supervisor: Sheila Beers. Make-up Supervisor: Penny Norton.
Studio Lighting: John Dixon. TM2: Dickie Ashman. Vision Mixer: David Langford.
Sound Supervisor: Chick Anthony. Grams Operator: Nick Ware.
Crew: 3.

Radio Times
Spencer Quist and finny friend. 'Navy people envy its marvellous radar. A dolphin has been trained to choose – blindfold – the larger of two objects that seem identical to the man's eye.'

The Story
'They're world problems, Minister. It's about time we stopped thinking in terms of national interests. Nature doesn't draw dotted lines over mountains and across oceans. We need a Doomwatch in every country. With international links.' – Quist.

There have been reported shark attacks off the Italian coast in which no-one survived, but one victim, before he died, claimed it was a dolphin. 'But how can dolphins be killers?' asks Quist. According to Professor Fillipo Balbo, there is no record of a dolphin ever attacking a human being unprovoked. Balbo is at Doomwatch because he wants to set up an Italian equivalent: La Sentinello del Destino, or 'Sentinel of Destiny.' Italy has the Club of Rome but no investigative unit, so Balbo wants Quist's help in these attacks. He is interested in the Oceanography project that Bradley has been working on. All the pollution from the world's rivers ends up in the sea, like one big dustbin. A ten-year projection of the Mediterranean and the American seaboard terrifies Balbo; the Mediterranean could be dead by the end of it. The attacks occurred in an area near a number of naval bases, including one manned by NATO. Have these dolphins escaped from a military establishment?
The news of Balbo's visit and the dolphin attacks troubles an unknown caller to the Minister. 'They' want no link to be made between recent naval exercises and the attacks. Quist calls in Stafford – who has already been forewarned by the Minister. Quist asks Stafford to look into the matter, as it is right up his street, but notes that he isn't very keen on the idea. Quist accuses the Minister of 'nobbling' one of his staff behind his back and explains that all Balbo wants to do is set up an Italian Doomwatch. The Minister reminds Quist that Balbo is well known as an ecological activist, as was his late father. Doomwatch can't afford to be lined up with cranks and the Minister warns him not to get involved.
Two days later, Stafford reports he has been stonewalled in his investigations, probably from fear of negative public reaction. He suggests that he takes a week's leave and spend a few innocent days in the Mediterranean. Quist agrees with a straight face that Stafford looks like he's been overworking, and a bit of Italian sunshine is required.
The latest victim to be attacked is Paola Maria Totti, swimming just off the Gulf of Spozin whilst trying to break a world record. The Gulf of Spozin has a naval base. Stafford wastes no time and goes to the bar of the

Club Galileo Galilee, the haunt of Naval officers, and finds Bill Manzaro, an Italian-born New Yorker, who is an old colleague. Stafford tries to steer the conversation to the attacks but gets nowhere. Quist and Balbo visit Paola in hospital, where she describes being rammed by what she felt could not have been a shark. She is invited to visit Balbo's Sea-Lab to meet some real dolphins.

At Sea-Lab, Quist has to arrange a cover story for the Minister as to why he is in Italy and sends over some samples of ocean water and plankton. Balbo and his assistant (and probably his lover) Giulia want to stop whoever it is training dolphins to attack people. The Minister tours the Doomwatch labs and is told about the ocean project by Bradley, but a phone call alerts him to the news that Stafford is also in Italy. He sends a telex to Quist, recalling him immediately. It has to wait. Paola has turned up for a swim with the dolphins. Although she cannot bring herself to do it after her ordeal, she feels the skin of one – it is the same as whatever attacked her.

Stafford is due to have dinner with Manzaro but is intercepted by Commodore Aylwood, who cryptically reminds him that they are supposed to be 'the Silent Service'. The Minister is angry with Quist, accusing him of trying to pull the wool over his eyes. What is Stafford doing snooping around NATO? When Quist is told by Balbo that a school of aggressive dolphins have been caught, he is back on a flight to Italy. Intriguingly for Stafford, a man named Calvelli knows who he is, that he was thrown out of the officers' club, and offers to show him Naples. Quist and Balbo study the dolphins; under-nourished and apparently untrained to be fed by hand, which would have made them more friendly to man. One flashes past and Quist is knocked into the pool. The water thrashes violently, the dolphins screech and Quist cannot be seen. Franco and Stafford dive in and Balbo and Giulla use poles to ward off the attack from furious dolphins. Quist is rescued, and remarks 'Nothing like getting close to the problem.'

Once again, the Minister is put under pressure to stop Quist's links with Balbo, fearing an international incident. Putting the phone down, the Minister wishes that 'they' would do their own dirty work. Stafford takes Quist to Cavalli's palazzo, where the wealthy man is holding a party. It soon becomes clear he is willing to buy detailed information of NATO's dolphin training programme. Stafford agrees to one hundred thousand dollars. Cavalli is satisfied, and Quist and Stafford leave. Stafford has taped their conversation and hands it over to Naval Intelligence, who had loaned him the recorder – the Italians had been keeping an eye on Cavalli for some time. Back at Sea-Lab, there is some good news. The aggressive dolphins have calmed down enough to be fed by hand, having previously been living off their own body fat.

Quist brings samples of excreta for analysis back to London, and Bradley is concerned by the results. Aside from the usual pollutants, the only thing that they find is choline chloride, and that would only make the dolphins ill. But then realisation strikes: it would also interfere with their sonar system: they would get lost, become panicky, attack anything they ran into. Choline chloride is used in poultry farming, and effluent containing the substance flows down from major rivers into the sea. It kills plankton and consequently the fish that feed on the plankton. The dolphins, in turn, are deprived of fish to eat and instead begin to live off their own body fat, where the choline chloride has already built up. As Quist describes it, 'The moment eventually comes when the ecological balance is upset and ... killer dolphins.' He admits that were not on the right track with NATO, but it's more ammunition for Doomwatch.

Quist tells a relieved Minister that the problem was ecological, not military. Relief is not the reaction Quist wants. It could be Britain's coastline next. Investment is needed: 'It's money, or our lives.' The Minister promises to back him to the hilt over a multi-national agreement. Quist still knows something is being concealed about dolphin training by the military. Stafford had been offered a fortune for information, not to mention the pressures put upon the Minister from on high.

MINISTER: That's quite another story.
QUIST: And this isn't the end of it, either.

Behind the Story
A very rare example of foreshadowing in *Doomwatch* happens at the end of 'Without the Bomb' when Quist asks Bradley rhetorically about the death of plankton in the Med. This episode deals with the consequences. Dolphins are becoming savage killers. There are rumours of dolphin training camps, and the Royal Navy or NATO is experimenting, or benefiting from such experiments, and fears Quist is on their fin-shaped trail. This does happen. The Americans have a marine mammal programme, for good purposes as well as the more sinister. The Russians abandoned theirs when the Cold War ended (and sold the creatures to Iran in 2000).

It angered Kit Pedler. He let his feelings be known in a syndicated press interview in 1967. The interviewer wrote: 'The dolphin, by means of a small box strapped to its back, is being converted by science into a living bomb, capable of attaching mines to the hulls of ships. At the mention of this, all benevolence fades from the face of Dr Kit Pedler. "This is prostitution of the world we live in," he says. "The dolphin is a most elegant, beautiful and benign creature that never did anybody any harm, with a learning rate for some tasks than man. Yet here are these wretched, soulless scientists prostituting one of the most elegant creatures on the earth."'

The Mediterranean

Balbo, with his famous father, were probably based on the Piccards, another father and son team who were fascinated by marine life and had the technical skill to actually get down into the depths of the oceans. Jacques' father, Auguste, was a physicist who was interested in cosmic ray research and built a pressurised cabin allowing him to reach an altitude of 50,000 feet in a balloon, becoming the first person to reach the stratosphere. He was also interested in what lies under the sea and invented a submersible to withstand the enormous pressures, breaking records as to how far down a man could go. Jacques worked as a consultant to the US Navy, who were interested in the strategic value of such a submersible. Having such an affinity with the sea, it is hardly surprising that in 1966 Piccard created the Foundation for the Study and the Preservation of Seas and Lakes. Stafford mentions him in his first chat to Manzaro. Piccard's prediction that life in the Mediterranean could be extinct by the end of the decade is echoed by Bradley.

It is hardly surprising that this was the view at the time. The enclosed 970,000 square miles of the Mediterranean Sea was the dustbin, as Quist put it, of Europe and North Africa. At first, concern was raised by the untreated raw sewage it received, linked to the rising levels of infective hepatitis in cities such as Rome. Oil is brought to the Mediterranean from the rivers Rhone, Ebro, the Po and the Nile, as well as dumped either on purpose or accidentally by tankers. There are oil fields in Algeria and Libya with refineries bordering on the sea. Add industrial effluent to the mix, and there were concerns over the shrinking levels of oxygen production in its waters. The Italians were concerned the effect pollution would have on their tourism industry and introduced a bill in August 1971, banning oil dumping in their territory.

International Doomwatch

It is a fitting episode with which to end the series. Doomwatch, once just an unwanted electoral nuisance, is now starting to look at the global implications, something this third series explores. The Americans have been setting up their own department, and now the Italians are pushing for it. Rightly, Quist argues that the issues are of a worldwide concern, and the Minister agrees, but, as we see, he is trapped in his world of national and international politics. Echoing the sentiment of the second series finale, 'Public Enemy', Quist once again urges 'It's our money, or our lives.' The episode is not a conclusion, with Quist riding off into the smog-obscured sunset and perhaps working on a United Nations- funded project, but the hints are there that this is the direction he would like to go in.

Production
Script Development
'The Killer Dolphin', as the episode was originally called, was the seventh script commissioned for the series, on 11 August 1971. Although it was due for delivery on 4 October, Roy Russell asked for a few extra days to iron out some problems he was having with the final scenes.

Casting
This was the first of Darrol Blake's episodes for the third series. 'I did an episode of *Paul Temple* which had two Italians in it and I cast London actors, and they really were inexperienced, not very good, but they were real Italians. I insisted on having real Italians in that episode of *Paul Temple*. Everybody said you could get a good English actor and put on a fake accent and I said, "Yeah, and they'll sound exactly like that." Come the *Doomwatch* episode, which was so much about dolphins and Italians, that I said I knew there was nothing in London I could use. My wife had a friend who went out to Italy and carried a spear in the movie *Cleopatra* and stayed to become king of the dub in Rome, so I knew I had a free bed there. I said, "Terry [Dudley], if you pay the airfare, I'll go and find somebody." I saw several Italian actors and settled on Angelo Infanti. Then, there was a tremendous long period where we tried to get him a work permit, and the thing was the Ministry would send it to Equity and say, "Is this okay? Can we import this actor?" and for five weeks it was rejected. The council met every Tuesday and rejected it, rejected it, rejected it. Terry said, "The tail will not wag the dog. We'll try again." And we tried a sixth time and they said, "Yeah, OK."' Infanti had appeared in *The Godfather*, which had yet to be released, where he played Fabrizo, one of the bodyguards hired to protect Al Pacino's Michael Corleone when he flees to Sicily. 'In Sicily, women are more dangerous than shotguns.' Viviane Ventura, playing Paola, on the other hand was born in London, as was Rita Giovanni, whereas Frank Duncan, playing the Commodore, was born in Switzerland.

Filming
Darrol Blake performed a recce of his selected locations with film cameraman Fred Hamilton on 4 January 1972. The director had just finished his episode of *The Regiment*, 'Fortunes of Peace'. Infanti arrived in the country on Sunday, 16 January, a day before the film unit travelled down to Brighton for a week's filming. 'We shot at night up at the Brighton Aquarium & Dolphinarium because it was open to the public during the day. The dolphins were wonderful, of course. They're so intelligent. I said

to the chap in charge of them: "What would happen if an actor falls in?" "They'll watch what's happening and then if he's floundering, they'll come forward and help him. But most of the time they'll stand back until they've assessed the situation." It was John Paul who fell in, we didn't have any stunt men on that. It wasn't that deep and he was a fit man at the time. So we needed them to swim left to right, play about or whatever. Two or three nights we shot up there. I was told that the next day, the dolphins wouldn't do anything because they did a show on the hour every hour to Joe Public. Apparently they wouldn't do anything if there were just three or four people, because we had a big unit, with the lights and everything, and we applauded and loved what they were doing. They had a whale of a time. The vaults underneath the Dolphinarium we used as the hospital.

'We stayed at Dora Bryan's hotel, I remember. She and her husband had a hotel and I remember there was a huge picture of her in the entrance hall, playing the lead in *Hello, Dolly!* at Drury Lane. We also went up to Sussex University's Gardener Centre, which was not far away, to do the exterior of the Italian research centre.' The Dolphinarium had been open since 1968 and it closed in 1990. It is now the Sea Life Centre, with the dolphins long since gone.

The film was edited the following Monday and Blake then concentrated on further casting and preparation for the rehearsals due to begin on Monday, 14 February.

More Casting

Bruno Barnabe had been the Head Waiter in 'Spectre at the Feast'. This would be Maria O'Brien's first appearance (in production order) as Susan, and she was contracted on 11 February 1972, very close to the studio days. Although she is listed in the camera script as appearing, Susan does not actually feature in the script itself, nor the running order at the top of the script which lists the order in scenes are to be recorded, and the actors needed for a scene. Barbara has little to do other than her usual secretarial duties, so it is probable that Susan was given some of these and a nondescript line or two. She was not listed on the credit slides for the end of the episode. Hardly an auspicious start! Richardson Morgan had appeared in 'The Plastic Eaters'.

Studio

'The Killer Dolphins' was the second story to be recorded. It was videotaped in TC1 on Wednesday, 18 February 1972. This was the first recorded episode of the third series to use the composite set for the new Doomwatch offices. Also making their first recorded but last transmitted appearances are David Ianson and David Pelton (the latter was married to a school friend of Darrol Blake, Patricia Healey). They were two of the background laboratory assistants working in the Doomwatch offices in most of the episodes featuring the set. The episode was recorded in story order with the exception for one car scene involving back projection, which was taped at the start of the evening. This was Cavalli contacting Stafford for the first time.

Stock Footage

Augmenting the specially shot dolphin film was some stock material for the first scene where Quist and Balbo watch the dolphins from Sea-Lab. The extra silent film of playful dolphins and a brief establishing shot of Naples harbour came from a variety of sources, such as World Background, BP, Anglia TV's *Survival* programme, BBC2's *Horizon* (which would shortly transmit an instalment called 'Whales, Dolphins and Menon' 6 March), the US Navy and the Italian public television station RAI.

Stock Music

The background music for the bar scenes came from an HMV record (HMV CLP 1768) called *Holiday in Italy*, with short extracts from 'More', sung by Tony Renis and Orchestra, and 'Roma Nun Fa' La Stupida Stasera', played by Nino Impallomeni and Group. The Golden Guinea LP *Italian Hits* (GGL 0112) provided 'La Dolce Vita' performed by 101 Strings. As if all that wasn't enough to make sure the viewers knew they were in Italy, some 'Mandolin Magic' came courtesy of *La Banda del Mandolino*, directed by Norrie Paramour, who provided 'O Sole Mio' (Polydor 2489 038). Finally, over four minutes were used of John Mayer's *Indo Jazz Interpolation No. 4* (KPM INT 01).

Editing

The episode was edited on 21 February between 9 am and 1 pm.

Publicity

With an episode featuring dolphins, the episode received some publicity on the morning of transmission. The *Sun* said that the episode would show Quist discovering that somebody had trained dolphins as a military weapon. *The Stage* printed a photograph of Quist sitting on the edge of the dolphin tank, reminding readers that a fourth series had not been commissioned.

Reviews

Richard Last in the *Daily Telegraph* hoped that the series would return – providing Ridge didn't – but was less than impressed with the episode: 'Last night's close of the season episode, 'The Killer Dolphins' was a fairly mediocre affair in which the barely suppressed melodramatic elements finally showed in an absurd confrontation at what appeared to be a Neapolitan orgy. The story would probably have done better as pure science fiction, perhaps as an *Out of the Unknown* tale.' Nancy Banks-Smith from the *Guardian* had a similar reaction: '*Doomwatch* ... was going on about demented dolphins. I did not have much hope of it after actors started staring at each other and ejaculating "you mean..." as if they meant it.' She preferred that night's *World in Action* on industrial noise pollution for doomwatching ...

Programme Review Board

The Board saluted the end of the series, with at least Monica Sims enjoying the episode.

Audience Research Report

Only 10 per cent of the viewing population watched this episode, compared to the 25 per cent who saw *Man at the Top* on ITV. However, it scored highly amongst the 126 viewers questioned, with 80 per cent highly entertained, making this the third most enjoyed episode by the sample after 'Flood' and 'Say Knife, Fat Man':

> 'The fact that dolphins (albeit not very friendly ones) featured in this episode evidently added to its attraction for some viewers, and the majority in any case enjoyed it very much. But beyond occasional remarks to the affect that the plot was unusual, although "kept within the bounds of possibility" and "showed what could happen" they had little to add in the way of specific comment about the story itself. A small proportion of those reporting seemed to agree that it was rather far-fetched and not one of the best in the series, and a few complained that the solution to the mysterious behaviour of the dolphins was "not explained properly" and that the episode was rather confusing, especially towards the end. There were scattered claims that the minor characters were not very well acted and that a general tendency to "ham" made all characters unconvincing. But apart from this, and for occasional complaints that the action jumped about too much, presentation apparently left nothing to be desired, many agreeing that the setting was as usual of a high standard.'

4
Reaction To The Third Series

'I implore the BBC to bring back Dr Pedler or forget *Doomwatch.*' Shane
Fahy, *New Scientist*

It has become fashionable to look at the third series as a series of
unfortunate episodes in comparison to the first series. Without doubt, it
certainly has a different feel and approach. It is difficult to look at
'Tomorrow, the Rat' and 'Waiting for a Knighthood' and realise that they
are both by the same author, Terence Dudley. He also wrote and directed
'Fire and Brimstone', an episode he must have hoped would shock the
audience in much the same way as 'Survival Code' did a couple of years
earlier. Instead, he received negative reactions from the press and viewers
who couldn't understand why a much loved (except by Richard Last of the
Daily Telegraph) character would behave in such an atypical way. It didn't
help that Kit Pedler and Gerry Davis launched their broadside a few days
later against the programme which they had created but no longer had any
control over. This was certainly something they had been planning to do
for a few months at least, and it played into the hands of the critics who
disliked the anthrax episode and, as the weeks went by, the new approach
to the programme. They wanted the shocks and thrills of the first series,
not wordy and worthy debates played out though the conventions of an
average crime thriller plot.

The debate kicked off in the pages of the *Radio Times* and *New Scientist.*
Terence Dudley bravely fought a rear-guard action and defended 'Fire and
Brimstone' in very polite and respectful tones in the 22 June edition. His
stance was challenged quite forcibly in a July edition of the *Radio Times*
where a Mr M Shaw responded to Dudley's defence of his opener: 'Quite
clearly Terence Dudley ... aims to defend the present series at all costs.
Suspense plots were the least important angle of the approach of Kit Pedler
and Gerry Davis. In a nutshell, the originals seemed logical extensions of
present scientific short-sightedness; the present series depends on a TV-
orientated, criminal approach to catch the attention of the viewer. (Student
theft of plutonium, for instance.) Mr Dudley's biased re-collections exhibit
his shallow-mindedness. The fact that a plastic-eating virus may not exist
is quite irrelevant. The episode in question focused clearly on non-
biodegradable plastics and loose laboratory security. The Hastings atom
bomb was merely an extension of an actual event concerning the USA and
Spain, where the bomb fell. Suspense indeed! Doubtless Mr Dudley would

recommend the "Hallelujah Chorus" as a will-they-ever-sing-it-for-the-last-time suspense plot. More seriously: I am a physics teacher, and I could quite confidently have recommended my pupils to the early series as an almost essential part of their education. The present cannot be recommended to any scientist, budding or otherwise. I suppose it is suitable as standard suspense fodder for the fashionably pollution-conscious.'

Dudley replied 'Mr Shaw commands my deep respect: my memory couldn't possibly span well over two years in such detail. But he really can't have it both ways. If a non-existent plastic-eating virus is "quite irrelevant" surely he diminishes the "extension of an actual event" with an atomic bomb? And not all scientists are short-sighted: certainly not the 24 of different disciplines who have contributed to the current series.'

The *Daily Mirror* felt that '*Doomwatch* had some authority and bite when it started. It tackled the growing pains of what has become a modern monster -- the mess we are making of our world and the nasty, scientific developments that the back room boys are playing about with and we wot know nothing of [sic]. Alas, those promising, if straightforward scenes are no more. The writers have gone in for the tall story market and each succeeding episode seems to be trying to cap its predecessor.'

New Scientist, in their issue dated 12 July 1972, published an angry letter from schoolboy Martyn Dryden: 'Concern has been expressed in the media, and in our school staffroom, over the poor storylines and low excitement-value of the current BBC-TV series of *Doomwatch*. We know, of course, that Dr Pedler and his associate are no longer responsible. A recent letter on this subject in *Radio Times* provoked an editorial disclaimer to the effect that the earlier series were just as boring: we are supposed to be suffering, collectively, from the psychological repression that makes all our childhood summers sunny in retrospect. I doubt this. Early *Doomwatch* had teeth; this one doesn't. People died in hundreds from Pedler's ingenious scourges; now, millions are saved – nothing is allowed to happen. I also detect an air of "it can't happen here" recently, especially in the fake TV programmes about population and the environment which have been so overdone as to be blatant self-parody. *Doomwatch* has sold out to its ultimate controllers: industry and (if, as I imagine the programme is sold to America) the CIA. This is nothing new, but, for the viewer who likes a scare on a Monday night it's still a shame.'

In the following week's edition, a Mr Shane Fahy wrote 'After an apocryphal first episode involving the good old "Frankenstein Complex", as Asimov once called it, the fictional government, and the not-quite-fictional BBC have decided to pull out the teeth of this programme and leave it a toothless, senile idiot that would do credit to the media of Huxley's *Brave New World*, or, equally, to the propaganda of Orwell's Big

Brother. Properly handled, by Dr Pedler, *Doomwatch* could have been a very valuable vehicle for members of both the establishment and the anti-establishment who would like to see people take a serious interest in affairs which could critically affect not only our civilisation but also our species. I sympathise heartily with Mr Dryden and his feelings about the "it can't happen here" attitude. Naturally this sort of programme, especially after the "no punches pulled" first series, must affect a great section of the viewers, by lulling them into a false sense of complacency, the results of which do not bear thinking about. Undoubtedly, if the viewing public are bombarded by "eco-nuts" screaming prophecies of doom and Armageddon the result (after some initial stimulation) would be utter boredom. Thus the two extremes of meekness and ferocity must be avoided which means steering a careful middle course, which so far only Dr Pedler has managed to do. Therefore, in conclusion, I implore the BBC to bring back Dr Pedler or forget *Doomwatch*.'

Cancellation

The BBC did not want Pedler or Davis back, and so they took Fahy's advice. They only had to glance at the viewing figures to confirm their decision. They averaged only five million, for which it is tempting to blame the time of the year at which the programme went out, but the ITV programme *Man at the Top* had double that number. Well over a year had passed since 'Public Enemy', and with 'doom so fashionable it is fast becoming an election issue', as Richard Massingham puts it in 'Waiting for a Knighthood', *Doomwatch* was no longer one of a kind and had lost its unique position as well as its audience.

Just over half of the viewing panel who reported on 'The Killer Dolphins' had watched most or all of the series, and they felt that it had not started well, had some good episodes, some boring, and that pollution control was a cliché now. There was some comfort to be gained in that the comments regarding the series as a whole were encouraging. Although it lacked the punch of the first series, *Doomwatch* was still a worthwhile programme to have on the air. The most popular episodes had been 'Flood', 'Say Knife, Fat Man' and 'The Killer Dolphins'; the more debate-filled and action-free episodes 'Deadly Dangerous Tomorrow' and 'Without the Bomb' came bottom. The report showed how many of the audience missed the colourful figure of John Ridge, and none of the new intake of characters had really caught the imagination in the same way as Ridge or Toby Wren.

In the last audience research report, a printers' error meant that it wasn't possible to assess how many would like to have seen a fourth series. It didn't matter. By the time that report had been compiled, Terence Dudley was preparing for the last series of *The Regiment*. It may have given him some small satisfaction, following the attack launched by Pedler and Davis, to see how the *Doomwatch* film failed to make much of an impression either.

One of the reasons for cancellation was, as Andrew Osborn pointed out to his colleagues on the Programme Review Board in July, many of the obvious and more dramatic situations had already been explored. There was not much else left to cover. A commentator in *New Scientist* agreed after commenting favourably on 'Deadly Dangerous Tomorrow'. That said, amongst the few reactions to the third series which survive in the Programme Review Board minutes, Desmond Wilcox said that he wanted to be a fan again but that the first five episodes just hadn't engaged him. Even Osborn admitted that the series had been 'patchy', but that there had been some very good episodes. *Flood* was the only episode to gain a mention during the second half of the run before the end. However, the Board did pay tribute to the series when it came to an end. It was noted that the programme had given a new word to the English language: *Doomwatch*.

After *Doomwatch*

John Paul's next job after *Doomwatch* was the play *The Garden* at the Hampstead Theatre Club. He continued to make regular appearances on television and stage for the rest of the decade, most notably in the opening episode of *I, Claudius* as Agrippa and the film *Cry Freedom* in 1987. One of his last appearances was in the ITV mini-series *Selling Hitler*, about the Hitler diaries hoax, where he played former Nazi Karl Wolff. He died in 1995.

John Bown and Elizabeth Weaver made occasional appearances on television until the early 1990s. Joby Blanshard was also no stranger to television viewers after *Doomwatch*, appearing in *When the Boat Comes In* (which Glyn Edwards also worked on), *All Creatures Great and Small* and *Juliet Bravo*. He was a good friend of Kit Pedler and saw for himself the various projects and experiments Pedler worked on. Joby may have been pleased to have learned that when the Pedlers were thinking of getting a new puppy, to fill the gap left by one that had died, Kit agreed, but only on the proviso that he could name it. He chose Bradley. Joby Blanshard died in 1992.

Vivien Sherrard resigned from Equity a couple of weeks after recording 'Waiting for a Knighthood', ready to get married and begin a new life in America: 'I do not remember the fuss in the press caused by "Fire and Brimstone". That must be because I was consumed with preparations for my wedding. Since Frank had to return to the United States, and no family members were available to help, all the work involved fell to me. It was an exhausting but happy time. I do remember being glad that *Doomwatch* was ending at precisely the same time that I was about to emigrate. Frank and I were married on September 9, and we left for the US a few days later. Terry Dudley attended our wedding and he brought little Stephen to our wedding, and evidently urged him to come up to me after the reception just as Frank and I were about to leave, to wish me every happiness! This was one of the most memorable incidents of the entire day, and the photographer caught it on camera. John Barron could not come to our wedding, but sent a telegram which read "Ministerial good wishes"!

'Frank would tell you that I have not become an American. He says I never got off the boat. Although I eventually gave way and took on US citizenship, largely because my father-in-law, a retired lawyer, wanted to be sure I would not run afoul of tax laws, should Frank pre-decease me. Now I have dual nationality. In England they say I sound like Katharine Hepburn, but in the United States my English accent is greatly admired. I do have a little trouble with spelling and pronunciation on occasion, but not that much.'

Simon Oates continued acting both on stage and screen, but his absence from the television screen in another leading role was remarked upon from time to time. He told the *Coventry Evening Telegraph* in 1974. An East Anglian theatre critic described Oates as 'one of those television actors who occasionally deigns to appear on stage,' which stung Oates as out of twenty year career, only four of them were spent on television for any great length. 'I can be out of work in more jobs than anybody I know.' Yet he was in great demand in the theatre and cabaret circuit. 'If anybody offered me an interesting series with a good script, of course I'd go back to television. It just does you good to get back to the stage.' In the early 1980s he was thinking of emigrating to Canada, having appeared several times in theatrical productions in Calgary.

Of all the productions he had ever worked on, *Doomwatch* was a firm favourite; he was always happy to talk about it and took part in the BBC4 documentary *The Cult of ... Doomwatch* in 2006. But the one role he would love to be remembered for, as he told Alan Hayes of the *Avengers Declassified* website in an interview conducted shortly before his death in 2009, was the cross-dressing Captain Terri Dennis in the stage show *Privates on Parade*.

That he was held in high esteem by his colleagues, both professionally and personally, is illustrated by this lovely recollection from Jean Trend: 'Simon was at a birthday party and David Jason was there. Simon was on sticks, he looked so poorly. He is a beautiful man. Simon actually stood up and told stories, and his timing was as immaculate as ever, and what David Jason did was get up and do a eulogy. Instead of waiting for the man to die, he actually said in front of Simon, surrounded by his friends, all the funny things and how he had helped David on his comedy career.

Even so close to death, Simon had that spark. Give him an audience and he was away! He was a darling man.'

Perhaps the last word should go to Simon Oates himself: 'I've had a life to die for. I've had ups and downs personally, just like anyone, but I couldn't have asked for a more satisfying life than the one I've had in theatre, television and film. I've been so lucky and I'm so grateful to have had the opportunity.'

5

Aftermath

'Inundated as we are by continual television repeats, I have often
wondered why we have never been treated to a re-run of the excellent
Doomwatch series. The recent exposures about salmonella and listeria and
the cover-up by the government must now pose the question however,
were TV producers too slow to see that *Doomwatch* was a potential money
spinner or did the programme get too near the bone for the comfort of the
Ministry of Agriculture.' Eric B Cranston, Glasgow, writing in the *Evening
Times* on 21 February 1989.

In December 1972, the *Daily Mirror* announced that 26 year old student
Jane Gower had become's Britain's first trained 'Doomwatch girl' after she
won a Master of Science degree in environmental pollution at Leeds
University. Just in time.

The hundred-plus recommendations put forward by the United
Nations Stockholm Conference were accepted by the General Assembly in
December. The result – a world monitoring system for pollution, launched
in the autumn of 1973. This was the UN's Environmental Programme
(UNEP) and was based in a thirty-two-storey conference centre in
Kenyatta, Nairobi. Kit Pedler's dream of a real Doomwatch would have
mirrored what they hoped to achieve: 'A team of international scientists
will evaluate information on pollution levels, fed to computers by space
satellites and land-based agencies from all over the world.' A former
Canadian businessman, Maurice Strong, was to be the programme's
executive director, and his assistant executive director was a theoretical
physicist, Dr Robert Frosch. A programme called Earthwatch was
designed to implement the recommendations made by the conference. The
pessimists, inevitably, called it Doomwatch.

The industrial juggernaut ground on. Even the energy crisis of the
1970s didn't stop it. Britain had discovered its own reserves of oil and
nuclear power and showed that it could have as much energy as it would
ever need – for the time being. Economic priorities meant that
governments did not want to scale back. Greenpeace and Friends of the
Earth took up the cudgels for the environment with direct action and well-
publicised confrontations, themselves targeted by the State as the crew of
the *Rainbow Warrior*, sunk in New Zealand by the French, would attest.
Criminals or justified activists: a matter of distinction. The Green Party,
created from the need expressed in *The Ecologist* landmark issue 'A

Blueprint for Survival', began to win council seats; a small step. However, the responsibility of a scientist towards the citizen and to the world was an idea that never went away and is still relevant in today's cynical age.

In Britain a small movement tried to argue for the need of a less harmful alternative technology which did not necessarily have to be regressive or primitive. They were not advocating a return to huts or caves but instead looking towards the post-industrial age. There were predictions of the end of industrial civilisation as the world gobbled up its natural resources including reserves of oil. Kit Pedler would confidently make such predictions and was frequently in the newspapers or on television, discussing his views or displaying his vision for what we would now call ecologically sound housing, something his daughter Lucy is now professionally involved with as an architect. He even designed and built a wooden chassis for the car. He became frustrated with the slow progress of the environmental movement and its motivation as the decade passed by. Self-sufficiency, and a scaled-down society based on smaller, localised units, was a fashionable area to be involved in. Its advocates were accused of being middle-class drop-outs, as epitomised by the BBC sitcom *The Good Life*. Pedler's line of reasoning led him to write *The Quest for Gaia*, published in 1979, a distillation of his thoughts and of the way he ideally wished to live.

Other TV Ideas

Pedler and Davis wanted to continue pursuing the *Doomwatch* theme in other television and film projects. Davis tried to interest Pedler in collaborating over a stage play revolving around a computer, but Pedler was not keen on the theatre and this idea floundered. At first, they began developing ideas for ITV, which they had hinted at during the 'Fire and Brimstone' saga.

One of these ideas might have been '1999: The Year of the Rat', which showed the results of Man ignoring the warnings of the early 1970s and treating the environmentalists as if they were crying wolf. By 1999 life was intolerable as a result of the accumulated filth and debris of unrestrained technological and industrial growth. An artificial virus escapes from a lab in 1978, carried by poison resistant rats and society collapses as no antibiotic could cure the epidemic. The series would follow the development of a successful vaccine and see which path the world would take: either a post-industrial one or a return to the old ways, with the virus ready to strike again. 'The city animal only just walks,' wrote Pedler in hand written notes. 'It's complexes are poised on a knife-edge and small breakdowns can lead to the most horrendous consequences. In New York, for example, a nineteen hour blackout led to street looting within a day.' The series would have followed the adventures of a *Dr Kildare* type character, and people living in an alternative technology commune. They were surviving, but only just.

This premise may sound familiar ... In 1975 Terence Dudley's final project as a BBC producer was the post-apocalyptic series *Survivors*, often seen as a companion piece to *Doomwatch*. Here, the dreadful has most certainly happened: a flu virus developed in a foreign lab is accidentally spread across the world by aeroplane, and the population is reduced to barely a fraction of what it was. The series showed how a group of survivors tried to get back to an agriculturally based life, working to the maxim of not using what they couldn't replace, whilst trying to protect modern sensibilities and social achievements in a new world that wasn't easily going to sustain them. By the close of the third series, a group had got a hydro-electric power station working again and were even using a form of currency. The ending was much criticised by some followers of the series, but it was logical that the wholesale abandonment of technology was never going to happen in the immediate aftermath of such an event. It would be needed to cushion the transition.

In many ways Kit Pedler would have been an ideal adviser for such a series, with his great interest in the technical challenges of self-sufficiency. This was Terence Dudley's last programme as producer, and he returned to directing and writing, working on programmes such as *All Creatures Great and Small*, perhaps his happiest time, and made some notable contributions to *Doctor Who*. He died on Christmas Day 1988.

Gerry Davis wanted to get an American version of *Doomwatch* made and used the feature film and a few episodes of the original series to generate interest. One format he pitched was *Worldforce 5*, based on Pedler's own ideas about a national disaster force, which followed on from the 'drums of death' that washed up upon the Cornish shore in 1972. This was the Disaster Squad, a team of people who went in following a calamity in an attempted to reduce the environmental and human impact afterwards. They appear to have been a United Nations outfit, based in a chalet on a lakeside in Geneva, created by millionaire businessman Arnold Kramer, whose daughter had died from mercury poisoning after swimming in the sea. Kramer discovered that the effluent which killed her came from one of his own subsidiaries. This Quist-like guilt trip inspires him to finance a new computer designed by scientific genius John Whale. It would function in the manner of the old Doomwatch computer, coming up with strategy and information on tackling or preventing environmental disasters. The Squad would be a ruthless outfit: a suggested example involved a crashed munitions train on a viaduct beside a village; they decide to dynamite the viaduct, killing the train crew but saving the village. Kramer (probably named after a similar character in the book *Mutant 59: The Plastic Eater*) would not think twice about kidnap, assassination or blackmail as they fought 'villainy and stupidity'. The issue at stake, the format read, was our own very survival. This was strong stuff. Davis and Pedler did not want another watered-down version of their message. When Gerry Davis moved over to America in the late 1970s, he tried to interest successful film producer and writer Carl Foreman in the series. Raymond Burr's name was linked to the role of Quist.

Without Davis, Pedler abandoned writing fiction other than for his own amusement and was busy lecturing, broadcasting and advising on environmental issues. Towards the end of the 1970s he experienced an upswing in his professional life when he collaborated with entrepreneur Nigel Tuersley on the Earthlife foundation, a project to build an ecologically sound centre in the heart of London. His interest in physics and alternative philosophies led to a documentary series called *Mind Over Matter* being commissioned by ITV. As the series was being transmitted, and Pedler was about to go over to America to research a potential film adaptation of Pedler and Davis' novel *The Dynostar Menace*, he suddenly died at his home in May 1981.

Gerry Davis continued pushing for an American version of *Doomwatch*, and by 1986 remained positive that it would happen. Sadly it wasn't to be, and he died in 1991.

Interest in the Programme

For a programme that has never had a terrestrial repeat, only one airing on a cable television channel in 1994, just two BBC videos and a single DVD release, *Doomwatch* is still very much remembered to this day. Certainly, Robert Powell's character of Toby Wren and his shock death has a lot to do with this, and some of the more interesting subjects of the first series (cannibal rats, melting aircraft and killer noise, for example) are well remembered. Aphrodisiac contraceptives, less so. Those involved in the ecological movements of the time felt that *Doomwatch* had an impact and a lasting value. Jonathan Porritt, Director of Friends of the Earth, was quoted in *The Listener* in 1988 as saying '*Doomwatch* was hitting the populist button, and became a particularly powerful catalyst in the early Seventies, even if it was true to the rather apocalyptic vision that prevailed then.'

During the 1980s the odd clip from an episode would appear on a nostalgia programme or quiz show such as *Telly Addicts*, or as a reminder of how Robert Powell's popular appeal was launched (with an inevitable look at that rat attack). The programme would sometimes appear as a retrospective in magazines such as *The Listener* or in more specialised publications such as *Starburst*. An interest began in the wake of a growing awareness of what was described as tele-fantasy or cult TV, helped by the burgeoning adoption of the domestic videotape recorder. Bootleg copies of virtually any surviving series which was slightly out of the ordinary began to circulate. *Doomwatch* was one of these, and, despite the almost unwatchable nature of some of the copies ('Sex and Violence' was particularly awful, but that added to its mystique of being a banned episode), it soon found a small but appreciative audience.

After the success of their *Doctor Who* and *Blake's 7* ranges, BBC Video dipped its toe into the programme and released four episodes over two cassettes, one containing 'The Plastic Eaters' and 'Tomorrow, the Rat', the other, 'The Red Sky' and 'You Killed Toby Wren'. These did not sell well and no more were issued. The same was true for a very early DVD release of 'The Plastic Eaters' and 'Tomorrow, the Rat'. This was the time before box sets became the only way to sell a programme.

Nevertheless, the interest and availability of 'classic' science fiction on video (legal or otherwise) was encouraged by several magazines which dealt with telefantasy, such as *Starburst, TV Zone*, the very short-lived *Fantasy Zone* (which featured a *Doomwatch* article in its very first issue), *Cult Times, SFX* and *Time Screen*, some of which suffered from paucity of information about the making of the series, unintentionally propagated myths or misremembered moments from the episodes. It was from these magazines that those fortunate enough to have watched and enjoyed the stories which had survived tried to glean what may have happened in those which had not. *TV Zone* covered a couple of these, but it wasn't until the late 1990s that a website run by C P Smith published storylines from later missing series one episodes. At last you could find out what was behind the food poisoning in 'Spectre at the Feast', just how Quist turned the tables in 'Hear No Evil' and what happened in the first forty-six minutes of 'Survival Code'. Alas, Smith did not have access to any third series scripts and could not continue the story.

Doomwatch does not have an active fan base, unlike other popular BBC dramas such as *Survivors* or *Blake's 7*, but the programme is remembered and is still being discovered by fans of 1970s television drama. There was a website, doomwatch.org, edited by Scott Burditt, which has not been updated since the first publication of this book in 2014, and it can now be found at a different address which is listed in the bibliography section of this book.

DVD
It doesn't help that the BBC kept few episodes in its vaults, with a handful of fuzzy 525-line copies recovered from Canada. The first series has eight episodes left, the third series only three (including the infamous 'Sex and Violence' which was never transmitted). The second series survives in its entirety. 2|entertain, the main publisher of BBC DVDs at the time, had plans for the programme following the release of *Adam Adamant Lives!* and the two *Andromeda* serials. Neither of these box sets sold as well as hoped,

and *Doomwatch* was dropped from the schedules. No remastering work had been carried out on the original tapes. With that went the possibility of seeing the scripts from the missing episodes appended as PDFs (which had been included in the case of the box sets mentioned above), not to mention a decent documentary and commentary tracks. The closest we came to a documentary was as part of *The Cult of ...* series on the digital channel BBC4 in 2006, which also covered *Adam Adamant Lives!*, *Star Cops*, *Survivors*, *Blake's 7* and *The Tripods* in its first series. The *Doomwatch* instalment featured contributions from Martin Worth, Robert Powell, Jonathan Alwyn and Jean Trend. Although the programme barely scratched the surface of the subject, it was a very well put-together piece. It can be found on the DVD release of the surviving episodes which was released in 2016 by Network to everyone's surprise. The Canadian 525 line episodes had undergone a process to make them as watchable as possible, but the condition of picture reflects the age of the tapes. It is better than nothing, and was warmly welcomed.

The *Cult of ... Doomwatch* also tackled something rather extraordinary which happened in 1999: the year when *Doomwatch* came back, not as *1999: The Year of the Rat* (which would have been fitting) but as *Winter Angel*.

Doomwatch: Winter Angel

Yvette Vanson, a major documentary producer, also developed dramas for television and film. She knew Kit Pedler's daughter Carol Topolski from Topolski's days as a censor, and they had collaborated on a film Vanson produced called *Violence and the Censors*. The idea of making a new series of *Doomwatch* appealed enormously. 'Carol let me have the rights for tuppence ha'penny.' Yvette Vanson and Simon Wright were executive producers whilst Peter Lee Wright was the producer. It would be a co-production between Working Title Television and Vanson Productions. A new company was formed: Doomwatch Productions Ltd.

Notable science fiction author Ian McDonald was asked to present ideas for the revival, and he pitched a number of 'cutting edge scientific ideas' only to find that the original series had been there first. John Howett was McDonald's co-writer. An awful lot had happened in the world of science and the environment between 1972 and 1998, when the script for *Winter Angel* was written: AIDS, food scares, the depletion of the ozone layer, imbalances between the haves and the have nots, a renewed nuclear arms escalation and de-escalation, waste disposal of all types ... an awful lot to concentrate the ecologically inclined mind of an author. There was good potential for a new series.

Rather than start from scratch, the film was going to be a continuation of the TV series (or the film, if you prefer), and Dr Quist would feature in the transition. We would learn how *Doomwatch* was closed down in 1979 under the new Conservative government, and meet two of Quist's former students. The BBC turned down the project, feeling it was not the kind of subject matter they were pursuing, but fledgling terrestrial channel Channel 5 took it on, much to contemporary critics' surprise. A two-hour ecological thriller was hardly Channel 5's style. Roy Battersby – 'a great political director', in Vanson's words – was hired. At a cost of £1.5 million, this was a very expensive project for the young channel.

Trevor Eve played astrophysicist Neil Tannahill, former student of Quist and the man who would assemble a new *Doomwatch* at the end of the film. As John Paul had died in 1995, Philip Stone took over the role of Quist, who was trying to draw Tannahill into a network of eco-warriors. Tannahill wished to remain neutral but was gradually persuaded to act when he discovered another of Quist's protégés, Dr Toby Ross (Miles Anderson), had succeeded in creating a black hole, feeding it nuclear waste from the Soviet bloc to keep it stable. Tannahill is assisted by computer genius Hugo Cox (Dallas Campbell) and environmental scientist Teri Riley (Allie Byrne). The TV movie was about as far from the original *Doomwatch* team of investigative ombudsman as could be imagined. Instead, we see a depiction of an authoritarian government, assassinations and media cover-ups. Adam Sweeting of the *Guardian* thought *Winter Angel* owed more to *Edge of Darkness*, BBC1's 1985 ecological thriller, than it did *Doomwatch*.

It was transmitted on 9 December 1999 at 9 pm. There were hopes it would be picked up for a series. 'All the reviews said this should be a series' said Yvette Vanson. 'Bring back *Doomwatch*, fantastic. Unfortunately, Channel Five didn't have the money or the inclination. But it was good fun to do.' It was released on DVD in 2010.

Could *Doomwatch* ever return?

Rights issues have been described as 'complicated' but not insoluble. There were attempts in the early 2010s to develop a new series, and a series of audio adventures were mooted but abandoned. However, it would be better to create something new and relevant rather than resurrecting the programme with tenuous links to the early 1970s. The themes, however, are as relevant today as they were forty years ago. But we are living in an age where drama is more inward-looking and doesn't like to explore issues further than the edge of the garden; or it tries to resurrect previous formats, or 'property', if you like, and turn them into modern 'product' with 'emotion', which usually means complicated relationship issues, rather than how we relate to the world around us, and what we are doing to it. A modern *Doomwatch* would spend more time on the emotional lives of the regulars than the issues we ordinary people don't realise we face every day, as society conditions us further and further into accepting the intolerable. Ridge's tangled love life would take precedence over the horrors of misapplied genetic engineering. Although, the two themes could go together ... However, a modern *Doomwatch* would certainly not contain the blind spots identified in the original, and a far more multi-cultural, and less masculine dominated set-up would be created, reflecting modern societies desire for inclusiveness. Above all, a new *Doomwatch* would simply have to be international, as we impact upon each other. Build our chimneys high enough, and we pollute Scandanavia ... A nuclear reactor melts down in Russia and we have contaminated milk in Scotland.

Drama is more expensive than it was under the old studio-based system that the BBC and regional ITV companies used to employ. The Channel 5 film showed that. Television executives seem to think that they must compete with the cinema for visual impact, and since our television sets can be mounted on the wall and rivalling the big screen, this is hardly surprising. Ecological disasters are a common theme for the cinemagoer, but they rely on spectacular special effects at the expense of any sensible message that a writer may be trying to impart.

Yet, the original premise of *Doomwatch*, formulated by Pedler and Davis and Dudley, the idea of a scientist's moral responsibility to us, the citizen, however, and the duty of governments to prevent technological hazard from runaway scientific and commercial development swamping and harming us, is evergreen.

Who is right?

Doomwatch ought to be remembered for being one of the more innovative series of its time, tackling the urgent problems of modern technological society in a shocking and direct manner, but the public disagreements between Pedler and Davis on one side, and Terence Dudley and Andrew Osborn on the other also raises comments. The split only became public once Gerry Davis had left the BBC and was looking to promote their forth-coming film. Their criticism of 'Fire and Brimstone' did damage the programme, but their stance received a lot of support from viewers upset over the treatment of Dr John Ridge. The scripts for the third series were professional and polished pieces of writing, but with exceptions such as 'Hair Trigger', 'Flood' or 'The Killer Dolphins', they did not have the attack or bite of their first series counterparts. The Doomwatch organisation and its characters became observers to police investigations, rather than in the field of battle. *Doomwatch* had also lost its unique science faction flavour for more realism. It is true that the novelty of the subject had diminished since the first series, and Dudley was aware of this. The series needed more than ever Pedler's imagination and Davis' drama-documentary approach to hold an audience, rather than the stage play exploration of a moral theme in a drawing room setting favoured by Dudley. But it must not be forgotten that Terence Dudley wrote 'Tomorrow the Rat' which for its time was the most controversial and shocking episode of the first series with the exception of 'Survival Code'. He, together with Davis and Pedler, produced the first successful series and kept his writers in check. They were a superb team when they worked in harmony and produced memorable television which is still enjoyed by its fans today. That should perhaps be their memorial, rather than what happened in 1972.

Part Four
Character Profiles

1
Spencer Quist, PhD, FRS

'At the time I felt about the Bomb as I do now: that with the threat of Hitler developing it, one did not have much alternative. But it was shattering when it was dropped on civilian populations in Japan; one realised that that was a mistake. One felt disillusioned about physics being used in this way.'

The above quotation could have come direct from the lips of Doctor Spencer Quist, who once said 'We thought it would never be used ... We wrote to the White House, all 130 of us. Explode it in the sea, we said. Demonstrate it. Don't drop it on Japan, demonstrate it.' Instead, it comes from Nobel Prize winner Professor Maurice Wilkins (1916-2004), the first president of the British Society for Social Responsibility in Science, founded with Steven and Hilary Rose on 19 April 1969 at the Royal Society in London.

His life bears some uncanny resemblances to Quist's. After reading physics at Cambridge, Wilkins worked on radar research during the war before joining the Manhattan project in California, where he contributed in a small way, separating isotopes. This was a man who as a student had been a member of the Cambridge Scientists' Anti-War Group but was convinced of the necessity of the work in stopping Hitler. Following the close of the war, issues with the atomic bomb pushed him away from physics and into molecular biology. Along with Crick and Watson, his researches helped to unravel the structure of the double helix of the DNA molecule, for which he was awarded the Nobel Prize for medicine in1962.

One of the first targets of the BSSRS was secret research being conducted into chemical and biological weapons at Porton Down, the government's research laboratories. Whether or not he was an influence for Quist, he was certainly emblematic of the type of scientist the post war period was beginning to produce: one with an ability to see a scientist's inherent responsibilities to the public and who could no longer blame outside forces for the dangerous application of their work. Quist also bears an uncanny similarity to another doctor. According to the original series format, Quist taught at the New Ipswich University from where he had originally graduated (changed to Oxford in the publicity material); Dr Kit Pedler went to public school in Ipswich for ten years. Quist enjoyed sculpting, as did Pedler, who also painted in his spare time. Both had mothers who were painters. Both could see the General Post Officer Tower from their office window. It is hardly surprising that a few of Pedler's real-life biographical details would find their way into his fictional creation. Quist was christened by Pedler and Davis after Adrian Quist (1913-1991), the Australian tennis champion.

Quist's Early Life

The background notes for Quist, which appear in the original format and are later embellished in publicity material, reveal the drive of the man. Quist's father was a lecturer in Social Sciences at Durham and, like Quist's mother, was not particularly political. He was an only child and graduated from Pembroke College, Oxford. His doctoral thesis was on the topology of the Riemann space, and his post-doctoral research was on critical mass relationships. A brilliant mathematician, he joined the 'Tube Alloys' team, which contributed to the Manhattan Project during World War II. His work led to the correct design of the critical mass shapes in the first four nuclear bombs manufactured by the Allies. This was where he met his first wife, Helena Weill, who was an American nuclear physicist. After the war, Quist continued refining his work.

The publicity material states that Helena died from leukaemia (the fate of Gerry Davis' first wife), believed to be a result of her work at Los Alamos. Her illness lasted seven years, during which Quist withdrew from work and cared for her. As we later learn, her last words to him in 1957 were 'Start again. Put it right.' 1957 was the same year Quist received the Nobel Prize for his mathematics in original solutions to complex topological functions. His guilt over the deaths of a quarter of a million Japanese, and his wife, drove Quist back to academia at the New University of Ipswich, reading pure mathematics. He is a withdrawn and sardonic man. The publicity material decided that Quist joined and headed the Pure Mathematics department shortly before his wife died. By the time he is asked to become director of Doomwatch by the newly re-elected Prime Minister, Quist is determined to make scientists face the moral and ethical consequences of their work before it is too late.

The description of Quist sees him as a powerful and strong man with a huge thirst for knowledge, but the guilt which has been gnawing from within has made him outspoken and aggressive. The format makes it quite clear that he has made a special study of leadership, which he believes is composed of rigid personal discipline, objectivity, command of feelings and total application to the matter at hand. He does not tolerate negligence and can drive his team to breakdown, but he will also stand up for his staff to the point where his own job or liberty is at stake. All this would be emphasised in scripts written by Pedler and Davis. In Dennis Spooner's 'The Logicians' he approves of the school's teaching of logic, believing this is what the world needs – clear headed thinking, uncluttered by emotion.

The publicity material describes Quist as having contempt for political dogmatists, devoutly atheist and a non-drinker, although this later point doesn't seem to have been followed through: he downs a pint very quickly in 'Invasion' and accepts half a pint of bitter from Bradley in 'The Inquest'.

Director of Doomwatch

When we first meet Quist in 'The Plastic Eaters' we see a man disillusioned with his post – as the format wanted – and faced with inter-departmental obstructionism, especially from his own Minister. He is almost prepared to resign but knows it would be accepted far too willingly. He refuses to countenance turning Doomwatch into a quasi-MI5 just to get basic information. With a number of successes notched to Doomwatch's name, the small department of ombudsmen has a reputation that Quist is keen to protect. There also seems to be a large slice of vanity on display; Ridge was correct in 'The Red Sky' in thinking that Quist would get more satisfaction running the whole place on his own. His loyalty to his team only goes so far and not when it threatens Doomwatch as a whole. Quist appreciates the importance of the department and knows how easily it could be finished. We see both sides to this in his dealings with Toby Wren. He was prepared to resign over Wren's suspension (perhaps he saw in the young man a potential protégé), but when he has to sack him for letting emotion get in the way of his work, he does it quickly and without ceremony. He has to do it to save Doomwatch.

The relationship between the emotional, instinctive Ridge and the brooding Quist is a fascinating dynamic during that first series. John Ridge, who originally knew Quist at Ipswich, understands him the most. In 'The Plastic Eaters' Ridge knew that guilt made Quist accept the Doomwatch brief. He reminds him of the atomic bomb to force him into action (such as authorising a break in to the Minister's office). When Ridge shouts at Quist that he is a murderer after the death of Toby Wren, Quist's furious reaction is simply because, deep down, that is how he feels but will not show it. Quist must have realised that he was cracking under the strain at the beginning of 'The Red Sky' but again refuses to admit that Ridge's diagnosis is correct in every detail. They may have had a huge respect for each other's abilities but Quist disapproves of many of Ridge's characteristics – the tendency to sneer, to crack jokes at the wrong moment, not to mention his rather open private life, though he unleashes Ridge onto Dr Mary Bryant to discover the secret of her research. In the right humour he is almost amused by him, but we seldom see them in a relaxed or even social situation.

Perhaps the early scenes in 'The Battery People' are the closest we get. Ridge, on the other hand, feels that Quist has an elegant scientific mind but is frustrated by his boss' reluctance to act as impulsively as himself. It is fair to say that Quist did not understand Ridge; he even admitted as much to Barbara Mason in 'Cause of Death'. What is it with that man that women seem to like?

Quist does not always see the need to get involved in a case. 'Quist doesn't usually like hunches', Ridge explains in 'Friday's Child', but when Quist suspects a cover-up or realises he is not being told the whole truth, he will unleash Doomwatch with his dogged determination to get to the heart of the matter, and when he does, he goes for the kill. Quist is not afraid to act as a moral judge, wagging a finger at the 'bad guys' as Ridge observed. He puts Duncan and Reynolds in danger (but not without warning) to show them the terrible side-effects of the T9 experiment, as there was no other way of persuading them. Quist needs to put up a token moral objection to, for example, tapping the phones at Falken's office in 'Hear No Evil', but has no qualms at further intrusive surveillance in the man's house. Likewise, he gets Ridge to break into the Beeston laboratories and the Patrick lab once he thinks the ends justify the means.

Colin Bradley is one whom he is certainly fond of, as he is the most dependable and level-headed of his three staff and closer in age. Pat Hunnisett is a reminder of the ordinary person, someone without a scientific discipline, of the consequences of their investigations. When she falls ill in 'The Devil's Sweets' we see the side of Quist that does not like to be helpless. He is concerned but will not show it, and then uses her recovery as a tool by keeping it secret and manipulating it. Quist uses Ridge's feelings to act as a weapon to break down the three businessmen he believed were stonewalling over their involvement in the poisoned chocolates. To be fair, Quist did not know that it would be Ridge who would pick up the telephone and be told by Wren that Pat was dead. But it took a while before he corrected the assertion. 'You bastard', indeed.

Emotions
Quist does not, or at least tries not to, allow emotion to cloud any issue. For a man who wants to be in command of his feelings, he is quick to anger and is frustrated just as easily. A rare fit of frustration in the Sussex psychology laboratories sees him throwing a flask of reacting chemicals to the floor, and, when he confronts Falken at the end of 'Hear No Evil', the amount of pent-up bile he unleashes on the man is astonishing. In 'By the Pricking of My Thumbs …' Quist refuses point blank to help journalist Oscar Franklin due to over-simplification of scientific matters in an article by Franklin concerning the XYY genetic theory – a theory which now threatens the future and even life of Franklin's adopted son. His even greater dislike of Professor Ensor in the same episode seems to be his primary motive when he changes his mind. Fay wonders about this several times. In some cut dialogue, Quist tells her 'I feel for the boy. I feel even

more for the fact that I was deceived.' Fay asks him how he can be so cold. 'Am I? You need a clear head, Fay, to stay unaffected by the world's only too general stupidity.' He can get it wrong, but, as Ridge once pointed out to the rest of the team, he doesn't like to admit it.

By 'Survival Code' Quist is finally face to face with a situation involving a nuclear bomb. Ridge once again correctly identifies the real problem as Quist having to face Los Alamos all over again. 'Because you made the first bomb, all the others are your responsibility. We're doing a job, not running a psychotherapy unit.' Meeting Dr Anne Tarrant for private counselling sessions in the following episode 'You Killed Toby Wren' makes him face up to the indulgence of guilt and realise that this time he had indeed done the right thing and could admit it. When Quist gets involved with the plutonium theft in 'Say Knife, Fat Man' or the secret test explosions in 'Flood', he is nowhere near as fraught as in 'Survival Code'.

In the second series he has become used to the demands of security and puts Dr Fay Chantry in a situation to exorcise a potential problem. His vision of Doomwatch rapidly becomes messianic. He speaks of taking the vow. His relationship with the various Ministries he has to deal with seems to be improving. He is certainly on good terms with Duncan, the Minister's assistant (having nearly sent the man over the edge of a cliff), and starts to see the Minister as a necessary prop by the time of 'Flight Into Yesterday'. Despite his problem with vested interests, Quist realises how much they need the Government – any Government – to push the environmental agenda. In the third series, this argument within Government has been won and Doomwatch has been vindicated, although the issue of 'who pays?' in order to clean up the mess is still unanswered. Quist also knows that only government and legislation can stop the pollution he is fighting and keep the scientific community in check.

Second Series Development
The second series Quist is more relaxed though he still has mountains to climb. He is less prone to emotional outbursts but still gets it wrong at times. In Invasion he can't tell the pub landlord the truth – that he will never see his village again. Instead, he is almost snide. He supports the cause of The Islanders, stuck in their huts far from home (a nice parallel to 'Invasion'), but is not above using them as a handy source of experimental data. When briefing Bradley on the shooting of Geoff Hardcastle in 'The Inquest', he is surprised when it sounds as if he is not terribly concerned. At the end of the series, it is a personal dislike of a young professor who insults him which creates his only on-screen argument with Geoff Hardcastle. He uses the suspected yellow fever outbreak and a quarantined Minister in 'The Web of Fear' as an excuse to get his flood

data analysed. He still needs to be absolutely sure that there is a case for Doomwatch to become involved.

The introduction of Dr Fay Chantry softened Quist's nature a little. Although there was never any hint of a possible relationship, he got on very well with her and was able to relax a little and express some of his deeper thoughts, some of which were cut from 'By The Pricking of My Thumbs...', though they were very revealing. After Fay wonders how he can be so cold about the Franklin case, she asks him if he hates people. Quist replies with difficulty 'Almost. They pollute themselves so eagerly. Perhaps it's because I've tried to love them, and failed? My responsibility entirely, I'm not blaming them. So now I talk of "truth" instead, as if it were...immutable.' The only time he was impatient with Fay was when he thought her work on the Ampleforth Project was making Doomwatch's reputation a laughing stock. Only at the end did he realise the true nature of her suffering.

Dilution of the Character

Quist's character did certainly change during the second series, but during the third, he is barely recognisable as that fierce fighter from the first. He no longer has his demons to drive him, his situation is much easier, and on occasion he is dwarfed in story terms by the Minister and sometimes Commander Stafford. By now, Doomwatch is definitely the arm of state that some American businesses feared it would become. Quist doesn't have to struggle as much as he used to, but that is not to say he is now complacent. The kind of stories the third series presented saw Quist observing and reacting. In the opening four episodes he is a bystander in other people's stratagems. This was a deliberate move by Terence Dudley, who wanted to make the character less of a demigod and less of a prig. The removal of Quist as the important central figure can be seen in 'Waiting for a Knighthood'. He is told things by Stafford, browbeaten by the Minister, gets help for Ridge, discusses diarrhoea over the dinner table with his new wife, has relaxing weekends in her cottage and ... that's about it.

The anthrax business in 'Fire and Brimstone' shook him to the core, but he had a certain sympathy with Ridge's actions. The environmental situation was not getting any better, and government action around the world was slow. Quist was prepared once again to resign and return to academic life, but the political realities of the event and the need for a cover-up forced the Minister to keep Quist on and improve the facilities for Doomwatch. As the series continued, the only real threat to Doomwatch was from the Treasury in 'Cause of Death', and the solution for the Minister was to make sure Quist was out of the way to prevent any scandal.

However, there are episodes such as 'The Killer Dolphins', 'Enquiry' and 'Flood' where Quist's full investigative best comes back to the fore. He is quite happy to drop sensitive issues, such as lead in petrol, because it is the brief that he is presented with which is all-important. Quist still has some issues which bring out the old fighter in him. He is appalled by the nuclear tests going on in the Barents Sea until he learns of the political trading that was going on, and he certainly felt the same zeal towards population control as Fulton.

By the end of the series, it is implied that an international Doomwatch is probable. One can only wonder if Dr Spencer Quist would have had a major role in its creation and implementation. It would have been the next logical step in his life. Failing that, then certainly a number of universities would have fallen over themselves to hire him – except for the ones he had exposed in the past, of course. He would have had to hand over the baton to another generation, but he would have inspired enough of them already. There are signs in the third series that Quist is losing his drive. At the end of 'Without the Bomb' he tells Bradley that he thinks it is now far too late to deal with the population problem, and in the final scene of 'Flood' he compares himself to King Canute (who drowned, as the Minister points out). One could see Quist becoming a bitter and disillusioned old man in his later years, as nothing appeared to improve around him. Or perhaps Anne helped him to find some peace at last and learn to start loving humanity once more. It would be a nicer conclusion to his story than the one Channel 5's film 'Winter Angel' gave him.

2
Dr John Paul Ridge PhD

'He's got a brilliant mind. Outstanding in many ways.' Barbara Mason,
'Cause of Death.'

Assuming writers have no imagination when it comes to the naming of
characters and just take them from real people or telephone directories, it
is possible that John Paul Ridge was named after a J. W. Ridge who
worked in the Ophthalmological Research Unit at Kit Pedler's Institute of
Ophthalmology in the mid-1950s and published a number of papers. The
'John Paul' part of the name was there from the very beginning, before the
role of Quist was cast, which was quite prescient on the part of the writers.

Original Ideas
The original format document describes Ridge's background in some
detail. He got his degree in Organic Chemistry at Cambridge and
proceeded to make a name for himself through a 'brilliant' line of research
into antibiotics. After collecting his doctorate, he turned down an
invitation to take a chair at Keele University and went off on a scientific
expedition to Brazil, where he ended up fighting for a lost cause with
Bolivian guerrillas, only just escaping with his life. He was signed up by
MI6 to spy on an Iron Curtain country. Thoroughly trained, his first
mission was successful, but his second was abruptly cut short when he
returned to Britain and resigned the service. This was regarded with
suspicion as he relates in 'Project Sahara'. The reason given was that he
was thoroughly disillusioned with the spying game and with his fellow
scientists on both sides of the Cold War. Quist met him at Ipswich while
Ridge was unsuccessfully readjusting back to civilian life. He was selected
for Doomwatch because of his 'amoral approach to any given problem'.
Ridge sees his loyalty as being to mankind rather than class, nationality or
race. This makes the security services suspicious. By now he is 38 and
suspects that he may be slowing down, and he is incapable of forming
permanent relationships with man or woman. 'This bothers him' because
underneath his 'hard' exterior, he is a nice, kind and charitable man.

The press pack elaborates on some more details and looks at his
character as if it was the result of a security investigation. His Ph.D in
Chemistry was taken at Trinity College. After resigning from MI6, he was
under surveillance until it appeared that he wasn't doing anything to
justify it. He is a womaniser 'almost to the level of compulsion, although

there is evidence that he is now dissatisfied with this situation and would like to form a more long-lasting relationship'. He has a total distrust of authority, a desire to attack organised activity, yet has a confused (at least from the point of view of the security-report compiler) idea of being of service to his country. He is best described as a 'mixture of schoolboy, intellectual and thug. He nevertheless retains an excellent front manner of great charm.' The report on Ridge somewhat predicts events in the third series: 'This rather incompatible mixture of qualities will, we think, lead to instability.'

The report also suggests that Ridge had killed three people, something that will be hinted at in 'Friday's Child' and confirmed in 'Fire and Brimstone', where some more details of Ridge's espionage days emerge. It seems that he once had a relationship with someone called Ilse, who he believes was deported by Special Branch. She died a year later in Dresden. One of the people involved in the case was Commander Neil Stafford. The only other references we get in the series to his MI6 days are of the 'back streets of Cairo' and a favour in Tripoli for a man called Willie. In the first series he is often to be seen breaking into offices, scaling fences, taking photos or planting bugs. Another side to his MI6 heritage was the slipping in and out of 'roles'. He made for a convincing civil servant in those episodes where he pretended to be from the Export Advisory Board and other similar outfits.

Doomwatch was a perfect vehicle for John Ridge. He passionately believed in the work that they were doing. He was fearless of the consequences and happy to stand on the moral high ground to berate others (in a manner he once criticised Quist for doing). 'In the Dark' sees him 'captured' after trying to break into McArthur's island house, but he is quick to point out to Andrew Seton that they were possibly concealing McArthur's death. What we see is Ridge trying to emulate Quist, but not always with correct judgement. Ridge will allow emotion to get in the way of his viewpoints, especially in matters of biology. He is disgusted with Dr Patrick's experiments in 'Friday's Child' whilst Wren and Quist marvel at the achievement. He keeps his opinions about the rat experiments subdued, but, by the time of 'You Killed Toby Wren', he is unbalanced by Toby's shock death and judgement goes right out of the window.

Relationship with Quist

Quist was a man whom Ridge admired and whom he thought had the most elegant scientific mind he had ever encountered, but his frustration with Quist was over the man's sense of caution. Ridge knew enough of Quist's background to know how to manipulate or shock him into taking action. This led to tension which was normally contained, but once in a while it would come to the surface. The first occasion was in 'The Red Sky', in which Quist was overworked, overtired and 'full of hate'. Ridge managed to persuade him to go on a holiday and not to take the whole work load on his own broad shoulders. Quist turned this around as if it had been his own idea. 'He's a clever bastard', Ridge sighs. But it goes back to the idea that Doomwatch is important and more than just one man. The next big clash happened in 'Survival Code', where Ridge would rather leave the recovery of the missing atom bombs to the Navy and the RAF and felt Quist was over-compensating for his part in the Manhattan Project. Even when Quist was proved right to be concerned about the bombs, it led to the death of Toby Wren.

Ridge was more upset by the death of someone he liked than he cared to admit. We see him spending the next few days needling Quist with a huge photograph of Wren and making cutting asides, and when Quist refuses to investigate the animal-human hybrid experiments in Norwich, Ridge loses it. He accuses Quist of indulging in a morbid sense of guilt and calls him an emotional hypocrite; a filthy, self-indulgent murderer. He then proceeds to indulge his own morbidity until Judith Lennox pulls him up sharp. Thus when Ridge gives his evidence before the tribunal, he stands up for Quist's actions. He now recognises that without Quist there would be no Doomwatch. He begins to call him Superman...

For the rest of the second series, Ridge and Quist get on much better. There is a little dig here and there but the conflict is gone. The only time Quist is really cross with Ridge is in 'Flight into Yesterday', when he manipulates the Minister into flying out to an ecological conference. 'I'm holding you personally responsible for the success of the Minister's visit...Or it's exit Ridge.' Ridge was fighting to keep Quist in Doomwatch by playing dirty, and this telling-off leads to a rather long sulk on the flight. 'In the Dark' shows a softer side to Ridge as he tries to persuade Quist not to get involved in whatever ethical minefield McArthur and his family have found themselves. It's done in a jocular (though perhaps slightly insulting) manner. 'He has no friends!' he tells Fay. Except for the nuclear physicists who built the Bomb, of course.

Ridge and women
Ridge's serial seducing probably played a large part in his espionage too, which became rather handy for Doomwatch. Explaining away his compulsion as 'mere nervous tension' in 'Tomorrow, the Rat', Quist found it useful to set him on Dr Mary Bryant, and even Geoff Hardcastle, on first impressions, felt that Ridge was the sort of man to appeal to Judith Lennox. Ridge once asked Dr Fay Chantry whether he disgusted her, but she replied that it was only when he was childishly proud of his latest conquest. Fay was one of the few women immune to his charms and survived any attempts at sledge-hammer seduction. Pat Hunnisett found it

easy to resist his almost constant flirtations. Barbara Mason, on the other hand, was something of a grey area. Although there was never any hint of an affair in the second series, she did seem quite fond of him, even kissing his cut forehead in 'No Room for Error'. She was also keen to keep in touch with him after he left hospital and was a shoulder for him to cry on in 'Cause of Death'.

One of Ridge's greatest assets, and something which Simon Oates instinctively developed, was his sense of humour. The character notes wanted him to be a cold fish, but after 'The Plastic Eaters', Ridge became a warmer and funnier character when the mood was right. Often his sense of humour was sharpened to contrast with a tragedy at the end of episodes such as 'Tomorrow, the Rat' and 'The Devil's Sweets'. He had a fine turn of phrase – 'How does that grab your apples?' 'Any joy at the morgue?' 'I'm a thug, darling', he says in response to a gentle insult from Fay. 'How can you expect me to understand all those polysyllabic, Latin derivatives?' After Geoff stings Quist about behaving like a domineering father, Ridge breaks the ice. 'Shall I throw him up against the wall, see if he bounces?'

Ridge's character is dramatically downplayed in the second series. He does not always have a large a role in the stories, and does not appear at all in 'The Inquest'. The gradual redefining of Doomwatch during the second series, from dangerous science-fiction imaginings to a discussion of social ills, saw the removal of the espionage elements, not to mention that the conflict between Quist and the government meant that Ridge's character was redundant. Ridge was also developing a slightly annoying tendency to put people off their job. 'Just don't make any mistakes', he very unhelpfully tells Dr Godfrey as he is about to wipe the memory core in 'The Iron Doctor', having said something similar to Bradley when he was about to perform the same procedure a few minutes earlier. The Ridge we know from the first series isn't there anymore; he is almost a caricature at times.

Third Series
The next time we see Ridge, he is stealing anthrax and sending six phials to major capital cities across the world. We later find out that his mental imbalance had been caused by lead poisoning, but the frustration with the slowness of state action to control pollution in all its forms had pushed him over the edge. Coupled with the complacent attitudes of commentators and perhaps people in general, he thought that they needed a shock. Ridge falls for the stratagems devised by Stafford and Dr Tarrant; when faced with a potential MI5 interrogation (which is simply a bluff), he tries to kill himself. His last words in the episode, as he slips in and out of consciousness, are 'Goodbye... Goodbye...' They could have left it there, but Ridge returns in 'Waiting for a Knighthood', having recovered his

sanity, and is itching to get out. At the end of the episode he is released but unable to return to the team.

Ridge's actions nearly destroyed Doomwatch. Quist offered to resign, and the Minister was happy to see its expertise at last deployed without Quist. But by the end of 'High Mountain', the department had doubled in size and Quist was untouchable. Ridge, therefore, saved Doomwatch, which became a department with far more authority than before. The next time we see him he has been working for aid organisations in Asia and has developed a view that what the East needs is Western advances. The last half of the episode is spent dismantling Ridge's new belief and suggesting that now he is outside Doomwatch he has a need to pick a fight with some other authority. The last we see of Ridge in this episode, he is being lectured by Quist and Tarrant in a holiday cottage over cultural differences. This episode is Quist's only on-screen encounter with Ridge after 'Fire and Brimstone'. He did visit him in hospital to have lunch from time to time, and at the end of 'Deadly Dangerous Tomorrow' tries to fix him up with a job, but Ridge never turns up for the appointment. He doesn't want charity, Anne diagnoses.

Ridge's best episode of the series, 'Cause of Death', was also his last, and it is also a very definite conclusion. He is now thoroughly disillusioned with Doomwatch and what it stands for. This is possibly an overreaction to his father's plight, which we learn of in this episode, and to how he had overlooked personal matters during his time in the department. His brother-in-law dismisses his previous career as 'Doomwatch nonsense', and his sister clearly resents Ridge's place in their father's affections. Neither of them seems to be interested in his recent illness, either. Quist describes him as a crusader who takes the world's problems upon his shoulders, which is almost the flip side of something Ridge said to Quist in 'In the Dark'. But this week Ridge is more concerned with his father than in saving the world. He nearly takes direct action in the matter of an unethical doctor and voluntary euthanasia – nearly does…but doesn't.

We also learn a little bit about his background, which was in a South London terraced community that was subsequently bulldozed and replaced with tower blocks. In a moving scene, Ridge tells Barbara Mason (who has clearly forgiven him for planting a phial of anthrax on her) how he feels that the world deserves all it is going to get. This time Quist wants to fix Ridge up with a job at a university, but Ridge still doesn't want hand-outs from Quist or Stafford or anyone. He tries to find a place for his father to be looked after with dignity. When he fails, he decides to take him in himself to care for. He says he'll learn how to do it, but it is too late: his father dies from a heart attack.

Perhaps Ridge does take that job in the university after his father's funeral, fading into academia with all those 'pretty birds' knocking on his door? After all, he does tell Barbara that he has been taking the wrong actions recently, thinking perhaps of 'Deadly Dangerous Tomorrow' (not to mention the anthrax business). That's where we leave Ridge – standing by the bedside of his dead father.

'I'm finished with Doomwatch and everything it stands for. No, I mean finished.'

3
Tobias Henry Wren, MA

'You're a physical chemist, first class honours Cambridge, single, and I'm told you're keen to join us... Well you have. This is your first effort. Let's see how you tackle it.' Quist to his new recruit, 'The Plastic Eaters'.

Toby Wren was designed to represent, to a small extent, the audience of the series. Not as experienced as the others in the Doomwatch team and without a title, he is neither as opinionated nor as haunted by demons as Quist and Ridge. He was to be a nice, fashionable, non-threatening and sensitive young man. In the event he became a highly popular character, with a huge number of female fans, and had one of the most memorable exits of any character on television.

Background

In the original format it is explained that he joins the department overawed by both the outfit and the reputation of Dr Quist. He was described as being average in both looks and personality and hesitant in front of the clashing egos of Quist, Ridge and Bradley. With Ridge designed to be the logical, cold, action man, Wren was to be the warmth and sensitivity of the group, and this sensitivity would attract Pat Hunnisett to him. It was planned for him to grow in confidence as the series progressed. The publicity notes went further into his character. Pre-doctoral studies at King's College, Cambridge, he held an MA and researched particle physics at the Cavendish Laboratories. His work was received with a mixture of regard and criticism because while 'undoubtedly original' it often lacked 'rigorous proof'. He is intuitive and abnormally sensitive to small character traits of those people with whom he is in contact. He is an idealist and a romantic and 'remains to be convinced that there is a strategic plan to life which he would be able to accept.' He can also be wrong in his ideas with conviction.

It was the imagination employed in his research thesis that caught the attention of Dr Quist. Pedler, by this point in his thinking, believed that as well as a social conscience, a scientist should have a creative imagination. 'An intuitive artist' suggested the format, and we see flashes of this during the series with his lighter-than-air bricks design in 'The Battery People' and his struggle to prove the link between the Somerset deaths and Alminster Chemicals in 'Train and De-Train'.

Our First Meeting

It is through Wren that we are first introduced to the Doomwatch set-up, as he arrives for what he thinks is a job interview – but he has already been accepted for the job. Within five minutes we discover that he disapproves of Ridge's sexist attitudes, and any awe he felt at being in Doomwatch quickly evaporates when the staff, absorbed in their work, ignore him. He is quite happy to walk out until Quist challenges him and gets a smart reply. He is then plunged into his first investigation: to discover the cause of a plane crash in San Pedro. Unwittingly he puts his return flight in peril by bringing on board a piece of contaminated wiring full of the Variant 14 virus. It is unusual to separate one of the main cast from the others so early in an introductory story, but we get the chance to see Wren face a potentially terminal situation, trying to remain calm as the plane dissolves around him.

This was not to be his only brush with death in the series – the young scientist has tragedy written all over him. In 'Burial at Sea' he touches a nerve agent, which causes a hallucination and a near-coma. The genetically altered rats attack him in the Chambers' kitchen, as they perceive him to be a threat – and possibly supper. A security department decides to suspend him on account of his heavy drinking. He nearly loses his job when he finally lets his feelings get the better of him, outraged by the callous behaviour of Mr Mitchell towards his ex-tutor from Cambridge, the likeable Mr Ellis.

Approach to Work

Wren's approach to work is usually calm and methodical. The imagination described in the format allows him to develop his hunches and act upon them, and he is often the one to discover the truth behind a situation. It was he who was suspicious of Doctor Patrick's evidence in court during Friday's Child, but his detachment from sentiment lets him step back and admire the scientific breakthrough Patrick has achieved. Wren works out the nature of the new breed of rat just by letting logic dictate to his imagination what he and Brad have just observed in the Chambers' kitchen. This deduction from observation occurs again in 'The Red Sky', with the passing overhead of a rocket-fuelled jet and the discovery of the collapsed Mrs Knott inside a lighthouse. Talking to Mrs Larch in 'Re-Entry Forbidden' unlocks the secret paranoia that gripped her husband. Last but not least, he discovers the secret of the sanctions-busting ship, the Helena, which gives Quist all he needs to blackmail Falken in 'Hear No Evil'.

With the small department surrounded by civil service and governmental enemies, Wren forms a close bond with Dr Quist and admires him. When Quist praises the very ill Wren in 'Burial at Sea', after he manages to pass over the sample jar containing the nerve-gas agent, the script describes the marvellous effect this has on him. Wren quickly learns how to interest Quist in a troubling case by not just coming up with a hunch, but by laying down grounds for suspicion until his boss is intrigued. 'I was suitably diffident', he later says to Ridge. Yet his faith in Quist allows him to tell Ridge over the telephone that Pat Hunnisett had died, when in actual fact she was recovering from her poisoning. He also approves of his 'dirty tactics' in 'Hear No Evil', threatening Falken with a blank spool of tape.

Though a clever and intuitive a scientist, Wren is never very comfortable in Ridge's line of work – a spot of espionage. His high-pitched voice during the chocolate factory scene in 'The Devil's Sweets' arouses suspicions in the manager; the pathologist investigating Ellis' death in 'Train and De-Train' also picks up on Wren's nerves, as lying never comes easily to him. When faced with the callous injustice of Mitchell's treatment of Ellis, he can barely conceal his dislike of the man and handles the situation badly. Unlike Ridge in later scenes, Wren plays it straight – no subterfuge or pretence. With their second encounter, which leads to Ellis' sacking, Wren can no longer contain himself and tells Mitchell what he thinks of him. Whether or not he did kick the booze, as was suggested at the end of 'Project Sahara' (doubtful, since he was looking forward to a drink in 'The Red Sky'), one can only imagine how much he drank after this incident.

Weaknesses
When Wren faces gross injustice or despair, he hits the bottle. 'Doesn't happen often, though', Quist confides to Stella Robson. Wren's drinking only ever manifested itself on screen during 'Project Sahara'. Quist knows how suspension from work would affect the young man and is deeply concerned – but only up to a point. Nevertheless, as Wren falls to pieces, Quist works hard to have him reinstated. Wren would stand up for Quist, too; in 'Survival Code', he feels Ridge has gone too far in trying to make Quist realise that they are in the way of the Navy's attempt to recover lost bombs. He even calls him a bastard.

The clouding of judgement by emotion is often touched upon in Doomwatch, as scientists who let that happen cannot do their job properly. Indeed, Wren accuses Ridge of this very matter in 'Friday's Child'. In 'Train and De-Train' Quist has no choice but to sack Wren, something Ridge warned him would happen earlier in the episode. Wren does not even try to justify his outburst to Quist when he hears the recording. (It must have given Wren some pleasure when a tape recording is used to bring down Falken two episodes later.) Quist is not vindictive, offering to give him a 'damn good reference'. But later, the next time we see them together in Mitchell's office, Quist is completely thrown by Toby's arrival.

He doesn't even make eye contact with him until they are out in the car park. Wren respectfully holds open the door for him, but they stand around, unable to talk to each other, just exchanging glances by their respective cars. Quist is obviously caught in a dilemma. Perhaps he sees a future him in Wren? He uses the Greenland lice report Wren had been working on to reinstate him, with a snappy 'Don't you go self-pitying on me!' Wren's tiny little smile says it all.

Wren's luck runs out under the timbers of the Byfield Regis pier. When he first comes face to face with the bomb, he pushes himself as far away from it as he possibly can, but then willingly takes over from Quist in removing the detonators – his ultimate show of faith. He thinks he has successfully removed all the explosive detonators from the nuclear bomb, but he has overlooked one last wire. His wire cutters have fallen into the sea, and as he follows the wire back to its terminal using a propped-up mirror, he is unaware that the final countdown motor has reached zero. And he so nearly succeeded, too.

The impact of Wren's death affected Pat Hunnisett so much that she fell ill and did not return to the department. 'The Devil's Sweets' implies that there was a mild romance in the offing, but her headache prevented her from having the drink that she had offered to buy him. Of all of the team, Wren was closest to her in age and she was clearly comfortable around him. Ridge could not conceal his anger for very long and blamed Quist directly. Their explosive argument and Ridge coming face to face with his own hypocrisy lanced the festering boil between them. What Ridge did with the huge 'blown up' photo of Wren we never find out. Only Bradley kept his feelings to himself. He too liked Wren, although occasionally had to remind him of how scientists were supposed to operate. In the aftermath of Wren's death, Quist visited his family. 'Quiet, normal, decent people', they told him how proud their son had been to work for him, how he always talked about him. Quist did feel guilt, how could he not? But once he came to terms with Wren's death, and that what had to be done that terrible night had to be done, he was healed.

Fans of Toby Wren took a lot longer to recover from the death of their hero. Even to this day, members of the public remember their TV heartthrob, and some are still quite annoyed to be reminded of what happened to him that night on the south coast.

4
Pat Hunnisett

'Free offers, I can never resist a free offer.' Pat, 'The Devil's Sweets'.

All the series format says about Doomwatch secretary Pat Hunnisett is that she is 'attractive, quick-witted, [and] loyal...Tea-maker, mother and potential mistress to the group. Pursued by Ridge she, in fact, favours the unresponsive Wren.' On screen, she is used to occasionally ask questions and have elements of the plot explained to her. And that's about it. As the youngest of the team, and therefore the 'hippest', she knows about the pop group, who are dying in a Plymouth hospital, in 'Burial at Sea'.

Occasionally Pat is allowed out of the office in order to do something other than sit behind the typewriter or fight off Ridge. Terence Dudley wrote for her to accompany Wren to the Chambers' household in 'Tomorrow, the Rat', presumably to help comfort any hysterical women. In 'Spectre at the Feast' it is clear that she is quite keen on George Pravda's character and that the age difference does not bother her. However, poisoned lobster bothers Egri, and he sees Pat as a wizened old crone, giving him a mild heart attack. Although it was nice of Dudley to try and give Hunnisett something additional to do apart from bitch about any other women who enter the Doomwatch office (see 'Project Sahara' and 'Re-Entry Forbidden'), it is quite unforgivable to reduce her to stupidity in 'Tomorrow, the Rat', where she is trying to work something out only for Quist to patronise her twice. And being a woman, she is therefore in charge of cooking lobsters during the investigation into the so-called Millionaires' Shakes in 'Spectre at the Feast'.

Pat finds Ridge a bit too forward for her tastes. We learn almost immediately in the series that he is interested in her, as he pinches her bottom. Normally she teases him and quite enjoys picking holes in his character. Ridge's flirtation reaches its peak in 'The Devil's Sweets', but this is used simply to contrast his grief towards the end of the episode, where he thought she had died. In the same story the 'unresponsive' Wren suggests that Pat take him out for the drink that she had promised him, but by then she had become ill from the drugged chocolate. Wren simply shrugs and walks off. However, the pair, probably similar in age, do get on quite well, as seen in 'Train and De-Train', with some mild joking and banter.

But with Dr Quist, she is far more circumspect and respectful, never sure whether she is going to be barked at, patronised or humoured.

However, as an efficient secretary, she knows in which direction Quist prefers to face when travelling by train. Quist probably hadn't given her a second thought until she falls ill, possibly as a result of the tests they were subjecting her to during the episode. 'Why don't we have a male secretary?' is, hopefully, an expression of his concern. When her illness becomes very serious, he is extremely worried but does not show it until he confronts Dr Benson in his lab. Even then, he uses her recovery as a tool by keeping it secret and manipulating it. However, her 'considerable sexual assets' were something Quist was not blind to, finding them useful in order to get co-operation from the manager of Jayson's hotel in 'Spectre at the Feast'. Since the episode no longer exists, one can only imagine the face the actress was directed to pull at that little comment.

She is certainly interested in the work of Doomwatch, although she finds their animal experiments hard to take and wonders whether the money spent on the American rocket programme could have been better used elsewhere. In these rare opportunities for a spot of characterisation, her opinions are usually slammed down, probably quite an accurate reflection of how a scientist might behave with an 'ignorant' member of the public.

Pat's zenith is in 'The Devil's Sweets', and at last she has something more to do than giggle in the office and look good in a mini-skirt. She is even on location at the top of the programme. She has a chance to be ill, upset, confused and frightened. In the script, when she has lit up a cigarette, she notices that Quist, Ridge and Wren are all staring at her. 'She swallows hard; she tries to find amusement in her ejaculation of perplexity and nervousness… Then a sudden taut movement of her head in close shot as she looks in fear of Quist.' She later stands up to Quist, and he realises he owes her some explanations and relaxes. In her final scene, the director is trying to make us think we are looking at her death mask – no make-up, head slumped forward – before she looks up and a jaunty soundtrack tells us all is well.

Her final scene in *Doomwatch* is her premonition of the Byfield Regis bomb killing off Quist, Ridge and Wren all together. She took Wren's death badly and was hospitalised. 'Fancied him rotten', explains Ridge to the new secretary, Barbara Mason. 'Still, no taste.'

We would have heard about Pat one more time in 'The Web of Fear' had it not been edited out. As Barbara complains of being treated as a coffee slave by Bradley, Geoff asks was the 'last one, Pat, as cheeky?' 'Not to start with', Bradley says. 'They get that way. It's having John Ridge around.'

5
Colin Bradley, BSc

'I'm the chief cook and bottle washer around here.' Bradley, 'You Killed Toby Wren'.

Colin Bradley is described in the format as a 'highly skilled instrument designer with a pass science degree.' The press notes added 'He is 39, slow but by no means stupid, and apparently able to do almost anything with his hands.' From the start he was to be a working-class north countryman with a class chip on his shoulder. He was to be the ordinary man with clear, traditional loyalties and views. Thankfully the way Joby Blanshard played the role ensured that this was to be no stereotype, and a warm, even lovable, characterisation emerged. Pat Hunnisett liked to tease him for his Yorkshire roots, but the biggest jokes at his expense came from himself. He tells Dr Quist in 'Hear No Evil' that he is looking forward to his trip to Flyingdales in Yorkshire because he came from those parts. He says his old friends think of him as a kind of superior technician, maintaining electric kettles for the typing pool. 'There's always a welcome back home for a failure.'

Bradley is usually to be seen operating the monolithic Doomwatch computer, which he helped to design and build. He sets up and monitors experiments, and he analyses and compiles data, sometimes throughout the night. The word for Colin is 'dependable'.

He is a straightforward man. Married, and with children, he is dedicated and only prepared to speak his mind when it is safe to do so. He is perhaps the only member of the Doomwatch team with whom Quist can relax and not have to be on guard as he is with Ridge, or cautious as he is with Wren on occasions. Bradley is very loyal to Quist; perhaps too loyal. He is prepared to turn a blind eye to Quist's bad temper in 'The Red Sky' and makes excuses for him in public, even though he privately agrees with the rest of the team in thinking that his boss badly needs a holiday. He also cut through Quist's apparent blasé reaction to the news Geoff Hardcastle had been shot in 'The Inquest'. Quist apologises for appearing callous, and then gets in his revenge by scolding Bradley for not keeping up to date with their work load.

Quist calls him 'Brad' from time to time; no other member of staff gets this familiarity. Bradley always calls him 'Doctor Quist' and never gets over-familiar, though sometimes he will have a drink with him after work or offer some company during stressful occasions, such as in 'Survival

506

Code'. After Wren's death, Bradley tries to protect Quist from Ridge's needling and, once that situation has passed, offers a few crumbs of comfort.

With Ridge he is less circumspect, even though the man technically outranks him. He doesn't approve of Ridge's behaviour, seeing him as 'too damn rude', and is frequently appalled by his willingness to say the unthinkable. With Wren he has a younger man to deal with, and they normally get on quite fine, although in 'Train and De-Train' he tells him off for leaping to conclusions over the cause of the Somerset deaths. 'Scientists don't bet.'

Colin Bradley does not like humbug. He dismisses Pat's concerns about the cost of a rocket programme versus the cost of feeding starving children, likening her to someone who puts out a collection box on her mantelpiece but puts nothing in herself. He also has no time for showing around celebrity guests, such as astronaut Dick Larch, especially when there is work to do. He is in favour of animal experimentation, having performed a few himself in the series. His attitude mirrors that of Dr Pedler's in the 1950s and early 1960s. 'It's either them or you', he tells Pat in 'Train and De-Train'. On other issues he will guard his feelings.

After Wren's death, it is as if nothing has happened when he introduces himself to Barbara Mason and puts her at her ease, but the moment he sees the huge picture of Toby he tells Ridge not to be so childish. Whatever feelings he had, he kept them strictly private and probably at home. Likewise, after the anthrax business, Colin stops Barbara from handing in her resignation when it seems that Doomwatch is finished, telling her to sleep on it, and takes her for a drink to cheer her up. He would stick with Doomwatch until the bitter end. Barbara likens him to an engineer in a sinking ship with the waters closing in over his head. Bradley doesn't play politics and certainly does not want to antagonise the Minister. He has a family to think about and support.

The only occasion in the first series where Colin Bradley takes centre stage is in 'Hear No Evil'. The 'failure' returns home to make some routine tests but soon uncovers sinister goings-on at the Jedder factory. His tact ensures that there is no sudden disclosure, and he brings the scandal back to London to be dealt with. From being the general technician and lab assistant in the first series, he starts to become engaged in Doomwatch projects and investigations in the second. He is quite excited in his only scene in 'The Islanders' over the data being produced from their tests on the exiles, has to re-programme the dangerous computer in 'The Iron Doctor' and takes centre stage for most of 'The Inquest'. Here, his blunt speaking and perfectly logical views create an uproar which causes more than a little embarrassment in the pub later on when he has to confess all to Quist and Hardcastle.

Colin Bradley is not in every episode. In the first series he is only absent for 'Friday's Child', but in the second series he is missing from three episodes, and in the third series, two. Even when he does appear it can sometimes be for just a scene or two, such as in 'The Battery People', 'The Islanders' or 'The Web of Fear'. However, by the third series he is a senior member of the team. The department doubles in size, and when he is faced with of a team of assistants in 'Say Knife, Fat Man', he doesn't quite know what to do with them. It is his report in 'High Mountain' that the Drummond group wish to suppress; it is his investigation into the 'crazy vicar' of 'Waiting for a Knighthood' that leads to the theory explaining Ridge's anthrax incident; and he gets to ride in a helicopter to see just what NATO have been getting up to in the North Sea in 'Flood'. He is also used as a handy information point for Barbara Mason, with whom he becomes quite close to in the third series. By the final episode, he is engaged in a long-term project, monitoring the pollution in our oceans.

In the early days, he rarely expresses an opinion on the issues that the Doomwatch team face, sometimes because he is hardly there, at other times because Quist, Ridge and Wren have already covered the angles, but probably most often because he 'knows his place'. By the time of 'High Mountain', Brad is the second-longest surviving member of the team, and the writers start to make him a mouthpiece for a particular side of an argument, sometimes representing an old-fashioned or conventional point of view, and it can get heated. In 'Without the Bomb' he is opposed to the free availability of Joyne, an aphrodisiac contraceptive ('It's downright disgusting'), agreeing with Anne Tarrant that he is a square. He said it himself in 'Flight Into Yesterday'. But as he tells Barbara Mason, he is concerned by the behaviour Joyne would promote in teenagers, reflecting a common middle-aged refusal to condone social freedoms that were unthinkable in the past. Perhaps he came from a Methodist Tabernacle tradition, as did some of his contemporaries.

Colin Bradley was popular with viewers, according to audience research reports for the third series, with some unaware that he had been in it since the beginning and who thought he was an interesting addition to the team. A 'blunt, plain speaking Yorkshireman', Hardcastle called him, and he was about as close to ordinary as the Doomwatch team ever got. It is fitting that he was there for the very end of the series

6
Geoff Hardcastle

'The boy who resigned from Norfolk last week. Was in all the papers. Remember? ... Biologist. Extra-uterine conception. Test tube babies. He resigned in protest.' – Quist, 'You Killed Toby Wren'.

1970 was a good year for taking responsibility in the biological field. The year began with James Shapiro, a 'brilliant young biologist', who only the previous November had announced the first isolation of a pure gene. He had withdrawn from further research for 'moral and ethical reasons'. The announcement was made in 1969 by Shapiro, Lawrence Eron and Jonathan R. Beckwith, and it was seen by them as an opportunity to heighten public awareness of the potential social consequences of research into genetics. Earlier that same year, the Harvard Educational Review had published a paper by biologist Arthur Jensen, who claimed that blacks were genetically inferior to whites in intelligence. Articles based on studies such as this soon prompted a group of physicists and biologists to form Scientists and Engineers for Social and Political Action, soon renamed Science for the People. Making public their concerns was as controversial as their work. Defending their 'alarmist' stance in a letter to Nature magazine, they wrote 'Let us simply point out to those who feel we have ample time to deal with these problems that less than 50 years elapsed between Becquerel's discovery of radioactivity in 1896 and the use of atomic weapons against human beings in 1945...If we do not [work for radical change], we will one day be a group of very regretful Oppenheimers.'

Peter Harper, whom we met in the chapter on 'Tomorrow, the Rat', spoke at a conference called 'The Threats and Promises of Science' at Imperial College London in August the same year. Aged 25, he was working for a Ph.D in experimental biochemistry on memory. 'He is one of a group of 80 young academics from 15 nations with growing misgivings over science's role in altering the way we live. They hope the conference will lead to the establishment of a permanent organisation to focus the attention of people on the influence of science and technology' reported *The Times* in July 1970.

Harper would later coin the phrase 'alternative technology' and he went on to become one of those at the forefront of the movement, later founding the Centre For Alternative Technology in Wales. He was also amongst the theosophists who had formed LASITOC a few years earlier. Standing for 'Look At, Search In, Try Out Committee', this international group of students had a fine aim: to discover the 'source of our present ills and to remove the source and then to make such a use of the technology we have and could develop, that we may achieve a new level of civilisation that protects the environment and guards the life-support systems of this planet that look, suddenly, very fragile'. LASITOC had organised the conference at which Harper had spoken. He told *The Times* 'I think there are certain things it is just as well not to know and I wrote out my resignation. The Professor told me I think you are mad but the best of luck. I finish at the end of term but my views have not changed. Most science is a waste of time and sometimes it is positively harmful.'

Later that same year, Harper would join Kit Pedler and other concerned people in the small London New Science Group, where they shared and formulated views. Out of this, the seeds were sown for alternative technology and the next exciting phase in Kit Pedler's life.

In Search of a Character
Whether it was Shapiro or Harper that was the origin of Geoff Hardcastle is hard to say without a glimpse at a writers' guide for the second series. It is more likely to be Shapiro, with the added element of Geoff's resignation thrown in. It was a logical step for a new character to take in the series. Toby Wren did not seem to have any particularly grievance when he joined the Doomwatch team. Geoff had an outlook (grievance is perhaps too strong a word) which at first excited Quist, though he later found it to be self-indulgent. Fertility research during a population explosion seemed to Hardcastle to be as equally self-indulgent. *The Population Bomb* had set the agenda in environmental concerns and would continue to do so for some time, in much the same way that global warming dominates now.

In his first episode Geoff Hardcastle is presented as a calm, clinical professional who dislikes sentimentalists. He is a humane man who does not want to see Professor Hayland and his work 'crucified' by the 'morbid media'. Geoff initially had no thoughts of joining the Doomwatch team, and after witnessing the clash between Quist and Ridge it is a wonder that he eventually agreed to. We do not see any formal 'taking the vow' scene as we do with Fay. There he is the following week, carrying lots of equipment up a craggy Yorkshire cliff face, being the butt of John Ridge's jokes. 'Invasion' sees Geoff as an established member of the Doomwatch team with Quist's full confidence.

He spends the first half of the story in Ridge's shadow but is full of the moral outrage and frustrations that marked Toby Wren at times. He is tenacious in trying to find the missing potholers that they had sent down into the caves. Later in the story he spots a vital clue that shows the boys had been inside the sealed-off Grange and were thus infected with a lethal virus. It's a good start for the character. We don't see him again for another two weeks.

The next time we see Geoff it is half way through the fifth episode, 'By The Pricking of My Thumbs....' He is doing some exceedingly dull work for Fay, snipping out pictures of chromosomes, before he is sent on the case of the missing schoolboy, Stephen Franklin. Geoff gets a chance for a tense stand-off at Gatwick Airport. In the episodes that follow, Geoff is fighting for screen time amongst a set of characters who were probably more interesting to write for. Stories such as 'The Web of Fear' and 'In the Dark' leave Geoff back in the Doomwatch office whilst Quist, Ridge and Fay go off to the Isles of Scilly or Scotland. He is very much the junior. He gets a bit of investigating to do, such as interviewing the designer of the computer in 'The Iron Doctor' or digging out dirt on the public relations firm set up to destroy Doomwatch in 'Flight Into Yesterday'. When he does have a chance to take centre stage in 'The Inquest', he gets shot and Bradley – an even more underused character – takes over.

After standard fare for him in 'The Logicians', Geoff Hardcastle finally comes to life as a character in 'Public Enemy'. But this the end of the second series and indeed of Geoff. He is able to play the generation gap card by understanding, if not necessarily supporting, Geoff Lewis' stance. It leads to the only argument he ever had with Quist, but it doesn't last long. The episode at least gives the chance for Geoff to do some detective work, climb a ladder, and get shouted down at a public meeting.

The last we hear of Geoff is in the third series' 'High Mountain', where the Minister makes it clear that he couldn't be trusted to keep silent about the Ridge affair and has arranged for him to take a job in industry. Presumably, this means he was still working for Doomwatch up to 'Fire and Brimstone'. Precisely what the job in industry was, we are not told. Chances are it was not Carlingham Alloys. Geoff Hardcastle was a character designed to replace, though not emulate, Toby Wren, and for that he has sometimes been judged lacking. This is not the fault of the actor but simply a lack of imagination on the part of the time-pressed production team during their script wars. Within the programmes they did make, Geoff Hardcastle was not given any real development or a chance to show his potential. It is no wonder John Nolan reportedly found it difficult to find any substance in the character, as Darrol Blake remembers. Apart from references to studying at Durham and Norfolk (and having an uncle who died of a lung disease), that's it.

John Nolan was not given the opportunity to shine as brightly as he could have done, but what he did do, he did very well indeed.

7
Dr Fay Chantry

'You're a person who needs to feel totally committed. That's one of the
qualities that earned you the job. And that's the reason you're here now,
for reassurance.' Quist, 'No Room for Error'.

The character that was designed to address the cries of sexism in Doomwatch
turned out to be a far more interesting person than the one who was supposed
to follow Robert Powell. An expert virologist, Fay Chantry had a successful
career researching new cures at a pharmaceutical concern. She was divorced
and had a young daughter (as indeed did her eventual replacement, Dr Anne
Tarrant). She applied to join Doomwatch after Quist realized that he needed
someone with a medical background because they were being swamped with
those sorts of enquiries. She needs to feel committed and tries not to let feeling
get in the way of investigations or decision making.

Fay's first episode was 'No Room for Error', one of those episodes where
coincidence is given a little stretch. The problem concerns a new drug that Fay
has helped to develop. It allows Quist the chance to address the one issue
raised by her security report – her relationship with Nigel Waring. Their fling
only happened after he had separated from his wife, but it seems that the
relationship became too intense, and Fay had to leave her job and re-enter the
NHS wards. As the episode proceeds, it seems that Fay may well abandon any
thought of working for Doomwatch, as she is quite impressed with the
changes at her former laboratory and with the new Nigel Waring.
Unfortunately, the investigation into the new drug's side effects points the
finger at the carelessness of Waring, and Fay has no compunction in being the
one to do the pointing. It cost her her relationship, and so she takes 'the vow'
with Doomwatch.

In her next episode, 'By the Pricking of my Thumbs...', Fay Chantry is a
different character from the one we had seen the previous week. Less prim
and proper, she seems to have relaxed into the Doomwatch team enough to be
quite aware of Ridge's womanising. Her character is given a little nudge with
the almost throwaway revelation that she is lonely. Once again she is prepared
to stand up to another professional – this time Ensor. Her sense of ethics is
very well rounded, and she is a delight. Why she wasn't introduced earlier in
the series is lost to history – probably budgetary reasons. Had the script not
been edited, we would have had a scene where Fay questions Quist about his
attitude to mankind, showing that even her boss was prepared to open up his
soul to his latest recruit.

Relationships

Dr Fay Chantry comes across as a warm, empathic character, who fits in remarkably well with the Doomwatch team. Fay is used as one of the major players of the team. Even when it is an episode to which she does not really contribute much, such as 'In the Dark' or 'The Logicians', she is around and takes part. Colin Bradley's first assessment that she 'seems like a nice kid' proves correct.

Fay's relationship with Ridge is quite interesting. Ridge is given a close-up when Fay makes her entrance, the suggestion being that he didn't realise that the new candidate for Doomwatch was to be a woman. But never again was there any hint that he might try his legendary charm on her. 'Simon and I were very good friends before I joined the Doomwatch cast, and we wondered if there should be a relationship between us, deciding no, Fay had enough on her plate!' remembers Jean Trend. But the on-screen relationship that they developed was one of mutual respect and playful teasing. Fay was certainly amused by Ridge's behaviour, smiling at news of his latest conquest. She was also pleased to call him 'a thug' when she overheard his phone call to Willie in 'Public Enemy'. As for Ridge's tour-de-force description of Mrs Griffiths in 'The Web of Fear', Fay can't resist a little grin every time he nearly gets round to describing her nice pair of – well, Fay cuts him off both times with a superbly timed interjection.

'In the Dark' was the closest Fay came to being a Ridge comedy stooge, building a bonfire in the woods to allow Ridge a chance to break into the McArthur island home. In 'The Logicians' she gets to do a double take when Ridge, phoning from the school, calls her mother and makes his report in coded language so as not to be overheard. She also has a mild flirtation in this episode with the elder Priestland. Obviously she has a thing for single parent fathers working in pharmaceutical laboratories. Her last episode, 'Public Enemy', sees her playing the detective, talking to residents around Carlingham about their problems living next to a factory as well as having 'joy at the morgue.'

Her relationship with Dr Quist mellows quite considerably after the first episode, where she puts her foot right in it. She thinks that Doomwatch has been withholding permission for Stellamycin to be used to fight the latest typhoid outbreak but has to backtrack quite spectacularly when it turns out to be a Ministry delay instead. Quist doesn't mind – further evidence that she is the right person for the job. She is the only one of the regular team not to have had a major disagreement with Quist, and the pair get on very well indeed, working very closely in 'The Web of Fear', and she tries to protect him from Ridge's psychoanalysis in 'In the Dark', the only time she ever snaps at Ridge.

There isn't much to say about her relationship with either Geoff or Colin;

they had very few things to do together on screen. Geoff is clearly considered her junior as he is given some very dull and tedious scissor work in 'By The Pricking of My Thumbs…', whilst she gets to assist Professor Ensor.

Skills

Fay's medical qualifications were fully exploited by the writers. 'The Iron Doctor', set in a country hospital, could have been written with her in mind, and 'Flight Into Yesterday' gave Fay the chance to write a report on the tests for jet lag. 'The Web of Fear' saw Fay Chantry use her expertise in viruses, which makes you wonder why she was not the lead in 'The Inquest', which had a similar set-up. Playing this sort of character did have a downside for the actress: 'All that scientific jargon I had to learn. It was a nightmare, I remember, and it seemed no-one else had that type of script but me. It was very hard. Simon used to say to me, "You need to bring in more humour to your part," and I said, "Well, you give me the humour when all I've got is scientific blurb and make humour out of that!" Looking back, I would think how differently I would do it now with the benefit of hindsight, and how sophisticated television has become since then. Humour would have been nice.'

The best episode for Fay was 'The Human Time Bomb', specifically written to give her centre stage. Fay starts the episode in a high state of nervous tension, and it builds up from there to her eventual nervous breakdown. She witnesses a road accident, a psychotic fit, is subjected to jeers from drunks, claustrophobia, dirty phone calls – but, above all she misses her daughter. The smashing of her daughter's picture helps to alienate Fay even further as well as making a symbolic point. The lack of sympathy shown to Fay by Quist and Ridge is quite shocking. Quist thinks Fay is becoming prejudiced and that she is playing into the hands of Langly, who will have any report of hers laughed out of court. She has become a part of the urban neurosis around her, seeing plots everywhere, witnessing the disintegration of the human condition. She saves Quist from being attacked by a small child with a hammer at one point by nearly running him over, although he doesn't see it quite as that.

It is a great shame that Fay was dropped from the team for the third series, for which the actress received no explanation. Just imagine, had Fay stayed on instead of Dr Tarrant taking over, would she have started a relationship with Quist, or married him? Both characters were divorced and had a daughter from a previous relationship.

The last we hear of Dr Fay Chantry is that she has returned to the NHS. In the rehearsal script for 'High Mountain' the Minister is pleased in view of Fay's history of 'instability'…

8

Ministers And Sir George Holroyd

'Don't give me trouble. My predecessor, now you riled him, but me, I'm not easily riled.' Davies, 'The Battery People'.

It is a safe bet to say that the Minister for National Security played by John Barron in 'The Plastic Eaters' is a totally different person to Barron's verbose, witty and erudite Minister first seen in 'You Killed Toby Wren' (whose forename, George, is only referred to once that season, and in his very first scene). Otherwise, what on earth could have happened to the sly, almost sinister character from *Doomwatch*'s opening episode to turn him into this jolly chap?

When being cleared for his internal commission to write 'Waiting for a Knighthood', Terence Dudley made it clear that he had created the latter character. The former was the sort of politician that Pedler and Davis wished to portray, but it was also the kind of apparently simplistic characterisation which Dudley deplored. George became Sir George Holroyd in the third series and appeared in all but one of the twelve recorded episodes. Interestingly, Holroyd was also the surname for Barron's character in 'The Plastic Eaters', but Geoffrey was his first name. This was never mentioned on screen, only in the draft script and in notes for the rejected storyline of Jan Read's 'The Pacifiers'.

If the above speculation is correct, Geoffrey Holroyd moved on, having been keen to get rid of Quist from Doomwatch, and was replaced by John Timothy Davies in 'The Battery People' as Minister for National Security. He too doesn't last very long in the job before Sir George Holroyd takes over. It is implied in 'You Killed Toby Wren' that this new Minister has been in the job for some time. Air Commodore Parks tells him that it has been standard practice to call in Doomwatch to investigate matters of technological hazard 'ever since you made it so', and Barbara Mason speaks of a recent Cabinet reshuffle which Sir George was anxious about in 'Flight Into Yesterday'. (A Cabinet reshuffle, where the Prime Minister moves around, promotes or sacks Ministers, would explain why Hamilton Dyce's Minister seems to be in two different areas of government in 'Tomorrow, the Rat' and 'Survival Code'.)

We do not get any sense of time scale in *Doomwatch*. With episodes recorded in summer and winter, and then transmitted in a different order, we get the cold winter trees of 'In the Dark' followed a few weeks later by the summer lushness of 'The Logicians'. Any amount of time could have passed since 'The Battery People'.

Second Series Ministers

In both of his second series episodes the Minister states that he supports the idea of Doomwatch, but his problem is with Quist, who is too independent from Government thinking in his view. He sees the political advantage of having such an organisation, especially if the Americans are thinking of setting up something similar. The theme of co-operation with America is highlighted in 'Flight Into Yesterday', where the Minister and Quist gain a better understanding of each other, even though they only meet briefly in the very first scene. Quist tells Ridge that Doomwatch doesn't stand a chance of surviving without the Minister, whilst the Minister learns that Quist is not so irresponsible as to launch a major attack on governments at a congress of scientists in America. This is a very different dynamic from the one Kit Pedler and Gerry Davis had in mind and was a signal for the future. This does not stop the Minister from acting against the advice of Quist's department in how to avoid succumbing to the dangers of jet lag, however. As the episode unfolds he is manipulated and stressed out to the point where he collapses from a heart attack.

John Savident's Minister, seen in 'The Web of Fear', is the Minister for Health, presumably seconded to National Security whilst Sir George recuperates. Richard Duncan is with him as his assistant, discussing the London flood menace. However, in the rehearsal script, it is made clear that Savident is not in charge of National Security and needs to liaise with that department's Minister. This scene was cut out of the finished episode, probably in rehearsals.

Third Series

In the third series the Minister was finally to become a regular and is described as such in the format document. He is 'of an age with Quist. A handsome, clever, cultivated man. Every inch a professional politician with a sharp mind and a pretty wit. Committed rather than dedicated he is the master of creative compromise and this is the crux of his conflict with Quist. In short, a man of immense cunning who intimates alone have the right to call him devious.' Quist, it is noted, 'is unable to compromise'. We never learn anything of his background other than a brief anecdote about his war years, where he was a Major in the Army, and that he had been in India.

After the first two episodes of the third series, Sir George no longer tries to neuter Doomwatch or regard Quist as anything other than a necessary but powerful nuisance, one he was forced to retain just when he thought he was finally getting rid of him. During the second episode, 'High Mountain', the Minister does not appear, at least in the script, to be gloating at the possibility of removing Quist. He does not accept his resignation immediately, wanting Quist to find a job worth leaving Doomwatch for as a face-saving exercise for the Government. Doomwatch has become accepted by the State, so much so that the Government questions the need for the department when its thinking is now factored into every other corner of policy by the time of 'Cause of Death'. The Minister brings Quist in to investigate during 'Enquiry', occasionally warns him off from others with little success and, as in 'Flood', uses Quist to fight his own very necessary battles. So much pressure was put on him to find out what Quist was looking into in 'The Killer Dolphins' that he made a rare appearance in the Doomwatch offices to see for himself.

The Minister and Quist were certainly not friends. All Quist can see in Sir George is the safe politician. They spar together in 'Without the Bomb', 'Flood' and especially 'The Killer Dolphins'. When Quist is recalled to London, he says to another character that he might throw some samples of dolphin excreta into the Minister's face. On the whole, the Minister is supportive, and Quist is almost knee-jerk in his reactions and assumptions. At times this almost seems unfair until you remember the battles Quist has had to fight, how Holroyd wanted him out by the time of the Byfield bomb affair and that he called him unstable in 'Flight Into Yesterday'.

As early as 'Flight Into Yesterday' Sir George tells Ridge that he agrees with Quist's views on the environment but will never say so in public. He expresses sympathy for Ridge's motivations in the anthrax scare, with the stunt he pulls in St James' Park in 'Deadly Dangerous Tomorrow' and over the state of care for the elderly in Britain in 'Cause of Death'. But he is a politician first and foremost; he can see the cost sheet dangling in front of his nose. That was his concern after reading Ridge's manifesto: the amount of legislation and expenditure needed to clean up the country. The political will to argue the case was just not there. This conflict of realities comes out in Waiting for a Knighthood, in which Sir George is quietly lobbied by Massingham to discover the Government's view on car pollution. Sir George expresses surprise at Massingham's pragmatic attitude towards pollution (which is along the same lines as the industrialists in 'Spectre at the Feast' or 'High Mountain'). He is only concerned that Quist is not investigating lead in petrol simply because everybody else seems to be. But he is clearly not on the side of the industrialists. Even when Massingham makes an emotional appeal for Sir George to make an announcement that lead in petrol is safe, to try and persuade his son's abductor that he is not to blame for her own child's death, he won't do it.

In the next episode, 'Without the Bomb', we meet his French wife Janette, played by Katherine Kath. We discover his lack of sexual appetite – a result of channelling his energies into his career. Janette doesn't mind. Their marriage has been successful and they are compatible. He has ambitions to rise to the top and become Prime Minister. We also find out that he won't let his own feelings interfere with the decision to make the aphrodisiac contraceptive Joyne available over the counter without a prescription. He knows too well the moral outrage Joyne will cause and is looking for a way to prevent a political explosion. Likewise, in his only scene in 'Sex and Violence', he tells Quist that not once in his political career has he appealed to the voters' more base instincts. He is no Enoch Powell, whose infamous 'Rivers of Blood' speech a few years earlier in which he criticised immigration, saw him sacked from the Shadow Cabinet and later leave the Conservative Party. He does not want to legislate for the sexual behaviour of the country and decide what is moral or indecent.

As a Minister, Sir George Holroyd is almost too good to be true, and at times he comes close to dominating his episodes, making Quist a secondary character. In part this is due to the wonderful performance delivered by John Barron, who made a career from playing establishment figures. He was a great favourite with the public and was often singled out for praise in the audience research reports and by critics in the media.

9
Which Government?

'Why our so called leaders cannot face the truth, I don't know. They lie, they push, they sell the future down the river … Immediate advantage and to hell with the long term consequences.' – Quist, 'The Red Sky'.

The Department for Observation and Measurement of Scientific Work, or Doomwatch, is a branch of the Ministry of National Security, although it can be seconded to any governmental department that needs their help or expertise. The department was created by the Prime Minister, who appointed Dr Quist to be its director. There is a Minister to whom they are answerable. He may be a junior Minister rather than a Secretary of State in charge of a number of departments within his overall Ministry. For example, the Ministry of National Security could be a branch of the Ministry of Defence, and in fact the original idea was for them to be attached to the MOD. A department like Doomwatch would have access to information of the most sensitive and secret nature, and a very high security clearance would be required. Although direct access to the Minister is available, they would normally go through his civil service or political staff. The department has a wide brief to investigate technological hazard. They act as watchdogs but have powers to hold inquiries, so a recommendation for action would be taken seriously.

When 'The Plastic Eaters' was made in 1969, the Labour Government was towards the end of its second term in office and was expected to win a third the following year. Hence, in 'The Plastic Eaters', Quist mentions how the Government was practically re-elected on the issue of Doomwatch. However, in a fictional drama programme, it was absolutely forbidden for a government to be knowingly based on one currently sitting, although that sort of thing isn't frowned upon as much these days. So was the Government intended to be a Labour one? It might explain why there is a Welsh MP, Davies, as Minister for National Security in 'The Battery People'. Conservative Welsh MPs existed in the 1960s of course, but mining communities more often than not sent Labour MPs to represent them in Parliament.

While writing was underway for the second series, Edward Heath's Conservative Government was voted in. 'You Killed Toby Wren' was written and produced during that first year in office, and the Minister here simply oozes Conservativeness. His knighthood is not referred to at this point. There were not many knighted Labour ministers at all in the 1960s and 1970s, although there were unelected ministers from the House of Lords in the Conservative government of the time.

In the format document for the third series, Dudley told his writers that 'the first series anticipated the creation of The Department of the Environment, in its Ministry of National Security. Care was taken during the preparation of Series II to avoid explicit reference to the Ministry and the Minister. If we continue to preserve the anonymity of the Ministry we allow the assumption that our Ministry is the Department of the Environment. This is yet another reason for our fiction to stay clear of irresponsibility.' References to the Ministry of National Security were phased out although Dudley forgot that they did still appear in the second series.

10
Anne Tarrant, PhD

'You're the serenest person I know.' – Quist, 'Fire and Brimstone'.

Dr Anne Tarrant was brought into the series as a one-off character who was going to help Dr Quist come to terms with the death of Toby Wren and help him with his guilt over the Manhattan Project. She certainly makes an impression on him, and Quist asks to see her again – but not in a professional capacity. The idea of never dating your shrink was obviously not in vogue in the early 1970s, and Dr Tarrant certainly has no problem with it. She ascertains that Spencer Quist is single and heterosexual, and that is probably the most important thing. If is sounds oddly self-evident, it is mainly because, in her entry in the third series writers' guide, it is explained that the 32-year-old Anne Tarrant had been deserted by her husband after the birth of her daughter. He had been a latent homosexual. Professionally, this might have intrigued her; personally, it must have devastated her, especially back then when it was considered a condition rather than a natural part of life.

Damaged relationships were a hallmark of the Doomwatch team. It may have been her fears of desertion that led to the original idea of Anne and Spencer 'living in sin'. Although this was no longer the 1950s, sensibilities were still touchy about unmarried couples daring to cohabit. Terence Dudley played it safe and advised writers not to dwell on this aspect of their relationship: on-screen chastity was the way. That is, until someone lost their nerve, and either Dudley or Andrew Osborn made sure that their relationship was solemnised (probably with a registry officer to assuage Quist's atheism) in the last episode to be recorded, 'Waiting for a Knighthood'. Anne is as middle-class as they come and insists that the vicar's wife is brought up to date on her private life, not giving her anything extra to worry about.

Anne Tarrant is a busy woman, part-time consultant psychiatrist to Broadmoor and to the civil service when required, and considered important enough to be asked to sit on the Purvis Committee in 'Sex and Violence'. The Minister himself has no problem in listening to her advice in 'Fire and Brimstone'. She has her own rooms, although whether she works independently or as part of a team is unclear. She also works at a marital aid clinic. With Quist's department expanded, he is allowed to hire any consultant he needs on whatever basis he requires, so it gives Quist (and the writers) an excellent chance to employ her expertise as a psychiatrist.

Quist uses her to assess the impact of Joyne in 'Without the Bomb' and on the condition of Michael Clark in 'Enquiry'. But generally she acts independently and only brings in Doomwatch because of her husband as in 'Waiting for a Knighthood' and 'Hair Trigger'. And sometimes their paths cross more coincidentally, as in 'Cause of Death'.

That she cares deeply is not in doubt. Anne's conflict with McEwan's mechanistic approach in 'Hair Trigger' is dismissed as academic jealousy, but she cares about the human being, rather than reducing that person down to reflexes and kicks. She gets angry over the incorrect diagnosis Dr Evans (which may have been deliberate) ascribed to Clark and is horrified by Stafford's proposal to torture John Ridge. She also gets quite heated with Colin Bradley over his old-fashioned views of sex in society, seeing the results of repressing the sex drive made manifest in her consultancy rooms.

Ridge knows enough about Anne's skills to suspect she is psychoanalysing him early in 'Fire and Brimstone'. It was her plan to fool him into thinking his blackmail plot had worked because she knew the possible mental consequences if Stafford pushed him too far. They don't seem to know each other well enough for Anne to visit him in his mental hospital until Quist suggests she go because he is 'always asking about you.' She is one of the 'weapons' used against him in 'Deadly Dangerous Tomorrow' to change his mind about giving a First World standard of living to a developing country. In the script Ridge and Anne seem quite friendly despite the serious intent of the weekend. It was probably Anne who developed the strategy to persuade him not to continue with his publicity stunt. But for once, there was no flirting – not even Ridge would dare attempt to seduce the boss' wife. In 'Cause of Death' she has been studying geriatric care in the country and will neither be lectured by him nor take any nonsense during one of his holier-than-thou outbursts. Anne never really formed an on-screen relationship with Stafford, Barbara or Colin as she was rarely in the office. But she was as hostile to Stafford in 'High Mountain' as the rest of them.

Relationship with Quist

It is with Quist that we see her the most, often at her country home (somewhere near Twickenham), where she would rather he spent his weekends relaxing. Quist admits to Mrs Simpson, wife of the vicar in 'Waiting for a Knighthood', that Anne has a habit of making the rest of the world feel it doesn't exist when he is with her. She knows that he was almost incapable of relaxing, describing him as a caged lion when he has to have a few days off with a bad cold in 'Cause of Death'. The writers' guide explains that Quist had been instantly attracted to her, not only by her looks but by her 'rare calm and detachment... To Quist she is Alexander

Pope's "reasonable woman."' She is his companion and confidante. As we have seen, their on-screen relationship was as close as 1970s BBC morality allowed. There are a few sly hints in 'Hair Trigger', but we normally see them relaxing together with a book or a paper, with some easy listening music or a spot of classical in the background. They chat lightly about Wilhelm Reich's *The Function of the Orgasm* as if it were a book on gardening and discuss the symptoms of lead poisoning (vomiting, diarrhoea) over dinner without pausing between mouthfuls.

That he depends on her comes out loud and clear in 'Fire and Brimstone': Quist is deeply troubled by the events that have unfolded, but Anne is able to see the situation with a cool and calm head. 'You're the serenest person I know' he says. Anne agrees: 'That's because I'm the most realistic.' One of the primary functions of the character was to make Quist less of a demigod and a prig, and it certainly succeeded. If 'High Mountain' is to be taken as an example, Anne may have preferred Quist to move away from government circles and out into the private sector. Her daughter only has one mention in the series (but it came in 'Sex and Violence', so it was never transmitted). Quist seemed fond of her. What he was like as a step-father is anyone's guess, but he was probably a good one. Anne brought out a new, softer side to Quist. He didn't need to fight any more.

11
Commander Neil Stafford

'What happens to people when they start working for you, Quist?'
Minister, 'Flood'.

Commander Neil Stafford can be described as a game-keeper turned poacher. His character brief in the third series writers' guide explains that he comes from Naval Intelligence but now works in 'Security' and may have been keeping an eye on the Doomwatch team for some time. As usual with these sorts of characters, he is described as 'the complete professional'. In addition, 'he's highly trained and deadly efficient. His mind is cold and his heart is colder but he can melt man, woman or beast with unforced, uncloying charm. A very dangerous man.' Some of the audience liked him. In the audience research reports he was seen as something of an enigma, initially unsympathetic, with hidden agendas. 'Deep and unpredictable' and 'the handsomest and most charming man on TV', according to one viewer.

Stafford's role in the plot was really to take over from Ridge but without the occasional forays into illegality. The idea for the character was that, since he was not a scientist, he could have the plot explained to him, which was a function normally reserved for the secretaries. He could penetrate establishments, act as an agent and be distinct from Quist's character as scientific investigator and the Minister's as political operator. He certainly wasn't to be a womaniser and had very few, if any, emotional outbursts. What we never learn in the series is that he had suffered a tragedy in his life five years earlier, when his wife and young baby daughter were killed in a car crash. His surviving son, now 14, is at Wellington.

First Appearance
Stafford's first appearance sets up the character well. He is simply the investigator trying to crack Ridge and discover the whereabouts of the missing anthrax. He is quite prepared to use drastic actions, including torture and subterfuge. He actually pushes Ridge too far with the implied threat of torture (a bluff, as it turns out, to get Ridge to effect an escape) and instead has to fight to save his life when Ridge bites through his own vein. Ridge's suicide attempt and Stafford's brusque manner with Barbara and Bradley in the Doomwatch offices don't exactly endear him to the team he has been seconded by the Minister to spy on. He knows this, yet in

some scenes in 'High Mountain' even does his best to wind up Bradley and Barbara. More importantly, he has to work hard to win over the trust of Quist, which brings us to his rather sudden conversion. We are expected to believe that, after listening to Ridge's outbursts about the state of the planet and having read some of his notes, he comes over to Ridge's thinking, or at least empathises to some extent. He tips off the French security services about the anthrax scare in 'Fire and Brimstone' in order to embolden the department he now has to work for and emphatically tells Ian Drummond 'I work for Doctor Quist' at one point in 'High Mountain'.

However, throughout the series we do not really get to see many examples of Stafford with a passion for the environment or the Doomwatch cause. It seems, and this is only conjecture, that his actions are merely to try and worm his way into the trust, if not affections, of Quist, Bradley and Barbara Mason. He has to report to the Minister, acting as his mole in the department, and does his best to get rid of the second spy in the nest – the unnamed laboratory assistant in 'Waiting for a Knighthood'. The script for 'Enquiry' wants us to believe he is appalled by lobotomin at the end of the episode as he tells Dr Quist that they have a report to write, and he suggests to the Minister how action should have been taken on the Cordell report in 'Cause of Death'. Even if he is a convert, he isn't going to be a tub thumper. If we accept his conversion on face value, Stafford has two masters to deal with – Quist and Sir George Holroyd – and flits between the two quite readily. He often has scenes with the Minister, sometimes trying to placate him. However, the Minister is exasperated by Stafford's arrest in Flood and furious that he is in Naples at a NATO base, investigating killer dolphins.

Relations with Quist

That Quist doesn't quite trust Stafford is plain very early on. He is not happy that Stafford is taking Ridge's place, and does his best to avoid him, but at the end of 'High Mountain' buys him a drink for helping to save Doomwatch. Quist will never forget that Stafford is the Minister's man and a spy, but he will use him when required. He is even pleased to call him 'Neil', but in the episodes that survive and the scripts, there is never a sense of warmth, understanding or even an occasional joke between the two. When Quist is away in 'Cause of Death', it is Stafford who takes his place and runs the shop. Although not quite a civil servant, Stafford is as close to the ideal man to take charge of the department in the Government's eyes.

To be fair, Stafford is not particularly consistent. He may call Quist 'our revered boss' in one episode, but then in 'Hair Trigger', having reported to Quist that Anne has been injured, he suddenly snaps that Sir George is waiting for an explanation for the incident. As late (in transmission order) as 'Flood', Quist is written as being suspicious over Stafford's co-operation. Whether this was carried through into rehearsals and onto the screen is, alas, something we may never find out, but it should be remembered that the script was one of the earliest written for the series. 'The Killer Dolphins' does suggest that Stafford is prepared to go that extra mile for Quist, going on leave to do some unofficial snooping into NATO's use of dolphins for military purposes despite the Minister wanting no investigation. During his digging, Stafford inadvertently discovers a spy ring, which at least partially mollifies the Minister.

If Stafford's relationship with Quist was iffy, it was nothing compared to his with John Ridge. We discover how the pair had locked horns before, over a woman who had to be deported. There is absolutely no love lost and a huge hostility. When ordered to get Ridge out of the mental hospital in which he has been incarcerated in 'Waiting for a Knighthood', their meeting is again tense and full of digs. But why does Stafford look around the hospital room as if planning an actual physical escape rather than assessing the state of his mind? He actually gives Ridge a lift home after his release and shakes his hand – a gesture that he is now also part of Doomwatch – but still, you can't help being suspicious.

Their next encounter, in 'Deadly Dangerous Tomorrow', is again as part of an investigation, this time over the mysterious appearance of a family of Indians in a tent in St James Park. By this time, the roles are slightly reversed. The caring, passionate Ridge has become a cynical 'realist' who wants India to have DDT to fight malaria. Stafford now thinks Ridge sees himself as a martyr and an innocent, but, as he tells the Minister later, he understands Ridge's cause because he too has been to India. It is Stafford who wants to save Ridge from himself; he suggests to Quist and Anne that they should take him down to the country for a weekend break and talk him out of his publicity stunt. The next time they meet is in 'Cause of Death'. Ridge is concerned for his father's welfare at the Cordell Clinic, where he may soon die. Stafford doesn't know this, and when Ridge visits the Doomwatch offices and tells Stafford where Quist can stuff the job he has tried to line up for him, Stafford takes offence and has to be calmed down by Barbara. He later admits to being inconsiderate. When he mistakenly believes that Ridge had stolen a report from Anne and given it to the media, Stafford admits to being wrong again, this time to Ridge himself, and is at the clinic to tell him of Cordell's forthcoming arrest. He is there when Ridge's father dies.

Stafford has an interesting relationship with Barbara, who can barely conceal her dislike for him and frequently tries to cut him down to size. Just the thought of having him working in the department is enough for Barbara to think about resigning. They have several notable conflicts: over the motives of a group of students who have stolen a shipment of plutonium; over the traditional role of a woman in society and her right to make the first move in sexual advances; and over Ridge, as we have seen. There cannot be any possibility of romance between these two, even when she teasingly comes on to him in 'Without the Bomb'. While Barbara puts Stafford in his place several times, and can make him embarrassed and on his guard, Bradley simply tolerates him, although he has to try not to feel intimidated on a few occasions.

John Bown played the role with quiet precision. In his three surviving episodes, we can see his character's relationship with the rest of the cast and the sinister air he sometimes brings. At times, Stafford dominates as much as the Minister, leaving Quist in the shadows to ask questions. And Quist is hardly seen in 'Cause of Death', unwell and packed off to his country cottage to recover. Nevertheless, Quist does appear in every episode of the third series. Of all the other characters, Stafford is the only one to do the same.

12
Richard Duncan

'The Minister is never late.' Himself, 'Flight Into Yesterday'.

Richard Duncan was first introduced as 'the Minister's assistant' – and, perhaps more pertinently, his 'hatchet man' – in 'The Red Sky'. He was a replacement for Barker, the Minister's PPS (which stands either for Parliamentary Private Secretary, which is a job for a Member of Parliament, or Principle Private Secretary, who is a civil servant). We first met the unctuous Barker, played by Robert James, in 'Project Sahara', but James probably was not available to reprise the role in 'The Red Sky', and Richard Duncan was created in his place. In his second appearance, Invasion, he is now a Parliamentary Secretary, which makes him an MP. The role in the script was an unnamed PPS, but Jonathan Alwyn cast Michael Elwyn for a second time and rechristened the character Duncan. In 'Flight Into Yesterday' Duncan seems to be active in the Houses of Parliament, which would appear to confirm his status as an MP. During 'The Web of Fear' he acts as assistant to the Minister of Health, who has presumably taken over the running of the Department following Sir George Holroyd's heart attack in the previous story. By the time of the first instalment of the third series, 'Fire and Brimstone', the camera script refers to him as the Minister's Private Secretary.

According to the man who played him, Michael Elwyn, not even the production team seemed to know exactly what Duncan was supposed to be. Elwyn decided that the character was an MP and not a civil servant. However, civil servants can become members of Parliament. Prime Minister Harold Wilson started his career within the civil service. The reason for this uncertainty is simply because Duncan came into life as a replacement figure for two other characters. Whatever his precise status, he is attached to the Ministry throughout the programme's run.

He is loyal to his Ministers yet supportive of Quist – but only up to a point. For example, he can see the merits of Dr Fay Chantry's report on Quist's jet lag experience in 'Flight Into Yesterday'. When we see him in Public Enemy he intervenes on what seems to be a local matter; however, if the local MP for Carlingham was a member of the party in government or the chairman was a party fundraiser, the Ministry would have been lobbied to put pressure upon Quist. The rather kindly hatchet man would have been dispatched.

Richard Duncan was given a new first name for the third series,

Anthony, but only in the writer's guide, which also briefly described him: he is a good listener and will go far because of it. We see him in 'Fire and Brimstone', but he has little to do, and we only hear of him in 'High Mountain'. In the rehearsal script of 'Deadly Dangerous Tomorrow', it was originally an anonymous civil servant who discovers the Indian encampment in St James Park; the role was slightly expanded and given to Duncan, which, considering it was his final episode, is rather fitting.

13
Barbara Mason

'I want you to come with me – as my PA' Quist, 'Say Knife, Fat Man'.

Had Barbara Mason only appeared in the second series, her character profile would have been marginally shorter than Pat Hunnisett's and probably a bit longer than Susan Proud's, for her involvement in the stories of that series was virtually negligible. Introduced as an office temp from the civil service typing pool, she hovers around in 'You Killed Toby Wren', where she acts as a handy device to reintroduce the surviving regular cast, gets confused over the phone system, is shouted at by Ridge ('Stuff it!') and then, six weeks later, fills in some plot background and develops a near-perfect memory in 'Flight Into Yesterday', but that's about it. Entirely due to the skills of Vivien Sherrard, who has the thankless task of bringing such a non-character to life, she provides a little light comedy with her nerves at meeting Dr Quist for the first time, followed by her relief when she gets a warm response. When suffering from jet lag, she does indeed 'look washed-up like a heap of seaweed', as John Ridge puts it. After her first episode we don't see her again until 'No Room for Error', and that is basically to kiss John Ridge's cut forehead better in a scene worked out in rehearsals. Vivien Sherrard does have a very expressive face (regardless of the amazingly square eyebrows she sported for a while); in one scene in 'Public Enemy' she has no dialogue, but her face says it all as she overhears Alderman Payne, completely reversing his attitude towards Carlingham Alloys, before she walks out of the office, disconcerting the angry Alderman for a moment.

With such a paucity of material, (she was even removed from 'The Islanders' to make way for Colin Bradley) Sherrard would have been forgiven had she done a Wendy Hall and not signed up for another series. But she did, and suddenly Barbara Mason comes to life. The brief character sketch written for the writers' guide describes her as being 'attractive, twenty-six years old… Her quiet, unruffled manner belies her brightness. Despite having no academic qualifications, she has done considerable homework in her time with Doomwatch as Quist discovers.'

Series Three
'Fire and Brimstone' shows how she has cemented herself in the affections of Colin Bradley, who describes her as 'the office squirrel' (in regard to the amount of stuff she keeps in her desk). She also becomes a carrier of a

phial of anthrax, secreted in her antiperspirant (she hates hot hands). For the first time in the series, Sherrard gets some location filming as we follow her passage through London, wondering whether she is going to infect the capital, not to mention herself.

With Doomwatch suddenly doubled in size and importance, she is promoted to Quist's personal assistant, with her old place at the switchboard taken over by Susan Proud, played by Maria O'Brien. This gives her a second chance to get out into the fresh air, as she stumbles across the group of students who have stolen the plutonium. In the end, she is the one who persuades them to call in the police.

Her basic role in the third series is to act as a handy way for the writers to express a point of view. She stands up for the Young Generation in 'Say Knife, Fat Man' against the more cynical views of Commander Stafford, agrees with the idea of the pheromone contraceptive aphrodisiac Joyne (and teases Bradley that it has made her sense of smell very precious to her), acts as the uninformed and potential 'moral midget' wanting to get her first small sports car in 'Waiting for a Knighthood' and stands up for Ridge in 'Cause of Death'. She has clearly forgiven him for what he nearly did to her with the anthrax, and, as she tells Quist, she wants Ridge to feel that someone from Doomwatch still cares about him. 'What is it about him?' asks Quist in amazement. The best she can come up with is 'He's got a brilliant mind. Outstanding in many ways.' That evening, despite Ridge cancelling their dinner engagement, she still turns up at his flat, and, after a frosty start, Ridge tells her of his problems: his father, his own depressing self-realisations, his disillusionment with Doomwatch and what it stands for. This, of course, forces the question (as it indeed must have done in the rehearsal room) were they at it?

Barbara's relationship with Quist changes in the third series, and she develops a confidence around him that she never had in the second. 'Although in awe of Quist,' says the guide, 'she isn't in the least timid.' She is prepared to argue with him whether students were responsible for the plutonium theft, pushing it heavily enough to the point where Quist tells her to come to the university with him. Stafford sees it as a kind of test, and she passes with full colours. As a PA, she is able to leave the office and join the rest of the active team in their 'Enquiry' at Longside Camp but, unfortunately, has few lines and does little more than take notes.

Commander Stafford is one she has very little time for. They did not get off to the best of starts during his investigation into the anthrax theft, but it must have been the idea of how far he pushed Ridge, to the point of attempted suicide, that made the idea of his permanent place at Doomwatch too much for her. She contemplates resignation as the department disintegrates around her, but Colin Bradley urges her to sleep on it. Despite Stafford's 'conversion' to Doomwatch she is still suspicious and distant with him and gets the odd opportunity to score a few points off him. Stafford, on the evidence of surviving episodes, doesn't quite know how to react to these digs. They are on opposite sides of the issues of Joyne as well. She sees his dislike of it is because the woman will no longer be passive. She takes the lipstick and advances on him, taunting him until he is trapped in a corner in, as she puts it, 'a state of male chauvinist panic'. By the time of 'Cause of Death', their relationship is such that she can calm him down when he is prepared to give up on Ridge.

Colin Bradley is her closest friend in the Doomwatch office. He was the one who noticed 'our Barbara' was suffering from jet lag in 'Flight Into Yesterday'. She has sandwiches with him in the lab, the occasional drink and gets the scientific aspects of an issue explained to her. It is only in 'Without the Bomb' that the generation gap causes the closest they ever get to an argument, and even then it is mild. Previously, her relationships with Geoff Hardcastle and Dr Fay Chantry were friendly enough, but not very deep. Geoff did have a habit of patronising her in exchanges, such as in 'Flight Into Yesterday' (and would have done so even more in 'The Web of Fear' had it not been cut), but she is still upset when he and Fay left the department.

With the experience she acquired over the years at Doomwatch, we can only wonder if Barbara Mason advanced up the civil service career ladder to a high position or whether she escaped into the freelance world, perhaps following Quist to his next job. You could see her as an influential president of a charity somewhere, possibly even married to John Ridge – well, for a while at least…

Part Five:
The Novels

1.1
Mutant 59: The Plastic Eater

The first of three *Doomwatch* inspired novels by Kit Pedler and Gerry Davis was released in late 1971 with a re-telling of their original and most intriguing premise, a plastic eating virus on the loose. No longer constrained by budget or Terence Dudley, they could allow their imaginations to run riot. They chose not to fictionalise the existing *Doomwatch* format and face potential BBC editorialising but to take a fresh approach.

Premise

The plastic-eating virus of this book is developed not in a government or commercial laboratory, but at home by a bacteriologist who works in a teaching hospital, where medical students scare him with their 'sense of youth and attack.' He had been looking into the problem of plastic waste disposal in his spare time and had hit upon a novel solution. He suffers from a fatal brain haemorrhage just at the point he realises he has made an exciting breakthrough with the virus, which is thrown into a sink during his death spasm. The virus lays dormant until it begins to feed on the rotting remains of a plastic powder, the residue of a recently developed bio-degradable plastic bottle called Degron. The license to mass produce the Degron bottles had been purchased by a soft drink manufacturer who 'wanted a new gimmick to sell the mixture of tartaric acid, citric acid, saccharin and colouring which he shamelessly called Tropic Delight.' The plastic bottle crumbles into powder when a small portion of it is exposed to sunlight, and the powder is washed into the sewers. The virus feeds and multiplies and gives off an inflammable gas, which builds up within the sewers. The subsequent explosions create devastation across the city. The first of these disasters occurs at King's Cross station in London, a place described as one of the most complex transport communication junctions in the world, and later the site of a real-life and terrible fire in 1987. The writers also finally get to sink a nuclear submarine, *HMS Triton*.

Interwoven into the plot are the adventures of a small, privately funded think-tank which made its fortune from licensing its brainwave Degron biodegradable plastic. The group was supposed to be providing useful scientific ideas to benefit mankind, but the profit motive had taken over. The consultancy's creator, Arnold Kramer, is himself killed when the plane he is travelling on falls victim to the virus and explodes over the Atlantic.

The book's hero, Luke Gerrard, spends much of the story investigating a suspected flaw in the Degron product itself, which may have contributed to a failure in microchips. They are unaware that there is a virus on the loose. The component failure causes havoc with London's brand new computerised traffic control network, a giant robot toy in a superstore grotto going berserk, and most seriously, a plane crash. Spores from the virus were found dormant inside the microchips until they warm up, absorb moisture and begin to feed on the plastic insulation of the surrounding wires.

Gerrard ends up trapped in the underground network as the explosions rock London. With him is Kramer's estranged wife Anne, with whom he inevitably forms a relationship – an element which occurs in all three *Doomwatch*-inspired novels. Trying to escape from the inferno in the tunnels, they soon discover the putrefaction created by Degron and the virus. An anti-viral agent is produced, but not before dormant spores hidden in microchips have reached Mars in the form of a Mars probe which has touched down.

A Combination of Styles
The novel is a mixture of Davis' narrative skills and Kit's experience of putting across a plausible scientific premise and points of view. Both writers perfectly compliment the other. Davis enjoyed writing situations within claustrophobic settings, and a large section of the book is set dealing with trapped survivors in the London underground. Pedler's solo contribution stands out from the plot as they are usually self-contained pieces detailing the background of a character or an event. There are several sections which takes us inside the mind of a scientist who has a 'good and original idea', how they are developed and the problems they face in getting them accepted and turned into practical expression.

Pedler explores his view that London was 'ground', rather than 'land', as he describes the complicated network of tunnels that are lie underneath people's feet at the King's Cross area, where the first major disaster occurs. He describes passengers entering the underground system escaping the polluting stench of car exhaust pipes 'from an area which has long since become intolerable for any real man-machine coexistence.' The area has dramatically changed in recent times.

Publication
The novel was published in February 1972 in hardback by Souvenir press and cost £1.80. The *Daily Express*, in a feature where Kit Pedler describes his work on constructing an eco-friendly house, called the book a chilling story 'in which plastic-eating germs, originally intended as a cheap way of disposing of old plastic bottles run wild'. Gerry Davis described it more accurately as 'topical and ironic. It's an illustration of what can happen when scientific research done in the name of progress backfires.' *New*

Scientist reviewed it and felt that today's sci-fi was suffering from a bout of gloom. 'The authors may be trying to tell us that we have got to be a bit more responsible in our scientific research (the hero never lets up telling us how responsible he is) but they mostly manage to prove how much society depends upon plastics. At least they have got away from the notion that man only has to fear the intervention of a Wyndham-like Kraken or some uncontrollable natural catastrophe. Man is more likely to bring doom upon himself. And the conjunction of two divergent scientific discoveries presented here offers Pedler and Davis the opportunity to work out their scientific detective story in a detailed and readable novel.'

The American edition was reviewed in *Literary Guild Magazine*, who thought that it was 'the most riveting novel of speculative fiction since *The Andromeda Strain* ... an edge of the seat thriller'. The back cover had the words 'London is melting!' across the blurb, whilst the French went with the book's original title: *La Mort du Plastique* (*The Death of Plastic*).

The *Guardian* promoted the paperback edition with a rare interview with both Pedler and Davis, where the origins of the story were discussed. 'It may seem unlikely that as the first biodegradable milk bottle goes on sale in their novel that another scientist working in the same area of self-destruct plastic should release a plastic-eating virus into the sewers of London. But then no-one ever thought the Americans would accidentally drop a nuclear warhead in Texas.' The paperback was published by Pan, price 40p, in the last week of December 1973 and reused the cover imagery originally used for the *Radio Times* promotion of the original series of *Doomwatch*.

Film rights were optioned by Tigon British Film Productions, and even Disney was mentioned for a possible adaptation in Gerry Davis' 1975 entry in the *British Film and Television Handbook*, but nothing came from it. The book has also been published in Japan, Italy, Germany and Russia, and some later editions cast the title in the plural as *Mutant 59: The Plastic Eaters*.

It is still available as an e-book, published by Souvenir Books, and is a darned good read.

1.2
Brainrack

Doomwatch had never touched upon the issue of nuclear power production nor of its waste disposal, only the Bomb itself. The building of any new nuclear power station was always steeped in controversy and protest. For their second book, Kit Pedler and Gerry Davis imagined the opening of the first private enterprise nuclear power station, built in Orkney and based on similar projects in the United States. At the same time, something is in the air, rotting people's brains and lowering their IQ, making them clumsier and under certain circumstances, lethal. The cause was something that 'Waiting for a Knighthood' would come quite close to doing, had it not chosen a more pedestrian route. Having said that, there was no way they could have afforded the visuals the book demanded when the power station experiences meltdown ...

Premise
The story features Alexander Mawn, who works in computing science at Plymouth University. He has been noticing how tiny mistakes by people involved in complex technological procedures are being covered up, leading to disaster in some cases. His researches anger the Gelder Consortium, who are aware of the issue which has plagued their projects. A group of industrialists plot to silence him. Mawn's assistant is killed by a hired spy, and Mawn goes on television, having been given data that has been deliberately corrupted in order to discredit him. With Marcia Scott, a psychologist, Mawn discovers that something in the air is reducing the intelligence of people.

One concern is the new privately owned nuclear power station due to be built at Grim Ness in Scotland by the Gelder Consortium, who had been responsible for a meltdown in Albania. The workers had previously had their intelligence measured by Marcia, and she is frightened by her findings. Colour blindness is a factor. They are unable to prevent the station from exploding the moment it is switched on, and meltdown occurs. Finally taken seriously by the government, Mawn discovers that the cause of the brainrack is cyclic pentane acetylide, which comes from petrol and is expelled as exhaust fumes. After an experiment in banning the motor car from London for a week, the pollutant is expelled, and the choice for the future of mankind is stark.

Behind the Story
On 14 February 1974, the *Daily Express* ran a story entitled 'New Warning

from *Doomwatch* Team'. It was really a promotion for the forthcoming, 'a real sizzler concerning a nuclear power station which explodes with great loss of life, making vast stretches of land uninhabitable'. At the same time, an exhibition was being held at Dunbar in Scotland, explaining the South of Scotland Electricity Board's proposals to build a new nuclear power station at nearby Torness Point. It was to be Britain's last second-generation nuclear power plant to be commissioned. This was at a time when the British Government, wanting to expand its nuclear power generation capacity, was investigating whether or not to buy under license the cheaper American designed light water reactor (LWR). The problem was that they did not have a good reputation, especially in America.

Earlier that month, the conclusion of the House of Commons Select Committee on Science and Technology on the choice of a reactor system came down firmly against the LWR. The Government's Chief Scientific Advisor (and who turned out to be its last), Sir Alan Cottrell, was concerned about possible fractures and their growth in the steel pressure vessels. Even the United States Atomic Energy Commission had admitted to 850 'abnormal occurrences' in 17 operating months of nuclear power stations, and two people had died. The Select Committee concluded that 'In view of the conflict of opinion on the safety of LWRs, it is, in our opinion, for the proponents of light water technology to prove its safety beyond all reasonable doubt, rather than for their opponents to prove the contrary. This point is particularly important in a densely populated country like Britain,' reported the *New Scientist* in February 1974. The *Daily Express* article also quoted Pedler as saying 'Besides design weaknesses there have been human failures in quality control … It could never happen with the British gas-cooled reactor. We've found no way to fault it on safety grounds.' They even go as far as to state this in the book.

Petrol Fumes
The most fascinating aspect of the book was the brainrack itself. Back in 1970 Kit Pedler conducted tests on the amount of carbon monoxide that city dwellers were exposed to on a daily basis. There were concerns at the time not just over the pollution being emitted by car exhausts or factory chimneys but also over the carbon monoxide which pedestrians inhaled on a regular basis, as well as smokers. Could this be the cause for bad, angry drivers? The term 'road rage' had yet to be coined. Lead in petrol was still a controversial topic, and the book mentions the issue in passing, but the cause of the degenerative atrophication of Betz cells in the brain (the thinking cells) was revealed to be cyclic pentane acetylide, a rare pollutant found in petrol. 'Self-induced idiocy from the motor car!' The book pointed out source material in a 1968 paper published by W N Sanders and J B Maynard in the research journal *Analytical Chemistry* which demonstrated

that over 180 separate chemicals were emitted from a car exhaust pipe.

There are some familiar ideas from the television series within the book: the idea of a professional covering up a mistake evokes 'Re-Entry Forbidden', whilst the humiliating demolition Mawn experiences in front of the TV cameras with his 'careless data' is reminiscent of Professor Griffiths' painful experience related in 'The Web of Fear'. The Palomares incident is referred to, concerning the way the contaminated soil had to be removed by the Americans. One also wonders if Kit Pedler's experiences on television debates and documentaries fed into the scenes set within the BBC. The hero of the book, Alexander Mawn, could have been based, however remotely, on Derek Bryce-Smith (see 'Waiting for a Knighthood').

Reviews

The Times of 14 March 1974 gave the book a brief but positive review: 'Although one wearies of the usual scientists who know it all, the whole theme of growing mental disintegration has the electric quality of real shock to it, especially when you realize the relevance of what is causing it all. The authors always seem to organize their ideas more credibly than their characters, and this particular ignition is a stunner which results in "millions of adults who are mentally retarded and are never going to recover". We need wolf-criers like this and we should take heed.' The *Guardian*, a few days later, was less enthralled: 'It is one of those admonitory tales about an ecological revenge on our runaway technology, relentlessly televisual in style. And indeed, as the Luddite scientist strives to alert the world to the eponymous brain-rotting disease, one longs for a film crew to bring the scenes to life. Slickly professional, though, and can be read at a gulp.' *New Scientist*'s Nicholas Valéry loved it, especially for its topicality. 'For me, the nuclear incident on a remote, windswept Scottish island, with the barometer falling, a blizzard raging, was as good as anything yet written by Hammond Innes, Alistair Maclean or Geoffrey Jenkins. A pity, I felt personally, that the story was not simply about this. With such a wealth of accurate technical detail, a much fuller account could have made a tremendous impact at the present moment and what a movie it would have subsequently made.'

The authors appeared on Radio 4's *Start The Week* on 18 February 1974, interviewed by Esther Rantzen, and on Radio 2's *Open House* nine days later, whilst Kit Pedler alone appeared on Radio 2's *Late Night Extra*. No movie was ever made from it, but 1979 brought the film *The China Syndrome*, which told the tale of safety lapses and cutbacks at a newly built nuclear power station. It was released in US cinemas not even two weeks before the nuclear accident at Three Mile Island.

The book was not as successful as *Mutant 59: The Plastic Eater*, but this didn't stop a third novel from being planned. Both Kit Pedler and Gerry

Davis would go on to campaign against further development of the nuclear power generating programme and, for their third book, turned their attention to what would come after nuclear power was abandoned.

1.3
The Dynostar Menace

The third and final *Doomwatch*-inspired novel, first published in 1975, was originally called *Starshock* before the more melodramatic title of *The Dynostar Menace* was settled upon.

Premise
The story takes place in 1986, and the events here are related to those in *Brainrack*. The disaster at Grim Ness and an exploding fast breeder reactor near Odessa in Russia have persuaded mankind to turn away from nuclear fission as a source of cheap power (coincidentally, the Chernobyl disaster would occur in 1986) and look instead towards nuclear fusion – the power of the sun. The problem lies in constructing something strong enough to contain the reaction process, until the scientists hit upon the idea of magnetic fields. With gravity being a limiting factor, they create a space station twenty-five miles in orbit – the Dynostar. The book also foresees an abandonment of space research: this was to be man's last adventure in space, sponsored by the Americans. Environmental safeguards are monitored by the Council of Twelve, a kind of successor to the Club of Rome. A week before the Dynostar is to be switched on for one second, they calculate that the magnetic field will balloon outwards and disrupt, if not destroy, the ozone layer protecting the planet from harmful solar rays. The order is given to close down Dynostar. A team of scientists and engineers, who have worked to exhaustion point getting the systems ready, now have to shut down the station safely – except one man is prepared to kill to prevent just that. In his mind the Dynostar is his project, it would work, and all it needs is that one second pulse to prove it. What do a few dead bodies mean in the light of saving mankind?

The three engineers in the Monitor Can on the Dynostar are murdered, but the authorities on Earth, headed by the American Lee Calder, the charismatic leader of the project, think it is an accident and send up former astronaut John Hayward to organise replacement scientists and monitor the close down. The activation of the Dynostar is automated, but it has to be shut down methodically to prevent any flare-up of the doughnut-shaped fusion reactor on top of the space lab. More accidents make it impossible to do this simply, and soon, with one of the crew found dead with his tongue cut out, they have to face up to the fact they have a deranged murderer on board.

Whilst Hayward investigates in space, Calder and Irene Andler, a psychologist, dig into the backgrounds of the scientists and their families, who have been living at the Clear Lake base whilst their husbands have been in space. One of the relief crew is irradiated with plutonium in the Monitor Can as the saboteur makes it impossible for an easy switch-off.

At first suspicion falls on Freeman, a homosexual who had been blackmailed some years earlier and tried to take his own life. Hayward is prejudiced against homosexuals, and, following the death of a man called Lyall, believes Freeman is guilty, as he was last seen with Lyall. A seal from a sabotaged spacesuit is found in his locker (although it transpires he had been given it to fix a fault). Freeman takes his own life, and Hayward's authority is over. Calder and Andler have more luck with the families and soon find out that one of the team was hiding a history of mental illness in the family. They had also harboured a deep hatred of one Dr Risbach, who had a habit of passing off the hard work of one of his underlings as his own, particularly with some of the essential maths for the project.

Calder gets Risbach to broadcast an announcement to the survivors of the space lab that he is taking over. It provokes a violent reaction from the guilty man, who sees a huge conspiracy spearheaded by Risbach against him and the project. It becomes a race against time to stop the power-up and escape back to Earth as the lab begins to disintegrate. The fusion reaction pulses for a fraction of a second, which is enough to disrupt the ozone layer above a park in Eastern Africa, killing a warden, blinding the wildlife and destroying the ecology of the area. The book concludes that, three years after the events, fusion research was abandoned and all further work was directed towards the exploitation of natural energy. A 'post-industrial millennium was assembled and waiting'.

Research

It is possible that, for some reason, Pedler and Davis are referencing Sherlock Holmes: 'Irene Andler' is very close to 'Irene Adler', Holmes' opponent in his first short story 'A Scandal in Bohemia'; and does 'Risbach' evoke 'Reichenbach', the name of the Swiss waterfalls where Holmes fought to the death with Professor Moriarty? In writing their book, Pedler and Davis conducted research with the astronauts and publicity staff of the Johnson Space Centre in Houston, Texas, drawing on the Skylab project, an orbital space station which was launched in 1973. The nuclear fusion side of things was handled by the staff of the Culham Fusion Research Laboratories in Oxfordshire. Rather coyly, the book acknowledged help from staff of a psychiatric teaching hospital in London.

Originally published in hardback by Souvenir Press in the UK and by Scribner in New York in 1975, Pan produced the paperback edition the following year. It was printed in Germany three years later as *Die Dynostar-Drohung*.

Reviews

New Scientist's John Gribbon did not like it at all. He pointed to a couple of plot holes (such as how was the power generated by the Dynostar going to be transmitted to Earth, and just how was the ballooning of the magnetic fields going to disrupt the ozone layer). He also wasn't terribly keen on a mad scientist and his thirst for recognition being at the centre of the plot. However, George Thaw in the *Daily Mirror* gave it a brief but positive write-up and earned himself a place on the back cover of the paperback edition. Martin Amis, writing in the *Observer*, thought it had 'lots of attractive technical know-how' and was 'an excellent read, poorly written but very well told'. *The Times* felt it was the best of the three books. By the time of Kit Pedler's death, *The Dynostar Menace* was going to be made into a film, and Pedler was to have been the technical adviser on the project.

Appendices

Appendix I
Storylines And Script Commissions

Series One
Storylines by Kit Pedler and Gerry Davis

DATE ACCEPTED	PROJECT No.	WORKING TITLE
18/12/68	2248/1229	'Check and Mate'
	2249/1286	'The Logicians'
	2249/1284	'The Devil's Sweets'
	2249/126	'The Battery People'
20/02/69	2249/1267	'The Pacifiers'
	2249/1285	'The Flames of Hell'
	2249/1287	'Rattus Sapiens?'
	2249/1288	'The Patrick Experiment'
01/07/69	2249/1349	'Hear No Evil'
	2249/1302	'The Synthetic Candidate'
	02240/0401	'Burial at Sea'
	02240/0402	'Re-Entry Forbidden'
10/03/70	02240/0519	'Pollution Inc.'
	02249/0504	'Train and De-Train'

Script Commissions

DATE	NO.	PROJ, No.	WORKING TITLE	AUTHOR
24/06/68	-	2218/1114	'Doomwatch'	Pedler/Davis
28/11/68	2	2248/1223	'Operation Neptune'	Pedler/Davis
17/12/68	3	2248/1229	'Check and Mate'	Hugh Forbes
28/01/69	4	2248/1267	'The Pacifiers'	Jan Read
29/01/69	5	2249/1269	'The Battery People'	Moris Farhi
26/02/69	6	2248/1288	'Friday's Child'	Harry Green
10/03/69	8	2248/1284	'The Devil's Sweets'	Don Shaw
18/03/69	?	2248/1302	'The Synthetic Candidate'	Elwyn Jones
12/06/69	10	2248/1349	'Hear No Evil'	Harry Green
?	?	?	'Rattus Sapiens?'	Terence Dudley
26/06/69	13	02240/0401	'Burial at Sea'	Dennis Spooner
22/08/69	7	2248/1285	'The Iron Doctor'	Harry Green
10/09/69	15	2249/0441	'Careless Talk'	N J Crisp
15/09/69	14	02240/0402	'Re-Entry Forbidden'	Don Shaw
15/09/69	16	2249/0446	'Survival Code'	Pedler/Davis
15/12/ 69	17	2249/0504	'Train and De-Train'	Don Shaw
?	?	?	'Spectre at the Feast'	Terence Dudley

Series Two
Storylines by Kit Pedler and Gerry Davis

DATE PAID	PROJECT No.	WORKING TITLE
26/05/70	02240/0599	'Darwin's Killers'
	02240/0570	'Lonely the House'
	02240/0600	'A Condition of the Mind'
	02240/0605	'Massacre of the Innocents'
3/07/70	02240/0583	'Death of a Sagittarian'
	02240/0607	'A Will to Die'
	02240/0615	'Inventor's Moon'

Script Commissions

DATE	NO.	PROJ, No.	WORKING TITLE	AUTHOR
02/04/70	1	02240/0565	'The Logicians'	Dennis Spooner
14/04/70	4	02240/0570	'Lonely the House'	Martin Worth
?	?	?	'The Pacifiers'	David Fisher
21/04/70	6	02240/0583	'Death of a Sagittarian'	Bill Barron
24/04/70	7	02240/0599	'Darwin's Killers'	Dennis Spooner
24/04/70	8	02240/0600	'A Condition of the Mind'	John Wiles
05/05/70	9	02240/0605	'The Iron Doctor'	Brian Hayles
06/05/70	?	02240/0607	'The Will to Die'	John Gould
?	?	02240/0608	'Massacre of the Innocents'	Roger Parkes
21/05/70	12	02240/0615	'Inventor's Moon'	Martin Worth
28/05/70	13	02240/0618	Untitled	Robert Holmes
28/05/70	?	?	'Public Enemy'	Patrick Alexander
28/05/70	15	02240/0620	'The Dove of Peace'	Louis Marks
01/07/70	16	02240/0638	'The Head'	John Gould
01/07/70	17	02240/0637	'Diplomatic Incident'	Dennis Spooner
13/07/70	18	02240/0641	'Green, Green Fields'	Tony Williamson
13/07/70	19	02240/0642	'Evil Inherited'	Robin Chapman
13/07/70	20	?	'The Misguided Missile'	Edward Boyd
20/07/70	21	02240/0651	'Home-Made Bomb'	Keith Dewhurst
?	?	?	'The Web of Fear'	Gerry Davis
?	?	02240/4417	'He Killed Toby Wren'	Terence Dudley
23/07/70	?	?	'How the Other Half Dies'	David Whitaker
11/08/70	25	02240/0659	'Desert Island'	Louis Marks
11/08/70	26	02240/0660	'Dangerous Cargo'	Elwyn Jones
27/08/70	27	02240/0668	'Your Body Will Never Forgive'	Malcolm Hulke
07/09/70	28	02240/0672	'St Anthony's Harvest'	Brian Hayles
11/09/70	30	02240/0675	'Cover All Over...'	Malcolm Hulke
15/10/70	31	02240/0695	'Jet Rag'	Martin Worth
03/12/70	32	02240/0709	'The Drugs Story'	Robin Chapman

Series Three
Script Commissions

DATE	NO.	PROJ, No.	WORKING TITLE	AUTHOR
04/05/71	1	02241/0475	Untitled	Terence Dudley
04/05/71	2	02241/0476	'The High Mountain'	Martin Worth
04/05/71	3	02241/0477	'Sound and Fury'	Martin Worth
18/05/71	4	?	'Flood'	Ian Curteis
04/08/71	5	02241/0528	'The Devil's Demolition'	Wolf Rilla
10/08/71	6	?	Untitled	Terence Dudley
11/08/71	7	02241/0530	'The Killer Dolphin'	Roy Russell
11/08/71	8	02241/0531	'Sex and Violence'	Stuart Douglass
13/09/71	9	02241/0553	'Without the Bomb'	Roger Parkes
13/09/71	10	02241/0544	'Birds of Prey'	Louis Marks
15/09/71	12	02241/0556	'Hair Trigger'	Brian Hayles
23/09/71	11	?	'The Mind Boggles'	John Gould
17/02/72	13	02242/0642	'Deadly Dangerous Tomorrow'	Martin Worth

Appendix II
Production Dates

Series One
Location Filming

DATE	EPISODE
w/b 03/11/69	'The Plastic Eaters'
w/b 10/11/69	'Burial at Sea'
w/b 17/11/69	'Tomorrow, the Rat'
unknown	'Friday's Child'
w/b 12/01/70	'The Devil's Sweets'
w/b 02/02/70	'The Red Sky'
w/b 09/02/70	'The Battery People'
w/b 23/02/70	'Train and De-Train'
w/b 16/03/70	'Hear No Evil'
unknown	'Survival Code'

w/b = week beginning

Studio Recording

DATE	EPISODE	STUDIO	PROJECT NO.
28, 30/11/69	'The Plastic Eaters'	TC3	2249/4079
10/12/69	'Burial at Sea'	TC8	2249/4085
20/12/69	'Tomorrow, the Rat'	TC3	2249/4081
10/01/70	'Friday's Child'	TC3	2249/4082
21/01/70	'Project Sahara'	TC6	2249/4086
31/01/70	'The Devil's Sweets'	TC6	2249/4083
11/02/70	'Re-Entry Forbidden'	TC1	2249/4087
20-22/02/70	'The Red Sky'	TC4	2249/4080
06/03/70	'The Battery People'	TC6	2248/4088
14/03/70	'Train and De-Train'	TC4	2249/4089
25/03/70	'Spectre at the Feast'	TC4	2249/4090
04/04/70	'Hear No Evil'	TC1	2249/4084
15/04/70	'Survival Code'	TC4	2349/4091

Series Two
Location Filming

DATE	EPISODE
w/b 29/06/70	'Invasion'
w/b 06/07/70	'The Iron Doctor'
w/b 20/07/70	'The Logicians'
w/b 17/08/70	'The Human Time Bomb'
27-28/08/70	'No Room for Error'
w/b 07/09/70	'The Web of Fear'
w/b 28/09/70	'The Islanders'
w/b 19/10/70	'By the Pricking of My Thumbs...'
unknown	'In the Dark'
unknown	'Public Enemy'

w/b = week beginning

Studio Recording

DATE	EPISODE	STUDIO	PROJECT NO.
03/08/70	'The Iron Doctor'	TC6	2240/4411
14/08/70	'The Logicians'	TC5	2240/4412
25/08/70	'Invasion'	TC1	2240/4413
04/09/70	'The Human Time Bomb'	TC6	2240/4414
15/09/70	'No Room for Error'	TC6	2240/4415
25/09/70	'The Web of Fear'	TC1	2240/4416
16/10/70	'You Killed Toby Wren'	TC4	2240/4417
27/10/70	'The Islanders'	TC3	2240/4418
06/11/70	'By the Pricking of My Thumbs...'	TC4	2240/4419
17/11/70	'The Inquest'	??	2240/4420
08/01/71	'Public Enemy'	??	2240/4421
19/01/71	'Flight Into Yesterday'	TC8	2240/4422
29/01/71	'In the Dark'	TC3	2240/4423

Series Three
Location Filming

DATE	EPISODE
w/b 03/01/72	'Fire and Brimstone'
w/b 10/01/72	'Hair Trigger'
w/b 17/01/72	'The Killer Dolphins'
w/b 01/03/72	'Sex and Violence'
w/b 03/04/72	'High Mountain'
w/b 24/04/72	'Enquiry'
w/b 01/05/72	'Deadly Dangerous Tomorrow'
w/b 15/05/72	'Waiting for a Knighthood'
unknown	'Say Knife, Fat Man'
unknown	'Flood'
unknown	'Cause of Death'

w/b = week beginning

Studio Recording

DATE	EPISODE	STUDIO	PROJECT NO.
08/02/72	'Fire and Brimstone'	?	2240/4581
18/02/72	'The Killer Dolphins'	TC1	2240/4582
29/02/72	'Hair Trigger'	?	2240/4584
10/03/72	'Say Knife, Fat Man'	TC1	2240/4583
21/03/72	'Sex and Violence'	TC1	2240/4585
31/03/72	'Flood'	TC6	2240/4586
21/04/72	'Without the Bomb'	TC1	2240/4587
02/05/72	'High Mountain'	TC6	2240/4588
12/05/72	'Enquiry'	TC1	2240/4589
23/05/72	'Deadly Dangerous Tomorrow'	TC1	2240/4590
02/06/72	'Cause of Death'	TC3	2240/4591
13/06/72	'Waiting for a Knighthood'	TC1	2240/4592

VIDEOTAPE NUMBERS

'The Plastic Eaters'	VTC/6HT/55040/ED
'Friday's Child'	VTC/6HT/56829/ED/D
'Burial at Sea'	VTC/6HT/55667/ED
'Tomorrow, the Rat'	VTC/6HT/55618
'Project Sahara'	VTC/6HT/56995
'Re-entry Forbidden'	VTC/6HT/57207/ED
'The Devil's Sweets'	VTC/6HT/57040/ED
'The Red Sky'	VTC/6HT/57360/B
	insert tape VTC/6MIS/57347
'Spectre at the Feast'	VTC/6HT/57940/ED
'Train and De-Train'	VTC/6HT/57793
'The Battery People'	VTC/6HT/57685
'Hear No Evil'	VTC/6HT/58388
'Survival Code'	VTC/6HT/58428/ED
'You Killed Toby Wren'	VTC/6HT/62604
'Invasion'	VTC/6HT/625035
'The Islanders'	VTC/6HT/62849
'No Room for Error'	VTC/6HT/61940/ED
'By the Pricking of My Thumbs …'	VTC6HT62929/ED
'The Iron Doctor'	VTC6HT61462/ED
'Flight Into Yesterday'	VTC6HT/64442/ED
'The Web of Fear'	VTC6HT62030/ED
'In the Dark'	VTC6HT64522
'The Human Time Bomb'	VTC6HT61859/ED
'The Inquest'	VTC/6HT/61551
'The Logicians'	VTC/6HT/61551
'Public Enemy'	VTC/6HT/64183
'Fire and Brimstone'	VTC/6HT/76772/ED
'High Mountain'	VTC/6HT/78624/ED
'Say Knife, Fat Man'	VTC/6HT/77543/ED
'Waiting for a Knighthood'	VTC/6HT/79244B
	insert tape VTC/6HT/79244A
'Without the Bomb'	VTC/6HT/78446/ED
'Hair Trigger'	VTC/6HT/77370/ED
'Deadly Dangerous Tomorrow'	VTC/6HT/78941
'Enquiry'	VTC/6IIT/78773/ED
'Flood'	VTC/6HT/77977
'Cause of Death'	VTC/6HT/79082/ED
'The Killer Dolphins'	VTC/6HT/76928

Appendix III:
Archival Holdings

Series One

'The Plastic Eaters'	625 VT
'Friday's Child'	missing
'Burial at Sea'	missing
'Tomorrow, the Rat'	525 VT
'Project Sahara'	625 VT
'Re-Entry Forbidden'	625 VT
'The Devil's Sweets'	625 VT
'The Red Sky'	625 VT
'Spectre at the Feast'	missing
'Train and De-Train'	525 VT
'The Battery People'	625 VT
'Hear No Evil'	missing
'Survival Code'	missing (final three and a half minutes exist as pre-credits of 'You Killed Toby Wren')

Series Two

'You Killed Toby Wren'	525 VT & B/W Film Recording
'Invasion'	525 VT & B/W Film Recording
'The Islanders'	525 VT & B/W Film Recording
'No Room for Error'	525 VT & B/W Film Recording
'By the Pricking of My Thumbs ...'	525 VT & B/W Film Recording
'The Iron Doctor'	525 VT & B/W Film Recording
'Flight Into Yesterday'	525 VT & B/W Film Recording
'The Web of Fear'	525 VT & B/W Film Recording
'In the Dark'	525 VT & B/W Film Recording
'The Human Time Bomb'	525 VT & B/W Film Recording
'The Inquest'	525 VT & B/W Film Recording
'The Logicians'	525 VT & B/W Film Recording
'Public Enemy'	625 VT

Series Three

'Fire and Brimstone'	missing
'High Mountain'	missing
'Say Knife, Fat Man'	missing
'Waiting for a Knighthood'	625 VT
'Sex and Violence'	625 VT (+ insert of 1'30" durn)
'Without the Bomb'	missing
'Hair Trigger'	625 VT
'Deadly Dangerous Tomorrow'	missing
'Enquiry'	missing
'Flood'	missing
'Cause of Death'	missing
'The Killer Dolphins'	missing

No audio recordings of missing episodes are known to exist.

Selected Bibliography

BOOKS

Allaby, Michael. 1971. *The Eco-Activists*. London: Charles Knight.

Beckwith, Jonathan R. 2002. *Making Genes, Making Waves*. Harvard: Harvard University Press.

Carson, Rachel. 1962. *Silent Spring*. Boston: Houghton Mifflin.

DeGroot, Gerard J. 2005. *The Bomb: A History of Hell on Earth*. London: Pimlico.

Dorril, Stephen and Robin Ramsay. 1991. *Smear! Wilson and the Secret State*. London: Fourth Estate Ltd.

Ehrlich, Paul. 1968. *The Population Bomb*. New York: Ballantine Books.

Fromm, Erich. 1968. *The Revolution of Hope: Towards A Humanized Technology*. New York: Harper and Row.

Hamilton, Fred. 2011. *Zoom In When You See The Tears*. Fantom Films Ltd.

Hay, George (ed). 1970. *The Disappearing Future*. London: Panther.

Herber, Lewis. 1962. *Our Synthetic Environment*. New York: Knopf.

McLoughlin, James. 1972. *The Laws Relating to Pollution: An Introduction*. Manchester: Manchester University Press.

Marshall, Kevin P. (ed). 1995. *The Making of Terry Nation's Survivors*. Fourth Horseman Publications.

Matusow, Harvey. 1968. *The Beast of Business*. London: Wolfe Publishing Ltd.

May, Elaine Tyler. 2010. *America and the Pill*. New York: Basic Books.

Pappworth, Maurice Henry. 1967. *Human Guinea Pigs: Experimentation on Man* (London: Routledge).

Pedler, Kit. 1970. 'Image in Capsule'. In Rosemary Timpereley (ed). *The Sixth Ghost Book*. London: Barrie and Rockliff.

— 1979. *The Quest for Gaia*. London: Souvenir Press.

— and Gerry Davis. 1971. *Mutant 59: The Plastic Eaters*. London, Souvenir Press.

— — 1974. *Brainrack*. London, Souvenir Press.

— — 1975. *The Dynostar Menace*. London, Souvenir Press.

Taylor, Gordon Rattray. 1968. *The Biological Time Bomb*. London: Panther Science.

— 1970. *The Doomsday Book*. London: Thames and Hudson Ltd.

Seely, Michael (ed). 2012. *Deadly Dangerous Tomorrow*. Tadworth: Miwk Publishing Ltd.

Troughton, Michael. 2011. *Patrick Troughton: The Biography of the Second Doctor Who*. Andover: Hirst Publishing.

Verwey, Will D. 1977. *Riot control Agents and Herbicides in War*. Leyden: A W Sijthoff.

Ward, Mark. 2004. *Out of the Unknown: A Guide to the Legendary BBC Series*. Bristol: Kaleidoscope Publishing.

Walker, Stephen James (ed). 2007. *Talkback: The Unofficial and Unauthorised Doctor Who Interview Book: Volume Three: The Eighties*. Tolworth: Telos Publishing.

Walsh, Gordon (ed). 1975. *Doomwatch: The World in Danger*. London: Longman Group Ltd.

Williams, Raymond and O'Connor, Alan (ed). *Raymond Williams on Television: Selected Writings*. London: Routledge.

PERIODICALS

Agarwal, Anil. 1978. 'Malaria Makes a Comeback'. *New Scientist* 2 February: 274-6.

'Anti-crowd Weapons Works by Causing Fits'. 1973. *New Scientist* 29 March: 726.

Anthrop, Donald. 1969. 'Environmental Noise Pollution: A New Threat to Sanity'. *Bulletin of the Atomic Scientists* May: 11-15.

Auger, David. 1984. 'Kit Pedler'. *Space and Time* 54: 9-10.

Barnaby, Frank. 1971. 'Time to Complete the Test Ban'. *New Scientist* 15 April: 131.

— 1972. 'Breeder Power Dangers'. *New Scientist* 24 June: 727.

Berry, Martyn. 1971. 'A Lethal Element'. *New Scientist* 18 February: 340-1.

Bonfante, Jordan. 1972. 'Lord Porn: A Noble Britain Leads a Battle Against Filth'. *Life* Vol 73. 18: 57-62.

Bonnell, J A. 1973. 'Lead Smelting at Avonmouth'. *British Journal of Industrial Medicine* Vol 30: 199-201.

Brown, Anthony. 1996. 'A Renaissance Doctor'. *In Vision* 62: 12-14.

Burn, Gordon. 1972. 'Does Quist Give a Damn'. *Radio Times* 1 June: 6-7.

Chappell, Mark. 1990. 'Doomwatch: The Iron Doctor'. *TV Zone* 16: 28-30.

Chedd, Graham. 1970. 'New Route to Hybrid Cells May Aid Genetic Carpentry'. *New Scientist* 31 December: 581.

— 1971. 'Doomwatch Incarnate'. *New Scientist* 18 March: 622-4.

Chepesiuk, Ron. 1997. 'A Sea of Trouble'. *Bulletin of the Atomic Scientists*, September-October: 40-44.

Clark, Anthony. 1992. 'Gerry Davis'. *Dream Watch Bulletin* 97: 30-1.

Comfort, Alex. 1971. 'Communication May Be Odorous'. *New Scientist* 25 February: 412-14.

Cowley, Elizabeth. 1970. 'The Honeymoon of Science Is Over – And Married Life Is Not So Rosy'. *Radio Times* 5 February: 2-3.

Darbyshire, Tony. 2010. 'Embryonic Nazis on Four Legs'. *Doomwatch Fanzine* 1: 3-17.

D'Arcy, Susan. 1972. 'Doomwatch'. *Photoplay*. Issue unknown: 57-59.

Dickson, David. 1973. 'From Molecules to Man'. *New Scientist* 9 August: 329-31.

Dixon, Bernard. 1972. 'Pornography and Science'. *New Scientist* 21 September:

467.

Fanning, M. 1967. 'Families in Flats'. *British Medical Journal* 18 November: 382-6.

French, Philip. 1970. 'Presenting the Deadly Dangers of Today'. *Radio Times* 10 December: 60-1.

Green, Luciea. 1972. 'Doctor Doom'. *Saturday Titbits*. Issue unknown: 28-29.

Gribbin, John. 1974. 'Dynostar Menace'. *New Scientist* 30 October: 293.

Gwynne, Peter. 1972. 'New York View Do Not Go Gentle ...'. *New Scientist* 2 March: 496-7.

Hearn, Marcus. 1992. 'Merchant of Doom'. *Time Screen* 18: 4-7.

Horgan, John. 2005. The Forgotten Era of Brain. *Scientific American* October: 66-73.

'Inside Doomwatch'. 1971. *New Scientist* 4 February: 261.

Kenward, Michael. 1972. 'Book Review: Mutant 59: The Plastic Eater'. *New Scientist* 20 April: 156-7.

— 1974. 'The Cloudy Issue of Reactor Choices'. *New Scientist* 7 February: 314.

Killick, Jane. 1998. 'In Production: Doomwatch'. *Cult Times* 37. Pages unknown.

— 1999. 'Allie Byrne Saving the World'. *TV Zone* 122: 56-59.

Leigh, Gary. 1988. 'Gerry Davis'. *Doctor Who Bulletin* 59: 10-15.

Lewin, Roger. 1971. 'Who Pays for Plastic Litter'. *New Scientist* 25 February: 440-1.

Loftas, Tony. 1971. 'Mediterranean Pollution – Another Year of Neglect'. *New Scientist* 15 July: 144.

Marson, Richard. 1987. 'Gerry Davis Interviewed'. *Doctor Who Magazine* 124: 8-12.

— 1988. 'Doomwatch'. *Starburst*. Issue unknown: 21-23.

Nabholz, Markus. 1972. 'Mapping The Genes of Man'. *New Scientist* 17 February: 368-70.

Pixley, Andrew. 1989. 'Doomwatch'. *Fantasy Zone* 1: 28-31.

— 1989. 'Survivors: A Writer's Tale'. *Time Screen* 14: 24-19.

— 1999. 'The Tomb of the Cybermen'. *Doctor Who Magazine* 281: 34-41.

— 2004. 'Good Vibrations'. *Doctor Who Magazine Special Edition: The Complete First Doctor* 11-16.

— 2004. 'The Times They Are A-Changing'. *Doctor Who Magazine Special Edition: The Complete First Doctor* 59-63.

— and David Richardson. 1989. 'Doomwatch: The World in Danger'. *Time Screen Revised* 4: 4-14.

Polan, Susan. 1989. 'Doomwatch – 20 Years On'. *DreamWatch Bulletin* 65: 24 & 29.

Richardson, David. 1994. 'Martin Worth: Doom Merchant'. *TV Zone* 55: 17-19

Rippon, Simon. 1974. 'The Probable Costs of Reactor Safety'. *New Scientist* 31 January: 252.

Salusbury, Matt. 2006. 'Father of the Cybermen'. *Fortean Times*. Issue unknown: 30-37.
Seely, Michael. 2010. 'When Will You People Learn Not To Interfere'. *Doomwatch Fanzine* 1: 22-24.
— 2011. 'The Plastic Eaters'. *Doomwatch Fanzine* 3: 2-19.
— 2011. 'Mutant 59: The Plastic Eater'. *Doomwatch Fanzine* 3: 24-28.
— 2011. 'Real Life Doomwatch'. *Doomwatch Fanzine* 3: 22-23.
'Testing Time Zone Effects'. 1969. *Flight International*: 729.
Valéry, Nicholas. 1974. 'Brainrack'. *New Scientist* 24 February: 496.
Tinker, Jon. 1971. 'Is Lead Blowing Our Minds'. *New Scientist* 27 May: 497.
Woffinden, Bob. 1988. 'Doomwatch.' *The Listener* 21 April: 10-11.

NEWSPAPERS
'Actor Took Over at Short Notice'. 1962. *Stage and Television Today*. 14 February.
'America's Submarine Rescue Plan'. 1969. *Coventry Evening Telegraph*. 21 January.
'An End For the Past and Future'. 1970. *Daily Mirror*. 11 May.
Banks-Smith, Nancy. 1970. 'Doomwatch'. *The Guardian*. 7 February.
— 1972, 'Television'. *The Guardian*. 15 August.
Barraclough, Peter. 1971. 'Beating the indestructible'. 1971. *Business Journal*. 26 May.
'BBC Drama All in Colour Next Year'. 1969. *The Stage*. 6 November.
'BBC Making No Strides in Series'. 1971. *The Stage*. 4 March.
Bedford, Ronald and Hellicar, Michael. 1970. 'First Assignment Case of the Tattered Tights'. *Daily Mirror*. 22 June.
Bell, Jack. 1971. 'Why Time Is Money'. *Daily Mirror*. 8 March.
'Bill of Rights Motion Accepted'. 1969. *Birmingham Post*. 23 July.
Black, Peter. 1972. *Daily Mail*. 7 June.
'Blitz Sirens Will Give Warning of Thames Flood Risk'. 1970. *The Times*. 18 August.
Brien, Alan. 1970. 'London: Of Man, Rats and the Absurd'. *New York Times*, 6 April.
Charleston, Michael. 1971. 'Birth Control Advice Should Be Free'. *Daily Express*. 14 October.
'Children Face Danger from Lead Deposits in Dust'. 1971. *Birmingham Post*. 16 December.
Clayton, James. 1968. 'Men Gaoled for Sex Offences Given Hormone Treatment'. *Coventry Evening Telegraph*. 28 November.
Clayton, Sylvia. 1970. 'Inventive New Science Fiction Series'. *Daily Telegraph*. 10 February.
'Clear Lead in December BBC'. 1971. *The Stage*. 14 January.
Comnew, Paul. 1972. 'Drums of Death Fear for 200,000'. *Daily Mirror*. 12

January.

'Control Science Says MP'. 1968. *Birmingham Post*. 8 July.

Cook, Judith. 1971. 'Doomwatch: A Show That Touches Reality'. *Birmingham Post*. ??

— 1971. 'Simon Oates: the Scientist with an Interest in Junk'. *Birmingham Post*. 14 April

— 1971. 'The Complicated Avengers'. *Birmingham Post*. 19 June.

'Dad's Racket'. 1971. *The Guardian*. 28 February.

'Darkness Slows H Bomb Search'. 1968. *Birmingham Post*. 24 January.

Darroch, Robert. 1972. 'Doomwatch Horror Shock Fact in Britain'. *Sydney Morning Herald*. 23 January.

Day, Langston. 1962. 'Teaching by Machine'. *Birmingham Post*. 1 August.

'Death of Two Tristan Refugees'. 1961. *Times*. 11 December.

De Salvo, Brian. 1964. 'Place the Face: Simon Oates'. *The Stage*. 28 May.

'Dolphins Join the Enemy'. 1972. *The Sun*. 14 August.

'Don't Hush Up Transplant Ops'. 1969. *Daily Mirror*. 1 September.

'Doomwatch Check on Farms'. 1971. *Daily Express*. 9 September.

'Doomwatch Is Back Chilling'. 1972. *Daily Mirror*. 5 June.

'Doomwatch SOS'. 1972. *Daily Mirror*. 17 January.

'Doomwatch TV Men Leave'. 1972. *Times*. 7 June.

'Doomwatch: What Is Worrying You'. 1970. *Daily Mirror*. 2 July.

'Dr Pedler's Survival Kit'. 1972. *Daily Mirror*. 21 June.

'Dumping Probe'. 1969. *Press and Journal*. 12 December.

'Entertainment But With a Message'. 1975. *The Stage*. 1 May.

Fazey, Ian Hamilton. 1967. 'Machine Gives Warning of Heart Attack'. ??. 19 August.

'File on Big Breadwinner Hog'. 1969. *Daily Mirror*. 18 April.

'Fifty Fifty Says BBC'. 1970. *The Stage*. 16 April.

Forwood, Margaret. 1972. 'Six Phials That Hold the World to Ransom'. *The Sun*. 5 June.

Gardener, Raymond. 1973. 'Prophets of Doom'. *The Guardian*. 13 December.

Garrett, Gerard. 1970. 'When Sci-fi Runs Wild'. *Daily Sketch*. 10 February.

— 1970. 'Last Night'. *Daily Sketch*. 17 February.

Gibbon, Alfred. 1970. 'The Killing Water'. *Daily Mirror*. 4 August.

Gibson, David. 1970. 'The New Word – Doomwatch'. *Evening News*. 14 December.

Goodman, Elizabeth. 1969. 'Not as Good as Usual'. *The Stage*. 4 September.

Grosvenor, Peter. 1973. 'Pedler of Dreams, Making His New Way of Living Come True'. *Daily Express*. 28 December.

Hadley, Katharine. 1972. 'The Slim Line Sex Symbol Still in Search of Love'. *Daily Express*. 10 August.

Hellicar, Michael. 1970. 'Don't Ask a Man to Smoke and Drive'. *Daily Mirror*. 1 October.

Hepple, Peter. 1970. 'Night Beat'. *The Stage.* 29 October.

Hobbs, Geoffrey. 1971. 'Hobb's Choice'. *Evening Standard.* 1 February.

'Hog Will Continue'. 1969. *The Stage and Television Today.* 17 April.

Holland, Mary. 1972. 'Ecological Overkilling'. *The Observer.* 11 June.

'Hooked on Slimming Pills'. 1968. *Coventry Evening Telegraph.* 30 November.

Hunter Symon, Penny. 1971. 'Few Fear Thames Flood Alert'. *The Times.* 4 October.

— 1971. 'Thames Lions Stay Dry as Flood Danger Passes'. *The Times.* 7 October.

Hutchinson, Tom. 1974. 'Brainrack'. *The Times.* 14 March

Ironside, Virginia. 1971. *Daily Mail.* 12 January.

Jackson, Martin. 1970. 'It's The Dr Who Team Again'. *Daily Express.* 30 January.

— 1970. 'Catch the Kids Bid by ITV'. *Daily Express.* 29 May.

— 1972. 'Allsop Gets a New Doom TV Show'. *Daily Express.* 1 April.

— 1972. 'Doomwatch Row Flares at BBC'. *Daily Express.* 7 June.

Kerrigan, Mike. 1970. 'A Very Familiar Face Gets Back in the Act'. *Daily Mirror.* 16 February.

'Kit Keeps Ahead of the Worst'. 1972. *Daily Mirror.* 19 January.

Lane, Stuart. 1970. 'Unorthodox'. *Morning Star.* 14 February.

Last, Richard. 1971. 'Doom Fact'. *Daily Telegraph.* 2 February.

— 1971. 'Doomwatch Should Study Its Own Ills'. *Daily Telegraph.* 12 January.

— 1972. 'Fighting Comeback by Doomwatch'. *Coventry Telegraph.* 13 June.

— 1972. *Daily Telegraph.* 18 July.

— 1972. *Daily Telegraph.* 14 August.

Lawrence, John. 1970. 'Boy's Own Fare'. *The Stage.* 12 February.

Leach, Gerald. 1971. 'Tuna Fish Scare Was Giant Red Herring'. *The Guardian.* 10 January.

Lean, Geoffrey. 2011. 'Ridiculed Scientist Saved Millions of Children from Brain Damage'. *Daily Telegraph.* 1 August.

Malone, Mary. 1970. 'This Horror Was No Laughing Act'. *Daily Mirror.* 17 February.

— 1971. 'Here Comes That Spooky Old Brain Again'. *Daily Mirror.* 16 February.

— 1972. 'Doomwatch Death Threat'. *Daily Mirror.* 20 June.

— 1972. 'Doomed But Who is to Blame'. *Daily Mirror.* 4 July.

'Manned Mars Flight Forecast in Ten Years'. 1966. *Coventry Evening Telegraph.* 18 July.

'Maplin Site C is Too Noisy'. 1972. *The Times,* 10 August.

Masters, Simon. 1974. 'John Gould'. *The Stage.* 2 May.

Melly, George. 1970. 'Into the Future With Voyeurs and Vegetables'. *The Observer.* 15 March.

'Menace of the Super Mice'. 1970. *Daily Mirror.* 31 July.

'MP acts to Stop Computer Prying'. 1969. *Birmingham Post*. 7 May.
'Mr Benn Sees 1800 Written Off'. 1968. *Coventry Evening Telegraph*. 22 March.
'Nature's Balance Upset'. 1970. *The Guardian*. 23 December.
'New Warning From Doomwatch Team'. 1974. *Daily Express*. 14 February.
'No Flies on Quist and Company'. 1971. *Daily Sketch*. 15 March.
Peacock, Bruce. 1971. 'Tube Talk'. *Leader Post*. 28 June.
'Perils of Wendy'. 1970. *Daily Mirror*. 9 February.
'Pest Killers May Cause Impotence'. 1970. *Birmingham Post*. 13 February.
Pincher, Chapman. 1972. 'Counter Attack the Only Way We Can Win This War'. *Daily Express*. 19 January.
Plaice, Ellis. 1970. 'Britain Backs US Plan for Dumping Nerve Gas in Sea'. *Daily Mirror*. 15 August.
'Prince of Wales Says Countryside is Regarded as a Dustbin'. 1971. *The Times*. 2 March.
Pritchett, Oliver. 1972. 'Creators Disown Doomwatch'. *The Guardian*. 7 June.
Purser, Phillip. 1971. *Daily Telegraph*. 21 March.
Reed, Arthur. 1969. 'Testing Time Zone Fatigue in Jet Travel'. *The Times*. 4 November.
Roberts, Frank. 1971. 'Flood Emergency Planning Review Urged by Ministries as London's Danger Period Starts'. *The Times*. 25 August.
'Rats Drive Out Two Families at Kenilworth'. 1968. *Coventry Evening Telegraph*. 16 October.
'Robots With Eyes'. 1969. *Daily Mirror*. 1 September.
Sandham, Bruce. 1969. 'Living in Self-contained Igloo of a Lunar City by 1989'. *Coventry Evening Telegraph*. 31 July.
Smith, Arthur. 1971. 'Down Doomsday Road'. *Daily Mirror*. 16 September.
Stuart, Malcolm. 1970. 'Tuna Declared Contaminated but Fit to Eat'. *The Guardian*. 23 December.
'Stream Pollution Causes Concern'. 1969. *Coventry Evening Telegraph*. 27 June.
Sutton, Arthur. 1969. 'More Funds for War on Super Rats'. *Birmingham Post*. 11 February.
Taylor, Geoffrey. 1960. 'Radioactive Waste A New Hazard'. *Coventry Evening Telegraph*. 28 November.
Teleletter. 1970. *Daily Mirror*. 27 April.
Teleletter. 1970. *Daily Mirror*. 15 May.
Thaw, George. 1975. 'Books'. *Daily Mirror*. 18 September.
Thomas, James. 1970. 'Don't Preach Doom at Me'. *Daily Express*. 10 February.
— 1971. 'TV'. *Daily Express*. 12 January.
Tristan Families Take Over. 1962. *Times*. 24 Jan.
Tucker, Anthony. 1970. 'Biologist Gives Up Gene Research'. *The Guardian*. 26 February.
'Uncanny Hints of Disaster'. 1971. *The Sun*. 4 January.
'Untitled TV Review'. 1970. *Evening Times*. 22 December.

'Viewers Protest'. 1970. *Daily Express*. 3 March.

'Violence and Sex Not the Cause of Delinquency'. 1970. *The Stage*. 21 May.

Wade, David. 1969. ',All Done by Voice'. *The Times*. 14 June.

'Wanted New Fee'. 1962. *Stage and Television Today*. 26 April.

Warman, Christopher. 1972. 'Wail of Sirens for First Time Since War'. *The Times*. 21 June.

— 1972. 'Models Test Feasibility of Maplin Sands Airport Site'. *The Times*. 16 June.

'Welcome To Westminster's Real Life Doomwatchers'. *Daily Mirror*. 22 April.

'Wellsian Setting for Project Earthwatch'. 1973. *The Times*. 7 September.

Wendy Hall. 1971. *Daily Mirror*. 22 April.

Wilkinson, James. 1971. 'Keep Britain Tidy With Plastic Eating Germs'. *Daily Express*. 7 June.

Williamson, E. 1968. 'Jumbo Jets'. *Illustrated London News*. 9 November.

'Winning the War on Rats'. 1967. *Birmingham Post*. 9 February.

Wright, Nicholas. 1969. 'Softly Softly Up The Ratings'. *Illustrated London News*. 20 September.

Wright, Pearce. 1970. 'Progress Towards "Test Tube" Baby'. *The Times*. 24 February.

— 1970. 'Scientists and Social Responsibility'. *The Times*. 24 July.

'Young Scientist Was Terrified of the Future'. 1970. *The Times*. 21 July.

WEBSITES
Links correct June 2018

Doomwatch.org has moved to https://variant14.wordpress.com. It is no longer updating and some of the information reflects the early stages of research being conducted into the programme. It still stands as the best website on the programme, run by Scott Burditt, whose encouragement and tenacity for detail made it a joy to contribute, and lead indirectly to this – and other – books on the subject.

Brand, Stewart. Other People's Mail. A 1969 letter written to Dr Carl Djerassi and his reply. Whole Earth Catalog.
http://www.wholeearth.com/issue/1030/article/211/other.people's.mail

Burgoyne, Chris. 2004. 'Interesting Application of Prestressing'. Winterton House. Department of Engineering, Cambridge University.
http://www-civ.eng.cam.ac.uk/cjb/4d8/public/winterton.html

Crandall, Kelly. 2006. 'Invisible Commercials and Hidden Persuaders: James M Vicary and the subliminal Advertising controversy of 1957'. Unpublished thesis. University of Florida.

http://plaza.ufl.edu/cyllek/docs/KCrandall_Thesis2006.pdf

Desrochers, Pierre and Hoffbauer, Christine. 2007. 'The Post War Intellectual
    Roots of the Population Bomb'. Article on two books which inspired
    Paul Ehrlich. The Electronic Journal of Sustainable Development.
https://www.researchgate.net/publication/253375313_The_Post_War_Intelle
    ctual_Roots_of_the_Population_Bomb_Fairfield_Osborn's_'Our_Plun
    dered_Planet'_and_William_Vogt's_'Road_to_Survival'_in_Retrospect

Flora, Michael. n.d. 'Project Orion: It's Life, Death and Possible Rebirth'.
    Article on nuclear propulsion systems. Island One Society.
http://www.islandone.org/Propulsion/ProjectOrion.html

Garb, Yaakov. 2002. 'Rachel Carson's *Silent Spring*'. Reproduction of an article
    from Dissent Autumn 1995: 539-546.
https://www.researchgate.net/publication/239930810_Rachel_Carson's_Sile
    nt_Spring

Hansard. n.d. 'Noise'. Speech in the House of Commons on 6 May 1970 by Mr
    Michael
McNair-Wilson, MP. Hansard Millbank Systems.
http://hansard.millbanksystems.com/commons/1970/may/06/noise

— n.d, 'Lead Content In Petrol', Debate in the House of Lords on 24 March
    1971. Hansard Millbank Systems.
http://hansard.millbanksystems.com/lords/1971/mar/24/lead-content-of-
    petrol

— n.d, 'Rabies Bill', Speech in the House of Lords on 22 November 1973
    proposed by Earl Fenner. Hansard Millbank Systems
http://hansard.millbanksystems.com/lords/1973/nov/22/rabies-bill-hl

Hansen, Robert. n.d. 'Then Volume 4: Chapter 1: The Early 1970s: Aardvarks,
    Wombats, Gannets, and Rats'. Book chapter on Eastercon in 1970.
http://www.ansible.co.uk/Then/then_4-1.html

Jones, Cheryl. 2010. 'Frank Fenner Sees No Hope For Humans'. Interview. The
    Australian.
http://www.theaustralian.com.au/higher-education/frank-fenner-sees-no-
    hope-for-humans/story-e6frgcjx-1225880091722

An Informal Conversation with Harvey Matusow and Friends, 18 December,
    1972. n.d. Recording of a KPFA-FM radio programme. Internet

Archive.
http://archive.org/details/AM_1972_12_18

Lee, Matthew. 2004. *The First Lady*. Episode guide and *Radio Times* features.
http://www.startrader.co.uk/Action%20TV/guide60s/firstlady.htm

— and Andrew Screen. 2003. *R3* episode guide and *Radio Times* features.
http://www.startrader.co.uk/Action%20TV/guide60s/r3.htm

Lopatin, Jeremy. n.d. 'Environmental Justice Case Study: Union Carbide Gas
    Release in Bhopal, India'. University of Michigan.
http://www.umich.edu/~snre492/lopatin.html#TOC

'Maurice Wilkins: A Brief Biography'. 2010. DNA and Social Responsibility.
    King's College London Archive Project Blog.
http://dnaandsocialresponsibility.blogspot.co.uk/2010/09/maurice-wilkins-
    brief-biography.html

Megan, Katie. 2007. BECTU History Project. Transcript of an interview with
    Yvette Vanson.
https://historyproject.org.uk/sites/default/files/HP0569%20Yvette%20Vans
    on%20-%20Transcript.pdf

Pearce, Fred. 2008. 'The Population Bomb: Has It Been Defused?' Yale
    Environment 360. Yale University.
http://e360.yale.edu/feature/the_population_bomb_has_it_been_defused/2
    042/

2013. 'Radiation Levels in Hurd Deep are Regularly Monitored'. Guernsey
    Government website.
https://www.gov.gg/article/107407/Radiation-levels-in-the-Hurd-Deep-are-
    regularly-

Soodyall, Himla et al. 2003. 'Genealogy and Genes: Tracing the Founding
    Fathers of Tristan da Cunha'. European Journal of Human Genetics.
http://www.nature.com/ejhg/journal/v11/n9/full/5201022a.html

Tower Bock. Watney Street. University of Edinburgh. Information on Gelston
    Point.
http://www.towerblock.eca.ed.ac.uk/development/watney-street-market-
    stage-2-block-7

Tristran da Cunha Association. 2005. 'Volcanic Interlude. A brief history of the

island 1961-3'. The Tristan da Cunha Government and the Tristan da Cunha Association.
http://www.tristandc.com/history1961-1963.php

Underwood, Ruth (ed). n.d. Articles. Collection of sources of information on the lost village of Imber.
https://foreverimber.wordpress.com/

Wilson, Duncan. 2010. 'Creating the "Ethics Industry": Mary Warnock, In Vitro Fertilization and the History of Bioethics in Britain'. 29 November. BioSocieties. Palgrave Macmillan. The London School of Economics and Political Science.
http://www.palgrave-journals.com/biosoc/journal/v6/n2/full/biosoc201026a.html

VIDEO
Doctor Who 'The Highlanders'. 2007. Michael Elwyn interview. Loose Cannon reconstruction (LC27).

Index

Episode titles appear <u>underlined</u>. '*' after an episode title denotes a working title; '+' denotes an unmade story.

About the Authors

Michael Seely lives and works in Norwich in a place *Doomwatch* very nearly investigated in the series …

He followed the original publication of *Prophets of Doom* with a well-received but now out of print biography of Dr Kit Pedler, one of the steering forces behind *Doomwatch*, and co-creator of the Cybermen in *Doctor Who*.

He also wrote the biography of renowned television director Douglas Camfield and recently assisted former *Doctor Who* actor John Levene with his autobiography *Run the Shadows, Walk the Sun*.

Phil Ware is a jazz pianist, educator, composer, arranger and producer. Born in London but resident in Dublin since 2000, he grew up in the wilds of Lincolnshire, an experience that haunts him to this day. Having initially decided on a career in TV, he became a professional musician instead after discovering that he could still enjoy late nights without that tiresome business of having to get up early the following morning.

Fascinated with genre television and film from an extremely young age, his first professional writing was for *Fear* magazine while still a schoolboy. More recently, he has co-written, overseen and edited various titles as a director of Miwk Publishing.

Other Cult TV Titles
From Telos Publishing

Back to the Vortex: *Doctor Who* **2005**
J Shaun Lyon

Third Dimension: *Doctor Who* **2007**
Stephen James Walker

Monsters Within: *Doctor Who* **2008**
Stephen James Walker

End of Ten: *Doctor Who* **2009**
Stephen James Walker

Cracks in Time: *Doctor Who* **2010**
Stephen James Walker

River's Run: *Doctor Who* **2011**
Stephen James Walker

Time of the Doctor: *Doctor Who* **2012 and 2013**
Stephen James Walker

The Television Companion (*Doctor Who*) Vols 1 and 2
David J Howe, Stephen James Walker

The Handbook (*Doctor Who*) Vols 1 and 2
David J Howe, Stephen James Walker, Mark Stammers

The Target Book (*Doctor Who* Novelisations)
David J Howe

A Day in the Life (Guide to Season 1 of 24)
Keith Topping

Inside the Hub (Guide to *Torchwood* Season 1)
Something in the Darkness (Guide to *Torchwood* Season 2)
Stephen James Walker

Liberation (Guide to *Blake's 7*)
Alan Stevens and Fiona Moore

Fall Out (Guide to *The Prisoner*)
Alan Stevens and Fiona Moore

A Family at War (Guide to *Till Death Us Do Part*)
Mark Ward

Destination Moonbase Alpha (Guide to *Space 1999*)
Robert E Wood

Assigned (Guide to *Sapphire and Steel*)
Richard Callaghan

Hear the Roar (Guide to *Thundercats*)
David Crichton

Hunted (Guide to *Supernatural* Seasons 1-3)
Sam Ford and Antony Fogg

Triquetra (Guide to *Charmed*)
Keith Topping

Bowler Hats and Kinky Boots (Guide to *The Avengers*)
Michael Richardson

By Your Command (Guide to *Battlestar Galactica*, 2 Vols)
Alan Stevens and Fiona Moore

Transform and Roll Out (Guide to The Transformers Franchise)
Ryan Frost

The Complete Slayer (Guide to *Buffy the Vampire Slayer*)
Keith Topping

**Songs for Europe (Guide to the UK in the
Eurovision Song Contest: 3 Volumes)**
Gordon Roxburgh

**All available online from
www.telos.co.uk**

Made in United States
Orlando, FL
23 September 2024